# *All in a Life*

# GARRET FITZGERALD

## AN AUTOBIOGRAPHY

GILL AND MACMILLAN

First published in 1991 by
Gill and Macmillan Ltd
Goldenbridge
Dublin 8
and
Macmillan London Ltd
Cavaye Place
London SW10 9PG
and Basingstoke
with associated companies in
Auckland, Delhi, Gaborone, Hamburg, Harare,
Hong Kong, Johannesburg, Kuala Lumpur, Lagos,
Manzini, Melbourne, Mexico City, Nairobi,
New York, Singapore, Tokyo
© Garret FitzGerald 1991
Index compiled by Helen Litton
Designed by Fergus O'Keeffe
Print origination by Seton Music Graphics Ltd, Bantry, Co. Cork
Printed by Colour Books Ltd, Dublin

**British Library Cataloguing in Publication Data**
FitzGerald, Garret
All in a life.
I. Title
920

ISBN 0-7171-1600-X

*To Joan*

*who has shared my careers as well as my life, and whose imagination and judgment, support and criticism, have made it possible for me to do far more and make many less mistakes than would otherwise have been the case.*

# CONTENTS

# PREFACE

Political autobiography is emphatically not history, but I believe it owes a duty to history: a duty to record the facts of political involvement as accurately and objectively as one can; to explain one's own contemporary motivation with as little abuse of hindsight and as much avoidance of self-justification as possible; and in the whole process to recognise that memory is a fickle guide.

At least from the time I started to study history at university I have been conscious of the importance of the contemporary record for historical purposes; and while I kept a diary of events only briefly and occasionally throughout my life I always conscientiously retained papers and documents, lodging them at intervals from 1977 onwards in the Archives of University College, Dublin, where they have now accumulated to some 450 boxes.

When shortly after my resignation from office I agreed to write an autobiography to be published jointly by Gill and Macmillan in Dublin and Macmillan in London, I secured the assistance of a qualified archivist, Mary Mackey, to whom I must express my deep gratitude. She spent a year indexing this material so that I would be able to draw upon it as required. The political sections of this book are firmly based on this archive, supplemented by my memory, of the fallibility of which in the absence of a contemporary record I am very conscious. On the Northern Ireland material I have consulted a number of the participants in the events described who are no longer civil servants, and John Rogers; to those concerned I am indebted for some very useful criticisms, but they also bear no responsibility for the text below. I am grateful too to Peter Sutherland and Patrick Honohan for their comments on the chapters dealing with domestic affairs during the periods when I was Taoiseach. In respect of the New Ireland Forum I am particularly indebted to John Fanagan, the secretary to the Fine Gael group in that body, who kept a contemporary record of events, upon which he has allowed me to draw, and who has also read the whole manuscript of the book and offered very many helpful comments.

I am also grateful to the staff of the Dáil Library and of Fine Gael head office for their assistance.

The material upon which I have drawn in relation to Northern Ireland and the Department of Foreign Affairs includes memoranda, notes of discussions, letters, and summaries of phone calls, as well as extensive reports, usually in dialogue form, that I dictated immediately after Ministerial meetings that I attended as Minister for Foreign Affairs in the absence of civil service participation, as well as similar reports of other meetings prepared for me by officials, including negotiating meetings in connection with the Anglo-Irish Agreement. In drawing on such material I have been concerned to provide as far as possible a balanced account of the contents of this material and have adhered closely to the actual language recorded in these reports. There is, however, an inevitable element of subjectivity involved, because I have had access only to the Irish accounts of such discussions. I have reason to believe, however, that in many instances the Irish reports are much fuller than those prepared for other participants.

I should perhaps add that inevitably the shape and balance of the book have been influenced to some degree by the availability of records in respect of various aspects of my life. This has certainly affected the balance between the external and domestic aspects of my political career; in the nature of things the latter are less fully documented, because so much of domestic politics is carried on by word of mouth without any written record being made. But, more generally, where I have no contemporary record and would have had to rely solely on memory I have had less to say about some events of intrinsic interest than about certain other episodes of which I made a full record at the time; these latter include the abortive attempt at a merger of Fine Gael and the Labour Party at the end of 1967; the 'Gentle Revolution' in UCD in the spring of 1969; and my attempt to achieve a Sunningdale-type solution to the Northern Ireland problem at the end of 1971, in advance of the abolition of Stormont.

There are no footnotes or references, simply because the material upon which I have drawn is not yet generally accessible. When it and other contemporary material becomes available from twelve years hence historians will be able to verify the extent to which I have handled the material fairly.

Relevant material has been omitted only where it involves genuine issues of national security; could create a risk to the safety or careers of individuals, especially people living in Northern Ireland; could, even at this remove, have damaging consequences for the national interest; or would be seriously hurtful to or libellous of individuals. I have endeavoured to ensure that the overall validity and balance of the account of events contained in this book are not affected by these necessary omissions.

Of course, while I have endeavoured to handle the *facts* of events objectively, I make no claim to objectivity in the views I express on events or people.

My three children, John, Mary, and Mark, have all contributed criticisms and corrections; I am very grateful to them for this help, and above all to Joan for her patience during the three-and-a-half years I have been working on the book and the very many hours in the course of which she listened to me reading the text to her and offered her criticisms and suggestions.

Finally, I owe an enormous debt to Louis McRedmond, who offered many useful suggestions in the course of most skilfully editing a text of about a thousand pages down to less than seven hundred; to my personal secretary, Clare Fallon, who has been indefatigable in deciphering the largely handwritten text with its multiple inserts and in typing it, not once but three or four times through various revisions; and to Michael Gill, whose patience and encouragement were undisturbed by the overrun of almost a year and a half in the delivery of the text. Like so many authors, I underestimated the time it would take to carry out the necessary research and also overestimated the share of my time I could give to the project during this period.

# Some Technical Terms and Abbreviations
## Used in This Book

Aer Lingus: the national airline

Aer Rianta: the national airports authority

Áras an Uachtaráin: the Presidential mansion in the Phoenix Park, Dublin

ard-fheis: national congress of a political party

Auxiliaries: an irregular force recruited in England and used to augment the
RIC in 1920 and 1921

Black-and-Tans: an irregular force recruited in England from among demobilised
soldiers and deployed in Ireland in 1920 and 1921, and issued with
mixtures of RIC (dark green) and British army (khaki) uniforms

Bord Fáilte Éireann: the tourist board

Bord Gáis Éireann: the national gas board

Bord na Móna: the peat development board

An Bord Pleanála: the planning appeals board

B Specials: a special constabulary of the RUC formed in 1921, associated with
Orange extremism

Cathaoirleach: title of the chairman of Seanad Éireann

Ceann Comhairle: title of the chairman of Dáil Éireann

CIE (Córas Iompair Éireann): the national transport authority

Córas Tráchtála: the export promotion board

Cumann Gaedhealach: the Irish-language society in the universities

Cumann na mBan: the nationalist women's organisation founded in 1913,
acting as an auxiliary to the Irish Volunteers and taking part in the
Easter Rising and the War of Independence

Cumann na nGaedheal: the government party in the Irish Free State, formed
in 1922 by the pro-Treaty section of Sinn Féin; it merged with other
parties to form Fine Gael in 1933

Dáil Éireann: the national assembly of Ireland, first elected in 1918 and formed
clandestinely in 1919; the name was retained for the principal chamber
of the legislature after the formation of the Irish Free State in 1922

DUP (Democratic Unionist Party): an extreme unionist party founded by Ian
Paisley and Desmond Boal in 1971

ESB (Electricity Supply Board)

Executive Council: the government of the Irish Free State from December
1922 to December 1937

Fianna Fáil: one of the principal political parties in Ireland, formed in 1926 by
the anti-abstentionist minority of Sinn Féin under the leadership of
Éamon de Valera

Fine Gael: one of the principal political parties in Ireland, formed in 1933 from
a merger of Cumann na nGaedheal and two other parties

GAA (Gaelic Athletic Association): the national sports and cultural association founded in 1884

Gaelic League (now Conradh na Gaeilge): a national organisation founded in 1893 to defend and promote the use of Irish

Gaeltacht: Irish-speaking districts

Garda Síochána: the national police force

GPO (General Post Office): the principal public building in O'Connell Street, Dublin, headquarters of the Irish Volunteers and Irish Citizen Army during the Easter Rising of April 1916

ICTU (Irish Congress of Trade Unions)

Intermediate Certificate: a national examination in a variety of subjects taken half way through secondary school

IRA (Irish Republican Army): a name first given to the Irish Volunteers during the War of Independence, then used by the anti-Treaty forces in the Civil War, and now by an illegal paramilitary republican organisation

Iveagh House: 80 St Stephen's Green, Dublin, seat of the Department of Foreign Affairs

LDF (Local Defence Force): a part-time military organisation established in 1940

Leas-Chathaoirleach: title of the deputy chairman of Seanad Éireann

Leaving Certificate: the national examination in a variety of subjects on the completion of secondary school, and the basis for university entrance

Leinster House: seat of Dáil Éireann and Seanad Éireann in Kildare Street, Dublin

Maynooth: St Patrick's College, Maynooth, Co. Kildare, a constituent college of the NUI

NET (Nítrigin Éireann Tta): the state-sponsored fertiliser manufacturing company

NUI (National University of Ireland)

Oireachtas: the parliament of Ireland, consisting of the President, Dáil Éireann, and Seanad Éireann

OUP ('official' Unionist Party): a name popularly given to the Ulster Unionist Party after the Unionist Party of Northern Ireland under Brian Faulkner had broken away in 1974

PR (proportional representation)

President of the Executive Council: head of the government of the Irish Free State

PRSI (pay-related social insurance)

rates: a tax on houses and other properties levied by city and county councils, abolished in 1978 but since partly replaced with 'service charges'

RIC (Royal Irish Constabulary): the armed police force formed in 1836 and disbanded in 1922

RTE (Radio Telefís Éireann): the national radio and television service

RUC (Royal Ulster Constabulary): the police force in Northern Ireland

SDLP (Social Democratic and Labour Party): a political party arising out of a section of the 1960s civil rights movement and including some elements of the former Nationalist Party

Seanad Éireann: the second chamber of the Irish parliament, partly elected from specialist panels and partly nominated by the Government

Sinn Féin: a nationalist party founded by Arthur Griffith and Bulmer Hobson in 1905, out of which grew both the Fine Gael and Fianna Fáil parties; the name is now used by the militant republican party associated with the IRA

Tánaiste: title of the deputy head of the Government of Ireland since December 1937

Taoiseach: title of the head of the Government of Ireland since December 1937

TCD (Trinity College, Dublin): sole college of the University of Dublin

TD (Teachta Dála): member of Dáil Éireann

UCC (University College, Cork): a constituent college of the NUI

UCD (University College, Dublin): a constituent college of the NUI

UCG (University College, Galway): a constituent college of the NUI

UDA (Ulster Defence Association): a loyalist paramilitary organisation formed in 1971

UDR (Ulster Defence Regiment): a part-time regiment of the British army formed in 1970 as a replacement for the B Specials

UUUC (United Ulster Unionist Council): a coalition of the OUP, DUP and Vanguard Unionist Party established in 1974 with the aim of bringing down the power-sharing Northern Ireland Assembly and Executive

UVF (Ulster Volunteer Force): an illegal loyalist paramilitary force formed in 1966, associated with sectarian murders

VEC (Vocational Education Committee): the committee under each city and county council that administers technical and other local authority schools

# PROLOGUE

I was four, or perhaps just five, playing on the study floor, my mother seated near me. I made a derogatory remark about the Protestant religion of the then Vice-President of the Executive Council, Ernest Blythe. He was a close family friend of almost twenty years' standing. My mother eyed me sternly and responded quietly, 'You do know that I'm a Protestant too, dear, don't you?'

I didn't.

Mother had taught me my prayers and the Catechism—I think I was then still on the Penny Catechism, and had not yet graduated to the more mature Twopenny. She had always accompanied my father, my elder brothers and myself to Mass, but, unobservant child that I was, I had never noticed that she did not receive Holy Communion. So her remark came as a shock. The religious bigotry that had somehow begun to stir in me, inculcated from God knows where (I hadn't yet started to go to school), was suddenly halted in its tracks. Life clearly was more complex than I had started to imagine.

It was in that study, with its lovely bow window of curved glass—we were always particularly exhorted not to risk breaking *that* glass, because of the extreme difficulty of replacing it—that I had already begun to learn to read, under Mother's gentle but firm tuition. Her tools—for she was an excellent teacher, with a practical bent—included her filing system for bills. As a way of learning the alphabet I was required to put each bill and receipt in the correct folder of the alphabetically designed filing box. And when I knew at least the commoner letters, there was a big word to decipher at the top of a newspaper—the *Irish In-dep-end-ent*.

The study was in fact our family room in what was quite a large house, surrounded by gardens and fields, a dozen miles south of Dublin, just beyond Bray, Co. Wicklow: a house with the enchanting name Fairy Hill. We had rented it for part of the summer of 1927 and had gone to live there in June 1928. My mother's father, John McConnell, had died three months earlier and, while he tied up most of his estate in a trust that was not distributed until after my mother's death some thirty years later, the immediate inheritance made it possible for us to move from a small house in Donnybrook to this much larger home.

John McConnell had been a Belfast businessman, and together with his brother James was a stalwart member of the unionist community in that city. In 1866 he joined the distilling firm of Dunvilles, of which he became a shareholder and director thirteen years later and in due course managing director. A major shareholder and co-director of Dunvilles was James Craig, the father of Lord Craigavon, Northern Ireland's first Prime Minister.

In the early 1870s my grandfather had been stationed in New York on behalf of his firm and, presumably as a result of this business involvement in the United States, became the representative of Alabama to the Grand Masonic Lodge of the United Kingdom. He was an intrepid traveller. Towards the end of his life, when, on a visit to London at the age of eighty-two, he took it into his head to fly to Paris, he was—so at least the family story goes—refused a place on board an aircraft at Croydon, on the unusual grounds that he was still dressed in his pyjamas! His own passport, however, shows that whatever he may have been wearing, he did in fact fly from London to Paris for a brief visit in September 1927.

Grandad, as he was known to us (to my mother he was 'the Pater', and her mother, our Gran, was 'the Mater', pronounced English-style), lived in College Green House, beside Queen's University. In 1878 he had married Margaret Neill of Robinstown House, near Aldergrove. She was a daughter of James Orr Neill, who had gone to America as a youth in the 1830s and is said to have prospered so well in the Chicago meat industry that by 1843 he had broken his engagement to the daughter of a meat baron, returned to Ulster, and purchased a wine-merchant's business. He also bought Ballyrobin Farm, near Crumlin, Co. Antrim, to which he eventually added two neighbouring farms. There he and his wife settled down. Sadly, all four of their sons were to emigrate to the United States.

John McConnell and Margaret Neill in their turn had five children. The two boys went to live in North America, as also did the eldest daughter, Elizabeth, who had been known as Lizzie in her youth but chose and retained into old age the Irish version of her name, Éilís. Like her younger sister, my mother (who, being born on 4 July 1884, was, to her everlasting chagrin, christened Mabel Washington McConnell), Éilís had been something of a rebel, espousing nationalism during her studies at Queen's College, from which she graduated through the Royal University in Dublin in 1904. My mother, who during her years at Queen's College had demonstrated *her* nationalism by joining and becoming a Committee member of the Cumann Gaedhealach, had her degree conferred by the Royal University two years later.

There is no evidence of nationalist proclivities in the case of the other daughter, Memi. She married an Englishman and went with him to Canada, where three girls were born, but the marriage was not a success, and she returned to live in Belfast in the 1920s.

Memi's three girls, together with various second cousins from the North, were frequent visitors to Fairy Hill at holiday-time, and my brothers and I spent some of our holidays with our cousins in Northern Ireland. Grandad McConnell had us all listed in his last address-book, where he meticulously noted the dates of birth, marriage and death of his own and his wife's relatives and friends; I myself featured there immediately after one of his friends, Sir Edward Carson, with whom I shared a birthday: 9 February. As it happened, I spent the first three months of my life in Bangor, Co. Down, with Aunt Memi and her three daughters, for my mother was very ill after my birth, which occurred when she was almost forty-two. She spent several months convalescing on the Continent—in part at least, I have been told, to recover from her disappointment that her fourth, and clearly final, effort at child-bearing had produced another son, instead of the longed-for daughter.

My mother's great friends in her youth were the Lynd girls, sisters of the essayist Robert Lynd, two at least of whom shared her nationalist sympathies, also became Committee members of the Cumann Gaedhealach in Queen's, and later settled in Dublin. One who remained in Belfast married Alec Foster, the socialist and nationalist headmaster of Instonians, at an age that left her junior to some of her husband's pupils. Another married Bill Lowry QC, father of the future Lord Chief Justice of Northern Ireland. Before the political division of the country split the Irish Bar, Lowry practised in Dublin, and his house in Leeson Park was an occasional refuge for my father when 'on the run' from the Black-and-Tans and Auxiliaries. Whether Bill knew this or only his wife, Ena, did I cannot say—but certainly safe unionist houses were thought best in those days by men in need of shelter!

After an uninhibited and happy childhood, involving a fair share of travel (to Dublin, to Scotland, and at least once to the south of France), my mother went first to Queen's and then, after undertaking a secretarial course and gaining some experience, including a brief period working for the President of Queen's, to London in 1908 to study for a postgraduate qualification in teaching. She lived in digs, and complained many decades later that her stamp collection was stolen by a landlady in whose charge she had left it when she was away.

After qualifying she stayed on in London, supporting herself by undertaking secretarial work for George Bernard Shaw and George Moore, among others, although her residence there was interrupted by a voyage round the world with one of her brothers—their father's idea of getting them to settle down!

Her interest in Ireland and Irish affairs, aroused in her youth and maintained at Queen's, continued in London, where she joined the Central Branch of the Gaelic League. There she met a young London-Irish poet some years younger than herself. He was aged about twenty at the time and named Thomas FitzGerald ('Tommy' to his mother, and to his brothers and sisters in childhood), but he had already taken the more romantic name of Desmond. (Desmond, from the Irish for 'South Munster', was one of the two earldoms that the FitzGeralds had held in Ireland in the Middle Ages.)

My father's parents were Irish emigrants who had met in London. They were married in St George's Cathedral, Southwark, London, in 1870. His father, Patrick FitzGerald, seems to have been brought up on a small farm near Mitchelstown, Co. Cork, and at the time of his marriage was a stonemason, living in south London; later he became a builder. My father's mother, Mary Ann, or 'Babe', was the second child and eldest daughter of William Scollard and Margaret Huggard of Castleisland, Co. Kerry, where William, who had worked on the Griffith survey of Ireland, had gone into private practice as a surveyor.

Patrick's marriage seems to have encountered difficulties, for after the birth of her first two sons in 1871 and 1873 'Babe' returned with them to her family in Castleisland for five-and-a-half years. My father, born in 1888 and christened Thomas Joseph, was the last of the second 'batch' of four children, two boys and two girls, born to the couple after my grandmother's return to London in late 1878 or early 1879.

The two elder boys, John and Patrick William, became a leather merchant and a journalist, respectively. John eventually settled in Brazil, where he died in 1958. William, as he came to be known, edited the magazine *Wide World*, which was supposed to publish only true stories of travel but which strained its readers' credulity with a story of an intrepid explorer crossing the Pacific on the back of a dolphin, as a result of which *Punch* published a cartoon showing my uncle, shipwrecked on a raft, spying a vessel in the distance and crying, 'A sale! a sale!' Later he offered his services as a public relations officer to various South American governments, apparently with some success, although the latter part of his life was spent as an invalid in London, where he died in 1942.

My father's other brother, France, an indefatigable dancer, ran a chemical works in Stratford, near his home in West Ham. During the Truce that preceded the Anglo-Irish Treaty of December 1921 he got into trouble collecting arms from barracks in London with the help of a drunken sergeant; he apparently tried his luck in one barracks too many. He cannot have spent too long in custody, since in early 1922, after the Treaty but before the Civil War, he became involved in providing arms and explosives to Michael Collins—a transaction that five years later was the subject of prolonged attention by the Public Accounts Committee of the new Irish parliament. In 1941 he died following a gas explosion at his factory, resulting from an air raid, and my father, with the help of my brother Pierce, who was an accountant, had to make a number of visits to Stratford during the remainder of the war to keep the factory going, producing chemicals for the war effort—a curious circumstance in which to return to his native east London after so many different careers as poet, nationalist revolutionary, propagandist, Government Minister, and philosopher.

Patrick FitzGerald died in 1908, but my grandmother, who was adored by her family, lived until 1927. After her death France and his younger sister Kate, the headmistress of a school in Upminster, who was my father's favourite sister and our favourite aunt, lived in South Kensington with their married sister Ciss (Margaret). Her house at 15 Cornwall Gardens was a mecca for all of us as children, whether staying in London or passing through to and from the Continent.

From an early age my father was interested in poetry. There is a story—presumably exaggerated, at least in relation to his age!—that when he was seven he walked from his home in West Ham six or seven miles into the West End in the hope of seeing W. B. Yeats going into the Café Royal. By the time he was in his twenties he was already one of the Imagist group of poets, which included T. E. Hulme, F. S. Flint, Hilda Doolittle, and Edward Storer, to whom he and Florence Farr introduced Ezra Pound when the latter spent some time in London in 1909 en route from America to the Continent. The Irish poet Joseph Campbell, then living in London, also belonged to this circle.

Desmond's interest in Ireland—which he may have visited once as a boy with his father—extended beyond the poetry of Yeats, for in 1908 he started to learn Irish at the Gaelic League class where he met my mother. She, having already acquired a knowledge of the language at university, had taken to using the Irish form of her name, Méadhbh Ní Chonaill. In 1910 my father made what was probably his second visit to Ireland, spending three weeks on the Irish-speaking Great Blasket Island off the coast of Co. Kerry and almost certainly visiting his relations in Castleisland.

Desmond and Mabel fell deeply in love, a fact that her father discovered in the spring of 1911. He summoned her back to Belfast: an understandable reaction to the involvement of his daughter with an impecunious London-Irish, Roman Catholic civil service clerk—the job my father had secured after leaving school, having for some reason turned down an offer by his elder brother William to put him through university. But a month or two later my mother eloped, returned to London, married my father, and went with him to Brittany. There my eldest brother was born. He was christened Desmond Patrick Jean-Marie, but was known as 'Demín'—little Dem—until as an older child the diminutive was dropped and he became 'Dem'.

My parents remained for almost two years in Brittany, for much if not all of the time at Saint-Jean-du-Doigt, near Morlaix, in the company of artists and writers. Then in February 1913, feeling, in my father's own words, 'for no tangible reason whatever . . . either that there was going to be a great movement in Ireland, or that it was necessary that some movement should be launched that would require the active work of everyone that was willing to assist,' they decided to move to Ireland, to Irish-speaking west Kerry. With my Belfast grandfather's help—he must by then have relented towards my father—they acquired a lease on part of the coastguard station on the peninsula opposite to the village of Ventry, seven miles west of Dingle, and there set about improving their knowledge of Irish. Within a couple of months of their arrival they had met Ernest Blythe, who had come there from Co. Armagh to learn Irish, working as a labourer on a farm, and shortly afterwards they also met The O'Rahilly, who was to be killed leading his men from the GPO during the Easter Rising three years later.

Within nine months of arriving in Kerry my father's presentiment proved justified: in response to the establishment of the anti-Home Rule force of the Ulster Volunteers a rival organisation, the Irish Volunteers, was formed in November 1913, and my father and Ernest Blythe enthusiastically set about recruiting Volunteer members and training them.

At Christmas 1913 my mother brought my father to visit her parents in Belfast. But my father did not neglect his political work even when he found himself in this unionist environment. He went to a meeting addressed by James Connolly and was invited back to tea by Connolly's daughters, Nora and Ina. As Ina told me half a century later, Nora brought my father back to their home while Ina, knowing that there was no food in the house save bread, went to buy tomatoes so as to take the bare look off it. My parents also met Roger Casement during this visit.

A few months later, in March 1914, my second brother, Pierce, was born in Kerry. In August the outbreak of the First World War precipitated a split in the Volunteers, the vast majority following the call of the Nationalist Party leader, John Redmond, to join the British army, while a small minority, including my parents, rejected this as a betrayal of the Volunteer movement. At a public meeting in Dingle to debate the merits of the issue, my father was knocked unconscious by an enthusiastic Redmondite.

My mother tried to recruit her old employer, George Bernard Shaw, to the cause. The ensuing correspondence—published as an appendix to my father's fragment of autobiography covering the years 1913–16—contrasts her passionate commitment to Irish nationalism with Shaw's cool and rational, but also very entertaining, reaction to her plea for support. He expressed 'some masculine sympathy with Desmond, whose head you are knocking against a stone wall'— thus accurately diagnosing that my mother rather than my father was the prime exponent of revolutionary fervour—and he ended one letter: 'Ireland is your plaything at present, because you are an educated woman trying to live the life of a peasant. You have put yourself out of the reach of Beethoven and the orchestra; so I suppose you must have something to play with. But you shan't play with ME, madam.'

In January 1915 my father was expelled from Co. Kerry. The proximate cause of the expulsion seems to have been my mother's decision to meet the exigencies of a war situation by keeping hens. From a Department of Agriculture leaflet she learnt that egg production would be increased if the hens were fed late at night, and the wavering light of her lantern, seen from the RIC station across the bay, apparently convinced the police that my father was signalling to German submarines.

Finding that Bray, twelve miles south of Dublin, was not among the areas prohibited to him, which included all major ports, my father decided to move there, and soon he was organising the anti-Redmondite Volunteers in Co. Wicklow. Later that year he was arrested and sentenced to six months' imprisonment for seditious speech and discouraging recruitment to the British army.

He completed this sentence just three short weeks before the Rising, in which he and my mother both participated, joining the garrison in the GPO. Although my father was opposed to an insurrection that had no prospect of success, he felt he could not let down men whom he had trained and who might be participating in it as a result of his encouragement.

On his arrival at the GPO he was appointed adjutant to his friend The O'Rahilly, who also disapproved of the Rising. During the days that followed he spent many hours discussing the moral justification for the Rising with Patrick Pearse and Joseph Plunkett (who was said to have met Chancellor Bethman-Hollweg in Germany the previous year when seeking support for an Irish rebellion). The two leaders told him of their belief—which was not, of course, their actual objective—that if Germany won the war the Kaiser's sixth son, Joachim, might be made king of an independent Ireland. Bulmer Hobson was also aware of this possibility, as he later told Ernest Blythe.

On the Thursday of Easter Week my mother was sent home from the GPO by Patrick Pearse to look after her two young children, but not before she had been given a dangerous mission: to carry a Tricolour flag, inadequately wrapped in brown paper, to be hoisted over Dublin Castle, which Pearse believed had been captured by the Volunteers. Faced with soldiers dressed in khaki pointing bayonets at her as she approached the entrance, she hurriedly turned about and returned to the GPO to report the failure of this rebellion—as of every other in Irish history since the castle was built in the early thirteenth century—to capture the seat of English power in Ireland.

In the following twelve months, having first sampled four Irish prisons or detention centres, my father was sent to Dartmoor, and then to Maidstone by train, chained to Éamon de Valera and Richard Hayes, as President de Valera reminded me more than once when I had occasion to meet him as Minister for Foreign Affairs in 1973. He was moved successively to Lewes, Parkhurst, and Pentonville, and from there was released in mid-1917. Less than a year later he was arrested again in connection with a fictitious German plot, and spent ten months in Gloucester Jail. He returned home in March 1919, three months after his election as MP for the Pembroke division of Dublin in the 'Khaki Election' at the end of 1918.

Some episodes from his prison career illustrate my father's character and temperament. He often enjoyed the company of non-political prisoners, preferring murderers to professional criminals because, apart from the single episode that had led each of them to their incarceration, they tended, he said, to be interesting people, sometimes quite generous with whatever small worldly goods they might enjoy. On the other hand he found the gregarious life of political prisoners sometimes hard to take. He objected in principle to the claims put forward by some of his colleagues to distinct political status, which seemed to him to contain a snobbish element in seeking to make a distinction vis-à-vis ordinary convicts and to diminish the honourable role of prisoner that they had chosen by virtue of their political actions.

He managed to get punished from time to time for various offences that he contrived in order to have temporary relief, through periods of solitary confinement, from his colleagues' company. These provided him with opportunities for writing poetry and for philosophical reflections, which later in life emerged in writings on scholastic philosophy that led to his appointment as Visiting Professor of Philosophy in Notre Dame University, Indiana, for parts of the years 1935 to 1938.

In April 1919, a month after his release from his third term of imprisonment, he was named Director of Publicity for the Dáil government, which had been established in January 1919 by the majority of Irish MPs, who had been elected in the Sinn Féin interest and who set up a separatist Irish parliament that was later driven underground. In this, his first, position of responsibility, he decided that the key to success in the propaganda war to come lay with mobilising foreign opinion in favour of the Irish cause. He returned to his native city, London, where, through his Imagist friend F. S. Flint—whom Ezra Pound once described as 'Frenchified'—he made contact with French correspondents in that city, and through them eventually with correspondents of papers from other European countries and the United States. Ezra Pound later celebrated the re-emergence of his poet friend in this new guise in a verse of Canto VII, which starts: 'The live man, out of lands and prisons, shakes the dry pods, Gropes for old wills and friendships . . .'

This concept of poet become man of action preoccupied Pound to such a degree that almost forty years later he was still persisting in efforts to have a biography of my father written around this theme—efforts that my mother resisted, on the grounds that anyone whom Pound would be likely to suggest as a biographer would be most unlikely to do justice to my father's profound commitment to Catholicism.

In November 1919 my father launched an underground daily newspaper, the *Irish Bulletin*, which was published from different locations without a break until after the Truce of July 1921. His insistence that nothing be published that could not be stood over in every detail infuriated many of his colleagues who were less meticulous in their concern for the truth. Virtue was rewarded, however, because within months journalists, finding the *Irish Bulletin* to be reliable, in marked contrast to the British propaganda machine, made increasing use of its material throughout the world. Growing international support for the Irish cause, flowing from this extensive and generally favourable media coverage, was a major factor contributing to the eventual British decision in July 1921 to agree to a Truce and to negotiations on the question of Irish independence.

Meanwhile my mother had remained active, working for Cumann na mBan for a period after 1916 and assisting my father with his work on the *Irish Bulletin*. In February 1920 my third brother, Fergus, was born, and just after his first birthday my father was arrested while visiting my mother in their flat; his Pimpernel-like success in evading detection until then had been helped by his English accent, which had enabled him when stopped and questioned to pass himself off as an English journalist. Fortunately for him—and perhaps ultimately for my existence also!—a passer-by saw the Black-and-Tans bringing him into Dublin Castle and told my mother. She telephoned the civil authorities in the Castle and succeeded in ensuring his safety; three months earlier several Volunteers had been shot while in custody there.

In July, following the Truce, he was released from what was to be his last imprisonment. He became involved in the Treaty negotiations in his capacity as Director of Publicity, a post which, during his absence, had been temporarily filled for a few months by Erskine Childers, later to be executed during the Civil War by the government of which my father was a member.

When the anti-Treaty members of the government resigned in January 1922, my father became Minister for Publicity outside the Cabinet. In August he entered the Cabinet as Minister for External Affairs. This was a logical extension of the role he had been playing as Director (and later as Minister) of Publicity, and indeed that department remained in existence, linked to External Affairs, until finally merged with it in 1924.

My father took up his new duties with enthusiasm, redeploying the talents of some of those who had been engaged in unofficial diplomatic activity on behalf of the pre-Treaty Dáil government and recruiting some others to form the small nucleus from which the Department of External Affairs (later Foreign Affairs) developed. In April 1923 he submitted Ireland's formal application to join the League of Nations, and in September Ireland became a member. In October he briefly attended the Imperial Conference. Also in that year he led a delegation to the Holy See to rectify the situation that had arisen as a result of an envoy from the Vatican arriving in Ireland during the Civil War and aligning himself with the anti-Treaty cause. In 1924 he registered the Anglo-Irish Treaty at the League of Nations, despite British protests that an intra-Commonwealth treaty should not be registered as an international agreement. In that year also the Irish Free State opened the first diplomatic mission abroad established by a Commonwealth country—a legation in Washington—and also asserted its independence in relation to treaty-making by refusing to be bound by the whole of the Lausanne Treaty with Turkey, on the grounds that the Irish state had not been represented at the negotiations.

In October and November 1926 the Irish team at the Imperial Conference, led by the Vice-President of the Executive Council, Kevin O'Higgins, fought a successful battle to secure recognition of the equal status of the dominions, a principle that my father had been particularly concerned to establish. This was the last major occasion on which he represented his country as Minister for External Affairs. In the government reshuffle that followed the election of June 1927, Kevin O'Higgins was appointed Minister for External Affairs, and my father became Minister for Defence.

At the time of his appointment he was gravely ill. An appendicitis operation had gone wrong, the wound had become septic, and a further operation was required a fortnight later to save his life, which nevertheless hung by a thread for many days afterwards. At this moment, tragedy struck. Kevin O'Higgins, the colleague my father most admired after the deaths of Arthur Griffith and Michael Collins during the Civil War, was assassinated on his way to Mass by a breakaway IRA group.

To prevent my father hearing the news—which in his condition could have caused him to lose his will to live—my mother spent every day from early morning until late at night at his bedside. At one point, hearing military aircraft overhead—the fly-past during the funeral—he recalled his new role as Minister for Defence and demanded to know what they were doing.

He recovered, and in the five years that followed tackled the task of reducing the size of the army and enforcing strict discipline, with a view to ensuring that when the time came for Fianna Fáil (which had been established in 1926 as a constitutional party, breaking away from the sterile abstentionist policy of post-Civil War republicanism) to take over government democratically after winning a general election, this transition would not be impeded by the army, which had defeated the anti-Treaty forces in 1922–23.

At the same time Patrick McGilligan, the new Minister for External Affairs appointed after Kevin O'Higgins's assassination, who was a long-standing friend and for a brief period in 1923–24 had been a member of the External Affairs staff, continued to draw on my father's experience, especially at the Imperial Conference of 1930, when the Irish and Canadian campaign to establish the sovereign independence of the dominions was fully brought to a successful conclusion, leading to the Statute of Westminster of 1931, which gave formal recognition to this new status. The sole Ministerial survivor from the Imperial Conferences of 1923 and 1926, my father, still only forty-two years of age, enjoyed at this Conference the improbable role for an Irish revolutionary of being the elder statesman of the Commonwealth. It proved to be the climax of his political career.

During these years his interest in literature had not waned. He was a co-founder of the Academy of Letters in 1923, where he enjoyed particularly the company of his hero, W. B. Yeats. He visited Joyce in Paris in early 1922 and suggested that the Irish government put his name forward for the Nobel Prize for Literature, a suggestion that Joyce felt was more likely to do my father harm than to do himself good. He was right; it came to nothing. My father defended, however, to his literary friends the Censorship of Publications Bill introduced by the government in 1927, trying without success to convince people like Ezra Pound and Francis Hackett that better results would be secured if highly educated people were responsible for taking decisions in this area than if they were left to the police. He proved strikingly wrong; in the following decades the Censorship Board brought lasting and merited obloquy on Ireland by banning many of the country's and the world's leading writers. Meanwhile my father continued to write poetry and had a book printed in France in 1926 containing some of his poems, a copy of which he gave to his friend Ina Connolly, who many years before had bought the tomatoes for tea in James Connolly's Belfast home.

In February 1932 the government found itself in a minority in the Dáil after a general election. The Labour Party supported de Valera, who formed his first government, and my father's party went into opposition—where they remained until after his death fifteen years later.

When my father had first been appointed a Minister in January 1922, he and my mother were in deep disagreement about the Treaty that had just been signed. He believed that it gave Ireland the possibility of evolving towards sovereign independence with other dominions, while she believed that the Treaty was an unacceptable compromise of republican principles. In the Civil War that began at the end of June 1922 my mother's sympathies were totally with the anti-Treaty side. Her deep love for my father and her intense loyalty to him restrained her from giving much practical expression to her strong political feelings. However, as is evident from my father's correspondence during the Imperial Conferences of 1923 and to a lesser extent 1926, he felt inhibited from discussing affairs of state with her because of her lack of sympathy. Indeed in 1926, three years after the Civil War and shortly after my birth, my mother wrote to a friend deploring the fact that her husband's government seemed unlikely to be defeated and expressing her disappointment that de Valera, by setting up Fianna Fáil, was taking the same path of compromise as her husband and his colleagues had taken five years before! However, the assassination of Kevin O'Higgins and her growing admiration for the integrity of the Cumann na nGaedheal government led her to modify her views radically in the late 1920s, so that by the time the Imperial Conference of 1930 took place my father, sure at last of her political as well as personal sympathy and understanding, took time to write to her daily and in detail about what was happening there.

When I was born, on 9 February 1926 in a nursing home at 89 Lower Baggot Street, Dublin, I was greeted in the ranks of Fianna Fáil as 'the child of the reconciliation', as Máire Cruise O'Brien recalls vividly. Her parents, Seán and Margaret MacEntee, were old friends of my parents; they had taken the anti-Treaty side in the Civil War, and it is said that when I was christened the pro-Treaty parish priest of Donnybrook was shocked to see me, a 'Free State baby', carried into the church by a republican like Margaret, who was to be my godmother.

Thus when in 1931 I learnt, literally at my mother's knee, my first lesson about religious bigotry, the political rift between my parents had been completely healed and my father was coming near the end of his period in government, of which I have no direct memory save for the armed soldiers who guarded us in the years after Kevin O'Higgins's death.

But as I grew up and came gradually to learn of my father's and my mother's roots in the two traditions of the island, and of their roles in the historic events of the years from 1913 onwards, I developed a growing interest in politics and international affairs, but also, above all, in the problem of the two communities in Northern Ireland. For, as a result of the events in which my parents had been so deeply involved, these two communities had with tragic results been left by the states that commanded their respective allegiances to fend for themselves for half a century within the claustrophobic confines of six counties of the island.

# CHAPTER ONE

# EARLY YEARS

Our house, Fairy Hill, was set in several acres of gardens and lawns and surrounded on three sides by fields, with two small woods and a complex of stables and outbuildings. The building itself was two-storeyed, with a bewildering and eccentric internal plan involving five different levels on the ground floor and three on the first floor.

Half way up the main staircase from the back hall was a spacious drawing-room, with steps to a conservatory opening onto a balcony leading to a walled flower garden. The back hall also gave access to a large dining-room and the kitchen quarters. The indoor staff comprised a cook and a maid.

Outside the kitchen was the vegetable-and-fruit garden, and beside it the stables with their lofts and mangers and numerous outbuildings, including a cow-shed and hen-house. Lawns broken by borders with rose bushes sloped down in front of the house to a tennis court, which served also as a croquet lawn, below which was a meadow and beyond that a small but mysterious wood. A gap in the trees revealed a dramatic view of the great houses of Sorrento Terrace on the sea at Dalkey four miles away.

All the groceries, the bread, and the milk—which came in a pony and trap containing a huge milk-can with a tap at the back, from which the milk was drawn in a tin measure—were delivered through the window of our play-room beside the kitchen. The weekday meat came by the same route, but the Sunday joint arrived somewhat eccentrically by post from Carlingford, Co. Louth. Three decades later I found myself canvassing a vote there for the Seanad from our postal butcher of the 1930s, who had become a county councillor.

A special attraction for a child was the hen-run. The hen-house door provided an easy route to the roofs of the stables, in the valleys of which cigarettes could be safely smoked, as my brother Fergus taught me when I was seven. Thereafter for some years I faced the difficult choice between deploying my threepenny pocket money in its entirety on five Players or reserving a penny for other purposes by slumming it with five Woodbines, until much later, at the age of fourteen, I took a rational decision to divert this nugatory expenditure, undertaken only because of peer pressure, into more enjoyable channels, such as chocolate and ice cream.

The gardens and lawns and their surroundings offered ample scope for my mother's gardening skills and enthusiasm, which she deployed with the aid of a gardener who lived in the gate-lodge and who, in the early years, was helped by an under-gardener. Flowers were in profusion—every conceivable shade of sweet-pea across the centre of the garden, new varieties of violets in a special border at one corner, and roses everywhere. In the neighbouring vegetable garden, fruit and vegetables grew in quantity and provided the raw material for the hundreds of pounds of jam and jelly my mother manufactured each summer—principally strawberry and raspberry, but also plum, damson and greengage jam and raspberry, loganberry, redcurrant and apple jelly.

Because my brothers were a good deal older than I, I was left much to my own devices, but my next brother, Fergus, faced with having brothers six years older and six years younger than himself, made the best he could of the company of a much younger sibling. He was a romantic and imaginative child. Under his guidance I learnt how to look after white mice and a grass-snake; played cowboys and Indians, but also re-enacted the legends of King Arthur and the fall of the Bastille; turned the garden paths into a simulacrum of the French railway system; studied astronomy; learnt Egyptian hieroglyphics; played airships, with a clothes-basket suspended by a rope from the branch of a tree; made quantities of toffee, trays of which, dyed bright pink with cochineal, tended to be left gathering dust on top of and underneath cupboards; and devised and acted plays.

Fergus also taught me to type with two fingers and a thumb—an art never lost, and never improved upon. At the age of thirteen he had gained access to the National Library, where he copied out in a red notebook the grammar, syntax and vocabulary (but only to the letter B) of the Quechua language of the Incas of Peru. Wanting a 'fair' copy of this material, and feeling that he had done his share, he required me at the age of seven to tap out his notes.

Fergus thus provided me with an eclectic supplementary education and rudimentary secretarial training. Other skills—bridge, poker, and the ability to walk up to seven miles—were learnt from an afternoon 'governess', Miss Cuddy, then in her late fifties, who lived to a lively one hundred, at which age she happily discussed with me my involvement in the Government formed in 1973. When I was five and went to school Miss Cuddy had replaced Nurse O'Neill, who had charge of me since I was a baby, and she remained until I went for a year to an Irish-speaking boarding school at the age of nine.

It would be very wrong to think from this account of events that my mother was somehow lacking in affection or care for me. Nothing could be further from the truth. But she was the product of a middle-class Victorian environment that involved extensive supplementing of parental care by nurses or governesses. She had never been able to afford such luxuries in the past when my elder brothers were young, my father was frequently absent in jail, and she was herself involved in revolutionary activities. It seemed natural to her to take advantage of a recent inheritance from her father by trying to give me the kind of childhood *she* had enjoyed. In fact she devoted a lot of her time to my education, both before and after I went to school. She was a gifted teacher, as I found to my benefit right up to the point when, many years later, I won as a result of her tuition a university entrance scholarship, with first place in English—a result that neither my school career nor my performance in school examinations had foreshadowed.

She also took on the whole burden of my Roman Catholic religious education, despite the fact that she was then a Protestant and my father was a devout and highly intellectual as well as orthodox member of the Catholic Church. Only in three small ways was her religious tuition inadequate. She taught me an incomplete version of the old Confiteor, apparently believing that the last two sentences were alternative endings rather than both being integral parts of the prayer. She never introduced me to the Rosary—of which, perhaps, she had not heard—thus creating intense embarrassment for me when I later went to an Irish-speaking school and failed even to observe that this form of prayer was being employed there until asked to recite it publicly in my second term. And she never taught me to make the sign of the cross on my forehead, lips and breast at the start of the Gospel—something I have ever since been too self-conscious to attempt.

Nonetheless her remarkable commitment to teaching me a faith to which she herself did not then adhere, backed by my father's undemonstrative piety, provided me with a religious foundation that saw me through into early middle age; only then did I begin to understand what religious doubt means, and by that time I was better equipped to cope with such problems, although not to overcome them completely.

My reading as a child was in some degree Victorian, or at least Edwardian. English and American children's books, the names of which are for the most part unknown today, the *Gem* and the *Magnet* magazines, which introduced me to Billy Bunter, Harry Wharton, et al, and the adventure stories of Rider Haggard and Jules Verne, were among my favourites. More modern works included Richmal Crompton's William books and Hugh Lofting's Dr Dolittle series.

My father made his contribution to my literary education in two ways: first, by reading both his own unpublished fairy stories and works by authors like Dickens aloud to me in the evenings, and second, by placing in 1937 a standing order at a bookshop for early editions of the *Boys' Own Paper*, which he had himself read avidly as a child in London. Eventually all the issues from 1879 to 1896 came my way, bringing with them the authentic aura of late nineteenth-century British imperialism.

I suppose this literary diet may seem slightly eccentric for the child of two Irish nationalist revolutionaries. But despite my mother's assurance to Bernard Shaw in one of her letters that she would bring up my eldest brother, Dem, to hate the English, and despite the fact that she had remained until after my birth a committed republican, neither she nor my father could sustain a narrow anglophobia. Dedicated Irish patriots all their lives, they nevertheless had a deep love of English literature acquired during their very different childhoods in the Belfast and east London of the late Victorian era. Moreover, their moral roots lay deeply embedded in the values of the Victorian period. It would have been inconceivable for either of them to have failed to pass on to their children these values, the glories of English literature, and, at a different level, their personal experience of late nineteenth-century English and American children's books and magazines—as well as their commitment to Ireland, to Irish nationalism, and to Gaelic culture. They saw no contradiction in transmitting the whole of this rich and varied heritage.

Thus my father's readings from Dickens were accompanied unselfconsciously by encouragement to speak Irish, especially after I had acquired what turned out to be a temporary fluency in the language at Ring College when I was nine years old. He took care to instil also a respect for the ancient culture of Gaelic Ireland, and he taught me about the revolutionary period by a wealth of anecdotes, which were not the less inspiring for being told very often in a humorous vein, for my father never failed to see the funny side of everything and everyone with whom he had been engaged.

Respect for the great figures of the national movement was something that my brothers and I imbibed from our earliest years—in my case all the more profoundly because, by the time I became conscious of their names, those whom my father had most admired and loved were all tragically dead: The O'Rahilly, killed within minutes of parting from him in the GPO in 1916; Griffith, dead of a stroke in the midst of the Civil War; Collins, killed in ambush ten days later; and the murdered Kevin O'Higgins.

The rich cultural background was further enhanced by my father's classical education and his deep involvement with, and intimate knowledge of, French literature and philosophy—although these latter influences reached me only later in my teens.

In describing some of the influences of my childhood, emanating from my mother and father as well as from my brother Fergus, I am partly anticipating. The years from the age of five onwards were, of course, primary-school years, when I was learning from teachers and schoolmates as well as from my home environment. After Easter 1931 I was sent to a small private school called St Brigid's, run by a Miss Lucy Brayden in a large house in Duncairn Terrace, Bray. Before long I found myself in a class that had ceased to have amongst its members any boy other than myself. Having three brothers and no sisters, I found the experience strange, but not unattractive. By the age of eight I had reached the conclusion that the right way to deal with the girl question was to select one and marry her as soon as possible. I even made my selection, and persisted with this choice until my second year at university, when it became clear that the affections of the girl in question were engaged elsewhere.

My interest in international affairs can also be traced back to this otherwise all-female class. One morning in October 1934 our teacher referred to the assassination on the previous day in Marseille of King Alexander of Yugoslavia and Foreign Minister Barthou of France. It turned out that a number of the girls had already heard the news, and I felt it must have been clear to all of them that I had not. I vowed never to risk such humiliation again: thereafter, for the rest of my life, I have read the newspapers assiduously every morning and so avoided any repetition of this shaming experience.

School was a morning affair; in the afternoon I went for long walks with Miss Cuddy. Sometimes we dropped into a house about three miles away in Shankill. This was the home of Dr Michael Tierney, Professor of Greek at UCD, who from 1927 to 1932 had been a member of the Dáil and was later to be Vice-Chairman of the Seanad, and whose wife, Eibhlín, is a daughter of Eoin MacNeill, Professor of Irish History and President of the Irish Volunteers from their foundation in 1913.

The Tierneys were friends of my parents, and the two eldest children, girls, were at school with me. I spent many happy hours at their house, the more so because in those years it was one of only two houses that I visited regularly—the other being that of Seán and Eileen Ó Faoláin, who returned from the United States in 1933 and whose daughter Julie (now Julia) was a couple of years younger than I.

When I was seven a radical change took place in our lives. Until 1927 Ministers had availed themselves of state transport only for official journeys to rural areas. My father, who never owned a car, travelled to and from his office by tram, even in the later stages of the Civil War. But after Kevin O'Higgins's assassination in July 1927 the army insisted on guarding Ministers. From early childhood, therefore, I had been accustomed to accompanying my father in an army-owned saloon car, driven by a soldier and followed by a car with three other soldiers. Each car was fitted with two submachine-guns, and each of the four soldiers carried a rifle, two revolvers, and a bag of ammunition.

The army guards were, of course, a great addition to the family, and particularly to my life. Companionable men, obviously fond of children, they ate the thickest sandwiches I have ever seen and did their best to help my mother—once digging up the grass bank outside the study window, believing this was her wish: in fact, having laboriously planted it with daffodil bulbs, she was furious, but carefully hid her distress. When we went to spend afternoons bathing at Jack's Hole, south of Wicklow, the soldiers acted as umpires for our game of 'manoeuvres', which involved all concerned—including on occasion bemused distinguished guests from Britain or further afield—crawling towards each other through the bracken, the object being for each to shout an identification of another before being identified himself or herself.

The change of government in February 1932, when Cumann na nGaedheal (soon to become Fine Gael) lost office to Fianna Fáil, and my father's consequent loss of his Ministerial position, had meant nothing to me at the time.

The dramatic change in my life came over a year later when the new government withdrew the guards from ex-Ministers. At one blow I lost these friends and my father lost the only car of which he ever had regular use during his life, becoming dependent on occasional lifts in a minute second-hand Austin Seven with which my eldest brother, Dem, had managed to equip himself two years earlier.

On the whole, however, politics intruded remarkably little in our lives, although of course my parents' friends included a number of people to whom they had become close during the period of the national movement. Most of these were still active in politics: Ernest Blythe and his wife, Annie, who was Fergus's godmother; Paddy (Tody) McGilligan and his wife, also Annie; and—from across the political divide—Seán MacEntee (Minister for Finance in the Fianna Fáil government after 1932) and his wife, Margaret, who was my godmother.

Friendship with the MacEntees went back to 1917 and transcended politics; in 1923 my father had helped to have Seán MacEntee released on parole from a post-Civil War internment camp so that he could inspect a public lighting scheme in Wexford for which he had acted as consultant, and had then secured his permanent release, providing him and his wife with passports so that they could celebrate his release with a holiday in Paris. Shortly after the change of government in 1932 Margaret MacEntee broke her leg while at Fairy Hill and had to remain in the house for three weeks. News of this stay got out and provoked a 'non-fraternisation' instruction from de Valera, which, however, the MacEntees ignored.

My mother's oldest friend, however, was Nancy Campbell, the estranged wife of Joseph Campbell, whom my parents had known since 1909 in London and who shared my mother's passion for gardening. Other regular visitors included Dr Richard (Dick) Hayes, who had taken part in the Battle of Ashbourne in 1916 and had later been sent from Dartmoor Prison to Maidstone chained to my father and de Valera; Sarah Purser, the painter and stained-glass artist, then in her mid-eighties; and Edward Longford and his wife, Christine, who, together with Hilton Edwards and Mícheál Mac Liammóir, had founded the Gate Theatre in 1928 and kept it going for many decades.

Among occasional guests of whom I have only vestigial memories were W. B. Yeats, T. S. Eliot, Desmond McCarthy, Frank Pakenham (the present Lord Longford) and Jacques Maritain from outside Ireland, as well as John McCormack, Professor Tom Bodkin, Oliver St John Gogarty, Seán Keating, and Bryan Guinness (now Lord Moyne).

But most of the guests were young people, friends of my two elder brothers, who were in their teens and early twenties when we lived in Fairy Hill. Some of them, such as Niall Montgomery and Don MacDonagh, had a literary bent; all were stimulated and entertained by my father's literary, philosophical and political conversation and by his endless flow of anecdotes and reminiscences. These at times overflowed into renderings of London music-hall songs from the turn of the century, which had been part of his childhood and which he sang with an authentic Cockney accent. My mother's immense and limitless hospitality and her sympathy for the young made her as popular with them in her own way as was my father.

Throughout the whole year, but above all in summer, the house was open to young and old alike, especially at weekends. Aunts, uncles, and cousins, and occasionally my Belfast grandmother and cousins-in-law of hers, born in the 1850s and 1860s, were occupants of the two spare rooms. Sometimes additional accommodation for an overflow of relatives was created by one or more of us sleeping on couches or on a chair-bed.

Summer activities centred around tennis and bathing expeditions to Co. Wicklow beaches; in winter there were walks, including hill-climbing—we called it mountain-climbing, but that exaggerated the size and steepness of the inclines we attacked. The tennis parties were accompanied by tea, home-made lemonade and cakes on the lawn—including my mother's speciality, a three-tier strawberry-and-cream sandwich cake. No alcohol was served either then or at lunch, or at 'late dinner'—the latter being a meal in which I did not participate. My father was not an absolute teetotaller, although, apart from a rather unsuccessful attempt to get him to drink stout medicinally after an illness, I cannot recall him drinking anything other than perhaps a glass of sherry at a reception. But he had a deep distrust of alcohol and distaste for drunkenness. He believed that drink had prejudiced many earlier Irish attempts to achieve independence of Britain. As a result the only alcohol—apart from that medicinal Guinness—that I ever saw in the house was a solitary bottle of Benedictine kept in the pantry off the dining-room 'in case a visitor came,' i.e. a visitor with the temerity to ask for a drink. I don't recall the bottle ever being broached. But the absence of alcohol never seemed to constrain the spirits of our guests of all ages, and I saw no signs of any acute sense of deprivation, not even among my elder brothers' university friends.

As each summer drew to an end and the evenings, and later the afternoons, grew shorter, the house itself came into its own. Drawing-room and dining-room, and for smaller groups the study, were centres of discussion, debate, and anecdote—the last being the only part I was old enough to enjoy. Sometimes in the evenings there were charades in the drawing-room, in which I was able, and more than willing, to participate, the house being ransacked for dressing-up materials and props. But winter, except for some weekends and, of course, Christmas, was on the whole a quieter time—that is if you ignored the sound of the family typewriters, for my parents both typed, as did some of my brothers; there were six typewriters in all.

Visits by relatives were not one-way traffic. While my first visit to my London aunts and uncles was in 1936, when I was ten, my parents and my elder brothers had always been regular visitors there either on trips to London or passing through London to and from the Continent. My brothers and I also stayed frequently with our relations in Belfast, and I particularly remember my father bringing me to Stormont and the shipyard when we were in Belfast after my grandmother's death. My only other journey outside the Dublin area during my early childhood was a summer holiday spent with my parents and Fergus at Derrynane in Co. Kerry shortly after the change of government in 1932.

My first holiday in London was an occasion for visiting all the traditional places, as well as some others in which my parents had a particular interest. With my mother I went to Ely Place to see the Mitre Inn with its cherry-tree beam, and I remember her telling me of its rural licensing hours as part of the County of Ely and its gates that were shut at night. My father took me to Westminster, wondering whether as a former MP from 1918 to 1922—abstentionist—he had any special rights there. Fergus initiated me into travelling underground for a penny from South Kensington to Gloucester Road via Charing Cross, Oxford Circus, and Notting Hill Gate.

Fergus's own travel ambitions extended far beyond London. At the end of the previous year, when my father was in the United States, he had run away from home for no apparent reason. His objective, he had confided in some sceptical school friends, was to join our allegedly rich Uncle Johnnie—my father's eldest brother—in Brazil. He had got as far as Stratford-upon-Avon, which he wanted to see before stowing away for South America, when the police found him, as a result of his decision to contact Ann Bodkin en route. Ann was a daughter of my parents' friend Professor Tom Bodkin, who had recently brought his family to live in Birmingham when he had become Director of the Barber Institute of Fine Arts there, and she felt in duty bound to tell her parents she had met Fergus, since she knew how worried my mother would be. The police lodged Fergus temporarily in a poorhouse, the inmates of which were apparently edified to find a schoolboy in the otherwise empty Casuals Ward reading the *Aeneid* in Latin aloud to himself. He was collected there by his two elder brothers, sent over to find him. Ann Bodkin was so upset by what she considered her betrayal of Fergus that she felt unable ever again to communicate with him, as I discovered almost fifty years later when I met her after Fergus's death.

As for Uncle Johnnie, that story reached its dénouement in 1963 when Fergus, on a journey to Brazil, visited his house in the countryside outside Rio de Janeiro. Johnnie, now dead, had married for a second time when in his late eighties, so that there would be 'someone to look after me in my old age,' as he had written to my mother. Fergus met his widow, a Brazilian peasant who had never heard of Ireland and thought our uncle was a German. The house showed no sign of wealth and was in bad condition, the only relic of Johnnie being a photograph on the wall of my father as Minister for External Affairs of the Irish Free State. In the village was a chapel that my uncle had built years earlier, dedicated to St Patrick in memory of his father. When the parish priest had refused to use the chapel, Johnnie had gone to the parish church and chased the priest and parishioners out of it with the aid of some shots from a revolver.

The year that Fergus ran away was also the year I spent at Ring College in Co. Waterford learning to speak Irish. The school at that time had about eighty pupils, boys and girls. There were no concessions to comfort—perhaps there never are at boarding school. Nevertheless I enjoyed it, although I found it hard to cope with the discipline. Fergus, who, like my elder brothers, had spent a year there, had warned me that when physically punished I must never show signs of my distress lest the other boys laugh at me. So on the first of many occasions when I had to queue up after supper for punishment by the headmaster, An Fear Mór—'the Big Man'—as he was known (father of Colm Ó hEocha, the President of UCG, who was to be chairman of the New Ireland Forum in 1983–84), I held back the tears, nobly as I thought. My reward was to be jeered at by the other boys on my way up to the dormitory for receiving what they assumed, from my lack of apparent emotion, to have been favoured treatment!

I learnt to speak fluent Irish that year, which subsequently, with the help of three Easter holidays in Ring, enabled me to coast through secondary school without making any special effort with the language. Ring, however, did not equip me with the vocabulary to cope later in life through Irish with issues like economics and politics.

I would not have accepted with good grace the period at boarding school if it had been scheduled to last more than a year. Day school suited me better, and I believe I benefited greatly from the stimulus of life at home with my parents during the years of my secondary education. I was launched into this phase of my life in the summer of 1936 when my mother brought me to be interviewed by Fr Coyle, the prefect of studies at Belvedere College, the Jesuit school on the north side of Dublin. He contented himself with a couple of rather unprobing questions before allocating me at the age of ten to the first division of first year in the senior school. There I found myself in a class where most of the boys were two years older than I. This kept me on my toes through-out the whole of my secondary schooling, which began that September.

In July 1936 an event had occurred that for the first time forced me to formulate, and then to rethink, my attitude on a foreign policy issue. The civil war had begun in Spain. My immediate instinct was to side with the Spanish government; this probably reflected an instinctive analogy with the situation in Ireland after the Treaty. Within a few days, however, I discovered that my parents, influenced by the failure of the Spanish government to protect churches, convents, priests and nuns from attack in the previous months, supported Franco. Out of loyalty to them I changed my position forthwith, but Fergus and Pierce supported the Spanish government throughout the war. Our family was thus divided on the question, as were so many others—although not as deeply, of course, as my parents had been divided by our own civil war thirteen years earlier.

We now underwent the traumatic experience of moving from Fairy Hill. The house had been well beyond our means since my father had lost his

Ministerial salary in 1932. After 1935, as Visiting Professor of Philosophy at Notre Dame University in America, he was able to eke out his Dáil pay, but long absences abroad put his Dáil seat in jeopardy: he was in fact to lose it in the 1937 general election. For a year after that he had no parliamentary pay at all until his election to the Seanad established under the new Constitution. The introduction of Ministerial pensions in 1938 also helped, but meanwhile we had moved to a house in Blackrock that we rented from Mrs Mitchell, mother of Charles Mitchell, the future chief newsreader of RTE. When my mother and I went to inspect the house Mrs Mitchell explained the presence of a motorbike on the bed of one of her sons (whether Charles or Alec I cannot recall): the young man apparently kept it beside him to prevent his mother from selling it.

My eldest brother, Dem, had got married around the time that we moved from Fairy Hill, but my two other brothers remained at home for a further five years, and their friends, together with my parents' friends, continued to come to frequent parties, although these were a lot less lavish than previously, as money was in much shorter supply.

The move to Blackrock brought about an important change in my own social life. For the first time I was living in an area with other children nearby. Soon I became involved with the boys next door and their friends in the area—all of them schoolboys in nearby Blackrock College, Belvedere's great rugby rival. We formed a 'gang', and before long we were defending our patch against rivals. Our defence was impregnable and lethal—and, in retrospect, incredibly irresponsible. Ensconced behind a stone wall, wearing Ned Kelly-type helmets made from large metal sweet-containers, three of us, each aided by a loader, could keep up rapid fire from three air-guns. Fortunately some sense of responsibility returned after the leader of the rival group was hit in the lip; hostilities then ceased. The victim is now a distinguished radiographer, of whose services my family and myself have had occasion to avail ourselves more than once.

These immediate pre-war years enlarged my horizons in other ways. In 1937 I went with my mother to stay for some days with one of her brothers, back from Canada for a couple of years with his wife and daughter, at a cottage in the English Lake District. The locale of Arthur Ransome's *Swallows and Amazons*, which I had read during the previous winter, came to life before my eyes. The second half of this holiday was spent in renewing my acquaintance with London, staying once again at my aunt's house in Kensington.

In the following year I visited the Continent for the first time when my mother arranged for me to stay with a French family in Melun, south of Paris. My brother Fergus had previously taken part in an exchange with the family, which comprised Mme Camus, the widow of a distinguished doctor whose death a dozen years earlier had deprived him of a Nobel Prize for which he had been designated, and her twelve children, half of whom were married, with children of their own.

En route to France with my mother, who was travelling on to Italy, there occurred an event that was to have far-reaching consequences for my future career. I had already become interested in aviation, having been conscious enough of this new form of transport at the age of five to have been aware of, and to have remembered thereafter, the R101 airship crash. In early 1936 at Ring I had skipped lunch one day in order not to miss a minute of Cobham's Air Circus flying over neighbouring Dungarvan. Now I found myself in the Italian tourist office in Regent Street, London, as my mother bought her tickets and made her reservations. While this lengthy process was taking place a bored child of twelve was collecting from various stands the timetables of the leading European airlines, to which I later added a copy of Cook's Continental railway timetable. In subsequent years these timetables (which, half a century later, I still have) became my most treasured possessions. While Europe was torn by war in the early 1940s much of my class time was secretly spent working out, for example, the shortest route from Narvik to Malta by rail or air—ignoring the fact that most of the airlines concerned had disappeared, and that many of the routes I was tracing ran across various battle lines. So was born the interest in air transport that led me in 1947 to join Aer Lingus, where I remained for the first twelve years of my working life.

But to return to my French exchange: on the afternoon of 8 July 1938 Mother handed me over to one of Mme Camus's daughters-in-law, who, after a brief stop at her flat in Place Vauban, drove me with her family to the house known as Le Bercail—'the sheep-pen'—near Melun.

At that stage of my life, despite my father's interest in French literature and philosophy, despite having studied French briefly at St Brigid's in Bray, and despite two years of quite good French teaching at Belvedere, I had no fluency whatever in the language. At the same time I had a strong predisposition in favour of France and things French, deriving from my father's francophilia. It was thus without any basic linguistic competence but with considerable good will that I faced the task of finding my feet in the unfamiliar atmosphere of a (very!) extended French family. For by the time I arrived at Le Bercail Mme Camus's married children had between them produced sixteen grandchildren. At any given time during that summer a fair proportion of them were staying in the house; on one occasion I recall that, including friends of the family, forty-five people sat down to lunch. In age I fell between the two generations, being a year younger than Mme Camus's youngest daughter, Marie-Paule, and two years older than her eldest granddaughter, Claude, both of whom soon became close friends of mine.

There was an extensive garden with a wood and a stagnant pool, into whose murky and strong-smelling depths I fell when I overbalanced on a home-made raft. We shot birds with air-guns—birds that at home would not have been regarded as fair game. And we drove to neighbouring houses owned by married children or friends of the family, fishing in their ponds for perch and carp. There were visits to Paris to see the sights and to shop. The same pattern was repeated when I went back to Melun in 1939, although that year I guessed as I returned home, on the day of the announcement of the Nazi-Soviet Pact, which cleared the way for the invasion of Poland, that there would be no third summer at Le Bercail.

But it was the quality of French family life, to which I was admitted as a privileged member, that I particularly appreciated. I was Mme Camus's 'petit lapin', accorded the same warm affection as her children enjoyed. I felt that my own family life, which had never involved so many other children, had been enlarged in an unforgettable way. The ties then established, interrupted during the war, have never been broken. Mme Camus died in the early 1960s, but as I write, almost all her twelve children (now ranging in age from their mid-sixties to their mid-eighties) and all but one of her twelve children-in-law survive, together with some two hundred descendants and descendants' spouses.

I was happy in Belvedere, and well adjusted, but not—as some of my schoolfellows will attest—very deeply involved. My emotions were engaged by my own family, and by my second family, that of Mme Camus, and I did not, as some children do, feel the need to overidentify with my school. Nevertheless I was happy there, stimulated by the teaching, which on the whole was good, and by competition from my older classmates, which ensured that I never obtained first place and rarely even one of the first four. Maths—as distinct from arithmetic—I found increasingly difficult. Manifest absurdities like the square root of minus one I could not tolerate, no matter how 'useful' I was told this fiction could be. Nor could I accept as reasonable the proposition that dividing a figure by nought produced infinity, for, as I painstakingly and unavailingly sought to explain to my maths master, dividing something by nothing must be the same as not dividing it by anything, and that—triumphantly!—must leave the figure in question unchanged.

Religion and politics exercised me, however. My resistance on the grounds of orthodoxy to a history teacher's proposition that Savonarola was a saint—how could he be, I asked, since the Pope had ordered him to be burnt at the stake?—got short shrift. I was put outside the classroom door and found there by my old friend Fr Coyle, prefect of studies, who, ignoring my protests, made me suffer the martyrdom of six strokes of his leather strap as a reward for my stubborn orthodoxy.

In one respect, however, I was heterodox. By the age of fifteen I had come to the conclusion, to which I have since adhered, that the disciplinary decision of the Council of Trent about the invalidity—as indistinct from the illicitness—of a 'clandestine' marriage, i.e. one not before a priest (or, in modern terms, a civil or registry office ceremony), was theologically unsound.

Even before the war began I was campaigning in the school-yard against the Nazi persecution of both Christians and Jews, using as my weapon Pius XI's powerful and now largely forgotten encyclical *Mit Brennender Sorge* ('with burning concern') and other anti-Nazi material. Resistance to my campaign came from boys who simplistically assumed that if the British were against them the Germans must be right. This issue became a dominant theme when we resumed school in 1939, a couple of days after the outbreak of war. Like my parents I was passionately pro-Allied; unlike them I had no time for neutrality, failing to appreciate their concern that our participation in the European war on the Allied side might, without greatly helping the Allied cause, precipitate a renewal with German help of the Civil War that a mere sixteen years earlier had divided them and the country so deeply.

With a couple of exceptions, such as the French master, the lay teachers who taught me were anti-British and accordingly appeared pro-German, as did a number of the 'scholastics'—those preparing for the priesthood; but only one of the actual priests, one of two Germans, was not a supporter of the Allied cause.

The Treaty and the Civil War also loomed large as subjects of controversy. I fought this issue endlessly, neither converting nor being converted. Later, in fifth year, my efforts in this and other political areas attracted the attention of a scholastic, Ronnie Burke-Savage, then in charge of one of the school debating societies. He suggested to me that at some stage I should envisage a political career, and to my recollection (but not to his!) suggested that I should aim at becoming Taoiseach. Whichever of us is right on that point, I had already felt vaguely that my career should have a political dimension, and this latent interest was now activated; thereafter I never entirely lost an ultimate political ambition.

I valued the absence of pressure in relation to sport at Belvedere, for I was aware that many schools made a fetish of it and that elsewhere I could have found myself isolated by my lack of athletic skills or interest in participating in organised games. I was unenthusiastic about the common practice of prayers for success in schools rugby; it seemed to me that prayers of intercession in such an area were either ineffective and therefore a waste of time or, if effective, unfair and unsporting. In this as in other areas of religious activity where I challenged the Jesuits they ignored my theological representations but did not seem to resent my individualistic views.

Tolerance, indeed, was a feature of the school. While discipline could frequently be painful, and inevitably from time to time unfair, it was not intrusive. On the whole, and within the reasonable limits required by the running of an institution containing six hundred boys, we were allowed to follow our own inclinations. The boys too were tolerant of one another: there was no bullying. And no furtive sexuality that I ever came across.

With their usual percipience, and despite my general orthodoxy and commitment to my religion, the Jesuits divined that I was not priest material, and refrained from ever approaching me on that subject. Although I was by this time fairly responsible, and on the whole supportive of authority, they also decided that I was not prefect material either. I was content to remain thus unrecognised by authority, having little ambition for school office.

It was towards the end of my school career that I developed, under the inspiration of Professor Tom Bodkin's brother Fr Matthew Bodkin, an interest in history. By contrast I never had any command of, or interest in, Greek, nor was I very comfortable with Latin. Science I did not study: a choice had to be made between Greek and science, and my parents chose Greek for me. I was moderately interested in English—although rather more in the grammar and syntax than in the literature—and I liked and, for reasons already mentioned, was good at French, in which I later calculated that I secured sixth place in Ireland amongst boys in the Leaving Certificate examination, the nearest I came to any kind of distinction in that national test.

During these later years at school we lived closer to town than we had done during most of my childhood. After the war started Mrs Mitchell, who normally travelled a good deal, wanted to return to Blackrock, and my parents therefore rented at £120 a year for the greater part of the war a large house in Temple Road, Rathmines, near where I now live. We were only the third Catholic family to come to live on the road, which until the 1930s had been an exclusively Protestant upper middle-class area, but we were made welcome by most of our neighbours, who did not seem to resent our presence even when I and my friends took advantage of the table-like surface of the roadway to organise roller-skating hockey during the virtually carless later years of the war.

Very shortly after our arrival in the house I answered the doorbell one day to an Englishman who asked to see my father. I discovered afterwards that he was the Marquess of Tavistock, later Duke of Bedford, who in pursuit of a peace mission had been told by a Northern family connection to contact my father as a possible channel to the German Minister, Eduard Hempel. It would have been difficult to find a less suitable channel for this purpose, given my father's views on the Nazis. However, my father must have put him in touch with someone else who could help him, for, as history relates, some kind of contact was eventually made, to the considerable embarrassment of some members of the British government, such as Lord Halifax, whose names were later brought into the affair.

Family life became quieter in this house, partly because my parents were now in their fifties, with less energy for social activity, and partly perhaps because of the war. New friends included John Betjeman and his wife, Penelope, attached to the British Mission under Sir John Maffey, later Lord Rugby, which was established after the outbreak of the war.

The privations that marked the war years were modest by comparison with those in Britain or Continental countries, involving rationing of clothing and of foodstuffs like butter, bread, sugar, and tea, but not of meat or sweets—items that in Britain continued to be rationed well into the 1950s. Petrol was in short supply in the later years of the war: as I recall it, only doctors, diplomats, Ministers and key civil servants qualified for petrol coupons, and this had profound social effects, putting almost everyone on an equal footing so far as mobility was concerned. It also involved a late revival of the horse as an agent of transport on a limited scale.

German aircraft dropped occasional bombs—all of which I slept through—and at breakfast one morning a dog-fight took place between British and

German aircraft, the sequence of which boys from different parts of the city pieced together by comparing notes later that morning in the school-yard. The Irish papers were censored rigorously, but we took the *Daily Mail* and, of course, had access to the air waves, and in particular to the BBC, and to Vichy, Brazzaville and, from the end of 1942, Algiers, thus helping to preserve the spoken French that I had acquired with the Camus family. Occasionally the voices of William Joyce ('Lord Hawhaw') and Ezra Pound were heard from Germany and Italy, but my father disliked listening to Axis radio stations and was so deeply upset that his old friend Ezra Pound should be spewing out anti-Semitic and pro-Axis propaganda that these broadcasts were quickly banned in the home. My absorption with the war was almost total, as is evidenced by the many scores of war maps that I drew—badly, but in accurate detail—and which survive.

In June 1940 my brother Fergus, then finishing his second year at UCD, together with most of his friends joined the army, the ranks of which swelled to almost 50,000. Insofar as the Civil War had up to then been a divisive element in Irish life, the coming together in the army in 1940 of the sons of the leaders of the national movement finally healed that division. With Vivion de Valera and Liam Cosgrave, Eoin Ryan and Fergus FitzGerald serving side by side in the army that seventeen years earlier had defeated the republicans in the Civil War, and with the leaders of the Fianna Fáil government and the Fine Gael opposition sitting together on the wartime advisory body, the Defence Council, where both were equally concerned to preserve formal Irish neutrality while supporting the Allied cause in many most unneutral ways, the Civil War episode was clearly closed.

In January 1942, although not yet sixteen, I joined the LDF, the part-time military organisation that attracted in all some 100,000 volunteers. Advised by Fergus that by joining a signals battalion I would learn Morse code, which, he said, would be useful to me later in life—it never was—and preferring sedentary to ambulant service (I have always disliked standing), I went to the recruitment sergeant of the 6th Communications Battalion in Parnell Square, a couple of hundred yards from school. I naturally hoped to bluff the question of age, and was disconcerted when the sergeant said, 'Garret, you needn't try to fool me about your age: I was one of your father's guards at Fairy Hill. But you can join anyway.'

The LDF was a broadening experience. I had never been much exposed to four-letter words before, certainly not at home and not at school, and it was something of a culture shock to have to disentangle and make sense of the words that occasionally intervened between these expletives.

Going to Gormanston training camp in summer involved a further educational process. Our captain assembled us before we left and delivered a talk in terms so guarded that I and my sergeant, Pádraic Mulcahy (a son of my father's former colleague in government, Gen. Richard Mulcahy, soon to succeed W. T. Cosgrave as leader of Fine Gael), were totally mystified. One allusion in his speech seemed to suggest that a health risk attached to cows, which, pre-sumably, we would come across in rural Gormanston; but having had experience of cows as a child I found this unconvincing. Later on, when I learnt of the existence of VD, I realised what the enigmatic health warning had been about; and indeed at Gormanston there were a number of female camp-followers.

In April 1942 Fergus had married his fiancée, Una. My father's own early marriage at about the same age, and with even less means, did not make him tolerant of sons following his example, as I was to find in my turn a few years later. Fergus's marriage was all the more disapproved of because it encouraged our elder brother, Pierce, to follow suit two months later at, for our family, the advanced age of twenty-eight but, like Fergus, with very limited means.

Pierce's honeymoon coincided with the temporary arrival of something like a menagerie at our house. My mother, who disliked animals, had felt con-strained, as during the First World War, to keep hens in order to ensure a supply of eggs—although with less drastic consequences on this occasion. A cat was also introduced to deal with a mouse problem, and I decided I wanted to keep a guinea-pig. (When I asked my father what I should call my new pet he suggested 'Ezra Pound', and when I pointed out that the guinea-pig was a female he countered with 'Mrs Ezra Pound', which I accepted.) My mother's dislike of animals received its come-uppance when to this collection were added simultaneously a hedgehog, which my father and I had found on the road, a second cat, which arrived to have kittens on top of our coal, and a shi-tzu or Tibetan lion-hound, which Pierce had acquired and left with us when he went away on his honeymoon to Glengarriff.

I should have left school in 1942, having passed the Leaving Certificate and NUI matriculation examinations in June of that year; but Fr Coyle's decision to put me into the secondary part of the school at the age of ten at last caught up with me. I was too young to enter UCD. And, of course, the war made it impossible for me to follow my brothers' example by going to school in Switzerland for two years between secondary school and university.

My mother's solution was to enter me for Trinity College, Dublin, which was less concerned than UCD about physical age. I was unenthusiastic, since my brothers had all been at UCD, but I went along with my mother's idea because I wanted to leave school. In the event nothing came of it. In those days Catholics were supposed to obtain the permission of the Archbishop of Dublin before entering Trinity. My father was too orthodox a Catholic to let me go there without this permission, but after initially agreeing to apply for it he changed his mind. For several years previously he had been a member of an ecumenical group called the Mercier Society, which had recently been the subject of an archiepiscopal ban. My father felt hurt that his efforts and those of his friends to bring Catholics and Protestants together had been impugned and that his own orthodoxy had somehow been called into question. In the end he was simply not disposed to seek a dispensation from the archbishop allowing me to go to Trinity.

I therefore went back to Belvedere for another year, an arrangement that involved joining with the new sixth-year pupils for most purposes but also studying Thomistic philosophy—an experience that I enjoyed and about which my father, given his deep interest in the subject, was naturally pleased. In the light of later events it is perhaps worth recording that amongst the seventh-year boys who had shared my sixth-year class was Dermot Ryan, and amongst the sixth-year boys whose class I shared when I was in seventh year was Des Connell: both later to become Archbishop of Dublin.

I was disappointed, however, about having to postpone entry to UCD for twelve months, all the more so because I knew that the girl whom at the age of eight I had decided I might marry was entering the college that year. But my schooldays were coming to an end nonetheless, and university loomed ahead. My mother decided that I should sit for the UCD entrance scholarship examination in modern languages, although there was nothing in my school career to suggest that this would be other than a waste of time. English, Irish, French and history were the chosen subjects. Mother decided to coach me in English herself, which she did with such success that, having been about 1,500th in Ireland in that subject in the Leaving Certificate examination, I secured first place in it in the scholarship a few months later.

As a result, to my astonishment I secured second place in the modern language group, which ensured that the financial pressure of my college career on my parents was relieved by a £100 scholarship. After a year of fairly spectacular idleness, again to my astonishment and almost irritation, in my first-year arts exam I secured a first honour in history, an exam I sat on the day after the distracting news of the invasion of Normandy. This was an honours subject that I had taken as an extra and in which I had done virtually no work—none at all in Irish history during the previous six weeks. (Incidentally, two other history firsts in that exam were Des Connell, now Archbishop of Dublin, and Declan Costello, later Attorney General in the Government in which I was Minister for Foreign Affairs.) This result determined my future course of action: I chose French and history as my main honours degree subjects, keeping Spanish as an extra.

History became my favourite subject. Our Professor of Modern History, John Marcus O'Sullivan, was a distinguished scholar who had been a colleague of my father's in government as Minister for Education from 1925 to 1932. His lectures were entertaining and stimulating: he had a certain nostalgic affection for the Austro-Hungarian Empire and disapproved of such name changes as that of Lemberg in Poland to Lwów, which he pronounced dismissively as if it were the bark of a small dog. He also had what I can only describe as a constitutional aversion to consonants. I still recall trying to discover the name of an Austrian statesman that he pronounced as O-a-u; I tracked it down eventually as Kollaruth.

The lecturer in modern Irish history was Robin Dudley Edwards, who had been taught history by my mother in Louise Gavan Duffy's Scoil Bhríde in

1917 and who, having lectured to Joan and myself in the 1940s, was my son John's professor when he took history for his degree a quarter of a century later. The UCD Archive, which he established towards the end of his career, contains my father's papers and my own, as well as those of many of my father's contemporaries. The reappraisal of Irish history that, together with Theo Moody of Trinity, he initiated made a major contribution to the development of more rational and objective attitudes towards the Northern Ireland problem and Anglo-Irish relations. 'Dudley', as he was known to so many generations of Irish students over half a century, had a slightly malicious sense of humour, which he was never inhibited from employing to take people down a peg or two. An ability to cope with this phenomenon was for history students over many decades a prerequisite for survival. He died while I was writing this book. One of his last engagements had been to attend the handing over of my father's papers to the UCD Archive; typically, he heckled my remarks on that occasion.

The Professor of Mediaeval History was also outstanding: Fr Aubrey Gwynn SJ, who came from a famous academic family associated with Trinity College. From him I gained a lasting interest in the Middle Ages and in particular in the continuities and discontinuities of European history between the Roman Empire and the modern age.

While I enjoyed work at college it certainly did not absorb much of my energy. I joined a large number of societies and concentrated on helping with the teas, having observed at an early stage that the preparations for these festivities, which followed language society meetings in particular, were under-taken by girls. Boys—oddly, I thought, having been brought up in a family of boys where all had to help with meals—regarded this part of a society's activities as beneath their dignity. I felt the loss was theirs, especially since after seven years at a single-sex secondary school the major attraction of university life, it seemed to me, was the company of girls. Before long I featured in the college magazine with the comment: 'Among the girls present was Sir Garret FitzGerald Bart.—and there he remained.'

I was particularly involved with the French Society, of which, indeed, I became secretary. In that position I had the opportunity to set the rules for a competition for a substantial cup presented by the French Ambassador in 1944, whether on behalf of Marshal Pétain or General de Gaulle I was not clear at that particular juncture. I naturally determined that the competition would be in oral French, and won it with a series of imitations, the accuracy of which few present were able to verify, of speeches in French by De Gaulle, Pétain, Laval, and Churchill.

I also joined the main debating societies: the Law Society, the Commerce Society, and, the most prestigious, the Literary and Historical Debating Society, or L and H, where I was able to carry on my pro-Allied crusade in an atmo-sphere of some hostility, for, as at school, the more vocal elements tended to be anti-British and consequently vaguely pro-German. My interest in statistics must already have been evident. When I rose to speak, Niall St John McCarthy, now a Supreme Court judge, used to heckle me with, 'Garret, say a statistic!'

I was not the only student of that period who later became involved in politics. Declan Costello, son of John A. Costello, who had been Attorney General in the government of which my father had been a member in the 1920s and was soon to be Taoiseach, was a friend, although his activities were centred in a law group. Charles J. Haughey was a contemporary whom I knew reasonably well, as in first year we studied several subjects together. Already he was moving in Fianna Fáil circles. I used to meet him with, inter alia, Harry Boland, Colm Traynor, and Peadar Ward, all sons of Fianna Fáil Ministers. His college centre of gravity seemed to be the Students' Representative Council and the Commerce Society; by contrast, mine was rather the L and H and the Law Society.

An element of student life in that period was the formal dance, most commonly in the Gresham Hotel and organised by the past pupils of a secondary school or by a charity, which included dinner during the evening. White tie and tails were appropriate for these occasions, with black tie for the five-shilling dinnerless Saturday night dances. Over forty years later President Reagan, at the end of his state visit to Ireland, allowed himself a moment of personal reminiscence, recalling how when he had been in Dublin as a fraternal delegate to a trade union conference shortly after the war he peered through the door of the Gresham ballroom one evening and had seen the men in white tie and tails and, he said, the girls in white dresses (only a minority in fact wore white) gliding across the floor. This, perhaps the only genuinely personal note struck on his official journey, was the one comment of President Reagan's that went unreported by the press. It was the one with which I could most readily identify.

A feature of these dances was that many of us travelled to and from them by bicycle, often with a girl on the crossbar, her ball gown packed away in a carrier-basket: it was necessary for girls to change at the dance if they were to have a safe bicycle journey home in a shorter skirt. Other forms of transport might be used. Joan recalls an evening when, emerging from the Gresham, she saw three young men about to take off by horse-cab: her next morning's nine o'clock lecturer, the future Senator Alexis FitzGerald, astride the horse, and the future Chief Justice, Tom O'Higgins, with Tom Crotty, a future county registrar, on top of the vehicle.

My partner at a number of these formal dances was Una Tierney, with whom I had been at school in Bray years before and in whom I had retained a romantic interest since the age of eight. Her home in Shankill was too far out for evening dances so she based herself at her grandparents' house in Upper Leeson Street. There I used to collect her, being received by her grandparents, Eoin MacNeill, Emeritus Professor of Ancient Irish History at UCD and a founder both of the Gaelic League in 1893 and of the Irish Volunteers in 1913, and his wife, Agnes. He too had been a member of the first government with my father, until his resignation after the Boundary Commission debacle in 1925.

These college years were spent against the ever-present background of the war. A diary for the summer of 1944 records hours spent listening to the radio as Rome was liberated and Normandy invaded. On 25 August there came the final stage of the liberation of Paris: by a happy chance, at 12.15 I picked up the underground radio station in Paris and was able to follow events throughout the day, culminating in de Gaulle's arrival at the Hotel de Ville in the evening. My devotion to the radio was such, indeed, that my parents sold it in March 1945 to remove what they considered a distraction from my studies.

Meanwhile I had met Joan O'Farrell; to be precise, I had met her on 25 November 1943 at a meeting of the French Society in the Music Room of 86 St Stephen's Green, formerly part of John Henry Newman's Catholic University and in our time the Student Union building. After the meeting I got talking to her and to an architectural student, and finding that neither of them had ever played three-handed auction bridge (which I had learnt as a small child with Miss Cuddy and Fergus) I instructed them in this art on top of the harmonium. Joan, then in her third year, was not impressed by this brash first-year student, and, except on a picnic the following April, our paths scarcely crossed again until the following summer, when we met several times at Sunday night informal dances or 'hops' in Belfield, then a student sports centre but today the centre of the college itself. As I recorded naïvely in a diary that I was keeping at the time, 'she was terribly nice and very helpful—lots of tips etc., but not in a condescending way.' (I was, and remained, a rotten dancer.)

Following a further picnic encounter (my diary recorded that 'she is very witty in a nice quiet way') I developed the habit of dropping in to see her in the Student Union building. She used to study there, with one or two other girls, for her September BA exam in the room where James Joyce had attended L and H meetings forty years earlier. By mid-July I was lending her an English history and had prepared for her a genealogical table to illustrate the War of the Spanish Succession.

For a long time the relationship remained casual. She had her own friends, all a good deal older than I, and I was conscious of being a fairly juvenile eighteen. Most of my companions were from my own year or were second-year students whom I had met through school contemporaries who had gone to college a year before me. Although by the autumn Joan and I were going to the cinema quite a lot with mutual friends, we both continued to circulate in our own sets: she had a number of boy-friends, and I had many other interests too, including Una Tierney.

It gradually became clear to me, however, that Una's interest was otherwise engaged. (In the event she married very happily shortly after leaving college, but tragically died in 1956 while still a young mother.) For my part, by the spring of 1945 I had begun to refocus my attention and to take the whole question more seriously. When on 7 May the news of the German surrender was broadcast it was Joan whom I rang to join me for the celebration, and we spent that dramatic—and, in Dublin, somewhat violent—evening together, with a large group of friends.

Ten days later I made up my mind that I wanted to marry Joan. She was quite entertained by this proposition, but did not take it too seriously; a proposal by a nineteen-year-old second-year student who had hitherto shown an interest in many different girls, with a long-standing predilection until quite recently for one in particular, must have seemed a bit frivolous. At the same time she was clearly fond of me and spent much of the following summer in my company. These were strenuous months for me as my determination grew in the face of her good-humoured resistance to my offer of marriage.

That she was not irrevocably opposed to the idea became clear one day when we were having tea together in the café of the Grafton Cinema. For the first time she told me her own history. Her mother and aunts had grown up in what is often described as 'straitened circumstances' following the death of their father, a Dublin brewery-owner whose tribulations in business left his family virtually penniless. After the Great War her mother married Charles O'Farrell, a colonial civil servant from an east Galway family who suffered a mental breakdown when Joan was a small child. When he recovered he took his wife and children to live in Sussex, where he broke down again. He tried to drown his son and to kill his wife: Joan, aged only five, had to run for help to save them. He was thereafter confined in a mental hospital, and Joan, her mother and brother went to live in Geneva with an aunt, an economist at the League of Nations who was also her godmother. They all returned to Ireland in 1933, and in due course, with her godmother's help, Joan was able to go to college.

Having told me this story, Joan explained that she was uncertain about the cause of her father's illness. It might have been a consequence of living in west Africa, or it might have been congenital. She was therefore uncertain whether she should marry and have children.

Ill-equipped though I was at that age to face a problem of this kind, it deepened my love for Joan, and during the remaining months of that summer I pursued my suit with determination in a manner that gradually broke down her double reticence to commit herself: her reticence about her own possible inheritance, and her reticence about my youth and immaturity. Early in September she conceded; six weeks later we fixed the date of our marriage two years on—10 October 1947—forgetting even to check what day of the week that would be. (It turned out to be a Friday—an awkward day for catering because of the Friday abstinence then in force for Catholics.)

There probably is not much point in trying to identify the reasons we fell in love; certainly I am in no position to say what moved Joan to accept my proposal. In retrospect I was not alone rather juvenile in manner and character but also somewhat full up with myself, not very sensitive to others and a good deal of a prig (some would say that I never entirely lost these characteristics!). For my part I can only say that Joan's warmth, vivacity and intelligence were part of the chemistry, together with the intangible element that can never be pinned down in any such relationship.

Whatever the explanation, by the autumn of 1945 we were deeply in love and very absorbed in each other; we had, indeed, become poor company for our friends, and remained so until some years after our marriage, not becoming sociable again until a good deal later. This was no problem for me, as I had never developed a bachelor-type life-style. I had never gone drinking with other men (indeed, I don't think I had ever been in a pub) and had only rarely attended sports events or other predominantly male occasions. Seven years at a single-sex school had cured me of any strong predilection for exclusively male company. On Joan's side the insecurity of her childhood probably encouraged her to establish an equally close and for a period quite exclusive relationship with me once she became convinced that she could rely on me without risking a further severe trauma in her life.

My mother had always had a shrewd idea of my romantic activities. When she saw me—uncharacteristically—devoting *all* my time, month after month, to one girl she was visibly worried. She was especially concerned about what my father would feel when he found out I was committing myself to an early marriage, especially as he had decided that he wanted me not merely to take the Bar exams but to practise as a barrister. This career was at that time con-sidered to preclude marriage for five or six years unless one had independent means, which I, of course, hadn't. Mother could not, however, prevent herself from sympathising with young love, and her concerns about a premature com-mitment were therefore balanced by a willingness even to finance our romance with occasional supplements to my pocket money. We ourselves engaged in some preliminary planning: how we might live on £350 a year if I became a third secretary in the Department of External Affairs or an administrative officer in the general civil service—or perhaps on much more exiguous amounts if I were to practise as a barrister, eking out the penurious early years with earnings from journalism or from the provision of genealogies to Irish-Americans.

While I had been so deeply engrossed in my own affairs, my parents had in fact been going through a very difficult time. In May 1944 the opposition defeated Fianna Fáil in a Dáil vote—most unwisely, as it turned out. De Valera called an election and won an overall majority. My father, who had lost his Seanad seat in 1943, stood for election to the Dáil in Co. Dublin, which had been his constituency for ten years until the party persuaded him to transfer to Carlow-Kilkenny in 1932. H. P. Dockrell, a son of the Unionist who had won the neighbouring Rathmines constituency when my father had been elected in Pembroke in the 1918 election, was also a Fine Gael candidate in Co. Dublin. A third candidate was 24-year-old Liam Cosgrave, son of W. T. Cosgrave, who had retired from the party leadership the previous year. Liam Cosgrave's nomi-nation came as a surprise, and was received with enthusiasm neither by H. P. Dockrell nor by my father. My father was not given to showing resentment, how-ever, and accepted the situation gracefully enough. My mother was less patient. Her comments were distinctly acidic, especially when Fine Gael won only one seat in Co. Dublin, and the single TD elected for the party was Liam Cosgrave.

Apart from filling envelopes in the election of 1943 and helping my father in his 1944 campaign, I myself had only one other involvement in politics during my student years. This was later in 1944 when I helped to define the party branch areas in the Dublin Townships constituency, which since 1969 has been my own constituency of Dublin South-East.

My father's political career of over thirty years thus ended at the relatively early age of fifty-six. At the same time his sister Kate, who was very dear to him and to my mother, became fatally ill with cancer. Her last eighteen months, from early 1944 to August 1945, during much of which she was in great pain, were spent with us, first in Temple Road and later in what had been Dem's flat in Donnybrook, which my parents took over when he moved to a house in Killiney early in 1945. There were also money worries. Since my father's defeat in the Seanad election of 1943 my parents' only income had been his Ministerial pension and my mother's small income from the trust fund set up by my grandfather. Moreover the chemical works in east London, for which my father had been responsible since his brother France's death in 1941, was in financial difficulties.

By a stroke of luck he found a buyer for the works during a visit to London in April 1946, and simultaneously my mother won £150 on the 'Spring Double', i.e. the Grand National and the Lincolnshire. She chose this moment to tell my father that I intended to marry Joan. In the discussion I had with him immediately afterwards he said that while he could not welcome this news he accepted it as a fait accompli, but that there could be no question of the marriage taking place for quite a number of years. It seemed better not to disclose that we had already decided on a date eighteen months hence.

At least the whole matter was now out in the open and Joan could be received, if not actually welcomed, as part of the family. My mother decided that an appropriate occasion would be in Kerry in May. With the proceeds of her racing win she had rented an island, Illaunslea, off Parknasilla, for that month. It had a house that could accommodate the whole family: my parents, my three brothers and their wives, seven young children, and Joan and myself. After we had got over the initial awkwardness inevitable on such an occasion, we found life on the island enjoyable. Journeys by boat had to be made to four different points on the mainland for the post, telephone calls, the bus service (actually a taxi), and to reach my brothers' cars on a nearby pier.

After that I settled down to a belated fourteen-hour work day for the following three months. But first I prepared the ground. Diligent analysis of past examination papers satisfied me that I needed to revise only selected topics, amounting to one-third of the history course and somewhat more in French and Spanish, in order to be able to answer fully in my finals. With the help of Joan, who prepared essay-type answers to potential questions in the various exams (she had herself taken history two years earlier), I found that I could concentrate in a specialised way on one-sixth of the history course and reduce substantially the work to be done in the two language subjects.

My results eventually validated this statistical approach. I secured a first in History and French—in the latter by virtue of a good oral exam only—and a second in Spanish.

During the following two months I applied for jobs in the civil service and in foreign airlines that were flying, or might fly, to Ireland. It may seem curious that I did not apply to Aer Lingus for a job. Dem had been appointed in 1937, at the age of twenty-five, to design the terminal at Dublin Airport, a building of some distinction. Pierce and Fergus, however, had both applied for Aer Lingus jobs much more recently and had failed, in circumstances that led them—and indeed our family—into the delusion that the company simply did not want FitzGeralds. In November, however, my French lecturer, Dr Louis Roche, pointed out to Joan—by then, after a period as a factory welfare officer, a cashier in the student restaurant in UCD—that Aer Lingus was advertising for administrative assistants. She immediately spurred me into action by sending a courier to the National Library, where I was amusing myself with desultory research. There were thirteen applicants for four places. At the interview in the Gresham Hotel I was asked a question about Pan American Airways. I recited that company's network, starting with its routes radiating from Boston, New York, and Miami, but when I reached New Orleans in my tour of the US coastline my interviewers stopped me, indicating they were satisfied that I was familiar with air transport.

I was appointed, with three others, at an annual salary of £300. We started work as administrative assistants on 13 January 1947 on the top floor of 39 Upper O'Connell Street in a room with a telephone, an electric fire, and no other furniture. We made phone calls sitting on the floor in front of the electric fire. That was the appalling winter of 1947, when Europe froze and much of it ground to a halt until the thaw came in late March.

While I was sitting my BA examination my father had developed angina, and his natural buoyancy and gaiety, already affected by the cumulation of factors I mentioned earlier, had been seriously undermined. He had therefore been in no mood to welcome my decision, a couple of months after the onset of his illness, to take up a position in Aer Lingus. He had wanted me to practise at the Bar, and attributed my acceptance of an Aer Lingus post solely to my desire to marry. He felt that I was throwing away the possibility of a distinguished career because of a frivolous romantic fancy. (None of us ever dared ask him to reconcile his precepts in this matter with his own example.)

When I went ahead with the Aer Lingus job he refused to speak to me. Given his precarious state of health at the time, this was very painful for me. I attempted to overcome his objections by calling in aid the Jesuit who at school had aroused my political ambitions, Ronnie Burke-Savage. He argued my case with my father, but to no effect. Happily, however, after a little while my father began to recognise from my enthusiasm, and from the way my work obviously stimulated me, that my interest in air transport was genuine. In mid-March 1947 he relented. Our relationship was restored, to my immense delight.

It was a timely reconciliation, for on the morning of 9 April my mother, returning to their bedroom after an early breakfast, called me frantically. He was dead of a heart attack on the floor beside his bed, at the early age of fifty-nine.

It was a devastating blow for us all, but above all for Mother. She never really recovered. In the eleven years that followed before her own death she certainly derived considerable pleasure from her children and grandchildren, but never hid from us the fact that she longed to re-join my father as soon as possible.

My brothers and I shared her terrible sense of loss. All of us had loved, admired and respected our father, and had found enormous stimulation in his company—drawing in different degrees according to our individual interests on his literary, philosophical and political talents, but all enjoying equally his company, his irrepressible sense of humour, and his extraordinary fund of anecdotes. To live up to his standards of integrity, emulate fully his patriotism and sense of public service, or replicate the combination of physical and moral courage for which he was so highly regarded by many of his contemporaries, would be impossible; but at least these qualities gave us something to which to aspire.

Lest this seem unduly hagiographical it should be added that there were other sides to his character also. He never succeeded—indeed I do not think he even seriously tried—to be objective about the 1921 Treaty, or the Civil War or its aftermath. While capable of warm friendship with people who had differed politically from him at that time, he never lost his bitterness about those events, and, like many of his contemporaries, was often reluctant to accept the good faith of some of the major political figures on the other side, tending to ascribe base motives to people who at worst may have had mixed motivations and many of whom had in fact acted with the same good faith as himself. He had little sympathy with, or understanding of, many aspects of Irish life, and suffered neither fools nor people with less elevated cultural interests than his own very gladly.

I felt his death particularly because of my age; I had enjoyed his company for a shorter period than my brothers, and although our relationship had been fully restored a few weeks before his death, it had been clouded in the preceding year or two by his opposition to my proposed marriage and to my choice of career. I was conscious also that I had missed an opportunity to get to know him better by trying to break through his reticence about his childhood and youth, which was a characteristic of many people of his generation.

Fortunately I had Joan to console me and the prospect of marriage as well as my future career in Aer Lingus to distract me. The Aer Lingus appointment had made it possible for us to make concrete plans for a wedding on our long-chosen date of 10 October 1947—which ironically, but fortunately, fell one day outside the traditional six months' mourning period.

By August I had saved £108, which, with £40 of promised wedding cheques and two £29 salary cheques to come (our salaries had been revised to £350 a year), and allowing £13 for a dance we were committed to, left me a total of £206 for two months' pre-marriage living costs, the furniture, my wedding expenses, and our honeymoon. In the event this sum proved inadequate by a margin of £18, which I had to borrow from Joan on the honeymoon; for a number of years afterwards all attempts by me to discourage particular expenditures on her part were met by the unanswerable—but, I felt, overplayed—argument, 'It can come out of my eighteen pounds.'

It had been decided that we would live in a flat in the upper portion of Joan's mother's house. The flat contained a sitting-room cum dining-room and two bedrooms, with a kitchenette and bathroom. We could not afford water-heating and depended on Joan's mother's sitting-room back-boiler for hot water for baths and washing during the first five years of our married life. In summer when there was no fire downstairs we had to depend on kettles and pots of water heated on our ancient gas stove. Because my mother gave us a bed (which my grandfather had bought second-hand in Bath in 1913 when my parents were coming to live in Ireland), and because we received several armchairs as wedding presents, our purchases of furniture could be limited to a sitting-room carpet, a dining-room table, a couple of kitchen chairs, and, later, a dressing-table for the bedroom.

The wedding itself, at 9 a.m. in Booterstown church, was a quiet family affair, both because of my father's recent death and because of Joan's mother's very limited means. Only one photograph survives—a proof copy, because by the time we could afford to pay for the wedding photographs several years later the photographer had disappeared.

Like most men on their wedding day I was appallingly nervous, Joan, by contrast, calm and radiant. Just after we got back to the house, and as the first guest was about to arrive, the wedding cake fell off its stand to the floor, and Joan had to receive the guests without me while in the next room I struggled to put it together again. The section of the cake that is customarily retained for the first christening suffered a further disaster when, during our honeymoon, it was eaten by mice.

We had originally planned to go to France, but when the time came this proved financially impossible. We switched to London, and the journey there was our first experience of air travel. Joan's godmother had rented a service flat for us in Bayswater. We benefited financially—if not gastronomically—from the postwar regulations that controlled meal prices in England. We were able to eat in places like the Savoy and Simpson's for sums of under £1 for the two of us—although in Simpson's we found that even arriving as early as 12.30 for lunch the chicken we had come for was already 'off' the menu.

To be truthful, London was a fairly depressing sight: so much of it destroyed and the rest dilapidated and unpainted. But there were many plays and shows to see and some pleasant outings to Hampton Court and to Epping Forest, to retrace a walk with my father eleven years earlier. Nevertheless, partly for financial reasons, we came home sooner than we had intended.

# CHAPTER TWO

# ALL ROADS LEAD TO POLITICS

Back in Aer Lingus after our honeymoon I set about inventing my work. As nobody quite knew what a research and analysis officer in an airline sales department was meant to do, some inventiveness was needed.

I set about estimating traffic flows, drawing up timetables, assessing the economic viability of routes, and so on. Of course there were other people in head office doing these things, but they did not seem to me, with the hubris of youth, to be doing them well enough, so I decided to try my hand, oblivious in my youthful naïveté of the tensions that this would create. Although no-one had asked for them, I prepared traffic estimates for our new transatlantic air route, due to start the following spring. I estimated that 8,500 passengers would fly on this service during its first twelve months, and that it would lose £1 million in that year. As the company had bought five 58-seat Constellation aircraft, any two of which would have provided a daily service with 42,000 seats a year, my forecast was not well received. A couple of months later a new Government, led by Fine Gael, cancelled the transatlantic service. I had nothing whatever to do with this decision. I had not communicated my doubts about the viability of the transatlantic route to anyone outside Aer Lingus; but the fact that I had a Fine Gael background probably did not help me in the company just then.

I also estimated that a direct Constellation service to Rome, to be started in December 1947, would have 92 per cent of its seats empty in the first two months, which turned out to be about right. That route too was cancelled. It had been intended that the Constellations would be operated on the Dublin–London as well as on the transatlantic and Rome routes; I estimated that the use of these long-range aircraft on this short route would cost £300,000 more than servicing the route with short-haul aircraft like the DC3. With the cancellation of the transatlantic route all the Constellations were sold, and this saving was effected. I then became involved in the process of arranging for the substitution of the much smaller DC3s on the London route.

The truth was that the company was going through a very bad patch. The Government had instructed it to buy not only Constellations but fuel-hungry Vickers Viking aircraft, and had instructed it also to open certain routes, not just that across the Atlantic, without any adequate research. Some 1,500 more staff than were needed had also been recruited as part of this ill-considered expansion. The subsequent contraction of fleet routes and personnel was painful.

By mid-1948 the company was again in good shape, however, and I had become fully involved, although still in a somewhat irregular manner, with the planning process. By 1949 I had persuaded the management to introduce mid-week fares to spread traffic demand through the week. These proved immensely successful: up to half the passengers switched their day of travel on some routes for fare differentials of between 60p and 90p. In 1950 I secured agreement on the introduction of special cheap fares during the busy summer months on the Dublin–London early morning and late night flights, or 'Dawnflights' and 'Starflights' as we called them. New routes were also being considered on the basis of my research into traffic volumes: we opened services from Dublin to Birmingham and Jersey in 1949, and planned others to be brought into operation to Edinburgh, Bristol and Cardiff in the early 1950s.

Our first child, John, was born on 27 October 1949. Like many young parents we soon wondered how on earth we had put in our time before the event. Both of us were well adapted to parenthood. Joan had intuitive good judgement in relation to many problems that arise in bringing up children, including an instinct for medical matters; there was no need for Dr Spock. And John was from the first an easy child. Then and thereafter parenthood was a joy.

Just before his birth I had been promoted, unannounced, to superintendent rank, and when this was finally made public in April 1950 the company transferred me to head office in O'Connell Street to carry on my planning work from a more central location. It took several years more for me to win acknowledgement that I was not just a back-room adviser but that my work was in fact managerial. Finally, in 1957, when my employers learnt that I was so frustrated by their reluctance to concede the point that I was thinking of taking on the editorship of a proposed liberal Catholic journal (which in fact never appeared), they caved in and appointed me commercial research and schedules planning manager. Perhaps the length of my title reflected their mild irritation at my persistence in demanding such recognition.

The company's general manager through my whole period on its staff was Jerry Dempsey, who was enormously liked and respected by the staff, a kind of father figure who inspired loyalty and affection. He managed a difficult team with great skill. In the immediate postwar years, with the rapid development of air transport technology, he needed the most competent people he could find to head the key commercial and technical divisions of the airline. He got them in two men in particular, each with a decade or more of experience in Imperial Airways: a stout Englishman called Max Stuart-Shaw, and a large Irishman called Jack Kelly-Rogers. They brought with them all the traditional incompatibility of the commercial and technical sides of aviation—to which was added a difference in national temperament. It made for exciting management, especially for those of us with front seats. Accompanied as they were by a number of others with external airline experience, they gave Aer Lingus a solid basis of professionalism.

As head of the Commercial Division, Stuart-Shaw was *my* boss. Impatient and peppery, he inspired terror and affection in equal measure—although not always in the same people. He was determined that Aer Lingus would be an efficiently run and highly professional commercial airline, and would brook no excuse for sloppiness or incompetence. It was the kind of leadership that the commercial side of an airline needed, and from which it still derives benefits over thirty years after his departure.

His professional instincts were so well developed that I could afford to let my imagination rip, proposing initiatives and innovations of all kinds, safe in the knowledge that he would unerringly sort out the possible from the unrealistic. Our relationship remained combative throughout, involving repeated cut-and-thrust on both sides with no holds barred, but beneath the surface there lay a deep mutual respect and affection. When, early in 1958, he left Aer Lingus, where I think he sensed that his nationality might be a barrier to reaching the top, I felt a great sense of loss. It was one reason, although not the only one, for my decision to leave the company myself a year later.

Jack Kelly-Rogers was a very different kind of person. He had piloted Churchill during the war and was understandably proud of this fact. He was less incisive than Stuart-Shaw but could be terrifying to his subordinates in his own way. He was, I felt, more the chairman of his team while Stuart-Shaw was certainly the chief of his. Whatever Stuart-Shaw's opinion of him—their relationship was a thorny one—the Technical Division that developed under Kelly-Rogers's leadership was extremely efficient and built up the high reputation for safety and punctuality that Aer Lingus quickly won in the airline world.

There were intermediate managers as well, of course, and I had many colleagues at my own more junior level. Gerry Giltrap was Kelly-Rogers's aide until he left to become Secretary to Trinity College, Dublin. Because of our fairly key positions in the Commercial and Technical divisions, Giltrap and I worked closely together, taking great care that our two bosses' attention was not unduly drawn to the fact. On his side there were several like-minded people of around the same age, such as Arthur Walls and George Bourke, now both with Guinness Peat Aviation. On my side I had Niall Gleeson, an economics MA who joined me in 1952 and is today managing director of the International Air Traffic Association in Geneva. About the same time another unrelated Gerry Dempsey (later director of Waterford Glass and organiser of the attempted bid by Grand Metropolitan for Irish Distillers in 1988) joined the Accounts Department and became a member of what might loosely be described as the junior management team.

The six of us represented a de facto planning group, developing information systems, co-ordinating commercial and technical policy, advising on the selection of new aircraft, planning new routes, and so on. For a group of young people in their twenties it was a great opportunity, and we made the most of it. We convinced ourselves that we, rather than our bosses, were running the company, and in turn they were probably entertained by our presumption—or, perhaps, at times a little impatient with it.

In my own area—or what I had set out to make my own area from the outset—I was concerned to secure a solid factual basis for decision-making. Exactly where were our passengers travelling from, and where were they eventually trying to get to when they went on our services? What was their newspaper readership pattern: did it depart from the average pattern in Ireland or Britain to any significant degree, and if so could we reach them more cheaply by a careful choice of advertising media? How did passengers react to higher or lower frequencies of service? Which would be more beneficial on our route network: a larger aircraft, bigger than needed for some routes or certain times of year but with lower seat-mile costs, or a smaller aircraft, costing less per flight but with higher seat-mile costs? What were the natural hinterlands of the places we served, and could parts of these hinterlands be better served by additional routes? Why did our planes take forty-five minutes to turn around at airports, and could this be reduced? How could aircraft seat densities be increased?

These were only a few of the questions to which I sought answers by various forms of research: analysing ticket sales, conducting sample surveys of passengers (one covering 5,000 customers was accomplished at a cost of £60), examining our accounts and distinguishing direct operating costs from indirect route costs and overheads, as well as experimenting with fares. Contacts had to be made with external sources of relevant statistics, with geography researchers and with other airlines.

In 1952 I read a paper on air fares to the Statistical and Social Inquiry Society, in the course of which I estimated the current price elasticity of air transport at 2, i.e. that a 10 per cent fare cut would create a 20 per cent extra demand. I believe that this figure was validated later in the 1950s by much more scientific researches than mine. However that may be, my paper led to my election, despite my youth, to the Council of the Statistical Society, and this in turn extended my horizons greatly, as I attended meetings and listened to papers and debates on much wider economic and statistical subjects and got to know economists and public servants.

I next turned my attention to a descriptive analysis of the economics of those activities in which a product has to be sold piecemeal and in which direct costs are relatively low, such as transport and theatrical and cinematic entertainment. In these sectors seats are sold individually but have to be produced collectively, as a vehicle trip or a performance. I proved, to my own satisfaction at least, that changes in costs were almost totally irrelevant to the optimal pricing of cinema and theatre seats and were relatively unimportant in certain forms of transport. A paper along these lines that I presented to economics lecturers and students in UCD caused some bemusement as those concerned endeavoured to translate my home-grown economic theory into what they were teaching or had been taught in their micro-economics.

This was not the first time I had stumbled over the science of economics accidentally. Earlier my efforts to develop criteria for deciding whether an individual round-trip or route would pay had led me not alone to insist on a radical reorganisation of the airline's accounts in order to display cost data in a manner meaningful for such decisions but to invent a concept of marginal costing that I was later both relieved and disappointed to find the subject of a book I came across: relieved because it confirmed the correctness of my theoretical approach, disappointed because I had naïvely thought that I had personally invented this particular wheel.

I had started tackling the professional exams of the Institute of Transport in 1949. In 1953 I sat for the associate membership examination. Our second child, Mary, was born at this time, just as the exams were taking place, and the two drawers of the cupboard in the nursing home room were filled respectively with baby clothes and my books and papers for the exam, which I passed, becoming an associate member of the institute. Later I became secretary, and then chairman, of the Irish Section. I was already lecturing part-time in the economics of transport at Rathmines School of Commerce, and by 1956 was doing so at my own college, UCD, as well.

During my later years in Aer Lingus I was involved with a new range of issues; increasingly I was preoccupied with scheduling aircraft and the associated rostering of air crew and with perfecting the equation of supply and demand on virtually a flight-by-flight basis, as well as co-operating with the Technical Division in the selection of new aircraft and in designing aircraft interiors in order to make optimum use of limited space. By the end of my time with the company I was also taking part in the preparations for our delayed but, because it was now timely, successful entry on the North Atlantic route.

One of the most demanding tasks I undertook was the scheduling of aircraft. This involved estimating traffic demand on each route on each of the 180 days of both summer and winter season, taking account of such factors as changes in the date of Easter and Whit Sunday, and of many special demands such as the rugby internationals in the early part of the year and the different holiday seasons in various parts of Britain.

My passion for matching as perfectly as possible supply and demand reached its culmination in 1958, in the months immediately before I left the company. That year was the centenary of the apparition of the Blessed Virgin at Lourdes. Since 1952 we had been building up a lucrative pilgrimage business to the French shrine, where indeed we had become by far the largest operator both of charter and scheduled services, with routes not merely from Dublin to Lourdes but onwards with traffic rights to Barcelona and Rome. (As the operator of the only Rome–Lourdes scheduled service I made a bid for the carriage of Pope Pius XII on his 1958 pilgrimage to Lourdes, and I drew from his decision to fly Alitalia the conclusion that the Papacy was more Italian and less universal than it was sometimes represented to be!)

The Aer Lingus predominance at Lourdes reflected, I had reason to believe, an irrational prejudice among some other airline managements against what they seemed to feel to be superstition: a feeling that made several airlines act perversely and non-commercially so far as Lourdes was concerned. Even our British shareholders up to 1957, BEA, showed hostility to our Lourdes operations, apparently suspecting that we were running these services for religious rather than commercial reasons, a belief that I found quite entertaining.

In any event, with the centenary year coming up I asked Stuart-Shaw to defer until autumn 1958 the sale of two of our Viscount 700 aircraft, which were being replaced with the larger and more economic Viscount 800 series. I told him I could use them profitably for Lourdes charters during the five months from May to October. He was sceptical: even *he* seemed to suspect me of a non-commercial, religious motivation! I persuaded him to agree, however, and as a result we achieved what I still believe to have been the most perfect supply-demand equation ever recorded in air transport. The two aircraft were used on that route twenty hours a day on *every* day of that five-month period, and we secured eighty-one of the eighty-two pilgrimages from Ireland and Scotland to Lourdes that summer.

What made our work in Aer Lingus so interesting was that much of it was in effect pioneering. We were in many cases first in the field: we simply *had* to be first, because we were operating in less favourable conditions than any other significant airline and we could survive only if we became more efficient than any other. The atmosphere in which we worked was thus extraordinarily stimulating, especially as we belonged to an industry at the edge of current technology, still in course of rapid development. The economics of transport was an underdeveloped discipline, and the very specific subdiscipline of air transport economics was quite unexplored; there was in fact almost no theoretical underpinning for many of the decisions we had to take.

Thus our peak-valley ratio was one of the highest in the world, traffic in the peak week being over eight times the winter valley level; our stage lengths were short—mostly routes to Britain—and correspondingly uneconomic; and an average fare per mile by sea and rail with which we were competing was *half* that from Britain to the Continent across the English Channel.

I might add, in the present era of enthusiasm for privatisation, that an extra spur for those of us in management and for many of the staff was the fact that Aer Lingus was our *national* airline. I make this point about my commitment to the public sector because it was an important factor in my life at that time; it is not intended as a prescriptive comment, for I recognise that the spirit that animated us in the 1940s and 1950s does not exist in quite the same form today and that some—although not all—state companies in Ireland (and no doubt elsewhere also) lost their pioneering dynamism in later decades and became prone to feather-bedding. Indeed some even became viewed by their staffs as 'soft touches', seen as existing primarily to provide them with secure, well-paid jobs rather than to serve the national interest or the needs of the public.

Before explaining why, against this background of commitment to the airline and enthusiasm for my work, I decided to leave Aer Lingus, I must first turn back a decade in order to say something of the other activities in which I was engaged during the ten years after 1948. In the general election of that year, under the direction of Alexis FitzGerald, son-in-law of John A. Costello, who was to become Taoiseach of the 1948–51 Coalition Government, Joan and I had canvassed for Fine Gael from door to door in Mr Costello's constituency of Dublin Townships (now Dublin South-East). My understanding—for which Alexis was always to deny responsibility—was that Fine Gael supported Commonwealth membership, and Joan and I canvassed accordingly; we particularly remember reassuring the inhabitants of Waterloo Road on the point.

After the election all opposition parties and independents joined together to form a coalition to replace Fianna Fáil after sixteen years of unbroken rule by that party. A new party, Clann na Poblachta, led by Seán MacBride, was included in this coalition, and MacBride became Minister for External Affairs. I still recall my disillusionment at this development. I had been brought up to regard MacBride with deep hostility; a member of the IRA from the Civil War onwards, he had been its chief of staff in the mid-1930s just after some particularly shocking murders had made a profound impression on me, including one near Ring College when I was at school there. His later conversion to constitutionalism had seemed to me ambivalent. Not having adult memories of the sixteen years of Fianna Fáil government, I did not fully share the conviction of older people in the opposition parties that an alliance with MacBride's party was a price worth paying in order to provide an alternative Government.

My unhappiness was intensified when, a few months after the 1948 election, the Taoiseach announced the Government's intention to declare a republic. At that time this clearly meant leaving the Commonwealth, for the evolution of which into a body of sovereign, independent states John Costello, as Attorney General, with people like my father, Paddy McGilligan, and Kevin O'Higgins, had worked so successfully in the years before 1932. Moreover, in the months that followed that announcement the Government also decided not to join NATO, which was then being set up in the wake of the Prague coup of February 1948, which marked the last stage of the absorption of eastern Europe into the Soviet bloc. I attributed the dynamic of this decision to MacBride also. Fergus and I responded by initiating a pro-Alliance correspondence in the *Irish Independent*, which eventually ran to over eighty letters.

About the same time, provoked by the British Labour government's reaction to the declaration of a republic, and concerned not to be outflanked politically by de Valera's worldwide campaigning against partition, the Coalition Government launched an all-party propaganda campaign on this issue, which I viewed as counterproductive.

These events, together with my progression to a more responsible role in Aer Lingus, led me to drop out of political activity until the mid-1960s. At the same time another area of activity, compatible with my position in Aer Lingus, opened up.

My father's journalistic involvement as editor of the underground *Irish Bulletin* between 1919 and 1921, and later activities of his as Irish correspondent of the *Catholic Herald* and the *Tablet*, had predisposed me towards freelance journalism. In 1946 and 1947 I had written a few articles for Irish publications on a remarkably heterogeneous range of subjects: air transport, dietetics, the Aztecs, Azerbaijan, and a Russian adventurer in post-Great War Latvia—as well as university notes, a couple of book reviews, and several translations of articles from French and Spanish.

When I moved in October 1947 to the Aer Lingus Sales Department in Abbey Street, which housed Publicity as well as Sales, I found a vaguely literary atmosphere there. Séamus Kelly, the company's PRO, wrote 'An Irishman's Diary' in the *Irish Times* as 'Quidnunc', and the publicity manager, Major Éamonn Rooney, was something of a stylist, from whom I learnt a good deal.

In February 1948 I was confined to bed ignominiously for several weeks with chicken pox during part of the general election campaign. My mother's very practical birthday present was a copy of the current *Writers' and Artists' Yearbook*, which contained details of many newspapers in English-speaking countries. Inspired by this, and by boredom in bed, I wrote several articles on the election campaign and sent them to a number of foreign papers. They were published in Bombay, Cape Town, and Johannesburg. This galvanised me into action. Within six months I had published articles on Ireland in the *Standard* of Buenos Aires, the *Ottawa Citizen*, and the *Montreal Gazette*, and had negotiated a weekly column in the *South China Post* of Hong Kong, to be followed within the year by a fortnightly column in the *Montreal Star*, a monthly one in the *East African Standard*, and less frequent contributions in the *Auckland Star, Melbourne Age, Adelaide News, West Australian, Statesman of India,* and *Cape Times*, as well as in Britain the *Eastern Daily Press* of Norwich, the *Western Mail* of Cardiff, the *Birmingham Post*, and the *Glasgow Herald*. Because in several countries I was writing for more than one paper, I usually prepared three versions of each article, one after the other. Occasionally I contributed pieces on non-Irish subjects, such as the Soviet economy, or air strategy in the atomic age. On one occasion, inspired by the relative concentration of my ad hoc newspaper 'chain' around the Indian Ocean, I wrote an article on the uninhabited island of Kerguelen in that sea, which netted me the remarkable sum of £28!

This external journalistic success, in which Joan helped me with perceptive critical comments to which I soon learnt to listen, did not go unnoticed back in Ireland. My unhappiness with the declaration of a republic, the anti-partition campaign and the decision against joining NATO was apparent in my articles and came to the attention of the Coalition Government. That Government had meanwhile established the Irish News Agency in 1949 under Conor Cruise O'Brien, who was seconded from the Department of External Affairs for the purpose. By the time this got going I had already 'sewn up' the Commonwealth journalistically, while completely failing to penetrate the United States, where the anti-partition line of the Government news agency found a more ready response. I recall the answer to a parliamentary question about the volume of publicity achieved by the Government news agency, which gave column-inch figures for the Commonwealth. I was delighted to find that their Commonwealth coverage was one-fifth of mine.

It must have been extremely irritating for the Government to find its propaganda efforts in a number of English-speaking countries blocked by the freelancing son of a former Cumann na nGaedheal Minister. My identity emerged when the accumulation of cuttings from various Commonwealth papers under my name caused the Taoiseach to enquire who was this Garret FitzGerald. His private secretary, Paddy Lynch (soon to become chairman of Aer Lingus and later for many years my academic colleague and friend in UCD), enlightened him. Mr Costello was then able to place me, as his son, Declan, had been a friend of mine since we had met at an inter-schools debate and later in college.

I had also been spreading my journalistic wings at home during 1948 and 1949, writing on economic subjects for a short-lived trade magazine, and I had started to write on air transport subjects for specialised journals abroad. A 'coup' that gave me particular satisfaction was the publication in February 1949 by *News Review* in Britain of a piece I had written about the Soviet airline, Aeroflot, which they featured as their lead article. In an early and unusual example of glasnost, Aeroflot had published their entire network timetable. Using my knowledge of airline scheduling I reconstructed the size and location of the company's fleet from this timetable, thus revealing that Aeroflot then had the world's largest fleet: 250 aircraft with 8,000–9,000 seats. I ended the article with the challenging statement: 'If their air force bears the same relation to that of Great Britain (viz. virtual parity) as their commercial air fleet, it will certainly be a factor to be reckoned with in any future conflict.'

At about the same time I broke into the Irish market for articles on foreign affairs. The *Irish Independent* had introduced a foreign affairs column known as 'World Spotlight'. The paper's assistant editor, Michael Rooney, was a brother of my colleague in the Abbey Street Aer Lingus office, Major Éamonn Rooney. A meeting was arranged and I submitted some articles, which were accepted. Thenceforth for five years I wrote regularly for this column, quickly developing an efficient technique. I would go in the evening from Aer Lingus to the National Library and consult the *Encyclopaedia Britannica*, from which I would extract relevant background up to 1945 on the country about which I was going to write. Then I would trace events forward to the present time, using *Keesing's Contemporary Archives*. My notes taken, I would go home, have a quick meal, and hammer out an authoritative article on wherever it was. By 9.30 p.m. I would be in Michael Rooney's office with the finished text. My knowledge of foreign affairs must have appeared to the readers, with more justification than they perhaps realised, to be encyclopaedic.

During this period I had remained very much under Fergus's influence. His period in the army, and especially in Military Intelligence, had pushed him sharply to the right. He—and therefore I at that stage of my life—saw communists under every bed. In 1949 I wrote an article for a British news magazine, *Cavalcade*, in which I imputed communist leanings to several quite innocent organisations, such as the Irish Housewives' Association and the Irish Association of Civil Liberty. I included Owen Sheehy Skeffington, a lifelong liberal, in my indictment, as well as by implication Christopher Gore-Grimes, a solicitor who was a brother-in-law of my eldest brother, and whom I described as 'a non-Communist stooge'! This outrageous diatribe appeared over my initials. Some time later Christo Gore-Grimes asked me to call to see him, and confronted me with my handiwork. I could not deny the indictment. There followed a series of solicitors' letters threatening libel actions. I settled with apologies, and learnt a well-deserved lesson that I never forgot. Those whom I had libelled were extremely forgiving. Sheehy Skeffington in particular proved very kind to me later when we served in the Seanad together. Although avowedly agnostic, his behaviour was of the kind commonly called Christian, although not universal amongst people of that faith.

This aberration aside, my freelance journalism proved remarkably successful. After 1949 I could count on about £350 a year from this source, which, together with the income from some Prudential shares my Belfast grandfather had left to us, almost doubled my Aer Lingus salary. Towards the end of 1954, however, there was a significant change in the pattern of my journalistic activity. The *Irish Independent* dropped its 'World Spotlight' series. Around the same time it turned down as 'too controversial' an article of mine on the decline in the number of university students taking Irish as a degree subject, and as 'too dull' a series I had written on tourism. I offered them to the *Irish Times*, where they were accepted with alacrity by the features editor, Jack White. He asked me if I could write a series on university finances, which I did; then he sought articles on the Government finances, and next, one on the national accounts.

I knew nothing of these subjects but was happy to undertake the necessary research, and soon my articles on economic subjects, written under the pseudonym 'Analyst', were arousing interest. No-one else was writing for the press on economic subjects, and the evident failures of economic management by successive Governments during this period was creating a frustrated interest in economic issues that I was starting to satisfy. While I used a pseudonym in order to minimise any possible embarrassment to or objections by Aer Lingus, I made no attempt to hide my light under a bushel. Such is the power of the press that within a couple of years I came to be regarded as an economist. This profoundly affected my future career, by opening up possibilities that I had never dreamed of.

But to return to my decision of March 1958 to leave Aer Lingus: I had never abandoned the hope that one day I might be able to enter politics, and clearly that could not be combined with a managerial position in a state company. Moreover, my life had already broadened out considerably beyond Aer Lingus. Lectures in the economics of transport, which I was giving on a part-time basis at UCD, were providing the required course in that subject for the bachelor of commerce degree. This was putting me in touch with students again a decade after I had left college, and I made the most of the opportunity to benefit from the stimulus of younger minds. Each week I took a batch of my students to the Country Shop tea-room after my lecture. Academic life was starting to attract me.

Moreover my modest denials of being an economist, given my quite different academic formation and lack of any grounding in economic theory, were usually brushed aside by people outside academic life in the light of my writings in the *Irish Times*. Even amongst academics I was generously received: in particular Professor George O'Brien, Professor of Political Economy in UCD since 1926, dismissed as irrelevant my lack of qualifications in the subject, pointing out that he himself had no degree in economics and naming a galaxy of similarly unqualified economists of great fame, going back to Adam Smith.

I had no illusions about my capacity, actual or potential, as an economist, however, for I knew I did not have any real grasp of more than the rudiments of economic theory, and that my blind spot in mathematics ruled out even an elementary understanding of econometrics. But the studies I had made of the Irish economy in connection with my *Irish Times* articles had satisfied me that I had some intuitive feeling for the actual working of the economic system in Ireland; and my lack of training in the subject had at least enabled—indeed forced—me to write about it in language free of economists' jargon and correspondingly more comprehensible to the lay reader.

By 1957 I had also published several serious economic articles in the quarterly journal *Studies*, then edited by my old friend Fr Ronnie Burke-Savage, who had encouraged me when at school to think of entering politics later in life, and who had tried to reconcile my father to the idea of my taking a job in Aer Lingus and to my marriage. One of these contributions was the first serious comparative study of the economies of Northern Ireland and the Republic, using national accounts estimates as well as industrial and agricultural output figures, and the other was an attempt at a broad-stroke analysis of the Republic's economic problems as they appeared in 1957.

My work in this area convinced me that the Irish economy had an unrealised potential in both the agricultural and industrial areas: the former inhibited by dependence on the cheap-food British economy, which access to wider markets alone could cure, and the latter by the continuance of protectionist policies long after their original function of encouraging the establishment of infant industries had disappeared.

The creation of the EEC by the Treaty of Rome in March 1957—when I got around to noticing it, for it made curiously little impact on me until the negotiation to establish a European Free Trade Association linking the rest of western Europe with the Community began—seemed a providential answer to this particular Irish question. Such an association implied the removal of protective barriers. There seemed therefore to be an opportunity—and indeed an urgent need—to make economic expertise available to Irish industry to meet this challenge. In the absence of almost anyone working in this area, and despite my lack of formal qualifications in economics, I believed that I might have a useful role to play.

In preparing Irish industry for free trade it was going to be vital that the inefficiencies inevitable in a highly protected industrial environment should not stand in the way of creating freer access to the Irish market as a trade-off for the possible opening of other European markets to Irish agricultural products and to the output of existing and new Irish industries.

Accordingly, early in 1958 I started to sketch out an alternative career, involving a complex combination of intensified journalistic activity, economic consultancy directed especially but not exclusively towards the manufacturing sector, and hopefully some kind of academic career in the area of economics—with, as a possible eventual outcome, a move into politics. But given that I had a wife and (since June 1957, when our family had been completed with the birth of our younger son, Mark) three children to support, I would clearly have to secure in the first instance supplementary income beyond my existing journalistic earnings.

In proposing such a gratuitous leap in the dark I had Joan's willing support. Even though she knew that a political career—a prospect that she disliked intensely—was in my sights and that this job upheaval might ultimately facilitate the switch to such a career, she did not demur. One factor that influenced her to accept, perhaps even to favour, a change of career was her growing dislike of flying. She had not flown herself since summer 1956, and her fears had led me also to travel by train and boat on occasion when going to Britain on Aer Lingus business, although this obviously caused some problems with the company. These occupational pressures to fly would disappear if I changed my career, and part of the 'deal' we agreed was that I would in fact travel by sea and land in future—an agreement that I adhered to rigidly for fourteen years.

In the hope of securing additional income before taking up my new career, I went to London in March 1958, first preparing the ground by letters to various organisations and institutions. My approach to the *Financial Times* proved fruitful. Freddie Fischer, then diplomatic correspondent, interviewed me and, on the strength of some sample contributions I had sent beforehand, appointed me Dublin correspondent on the spot. That afternoon I was appointed Irish representative of the Economist Intelligence Unit, on the strength of my role with the *Financial Times*; I am not sure whether I thought it appropriate to divulge to them the very recent character of my *Financial Times* appointment.

When I got back to Dublin I found that the Government wanted me to accept appointment to a Commission on Workmen's Compensation, but when I raised this with the general manager, Jerry Dempsey, he responded negatively, saying that I had already taken on too many outside activities and that my health could suffer. He suggested that I turn down the invitation. Faced with this dilemma, I decided on the spur of the moment that the only thing to do was to tell him that I intended to leave the company in September and that I therefore proposed to accept appointment to the commission. This understandably took him aback, but I had burned my boats and had no choice now but to go ahead with my plan and leave Aer Lingus, although the additional income I had so far generated represented only a fraction of the salary I was then being paid: £2,250 a year.

Finding alternative employment immediately became a very urgent priority. I talked to Professor George O'Brien, whom Joan and I had known for many years; he had been her Professor of Political Economy in UCD. He said he would be delighted to have me as a member of his staff, adding that the President, Dr Michael Tierney, would have to approve such an appointment and recommending that I, rather than he, should make the approach, particularly as Michael Tierney was someone I had known since my childhood.

Michael Tierney was well disposed but told me that no post would be available in the coming academic year. Shortly afterwards I mentioned my situation to Louden Ryan, lecturer in economics in Dublin University, or Trinity College, as it is usually called, and he proposed that for the next academic year I seek an appointment there as Junior Rockefeller Research Assistant, at £800 a year. I did so with success, my project being a study of the source of inputs into Irish industry as a contribution to input-output analysis, then in its infancy in Ireland. Apart from its intrinsic value, this project promised both to help me understand better the working of Irish industry—necessary if I were to undertake my self-appointed task of preparing Irish industry for free trade—and also to provide me with a valid reason for approaching and thus making myself known to several hundred industrial firms to obtain detailed information. This process, I felt, would yield the useful by-product of alerting those concerned to my interest in Irish industry, an interest that hitherto only Louden Ryan amongst Irish economists had evinced.

Feeling that Michael Tierney would be pleased to hear that my employment problem was temporarily resolved, I went to see him with the good news. To my surprise he was deeply upset. I had not sufficiently allowed for his intense, irrational dislike of Trinity College. He announced that I would be absorbed by that institution: they would swallow me up and I would be permanently lost to my own university. I reassured him, in words that I came to regret, that such was my loyalty to UCD that if a job turned up there, even at the bottom of the lowest salary scale, I would accept it. That was precisely what happened a year later: he offered me a post at the bottom of the assistant grade 3 scale, at £650 a year, which I could not turn down after my protestation of loyalty; and on that scale—normally limited to postgraduate students—I was to remain for ten years.

The income gap remaining after my departure from the airline was soon filled, however, as a result of a number of consultancies that I arranged. Aer Lingus decided that it would require my services on a part-time basis for at least another six months. I was also employed by Córas Tráchtála and the Central Statistics Office. And the *Irish Times* agreed to take my 'Economic Comment' weekly. So, at the end of September 1958 I retired from my position as research and schedules manager in Aer Lingus and started a new and, as it turned out, hectic life comprising basically three careers, in academic activity, consultancy, and journalism, to which, in 1965, I added the fourth dimension of politics.

While I had been engaged in my preparations for this radical change of career, my mother had suffered a stroke. For six months she remained in a coma, until her death in April 1958.

Her life since my father's death eleven years earlier had been centred on her family and a few very old friends, although she enjoyed frequent visits to Italy, where Fergus and his family had been living since he had secured an appointment with the UN Food and Agriculture Organisation early in 1951. She was the last survivor of her own family but she had lived to see the birth of her sixteenth and last grandchild, our Mark. Her religious faith sustained her in these years because of the promise of being reunited with my father. After her reception into the Catholic Church in 1944, however, she had found the adjustment from austere Presbyterianism to the baroque Catholicism of the pre-Vatican II period difficult to take. My last conversation with her before her stroke had been on this subject; I had tried to reassure her that it was not necessary for salvation to respond to the flowery sentimentality of many Catholic devotions—something she was finding impossible to do.

Her death terminated the trust that had continued to hold the bulk of my Belfast grandfather's estate, in which he had left his irresponsible children (as he saw them!) only a life interest. Robbie Lowry, the son of my mother's old friend Ena Lynd, helped to unravel the legal complexities; he was later to become Lord Lowry, Lord Chief Justice of Northern Ireland, and in that capacity features in later chapters. Although my one-twentieth share of the estate was modest, it enabled us to move to a much larger house in Eglinton Road with an unusually extensive garden. The house had a garden-level flat for Joan's mother, as well as three other rooms on that floor, four reception rooms above (one of which I used as an office), and six bedrooms on the top floor. There we remained until my appointment as Minister for Foreign Affairs in 1973 forced us to move temporarily to a much smaller house in a more distant suburb.

The fact is that in 1959, with a total income by then much bigger than my Aer Lingus salary, we adopted a standard of living which, although unaccompanied by any particular extravagance, exceeded the means we could reasonably hope to have available to us later on, especially if I were to enter politics and attain relatively underpaid public office.

Meanwhile I had enjoyed my year at Trinity. Junior and temporary though my status was, I found myself nevertheless admitted fully to the life of the college—even, indeed, to the almost sacred rite of wine-tasting by which the Trinity cellars were replenished. My fame as an amateur (and never very percipient) authority on wine had been unintentionally conveyed to the nation at large through confusion on the part of the *Irish Times*, in which a couple of frivolous articles of mine on wine-tasting, intended to appear anonymously, were in error published over my name (the corollary being that three serious economic articles on food subsidies appeared without attribution). It was on the spurious grounds of my supposed skill that I was invited to join senior members of the Trinity staff in serious wine-tasting. This ceremony, otherwise informal, ended strictly in accordance with protocol: the untasted remains of each bottle became, according to the ranking of the wine at the tasting, the perquisite of the tasters, in order of seniority, and in this order they departed. I consequently came home with the residue of the worst wine, which, nevertheless, Joan and I were content to consume later in the evening.

All my time that year was not spent in Trinity, however. The basic data I needed for my research was in the Central Statistics Office. The Director, Dr Dónal MacCarthy, was well disposed to me as by far the most prolific Irish writer on statistical data. On my resignation from Aer Lingus he had commissioned me to undertake a study of Irish external trade from 1933 to 1957 and, on grounds of this commission, had me appointed by the Taoiseach as an 'officer of statistics', which gave me access to the confidential Census of Production data on industrial inputs that I needed for my TCD research project. I suspect this was the only such appointment in the history of the state.

The visits to firms that I undertook in pursuit of my research introduced me for the first time to Irish industry, and (since Joan and the family often accompanied me) introduced my children for the first time to Irish hotels. The children decided that the essential feature that distinguished hotels from mere guesthouses was the existence of two staircases, which enabled them to circulate rapidly inside the building. Within a couple of years they were able to name over fifty hotels, so defined, in which they had stayed.

My growing involvement with the public service, which had started when I joined the Council of the Statistical and Social Inquiry Society in 1952, had taken a further turn in 1958 when I was asked to join an informal Economics Club drawn mainly from the public service that discussed contemporary economic issues. Arising from these exchanges members of the group launched proposals for an Economic Research Institute, which was established in 1960 with Ford Foundation money. At about the same time I attended the foundation meeting of another new body, the Institute of Public Administration. I soon found myself on its Executive Committee, of which I remained a member for twenty years, attending its meetings even when I was Minister for Foreign Affairs.

For a potential, and afterwards actual, politician, all this proved to be of great benefit. I found in later years that most politicians, even those who had been Ministers, had a curiously limited view of public servants, frequently crediting them with a party political bias, which in fact is extremely rare, and taking an 'arm's length' approach to them as if they were alien beings. Having worked with many civil servants in and through the Institute of Public Administration, as well as in bodies like the Committee on Industrial Organisation, the National Industrial Economic Council, and the Transport Advisory Committee, I had a quite different perspective. While I was well aware of the capacity of some of them, although happily far from all, to defend skilfully the interests of the civil service and its members, I also came to appreciate the dedication of so very many of them to the public interest. I learnt to understand something of the positive rationale of bureaucracy: for example the concept of preserving equity between beneficiaries of state assistance that underlies so much of the rigidity of the bureaucratic process and of the resistance by public servants to the exercise of discretionary powers. I came to appreciate also the commitment to thoroughness, which, while sometimes frustrating in the slow tempo it imposes on change, protects the system against egregious error.

At the same time my appreciation of the public service ethos carried with it a sensitivity to the duty of civil servants to maintain the highest standards, and I developed a critical attitude towards occasional failures to live up to the principles I had come to hold in high regard. I suspect this made me a demanding and impatient Minister, especially when as Taoiseach I had to deal with so many different departments of state, not all of equal calibre.

Although my consultancy work during the years from 1959 onwards brought me into touch with almost every industry in the country, and with many non-industrial business interests, my close involvement with the public service ensured that my orientation towards business remained in large measure a public service-type approach. During my political career I never developed the natural empathy with the private enterprise sector that many politicians, coming themselves from business or farming, instinctively feel. While this certainly ensured that as a politician I did not easily succumb to business pressures, it may also have deprived me of the full understanding of the business mind that alone secures for a politician an easy relationship with the private sector.

Another by-product of my involvement with the Institute of Public Administration was a commission to write a short book on 'semi-state bodies': state enterprises and non-commercial state boards. In retrospect, this book was a naïve analysis of the structure and features of that sector of the economy, although in the absence of any other work on the subject in Ireland it remained for many years the standard text. I received £15 for the first edition in 1961, somewhat more for a revised edition two years later. The book reflected, I believe, the positive orientation towards state enterprise that I had developed when in Aer Lingus.

During the course of this, for me highly significant, academic year 1958/59 I had also found myself unexpectedly installed as chairman of the Irish Council of the European Movement, which was reconstituted in April 1959 by a young barrister, Denis Corboy, whom I had met at a debate in the King's Inns. I found myself editing and writing the council's monthly news bulletin on European affairs—a heavy task because of my somewhat manic determination to include *all* information on the EEC on which I could lay my hands. Joan, whose upbringing had made her francophone also, happily shared my enthusiasm and my interest in a European involvement for Ireland.

The council's first visitor from Brussels was the Community's first President, Dr Hallstein. When I met him at Dublin Airport one young journalist present asked a single question, the ignorance behind which clearly disconcerted Hallstein: Was Ireland a member of the Common Market? Another early visitor was the Agricultural Commissioner, Dr Mansholt. I enjoyed the bemused faces of four members of the Government sitting in the front row as Mansholt, with a twinkle in his eye, congratulated them on their success in getting farmers off the land.

Two years later, in April 1961, I paid my first visit to Brussels, as an economic journalist on that occasion, representing the *Irish Times*, together with colleagues from the other two Dublin dailies. In view of the state of the Irish economy after the stagnation of the 1950s my two friends felt I was behaving oddly in posing questions about possible Irish *membership* of the Community, as distinct from mere association with a very long period of transition to membership. The unprepared condition of the protected Irish industrial sector had meant that hitherto the Irish Government had publicly aspired only to association with the EEC. Before leaving for Brussels, however, I had gone to see Ken Whitaker, Secretary of the Department of Finance and author of the First Programme for Economic Expansion, launched in 1958, whom I had got to know through the Statistical and Social Inquiry Society. I asked him if there was anything I could usefully do in Brussels, and he told me that it would be helpful if I were to test reactions to the possibility of Irish full membership. I had the last laugh on my colleagues when, three months later, the Taoiseach, Seán Lemass, announced Ireland's application for membership of the Community to a surprised Dáil. He had decided that the economic progress following the Whitaker First Programme initiative and Lemass's own emergence as Taoiseach in succession to de Valera justified what many then felt to be a gamble.

This Brussels visit inaugurated a series of journeys to Europe's new capital, and to neighbouring Luxembourg, sometimes three times a year and never less than annually, during which the number of different hats I wore bewildered and amused my new Eurocrat friends. After my appearance as a journalist in April 1961 I came variously as a university lecturer, as vice-president of the European Movement (to which position I was elevated after my period as chairman), as an economic consultant, and eventually in 1966 as a member of the opposition front bench in the Seanad.

In October 1959 I had become, as I have related, a full-time—as distinct from whole-time!—assistant in UCD. I enjoyed every moment of this new life: the contact with the students; getting to know as colleagues the staff, many of whom not so long ago had been my teachers; and the challenge of lecturing on subjects peripheral to economic theory in which I had some competence, such as the European Community and transport economics.

My great deficiency as a lecturer was my rate of speech. Despite efforts to slow down, I never managed a pace that my students could cope with. I endeavoured to compensate for this by making each point several times in different ways, and by enlivening the lectures and the seminars with anecdotal references. I was, moreover, genuinely interested in my students, and despite my many other activities tried to ensure that I was accessible to them. For the smaller honours classes I revived the social arrangement I had introduced for my economics of transport students when I had been a part-time lecturer, but now I invited them in small groups to my home rather than to a tea-shop, as the move to a larger house nearer to town had made this feasible. I also lured various members of the economic establishment, like Ken Whitaker, to join us for some of these occasions. In all this Joan joined enthusiastically; she was delighted to find herself re-involved in the life of the college where both of us had spent such happy student years.

For me the benefits of this socialising were, to say the least, two-way. Many of my conservative attitudes and prejudices simply did not stand up to the challenges the students—and my own children—posed; even as early as 1961, when the process of economic growth after the stagnation of the 1950s had barely got under way, some of the students were already beginning to ask very pertinent questions about the purpose to which the additional resources being created would be put. This challenge in particular was useful, for the danger certainly existed that those of us engaged in trying to pull our country out of inertia and economic stagnation and prepare it to take its place in a wider Europe might become so absorbed in these tasks that we would ignore the social implications of growth.

By 1964, under this intellectual pressure, I had not only re-examined my inherited prejudices about the adequacy of our traditional economic and social structure to secure a just distribution of expanding resources but had incorporated this rethinking fully into my frame of reference as I approached the point when entry into politics was starting to become a real issue for me. Nor was this intellectual revisionism—if so one can describe it—confined to issues of social justice: the religious conservatism that I had retained from childhood was also giving way to an acceptance of the positive value of religious pluralism and to a much less rigidly conservative personal theology.

Since its foundation in 1908 as a college of the National University, in succession to Newman's Catholic University of 1854 and the subsequent Jesuit University College, UCD had been a kind of benevolent academic dictatorship, both under its wily first President, Dr Denis Coffey, and then, after a brief interval with Arthur Conway as President when Joan and I were students, under Michael Tierney. A scholar, a genial friend, and very much a family man, Tierney had nevertheless a gruff exterior. He suffered fools not at all, knew how he wanted the college to develop, and was dismissive of anyone who opposed his regime. No-one could dislike him, but few had the courage to argue with him. It had been the custom of the Governing Body to accept his proposals without demur.

His term of office expired when he reached the age of seventy in 1964 and he was replaced by the Professor of Modern English Literature, Jerry Hogan. The tradition of an authoritarian presidency imposed itself on Hogan, but the times, and his own different style, were against him. A growing demand amongst the staff, and later (although only briefly) amongst the students, for greater involvement in the running of the college were features of the 1960s.

The appointment by the Government in 1960 of a commission to report on university education gave the spur to a staff initiative. Wishing to respond to a request for submissions, and also seeing an opportunity to get a staff organisation under way in non-contestatory conditions, a committee was formed of which I was a member and which resulted in the establishment of an Academic Staff Association. Thenceforward I was actively engaged in college and university politics: an excellent training ground for the much less emotionally strenuous world of national politics.

In 1964 I took an initiative in relation to the Governing Body of the college that secured the election of Professor Desmond Williams and Professor John O'Donnell—distinguished historian and chemical engineer, respectively—as well as the return of four candidates, including myself, to represent the graduates on a 'reform' platform. We already knew that three of the four Fianna Fáil Government nominees—Dr Éamonn de Valera, son of the President, Judge Brian Walsh of the Supreme Court, and Máirín Uí Dhálaigh, wife of Chief Justice Cearbhall Ó Dálaigh—shared our contestatory approach to the college establishment.

The nine of us used to meet in our house before each session of the Governing Body with a view to concerting tactics. We were not, however, a very effective opposition, at any rate during our first 1964–67 period. Our problem lay in the group dynamics of the Governing Body—or rather, perhaps, the lack of group dynamics. The practice was for the President to introduce each item, usually asking the Secretary-Bursar, Joe McHale, to develop the detail of the issue. The President would then seek approval, which most members immediately nodded. As soon as any of our group sought to speak, most of the traditionalist majority would turn to look in evident, if somewhat exaggerated, astonishment at the impertinent intervenor. If another of our group supported the first speaker the remainder would look quite shocked at this evidence of conspiracy. The psychological pressure to accept the establishment view without dissent was thus enormous.

I was also active within the Political Economy Department itself. In 1962 I organised a visit to Brussels by university lecturers in economics, including economists from Queen's University, Belfast, and Magee College, Derry. In the event the Northern contingent outnumbered that from the Republic. It seemed a pity not to maintain this North-South contact; accordingly I initiated a conference of Irish university economists at the Ballymascanlon Hotel outside Dundalk, just south of the border, which became an annual event. After it lapsed for a couple of years it was revived later in the 1960s and has since continued in an enlarged form, including the attendance of research economists.

In 1960 I had attained my objective of acquiring a role in industrial policy-making in preparation for free trade. Seán Lemass, after his election as Taoiseach the previous year, had told the Confederation of Irish Industry that they should study the problems that different sectors of industry would face as trade began to be freed. The confederation accordingly asked a fellow-economist, Gerry Quinn, and myself to carry out a pilot study of the highly protected woollen and worsted industry. We visited every firm involved, and concluded that the industry would face serious difficulties under free trade conditions, with many firms likely to disappear unless they made drastic improvements in their productive efficiency and above all in their marketing.

The fact that we had taken a year to complete this study, admittedly on a part-time basis, suggested the need for a much more radical approach if the whole of Irish industry were to be reviewed within any reasonable time-scale. This seemed all the more necessary since our report coincided with Britain's and Ireland's first application for EEC membership. Accordingly we recommended that the Government be approached to co-operate in, and help to finance, such a general review.

An Economic Planning Division had been established in the Department of Finance two years earlier, with my TCD friend Louden Ryan as a consultant economist, and in off-the-record discussion with him and his boss, Charlie Murray, it was agreed that Gerry Quinn and I would propose in our report that the review of industry be undertaken jointly with this branch of the Department of Finance. It might have seemed more logical to have proposed a joint effort with the Department of Industry and Commerce, but despite the fact that the former Minister for Industry and Commerce was now the Taoiseach and was promoting free trade, that department had remained protection-oriented and seemed unlikely on its own to be an adequate partner in the kind of exercise we contemplated.

After some initial hesitation—such a close partnership with the state would be breaking new ground for Irish business—the Confederation of Irish Industry accepted our proposal. In advance of a meeting between the confederation and the Secretary of the Department of Finance, I briefed Ken Whitaker privately; this led to immediate agreement on our proposal at the meeting.

A Committee of Industrial Organisation was thus appointed by the Government to mobilise the necessary resources and supervise the project. Over the following four years this committee's studies covered the whole of Irish manufacturing, with the involvement of every firm of any size in each industry.

The only hitch—and it proved of short duration—was a demand by the Irish Congress of Trade Unions to participate in the exercise; in our anxiety to get the project launched, both Whitaker and I had overlooked the trade unions. This was rapidly agreed, and they proved to be most constructive partners. Indeed, insofar as tensions existed within the committee they proved—as I had anticipated—to be between the Department of Industry and Commerce on the one hand and the rest of us, with Finance, the CII and ICTU endeavouring as a troika to nudge that department into psychological acceptance of free trade.

Meanwhile I had become the economic consultant to the CII. This in turn led to my participation in the National Industrial Economic Council, set up as an element in the planning process for a Second Economic Programme in July 1964. I thus became de facto a full participant in the planning process, which involved detailed consultations with all sectors of industry on quantified targets for consumption, imports, production, exports, and employment.

This planning was, I believe, valuable for more than one reason. It forced firms to think of themselves, in most cases for the first time, not just as individual production units but as components in an industry within which they had a market share for which they had to compete against domestic and external rivals. It forced state enterprises, in many cases also for the first time, to think of themselves as enterprises rather than institutions with a right to free state capital and protection against competition. And it forced Government departments, if not always Ministers, to consider seriously the extent to which various impediments to enterprise arising from political considerations were obstructing competitive enterprises that were trying to succeed in a free market environment.

Planning of this kind had a short life, however. Disconcerted by a relatively minor recession in 1966, as a result of which the Government feared the plan targets for 1970 would not be met, it dropped the Second Programme in 1967 and substituted a far less detailed Third Programme, designed to fudge all the key issues as a preliminary to dropping altogether the concept of quantified targets at the end of the decade.

I had benefited from these activities in two distinct ways. First, I had been able to use the insights I had gained as material for a doctoral thesis, on which I obtained a PhD in 1969. I turned this into a book, *Planning in Ireland*, published by the Institute of Public Administration and by PEP in Britain. And on the strength of my PhD I secured belated promotion to college lecturer grade in UCD after ten years as an assistant—a promotion that had been held up because I had no degree in economics. Secondly, the detailed understanding of the structure and working of Irish industry that I achieved during this period stood to me in opposition politics and later in Government.

At about the same time as the CIO was established I had made the transition from providing economic consultancy on a personal basis, while also representing the Economist Intelligence Unit in Ireland, to becoming managing director of an economic consultancy company owned 50-50 by the EIU and myself, namely the EIU of Ireland. The board comprised Sir Geoffrey Crowther and John

Pinder from the EIU and my UCD colleague James Meenan, Joan, and myself, with Professor George O'Brien as chairman. During its eleven-year life the EIU of Ireland undertook consultancy or research work for some 150 clients, including a score of state boards or public boards, a score of industrial or trade organisations, over fifty individual firms, fifteen trade unions or bodies representing workers' interests, half a dozen stockbrokers, and over a dozen foreign interests.

In thus merging my consultancy work with EIU representation I hoped that the new company would develop a life of its own so that it would be able in due course to continue without me—and thus provide in the form of dividends the supplementary income Joan and I would need to maintain our way of life if I were to enter politics and be appointed to office. The theory was good, but in practice the company remained dependent on me and, while generating a good income to supplement my small salary from UCD, it never developed in the way I had hoped.

During the years from 1958 to 1961 I also served on two commissions: the Seanad Electoral Law Commission and the Workmen's Compensation Commission. I have already described how the latter appointment had precipitated my resignation from Aer Lingus. The Seanad Electoral Law Commission reflected de Valera's interest, towards the end of his period in Government, in revising the composition of the second house. Under the 1937 Constitution, eleven of the sixty members of the Seanad were appointed by the Taoiseach and three each were chosen by the graduates of the two universities. The remainder were given a vocational veneer by being elected from five vocational panels—agriculture, labour, and so on—but as half of these were nominated by the members of the new Dáil and outgoing Seanad, and as all of them were elected by a completely political electorate consisting of members of the Dáil, Seanad, and county councils, this vocational veneer was thin.

The Seanad Electoral Law Commission, comprising ten politicians, ten non-politicians, and a judge as chairman, had to review this electoral system. Ralph Sutton, a barrister friend and son-in-law of John A. Costello, suggested to me that we should present a hard-man/soft-man act: he, as the hard man, would propose that all forty-three panel senators be elected directly by vocational bodies while I would deprecate his extremism and recommend a middle course between political and vocational election. This ploy proved remarkably successful: the politicians fell into our trap and almost unanimously signed a report recommending that twenty-three of the forty-three be elected as well as nominated vocationally. Ralph and I later derived considerable malicious pleasure from hearing the Seanad leaders of the two main parties—both of whom had signed the report—denouncing it in the Seanad as the work of political illiterates. Nothing ever came of all this. De Valera had resigned and been elected to the Presidency; while the commission was meeting, his successor, Seán Lemass, was preoccupied with other matters and lacked any interest in Seanad reform.

In 1961 I was appointed chairman of the ESB General Arbitration Tribunal by Erskine Childers, then Minister for Transport and Power as well as Tánaiste. (My father had been a member of the government that decided that his father, Erskine Childers senior, should be executed during the Civil War for possession of a pistol given to him by Michael Collins. As a boy in 1942 I had observed the amicable relationship that nevertheless existed between Erskine Childers junior and my father when they met in Leinster House. The son had taken literally his father's Christian injunction to shake the hands of those responsible for his execution.) Childers described the appointment to me as a 'sinecure' involving, perhaps, seven meetings a year with a fee of £750 per annum. In fact there turned out to be over twenty meetings a year but even at that the chairman was well rewarded by the standards of the time.

Two years after my appointment to this position Joan saw an advertisement for an economic consultant to the Garda Representative Body, the organisation that was officially recognised as representing the basic rank for negotiating purposes. I applied, and was appointed. Shortly afterwards Erskine Childers called me to his office. In the presence of the Secretary of his Department, Dr Thekla Beere, he told me that they both saw a possible conflict of interest because a claim that I might prepare for the Gardaí could conceivably be quoted to me in a dispute that I might have to arbitrate in relation to the ESB. While this contingency seemed remote, I had to admit that it was theoretically possible and that I had failed to advert to it. I agreed, therefore, to tell the Garda Representative Body immediately that I had to turn down their appointment. While I regretted this outcome, I privately admired the careful concern of civil servant and Minister for the public interest.

Ten days later I was called to Childers's office again. An embarrassed Tánaiste told me that my refusal of the appointment with the Garda Representative Body had led to a near-mutiny, since it was interpreted as evidence of Government interference at a time when there was already unrest in the force. Childers went on to say that in the absence abroad of the recently appointed Minister for Justice, Charles Haughey, the Taoiseach had told him to direct me to take up the position that ten days earlier he had required me to turn down! I would, of course, have to resign from the chairmanship of the ESB tribunal.

I accepted this direction (as it was somewhat curiously described), but I commented wryly to Childers that this was the end of his 'sinecure', the fee for which was several times more than the Garda Representative Body proposed to pay. He responded at once that the Taoiseach and he had recognised this and that accordingly I would be paid a £500 fee for my participation in the Transport Advisory Committee, to which he had some time previously decided to appoint me. Virtue was ultimately rewarded, for the Garda body, pleased to have down-faced the Government on the issue and to have secured my services, were concerned that I should not be at a loss and more than doubled their proposed fee, to the same level as that for the ESB tribunal chairmanship.

I was exceptionally fortunate to have had all this experience of the public service—in such diverse areas as industrial policy, transport policy, industrial relations, and European integration—not to speak of university affairs, before entering national politics. Few Irish politicians have ever had the opportunity to acquire such a wide acquaintance with public affairs before entering political life. Insofar as my subsequent performance in politics fell short of the standard of achievement I should like to have attained, the fault clearly lay with my character rather than with the experience that I brought to the political arena. Of course the multiple activities that I was undertaking during these years, as lecturer, journalist, and consultant, were demanding, and were to become even more so when I added to my three careers a fourth, that of politics. But I was young and energetic enough to take the strain, and I enjoyed the variety of my life. Moreover, much of my work—preparing lectures, writing articles, conducting research for consultancy clients and writing reports for them—could be done at home; the house to which we had moved in Eglinton Road was within two miles of UCD and of my EIU of Ireland office. Thus despite the pressures of my work I probably saw more of Joan and the children than previously when I had been working in the Aer Lingus head office in O'Connell Street and living farther out of town in Booterstown Avenue.

We made one family trip to the Continent around 1961, when I had to address a tourism conference in Lausanne and Montreux on behalf of Bord Fáilte. I had hoped to introduce the children to Mme Camus when passing through Paris—almost a decade had passed since Joan and I had last seen her and her family, because we had not been able to afford Continental holidays during the intervening years—but unhappily she was too ill, and died shortly afterwards. In Geneva, however, Joan was able to show the children where she had passed part of her childhood.

## CHAPTER THREE

# POOH-BAH IN THE SENATE

My life up to 1964 had increasingly become a conscious preparation for politics. But I had no particular plan as to how I would go about becoming a politician. I had not even fully made up my mind as to which party I would join, although this decision may at an unconscious level have been more predetermined than I admitted to myself.

In the late 1950s Fine Gael had been going through a renewal of intellectual vitality, albeit in circumstances of minimal public support for the party. A Research and Information Council had been established, which organised a series of public lectures in the Oak Room of the Mansion House. I myself spoke to this group on several occasions, including once on the need for the party to have the courage to adopt an imaginative position clearly distinguished from that of Fianna Fáil on questions such as Northern Ireland. Detecting the emergence in the North of a new, moderate nationalist movement many years before the Civil Rights campaign, I suggested that in our own state a challenge to the shibboleths of traditional anti-partitionism by a fresh, open and liberal approach could lead to something quite different, transcending the sectional attitudes of past decades. More than twenty years later I was to promote this vision as Taoiseach.

It seemed to me at that time that Fine Gael in its current incarnation was still not my cup of tea, despite its new attitude to some of our economic problems. When Lemass took over as Fianna Fáil Taoiseach from de Valera in 1959 he undertook preparations for free trade with the same vigour with which he had undertaken the protection of infant industries a quarter of a century earlier. His command of economic policy-making was unequalled, and whatever my prejudices against Fianna Fáil—and these remained strong—I had to admit to myself that he was the best Taoiseach available for the purpose of initiating a long-overdue process of economic growth. His partnership with Ken Whitaker (who, since the adoption by the Government of his Economic Development Programme in 1957/58, commanded great authority) was remarkably constructive. Reluctantly I felt obliged in 1961 to accord him the support of my vote, giving my number 1 preference in Dublin South-East to Seán MacEntee, the only occasion I ever voted Fianna Fáil.

Although Fianna Fáil failed to secure an overall majority in that election, this did not prevent Lemass from governing in an unusually effective manner, despite his need to rely for the next four years on the support of independents. Shortly after the election Charles Haughey approached me to ask if I would carry out an analysis for Fianna Fáil of why they had not done better in the election. I suspected—rightly, I subsequently found out—that this was an attempt to draw me into the maw of the party, and I replied by proposing a fee, thus making it clear that I was determined to maintain my political independence. He responded with a letter saying that this was not what he had in mind.

I had one other contact with Fianna Fáil two years later when I was asked if I would contribute to a seminar on Irish-language policy to be organised by the party. I welcomed the opportunity to express my strong views in such a forum. I found myself flanked by two enthusiasts who favoured the revival of the language by continuing to make Irish essential for school-leaving examinations and public appointments: Seán Ó Tuama and Dónal Ó Móráin. This stimulated me to an eloquent attack on this policy, not least because it was in my view clearly incompatible with any serious attempt to achieve Irish unity by consent. The Irish-language requirement was, I believed, an insurmountable obstacle to Northern unionists, to almost all of whom the language was alien and many of whom saw it as a means of ensuring that they would be excluded, by virtue of their ignorance of the language, from full participation in the life of an Irish state comprising the whole island. To my surprise I found that a significant minority of the participants agreed with me. Perhaps on this account it was the last time I was invited to address a Fianna Fáil meeting.

During the 1950s I had had some contacts with Northern nationalists who were dissatisfied with the sterile anti-partitionism of the moribund nationalist parties: people like J. J. Campbell and Paddy Gormley MP. In 1959 Michael McKeown, founder of National Unity, a constitutional nationalist group that preceded the National Democrats (themselves a precursor of the SDLP), invited me to address a meeting in Belfast, together with Harry Diamond, a Republican Labour MP. As they could not afford to pay me for my talk, Michael offered me honorary membership of National Unity, which I accepted: this was therefore the first political group I ever joined.

During these years my childhood ambition to follow in my father's political footsteps, and my long-standing urge to challenge from within the political system the counterproductive irredentist anti-partitionism that defaced our politics, were reinforced by several new political aspirations. My experience of the efforts then in progress to prepare our industrial sector for free trade and to introduce a form of economic planning was bringing home to me increasingly the limits on administrative action as a means of effecting radical changes—and

I believed that such radical changes were needed in attitudes and policies in order to prepare our society to take its place successfully within a dynamic European Community. I was coming to realise that only through politics could the necessary breakthrough to an efficient, open economy be made in Ireland.

At the same time, as I indicated earlier, my social ideas had been undergoing something of a revolution. The conservatism and indeed clericalism of my youth had given way gradually to a much more liberal and progressive outlook. By 1964, instead of rejecting liberalism and socialism I was concerned to incorporate them into an integrated Irish philosophy of life.

The views I had come to hold on these issues were set out in late 1964 in the journal *Studies*, edited by my old friend Fr Burke-Savage SJ. Part of my motivation in publishing this article was a feeling that I ought before entering politics to give notice to my future colleagues of my basic political stance.

In this article I summed up in a typically long and convoluted sentence the views I had come to hold: 'Whether or not we succeed in developing a healthier and more positive relationship with our history and in deriving a more positive inspiration from our past than is commonly the case today, the fact remains that we will have to look to more universal philosophies and wider traditions; first of all to the Christian tradition from which we derive the basic structure of our thought; to such traditions as British liberalism, whose emphasis on tolerance provides a new insight into the meaning of Christian charity; and to the socialist tradition which has helped to develop the sense of social consciousness inherent in Christian thought which has been overlaid at some periods by over-emphasis on the individual and the family at the expense of society.'

I went on to say that two negative features of Irish life particularly concerned me. First, the materialism of a society in which preoccupation with property loomed large, and, second, what I described as 'the strong anti-cultural bias of a large part of the community'.

I criticised the Catholic Church's excessive emphasis on the right to own private property—'which no one in this all-too-bourgeois island challenges,' suggesting that it might be 'even more appropriate to emphasise the corrupting power of property whose effects are at times glaringly evident among our farming community and among the middle classes . . . Besides these materialistic preoccupations even the bitterness of members of the working classes—and surprisingly few are bitter—appear in a favourable light.'

In 1968 I was to return to this issue of attitudes to property in an address on socialism. This was later republished in the *Irish Times* supplement commemorating the meeting of the first Dáil in January 1919 and its radical Democratic Programme, in the drafting of which the leader of the Labour Party, Thomas Johnson, had played a leading part. In this paper I raised the question of the compatibility of the accumulation and transmission of substantial volumes of property by inheritance with the attainment of equality of opportunity in society. Recognising the extreme difficulty of tackling this fundamental problem by an evolutionary process, I nevertheless rejected the revolutionary approach, both on the grounds that any benefits in the form of greater equity might be outweighed by the misery such revolutions created and also because any attempts at radical social change by such methods would disrupt our small open economy, which was dependent upon our ability to compete in world markets and to attract foreign investment. Accordingly I preferred to rely on education to change social attitudes in the direction of equity—as public attitudes had already in my view been fundamentally modified on many other issues in the preceding generation. In the meantime moves towards profit-sharing and worker partici-pation in industry and the introduction of a wealth tax applicable to perhaps five thousand large estates, as well as of capital gains tax, would be small steps in the direction of social equity.

On the anti-intellectualism of Irish society I had said in the 1964 *Studies* article that 'this attitude finds expression in the flagrant pressure towards con-formism in the schools, the discouragement of original thought or effort, the cult of the second-rate, the recurrent disregard for an instinct to destroy things of beauty,' to which I added reference to 'the elevation of sport and drink to leading roles in society; the weakness of some aspects of family life in what is still a male-dominated society, and the lack of any adequate appreciation of the public as against the private interest.'

The Irish culture that I espoused would, I had gone on in this article to say, reject these attitudes; it 'would draw on the mixed origins of our society, Gaelic, Anglo-Irish and English, and would be neither exclusive nor sectional. It would glory in our mixed inheritance, despising none of it and elevating no part to a position of pre-eminence over the rest . . . Relations between North and South would be based on whole-hearted acceptance of the principle that political unity must be preceded by a unity of hearts; the Government of Northern Ireland as a provincial administration would meanwhile receive the unequivocal recognition that is its due.'

This *Studies* article appeared some months after my decision to cross the Rubicon and enter active politics in April 1964. There was no immediately precipitating factor for that decision. It was just that the time had come, I felt, to make up my mind. I considered the choices: Fianna Fáil, Fine Gael, or Labour. While I admired Lemass and felt that he was the best person to lead the Government at a time when economic growth was still the first priority, I felt that the future of that party was now falling into the hands of two younger groups of politicians, conservative materialists and traditional nationalists, neither of whom were in tune with what seemed to me to be the needs of late twentieth-century Ireland, namely social justice, conservation of our cultural and natural environment and a pluralist society at home, together with a policy vis-à-vis Northern Ireland that would be designed to remove the fears of unionists and to secure the rights of nationalists.

Those who seemed most likely to inherit the Fianna Fáil leadership, and who were already forming a hard core within the existing party structure, struck me as precisely the wrong people for these increasingly urgent tasks, although there were of course others in or near the leadership with a concern for some of these issues and for integrity in politics. These latter, however, seemed unlikely to come out on top in the ruthlessly competitive environment of Fianna Fáil, and in any event few of them shared the whole range of my concerns.

In theory at least Labour was far more compatible from my point of view. Its dependence on the trade union movement was, however, a negative factor so far as I was concerned. It is true that I had developed considerable respect for a number of the trade union leaders, but I did not like the idea of a political party being tied to a sectoral interest, even one representing as large a group as the organised labour force, an interest that in many respects was a conservative force in society. Moreover, as in Britain, the Irish Labour Party had a left wing that—as was particularly clear in relation to the issue of EEC membership— tended to take up an isolationist and at times narrowly nationalist stance, with which I certainly could not identify. The realist in me also recognised that under Irish circumstances the Labour Party could become effective in government only if linked to a larger party with at least a bias in favour of a socially more just society.

That left as a candidate for this role Fine Gael—towards which, of course, my inclinations in any event led me. Although in many ways conservative and, until recently, notably clericalist, in several other respects it came closer to my model than any alternative party. Thus it had a tradition of less aggressive nationalism than Fianna Fáil, even if since 1948 it had temporarily fallen under the spell of Fianna Fáil's irredentist anti-partitionism, and it had a strong tradition of integrity—including a revulsion, which I shared, against the use of public office for private advantage. There were reasonable grounds therefore for believing that Fine Gael had the potential to resist both aspects of the materialist- nationalist axis emerging in the Government party.

That Fine Gael could become a force for social progress seemed less probable in 1964. Yet there had always been more radical elements within the party: at that time Patrick McGilligan was still a TD, and my contemporary, Declan Costello, committed to social justice, was a potential force within the party. Accordingly, I made my decision in favour of Fine Gael and, having secured Joan's reluctant and at best half-hearted concurrence, I took three initiatives— although at this distance in time, and in the absence of any contemporary record, I cannot be certain of the order of these steps.

Taking the opportunity of a lift back from a reception in the German embassy I sounded the Fine Gael leader, James Dillon, on what to me was a crucial issue: if I joined Fine Gael, would I be free to continue to reject the irredentist nationalist thesis that Northern Ireland had no right to remain outside the Irish state and that the future shape of Ireland should be determined by a majority in the island as a whole without regard to the wishes of a majority in the North? Dillon's response was reassuring; I believe that he shared my view on this issue and was himself unhappy with the irredentist thesis.

A second move was to inform Ken Whitaker, who since the late 1950s had become in a sense my mentor, of my intention. He was shocked, and markedly hostile towards my proposed move. He said that if I entered politics I would lose the considerable power to influence events that I had acquired through my writings and my involvement with public affairs. He did not believe that this loss of influence would be compensated by any corresponding gain through playing a role in party politics or, eventually, in government. I tried to rebut his pessimistic view by suggesting that in the longer run I might have even more influence on events as a politician in government than as an independent economist; this argument he greeted with evident scepticism. I was naturally flattered at his assessment of the role he felt I was then playing, but he did not convince me that I should change my mind.

The third contact I made was with Declan Costello, whom I knew well and who had been a TD since 1951. We met for lunch in the Unicorn Restaurant. He told me that he was at a critical point in his own relationship with Fine Gael. He had recently almost abandoned hope that it might become a progressive party, but his father had said to him that before leaving it and joining Labour he should at least give Fine Gael a chance to decide where it stood by putting to the party the issues that he wished them to adopt as policy, so that they could make a clear decision for or against. Accordingly, he had listed eight points, and was now awaiting the party's reaction. He counselled me to postpone a decision until the results of this initiative emerged. I agreed.

Shortly afterwards, on 26 May 1964, the party, fearful of the effect of Declan's departure, announced its acceptance in principle of his eight points, authorised him to produce policy statements to flesh them out, and appointed a Policy Committee under the chairmanship of Liam Cosgrave to examine and review the documents as they emerged. Declan asked me to join the group helping him to prepare his material. I did so, postponing any decision on joining the party itself until the result of this exercise became clear. The following nine months were a busy period as our somewhat heterogeneous group, which was bound together by one common factor—admiration for Declan Costello and for his effort to give a new, contemporary relevance to Irish politics—struggled to produce a set of coherent policy documents covering a wide range of issues.

My own principal contribution was a paper favouring the introduction of a wealth tax, with the double objective of encouraging a more productive use of capital—an area in which the Irish economy was notably weak—and of improving, at least marginally, the distribution of wealth. This proposal was submitted to Liam Cosgrave's Policy Committee, and because of its relative complexity I was allowed to present it personally to that body. (Normally policies, by whomsoever drafted, were submitted to the committee by Declan himself.) I found the committee members resistant to my arguments and, as I was quite convinced of the compelling logic of my position, I emerged frustrated by their failure to grasp what appeared to my politically innocent eyes to be the self-evident economic, social and political merits of my proposal. I had fruitlessly argued that there *should* be wide political support for a policy from which many would benefit and that could affect adversely only a tiny minority. Subsequently, in the 1970s, I was to discover just how naïve I had been on this issue.

Most of the policy papers that reached the committee in late 1964 and early 1965 were, however, those for which Declan himself was personally responsible; unlike the rest of the group, *he* had started off with a clear idea of his priorities and with the benefit of political experience. And when in March 1965 Lemass called an election unexpectedly—partly, we believed, to pre-empt the publication by Fine Gael of a fully fledged Just Society policy—it was in effect these initial proposals of Declan's that formed the great bulk of the material put to the parliamentary party at once for acceptance. The 30,000-word document eventually issued covered economic planning, prices and incomes policy, banking and monetary policy, social capital investment, taxation, social welfare and health, and youth policy.

Despite the qualms of many less adventurous spirits, Declan's proposals were largely adopted by a party that at that time had nothing else to offer to the electorate; his move filled a policy gap. He was naturally pleased that his policies had been endorsed by the party and that Fine Gael was to fight the election on this basis. But he remained sceptical about the full-hearted conversion of the party to his ideas. Some of this scepticism spread to me. I was approached to stand with his father in Dublin South-East. Initially I accepted, but then, within thirty-six hours of the deadline for nomination, influenced perhaps by Declan's doubts but also by Joan's unhappiness about my entering politics, I withdrew. As a result my name did not go before the constituency convention, and no-one other than those immediately involved was aware that I had been so near to committing myself.

Having thus pulled back from the brink, I transferred my attention to a different kind of election challenge: the presentation of the results on television. I had already had some experience of this medium following the launching of Irish television at the beginning of 1961. Indeed, with Kevin O'Kelly—already in the 1950s a familiar figure to radio listeners and soon to be RTE's religious affairs correspondent—I had contemplated setting up a television production company in 1961, but nothing had come of it. I had, however, appeared as an economic commentator in the early television news bulletins (until I discovered that there was no provision to pay me for appearances under the auspices of the News Department!). I had prepared and presented a series of programmes on the EEC, including interviews with the Taoiseach and other party leaders; and I had also participated in a programme mounted by RTE for the British general election results in 1964.

Now, in April 1965, I was anxious to play a full role in the first television coverage of an Irish general election. I knew that because of our PR system—which can involve up to fifteen or more counts in a constituency as surpluses are passed on from elected candidates and as the votes of eliminated candidates are distributed—the preparation and presentation of electoral results visually would give rise to special problems. As I had kept not only election results since 1943 but also, possibly alone in the country, had details of the times at which individual counts in some elections had been declared, I was in fact unusually well qualified to undertake this task.

RTE agreed to employ me not only to comment on the results but also to help prepare the programme. For rehearsal purposes I drew up likely 'shadow' results of the first seventy counts, which would bring us from a 5.00 p.m. start on the day after the election (by which time only a few early counts would be available) to beyond the peak period for the flow of results, which is around 6 to 7 p.m. At 10.30 a.m. on the day after the election we all gathered in the studio to rehearse the election programme on the basis of my fictitious results. Everything went wrong, including, particularly, the computer. Finally, at 12.25, the first 'shadow' result started to come in and we made our first comments. But at 12.30 a loud whistle blew and the staff all rushed to the exits. 'Fire?' I asked, alarmed. 'No, lunch,' said an RTE man, moving at high speed towards this repast.

So our rehearsal never actually took place, and my laboriously produced 'shadow results' were never commented on in rehearsal, as I had planned. Nevertheless the exercise proved of value, for in those two hours in the morning the 'bugs' had been got out of the system, and from five o'clock onwards the results flowed smoothly. Over twenty years later my economist son John was to be involved in providing a much more sophisticated computer service to the election programmes of 1987 and 1989.

A week or so after the 1965 general election, which Fianna Fáil won by the narrowest of margins, we were dining in a restaurant with Alexis FitzGerald and his wife, Grace (Declan Costello's sister). During dinner the restaurant phone rang; it was Declan calling from Leinster House to say that James Dillon had just announced his resignation as party leader at successive front bench and parliamentary party meetings and that Liam Cosgrave had immediately been elected in his place. We were all taken aback; insofar as James Dillon's retirement had been anticipated—and most of us had not, I think, seriously expected it so soon after the election—it had been assumed that an interval would follow before the election of a successor, in order to give time for candidates for the leadership to emerge, and that in those circumstances Declan would have had a good chance of being elected by the parliamentary party.

Shortly afterwards Declan and Alexis approached me to run for the Seanad, the election to which occurs about two months after a Dáil general election. I demurred, as my professor, George O'Brien, would be standing again for one of the three National University seats and I did not want to put his election at risk. For some reason it had not struck me that I could stand for election by another route, but my friends suggested that I should seek nomination as a Fine Gael candidate from a vocational body, and thus stand on a nominating bodies sub-panel for election by the members of the incoming Dáil and outgoing Seanad and county and city councillors—an electorate of 872 people at that time, of whom some 300 plus were Fine Gael. Liam Cosgrave favoured my candidature.

Having discussed this proposal with Joan and secured her reluctant consent, I set about seeking a nomination from a vocational body. I was rather late in the field, and most of the organisations with which I had some contact in the preceding years had either already made their nominations or decided to make none.

After a couple of days of fruitless phone calls I rang the secretary of the Irish Hotels Federation, F. X. Burke, who called a special Council meeting. I was helped by, among others, Todd Andrews, chairman of Bord na Móna, a radical Fianna Fáil republican with whom I had a good relationship, despite the antipathy he had felt towards my father since the Civil War; at my request he asked his hotelier son, Chris, in Limerick to support me. I was chosen for nomination by a margin of one vote over a non-political candidate, the president of the federation. One of those who voted for me was an apolitical hotelier, Billy Kelly, who would, I am sure, have voted for his president but for the fact that in 1964 we had abandoned our holiday pattern of previous years (when we had spent a month every summer in a rented seaside cottage at Bettystown, Co. Meath) in favour of a more gregarious holiday at his Strand Hotel in Rosslare. Our consequent friendship proved the marginal factor securing the nomination for me.

The nomination secured, during the month of May I set about canvassing votes personally, for it is a well-established fact that without personal contact with the individual members of the political electorate throughout the country a Seanad candidate has no hope of securing support. In twenty-nine days I made ten sorties from Dublin, driving some four thousand miles across the country, calling on well over 250 Fine Gael county councillors and almost a hundred others. (Most of the TD and senator votes had already been committed at that stage, so that I had to depend mainly on the county council vote for my election.) I had plotted the dwellings of these county councillors on half-inch-to-a-mile Ordnance Survey maps, pinpointing the precise location of each councillor with the aid of an administrative atlas and gazetteer of Ireland that my father had purchased when Director of Publicity for the Dáil in 1920, and with the help of local TDs in a number of areas. This preliminary mapping made it possible to devise route plans that would minimise the driving involved.

The canvass was, incidentally, greatly facilitated by the fact that over 80 per cent of the voters were at home when I called, regardless of the hour of the day. This reflected the fact that very many of them were farmers, shopkeepers, or publicans, living at their places of work—as well as, perhaps, a combination of courtesy and curiosity that encouraged them to make themselves as available as possible to the dozens of Seanad candidates seeking their votes. Part of my canvass was undertaken in the company of my friend Alexis FitzGerald, who at my countersuggestion had secured a nomination on another panel. Joan accompanied me on most of the journeys, as did our children on several occasions.

I did not quite know what to expect on this canvass; I had heard many stories about Seanad campaigns, but did not know enough to distinguish fact from fantasy, truth from reality. In the event many of the more alarming stories turned out to be myths; for example, although I was offered countless cups of tea only six alcoholic drinks were pressed on me. One story turned out to be well founded, however: that the number of first-preference votes I would receive would be 90 per cent of the number of which I was 'certain' and 50 per cent of the number I thought I *might* get. Since I felt hopeful about 130 voters, who had not turned me down, and 'certain' of just over 70, I looked like getting an actual vote of 65. A not insignificant proportion of them I owed to my appearance on the general election television programme. I became sufficiently confident of this formula to cease canvassing when I reached this point—an unprecedented act of presumption—for with anything over 55 first preferences I should be reasonably certain of election. I pulled back at that stage, because I had reason to believe that many of the votes were coming to me at the expense of a sitting Fine Gael senator, Ned McGuire; and given his importance as a frontbencher and party fund-raiser I did not wish to deprive him of his seat unnecessarily. My self-denial proved fruitless: with only 40 votes, he lost; his campaign had suffered from newspaper reports that he had spent part of the campaign period on holidays abroad.

I should add that the standard not merely of courtesy but also of honesty among the voters was very high. Half the Fine Gael people whom I approached told me that their first-preference votes were pledged to other candidates, and a further quarter, while friendly enough to enable me to mark them in as 'possibles', had been careful not to commit themselves unequivocally. Only a quarter were firm promises, and my eventual vote of 64 equalled 90 per cent of this latter figure: exactly in accord with the advice I had received when I started my campaign.

I was declared elected on 10 June. I attended my first Seanad meeting several weeks later. In the meantime Liam Cosgrave had appointed me as one of six Seanad front bench members, with full participation in Fine Gael front bench meetings; as a result, my first time ever to sit on the back benches was after I resigned from the leadership of the party in March 1987, twenty-two years later.

My entry into politics through the Seanad rather than the Dáil had several advantages. First, the election process brought me into immediate touch with elements of the party—and indeed of other parties—throughout the country. For a Dubliner with limited experience of the rest of Ireland this was a great bonus; I was sensitised straight away to a whole range of problems and issues with which I was either unfamiliar or which, if I already knew of them, had dimensions that I had not fully appreciated. I learnt much about regional differences, in temperament and character as well as in interests. And I rapidly came to appreciate the kindness and courtesy of members of the party throughout the country.

Secondly, the less partisan atmosphere of the Seanad as compared with the Dáil suited a political neophyte like myself. I was neither required nor expected to make propaganda speeches, nor to spout political rhetoric in the House. In respect of the great bulk of legislation my task was rather to examine it critically but constructively; the former accorded well with my argumentative disposition, the latter with my natural instinct as an academic.

Much to my disappointment, Declan Costello had withdrawn from the Dáil front bench while I had been campaigning for the Seanad. A combination of health problems and unhappiness with what he perceived as an inadequate commitment amongst his colleagues to his Just Society policy had prompted this decision, which left me in something of a vacuum. I found the party leader, Liam Cosgrave, open to some of my ideas, however, and before long I was working closely and harmoniously with him and with progressive elements among the senior members of the party.

Thus in 1966, around the time when a second attempt to achieve British, Irish and Danish membership of the European Community was initiated, I persuaded Liam Cosgrave to accompany me on a visit to the European Commission in Brussels. During this visit Sicco Mansholt and Robert Toulemon (the official in charge of the negotiations) emphasised to us the importance from Ireland's point of view of getting our negotiation virtually completed before the British negotiation got under way, a point that Cosgrave stressed in the subsequent debate in the Dáil. We also found Commissioner Jean Rey very well informed about the Irish situation: he quoted liberally from a recent Seanad debate on the Community that I had initiated. This debate had persuaded the Government to establish a separate diplomatic mission to the EEC, something that the Minister for External Affairs, Frank Aiken, had turned down when proposed at a Fianna Fáil parliamentary meeting a week or two earlier.

I was now beginning to find my feet in the Seanad as a member of the Fine Gael front bench in that assembly. The two other active members of this front bench were Ben O'Quigley, the party's leader in that House, who was a barrister from Co. Carlow, and Jim Dooge, Professor of Civil Engineering and a hydrologist of world reputation, who was also Leas-Cathaoirleach of the Seanad. Because Jim had frequently to be in the chair, and because by convention as Leas-Chathaoirleach he was expected to avoid serious controversy, the brunt of opposition fell on Ben and myself. But in the month of July every year, when the Seanad usually had to handle a rush of legislation from the Dáil after its summer adjournment, Ben had to go on circuit to Mayo. And if, as happened occasionally, Jim was away as well, lecturing in the United States or Australia, I could find myself handling *all* the legislation coming to the House; on one occasion I dealt with seven different Bills in a single day!

In all this I was accorded a wide discretion. Most legislation does not involve matters of party policy, and one is free to tackle the task of constructive opposition, trying simply to improve the quality of the legislation. A common thread tended to run through many of the debates, however: Fianna Fáil, possibly because it had been in office for twenty-seven of the previous thirty-three years, tended to favour an approach that gave maximum power to the executive, a position that most civil servants also tended to favour. Fine Gael by contrast had, and has retained, an instinct for a more open and democratic approach, and for conceding a greater role to bodies independent of government. Sharing this instinct, I found it easy to pursue a fairly consistent opposition line in the Seanad, and enjoyed the mild rough-and-tumble of debates, especially when they centred on this kind of issue.

I soon found the self-confidence to strike out on my own on certain matters, for example arguing in connection with the 1966 Broadcasting Bill that if we believed in a united Ireland, RTE should be expected to give a third of its current affairs time to Northern Ireland politics and almost a quarter to the views of Northern unionism. This *jeu d'esprit* evoked no response from the Government side, but equally no-one on my own side demurred at my expression of such heterodox views.

There were lighter moments too. In a debate on corporal punishment a Fianna Fáil senator repeatedly asserted that although he had frequently been 'bet' at school it had never done him any harm. He said it once too often for Senator Bedell Stanford of Trinity College, normally the kindest and most courteous of men, who rose to remark that if corporal punishment had not done the harm to the senator, he wondered what exactly had done it!

My entry to politics through the Seanad had left me ill prepared for two aspects of politics: making partisan speeches at public meetings out of doors, and involvement with the party organisation. But a year was in fact to elapse before I had to face these two challenges.

It was indeed only the approach of a Presidential election, in May 1966, that brought me to a realisation of the curious fact that although by then I was a well-established member of the Fine Gael front bench I had never got around to *joining* the party itself. Clearly I had to find my local organisation, and through it join the party. Accordingly I went to see my local TD, John A. Costello, to ask him how I should go about joining Fine Gael in Dublin South-East. His response was, as usual, forceful, blunt, and idiosyncratic. 'Forty years in politics; twice Taoiseach; never joined Fine Gael.' Somewhat timorously I suggested that times were changing and that his precedent might not necessarily be the best one for me to follow. With apparent reluctance and perhaps with a hint of disappointment at my conventional approach to politics, he conceded that there *was* a Fine Gael organisation in Dublin South-East and that if I turned up at the Morehampton Hotel on the following Thursday I would find the constituency executive meeting there. I followed his directions, and so found my local organisation. It was a small meeting, consisting mostly of fairly elderly people.

To my dismay at this point I was called on to play a small part in the larger campaign at national level by joining our Presidential candidate, Tom O'Higgins, on the trail through Co. Wicklow, making speeches in Bray, Wicklow and Arklow as well as later on at a final rally outside the GPO in O'Connell Street. While during the previous decade I had acquired considerable experience as a public speaker, especially about the EEC, the idea of addressing outdoor meetings as a partisan political speaker terrified me; indeed I never acquired a facility for this kind of oratory, and throughout my whole political career I remained as uncomfortable at outdoor political rallies and meetings as I was happy to speak at indoor meetings, especially those of a non-partisan character.

Whether my unhappiness at outdoor meetings was due to the acoustic problem arising from the lack of resonance out of doors or to the sense of a fugitive and non-captive audience I never discovered. But at my very first such meeting in the course of the Presidential campaign my discomfort was magnified several times over by virtue of the fact that the meeting was held outside the Royal Hotel in Bray and that friends of mine, Tony and Éilís McDowell, had chosen to come to listen while dining in comfort at a window table in the hotel dining-room, right beside the platform, in front of the courthouse where my father had received his first jail sentence over fifty years earlier.

In Tom O'Higgins' second Presidential contest in 1973 another young man, Peter Prendergast, a marketing consultant active in Dublin constituency politics, acted as a personal aide-de-camp and unofficial manager during the campaign, gaining experience that proved very relevant to his subsequent career. In 1977, after I became leader of the party, he was appointed general secretary and national organiser and was responsible in very large measure for the remarkable recovery of Fine Gael between 1977 and 1981, which brought me into Government as Taoiseach in June 1981.

Michael Sweetman was a cousin of Gerard Sweetman, Fine Gael Minister for Finance in the 1954–57 Coalition Government and a leading front bench member of the party. Michael was poles apart from his much older cousin, however; he was a liberal intellectual whereas Gerard was a pragmatically conservative businessman. A member of their family who had been politically prominent at an earlier period was Michael's grandfather, Roger Sweetman, a pre-independence MP whose home at Derrybawn, near Glendalough, had been a shooting lodge that had been rented by Joan's brewing grandfather late in the previous century.

Michael was a somewhat improbable figure in politics, especially because of his deceptively languid manner, which had certainly fooled Joan and myself when we had first met him as a representative of Córas Tráchtála at a conference in Copenhagen in 1963. But in the interval between 1963 and 1966 I had got to know him better and to admire enormously the skill with which, as a policy adviser and speech-writer, he sought to centre this Presidential campaign around the concept of a pluralist society. He had a markedly original mind, an unself-conscious lack of convention, and a mischievous sense of humour. He had no time for the conventional pieties or sacred cows of Irish politics. He was, to those who knew him well, a unique and very attractive figure.

The combination of Tom O'Higgins as candidate in 1966 and Michael Sweetman as adviser and speech-writer presented a major challenge to Éamon de Valera, who was seeking a second seven-year term of office at the age of eighty-four. As retiring Taoiseach, de Valera had achieved a convincing win in 1959 over Gen. Seán Mac Eoin, Fine Gael frontbencher and hero of the War of Independence. But seven years in the relative obscurity of the Presidency, with only one major highlight—the visit of President Kennedy in 1963—had left him more vulnerable, especially with the younger generation of voters, to whom Tom O'Higgins, in his late forties with a large young family, seemed a more attractive candidate. The tone of Tom's speeches, with their emphasis on moving away from a traditional inward-looking nationalism to a more open and pluralist concept of Irish society, struck a chord with that generation also; he was a candidate for the 1960s, and in this election he came within a half of one per cent of defeating de Valera.

This Presidential election had a significant impact on Fine Gael. It strengthened the progressive wing within the party, for it showed that more adventurous policies *could* attract votes, contrary to the conventional wisdom of the old guard. And it added to Declan Costello's social-democracy a liberal element that was to remain an enduring factor within the party. This need not have proved divisive: parties like Fine Gael and Fianna Fáil can usually accommodate significant ideological differences without undue tension. In the event, however, it worked out differently and rather divisively, for reasons that must remain at least partly speculative.

One theory prevalent within the party has been that in the aftermath of the Presidential election—during the summer of 1966—something of a vacuum developed within the top level of Fine Gael. Tom O'Higgins took a well-deserved long holiday. At the same time my close relationship with Liam Cosgrave seemed to alter. There has been speculation that this may have been due to the invention by a political columnist, 'Backbencher' (John Healy) in the *Irish Times*—then approaching the height of his fame as a commentator on the political scene—of the term 'FitzCosgrave' to describe my relationship with the party leader.

Into this temporary vacuum, so the conventional wisdom in Fine Gael runs, stepped a forceful character: Michael Sweetman's cousin, Gerard Sweetman. His relationship with Liam Cosgrave during the preceding decade was said to have been clouded because of some disagreement about his treatment of Cosgrave's father, W. T. Cosgrave, when Minister for Finance a decade earlier. But now, in the summer of 1966, whatever coolness had existed between the two men seemed to evaporate. Certainly by the autumn Sweetman was firmly installed as organiser of the party, a position for which his forceful personality well fitted him.

He was not an ideological right-winger but rather a politician with a business orientation and a practical interest in winning power for his party. He was tough, and had little instinctive sympathy with the younger generation, least of all with the liberal youth of the 1960s. He had no malice in him and did not bear grudges, but in what he conceived to be the interests of the party he could be quite ruthless. My relationship with him was combative but not unfriendly. When from time to time we were in agreement on an issue he would tell the rest of the front bench good-humouredly that when we two agreed, no further argument was necessary.

Thus from autumn 1966 onwards a certain tension began to develop. It would be wrong to exaggerate its significance in this early period; only in retrospect, when some years later a fairly clear-cut division emerged within the party, were the roots of division traced back to this period.

It was in November of that year that I had my first experience of a by-election. Thady Lynch, the Fine Gael TD for Waterford, had died and we were contesting the election with a young candidate, Eddie Collins. Waterford city had remained a Redmondite stronghold during the half century after the 1918 defeat of the Irish Party and the death of its leader, John Redmond. So strong was this Redmondite factor that when I arrived in Waterford, accompanied by Alexis FitzGerald and a number of UCD students, including Maurice Manning, now Fine Gael leader in the Seanad, and Vincent Browne, now editor of the *Sunday Tribune*, we were told that in a number of areas we should seek votes for 'Eddie Collins, John Redmond's man', without stressing the Fine Gael connection. I still remember the response in one house when the door was opened by an elderly woman: 'Of course I'll vote for Eddie Collins; haven't I got John Redmond's picture at the top of the stairs, beside the Sacred Heart!'

My personal relationship with Liam Cosgrave seemed to me to disimprove further after an incident in 1967. Brendan Halligan of the Labour Party had told me about growing support in that party for coalition with Fine Gael, but said that Labour would not serve under Cosgrave as Taoiseach. Loyalty to my party leader seemed to require that he be made aware of this assessment, which could reasonably influence his thinking about any relationship with Labour. I naturally disliked being the messenger with bad tidings, however, and it was only after consulting James Dillon—and acting on his advice—that I told Cosgrave what I had heard. I doubt that it helped our relationship.

In October 1967 I was appointed to an electoral strategy committee to make recommendations on the whole field of policy and tactics. Because I feared we were drifting rather than preparing for an election, I had already written a draft proposal for such a committee and put it to Tom O'Higgins and Jim Dooge during a by-election in Cork. Jim had rewritten it and put it to the front bench. The most urgent matter seemed to us to be the possible consequences of a further Fianna Fáil attempt to reverse the negative decision by the electorate on that party's 1959 proposal to substitute the 'X' voting system in single-seat constituencies (as used in Britain) for the Irish system of proportional representation by preferential voting in multi-seat constituencies.

Jim Dooge prepared an analysis of the likely electoral effect of such a change. I worked with him on this. We concluded that, as compared with 72 seats in the 1965 election under PR in a single-seat constituency system, Fianna Fáil would get 80 of the 144 seats even if the alternative vote were retained, and something like 96 if their proposal for the X-vote system were introduced. Cosgrave agreed that we should open talks with Labour on how to confront this threat.

During the following weekend I discussed the situation with Brendan Halligan. Whatever chance there might be of persuading Labour to co-operate with Fine Gael, he said, a short-term link would certainly be of no interest; only a long-term or permanent link—perhaps even a merger—would have any chance. Those in Labour favouring an alliance or merger, according to Halligan, were Barry Desmond, Noel Browne, Seán Dunne, Stephen Coughlan, and Michael Pat Murphy, with Micky Mullen perhaps persuadable. Michael O'Leary was thought to be hostile, for tactical reasons, until after the next election. Jimmy Tully too was hostile, but his attitude could change in the event of a referendum on PR.

As it happened, the expected Government decision did not come on Friday 15 December, and as a result it was clear that no announcement on possible Labour-Fine Gael plans would need to be made until after Christmas. In the interval I had further discussions with Brendan Halligan and Barry Desmond. Halligan repeated that a merger of the two parties was a much more likely starter than a coalition. A merged party would be much better placed to contest elections in single-seat constituencies with the X-voting system. A coalition would be at risk all the time as a result of the pressures to agree which party would stand in which constituency: the same problem that faced the Liberals and Social Democrats in Britain before the 1987 general election there. Later it transpired that, contrary to an earlier impression, Michael O'Leary shared this view.

On 3 January 1968 a crucial meeting of the Fine Gael front bench took place, which continued from eleven in the morning until five in the afternoon. Mark Clinton suggested a merger, although he knew nothing of the views on this subject that had been expressed by Halligan and O'Leary. Jim Dooge and Tom O'Higgins supported the idea of exploring this possibility. Gerard Sweetman opposed it, and three others expressed reservations; but at the end only Maurice Dockrell demurred at the proposed talks, seeing them as dangerous, but not entering a formal objection to them.

On the separate issue of whether to reject a Government proposal, should it arise, to replace PR by a single-seat system with an alternative vote (marking the candidates 1, 2, 3, etc.), which would reduce the need for agreement with Labour on candidates, a private sounding that I carried out at Liam Cosgrave's request during the meeting showed ten members in favour of retaining PR—two not strongly—as against eight favouring the alternative vote in single-seat constituencies, including Cosgrave himself and Sweetman.

On the following Tuesday, Liam Cosgrave phoned me to say that he had raised the possibility of a merger with the Labour leader, Brendan Corish, who was not encouraging, but sought a proposal in writing. However, a few minutes after they had parted Corish had rung to withdraw this request, saying that he was making a speech that night that would cut across the proposal for an arrangement between the parties.

I rang Halligan, and at his suggestion went to see Corish in Leinster House. He was discouraging, fearing that word of talks would get out and would damage Labour. He would be glad to see people like Declan Costello, Tom O'Higgins, Paddy Harte, Oliver Flanagan (in my contemporary notes I placed an exclamation mark after this name) and myself in Labour, but a merger of the two parties would be very difficult. However, he would put it to his front bench on the following day and would ring me afterwards.

He did so the following afternoon, saying 'Nothing doing,' adding that he hoped there would be no more approaches from us, as in that event they would have to issue a denial. Subsequently Jim Downey of the *Irish Times* told me that the proposal had been defeated by a small majority, but I never got confirmation of this.

And so Fine Gael and Labour went their separate paths as parties, although they have served in coalitions together on three subsequent occasions. Had this move succeeded, the political history of the succeeding years would surely have been very different.

As we had foreseen, Fianna Fáil went on to launch a referendum in 1968 to change the constitutional provisions on the electoral system. A television programme prepared and presented by Professor Basil Chubb and David Thornley of Trinity College showed that, as Jim Dooge and I had calculated, the introduction of the proposed British-type system would, given Ireland's particular political geography, provide Fianna Fáil with a clear majority even with as few as 40 per cent of the votes—a figure they had never failed to exceed since 1932—and that they would win almost 100 of the 144 seats with the share of the vote they normally secured. When the referendum was held, after a hard-fought campaign in which Fine Gael and Labour defended PR, the Government proposal was defeated; not by the narrow margin of 1959 but by a majority of almost 235,000 out of 1,080,000 valid votes: in other words, over 60 per cent voted against it.

After the election of 1965 the process of policy formulation had been resumed in Fine Gael, widening the core of Just Society policies. I had prepared, with the help of a committee of experts, an extensive document on education, which was published in 1966. So also was a policy statement I wrote on Irish, proposing removal of the provision dating back to 1934 that the Leaving Certificate be awarded only to pupils who passed in Irish, as well as abolition of the Irish-language requirement for entry to the civil service; eight years later our Coalition Government was to effect both of these reforms.

Another policy statement, issued for the 1967 local elections, proposed the removal of planning appeals from the political arena, and the making of state appointments on merit alone. Following the foundation of the state, political patronage had been eliminated from the vast majority of state appointments through the establishment of the Civil Service Commission and the Local Appointments Commission; but several categories—such as rate collectors, and teachers in VEC schools—had been excluded from the remit of the Local Appointments Commission, and the appointment of judges had also remained political. The latter was eventually put right in an ad hoc manner from the late 1970s onwards.

As we approached the general election, expected in 1969, a special front bench meeting in the Montrose Hotel approved with some amendments a series of policy documents which, with other people, I had been preparing. The range of areas covered was wide: public enterprise, industrial democracy and industrial relations, estate duty, social welfare, public administration and public morality, agriculture, foreign policy, and development aid. Together with the original Just Society policies of 1965 and the education, Irish-language and local government policies published in 1966/67 they represented a significant corpus of social-democratic and reforming proposals. For the second time, however, my suggestion for the abolition of estate duty and the substitution of a wealth tax was rejected at this meeting.

During these years from 1965 to 1969, when I was finding my feet in politics, I was also keeping my other activities going: journalism, consultancy, and university lecturing. Combining politics with journalism did not create any serious problem for me, although I was conscious that in my determination to retain journalistic objectivity I probably pulled punches when writing about issues that involved Government policy. Not everyone accepted that this was the case, however. One departmental secretary who had been closely associated with Seán Lemass told me that he had ceased reading my weekly economic column in the *Irish Times* because he 'knew' it was biased. When I asked him innocently how he knew this if, as he said, he had ceased reading it, he said he did not need to read my articles to know that they were biased!

By contrast, a number of Fianna Fáil politicians approached me individually in Leinster House to ask me to criticise various aspects of Government policy in my economic column. I counted seven such approaches during my first six months as a senator, from five Fianna Fáil politicians, including the Tánaiste, Erskine Childers, who had for long been a fan of my economic writings. He wanted me to criticise more vigorously the Government's approach to inflation, with which he—I think rightly—was unhappy. Neither he nor his colleagues were at all satisfied when I explained my concern to keep my reputation for journalistic objectivity by restraining my criticism of Government policy in the *Irish Times*, nor were they impressed by my offer to make in the Seanad the critical comments they proposed! I have to add that no similar pressure to politicise my column came from any of my colleagues in Fine Gael.

In the spring of 1964 I became BBC correspondent in Ireland, and I took on the *Economist* shortly afterwards. The *Economist* was the only paper with which I ever had trouble. Proud of their 'house style', they rewrote their correspondents' contributions. Up to a point this is acceptable; but sometimes they went too far in my view. I was moved to protest strongly when they added a first paragraph of their own to a piece they had asked me to write about the fiftieth anniversary of the 1916 Rising, which they published over the by-line, 'By our Dublin Correspondent.' It read, 'This week fifty years ago a group of hotheads seized the GPO in Dublin,' and was accompanied by a photograph of de Valera being escorted under arrest by two British soldiers, our President being described under the photograph as 'one of the hotheads'! On that occasion I got an apology from the paper.

My consultancy business, the EIU of Ireland, also kept me busy, but my heart remained mainly with UCD. In 1967 the college became involved in a major controversy. The issue was a proposed merger of UCD with Trinity College to form a new university. Even today the origins of this proposal remain obscure. It appears, however, that following publication of a summary of the Report of the Commission on Higher Education that had been appointed in 1961, which itself made no such proposal, the energetic Minister for Education, Donagh O'Malley, decided to embark on a merger. The UCD authorities apparently got wind of what the Minister intended to do, however, and, it seems, decided to pre-empt it by publishing a merger proposal of their own. This proposal would have had the effect of submerging TCD totally in UCD by means of a complete merger of every individual faculty and department: UCD, being the larger college, would have had a majority of staff in almost every merged unit. The Minister in turn apparently learnt of this UCD estab- lishment ploy and instead suggested 'one University of Dublin, to contain two colleges, each complementary to the other'—wording that did not fit in with the UCD authorities' 'total merger' concept.

The UCD staff, who, since the previous year, had been linked with TCD and other colleges in the newly established Irish Federation of University Teachers, were divided on the merits of a merger, but they overwhelmingly— and generously, it must be said—rejected the 'total merger' concept that would effectively have wiped out TCD. The battle within the college went on until the end of October 1967, when a motion was put to the Governing Body that included the clause, 'The Governing Body is prepared to explore the principle of unified Departments and Faculties in one college or the other'—which would have left TCD staff in a minority in both the transformed colleges.

The group on the Governing Body that I had brought into being in 1964 proposed an alternative motion, citing the divergent views of various faculties and couched so as to make it clear that the approach envisaging unified facul- ties and departments was not necessarily seen as the best solution, and that the college would consider other possibilities. We were defeated, and subsequently submitted to the Government a minority report setting out our reasoning and our preference for two colleges, each of which would have a core of key arts subjects together with physics and chemistry. This action was denounced as disloyal. We were told that there simply could not be such a thing as a minority report from the Governing Body: that only the majority view could be expressed. The atmosphere at subsequent meetings became even more tense than in the past.

In the event the proposed merger was not proceeded with, partly because of the sudden, tragic death of Donagh O'Malley in February of the following year. For my part I regretted that a federal link was not established between the two colleges, which I felt would have ensured a better balance between them, given the long-term problems that UCD could face in attracting, under straight competitive conditions, a fair share of the better students to a larger and more anonymous campus on the suburban site to which by this time it was committed to moving. But I do not regret having won the battle to prevent TCD being submerged in UCD.

At the time that this controversy erupted the UCD Arts Faculty was still located in the city, at Earlsfort Terrace, although Science had just moved to the suburban Belfield campus. In 1968 concern began to emerge that the planned move of the Arts Faculty to the Belfield site in September 1969 would precede the availability of library facilities in the Library Block being built beside the new Arts Building. The authorities handled the students' genuine concern ineptly, and in February 1969 the library issue became the catalyst for a UCD version of the 'Days of May' revolt that had broken out in so many universities around the world during the previous year. A radical group called Students for Democratic Action occupied the administration offices, and a more moderate element organised mass meetings elsewhere in the college. From the outset I involved myself in efforts, which proved successful, to channel these developments in a constructive direction. I also helped to influence the Academic Council against disciplinary measures, which would only have made matters worse: this stand, while successful, did little to endear me and my friends to the establishment. And I encouraged, through resolutions I got through one of the mass meetings, serious discussion by students on the function and structure of the university in the contemporary world. Many staff were drawn into these student debates, which went on over several days, and were deeply impressed by the students' evident concern to have the benefit of their participation, views, and guidance. At an ad hoc staff meeting the sharing of experiences by academics who had become involved reinforced the resolve of most of their colleagues to join in this exercise of self-education.

The contrast between the almost uncontrollable and negative attitudes of students at earlier mass meetings and the constructive approach of all concerned in these seminars, organised on an individual class basis, was very striking. Some of the student discussion in these meetings turned on the need to raise standards, with staff members seeking to head off student enthusiasm for measures that would have drastically increased the failure rate! The weaknesses of college structures, especially the Governing Body, were probed, and the role of the university in society explored.

I endeavoured to encapsulate something of the emotion of the moment in a statement I drafted and which was signed by over seventy staff members. It recorded the emergence of a climate in which traditional barriers to communication had been removed in a mood of determination to avoid the disruption and bitterness that had occurred in other countries where student revolts had taken place, and noted that students had demonstrated extraordinary confidence in the staff.

Much more was to follow. But from then on it was anti-climax as students gradually lost interest in their own 'Gentle Revolution', as it come to be known. The move to Belfield was accomplished reasonably smoothly, the interim library problem being resolved by using space in the basement of the Arts Block for a temporary library rather than requiring the students to travel back into the city every time they wanted to consult a book. The threat of disciplining the occupying students evaporated, and in the years that followed the college evolved fairly rapidly towards a more open society with a more relaxed relationship between the administration, staff, and students.

Little else remains save the memory shared by some thousands of people now approaching middle age or, in the case of the staff, already past that point, of an exhilarating moment when barriers disappeared and, for a brief instant, a different kind of academic community of students and staff seemed possible.

Before moving back to the political arena I should, perhaps, record a brief excursion into theology in 1968.

At the end of July that year we had gone on a family holiday to France, and it was on the ship as we approached Le Havre that we heard about the publication of the encyclical *Humanae Vitae*. When we got the text I found that on reading it my reaction was quite negative, as was Joan's. I had always been opposed to artificial contraception on what I had thought were moral grounds, but study of the encyclical convinced me that the moral argument was not sustainable. I came to the conclusion that my objections to artificial birth control had been aesthetic rather than moral.

When we returned home at the end of the month we heard of a conference to be held in Co. Wexford later in September at which theologians, doctors, academics, journalists and others were to discuss the encyclical. Joan arranged for us to attend. It was a stimulating and indeed inspiring occasion as all concerned strove to address the moral and medical issues involved. With the help of religious affairs commentators from the national media, and at least one newspaper editor, we produced a report that we submitted to the Irish bishops. This stressed the great problems the encyclical created for a significant number of people in relation to contraception itself, in relation to ecclesiastical authority, and in relation to developing ideas about the nature of the church. It also expressed concern that a document that demanded internal and external obedience to its teaching should contain apparent inadequacies and inconsistencies. It recorded that the members of the medical profession present stated that the biological premise upon which its recommendation of the safe period was based was scientifically untenable. We added that these 'natural' methods were frequently disruptive of the harmony of married life, whereas the contraceptive methods condemned by the encyclical had been often found to foster conjugal love and to help towards the attainment of maturity in marriage relationships— a view which, the report recorded, was endorsed by married couples present.

Reactions by the hierarchy to this report, transmitted to them by a lay participant, Vincent Grogan (at the time Supreme Knight of the Order of St Columbanus, which was then passing through a brief liberal phase), were varied. One bishop described it as 'most useful', 'understanding', and 'reasonable'; another remarked that we would appear to have had 'a very interesting and stimulating week-end'! The reply from the Archbishop of Dublin, John Charles McQuaid, was characteristically brief and pungent: 'I thank you for your manifesto. I feel sure that you would prefer to go to your judgement with the knowledge that you had done all in your power to secure full assent to the teaching of the Vicar of Christ.'

The deeper interest that Joan in particular, and I to a lesser extent, developed in theology in our later years was considerably stimulated, I believe, by this remarkable conference.

# CHAPTER FOUR

# A NEOPHYTE IN DÁIL ÉIREANN

Although Jack Lynch could have postponed a dissolution of the Dáil until 1970, an election seemed likely in 1969. The prospects for the opposition were not good. Labour's sharp shift to the left, in the belief that 'the seventies will be socialist,' and its public rejection of a coalition with Fine Gael had widened the gap between the two opposition parties. This was a positive factor for Fianna Fáil, because preferential voting between the non-Fianna Fáil parties (e.g. voting numbers 1 and 2 Fine Gael and number 3 Labour) is important and can influence the outcome against Fianna Fáil in marginal seats. Moreover, a swing against Fianna Fáil, which might perhaps have been expected since they had been twelve years in office, was likely to be inhibited by what public opinion would perceive as a prospect of instability if that party were to be defeated, when, at best, Labour would then be supporting Fine Gael in Government from outside rather than participating in Government within a coalition.

Fine Gael had the advantage of a vigorous and quite ruthless organiser in Gerard Sweetman; and the policy work with which I had been so closely involved since 1965 had provided the party with a more solid and extensive platform than any Irish party had ever possessed in the past. But I had still to learn that Irish elections are rarely won or lost on a wide range of policy issues. At best, one or two key subjects may influence the result.

By this time I was actively involved in the Dublin South-East constituency and was accepted as the automatic successor to John A. Costello on his impending retirement. Attention had, indeed, become concentrated on the question of a second candidate in Dublin South-East on the assumption that I would be the principal one. One possibility was Alexis FitzGerald—not my friend the well-known solicitor but his young nephew of the same name, who had joined the party in Dublin South-East at the same time as myself and had become an effective organiser there. However, he was reluctant to stand in Dublin South-East with me, believing it would be a mistake for the two Fine Gael candidates to have the same surname, even though not related to each other. He proposed Fergus O'Brien, a salesman in the ESB in his late thirties who was vigorous and energetic. Unfortunately this question of candidates had been faced too late, and when the election was called for June 1969 Fergus O'Brien had had no chance to build up support for himself before the campaign started.

In those days there were still public meetings in Dublin. I recall a delightful Saturday afternoon at Sandymount Green when I addressed a friendly crowd of some three hundred in brilliant sunshine, as well as another occasion at Ringsend where I first met Noel Browne, who was speaking from a Labour platform. There was also a final rally at the GPO, at which I spoke. It was the last major outdoor meeting of this kind in the city centre: thereafter the danger of loyalist paramilitary bombs, the first of which exploded in Dublin in 1972, made such large political gatherings in public too much of a security risk.

When the votes came to be counted I was found to have topped the poll in Dublin South-East, with Fianna Fáil and Labour securing the other two seats; but the outcome of the election nationally was disappointing. True, Fine Gael, with a fractional increase in its share of the vote, gained three seats—but so did Fianna Fáil, which, after providing the Ceann Comhairle, had a majority of five. Labour and independents were the losers.

On election day I had had an unexpected shock. Normally a candidate spends the day visiting polling stations, and I had started out on this tour before they opened at nine o'clock. By eleven, however, I had developed a migraine, and I returned home to get a couple of hours' rest. In the meantime the post had come, and Joan had opened it. One document was the agenda for the next Governing Body meeting; it included a proposal that any UCD staff members elected to the Dáil should be sent on leave of absence without pay.

I had never foreseen such a possibility. Since the foundation of the state, UCD staff had been allowed to be members of the Dáil, without prejudice to their posts, taking leave of absence only when holding Ministerial office. The roll-call of such academic politicians was long and included some of the most distinguished academics and notable politicians of the period since independence: Eoin MacNeill, John Marcus O'Sullivan, Patrick McGilligan, Michael Hayes, Michael Tierney. To propose to change a policy that had permitted such a fruitful relationship between the college and national politics was certainly a startling innovation, and, as I remarked to Joan, to propose it at a moment when it was too late to prevent oneself from being elected seemed particularly unfair!

I rang Alexis FitzGerald, friend, political adviser, and solicitor; he said he would do what he could. In the event he rang his father-in-law, John A. Costello, to whose former seat I was about to be elected, and he in turn, I discovered later, rang the Taoiseach, Jack Lynch, who was horrified at this proposal and said that he would ask the Fianna Fáil county councillors on the college's Governing Body to oppose it. In the event, a subcommittee headed by a distinguished medical professor (himself a practising consultant and therefore a somewhat odd choice as chairman of a subcommittee to investigate academic pluralism), decided that honour would be satisfied if my salary were reduced by 20 per cent on account of my absences from the college during part of the working week—absences that would be slightly longer as a deputy than they had been as a senator. To ensure that no-one could complain about my service as a lecturer-deputy I arranged to give one *more* lecture or seminar each week than any of my colleagues in the Department of Political Economy.

A brief Dáil session before the summer recess followed the election. This session opened on 2 July with the re-election of Jack Lynch as Taoiseach and a debate on his new Government. I spoke in this debate, which was probably somewhat unusual for a new deputy. Moreover, on 9 July there were three Bills that interested me: an Air Companies Bill, a University Bill, and a Decimal Currency Bill. Although my Dáil front bench portfolio was education I spoke on all three Bills that day and in detail on the Finance Bill in the following week, as well as putting down questions to the Taoiseach and nine Ministers.

When the Dáil resumed in October I made lengthy contributions of two to three hours in each case on foreign affairs, Northern Ireland, and the Department of Labour estimates. Finally, when a supplementary estimate for the Department of Education was introduced towards the end of the year, I had a chance to speak on the subject actually allocated to me on the opposition front bench, and in April 1970 I led the opposition side in the debate on the education estimate for 1970/71, speaking for almost four hours on the forty-odd aspects of education that seemed to me to be matters of concern or controversy at that time.

The frequency, variety and length of my interventions in the early period of this Dáil were the product, in part at least, of the Pooh-Bah role I had been required to play in the Seanad—but also, I have to admit, of a somewhat bumptious conviction that I had something significant to say on all these issues. My intense activity in debate provoked comment; the most pointed (and it had a certain impact on my subsequent Dáil behaviour) took the form of an *Irish Times* cartoon showing a Fine Gael front bench consisting of twenty-one Garret FitzGeralds. But of the tensions thus created with some of my colleagues I was only partly conscious at the time.

Within the educational area itself I also trod on some corns, including those of people who had not been accustomed previously to radical views on education from Fine Gael speakers. My April 1970 education speech strongly criticised the excessive time given to Irish in primary schools, the adverse effect of which on educational standards had been demonstrated by an academic study in the mid-1960s; and I also raised the question of parents' involvement in decision-making, a concept popular neither with teachers nor the clergy who managed Catholic primary schools. My criticism of the threefold division of second-level schools (between Catholic and Protestant, secondary and vocational, and boys' and girls') was also controversial at that time, as, in a quite different way, was my support on educational grounds for the merger of small one-teacher and two-teacher national schools in rural areas: such schools were seen locally as cherished symbols of community identity. Finally, I offended conservative clericalist elements by defending the new category of community schools, which had arisen from the need in smaller centres to rationalise religious and local authority schools, and by pressing the case for the independence of these new schools from a measure of Catholic clerical control that would have made them unacceptable to Protestant parents.

In 1971 I was moved to the shadow Finance portfolio—a promotion which, although it may have been due to what were seen as my radical views on education, I nevertheless welcomed; and it was in that capacity that I served out my last two years in opposition.

Meanwhile in my geographically small constituency I had been helping to build up a strong, young and lively organisation. Within a short period there were twelve active branches, nine of them covering various districts while two others were university branches, in TCD and UCD, and the twelfth was a unique School Students' Branch. As students were supposed to be, and often were, also members of geographical branches, and as some of these students were elected as constituency delegates for these geographical branches for a number of years, some one-third of our constituency executive members were very young people, who provided lively and good-humoured debate at that level.

At the same time with my fellow-candidate, Fergus O'Brien, I was undertaking a methodical door-to-door canvass of the very many council flats and houses in the constituency, simultaneously establishing weekly clinics in three centres. The reward for all this work came in 1973 when Fergus and myself were both elected, winning two of the three seats with the help of between a quarter and a third of the vote in working-class areas.

Since the Derry march of October 1968 Northern Ireland had been casting a shadow over the whole island. Now, with the large-scale rioting of mid-August 1969, it threatened the whole island's peace. Joan and I were on holiday in France with the children and with a number of friends when these dramatic events occurred, but as soon as I got home I set about drafting a Northern Ireland policy statement. Despite my long-standing concern about the attitude of political parties in the Republic towards the North, I had not hitherto intervened in this policy area. I was now disturbed at the extent to which even moderate-minded people in the party leadership had been moved by the dramatic events of the preceding weeks to react in what seemed to me to be a somewhat extreme manner. The absence of any clear framework of party policy in relation to Northern Ireland had, I felt, left a dangerous vacuum, the atavistic filling of which in conditions of great tension carried evident dangers.

For me the crucial issue was to get acceptance by the party of the principle that, whatever we might think of partition, and however much we might feel that the division of the island had been damaging to its peace and prosperity, given that this division had become an established fact it could and should be ended only with the consent of a majority in Northern Ireland.

This had never been accepted, overtly at any rate, by Fianna Fáil as a party, to some extent perhaps because of a feeling that to do so would have been to weaken their hold on a segment of republican opinion that might then have drifted towards support for the IRA. I had always believed, however, that Fine Gael had the duty to take an unambiguous stand on the issue. In fact, the party had participated in—and from its vantage point in Government in 1949 had even led—an anti-partition campaign that echoed the traditional republican slogans, 'The North has no right to opt out,' 'Ireland has a right to its six north-eastern counties,' and so on.

I did not believe that this approach would ever bring about Irish unity; Britain would neither be cajoled nor intimidated into 'handing over' the North against the wishes of a majority of its inhabitants, and the more we expounded this thesis the more we alienated Northern unionists, thus postponing any possibility of reunification by the only feasible route: that of the eventual consent of a majority in Northern Ireland.

I had welcomed the civil rights movement enthusiastically as a radical departure from republican irredentism, refocusing the energies of Northern nationalists, and the sympathies of fair-minded people everywhere, on the hitherto neglected issue of the legitimate grievances of the Northern minority. This movement, as I saw it, and still see it, represented a belated and realistic 'opting in' to the Northern Ireland system by the minority there, seeking their rightful entitlement to participation on a basis of equality in the society of Northern Ireland. It represented, I felt, the first step towards a normalisation of politics in Northern Ireland from which might eventually spring a new climate in which the relationship between North and South could be addressed afresh, with objectivity.

In the event I proved grossly overoptimistic; unionist opinion was unable to adjust constructively to this kind of 'opting in' by the nationalist minority. Unionists' sense of being themselves the real minority in the island as a whole, with all the deep-seated fears of a permanent minority, was too strong. Apart from a few leaders like the Prime Minister, Terence O'Neill, they thus lacked the self-confidence to respond positively to this radical change of emphasis by Northern nationalist opinion. And so by August 1969 what could have been a most fruitful development had been converted by intransigent unionist opposition into an inflammatory one.

To damp down the flames seemed urgent. This had to involve reforms that would restore normality to the security situation in Northern Ireland and accommodate the legitimate aspirations of the Northern nationalists, who had been excluded for fifty years from any role in the affairs of the part of the island in which they found themselves. But it must also involve reassurance for the unionists who for half a century had felt threatened by Southern political demands that Britain reunite the North with the rest of the country regardless of the wishes of the Northern majority.

These considerations provided the parameters for my draft policy statement on Northern Ireland. It began by identifying the problem as the mutual fear by the two sections of the Northern community. Unionist fears had been intensified by the Republic's pursuit of policies intended to persuade or force Britain to 'hand over' the North and by plotting on the part of subversive elements in the Republic. Nationalists, in turn, feared attack by Protestant extremists. I went on: 'Force as a weapon of policy having been rejected by responsible political groups in the Republic, the only way in which the present divided state of this island can, or should be modified is with the consent of a majority of the people of Northern Ireland.'

*This*, as I saw it, was the key sentence in the document; although not everyone who read it, nor all those who joined in adopting it at the time, may have appreciated its full significance.

The draft went on to recommend consultation between politicians in the Republic and those of their Northern counterparts opposed to discrimination. It favoured diplomatic efforts by the Irish Government to persuade Britain to promote 'normal democracy and a just society in Northern Ireland'; reconstitution of the RUC; disbandment of the B Specials (who were effectively a unionist militia); and guarantees against the gerrymandering of electoral areas. It sought the creation of a body similar to the Council of Ireland envisaged by the Anglo-Irish Treaty of 1921, and said that the parties in the Dáil should repudiate force as a means of reunification while at the same time dedicating themselves to work towards voluntary reunion. It advocated study of the Constitution and laws of the Republic to see what changes might make them acceptable 'to the widest spectrum of opinion in Ireland,' as well as the pursuit of economic prosperity so that social welfare services might be provided in our state comparable to those in the North. And it advised the immediate establishment in the Republic of an all-party parliamentary committee for Northern Ireland affairs.

The document included a clause that urged the Government, 'after appropriate consultation with Northern opinion,' to press Britain to provide for minority representatives in the government of Northern Ireland as a guarantee of fair treatment for all. This policy statement thus put forward what was, I believe, the first suggestion of power-sharing on either side of the border, for Northern nationalists were not at that time yet able to envisage a process of working with unionists in government; over a year was to pass before they even began to entertain the concept.

Recognising that because of domestic divisions in Fine Gael (to which I shall come later) a policy document drafted by me might receive less than a warm reception from some members of the front bench, especially as Northern Ireland was outside my area of responsibility, I asked Paddy Harte, the TD for Donegal North-East, who was known to be deeply concerned about the North, to submit it on his own account to the front bench, having first of all, during the weekend of 7–8 September, sought the opinions of John Hume and Austin

Currie. These two had secretly met Liam Cosgrave, Gerard Sweetman, Paddy Donegan and Mark Clinton of Fine Gael at Virginia, Co. Cavan, on the previous Monday. I hoped that contact with three leaders of the civil rights movement might have helped the leaders of our party to appreciate the shift that had occurred in Northern nationalist opinion away from sterile anti-partitionism towards a realistic attempt to tackle the roots of the problem inside Northern Ireland itself. Unsure, however, of the impact of these discussions on my colleagues, I awaited with some trepidation the front bench meeting of 11 September, at which Paddy Harte was to produce the draft policy, which John Hume and Austin Currie had by then approved.

As it happened, two of the four more traditionally anti-partitionist members of the front bench were absent abroad on that day, making traditional-type anti-partition speeches, and when we came to discuss the policy statement in the afternoon both Liam Cosgrave and Sweetman had to leave the meeting, for different reasons. The policy went through without difficulty. I wanted it published at once, but our PRO had standing instructions—reasonably enough!—that nothing should be published unless Cosgrave had an opportunity to see it first. I awaited the outcome of this clearance process like an expectant father. When the PRO emerged from his discussion of the document with the party leader he told me that it was cleared save for one inessential paragraph.

The principle of 'no reunification without consent' was soon adopted also by the Labour Party. And after the 1970 Arms Crisis had changed fairly radically the composition of the Fianna Fáil Government, Jack Lynch edged Fianna Fáil gradually towards the same stance, so that when the Sunningdale agreement, incorporating this principle, was signed in December 1973 he was able to get his party to accept it.

This did not mean, however, that traditional anti-partition rhetoric vanished overnight from Fine Gael or Labour, let alone from Fianna Fáil. Indeed, two years later it was to cause problems in Fine Gael, as I shall explain further on in this chapter.

Meanwhile I made my first personal contact with John Hume. Accompanied by Tom O'Higgins, Alexis FitzGerald, and Michael Sweetman, I went to Derry and had a long discussion with John Hume and Ivan Cooper in the latter's house. It was the beginning of a relationship with John that endured thereafter, even when at times policy differences emerged between us, as in the late 1970s.

But before coming to the way in which, in May 1970, Northern Ireland exploded into the politics of the Irish state with shattering consequences for the Fianna Fáil Government, I must turn back to the end of August 1969 to describe a series of events in which I was involved within Fine Gael itself.

On my return from France I had found myself faced with an evening newspaper headline announcing that six young members of Fine Gael, friends of mine, had been expelled from the party by the organisational and disciplinary body,, the Standing Committee. The expulsions arose from a row about candidates in the Dublin South-Central constituency during the June general election. The name of Maurice O'Connell, a young candidate chosen by the local convention to contest the constituency with the sitting TD, Richie Ryan, had been deleted by the Standing Committee before the election and replaced on the ticket with that of the late John Kelly, Professor of Roman Law and Jurisprudence in UCD. Maurice O'Connell had been a member of the committee that had drafted our educational policy under my chairmanship three years earlier, and his summary removal from the ticket and replacement with another candidate, albeit one of great distinction, had been badly received by many in Fine Gael, especially amongst the young. O'Connell had, however, breached party rules by standing in the election as an independent, and disciplinary action had been initiated by the party organiser, Gerard Sweetman, against him and five others who had supported him. These included John Maguire, a postgraduate student who had played a constructive role in the UCD 'Gentle Revolution' some months earlier (and now Professor of Philosophy in UCC), Vincent Browne (then editor of a Fine Gael youth magazine and now editor of the *Sunday Tribune*), and Henry Kelly, of television fame.

Their expulsion at the end of August nevertheless came as a shock, and defects in the procedure adopted seemed to me to call for action. The Standing Committee was obviously not going to be persuaded by political means to reverse its disciplinary decision, and the parliamentary party had no role in a matter of this kind. The only course open was a legal one. I sought advice; within a few days a letter was on its way to the party's trustees, calling on them to preserve the rights of the six to the party's property by rejecting the decision of the Standing Committee on the grounds of a series of procedural irregularities. This ploy succeeded. Sweetman had to admit defeat. On Cosgrave's proposal, the Standing Committee reversed its decision before the end of September.

The tensions within the party at this stage came home to me very forcibly when I was called to a meeting—it may have been a subcommittee of the Standing Committee—apparently to account for my support of the six. For two-and-a-half hours I had the eerie experience of listening to myself being referred to exclusively in the third person. 'We all know he's a communist, don't we?' 'Oh, yes, we all know about *him*.' And so on and so on.

On 6 December, however, Cosgrave and Sweetman asked me if I would help to end the discord by inviting Maurice O'Connell to transfer to my constituency of Dublin South-East from Dublin South-Central, where Richie Ryan apparently still considered him a threat. For the sake of peace, I agreed, but it did not solve the problem. Richie reacted to the news of the transfer by denouncing what he called 'an anti-party group', which, he said, was trying to destroy Fine Gael. Some of the group believed in confiscation; the Irish people were not going to abandon their property to revolutionaries who wanted to bring doctrines into Ireland that had been rejected by most other countries. He added: 'Those of us who have for years, and when I say years I mean decades, fought for social reform in this country now find ourselves being accused of insincerity by people who have come along at the last moment to pretend that they are more revolutionary than those who have been providing and fighting for this reform.'

These extraordinary allegations, arising from my acceptance of a request from the leadership of the party to take Maurice O'Connell into my constituency, were neither contested nor clarified by the leadership, and while the row eventually blew over, relations within the party were damaged. A belief grew up that Liam Cosgrave was surrounding himself with a clique of 'loyalist' supporters. It seems to me in retrospect that this would not have been in character. But the fact that he did not appear to deal with the Richie Ryan outburst, together with vocal declarations of loyalty to him by a number of his colleagues during the aftermath, gave an impression that he had sided unfairly with one group in the party; and party unity suffered.

In justice to Richie Ryan it should perhaps be added that the resentment he expressed somewhat melodramatically was comprehensible. He had joined Fine Gael with a radical reforming approach in the late 1950s, and it must have been galling for him that Declan Costello (admittedly with much longer service in the party) seemed to have trumped his card in 1964–65 with the Just Society policy and that a newcomer like myself was by 1969 being seen as yet another new radical force.

For a period after the traumatic events of May 1970, which demanded and received a united response from Fine Gael, the divisions in the party disappeared, however. I shall recount these events as I experienced them.

On 5 May 1970 Jack Lynch informed the Dáil that the Minister for Justice, Mícheál Ó Móráin, had resigned. Liam Cosgrave asked whether this was the only Ministerial resignation the House could expect. The Taoiseach replied, 'I don't know what the deputy is referring to,' to which the Fine Gael leader responded, 'Is it only the tip of the iceberg?' He refused, however, to accept Lynch's invitation to enlarge on what was on his mind.

That evening I went into Cosgrave's office shortly before eight o'clock to find a number of members of the front bench talking with him in grave tones. The discussion was clearly confidential; I left them to it. Much later I learnt that Cosgrave had been consulting the people present about two separate reports he had received of a plot to import arms for the IRA, which allegedly involved Government Ministers. Fearing that these reports might have been a trap, he hesitated to take action, but Mark Clinton said he should present the information to the Taoiseach. He agreed, returning about an hour later to tell his colleagues, 'It's all true.'

At about ten o'clock, knowing nothing of all this, I walked into the Ministers' corridor in search of a member of the Government to whom I wished to speak. He was not there, but the door to his office was open and the television news was on. I stood in the door to watch; the news item was about the Kent State University massacre. The door from the Taoiseach's office at the end of the corridor opened. A glowering Kevin Boland—Minister for Local Government— came along the corridor, too preoccupied to notice me. I went home to bed.

In the middle of the night, at 4.00 a.m., the phone rang. It was Muiris Mac Conghail from RTE. Lynch had announced at 2.50 a.m. that he had sacked Neil Blaney and Charles Haughey, apparently for gun-running. Blaney I could understand; but Haughey? What on earth was he doing involving himself in an affair of that kind? The last thing I had heard about his attitude to Northern Ireland had been in the previous September, when he was rumoured to have been a moderating influence against Blaney.

And what should I do? I rang Tom O'Higgins and Alexis FitzGerald. They were equally shocked by the news; neither had any suggestion as to what could or should be done. Eventually, at about 5 a.m., I went back to sleep.

The Dáil assembled at 11.30 a.m., an hour later than usual because of the 1916 Commemoration at Arbour Hill that morning. There was a brief delay before Jack Lynch entered. He proposed an adjournment until 10 p.m. so that the Government and the Fianna Fáil party would have time to meet. Questions from Cosgrave revealed that Blaney and Haughey had not yet responded to the Taoiseach's call for their resignations—but, Lynch added, he was entitled to act on his request by asking the President to terminate their appointments. After a brief exchange between the party leaders on the possibility of an earlier resumption, an adjournment to 10 p.m. was agreed.

Boland had resigned in protest at the dismissals; when I had seen him the previous evening he had apparently just submitted his resignation to Lynch. Shortly after the Dáil adjourned that morning another resignation came: Paudge Brennan, Blaney's Parliamentary Secretary. By contrast, Blaney himself had said that he might not in fact be leaving the Government. Was he hoping to overthrow Lynch before his appointment was terminated?

By 7 p.m. rumours of a 'coup' of this kind were dissipated. The late-afternoon Fianna Fáil party meeting had ended in less than an hour, with Lynch in firm control. We heard later that the discussion had been skilfully confined to the single issue of the Taoiseach's right to appoint and dismiss Ministers.

A four-and-a-half-hour debate started at 10 p.m. on the motion to name Desmond O'Malley as Minister for Justice in succession to Ó Móráin. The Taoiseach in his opening speech announced that as neither Blaney nor Haughey would comply with his request to submit their resignations, the President had terminated their appointments on his recommendation. He then outlined a sequence of events beginning on Monday 20 April when, he said, the security forces had submitted to him information about an alleged attempt to import arms, which prima facie involved two members of the Government.

Cosgrave followed, describing how at 8 p.m. on the previous evening he had told the Taoiseach of information he had received about an attempt to import arms illegally through Dublin Airport, those involved including, in addition to the two Ministers, a brother of each of the dismissed Ministers and some of their friends. Following the failure of the Minister for Justice to give a directive to the Gardaí in relation to this matter, the Taoiseach had been notified and the attempted importation had been dropped; but although the question of dismissing Ministers had arisen, no action had been taken until the resignation of the Minister for Justice, Mícheál Ó Móráin, on 4 May. When Cosgrave had received information on Garda notepaper supporting information he already possessed, he had decided to put the facts in his possession before the Taoiseach.

I took no part in this relatively brief debate, but in the subsequent debate on the nomination of Ministers to replace those who had been dismissed or resigned on the fifth and sixth I found myself by accident closing on behalf of the opposition. This second debate was the longest in the history of the state, lasting for over thirty-six hours, from 10.30 a.m. on Friday 8 May to 11 p.m. on Saturday 9 May.

Initially no-one expected such a long debate. When in the early evening of Friday I was nominated to conclude for Fine Gael (by default, because it was realised at this stage that all our leading frontbenchers had already spoken), I expected the debate to end late that night. But every time I looked at the list of members wishing to speak it had grown longer, not shorter. All the members of our party now wanted to say their piece.

Around midnight I went home to work on my speech in more peaceful surroundings. At about 2.30 a.m. I was rung to come in at once, as it was believed that the Government intended to move the closure. This turned out to be a false alarm, but, as a result of a practical joke by a Government deputy, it resulted in the loss of the notes I had made for my speech. I went home and started again at 7.30 a.m., working until near lunchtime. My speech probably benefited considerably from being rewritten. It largely took the form of an attempt to reconstruct the extraordinary events of the preceding weeks from an analysis of all the statements and counterstatements that had emerged from those involved, between which there were many contradictions. Some observers noticed that while I was speaking members of Fianna Fáil, including Ministers, were listening with an attentiveness that suggested they felt they were now getting for the first time the facts of what had taken place.

The penultimate sentence of my speech—before a final phrase extolling the responsibility with which our party and its leader, Liam Cosgrave, had handled this issue—was a pointed contrast between the political bitterness displayed by Blaney and the total lack of resentment on the part of Erskine Childers, the Tánaiste, and his forgiveness of those—including my father—who had been responsible in 1922 for *his* father's execution. To my astonishment the Fianna Fáil benches erupted in applause, joined, somewhat uncertainly, by some of my colleagues behind me. I should of course have had the wit to sit down at that moment; instead I waited till the applause died down and proceeded unimaginatively to my planned final sentence and appropriate applause from our own benches.

On the following Tuesday and Wednesday there was a confidence debate. I was the penultimate Fine Gael speaker. One question that I pressed was whether the money to buy these arms had come from state funds. The Taoiseach had told the House already that there was no question of Secret Service funds having been used, nor was any money missing from the Department of Defence. I said that 'the likely place is the Department of Finance . . . there is no denial in respect of there.'

A couple of hours later, replying to the debate, the Taoiseach said that he had made specific enquiries as to whether any moneys could have been voted or could have been paid out of exchequer funds, or out of any public funds, in respect of a consignment of arms of the size in question, 'and was assured that there was not and could not have been' any such payments. It later transpired that this was an accurate, although not verbatim, account of what he had been advised he could say. However, many months afterwards, when the Committee on Public Accounts came to investigate the affair, it emerged that the money had in fact, as I had suggested, come from the Department of Finance, having been 'laundered' through the Irish Red Cross Society to bank accounts in false names. Moreover, the file on this 'Fund for the Relief of Distress in Northern Ireland', which had been examined as a preliminary to the advice to the Taoiseach that he could give this assurance, had contained a number of references to the money being needed by 'Jim Kelly's friends' or 'Kelly's people'—and during the previous week an Army intelligence officer, Captain Jim Kelly, had been featuring as a key person in the whole affair.

Months passed, however, before these facts on the use of funds authorised by the Minister for Finance emerged. I was a member of the Committee on Public Accounts that was given the task in December 1970 of investigating and reporting on this aspect of the arms affair. By that time the trials of the former Ministers and others accused of illegal arms importations were over; on the evidence the jury had found them not guilty. Our committee's inquiry went on for over eighteen months. We got little co-operation from many of those asked to give evidence to us. The Official Secrets Act was invoked to prevent publication of a memo that had been sent by the Secretary of the Department of Justice to the Secretary of the Department of Finance shortly after the Dáil debates and which had identified the Finance sub-head from which the money had come. A successful Supreme Court challenge was mounted on technical grounds against the committee's power to compel the attendance of witnesses.

Nevertheless, despite the problems such an inquiry posed for its Fianna Fáil members, the committee produced a final report that clarified to a degree the process by which state funds authorised by the Minister for Finance, Charles Haughey, had been used to finance an attempt to import arms illegally. On the basis of the evidence we had been able to unearth despite the uncooperativeness of some witnesses, we brought our Fianna Fáil colleagues on the committee to accept that if three Ministers, Neil Blaney, Charles Haughey, and Jim Gibbons, had 'passed on to the Taoiseach their suspicion or knowledge of the proposed arms importation' the misappropriation of part of the money spent on arms might have been avoided, with a rider to the effect that the committee was not satisfied that the decision of Charles Haughey as Minister for Finance to make available a specific sum of money from the Fund for the Relief of Distress in Northern Ireland was justified.

By the time the committee reported, in July 1972, much else had happened in Northern Ireland. Shortly after the Arms Crisis of May 1970 the British government had changed, and several weeks after that election came the Falls Road curfew, when the British army carried out mass raids on houses in nationalist areas, the character of which alienated many nationalists who hitherto had welcomed the army as protection against unionist pogroms. Throughout 1971 the situation in Northern Ireland kept on deteriorating.

These events reached a climax in August 1971. Joan and I had decided to take our summer holiday in Kerry. For the first week it rained almost without a break. Then we woke one morning to the news that several hundred nationalists had been detained in Northern Ireland with a view to internment. The reaction in nationalist areas was violent—especially as it quickly emerged that a large number of those detained were innocent of any IRA involvement, being the victims of the collapse of the police intelligence system after the RUC had been discredited in 1969. It also soon became clear that many had been brutalised after their arrest, and there was much bitterness at the selective character of detention. Moreover, no loyalist paramilitaries were included, an omission that I was later authoritatively told by a member of the Northern Ireland government had been justified by the security authorities to that government on the grounds that the files on the loyalists had been lost!

On the day that detention took place I was called to Dublin from Kerry to meet an SDLP delegation, which did not include John Hume, and to attend a front bench meeting. The SDLP representatives foresaw mounting violence and bloodshed following the detention—they proved right in this, as on that day alone twelve died—and they took what seemed to me at least a very hard-line attitude, insisting that they would now contemplate nothing except the abolition of Stormont. It later transpired that John Hume was not in full agreement with this; indeed, when I met him ten days later in Derry he was very upset to hear the line his colleagues had taken with us, which, he said, was very different from the position that had previously been agreed among them.

The reports of harassment of the nationalist population by the British army were deeply disturbing. An opportunity to ventilate this issue later presented itself when the British television programme 'World in Action' interviewed me on Northern Ireland. To ensure that the point would not be lost in the course of editing, I ignored the actual questions put to me and aired the harassment issue in *all* my replies. The programme was, however, banned by the Independent Broadcasting Authority, at the instance of a Northern cousin of mine who had been appointed to that body after retirement from the BBC in Belfast. The *Spectator* reported that the ban had been due to my comments on the behaviour of the British army, but I was never able to confirm this.

But to return to the events of August 1971: back in Kerry I received a phone call on the morning of Friday 13 August from a fairly recently appointed

Northern Minister, Robin Baillie, whom I had got to know in November 1970 before he had become a member of the government. He asked me to come to Belfast, and on the following day he met me at Portadown and drove me to his home. He had joined the government, he said, because he believed that Brian Faulkner, who had succeeded James Chichester-Clarke as Prime Minister of Northern Ireland, provided the only hope of a peaceful solution and that Faulkner would steer the North towards an agreement on full participation of the Northern minority in government. He still believed that Faulkner was prepared for 'proportional government', and despite the depth of the rift with the nationalist population arising from the form that detention had taken, he believed that progress on these lines might even now be possible. He added that in the light of the events of the preceding week even quite intransigent unionists were looking for a solution.

I told him that in this postdetention situation I saw little prospect of getting talks going again between the Northern Ireland government and the opposition unless the opposition could be satisfied in advance that a solution along the lines of proportional government would in fact be acceptable to Faulkner and his government and that internment would also be withdrawn. He said he would make further soundings, and we agreed to meet again in a week or so.

On my way back to Kerry through Dublin I went to my home and typed a letter to Liam Cosgrave telling him of my meeting with Robin Baillie, expressing great scepticism about whether anything could come of this initiative, however, and suggesting that while the fewer people who knew of my contact with Baillie the better, our shadow Minister for Foreign Affairs, Richie Ryan, must of course be told.

On the evening of Thursday 19 August I rang John Hume and he agreed to see me on the following day. I arrived in mid-morning to find the area around his house invested with British troops. John was out, but returned after half an hour. Furious at the army presence, which put his home and family at risk from the IRA, he rang the RUC, who declared themselves impotent in the matter. John then went down to the corner to persuade the British officer in charge to move away. I stood in a doorway beside a heavily armed soldier, watching the other soldiers in the little gardens opposite the houses listening to the argument. For about a quarter of an hour John got nowhere. Then he suddenly had a brainwave. 'Do you realise', he said to the officer, pointing at the soldiers in the gardens, 'that your men are standing on private property?' The officer, overcome with embarrassment at this apparently unanswerable thrust, responded at once. The men were told to move. I was enormously impressed with the courteous manner in which the officer conveyed his orders. To the soldier beside me he said, 'I say, please, would you mind moving away?'!

John and I went to a hotel; there I put to him proposals that I had worked out. First, the British government should, at the request of Faulkner, call a meeting bringing together government and opposition in Northern Ireland;

this formula would preserve Faulkner's position with the Unionists but would make it possible for the opposition to come to a meeting. Second, the meeting should agree to a new Northern Ireland parliament being elected by PR, and to a proportionately representative government being chosen either by that parliament or by the British government after consultation—but this should *not* be made a precondition. Third, the detainees should be released. And, fourth, a Council of Ireland with economic and consultative functions should be formed following discussions with the Republic. In other words, I proposed much of what actually emerged two years later before and at Sunningdale.

John believed that he could get his colleagues, with the possible exception of Paddy Devlin, to accept this. I then drove to Belfast and saw Baillie. He was prepared to try to 'sell' these proposals to his colleagues, of whom only Faulkner knew he had been talking to me. He felt that judicious preparation would be necessary, however, involving Ken Bloomfield, the Permanent Secretary to the Cabinet, and he even suggested that I might talk to the British Home Secretary, Reginald Maudling. On my return to Dublin I briefed Liam Cosgrave and Richie Ryan on my activities and left into Cosgrave's office a memo in which I expanded my proposals after consulting John Kelly and Michael Sweetman. I gave other copies of this memo to Conor Cruise O'Brien (who was going to a meeting in London on 1 September of the British and Irish Labour Parties, the Northern Ireland Labour Party, and the SDLP), both for himself and for John Hume—and, if he thought appropriate, for the British Labour Party.

This memo fleshed out my earlier proposal in considerable detail. It added the idea of a Deputy Prime Minister from the opposition, which was also to be a feature of the end-of-1973 settlement; a suggestion for a security force drawn from the whole community; a proposal for a Bill of Rights; and a suggested procedure for nominating the judiciary that would ensure a visibly balanced court, something not achieved even after the Anglo-Irish Agreement of 1985. It also included detailed proposals for an equitable grouping of the existing single-seat constituencies into three, four and five-seat units in order to facilitate an early PR election without a lengthy process of constituency review; this grouping was designed to ensure both proportionality of representation in each of three main regions of Northern Ireland and also some representation for both communities in every constituency. Although John Hume, Austin Currie and the SDLP leader, Gerry Fitt, saw virtue in my ideas, many in that party still favoured the demand that Stormont be abolished.

Early in September Jack Lynch met the British Prime Minister, Ted Heath, a meeting that marked a significant advance on the British side since it recognised the Irish Government's legitimate interest in a situation threatening the security of both parts of the island. The British also proposed a tripartite meeting between the Taoiseach, the British Prime Minister, and the Prime Minister of Northern Ireland, which would involve a much closer involvement for the Republic in the affairs of Northern Ireland than had hitherto appeared conceivable. Lynch at first reacted coolly to the suggestion of discussions involving the head of a mere provincial government, and asked that the Northern opposition also be invited. The British were not yet attuned to the possibility of quadripartite talks of the kind that would take place at Sunningdale two years later, but Maudling offered separate meetings in London with the Northern government and opposition.

Although the Taoiseach eventually agreed to attend the tripartite talks, the SDLP rejected diplomatic urging from various quarters, including its own leadership, to meet Maudling unless internment were ended and Stormont abolished. It made matters no easier that during these days the leader of the SDLP, Gerry Fitt, was incapacitated with back trouble in St Vincent's Hospital in Dublin. With the help of Brendan Halligan and myself he made valiant efforts from his bed to control the course of events and, at Brendan Halligan's suggestion, received numerous visitors for political consultations—including Jack Lynch, Liam Cosgrave, and the British Ambassador—but there were limits to what could be expected of him.

Meanwhile I had been in touch again with Robin Baillie, and it had been agreed that I would meet Peter McLachlan of the Conservative Central Office at Baillie's house. Gerry Fitt asked me to sound out Baillie at this meeting on the possibility of an intermediary being nominated between himself and Faulkner—someone like Maurice Hayes—and he asked me to call on him with news of my discussions on my return from Belfast and after his meeting with his colleagues had ended.

I found Baillie and McLachlan very depressed. The IRA bombings of previous weeks had evoked their intended reaction amongst unionists: a hard-line attitude demanding repression and no concessions. Nevertheless the two of them went over a re-draft of my memorandum, a copy of which I had left into Liam Cosgrave's office before leaving Dublin.

On my return Brendan Halligan and I visited Gerry Fitt after an SDLP delegation had left. Fitt reported that there had been no real discussion of the issues. We seemed to be stuck. After some discussion he agreed, however, to issue a statement denouncing the Provisionals, which Baillie had felt might help to soften unionist attitudes. But on the following Wednesday, just as Baillie and McLachlan were preparing to get positive reactions to this statement from Faulkner and Maudling, Faulkner signed 219 orders converting the detention of 219 men into indefinite internment—something which, it appeared, he had done without consulting London, giving the British government one hour's notice. That at least was the impression I received from the British embassy.

As I reported to Cosgrave (he was just returning from a week's holiday), in a letter telling him that I proposed to attend an impending Westminster debate on Northern Ireland at McLachlan's suggestion in the hope of lobbying Tory MPs, this made any further initiative by Fitt in advance of the debate rather pointless. I added that I had drafted a Commons speech for the SDLP leader. Because of his back problem Fitt had spent much of his time in St Vincent's lying across the bed with his arms and legs dangling on either side, the only posture in which he could secure relief, and he could not write a speech, but he had given me an outline of what he wanted to say. On arrival in London I found that Fitt could not read my typescript: the type was too small, he said. I wrote out the speech in capital letters—25,000 of them, finishing at 4 a.m.

On Monday 20 September I had mentioned in a speech in my constituency that a group of TDs was going to attend the Westminster debate. Next morning I read that Richie Ryan was also going, and I tried fruitlessly throughout the afternoon to contact him so that we might co-ordinate our plans. Then at 6.30 p.m. I was rung by a journalist to comment on a statement issued by Richie that criticised our proposed visit to Westminster in astringent terms. I put out an explanatory statement, clarifying some misunderstandings. This was to have a sequel a month later.

Maudling's speech during the debate showed some signs of a thaw in British attitudes towards the minority in Northern Ireland and of the beginning of movement towards the concept of power-sharing: he commented that it was difficult to reconcile a permanent government and a permanent opposition with the concept of democracy. He also indicated an openness to proportional representation as a method of election in Northern Ireland, and spoke of the possibility of a sharing of government through some new basis of representation, with a permanent place in public life for the minority.

When Gerry Fitt's turn came to speak, for about four or five minutes he stuck to the script I had prepared at his request. Then his feelings got the better of him and the script was abandoned. Although the speech he made was no less powerful than that which he had planned, for example in its denunciation of the manner in which detention and internment had been carried out and in its statement of the constitutional nationalist position, it lacked certain components of the draft which at his suggestion had been designed to evoke a response from Unionists in the House of Commons—at least one of whom, alerted by me, had been prepared to respond to the speech as planned.

That was effectively the end of this attempt to secure a Sunningdale-type settlement before rather than after the abolition of Stormont—an initiative that, had it succeeded, would have saved Unionists the trauma of that event. In retrospect it probably never had much chance of success. Even if Faulkner considered it seriously (and the involvement, albeit marginal, of Bloomfield suggested that he may have done so) his Cabinet was unlikely to have countenanced a move to power-sharing at that time. And it has to be recognised that the impact of the detention and internment decisions on the nationalist community meant that the SDLP would have found it very difficult to retain support if at that moment they had entered into discussions with the Unionist government. Moreover, the tensions between Fitt, essentially an independent who was never comfortable in the role of party leader, and the rest of the SDLP—tensions that eventually led to his resignation from the leadership—were already present; and his attempt to direct events from Dublin, at a distance from the realities of Northern Ireland and with the aid of Southern politicians, must have been difficult for them to accept.

The coincidence of the brief Anglo-Irish controversy over tripartite or quadripartite talks with Maudling's proposal for separate discussions with the Northern government and opposition also made acceptance of the latter invitation more difficult for the SDLP, because, at the critical moment, there seemed to surface the more attractive prospect of involvement in talks together with the two sovereign governments as well as the Northern Ireland administration.

These events were to have a curious domestic sequel in Fine Gael a month later. When the Dáil debated Northern Ireland on 20 October, Richie Ryan, specifically citing the authority of Liam Cosgrave, proposed that Northern Ireland be constituted an international protectorate under the British and Irish governments for a transitional period; this proposal had never come before the party or the front bench. Liam Cosgrave, for his part, called for a phased withdrawal of the British army from Northern Ireland. I shared his concern about the performance of the troops at that time, but then and since have seen no available substitute as a deterrent to civil war in that part of the country.

At the front bench meeting on 26 October John Kelly and I raised these two speeches and expressed concern about major departures from what we had understood to be party policy on Northern Ireland. Cosgrave's reaction was instantaneous and, to say the least, vigorous. He told the front bench with evident anger that I had been engaged over a period in discussions in the North about the situation there without his knowledge and that I had produced and given to people two documents, the second of which I had brought to the North before he had seen it.

I reacted as best I could to this unexpected onslaught—for it was an onslaught—mentioning four letters I had written to Liam Cosgrave setting out the details of my discussions in the North as well as my personal contacts with him and Richie Ryan during the period from mid-August onwards. Subsequently I circulated to the front bench a detailed account of all the events of the period in question, based on my letters to the party leader and a note that for historical purposes I had compiled on 11 September of events up to that time.

In retrospect it seems to me that while on the one hand Liam Cosgrave had not been prepared to instruct me to stop what I was doing—he was perhaps more inhibited about confronting me than I, never the most sensitive of people, realised—this very restraint, combined with some pressure from an aggrieved shadow Minister for Foreign Affairs, Richie Ryan, must have built up in him a head of frustration. And, as was to happen on several other occasions during those years, this had eventually exploded.

On Sunday 31 January 1972 Joan and I were dining out when we heard first reports of a massacre in Derry. We went home at once and listened to various news bulletins. Clearly the death of so many men and boys at the hands of the British army in Derry, whatever the circumstances—and so far as one could judge at that stage there appeared to have been little if any justification for the paratroopers' actions—could endanger peace in the island as a whole. To find out whether there had been any provocation before the paratroopers' attack I rang the City Hotel in Derry, which, until it was burnt down by the IRA, was the usual haunt of journalists. I got Simon Winchester of the *Guardian*, who told me he had been one of only three reporters on the spot when the paratroopers launched their onslaught and that he had observed no firing on them beforehand.

Racking my brains to think of what I could do to help defuse the situation, I decided, in the hope of getting support for an inquiry into this appalling event, to contact the editor of the *Guardian*, Alastair Hetherington, whom I had met. First, however, I got through to the *Guardian* newsroom to find out whether in fact they were running Simon Winchester's story. They were, and a sub-editor read it to me. When I got through to Hetherington I made the mistake of mentioning that their own news story was about an unprovoked attack. I had got off on the wrong foot. 'Where did you get that?' he demanded, and was not pleased to hear that it was from talking to Simon Winchester and to his newsroom. My approach received a correspondingly cool reaction, and proved totally abortive.

Three days later I set off with Tom O'Higgins, Alexis FitzGerald and Michael Sweetman for the funerals in Derry. I shan't attempt to describe the occasion; it was shattering. Everyone in the tight-knit nationalist community in Derry had lost a relative, a neighbour, or a friend. After the funeral we were brought back for a meal to a nationalist house. When I went into the kitchen a woman said to me, 'Isn't it great that so many are joining?' 'Joining what?' I asked, bemused. 'The IRA, of course,' another woman responded. I started the long journey back with my fears for the immediate future heightened; if that was the instinctive reaction of moderate nationalists—for I knew it was such a house—to the trauma of these events, what hope could there be for Northern Ireland?

On the way home we stopped several times, timing our halts to coincide with television news bulletins. The British embassy in Merrion Square was under attack, and before we got back to Dublin it had been burnt out. My forebodings about the impact of the Derry massacre on security in the Republic as well as Northern Ireland seemed justified.

Next day the Dáil debated the situation. The fourth speech after those of the Taoiseach, Liam Cosgrave and Brendan Corish came from Neil Blaney, ensconced high up on the back benches with three other Fianna Fáil dissidents. It was inflammatory, as I had feared it would be. But this speech, and those of Blaney's three supporters later in the debate, evoked an immediate, instinctive response from the Government and from the opposition benches: a response that demonstrated the strength of our democratic system and the ability of our politicians in a crisis to transcend their differences in the interest of the country. Every contribution was directed towards taking the heat out of the situation and reducing the tension. Instinctively, and without concert, all concerned resisted the temptation to hit out blindly at the authors of this tragedy; too much was at stake for that: peace itself, in fact. There were, it is true, some on the Fianna Fáil benches who were clearly restive at the restrained tones of the Government speeches, but party discipline was maintained.

There followed the Widgery Tribunal into the event in Derry, which evoked universal cynicism in nationalist Ireland, but there were signs that, while no-one in the British government would admit the truth of what had happened in Derry, nevertheless behind the scenes a radical review of British policy in the North was under way. Twice in less than six months—at the time of the detentions, when so many of those arrested had been ill-treated (some to a degree that was later described by the Commission on Human Rights in Strasbourg as 'torture', a phrase subsequently modified by the Court of Human Rights to 'brutal and inhuman treatment'), and now in Derry—the British army had acted in support of a subordinate civil power outside the control of Westminster in a manner unacceptable to civilised opinion in Britain or else-where. Men like Ted Heath, Willie Whitelaw and Peter Carrington were not likely to tolerate this any further. The days of Stormont were clearly numbered—as, indeed, I had already concluded six months earlier, when, after the detentions with a view to internment, I had endeavoured to secure a transition to a power-sharing administration in advance of what then appeared to me to be an inevitable abolition of the provincial government.

It was at this time that I first met Willie Whitelaw in the House of Commons, with whom inside a year I was to find myself dealing across the table as my opposite number so far as Northern Ireland was concerned. His openness and bonhomie impressed me; I did not then know that the decision had already been taken to establish direct rule in Northern Ireland if Faulkner refused a British requirement that responsibility for security be transferred back from Stormont to London, and that Whitelaw himself was in this event to be the first Secretary of State. Within days of this Faulkner had in fact rejected a trans-fer of responsibility for security to London, and had resigned. The Stormont parliament was technically suspended but in reality abolished, and on 1 April Whitelaw took over as Secretary of State.

Four months later, after the announcement of an IRA cease-fire, the new Secretary of State met the IRA leadership in London. None of us had foreseen such a development, believing naïvely that no British government would be so foolish as to encourage the IRA to continue their campaign indefinitely by giving them reason to believe that, if they went on murdering people long enough, Britain would negotiate with them. We should have been warned by Harold Wilson's visit to Dublin as leader of the opposition a year earlier when, behind the backs of the Irish Government and opposition, whom he was meet-ing, he arranged to see the leaders of the terrorists who, with support from only a tiny minority of Irish people, threaten our state as well as Northern Ireland. In retrospect it is clear that we should have protested more loudly in 1971 at what we saw as an act of treachery towards the democratic politicians of the Republic on its own territory, and should not have allowed concern about alienating a past and future Prime Minister of Britain to mute our outrage.

Whitelaw's initiative vis-à-vis the IRA came to an abrupt end following the breakdown of the cease-fire a couple of days later. I know that he recognised in retrospect that it had been a serious mistake. But I am not sure that British politicians even today understand the extent to which this and similar contacts— such as the discussions between the Northern Ireland Office and Sinn Féin that were initiated several years later by Merlyn Rees, and contacts in 1981 during the hunger-strike—have contributed to the continuation of IRA violence over such a long period by enabling that organisation to persuade its members that persistence in the campaign of terror will eventually lead to British-IRA negotiations for a British withdrawal.

Meanwhile the argument within Fine Gael about the party's Northern Ireland policy had been partially sidetracked by the row over my activities sparked off by Liam Cosgrave's remarks at the front bench meeting in October 1971. The disagreement simmered on, and differences between what seemed to have become two wings of the party, deriving primarily from disagreements on domestic issues, were intensified by different approaches on Northern Ireland. At times the tensions led to momentary flare-ups on Liam Cosgrave's part. One of those arose from a dispute over American bombing of North Vietnam which had been widely condemned by, inter alia, the Pope and the UN Secretary-General, U Thant. When Tom O'Higgins, Jim Dooge and I had raised this issue at a front bench meeting we failed to secure the support of our colleagues for a statement criticising the American action, but there had been no demur when we stated our individual intention of signing an appeal for support for the Pope and the Secretary-General. Subsequently I also spoke along these lines at our ard-fheis. Cosgrave's response in his ard-fheis speech was not merely to record his disagreement with our position but to do so by referring to 'people who allow their humanitarian instincts to lead them to become communist dupes'—which, as I commented privately at the time, seemed a little hard on the Pope!

Some time after this I found myself in public disagreement with Oliver Flanagan on the issue of jobbery, to which I was strongly opposed. Two councillors who had taken exception to Flanagan's support for 'jobs for the boys' then criticised Cosgrave for nominating Flanagan to represent him at the consecration of a bishop. When at a party meeting subsequent to this I listed amongst differences between Fianna Fáil and Fine Gael our parties' divergent attitudes, as I saw them, to jobbery and corruption, Cosgrave in his reply chose to attack the two councillors, whose comments had not otherwise featured in the debate, and referred approvingly to Flanagan's senior position in the party. This was seen as a disguised attack on me.

But the most publicised example of what was seen as tension between the leader and the liberal social-democratic wing of the party occurred at our ard-fheis in May 1972. In a departure from his script Cosgrave first launched an attack on a market research company that had carried out a recent poll, saying obscurely that 'those who organised it could now give back the thirty pieces of silver.' Those who knew of my keen interest in polls interpreted this as an indirect reference to myself, although I had had nothing to do with the poll in question. He went on, moreover, to refer to people who had joined the party 'after it had been built up and had then begun their attack' on the party. These enemies of the party, whom, in a hunting metaphor that came easily to him, he described as 'mongrel foxes', would, he said, be 'unearthed, and then I will let the rank and file of the party, the pack, tear them apart.' The tone of this unscripted attack was disconcerting, especially for those of us who were seen as its targets; for a moment, indeed, I wondered whether I should leave the platform, as I believe several others considered doing, but discretion out-ran valour.

The newspapers made much of this, also remarking on the support from the floor given to Declan Costello's speech in favour of social reform, and to Pat Cooney's support for legislation to legalise contraception. Moreover they also contrasted a reference of mine to 'a Fine Gael Government or one with the Labour Party, among whom we have many friends' with what they saw as Cosgrave's visible lack of enthusiasm for anything other than an all-Fine Gael Government. The political correspondent of the *Irish Times* described Cosgrave as having 'created a leadership crisis in the public mind where it did not exist.' Another feature of this ard-fheis was the election as vice-president of Tom O'Higgins, who had been narrowly defeated for this post in the last ard-fheis, as well as myself; Paddy Donegan, seen as representing the right wing of the party, came fourth in this election.

In early November 1972 tensions between Liam Cosgrave and his deputy leader, Tom O'Higgins, had become visible at a party meeting. This led to a very full, and unusually frank, discussion at front bench meetings on 8 and 14 November. Many speakers at these meetings questioned openly for the first time aspects of Cosgrave's leadership, and in particular expressed concern at what his critics perceived as a withdrawal of confidence on his part from some members of the front bench during the immediately preceding years, together with what was seen as undue reliance on a small group of 'loyalists' on the front bench.

At the end of the front bench meeting of 14 November Cosgrave asked for twenty-four hours in which to consider his position. But when the front bench resumed twenty-four hours later, he ignored the discussion of the previous day and proceeded as if it had never happened. If this was intended to disconcert those who had initiated this discussion, it certainly succeeded. But after consultation between a number of those concerned it was decided to leave the matter on one side for the time being, for in the following week we had to face a difficult decision on how to handle a Government Bill to amend the Offences Against the State Act, 1940, so as to include, among other things, a provision that would constitute as evidence a statement by a Garda chief superintendent that he believed a person to be a member of the IRA.

When the front bench met to consider this Bill on 27 November it became clear at once that differences on the legislation ran very deep. Eventually it was decided to refer a decision on our course of action to the parliamentary party meeting the next day, without presenting a recommendation from the front bench, as was the normal practice. This meant that the differences within the front bench were to be openly revealed to the parliamentary party.

When the parliamentary party met, Cosgrave favoured the legislation, whereas a majority wanted to oppose it on the second stage because they took exception to some of its clauses on civil liberties grounds, including the provision regarding a chief superintendent's evidence. Eventually, late that night, after a discussion in the course of which twice as many members spoke against the Bill as for it—including a number normally strongly supportive of Liam Cosgrave, such as Richie Ryan, Mark Clinton, and Oliver Flanagan—he most reluctantly agreed to go along with a proposal to oppose the Bill on the basis of a reasoned amendment, to be proposed by the shadow Minister for Justice, Pat Cooney, and seconded by the party leader himself. It was after midnight when the meeting adjourned. Cosgrave was reported to be distressed at the party's decision but, the press said, would nevertheless vote as the party had decided; there had, they said, been no threat to resign.

Pat Cooney's speech in the Dáil proposing the amendment argued that the Government had failed to fully use existing powers and that both the 'chief superintendent section' and another banning demonstrations that could be deemed to be interference with the course of justice were objectionable, especially when introduced by a Government that had, he claimed, abused powers given to it under an earlier, hotly contested Prohibition of Forcible Entry Act. However, the tone of Cosgrave's speech seconding this reasoned amendment disturbed many of his colleagues because of his emphatic statements about Fine Gael's willingness to give all the powers and machinery necessary to the Government to deal with subversives 'remorselessly', and his dismissal of expressions of concern for liberty and freedom. 'Communists and their fellow-travellers and soft-headed liberals are always talking about repression,' he said. He also referred to 'anti-apartheid protest marches which degenerated into a rabble and were a disgrace to all associated with them.' Given that a number of his front bench, including Richie Ryan and myself, were members of the Anti-Apartheid Movement, this was felt by some to have been a bit gratuitous.

The press reaction was that he had 'hi-jacked his own front bench, shot down the reputations of his own key men, and ended Coalition hopes.' I was reported as not having clapped him when he sat down; and Pat Cooney's applause for his leader was of such a modest character that ever since that time faint applause for a colleague by a Dáil deputy has been described as a 'Cooney pat'.

The party met again that night. The issue of how to vote at the end of the second stage was debated all over again, and the meeting ended with a somewhat narrower, but nonetheless clear, majority for a vote against the Bill at second stage. The party thought that, for good or ill, this ended the matter.

By Friday, however, as the debate continued in the Dáil some among the party leadership were concerned as to whether Cosgrave would feel able to vote with his colleagues. As a result, at lunchtime that day an approach was made to Fianna Fáil to seek agreement to several amendments that would have met our main concerns and enabled a united Fine Gael to support the Bill. These proposals were, however, turned down at an early afternoon Government meeting; by this time Fianna Fáil had smelt blood and were, understandably, looking forward to facing a divided and possibly even headless Fine Gael in a 'law and order' election on the issue.

When word of this was received at 4.30 p.m. Cosgrave called yet a further party meeting in the hope of persuading his colleagues to reverse their twice-taken decision. This proved too much for the members, who, just before eight o'clock, after several hours' debate in the party room and with Tom O'Higgins already on his feet in the Dáil for half an hour waiting to hear what line he was to take, voted by 38 to 8 to oppose the Bill. Six of the eight opponents of the Bill immediately rallied to the majority, leaving Liam Cosgrave and Paddy Donegan alone in their dissent. As some members tried to persuade an unyielding Cosgrave to change his mind and vote with his party, I went down to the House to put Tom O'Higgins out of his agony.

As he proceeded to reveal the outcome of the discussions with the Government that afternoon and to accuse Fianna Fáil of arrogance by refusing to consider any amendments to the Bill, word reached us that bombs had just gone off in Dublin. I think I whispered this news to Tom O'Higgins just as a Fianna Fáil deputy, Noel Davern, interrupted him to ask him if he supported the bombings. Tom replied to Davern that he was aware of them and told him not to be a 'bloody ass'.

I went upstairs at once to our party corridor and found a large number of our deputies engaged in heated discussion on the landing outside the party room. After a few minutes there was general agreement, albeit with some dissentient voices, that in view of the bombings, which at that stage some thought might be an IRA provocation (although in the event it transpired that they had been undertaken by loyalist paramilitaries from the North, leaving 2 dead and 127 injured), we should reverse our stand and agree to support the Bill. I returned to the House, where Tom O'Higgins had concluded—inconclusively—and had gone to look for Liam Cosgrave to tell him what had happened.

After consultations with the Government, Pat Cooney intervened in the debate at 9.45 to withdraw our reasoned amendment. Following two adjournments the House reconvened at 11.25 and passed the second stage. Two Fine Gael deputies, Oliver Flanagan and Eddie Collins, voted against, together with Labour and independents.

The committee stage debate continued until 4 a.m., however. When the House then adjourned many in Fine Gael, including past supporters of Liam Cosgrave, left for home believing that he would be replaced as leader the following week. But unknown to most deputies he had during the course of the evening appeared on television to great effect, and by Saturday morning he was widely seen as the hero of the hour: the man who had stood firm and had, in tragic circumstances, been proved right.

And so, in retrospect, he had. Our emotional opposition to this Act was not subsequently justified by the use actually made of it. All too soon, indeed, the 'chief superintendent clause', far from proving dangerous to the liberty of innocent people, was rendered ineffective by virtue of a change in IRA policy instructing members to deny on oath allegations of membership by a chief superintendent. If no other evidence of membership was presented to them, the courts came to accept this rebutting evidence. Moreover, in political terms Cosgrave was also right: had we opposed the Bill we would, I believe, have been severely defeated in a post-Christmas law-and-order election.

Why, in the light of this, did a majority of Fine Gael oppose the Bill? After a long period in opposition—sixteen years in this case—a party tends to become anti-authoritarian, and in this instance there was a belief that Fianna Fáil, some of whose members were ambivalent about the IRA, had not been enforcing existing laws adequately. This had indeed been an insistent refrain of the opposition for several years previously, and the new legislation was seen by some as a 'cover' for this perceived failure rather than as a genuine attempt to strengthen the existing law.

Moreover, within Fine Gael Liam Cosgrave's position had been weakened by the manner in which he had handled tensions with Tom O'Higgins and myself and in particular by what was seen as his failure to respond at the front bench meeting of 15 November to the criticisms of his leadership made at the two immediately preceding meetings. The unresolved problem thus created, and left in abeyance because of the need to decide how to handle the Offences Against the State (Amendment) Bill, hung over the stormy debates on this measure in the party a fortnight later at which Cosgrave's quite uncharacteristic vacillation, under what admittedly was extreme pressure, unnerved his own strong supporters in the party.

These dramatic events had profound effects on the political fortunes of the Irish state, for, although deprived by a matter of minutes of the opportunity to call a snap 'law and order' election, Jack Lynch nevertheless calculated that the aftermath of these bruising events within Fine Gael provided his best moment to seek and secure a further mandate a year and a half before this Dáil had run its term. This proved to be a major miscalculation, which put an end to Fianna Fáil's second sixteen-year period in office and replaced Lynch with the man who had seemed for a brief moment on the evening of 1 December 1972 to be on his way to the back benches: Liam Cosgrave.

The drastic change in Joan's life and mine that these events were to precipitate had been preceded by a major change in our family situation. John and Mary had both married in late 1972. John had secured a good degree in 1970 in economics and history—an extremely difficult combination—and, after completing an MA thesis on an aspect of eighteenth-century Irish economic history, had joined the Department of Finance as an administrative officer. In September 1972 he married Eithne Ingoldsby; that decision had been made several years earlier when they had been classmates in UCD, and Eithne had preceded him into the Department of Finance, where she had soon become an expert on health and social welfare economics.

Mary had followed John into UCD, where her degree choice had been English and philosophy; in December 1972, when in her final year and aged nineteen, she married a fellow-student, Vincent Deane, whose enduring interest proved to be Joyce studies, in particular *Finnegans Wake*. After some years teaching in a school Mary became a temporary assistant lecturer in English in Maynooth, and later in UCD. Thus by the time the 1973 election was held only Mark, aged fifteen, remained at home.

Meanwhile, in anticipation of a possible change of Government in which I was likely to be involved I had been shifting the emphasis of my mixed career. My burden had been somewhat lightened, to my relief, in 1969 when I had been replaced as correspondent of the *Financial Times* and the BBC. Moreover, following my election to the Dáil the Confederation of Irish Industry, on the prompting, I understood, of the new Minister for Finance, Charles J. Haughey, had indicated to me that the degree of my political involvement as an opposition front bench spokesman in the Dáil made it inappropriate for me to continue as consultant to the confederation and as one of its representatives on the General Purposes Committee of the National Industrial Economic Council. I regretted this change but accepted it as an inevitable part of my career development.

However, for several more years I continued my general economic consultancy work but with growing doubts as to the possibility of the Economist Intelligence Unit of Ireland remaining a viable entity after a change of Government in the absence of my continuing involvement. By 1972 it was clear to me that I was becoming more rather than less involved in keeping the company going; since I had ceased to be managing director in 1967 it had tended to stagnate rather than to develop, and while I still derived a useful income from my work for it I could have earned almost as much working on my own without the overhead of the small staff and office premises. Accordingly, in the spring of 1972 the EIU in London and I agreed to wind up the company. I entered into an alternative arrangement with an accountancy and consultancy firm, Stokes Kennedy Crowley, to work with them as an economic and market consultant, an arrangement that naturally ended when I became Minister for Foreign Affairs a year later.

As a result of these changes I was able to make the transition to Government in March 1973 without too much trauma and without upsetting too many clients. The fact that the Government was formed during the course of an academic year in UCD did pose some problems, but my colleagues in the Economics Department took over my seminars and, although I was given leave of absence and ceased to be paid by the college from that moment onwards, I returned after Easter to complete my lectures in the Trinity term.

As it happened, the last of my European Community lectures before I was appointed to office had been about the Council of Ministers, and I had the pleasure of starting my first post-Easter lecture in this course as follows: 'The actual operation of the Council of Ministers is somewhat different from what I described in my last lecture.'

The change of career had serious financial implications, however. The Ministerial salary added to my Dáil allowance was very much less than what I had been earning from my combination of academic, consultancy and journalistic careers; indeed our after-tax income fell by some 40 per cent. Expenditure is more difficult to reduce; over the next two years our overdraft rose exponentially. By 1974 a move to a smaller house was inevitable, and with two of our children married was in any event appropriate. Unable to find a suitable house in the locality we had to move farther out of town, but within eighteen months Mark, now an apprentice auctioneer, found our present home in Palmerston Road. As a result of planning permission for a dwelling in the rear half of the back garden the value of the house and what remained of the back garden had been reduced. Mary and Vincent offered to carry one-third of the mortgage in return for the garden flat, where they and the friends with whom they were sharing an apartment would live. This made the move back into town feasible for us, although we never succeeded in reducing our living standards commensurately with the drop in income.

CHAPTER FIVE

# EC: THE ENEMY WITHIN

It was on 31 January 1973 that Jack Lynch called an election, hoping, no doubt, to secure a further overall majority—perhaps even an increased majority—as a result of the disarray into which Fine Gael had been thrown by the dramatic events in the Dáil two months earlier.

The reaction amongst the opposition to this move must have disconcerted him, however. Not alone did Fine Gael close ranks around Liam Cosgrave but Fine Gael and Labour immediately opened negotiations for a National Coalition platform on which to fight the election. I was not involved in the initial stages of this operation, as my constituency called an immediate convention, but when I surfaced after being nominated I found that agreement had virtually been reached on a joint programme. It did not include my twice-rejected proposal to substitute an annual wealth tax for estate duties, but an additional clause designed to open the way to this was added at my suggestion and accepted without difficulty by Labour.

In the election Fine Gael gained four seats from Fianna Fáil, Labour one, and independents one. Fianna Fáil's six-seat overall majority was thus converted into a Fine Gael-Labour majority of two.

The only inkling about my future that I received before the Dáil resumed to elect Liam Cosgrave as Taoiseach came a week later. He asked me, without prejudice, which Government post I would prefer. I said I would be happy to continue in Finance, which I had been understudying as shadow Minister, but was, of course, prepared to accept whatever he might propose. He responded by saying that it would either be Finance or another senior post. I asked which other senior post he was thinking of; he hesitated, and then said, perhaps understandably, that he would prefer to leave that over.

As I waited for the Dáil to meet I began to take stock of what was involved in becoming a member of the Government. Apart from the sharp drop in income, compensated only in part by having a state car and driver, there was another side also: the security implications. All my life I had visited Northern Ireland on and off in order to see my many relatives there, and in latter years to meet members of the SDLP or other people involved less directly in politics. But after 14 March I would no longer be able to travel to the North without protection, and even on that basis access might be difficult. Irish Ministers had never been in the habit of visiting Northern Ireland.

I decided to pay one last visit as a free man to the part of Ireland where my roots were deepest—the only part where I had relations with whom I had maintained close ties. So I arranged to go on a sentimental journey to Belfast on Tuesday 13 March, the day before the Dáil met. I then took a second decision: to turn the trip to practical advantage by making informal contact with Unionist leaders, whom I had not previously met. Accordingly I arranged appointments at the Europa Hotel with three Unionist Party leaders and separately with a fourth, independent, Unionist politician. The meetings were cordial, and I was encouraged to maintain contact subsequently when in Government. I also called in to the SDLP headquarters, where I discussed PR with two members of their Executive.

Next morning, Wednesday 14 March, I was on my way to Leinster House when I passed a friend from the Department of Foreign Affairs, who said out of the corner of her mouth: 'Welcome to Iveagh House.' Shortly afterwards in the restaurant at lunchtime Brendan Corish, the Labour leader, called me over to his table as I passed by and told me not to be too disappointed if I were not appointed to Finance. 'What's the alternative?' I asked him. 'It could be Foreign Affairs,' he replied.

When Joan came into the House I told her of these hints. She was upset. She had not flown since 1956, nor had I since 1958, out of deference to her fears, save once, a year earlier, when I had missed the night boat-train at Euston. She hated the idea that I might have to fly frequently to fulfil my duties in Foreign Affairs.

At three o'clock the Dáil assembled to elect a Taoiseach. Liam Cosgrave was duly chosen and went to Áras an Uachtaráin to receive his appointment from the President, Éamon de Valera. We were told to be at the Taoiseach's office at 5.30 p.m.—half an hour before the Dáil was due to resume for the announcement of the new Government.

I waited in the corridor outside, expecting that we would be called in one by one, but at 5.35 p.m. I was asked to join others inside. As I entered, Liam Cosgrave stepped forward, shook my hand, and said, 'Foreign Affairs. Is that all right?' I assented.

The cabinet of fifteen had five Labour members, including Brendan Corish as Tánaiste. When the new Taoiseach read out the list of Ministers, confirming my nomination to Foreign Affairs, Joan in the public gallery burst into tears. Mark, then fifteen, tried to console her, pointing out that in the immediately preceding period the Minister for Finance had had to fly to Brussels more frequently than the Foreign Minister.

Several hours passed before we made our way to Áras an Uachtaráin to receive our seals of office. Because of uncertainty about when we were leaving, most of us had had nothing to eat. I was in the last car of the cortege with Pat Cooney. Along the quays we saw a sweet shop; we stopped the car, and I dashed in to buy several bars of chocolate from an astonished shopkeeper. We were still dining off them when we arrived at the Áras. After the formal proceedings we held, in accordance with custom, our first cabinet meeting at a table in the Áras, which had been that of the first government of which my father had been a member. The Secretary of the Department of Foreign Affairs attended on this occasion, as well as the Secretary to the Government. He told us that the British government was about to approve a White Paper on Northern Ireland, probably on the following morning, and that if we wished to make an input to their deliberations we would have to move very rapidly indeed. The cabinet decided that we should prepare a message to send to the British, and appointed a subcommittee to meet at 9.30 a.m. in order to consider a draft that I was to prepare during the night. This was then to be presented to the cabinet for consideration at eleven o'clock.

On my way home I first had to make some broadcasts and say farewell to the *Irish Times*, for which I had been writing for almost twenty years. When I eventually arrived home it was 2.30 a.m. During the next hour or two I prepared a draft message to the British government, which the ad hoc subcommittee approved, with some modifications, before the Government met at 11 a.m. Our London embassy delivered the message to Downing Street at 11.45 a.m., where the British Cabinet had been in session since 10.30, discussing the draft White Paper.

It was then decided that I should fly to London that afternoon to see the Prime Minister and the Foreign Secretary in order to explain our point of view more fully. By 2.30 p.m. I was on my way, and at 6.30, after a briefing session at the embassy, was in Downing Street with Ted Heath and Alec Douglas-Home.

Two things remain in my mind about this first contact with the British government. One was my attempt to persuade them of the value in Ireland of a judicial review of human rights. This feature of the constitutional system of the Irish state also existed in Northern Ireland during the Stormont period, when the High Court in Belfast had the power to declare legislative discrimination against the minority community in the North *ultra vires* the 1920 Government of Ireland Act—although the power had rarely been invoked. Ted Heath's response to this suggestion was unambiguous: 'Constitutionally impossible! Her Majesty's judges could not possibly overrule Her Majesty in Parliament.' It was the first time, but by no means the last, that I came up against the curious rigidity of Britain's unwritten constitution.

My second memory of this meeting is the initiative I took about visits to Northern Ireland. I told the Prime Minister and the Foreign Secretary about my recent visit and informed them that I would be going there regularly in my new capacity. I guessed that, given the obvious value of contact being deve-

*My parents in their late thirties.*

*Family Homes.* (Above) *Ballyrobin House in Co. Antrim about 1870 with the Neill family seated outside. My grandmother is on the extreme left and my great grandfather on the extreme right.* (Below) *Fairy Hill, Bray in 1928.*

*My father with* (above) *W.T. Cosgrave, President of the Executive Council and Ernest Blythe, Vice-President of the Executive Council and* (below) *with W.T. Cosgrave outside the Pro-Cathedral, Dublin.*

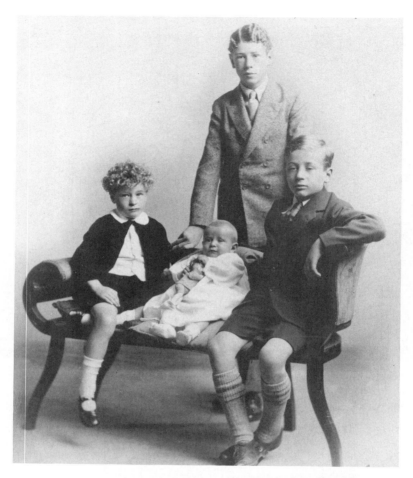

*Family Portraits.
Fergus, myself,
Dem and Pierce
in 1926* (above)
*and myself a year
later* (right).

*My enthusiasm for transport showed itself early. There was rapid progress from the motor car in 1930 to the sail cycle a year later and the much more powerful motorbike in 1932.*

*At Jack's Hole, Co. Wicklow, with Fergus in 1931, and at Fairy Hill with flags for the Eucharistic Congress a year later.*

*I meet the chimpanzee at London Zoo in 1936.*

*Only the proof survived of our wedding photograph in 1947—we couldn't afford to pay for the prints. (Below)* On holiday together three years later in London.

*As a young executive on the way up in Aer Lingus in the early 1950s.*

loped between the Irish Government and Unionist politicians, they could hardly object to what I was proposing, and I was right.

From then on I visited Northern Ireland several times each year, naturally notifying the Northern Ireland security authorities of my intentions, but not seeking clearance from, or giving formal notice to, the British government.

The EEC Foreign Ministers were to meet in Brussels the following day. By the time the Downing Street meeting finished it was too late to catch the last plane to Brussels, and no seats were available on the night sleeper via Dunkirk. Douglas-Home rose to the occasion, offering me a lift with him in an ancient Andover of the Queen's Flight, which took off from a dark corner of London Airport, illuminated by a single light—a departure that reminded me forcibly of films I had seen about the Resistance in occupied Europe during the war. The flight gave me the opportunity to establish a relationship with Douglas-Home, and assured me of a night's sleep in Brussels before my first encounter with the other Foreign Ministers of the Community.

The occasion was not in fact a meeting of the Council of Ministers of the Community but rather a meeting of the Foreign Ministers of the Nine on Political Co-operation, or foreign policy co-ordination. Among the topics for discussion was whether the Nine should recognise North Vietnam. This was the type of issue that Ireland had not hitherto had to face, because it has always been the Irish practice to recognise states, not governments, which avoided the awkward problem that could arise when one regime replaced another in non-democratic states. Recognition of North Vietnam was thus not an important question for us, and on this occasion I was able, without attracting attention, to remain silent. Nevertheless it was clear to me from the discussion around the table that a radical shift was required in the focus of Irish foreign policy now that we had joined the Community: henceforth we would have to fulfil our responsibilities in conjunction with other member-states, and for that purpose would have to develop, on the basis of *our own* information and *our own* assessments, policy positions on a whole range of global issues that had hitherto been of concern to us only in the more limited context of UN membership. This could not be done credibly without an extension of our representation abroad, in particular by establishing diplomatic relations with the Soviet Union. At that stage we were the only state in the world apart from Portugal and the Holy See not to have such relations, reflecting the extent to which Irish politicians had allowed fear of popular anti-communist prejudice to influence their actions irrationally in relation to foreign policy.

Back in Dublin on the following Monday morning I went into my department, effectively for the first time. I met the senior people, and was then brought on a tour of the building to meet the rest of the staff. Several incidents stand out in my mind. The first is a conversation I had with Seán Donlon walking up the stairs of the Anglo-Irish Division, in which he was then a counsellor responsible for relations with Northern Ireland. I asked him what contacts he had with Northern politicians. 'None at present,' he replied. 'We had contacts with the SDLP until last November.' I found this somewhat astonishing. Eventually I discovered that contacts with the SDLP had been maintained until the previous November by a senior official in the Anglo-Irish Division, Éamon Gallagher, but that Jack Lynch had apparently been dealing directly with Gallagher without keeping his Minister, Paddy Hillery, informed. Gallagher had thus found himself in an invidious position vis-à-vis his own Minister, and in November 1972 had asked to be transferred to the Economic Division. Because of uncertainties about Government policy, contacts with the SDLP had not been maintained after his departure.

I should perhaps add that during the previous three years the whole question of contacts between the Irish Government and Northern Ireland had been complicated by the extreme tension in that part of the island and by concern about British reactions to the maintenance of such contacts, especially after the Arms Crisis in 1970. At one period Gallagher had been told that he could go to Northern Ireland only outside office hours—in the evenings or at weekends—so that if his presence there were queried by the British, he could claim to be off duty!

I told Seán Donlon that he should resume contact with the SDLP immediately. I then asked him about contacts with Unionists. There had been none, he told me, and I had the impression that such contacts had not been encouraged. I told him that I did not see how we could hope to find a solution to the Northern Ireland problem without such contacts, and that he should follow up the informal discussions I had had with Unionists in Belfast six days earlier. I told him also that I would be visiting Northern Ireland on a regular basis.

The relationship between Iveagh House and Northern Ireland changed radically from this moment on. Contacts with political leaders of both communities in the North were developed in a structured way, with different officials designated to deal with each: initially Seán Donlon with the nationalist side and John McColgan with the unionist leadership. Our line to Ian Paisley, however, had to be through Paddy Harte TD, as Paisley would not talk to representatives of the Irish Government—a category in which he did not include Paddy Harte, who was a Fine Gael backbencher.

At the same time it also proved possible to intensify relations with British opinion-formers as a result of the academic, journalistic and political contacts I had established over the years. Foreign Affairs officials, both from our London embassy and from Iveagh House, became much more involved in activities in Britain related to Northern Ireland, thus in turn increasing our influence on British attitudes regarding the North.

Having met the staff in the Anglo-Irish Division I was brought to the Registry and shown the department's very first file, my father's personal file S/1 (S being for 'Staff'). It contained little except income-tax demands from the mid-1920s. Jack Perry, the boilerman, then brought me around the basement. As we explored the cellars it became evident that he was still distressed about some of the things that had happened after Lord Iveagh had handed the building over to the Government in 1939. In this context he referred obscurely to 'Queen Victoria's head under the stairs'. I subsequently elucidated this mysterious remark. When de Valera had taken possession of the house, his personal secretary apparently held strong views about remnants of British imperialism. According to the account I received, she ordered the destruction of anything containing what she considered to be a symbol of royalty or the British regime. Happily—and this was what Jack Perry had been hinting at—she had failed to observe that the badly lit but quite remarkable wooden carving along the lower edge of a balcony at the top of the main staircase contained at its centre a medallion with the head of Queen Victoria!

My own office on the first floor was a spacious, and gracious, room. It had eighteenth-century tapestries of silvan scenes inset along one wall, a huge fireplace in which on appropriate occasions a turf fire blazed, and two great windows overlooking the part of the Iveagh Gardens that belonged to the house, the remainder being at the disposal of UCD. In the UCD part of the gardens thirty years earlier I had been lectured on fine days, had organised a children's party, and had lounged around with friends discussing at times the kind of matters for which I now had Ministerial responsibility.

In the centre of the lawn outside my office was a small ornamental pool with overhanging shrubs, where in the spring a pair of ducks from Stephen's Green nested and hatched out their offspring, just as I had become accustomed since becoming a member of the Oireachtas to seeing another pair doing each year in the pool on Leinster Lawn. One Sunday when in conference with several senior officials on an urgent matter I saw the hatched ducklings struggling unavailingly to get out of the pond along an overhanging branch; I mobilised the officials to help me find a plank in the basement along which the ducklings could proceed with a view to following their parents out the rear entrance and down Earlsfort Terrace to Stephen's Green.

The other rooms on my floor of the main Iveagh House building included an ante-room with a connecting door to my office, used for pre-lunch or pre-dinner drinks when we were entertaining; a conference-room cum dining-room; and my private office, which had to close down temporarily to become a servery when lunch or dinner was being offered.

The balcony embellished with Queen Victoria's head outside the ante-room connected with the main staircase, by which access was gained to the ballroom, where up to a hundred people could be entertained for major occasions such as the annual St Patrick's Day dinner for the diplomatic corps, at which traditionally each table was hosted by a Minister, opposition leader, or senior judge. It is not surprising that a succession of Ministers for Foreign Affairs were said to be chary of hosting their Taoiseach in these surroundings, lest he decide to exchange his relatively spartan accommodation in Government Buildings for the magnificence of Iveagh House.

After my initial tour of the building I sat down to discuss foreign affairs with the Secretary and Assistant Secretaries, who constituted a 'Management Committee', the meetings of which on Mondays I soon arranged to join in mid-morning, after they had had an opportunity to review outstanding issues among themselves and prepare for discussion with me.

The Secretary was Hugh McCann, a diplomat with great experience who had been appointed Secretary of the Department ten years earlier after a period as Ambassador to the Court of St James. His Secretaryship had been extraordinarily fruitful. He had effected a gradual, fairly painless and notably humane transition from a system of promotion by seniority to promotion on merit. There had, of course, been objections to this important change in personnel policy, but on the whole they had been muted, and only one senior ambassador sought (without success) to persuade me to turn back the tide.

Of course, such an innovation takes time to yield results, and I was probably the first Minister to benefit fully from it. By the time I arrived at Iveagh House one-quarter of the ambassadors were under fifty and one-quarter of officials of counsellor rank were 'high-fliers' under forty years of age. There were in addition a number of young First Secretaries still in their twenties, on whose talents I was able to draw, promoting them to counsellor rank within a couple of years.

At the time of my appointment a reshuffle of senior posts in the department was in fact pending. I knew that Hugh McCann had been hoping after his strenuous decade as Secretary to be released for service overseas, but he agreed at my request to remain for a year to guide me in my responsibilities and to give me time to feel my way in relation to the staff. I found this immensely valuable. During the crucial early period in the job I had the advantage of his exceptional experience and wisdom in all I attempted.

As it happened I already knew personally over one-third of the fifty senior officials. Some had been at college with me and others I had come to know mainly through my interest in EC affairs. After my appointment I made it my business to brief myself from other sources on the capabilities of many of those whom I did not know personally. I was therefore far better placed than most Ministers in relation to my staff: many politicians have been appointed to Ministries where they have no prior knowledge of *any* officials. Happily Hugh McCann and his successor, Paul Keating, were both disposed to share with me their responsibility for staff promotions and postings, and, while I never sought to impose my views in such matters, it is fair to say that the disposition of staff while I was Minister was a joint responsibility, and one that absorbed many hours of my time at different periods in conjunction with the Secretary of the day.

After my first meeting with the Management Committee I decided to call a conference of all senior officials and ambassadors to discuss our foreign policy in the light of our very recent entry to the European Community. No such conference had ever previously been held (nor has one been held since). Fortunately I was too new in the job to know much about financial constraints or to be inhibited by precedent from organising this event.

The conference, which lasted three days, convened in Iveagh House in mid-April. I decided that our initial discussion should deal with the evolution of Europe towards unity, looking at the question in European terms, broader in scope than narrow national interest or even enlightened self-interest, for we were now members of the European Community, responsible with our partners for achieving its objectives. Knowing that other national bureaucracies had tended to take a narrow view protective of their national interests in the Community, and that this was holding up progress towards the economic integration that I believed to be in *our* interest, I was anxious to face the department bluntly with this issue. In most other areas I would have to learn from them, but in this I wanted to give a personal lead, based on my long involvement with the European ideal.

The implications of Irish neutrality came up during the initial discussion. One ambassador, who had participated in the negotiations for membership, remarked that the matter had been raised by the Commission during these negotiations and also by Community governments with the Taoiseach, Jack Lynch, during his tour of capitals in connection with our membership. This, no doubt, had influenced the previous Government to accept publicly that Ireland would participate in the defence of a fully integrated Community, a position supported by my own party.

In commenting after the first round of contributions I suggested we might be 'tilting at windmills' if we saw the defence issue as something likely to arise in the near future, a view subsequently proved correct. Given the slowness of the whole process of integration, I felt that European defence was some distance down the road.

It was clear from the discussion, however, that we should seek allies in support of the Common Agricultural Policy, already under threat, and that we should quickly produce our own ideas on regional policy.

I then directed the attention of the conference to the issues of supranationalism and democratisation of the Communities, which I felt had been glossed over in the opening exchange. Was it more important for us to have a veto to stop things happening or to seek support from others to get things done by means of majority voting? Was there anything in the fear that supranationalism—which meant less chance to veto decisions—would lead to big-power dominance? (For myself I thought that the opposite danger existed, i.e. big-power dominance in the absence of an adequate supranational decision-making system.) Were we to be inhibited from pursuing economic integration because of the fear that in a fully integrated Community we should eventually be involved in defence commitment? After all, we had accepted the logic of this commitment in the publicly stated positions of the previous Government and of my own party on EEC membership, and surely the matter was not likely to arise as a practical issue for a long time to come? Finally, was an economic and monetary union feasible, and if so would the Community not need much stronger democratic controls in that event?

These queries evoked a discussion that focused somewhat more sharply on the issues of supranationalism and democratisation. There was some scepticism about the desirability from Ireland's point of view of giving the European

Parliament more powers, and there were mixed opinions on the issue of the veto. But at least this exchange of views had ensured that Foreign Affairs staff were looking afresh at these matters, and I was satisfied, in the light of what had been said, that I would not face opposition from within the department in pursuing the kind of European policy that I had in mind. In winding up the debate I stressed the need for us to seek out issues in respect of which we could play a constructive role, not purely in the narrow interests of Ireland but in such a way as to demonstrate that we had a European philosophy beyond looking for what we could get out of the system.

A lively moment came during the discussion when I was told that Claude Cheysson had just been appointed a French member of the Commission. I did not know Claude Cheysson at that time; later we became friends. But I knew that the Rome Treaty provided for the appointment of Commissioners by the common consent of governments, which in my naïveté I thought meant what it said. And I had not been asked to secure the consent of the Irish Government.

'How has he been appointed?' I asked.

'By the French government,' replied Éamon Gallagher.

'But *we* haven't agreed,' I responded.

'It has been agreed,' replied Gallagher.

'By whom?' I enquired.

'By me,' said Gallagher, after a brief hesitation.

'But you aren't the Irish Government,' I responded. 'Don't let it happen again.'

The conference participants were highly entertained by this exchange—both by Gallagher's discomfiture and, I presume also, by my assumption that the Rome Treaty meant what it said on this matter.

The discussion moved on to the other topics on the agenda. I learnt much from the discussion on the Conference on Security and Co-operation in Europe (CSCE), which was due to convene in Helsinki in three months' time. My belief that we had to open diplomatic relations with the Soviet Union, strengthened by my experience at the Political Co-operation meeting in Brussels two days after my appointment, was reinforced.

We then discussed relations with the rest of the world, focusing particularly on the United States, China, and Japan. I took a poll on the priority to be given to the opening of diplomatic relations with further countries. This provided guidance for the expansion that I undertook during the following four years—an expansion that increased the number of our resident missions from twenty-one to thirty. A subsequent discussion on development co-operation showed the strength of departmental commitment to the expansion of our hitherto minimal volume of overseas aid.

After a brief review of our information and cultural activities, we turned to Northern Ireland. The publication of the British White Paper, to which the Government had sought to contribute on our first day in office, provided a focus. It represented a significant shift in British policy, involving a clear commitment to power-sharing in the North and acceptance of the need for an 'Irish dimension': some kind of North-South council. This development, together with the fact that our Government comprised two parties both of which were explicitly and unambiguously committed to seeking Irish unity *only* on the basis of consent by a majority of the people of Northern Ireland, created a new situation to which our foreign policy had to adjust.

Finally we had a session in conjunction with the state agencies responsible for the promotion of various Irish interests abroad: exports, industrial promotion, tourism. It emerged that past tensions between the department and Córas Tráchtála, of which I had been aware, had been resolved and a good working relationship established.

As I found out in the years that followed, some problems still remained with the Industrial Development Authority. Moreover, an ancient quarrel persisted between the Department of Foreign Affairs and the Department of Industry and Commerce, which, under the terms of the 1924 Act establishing the responsibility of Government departments, had been put in charge of 'trade'. Although in a new state that had yet to establish external trade links the word 'trade' had probably been intended to mean internal trade, especially as this same Act gave the Department of External Affairs (later Foreign Affairs) responsibility for the external relations of the state, the Department of Industry and Commerce had claimed and exercised jurisdiction in the external trade area. Now, with external trade an exclusive competence of the Community, that department's claim to control of this area of policy had been undermined; but this did not prevent a determined rearguard action by its staff. In the years that followed, my good personal relations with the new Minister for Industry and Commerce, Justin Keating, helped to damp down this persistent quarrel—although the two of us had to meet several times a year in order to sort out the conflicts that persistently arose at official level.

The conference behind me, I drafted a memorandum for the Government setting out the lines of our foreign policy. The five main themes of foreign policy that I identified in this memorandum, and which became the basis for my Dáil speech on the subject in May, were:

—To help maintain world peace and reduce tensions.
—To resolve 'even on a provisional and open-ended basis' the Northern Ireland problem and to pursue relations with the UK government to achieve this purpose.
—To contribute to the development of the European Community along lines compatible with Irish aspirations.
—To secure Ireland's economic interests abroad.
—To contribute to the Third World in a manner and to an extent that will meet our obligations.

On the EEC, having reviewed the pros and cons of alternative approaches, I concluded in this memorandum that our long-term interest would be best served by an evolution of the European Community towards a more democratic structure, involving a greater supranational element in the form of a strengthened European Parliament and possibly a move from unanimity to qualified majority voting. I warned against the unwisdom of allowing fear of getting involved in a defence commitment under any circumstances, even if the Community became a full federation, to determine the whole course of our foreign policy for decades ahead against our vital economic and social interests.

On the practical side I set out the need for additional staff both at home and abroad to undertake our new responsibilities, and proposed opening embassies in Luxembourg, Moscow, and possibly Vienna and Oslo—and at a later date, perhaps, in east Africa, Brazil, and China. The memorandum was approved by the Government on 7 May without difficulty.

It took me some time to get used to meetings of the Council of Ministers. I had imagined them to be intimate affairs: nine of us around a table. In fact there were scores of people, sitting in serried ranks around a rectangle of tables with a large space in the centre, into which at the start of each meeting hordes of photographers rushed, followed by a second wave of television cameramen. Around the room were the interpreters' booths. The delegations sat in alphabetical order, which means that we were always seated between France and Italy, with the United Kingdom diagonally opposite to us. The atmosphere was intimidating for a neophyte like myself; apart from my own staff there were no familiar faces, and the procedure was strange to me. At my first meeting I plucked up the courage to intervene on an issue that seemed to me to be going by default, relating to the tightening up of Community auditing procedures—something about which I felt strongly. My intervention clearly caused consternation, for this matter had already been settled at permanent representative level and appeared on the agenda merely as a formality.

It did not take me long, however, to come to feel at home in this curious world. My colleagues were for the most part relaxed and friendly, and because in these years fewer changes than usual took place in the composition of the Council, we got to know each other well. (The Foreign Ministers of the Benelux countries remained unchanged throughout my period, and only one change of Minister took place in the cases of Germany and Denmark, while throughout most of the period Mariano Rumor and Aldo Moro alternated in the posts of Italian Foreign Minister and Prime Minister.)

It is mainly in the Council of Ministers that conflicts of national interest within the Community are fought out; it is the least 'communautaire' of the institutions. I was surprised, therefore, to find that the members of the General Council (as the Foreign Affairs Council likes to be called, emphasising its co-ordinating role vis-à-vis Councils involving other Ministers) frequently went to considerable trouble to help each other where they could do so without prejudicing significantly their own interests. Indeed I found the Council to have a palpable sense of collegiality—a quality I had assumed to be found only within the Commission. Not unnaturally this sense of collegiality was most evident in the General Council's relations with the Council in its other formats—ECOFIN (as the Economics and Finance Council is known) or the Agriculture Council, for example—or, later on, with the European Council of Heads of Government.

It was, indeed, fascinating to see the extent to which in many subtle ways each of these bodies developed a corporate identity of its own, cutting across national loyalties and the collective responsibility of national governments. The Agriculture Council was, of course, notorious for its corporate loyalty to the interests of farmers throughout the Community, which often seemed to cut across and frustrate attempts by the European Council, the General Council and ECOFIN, not to speak of some national governments, to limit the cost of the CAP. (On the whole, during most of the period of Irish membership this feature of the Agriculture Council has tended to suit us.)

Twice during my Presidency of the General Council in 1975 I was sent by my colleagues to a simultaneous meeting of the Agriculture Council in another room in the Council's Charlemagne Building to urge the Agriculture Ministers to speed up their deliberations on some point, the settlement of which was a precondition of agreement in our Council on a trade issue. On each occasion I warned my colleagues that my appearance among the Agriculture Ministers would be unwelcome and counterproductive—and I was right! There was evident resentment at what was seen as an attempt by the General Council to interfere with their deliberations. Although in theory the specialised Councils such as Agriculture are technical committees of the General Council, this constitutional point has long been lost sight of by the Ministers of those departments meeting in this format.

But to return to May 1973: I had already initiated bilateral contacts in Brussels with some of my Community colleagues. I had a brief meeting with the French Foreign Minister, Michel Jobert. This aroused interest in the Quai d'Orsay, two officials of which approached me separately some weeks later to suggest a further discussion with their Minister. One of them referred to Jobert's 'inexperience' causing problems in the Council of Ministers—a remark I listened to with a straight face as a Minister of three months' standing myself— and to the official's hope that Gaston Thorn and I might help to sort out consequent problems.

More useful at that point were two meetings in Luxembourg in the margin of Council meetings there, first with the Netherlands Foreign Minister, Max van der Stoel, and later with the Luxembourg Foreign Minister, Gaston Thorn. In these discussions I suggested an early move to direct elections for the European Parliament and a strengthening of that body's powers. Our substantial identity of views suggested to me the desirability of a multilateral concerting of tactics by Ireland and the Benelux countries. Accordingly, Thorn and I agreed to arrange a quadripartite meeting together with our Dutch and Belgian colleagues during the forthcoming Helsinki Conference in order to discuss ways of promoting greater democratic control of the Community institutions. In the event it proved too difficult to convoke such a meeting at Helsinki; instead, luncheon discussions before the start of subsequent Council of Ministers meetings were arranged with a view to concerting our approach to the institutional development of the Community.

I believe these meetings were useful. At the end of the year, however, the Benelux countries became concerned about possible negative reactions elsewhere to our 'caucuses'. I had the impression that they might have been 'warned off', possibly by the French. Despite this setback van der Stoel and I agreed to try to maintain some cohesion among the smaller countries through bilateral Irish-Dutch contacts, he liaising thereafter with the Belgians, I with the Danes, and both of us with Gaston Thorn. This loose arrangement was less satisfactory than our joint meetings had been, but it enabled the five of us to achieve some measure of cohesion, for example in relation to a reported Franco-German move to establish some kind of '*Directoire*' in 1975.

Joan's fear of flying had persisted, and after my first unexpected visit to London and Brussels I sought to reassure her by travelling to EEC meetings by train and ship, a journey of about twenty hours in each direction. When Joan accompanied me on one such trip, to the OECD annual meeting in Paris in June, she found herself beside Christopher Soames, the Conservative politician who had become EEC Commissioner, at a dinner. Soames was so absorbed by his conversation with George Schultz that when they next met Soames failed to recognise her, at which Joan said in a pleasant voice: 'You forget, Sir Christopher, that we did meet before, at dinner in Paris, when you ignored me. I think you must be the rudest man I have met.' Soames was delighted with this; they became good friends thereafter.

When the trip to Helsinki loomed up, Joan raised the question of accompanying me, as I would be away for a week. I agreed, pointing out, however, that we would have to pay her expenses ourselves. (I worked on the principle that unless Joan was invited on a trip, as normally happens on bilateral official— as distinct from working—visits, or was required to co-host mixed functions, or was attending a conference such as OECD to which all Ministers normally brought their wives, we should pay her expenses. While a number of Ministers were bringing their wives to Helsinki, it did not seem that this would be the general pattern, for the dinners and lunches, as at the UN, would not include spouses.) To reach Helsinki by train and ship would take two-and-a-half days, with seven changes of train and ship in each direction. Joan conceded that this was excessive and agreed to fly, for the first time in seventeen years.

The conference at Helsinki provided an opportunity for a wide range of contacts with Foreign Ministers from non-Community countries—as well as for follow-up discussions with Jobert on regional policy. In addition to meeting William Rogers, the US Secretary of State, and Mitchell Sharp, the Canadian Foreign Minister, I had discussions with all the eastern European Foreign Ministers except the Bulgarian, and with Archbishop Casaroli, who represented the Holy See. I shall return in a later chapter to my discussions with him.

The meeting with the Czechoslovak Minister was in their embassy after dinner; I had another dinner engagement that evening but dropped in for coffee. Most of the guests had left by the time I arrived, and I recall my surprise at walking past the guards and their dogs into a building that at first seemed empty. I went from room to room shouting ineffective 'hellos' until I finally tracked down the Minister, a couple of his guests and some of his officials in an inner room. When the guests had left I raised the attempt to smuggle Czechoslovak arms to the IRA through Amsterdam several years earlier. I was told that the Czechoslovak government had been very upset by this affair; the arms had been sold to a dealer with whom they had had a good relationship for the preceding two years and were intended for the Middle East. They had terminated this relationship with him in view of what had happened.

The conference itself, the successful conclusion of which required a consensus of all thirty-five countries present, was deadlocked at the end of the week by a Maltese demand that the decisions reached should be applied in the Mediterranean region. Outside the air-conditioned conference hall itself the heat and humidity were intense, and at one point on Saturday morning I wandered into the hall in order to cool down. A man ran up the steps to me clutching a scrap of paper. 'Close the conference,' he said. As I looked astonished at this command, he reeled off the names of a number of countries. 'They've all gone home,' he said, 'and you're next. Take the chair and read out this,' pointing to a sentence handwritten on the scrap of paper, 'and close the conference quickly before anyone objects.' As he trotted away I asked someone who he was. 'Mendelevich, the Soviet representative,' I was told. 'He's been trying to break the deadlock.'

I took the chair, enjoying the astonishment of my officials as they entered the hall in answer to the resumption bell. When the conference had assembled I read out the key sentence, asked 'Is that agreed?' and after a fractional pause declared: 'Conference adjourned.' There was massive applause, and as I walked up the aisle congratulations showered on me from all sides—as if I had actually been responsible for the breakthrough.

I was in fact fairly sceptical about the whole Helsinki exercise. The Soviet commitment to respect for human rights did not seem convincing, and the subsequent negotiations leading to the signature of the Helsinki declaration by heads of government two years later yielded relatively little in the way of visible, concrete results until many years later.

The most important development from an Irish point of view was the meeting I had with Andrei Gromyko about opening diplomatic relations between our two countries. Gromyko was accompanied by a colleague and an interpreter, and he explained to me in English at the outset that, as his colleague did not speak English, he would speak in Russian and have his remarks interpreted. I then told him that the Government wished me to proceed with the proposal for an exchange of embassies, and I suggested that the matter be settled between us at the end of September during the UN General Assembly debate. What we had in mind, I said, would be an exchange of small missions, as we were a small country.

He responded in Russian, very vigorously. My reference to 'small missions' had annoyed him. His remarks, as interpreted, were a denunciation of the British, who had recently expelled over a hundred Soviet officials from London. He attributed my concern for small missions to British influence. The British, the interpreter went on to say, were not clean. At this point Gromyko interrupted in English; what he had said was that the British were 'unclean': they had spread slanders about the Soviet Union, which, he implied, had influenced the shape of our proposal. I responded that I had had no representations from Britain on the subject, and that my recommendation of small missions was made entirely on my own initiative.

He calmed down at this and went on, in English, to ask me if we had a mission in London—had we not withdrawn our Ambassador there some time ago? And had we embassies in Paris and Washington? At this and other points in our discussion he struck me as being badly briefed.

I told him that we had been disturbed at times to see that opinion in the Soviet Union—a polite reference to their press—appeared to view the Provisional IRA as a left-wing socialist group with which the Soviet people might sympathise, whereas in our view they were a dangerous right-wing group, who had in fact broken away from the official Sinn Féin and IRA on the grounds that the latter were unduly socialist and too friendly with Communists. When he responded by saying that Soviet papers simply reported facts I challenged this, saying that they also contained considerable comment, some of which seemed to be misguided. He went on to say that the Soviet people sympathised with Ireland over the Northern Ireland problem. I replied that I accepted this but that at times their sympathy seemed to be misguidedly directed towards the Provisional IRA rather than towards the Irish people and their Government. At the end of our discussion we agreed to meet again at the UN General Assembly session in New York in September and October in order to settle the arrangements for an exchange of diplomatic missions.

The August break was particularly welcome that year. We spent part of it in Donegal, where we stayed with Seán and Paula Donlon and spent much of the time with John and Pat Hume and other SDLP people, and then joined some friends who had rented a house in the south of France. This was the start of a new cycle of holidaymaking. Up to the early 1970s our summer holidays had all been family occasions, but now, with our children effectively grown up, we accepted an invitation from Denis Corboy, a friend of many years' standing who was now the EEC information officer in Dublin, to join a 'house party'; he had rented a house in a restored mediaeval village at Les Arcs in the Var. Ever since then many of our holidays have taken this form, with one or other of our children together with their spouses and their children joining our friends and ourselves from time to time from the late 1970s onwards.

We had a hectic fortnight in New York at the 1973 UN autumn session, during which I met over a dozen Foreign Ministers from various parts of the world and delivered my General Assembly speech. While there I concluded the negotiations with Gromyko for an exchange of diplomatic missions. The signing ceremony was much more jovial than our initial encounter had been. I referred to the loan of $20,000 given by the underground Dáil government in 1920 to the infant Soviet Union against a pledge of jewels that had been the property of a member of the imperial family, a loan redeemed some thirty years later. He appreciated my comment that the absence of provision for interest on the loan showed what poor capitalists we were.

I was particularly happy to make my debut at the UN under the auspices of our Ambassador, Con Cremin, then in his final year before retirement. Con was a classical scholar of distinction, a litterateur, linguist, and raconteur. He was also a most charming companion. My only problem with him was his very strong Kerry accent, which at times I found hard to penetrate—although I noticed that his UN ambassadorial colleagues seemed to have no difficulty with it. Fortunately the Cremins' family language was unaccented French, so that at home in the residence with his family Joan and I could understand him easily.

Joan had accompanied me on this trip also; by now she had completely overcome her fear of flying. As we were paying for her journey, and had decided to return by sea (travelling on the *France*, on what turned out to be one of the famous liner's last voyages), we travelled economy class on the way out by air. So, out of courtesy, did Hugh McCann and my personal secretary, Ita McCoy. A couple of years later when we were on our way to Brussels one day we were discussing another visit to the UN. Joan commented that the wife of the French Foreign Minister had told her that she sometimes reduced the cost of accompanying her husband by travelling on a charter flight, and suggested that we look in the newspaper to see if there were any charter flights to New York coinciding with the UN. We looked in the *Irish Times* and by a happy chance found a suitably timed charter organised by a Tipperary hurling team and a Limerick football team, and had a most enjoyable flight with them in both directions.

I have mentioned Ita McCoy. She had been present when the IRA murdered her father during the Civil War because of her brother's participation in the Free State government: her brother was Kevin O'Higgins, who, in turn, was murdered on his way to Sunday Mass by an IRA breakaway group five years later. Ita herself worked for the Fine Gael party and had been personal secretary to Richard Mulcahy as Minister for Education, to John A. Costello as Taoiseach, and later to her nephew Tom O'Higgins as deputy leader of the party. I think she was about to retire when I became Minister, but she agreed to come with me to Foreign Affairs as my personal secretary—that is, secretary for political as distinct from official purposes. I have to add that she was also an unofficial adviser, for her long experience and acute political mind were extraordinarily useful to a relative newcomer to politics like myself.

The relationship between Europe and the United States had become more problematic in the late 1960s and early 1970s. There were growing doubts in western Europe as to whether the United States would indefinitely maintain its scale of commitment to European defence, while the Americans for their part were showing signs of frustration with what they saw as unwillingness on the part of western Europe to contribute sufficiently to its own defence. Sections of western European public opinion had also become alienated in some measure from the United States as a result of the Vietnam War and the bombing of North Vietnam.

In an attempt to halt this drift in the transatlantic relationship, Henry Kissinger, then National Security Affairs Adviser, proposed on 23 April 1973 that a new Atlantic Charter should be drawn up in advance of a visit by President Nixon to Europe towards the end of the year.

Europe received the suggestion with less than enthusiasm, seeing it as a clumsy attempt to reassert American dominance. Apart from major reservations by Britain and France, American discussions with Europe ran into the problem of Irish neutrality, so that for some purposes Ireland had to opt out of the talks (with NATO members) while other subjects could not be raised without Irish involvement (as a Community member). War in the Middle East and the resultant first oil crisis ensured by the autumn that the unwelcome initiative had to be wound down as rapidly as was diplomatically possible.

One half of the winding-down process was arranged to take place on the occasion of a NATO meeting in Brussels in December; the second half at a meeting with the EEC Council of Ministers—i.e. the same personnel plus me. I told my colleagues that I would be in Brussels at the relevant time, chairing a conference organised by the *Financial Times* on trade and industry. During a morning coffee break at the conference a message came to ask whether, if the EEC Ministers and Kissinger came to my conference hotel at three o'clock, I could spare an hour for an EEC-US meeting.

I agreed, and just before three o'clock that afternoon I heard the noise of the police sirens accompanying the convoy of Ministers. Kissinger was the first to arrive in the room that had been booked for the meeting. As we awaited the others, he entertained me with a story about his arrival in Europe on a troopship during the war. Going up on deck he had found a disconsolate Irish-American private gazing into the impenetrable fog of the Irish Sea towards an invisible England. Seeing Kissinger approach, the private groaned, 'God, how I hate this place!' Kissinger had been deeply impressed at the depth of his Irish-American dislike of an England he had not yet been able to see.

The formal meeting involved relatively innocuous statements of position, during which, however, I stressed the divergence of European attitudes from those of the United States on certain questions, such as the Middle East. When Kissinger expressed a hope that consultative arrangements between the United States and Europe could be worked out that would enable the US to express a view before we in Europe took final decisions on matters of mutual concern, thus presenting the US effectively with a fait accompli, no-one seemed to feel it appropriate to respond by asking if the United States would reciprocate by consulting Europe before *it* took decisions. And so the Year of Europe was buried, and I went back to prepare the summing-up of my industrial and trade conference.

While Joan and I had been on our way back to Ireland from the UN General Assembly session, travelling on the *France*, the Yom Kippur War had broken out. The subsequent Arab oil boycott threatened the economic life and the financial stability of the industrialised countries; and because of the skilful way in which the Arabs enlisted the sympathies of the Third World, these events also endangered the relationship between industrialised and developing countries. The boycott, moreover, led to a deep split in the Community itself, owing to a lack of support amongst other Community members for Denmark and the Netherlands, which were threatened with an oil boycott by the Arab countries. It led as well to a French decision to opt out of a western consensus on how to face the crisis.

This split was already looming when the Council of Ministers met in Brussels on 6 November to consider the situation—a meeting which, contrary to the normal practice, was held in total secrecy, without officials or interpreters. The president for this occasion was the Danish Minister for Foreign Affairs, Ivar Nørgaard, who opened the meeting by telling us that if we spoke *very slowly*, in English or in French, we would understand each other. On his second repetition of this proposition, Jobert remarked, *'C'est de vous qui'il parle, Garret, et en anglais et en français.'* My speed of utterance had already become a byword in the Council.

It immediately became clear that oil was an issue upon which a frightened Community would be unable to maintain solidarity. There was a distinct air of 'every man for himself', and we were soon in inglorious disarray, and in this state we prepared for the summit meeting of heads of government to be held in Copenhagen in mid-December.

The political side of the preparations for this summit had been undertaken at a meeting of Foreign Ministers in Copenhagen on 19 November. I have to say that I recall more about peripheral aspects of this meeting than about the discussions themselves. I was engaged at that moment with the other members of the Government in the first by-election campaign of our administration, which we had to fight from a base in a small hotel in Ballybay, Co. Monaghan. We were holed up there because of a kidnap threat by a breakaway IRA group; the state of affairs in this area around that time can be illustrated by the fact that six months later the Provisional IRA murdered a senator of my party, Billy Fox, a Protestant, during an atrocious raid with sectarian overtones on the home of his fiancée.

My quick foray from the by-election scene to Brussels and on to Copenhagen was marred by a series of property losses due to my absentmindedness—an academic characteristic that I had carried into politics, where it is less tolerantly viewed. At different points along the way I mislaid my overcoat, the book I was reading, my pyjamas and toothbrush, and my watch: a trail of losses that took a month to retrieve.

In Copenhagen the Queen of Denmark gave a luncheon in our honour. As her children peered curiously down at us from a high balcony, I asked my neighbour, Alec Douglas-Home, what he thought of Nixon. 'Well, Garret,' he responded, 'you and I are very different people, from different backgrounds— you are Irish and I English, you are Roman Catholic and I Anglican—and we would disagree about the rights and wrongs of certain issues. But at least we know right and wrong exist; *that man doesn't.*'

The Copenhagen summit itself three weeks later proved a disaster. Pompidou was ill; Brandt not at his best. The 'fireside chat' of the heads of government— a real fire had been provided, at which the Foreign Ministers were allowed to peep—was an occasion of total confusion. My colleagues and I, charged with preparing a declaration, had to spend many hours trying to reconstruct what the heads of government might have said to each other; and a joint meeting of heads of government and Foreign Ministers proved less than happy; although it was the first of a number of such meetings at which I enjoyed improving the English of drafts prepared by the British delegation.

The most baroque feature of this least successful of summits was the uninvited appearance of six Arab Foreign Ministers, towards whom we felt about as welcoming as King Herod to the three kings from the east when they brought him news of the birth of a future king of Israel. Given Europe's parlous energy situation, we dared not refuse to hear them, but the only available time was after midnight. Any hopes that the lateness of the hour might encourage brevity were soon dashed. They were not going to let us off lightly in their moment of triumph, and it was almost three in the morning before they allowed us to stagger off to our beds.

There followed shortly afterwards the US proposal for a conference of oil consumers in Washington in mid-February. When we met to discuss this pro- posal, Jobert launched into the attack. He described this as the end of a process of political and economic degradation in US-Europe relations. We should not be in a hurry to reply, although we would have to go. But when we went we should go as a Community and speak with one voice. This was a little optimistic, given the depth of the divergence between those present as to what they wanted to emerge from Washington; and, in the event, member-states spoke for them- selves at the conference.

At Washington, France was basically opposed to the idea of a cartel of con- sumers, the emergence of which it felt would be counterproductive. It was not clear to me at first that France's mind was irrevocably set on non-participation in a projected International Energy Agency, and when the conference was about to break on this issue I got Norway to support me in putting forward a compromise. This disconcerted Kissinger, who had been about to wind up the proceedings on the basis of evident disagreement between France and the rest; and the conference had to postpone its conclusion by an hour. Although Jobert sent me a note across the table saying '*Merci pour votre aide,*' it became evident subsequently that I had been wasting my time, as Jobert apparently had instructions from Pompidou to reach disagreement. But my efforts probably did our relations with France no harm; and Kissinger at least had reason thereafter to remember that Ireland existed.

An issue that Kissinger had raised at our discussion in Brussels, about consultation procedures between Europe and the United States, remained to be settled. Early in April 1974, with the Year of Europe now out of the way, we considered this question at a Council meeting in Luxembourg. The debate focused on a somewhat abstruse point of procedure concerning the precise method to be adopted for consultations on a basis of reciprocity 'with an allied or friendly state' (the second adjective being added in deference to the Irish position outside the North Atlantic alliance). The French had one view, the rest of us another.

Jim Callaghan, making his first appearance at the Council after the change of government in the United Kingdom, and speaking as if he were at a NATO meeting—I had to point out that he was now in a different context—expressed astonishment that we should have to agree *any* text about the procedure to be followed for consultations with the United States, which he appeared to assume would occur more or less automatically, and he objected to any member-state having a veto in the matter. He did not yet seem to appreciate that respect for national sovereignty in foreign policy at that stage of the Community's development necessarily required unanimity in Political Co-operation matters, although he soon revised his position on this when he found the other member-states moving towards positions on particular issues that Britain did not favour.

It is fair to add that at this, his first, Community meeting Callaghan was fairly tense, as he had the task of presenting Britain's demand for renegotiation of its terms of entry to the Community, a proposition received with distinct lack of enthusiasm around the table.

The outstanding issue of consultation with the United States was eventually remitted to the first informal meeting of Foreign Ministers at Gymnich, near Bonn, in April 1974. There the question of consultations with 'allied and friendly states' was dropped in favour of the narrower matter of consultation with the United States, which seemed to be acceptable to all. In the event no such consultations took place during the French Presidency in the second half of the year. It was left to me, in January 1975, to inaugurate this process by undertaking a visit to Washington to meet Henry Kissinger.

The Gymnich meeting took place in the castle of that name, and its informality was emphasised by the presence of our wives. Jim Callaghan attended as British Foreign Secretary. I had met him in Dublin three years earlier when he was informing himself about the Northern Ireland problem, and had told him of Fine Gael's insistence that Irish reunification should be achieved only with the consent of a majority in the North; he had instantly parried, 'Acquiescence, dear boy, acquiescence.'

Much time at Gymnich was spent on the question of European union, the first discussion of the subject among the members of the enlarged Community.

The Paris summit in December 1972, on the eve of our membership, had decided that 'European union' should be achieved by 1980. Callaghan started our meeting by asking what this meant: he presumed it did not mean a union like that between Britain and Ireland, which, he suggested, had not been exactly a success; nor like that between England and Scotland. I asked whether it perhaps meant a change in the current structure of the Community with a view to modifying the need for unanimity in decision-making in the Council of Ministers, increasing democratic control by the Parliament, and minimising the division between the political and economic aspects, which had proved unsustainable in practice during the recent Middle East crisis.

Callaghan's rather negative question and my deliberately positive ones produced what might be described as a chorus of nescience: van der Stoel, Scheel, Thorn, Moro and Jobert all agreed that *no-one* knew what European union meant! The general feeling in the subsequent discussion was that the Community should move towards integration, which would involve as high a degree as possible of common policy; but the British and French showed a preference for a confederal Europe, in which, on major political issues, the attitudes of national governments would be fully recognised. However, an attempt by Jobert to delegate the further development of the concept of European union to representatives of governments meeting without the Commission was blocked by other Ministers, who insisted that the Commission be involved in any such exercise.

The social side of this meeting included, after dinner, a descent into the dungeons of the castle, where our host, Walter Scheel—who later that year became President of the Federal Republic, and whose singing voice had won him a golden disc—endeavoured to get a sing-song going. Only Jim Callaghan and Joan were prepared to join in, but this did not deter him. The shortage of a common repertoire proved a problem: when 'Tipperary' was proposed Scheel swept to one side Joan's lighthearted query about the suitability of a British Great War song for a German Foreign Minister, and we had a good rendering of it. I recall that Jobert and the late Aldo Moro, two small, slight figures, were seated on either side of their considerably larger and jolly host, a triptych illustrating gaiety surrounded by gloom. Before long the two of them had slipped off to bed, leaving us to what they clearly regarded as our quite unsuitable musical activities.

Next morning, sadly, Joan and I had to leave at first light; we had been phoned with the news that her mother had fallen gravely ill. She died a fortnight later, to Joan's deep distress and indeed to that of all our family. An extraordinarily reclusive person and very religious, she had been part of my life for almost thirty years, and the children were deeply attached to her. Given the traumatic background of her childhood, Joan had an extremely close relationship with her mother, whose death left a gulf it was impossible to fill.

After Gymnich, with the election of Giscard d'Estaing as President of France and the replacement of Jobert by Jean Sauvagnargues, the French Ambassador to Tunisia, the Community moved into a new phase. Frustration with its progress had been growing since the mid-1960s. When the process of removing tariff and quota restrictions between member-states had been completed, a common external tariff installed, and a Common Agricultural Policy inaugurated, further significant progress had been halted by the French refusal after 1965 to accept qualified majority voting in the Council. Decisions on many outstanding issues had been blocked by veto threats in support of various pressure groups, and the European Commission had lost its impetus as the initiating organ of the Community. In 1974, however, France was not yet ready to accept the need to restore the Community decision-making structure that had been abandoned at its insistence in 1965. The French government remained basically hostile to the Community's supranational institutions. Its new President sought to find another way ahead, one that would bypass the institutions by creating an inter-governmental system centred on the three larger member-states: France, Germany, and Britain.

On 16 September a further informal discussion by Foreign Ministers took place in Paris, at which Sauvagnargues developed ideas on the future of the Community that had been put forward by Giscard d'Estaing at a highly significant dinner discussion between heads of government at the Élysée Palace two nights earlier—a dinner to which the President of the Commission, François-Xavier Ortoli, had not been invited.

The French proposals as Sauvagnargues presented them involved the removal of the barrier between meetings on Political Co-operation (foreign policy co-ordination amongst the Nine) and Councils of Ministers. Regular combined meetings of the two kinds would be attended by heads of government and the President of the Commission. These meetings were to be private and would not be followed by any communiqué; they would be called 'Meetings of the European Community'. A 'light' secretariat would prepare the meetings and follow them up. In Political Co-operation only matters directly affecting Europe would be discussed.

Areas not of vital interest to member-states were to be identified with a view to getting away from the abuse of the veto in the Council. Discussions were to be held on such subjects as energy, aviation, transport, youth, the environment; apparently these were to be intergovernmental discussions, despite the fact that some at least of these areas already fell within the competence of the Community. Direct elections to the European Parliament were to take place in 1980 or before; the Parliament might have a right of initiative and a limited legislative role, but it would control neither the Council nor the Commission.

All this was to replace the 1972 Paris summit idea of European union, which was described as 'idiotic' by Sauvagnargues, provoking Gaston Thorn to whisper to me that this was the first time he had heard Pompidou referred to by a French Foreign Minister as 'idiotic'!

All those present except Jim Callaghan and the new German Foreign Minister, Hans-Dietrich Genscher, saw these proposals as a most serious threat to the internal institutional balance of the Community and to the balance between larger and smaller states. Smaller countries' interests would be less well protected if the key meetings were to involve heads of government, amongst whom the leaders of the larger countries tended to dominate and between whom the sense of collegiality (which, despite many conflicts and tensions, was a feature of meetings of the Council of Ministers) would be much weaker. The creation of a new secretariat to the heads of government, the proposed limitation of the Commission's participation to the President of the Commission, and the extension of a right of initiative to the Parliament, would all weaken the Commission's independent role. At another level the idea of limiting Political Co-operation to matters directly concerning Europe seemed to echo the 'region-alisation' proposal in Kissinger's Year of Europe initiative, to which all, and most especially France, had taken exception. This made sense only if, as some of us suspected, a move was envisaged towards wider foreign policy formulation by France, Germany and Britain without consultation with the rest of the Nine.

Finally, Callaghan's enthusiasm for the proposals and the docility of Genscher, who said he was 'happy' with them, convinced most of us that this was in fact an initiative preconcerted between the 'Big Three': a move towards the 'Directoire' or Directorate that some of us had begun to fear.

For my part, I did not accept that the Élysée discussion envisaged decision-making by the proposed heads of government meetings, and I said that if there were to be decisions on matters within the Community competence they could be taken only on an initiative of the Commission. When Sauvagnargues, who at that stage appeared—or perhaps pretended to be—unfamiliar with the institutional structure of the Community, contested this, Ortoli supported me, and Sauvagnargues had to accept my point. I added that if the executive power of the Community was to be strengthened by the proposed changes, then in order to maintain the institutional balance the Parliament should be given legis-lative power in parallel.

A month later in the margin of a Council meeting in Luxembourg we returned to these proposals. On this occasion Sauvagnargues presented the French 'European Council' proposal (this is what the suggested heads of govern-ment meetings had now been named by him) as the implementation of a 'decision' at the Copenhagen summit to hold two heads of government meetings a year. This was immediately contested by van der Stoel, who pointed out that the Copenhagen summit had agreed to the *possibility* of two such meetings, not to their being obligatory. Sauvagnargues went on to explain that such meetings were not intended to *replace* Council of Ministers meetings or to take decisions deferred by the Ministerial Council but only to 'mark the political globality' of Council of Ministers and Political Co-operation meetings. It had been envisaged that heads of government, meeting as the Council of Ministers, would deal with Community matters, and that in the Political Co-operation framework they would deal with political matters. These proposals were to form the agenda at the summit proposed for Paris in December.

Another tough discussion ensued. At the outset I said that, whatever might be thought in France, elsewhere another summit to discuss purely institutional questions would be unacceptable to public opinion, which, in the aftermath of the recent oil shock, was preoccupied with concrete problems. To be successful the summit would need to deal with such matters as regional and energy problems and the co-ordination of national economic policies. When Jim Callaghan remarked that this was an impossible condition, I retorted that if this were the case it would be better to have no summit at all.

The discussion eventually led to agreement on a number of points, including criticism of the French proposal for intergovernmental discussion of matters already within the competence of the Community; insistence that Political Co-operation should not be limited to issues relating to the European region; a recommendation that any secretariat be limited to taking notes and recording decisions and not be extended to preparing the meetings; and, finally, consensus—which did not survive—on dropping the term 'European Council'.

At the end of the meeting it was agreed to appoint an ad hoc group consisting of a joint meeting of the Committee of Permanent Representatives and political directors to examine these proposals further. It was also agreed that as a basis for the work of this ad hoc group the political directors would agree a record of conclusions of our meeting.

In the event the political directors' meeting a few days later failed to prepare any record of our conclusions, and on its own account established two *separate* subgroups, one, led by political directors, to deal with institutional change, and the other, involving the permanent representatives in Brussels, to prepare concrete matters for the summit. This would have limited the possibility, important to Ireland in view of the need for a decision on the proposed Regional Fund, of 'trading' concessions by us on certain aspects of institutional reform, against getting a decision on the Regional Fund, which seemed in some danger of being dropped.

I was furious at this development, and, after telephone calls to Ortoli and van der Stoel (neither of whom, I found, had been told about some of these failures to carry out our decisions), I sent a message on Monday 21 October to my colleagues proposing that the political directors do what we had decided should be done by belatedly preparing agreed conclusions of our meeting, and calling a meeting of the joint ad hoc group that we had formed so that it might report to our next meeting.

This initiative proved successful. The political directors met again three days later and produced for the ad hoc group a revised mandate that took account of our position in large measure, reflecting with a good deal more accuracy what had been actually agreed at our meeting. It also firmly established the unity of the ad hoc group. As a result, in the weeks that followed, the work of preparation for the Paris summit went ahead reasonably satisfactorily from our point of view both in the ad hoc committee and at Ministerial level.

When the heads of government met in Paris in December, Harold Wilson, who clearly enjoyed consorting with his fellow-Prime Ministers, started the bidding on the frequency of the proposed meetings of heads of government at four a year plus emergency meetings. Liam Cosgrave countered with a bid of two. The remainder proposed three, and that figure was agreed, with the addition of 'and when necessary'.

The name 'European Council' was reinstated after Giscard d'Estaing had clarified that when the heads of government dealt with Community matters these would be meetings of the Council of Ministers. The issue of the secretariat was settled by agreeing on an administrative secretariat 'with due regard for existing practices and procedures'; the role of the Ministerial Council's secretariat was thus protected. The role and powers of the Commission were also explicitly preserved.

A formula was agreed on the thorny question of limiting the veto or unanimity practice. In the event, however, despite my temporarily successful efforts during our Presidency in the following six months to give effect to this self-denying ordinance, the Council soon started to ignore again the Paris decisions on this matter and reverted to its old habits. Only in 1987 with the ratification of the Single European Act was this problem finally resolved.

On the issue of direct elections a proposal by Cosgrave that they should be held in 1978 was agreed in a slightly modified form, namely 'at any time in or after 1978'. We were happy with this formula, for, while we were anxious to see these quinquennial elections taking place soon, our particular concern had been to have them coincide if possible with our own quinquennial local council elections. It was our belief—which would be proved correct—that the coincidence of two different elections would boost the poll for each. Our next local elections were to take place in mid-1979 and we had calculated that, given some inevitable slippage in implementing this decision, we were more likely to achieve our 1979 objective if we named 1978 than if we named the year we really wanted.

All in all these decisions represented a reasonably satisfactory outcome to a situation that had seemed quite threatening three months earlier so far as both the integrity of the Community's institutional structure and the interests of the smaller countries were concerned. For the three larger countries, on the other hand, there had been something of a setback to their hopes of strengthening their position vis-à-vis the supranational institutions of the Community.

I felt, however, that it would be desirable to try to head off further efforts of this kind by making proposals for improvements in the actual working of the Council of Ministers. Accordingly, at the informal meeting of Foreign Ministers at Farmleigh in April 1975 I secured a mandate, as President of the Council, to prepare such proposals in consultation with the President of the Commission.

In these proposals Ortoli and I first identified what seemed to us to be the principal defects in the working of the Council:

—Because the time of the Council was devoted almost entirely to its legislative function, discussion of broad policy issues was minimal.

—The proliferation of specialist Councils (for example of Finance Ministers and Agriculture Ministers) without adequate co-ordination was giving rise to incoherence in Community policies and decisions.

—Meetings of the European Council were inadequately prepared.

To meet these problems we proposed:

—That a period be set aside at all or most Council meetings for discussing a major policy issue in depth.

—That policy discussions on matters involving the overlapping authority of Ministers take place at joint meetings of the Ministers concerned, with adequate preparation and restricted attendance to ensure more relaxed and confidential discussion.

—That prior to European Council meetings, special joint Council meetings be convened involving Ministers for Foreign Affairs and Finance and, where appropriate, other Ministers.

At the next informal meeting of Foreign Ministers at Lucca our proposals were considered. Sauvagnargues demurred several times at particular features of what we had proposed, and as a result Mariano Rumor, in the chair, had to summarise three times what seemed to him to be common ground. His final summary involved agreement on mixed Council meetings before European Councils and the making of reports to each General Council meeting on what was happening, or might happen, in other Councils. He also recorded agreement that policy aspects of budgets should in future be discussed by Foreign and Finance Ministers jointly.

An attempt was subsequently made to implement these ideas. In particular the idea of preliminary discussions on policy issues before we tackled the agenda at our meetings had some success, but the problem of coherence in Community decision-making remained largely unresolved: the Ministers in each specialist Council want to do their own thing; none of them want to be co-ordinated by Foreign Ministers—or indeed by anyone else.

During the following year there were signs that the idea of a Community Directorate was not dead. The relative ineffectiveness of the European Council, in which the leaders of the Big Three had to listen to the Prime Ministers of six other countries often speaking at some length, may have encouraged them to look to some other way to assert themselves. During the summer of 1975 we heard reports of discussions between Helmut Schmidt and Giscard d'Estaing about the possible establishment of a small executive committee of three member-states to carry on the work of the European Council between sessions. As originally envisaged in June it was said to consist of the three larger states— Germany, France, and Britain—but apparently they soon realised that this would be impractical and moved to the idea of a committee with seats for two of the three larger states and a third seat rotating between the smaller countries. My Benelux colleagues were concerned about this, and I alerted the Danish Foreign Minister, K. B. Andersen, to the danger during an official visit to Denmark in September 1975. He was grateful for the warning, which, he said, made sense of a remark by Schmidt to his Prime Minister that had not been understood at the time.

At the Lucca informal meeting of Foreign Ministers in October, van der Stoel warned against further weakening of the Commission, adding that the Netherlands would reject any move towards a Directorate. For my part I referred to newspaper reports about the possibility of a Directorate and to the frustration of the smaller countries at the unwillingness of their larger partners to strengthen the Community. Van Elslande, the Belgian Foreign Minister, expressed the hope that my fears would not turn out to be well founded.

After these further warning shots by the Netherlands, Ireland, and Belgium, the Directorate threat seemed to evaporate. Dissatisfaction with the actual working of the European Council soon re-emerged, however. It proved difficult to persuade the heads of government that Community procedures had to be observed. Thus, at the fourth European Council meeting in Luxembourg in 1976 Giscard d'Estaing presented a text on monetary policy that had not been brought forward by the Commission, and went on to claim that *only* the European Council was qualified to give 'orientations' to Community policy. Schmidt and Wilson tended to support Giscard d'Estaing's assertions of an authority never contemplated by the Rome Treaties.

At the informal meeting of Foreign Ministers in Luxembourg six weeks later a long discussion focused mainly on the deficiencies and dangers of the European Council, which had now met on three occasions. I opened the debate with a fairly lengthy statement and was strongly supported by van der Stoel, Rumor, and Thorn, while Ortoli agreed that the European Council threatened to weaken the institutions of the Community. Sauvagnargues went on the defensive, pointing to what he described as the 'achievement' of our Dublin European Council in resolving the British renegotiation problem—a point that Rumor conceded, although in my opening remarks I had described this as an issue on which the Community had been 'predoomed to success'.

Sauvagnargues went on to describe the European Council somewhat grandiloquently as the '*pièce maitresse*' of European Union, and more modestly as 'a balance between a procedure for consultation and a procedure for decision.' It was not a court of appeal, he said, 'but was competent to deal with all issues.' Thorn riposted that he found extraordinary the idea that the European Council in effect constituted European union, and Leo Tindemans recorded his horror at the implication that 'fireside chats' between heads of government would be sufficient to give Europe the authority it needed.

There the discussion ended, at least for the duration of my period as Foreign Minister. European Councils continued to meet, and at some of these meetings useful progress has occasionally been made on issues that have become deadlocked at another level. And over and beyond these 'court of appeal' achievements on matters that might have been—probably would have been—resolved by the General Council of Foreign Ministers if the European Council had not existed, it has to be said that it was the European Council meetings at

Milan and Luxembourg in 1985 that initiated and completed the negotiations for the Single European Act. But many of these heads of government meetings have been fairly humdrum affairs, accompanied by a good deal of media 'hype'.

The really important thing was, however, that the European Council failed to develop along the potentially dangerous lines proposed by Giscard d'Estaing and his Foreign Minister in 1974. In retrospect the diversion of this new entity away from its original intended shape and role reflected in significant measure, I believe, the determination with which the smaller countries resisted the original initiative, and, by insisting on the role of the Commission as the *sole* initiator of proposals for decision, headed off what seemed for a time to be a concerted attempt by the three larger countries to secure a dominant role for themselves in Community decision-making. When these larger states saw that the smaller countries were not prepared to go along with an erosion of the Commission's exclusive right of initiative, they opted instead for something never contemplated in the original Giscard proposals: European Councils comprising informal discussions leading only to 'orientations'.

Two other attempts were made while I was Foreign Minister to challenge the integrity of the Community structure. The first arose in the autumn of 1975 from a British problem in relation to a proposed global producer-consumer conference. Britain, of course, was starting to see itself at that time as a major oil producer and was legitimately concerned that the mandate to be agreed for the Community negotiations at the conference should, in relation to energy, reflect Britain's interests as a producer as well as the other members' interests as consumers. At the Council of Ministers meeting in early October, however, Britain suddenly sought separate participation at this conference, regardless of the mandate that might be given to the Community delegation.

I discussed the problem later that week with Henry Kissinger in Washington. The American view was that the problem lay in domestic British politics, and specifically in Labour Party politics; and Kissinger shared our concern lest a proliferation of Community countries' representation could explode the membership of the conference, doubling its size and threatening its effectiveness.

Shortly after my return to Dublin I was asked by the *Times* for an interview on Community issues, and I answered questions on this problem frankly. This interview made the principal headline in the paper and was reported on British radio and television. An informal meeting of Foreign Ministers at Lucca was to discuss the matter several days later. As we were assembling for the meeting Hans-Dietrich Genscher asked me what was wrong with Jim Callaghan, who had greeted his colleagues and even Joan with striking coolness, and me with scarcely disguised hostility. I told Genscher that I suspected I was in the doghouse because of the *Times* interview.

I was right. When our discussions turned to the producer-consumer conference, a number of those present spoke briefly about it, carefully avoiding the question of the British claim to a seat. Callaghan then enquired grimly whether anybody else wanted to speak. When no-one responded, he took a piece of paper from his pocket with a flourish, unfolded it, and began to declaim: 'I am grateful for the restraint *some* members of the Community have shown. *Others*, however [looking up at me], have expressed themselves with considerable freedom, using *our* newspapers and *our* radio to attack Her Majesty's Government. Those concerned have inflamed the situation.' And he went on to try to make a case for separate British representation at the conference. Britain, he said, was prepared to negotiate on these matters and would co-operate constructively, but it had to safeguard its own interests. There was no agreed Community policy, and it was quite unclear what such a policy would be. Britain must therefore represent itself.

When he left the room to fetch a document, I urged my colleagues to explain on his return what he appeared still not to have understood: that Britain could not be a member of the conference as well as the Community, because if Britain and the Community disagreed—and Britain's separate representation would be superfluous if it and the rest of the Community were in agreement— then there could be no Community position, and the other eight members would be disenfranchised. In view of his evident fury at my *Times* interview it would have been scarcely helpful for *me* to make this point, so I suggested that Thorn and Ortoli should beard the British lion. When they did so on his return, the British Foreign Secretary abruptly terminated the discussion, saying that the Community could go ahead with its own arrangements; Britain would look for separate representation. The discussion, he said, should end at this point; otherwise 'we would only get more bad-tempered'!

And so the storm was transferred to a larger tea-cup: the Rome European Council of 1 and 2 December. In his opening statement there, Harold Wilson overstretched the credulity—and the patience—of his listeners by telling them that British membership of OPEC was no longer a humorous idea but was now a strong probability. The discussion went on from mid-morning to late afternoon, and eventually a formula was patched up to save face for Wilson and Callaghan. It was agreed that the representative of a member-state in the Community delegation could speak at the Conference, but only (*a*) at the invitation of the Community President, (*b*) having first explained to his partners why he wanted to speak, and (*c*) having discussed with the other members what he was going to say, which (*d*) must not conflict with the Community mandate. Finally, (*e*) if there was no agreement with the Community on an issue the President would not invite anyone to speak.

I admired the skill with which Wilson and Callaghan sold this climb-down to part of the British press. By holding their press conference at the British embassy rather than at the conference centre they ensured that most of the British journalists would not cross-check the line they were being fed. Next day the *Times* and the *Telegraph*, as well as most of the popular papers in Britain, proclaimed a famous victory; however, the *Financial Times*, with a team of four journalists attending all the different press conferences, and the *Guardian*, because its single correspondent was less easily misled, told the true story.

The other challenge to the Community structure involved a prolonged battle over representation at world economic summits. This, like the Directory issue, ranged not one member-state against the rest but the large against the small, so it was potentially very dangerous.

At the Helsinki CSCE in July 1975 word leaked out that talks were taking place between some of the larger western countries present about a meeting to be held to arrange for a world economic summit. When questions were asked within the Community it was stated on behalf of the larger countries that these Helsinki discussions had been 'purely informal', that no decision had been taken, and that the relevant governments had merely agreed to 'keep in touch'. Nevertheless, some time later a preparatory meeting for such a summit in fact took place in New York, and the agenda for an economic summit to be held at Rambouillet in France was announced.

At Lucca, the subject was broached defensively by Sauvagnargues, Genscher, and Callaghan. These summit discussions, they said, would be 'very informal'; there would be 'discussions only': no decisions. Earlier at this meeting, when the European Council had been under discussion, I had referred to the lack of frankness of larger countries at Helsinki about this world economic summit. Now van der Stoel vigorously endorsed my earlier criticism, making a particular point of the fact that among the items now announced for the agenda of the new economic summit was trade, a Community competence. He was immediately supported by van Elslande and then, powerfully, by Ortoli, who said that he had hoped our discussions in Helsinki would have opened the way for Community action as others—gesturing towards me—had suggested there. A conference of this kind should not have been launched without consultation within the Community; while it could happen once without leaving traces behind, it could be highly dangerous if it happened again. I joined in to support my colleagues, pointing out that despite what had been said to us at Helsinki the first that a number of us had heard of this conference was what we read about it in the newspapers. If this happened a second time it could wreck the Community.

Despite efforts by the Big Three to pour oil on these troubled waters, the rest of us maintained our position, and the discussion ended after Ortoli had warned again about the dangers of any follow-up to the impending conference.

Our discussion had been a useful exercise in asserting the Community's role, and had been a warning to the larger countries of the dangers of purporting to act for others without their authority; but inevitably the whole issue surfaced again in relation to a second world economic summit, which it was proposed to hold in Puerto Rico at the end of June 1976. However, at the informal meeting of Foreign Ministers at Luxembourg in May 1976 the Big Three asserted their 'sympathy' for the idea of Community representation by the Presidency of the Council. After Ortoli had referred to the problems that would arise if the Community purported to speak as such on an occasion like this in the absence of the Commission, van der Stoel 'totally rejected' the suggestion of representation only by the Presidency of the Council plus the 'Big Four' (Italy was also to participate, as it had at Rambouillet). There was only one possible solution, he said: prior adoption of a Community position on matters of Community competence, and representation either by the President of the Council *and* the Commission, or by the Commission with the nine member-states.

The Council then fudged the issue, on the basis that the Four would make it clear at Puerto Rico that they could not discuss *au fond* any questions involving Community competence, as the Community would not be represented there. That was obviously unrealistic, however; and when a third economic summit was proposed for May 1977 the issue had finally to be faced. This was during the first British Presidency. Jim Callaghan was now Prime Minister. The Foreign Secretary, Tony Crosland, had died a few weeks earlier, and his successor, David Owen, was therefore in the chair at the Council of Ministers. Despite determined French resistance, the question of Community representation was referred to the European Council meeting of 25 March (held in Rome to mark the twentieth anniversary of the Treaties), and a cogently argued proposal that the Community should be represented by the President of the Commission as well as the President of the Council was adopted there without further argument.

The controversy did not end there, however, for the smaller countries and the Commission resented what they regarded as discourtesy to the President of the Commission, Roy Jenkins, at the London summit in May, when he was excluded from several important sessions. In a statement afterwards to the European Parliament Jenkins said that while at the parts of the meetings he attended the role and responsibilities of the Community were fully recognised by members and non-members of the Community alike, he could not pretend that the arrangements for Community representation were either logical or entirely satisfactory. He had not been admitted to the general economic debate when the very topics were discussed that had been dealt with at the last European Council and regarding which the Commission had been charged with certain tasks, nor had he been present at most of the discussion on energy.

Nevertheless, in this as in the other cases the battles fought by the smaller countries during the mid-1970s protected the Community against a real danger of erosion and enabled its institutions to survive until the mid-1980s, when a reversal of traditional French attitudes led to the Single European Act, with its commitment to the achievement of the internal market by 1992 and the accompanying revival of the Commission's key role in European development.

Before going on to the Irish Presidency I should, perhaps, refer to an aspect of Community affairs which, while it did not affect Irish interests significantly, was important to some other members. This was Mediterranean policy. The mid-1970s was a period in which the EEC was establishing new relationships with Mediterranean countries, opening its markets in some degree to their products and providing limited aid packages to some of the countries concerned. The negotiation of these agreements, which did not concern Ireland very directly, involved internal adjustments within the Community to compensate affected member-countries—Italy and France—for the diversion of trade resulting from improved access for foreign Mediterranean products.

The only Irish product that seemed likely to be affected adversely by such improved access was the early onion crop from Castlegregory, Co. Kerry. These onion-growers needed an extra fortnight each year beyond what was proposed by the Commission in order to dispose of their crop before Spanish onions were allowed into Ireland. Throughout a long and tedious debate I remained silent on this issue, calculating that my best chance of securing the extra fortnight was to wait until the final package was ready and then to whisper in the ear of the President, Jean Sauvagnargues—beside whom I sat, for alphabetical reasons— a last-minute request. He would, I felt, be so grateful to me for having refrained from adding to his troubles over two difficult days that he would be prepared to slip our 'onion fortnight' into the package at the last moment, without anyone even noticing. My manoeuvre succeeded. Castlegregory was saved without a word being spoken by me at the Council meeting.

At an earlier, inconclusive meeting on Mediterranean policy, in order to while away the time during the hours of discussion on issues in which I was taking no part I set myself the task of preparing a verse in rhyming couplets that would mention once, and once only (with the exception of new potatoes, of which I am particularly fond), every product referred to in the immense Commission proposal before the Council. This was the result:

> At a meeting of Foreign Mins.
> Decisions *weren't* taken about tins
> Of apricots and mandarins;
> New potatoes and capers in brine,
> Pimentos, bayleaves, and also thyme;
> Oranges, bitter; hinnies and mules;
> Watermelons, within the rules;
> Pectic substances and pigeon meat;
> Rose-bushes, but not to eat,
> Saltwater fish, excepting tunny;
> Horses for slaughter, and natural honey;
> Artichokes and aubergines;
> Cucumbers, melons, and also beans;
> Almonds provided they're not in shell;
> Canned orange hybrids, and prunes as well;
> Onions; grapes; and new potatoes;
> Strawberries; raspberries; and tomatoes;
> Comminuted citrus and Tarragona wine,
> Which taken together sound rather fine;
> Olives; peppers; and sowing seeds;
> Fish products of several breeds;
> Truffles preserved,

Properly served;
Anchovies dried;
Hake, grilled or fried;
Grapefruit juice and frozen fruit;
Plums and carrots cooked to suit
The tastes of gourmets of every guise:
That's what *should* have been in this compromise.

Having produced this *chef d'œuvre* I sent it across to Jim Callaghan for his entertainment. He and his colleagues appeared so taken with it that one of my officials, who obviously did not trust the British, became alarmed lest they publish this verse as their own and thus deprive me of the credit for it. It was accordingly passed immediately to the *Irish Times* correspondent and appeared in that paper a day or two later. I received no literary award, however. But fifteen years later Jim Callaghan asked me for a copy; he had mislaid the one I had given him at the meeting.

One aspect of Mediterranean policy that could have a bearing on our interests was the application by Greece for membership of the Community. I made two preconditions to our acceptance of that country's application—not because of any hostility to Greece but simply in order to protect Ireland's interests. The first of these preconditions related to the decision-making processes of the Community. I had remarked at an earlier Council meeting that the difficulties we were then experiencing in getting decisions amongst nine member-states in the absence of qualified majority voting suggested that it had been unwise of the original Six to admit the British, Danes and ourselves without having sorted out this majority voting question first. Now we were proposing to add a tenth member-state. I felt that the time had come to draw a rational conclusion from our experience and to move firmly to majority decision-making *before* any further enlargement. Accordingly, when the matter of Greek membership first came before us I made progress on this decision-making issue a first precondition for Irish acceptance of Greek membership. At the informal meeting in Luxembourg I stressed that this was not a precondition for the opening of negotiations but for their conclusion.

Our second precondition related to the availability of adequate financial resources. I made it clear that we could not accept that Greek membership—or that of any other later applicant—should water down the resources available to finance existing policies. Resources had to be increased commensurately with the net increase in budgetary requirements, after allowing for Greece's own contributions.

At the time when I raised this issue, other member-states had responded by saying that they could not commit themselves without consulting their governments, which, of course, I accepted, thus giving the green light to the *principle* of Greek membership while maintaining our preconditions for actual Greek accession. Now at Luxembourg, some time having elapsed, I suggested there should be no difficulty about countries agreeing to this entirely logical proposal.

When Tony Crosland, who had joined the Council less than two months previously, asked for clarification of my point, Gaston Thorn intervened to say that it was quite simple: the needs of ten members should not have to be met out of the funds available for, and appropriate to, nine.

While the conclusion of the Greek negotiations took place during the lifetime of the next Irish Government, I presume that this second Irish precondition must have helped to ensure the protection of our stake in the budget; the first precondition, about reforming decision-making in the Community, seems to have been quietly dropped, however. This question was not finally addressed until the negotiation of the Single European Act nine years later.

# CHAPTER SIX

# IRELAND'S EC ROLE

From the time we joined the Community the question of the first Irish Presidency loomed large in our minds. Given the extent to which we were likely to be net recipients of Community funds and our reticence about sharing in the defence of the Community until a much later stage in its development, it was clearly important for us to use the opportunity of our Presidency in the first half of 1975 to demonstrate our commitment to the Community and our determination to advance its interests.

In the latter part of 1973 we asked the Danish government if we could send some of our staff to Denmark to find out how they were tackling their Presidency, for which they had had only six months to prepare after entering the Community with Britain and ourselves in January of that year. And during 1974 we organised courses in chairmanship for the hundred or so civil servants who would have to preside over almost two hundred Community committees and working groups during our six-month stint.

In August of that year Joan and I were holidaying in the south of France in company with, among others, my fellow-Minister Justin Keating, Mary Robinson, then a senator and now President, and the EEC representative in Dublin, Denis Corboy. One day the four of us went off for a working lunch in the garden of a restaurant to discuss the Presidency, following which I drew up a memorandum for my department in which I pointed out that any proposals we might put forward would have most impact if visibly accompanied by changes in the style of the Presidency. These could include, I suggested, more frequent and regular attendance in the European Parliament by the Irish Presidents of the General (Foreign Affairs) and other Councils; a more free-for-all question-time procedure there; direct Presidential contact with the Economic and Social Committee; Presidential emphasis at Council meetings on the recommendations coming from the Parliament and this committee; and a more open and relaxed relationship with the press. All these proposals were, in the event, implemented. My decision to brief journalists *before* as well as after meetings ensured that they would less easily be misled by partisan national briefings following each Council. Moreover, during my term of office I attended all seven sessions of the Parliament, and I also initiated a question-time for Political Co-operation matters: hitherto the Presidency had answered questions only on Community affairs.

To these proposed innovations I subsequently added a meeting with the full European Commission before the start of the Presidency, with a view to concerting our joint approach for the next six months; this process had until then been confined to a meeting between the incoming President of the Council and the President of the Commission. Later on in our Presidency a state visit was arranged at my suggestion by the President of Ireland to the four principal institutions of the Community: Parliament, Council of Ministers, Commission, and Court of Justice. We also initiated during the Presidency the regular post-Gymnich series of informal weekends for Foreign Ministers, who were accompanied on the earlier of these occasions by their wives.

During this six months it fell to us also to organise the first European Council meeting in Dublin, in March 1975; to bring to a successful conclusion the first of the quinquennial series of Lomé negotiations with the ACP (African, Caribbean, Indian Ocean and Pacific) countries; and to launch in Washington a process of Political Co-operation consultations with the United States. Another improvement in Community practice during our Presidency was the introduction (on the occasion of preparatory meetings for the International Energy Conference) of a joint spokesmanship by the Presidency and the Commission in international negotiations—a practice that was repeated at the Euro-Arab dialogue in Cairo in June and later developed into a system under which, even in matters not strictly within the Treaties, the Presidency and Commission negotiate together for the Community. In these and the other ways mentioned below our Presidency was—and was seen to be—a period of considerable innovation.

Immediately after the Paris summit in December 1974 I had given thought to how I might carry out the heads of government decision 'to renounce the practice of making agreement on all questions conditional on the unanimous consent of the member States.' I devised a procedure for each meeting of the General or Foreign Affairs Council under which I would obtain from the Council's legal advisers a classification of agenda items that would distinguish decisions requiring unanimity under the Treaties from those that should be taken by qualified—or, more rarely, simple—majority vote, and distinguishing also items requiring a formal decision under the Treaties from those in respect of which the Council was really being asked only for an orientation or opinion. I proposed to read out this annotation of the agenda at the start of Council meetings and to ask the members whether any of them had difficulty because of a vital national interest in agreeing to make decisions by qualified majority in each case where this was provided for.

Before the end of the year I phoned my colleagues to tell them of my intentions. As I expected, no-one except Jim Callaghan demurred at my proposal. He objected strongly. I changed my draft wording in response to a valid point of detail that he raised, but I told him that I still intended to implement the procedure despite his objections.

I did so at our first Council meeting in Brussels, on 20 January. Callaghan lodged a protest, which I noted, and this pattern was sustained at each meeting throughout the Presidency. As it happened, many of the matters that came before the Council during the first five months required 'orientations' rather than formal decisions, and where decisions were called for they required unanimity under the terms of the Treaty of Rome. I began to think that my new procedure would never bring the issue of qualified majority voting to a head; but at the last Council meeting of our Presidency the opportunity to press a matter to a vote arose quite unexpectedly, and in the most favourable circumstances.

Jim Callaghan told the Council that the beef producers of Botswana and Swaziland were suffering severely from the impact of the levy on beef imports to the Community. (So also, I was told, were the big British companies that imported this beef.) Callaghan made a strong, and quite emotional, plea that beef from these states be allowed free entry to the Community. Everyone was in principle agreeable to an exception for these countries, but France and Germany could not agree on whether this should be done by exempting the countries in question from the levy or by refunding the levy to them. The proposal thus threatened to founder on a technical issue of procedure. I saw my chance and, looking down the table towards Callaghan at the far end, I proposed a qualified majority vote on which method of meeting the British request should be adopted. Callaghan's face was worth seeing as he saw the trap close on him. He had no choice but to concede the issue of principle with good grace in order to secure his immediate objective. Later that night a further qualified majority vote was taken on a matter concerning a trade agreement with Sri Lanka.

I urged my Italian successor in the Presidency to maintain this practice but, after a couple of half-hearted attempts, he dropped it, and the Council soon reverted to the practice of deciding all issues, however trivial, on the basis of unanimity.

One of the first engagements of our Presidency was a meeting in Washington on 8 January with Henry Kissinger to launch the process of political discussion between the US and the nine member-states of the Community, which had been agreed more than six months previously but had not been initiated during the intervening French Presidency. On my way to Washington for this meeting I decided that my best approach would be to find some controversial issue on which he and I would disagree; in this way I might ensure that he would remember our encounter.

Much of the discussion over lunch involved Henry Kissinger expressing his views, in part at least for the benefit of two congressmen present, with occasional interpolations from me. I found this interesting and useful but it represented something of a one-way process.

Issues that I raised at that stage, however, included the possibility of involving the PLO, whom we believed to be supported by the Palestinian people, in Middle East negotiations. Kissinger queried the ability of this organisation to establish itself as legitimately representative of the Palestinians, and doubted whether any effort should be made to involve them.

I was asked a number of questions on the European Community and was pressed about the role of the European Parliament. Kissinger asked how one could possibly imagine a common system of direct elections from Jutland to Sicily, but his scepticism seemed based on an inadequate appreciation of what had already been achieved in the Community; he seemed quite unaware that the existing Parliament was already organised on party lines, transcending national differences.

The serious discussion (part of it after lunch) concentrated on the proposed global producer-consumer conference. The US position as enunciated by Kissinger was that the United States would not go to a conference without prior agreement amongst oil-consuming countries on financial solidarity, energy conservation, and the development of new sources of energy. I explained that Europe, and most vocally France, had doubts about the wisdom of being seen to gang up on the producers, although, of course, the European countries would not want to approach the conference in disarray. I said that it was important to avoid a situation where the United States appeared to be telling Europe what to do. This prompted from Kissinger an assurance that there would be genuine dialogue between the United States and Europe: there was no possibility that the US would present its proposals on a 'take it or leave it' basis.

As it happened, however, on the previous day the EC Finance Ministers' meeting in London had agreed only to 'study' rather than to accept a US proposal for a financial facility to soften the economic consequences of the oil crisis. This proposal had followed on a recommendation from the International Monetary Fund, and may have been seen by EC Ministers as a US move to undermine the IMF approach. However that might be, Kissinger was annoyed at the relegation of his proposal by the EC to the status of a 'study', and said that unless it were accepted the United States would not participate in the conference. I sought to calm him down, pointing out that reports of the EC reaction in the US press had been quite misleading in several respects, and adding that in my view the two proposals were complementary, not competitive. Pointedly, however, I also said that the US side had contributed to the problem by their approach: the American way of putting things was often unfortunate—I would put it no stronger than that. I went on to add that it was a pity that the United States had not contributed to the UN special fund to help developing countries in the aftermath of the oil crisis, as the EC and Japan had done. The American attitude to that fund was not understood in Europe. Kissinger replied defensively that there was some division in the US government on the issue.

This gave me my opportunity to go on the attack, as I had decided to do during my flight to New York. I queried the wisdom of the aggressive and confrontational approach by the United States towards the Third World during the recent United Nations session, which had made it unnecessarily difficult for the Americans to get support for their policies. Psychology was important, and they should not underestimate the neuroses of ex-colonies; Ireland had spent the last fifty years working its way out of a neurosis of this kind. The United States might do better to let countries like Ireland, which understood the psychological problem, influence the Third World in a constructive direction. Even the former colonial powers might in some cases be better equipped to deal constructively with their ex-colonies than the United States.

Kissinger's initial reaction to this onslaught was, as I had expected—and hoped—one of irritation. But, somewhat surprisingly, he soon became defensive. American timing in criticising Third World countries at the recent United Nations sessions might not have been correct, he said, and the words used might have been better chosen. On the other hand there was a real problem, and the softer European approach might be regarded at times as an evasion of the issues. However, the United States should perhaps talk to its allies before the next United Nations session.

It became clear during later discussions that my decision to 'pick a fight' at our first formal bilateral session had been well judged. Kissinger enjoyed our somewhat combative discussions on this and other occasions, and years later in conversation contrasted them with his meetings with a number of my more cautious European colleagues.

A few days later the first of two final negotiating conferences with the ACP countries took place in Brussels. These discussions had begun in 1973 at a meeting that nearly collapsed before it started. On that occasion I had had an appointment with Commissioner Briggs of Nigeria an hour beforehand, in the course of which it emerged that the African delegates considered themselves an Organisation of African Unity group; I also learnt that it had been decided at a meeting of the group in Lagos that they should be serviced by the OAU secretariat. It seemed to me that unless a place were provided for the secretariat near to Briggs as spokesman for the group, our first session might be disrupted. I passed this on to the Danish Presidency, and an earlier decision against such an arrangement was accordingly rescinded, with the result that the conference was smoothly launched.

Just before that first conference had got down to business I had walked around the table introducing myself to the delegates. I was disconcerted when one ACP Minister asked me what I was doing there. 'I'm an EC Minister,' I responded. 'But Ireland isn't a member of the EC,' he said, and he went through the nine member-countries, naming Sweden, however, in place of Ireland. I told him Sweden was not a member, reiterating that Ireland was. His face fell. 'I told my President it was Sweden,' he said sadly, adding with, I thought, some trepidation, 'I'll have to tell him I was wrong when I return.'

Unfortunately, the negotiations then started had not, as intended, been completed during the French Presidency in the second half of 1974. A new deadline of the end of January 1975 had been set, which I was expected to meet. Fifty separate issues, some of them highly controversial, remained to be settled between the nine EC and forty-six ACP countries. At first I despaired of ever grasping such a formidable body of negotiating material, but I was extraordinarily fortunate in the official who had been in charge of the negotiations on our behalf up to that point: a young First Secretary, Hugh Swift, who later served as EC delegate in Zambia. I soon found that he enjoyed the confidence and trust of the far more senior Ambassadors who represented most of the other countries. He inducted me into the mysteries of the negotiation, so that after two days I had some grasp of the issues that remained to be settled.

Ireland had a clear advantage in presiding over this negotiation. The ACP countries knew that we were sympathetic to them and that, as it happened, we had no national interests to defend. Even on the vexed issue of the scale of aid to be provided I had a free hand, because of our Government's commitment to increase our own aid programme rapidly; this enabled me to press for the acceptance by our EC partners of as high a figure as possible. At the same time our EC partners knew me well enough by this time to understand that I would not betray *their* interests. Finally, given that this negotiation involved the incorporation of former British colonies into a framework—that of the earlier Yaoundé Agreement—that had hitherto been confined almost exclusively to former French colonies (plus Zaïre and the Netherlands Antilles), the fact that I could negotiate in French was helpful, reassuring the former French colonies linguistically that I was not oriented primarily towards the former British colonies.

After two days the meeting was adjourned for a fortnight, towards the end of which I flew on Monday 27 January to Abidjan to attend and address a parliamentary conference between the EC and Yaoundé Agreement countries.

I was impressed with Abidjan: a most attractive mixture of modern and traditional in this, the most prosperous of African states, the Ivory Coast. What remains most strongly in my mind is the President's guard of honour, well over six feet tall and dressed in gold and silver helmets and breastplates, white breeches, and scarlet cloaks: like Rome's African legions, as I imagined them, come to life.

In my speech to the joint parliamentary assembly I naturally made the most of the parallel colonial experiences of Ireland and the African countries: colonisation, dilution but also enrichment of our cultural heritage, excessively close post-colonial links with the former colonial power: '*dépendance durable et néfaste . . . relation à la fois trop avantageuse et trop exploitative . . . période néo-coloniale dont nous autres irlandais avons pour notre part une expérience particulière.*' It wasn't the speech the Council secretariat wanted me to make, and it may not have brought joy to the hearts of the French and British Ambassadors, but it got a good reception from the audience.

On the way back to Brussels I stopped over in Rome on Wednesday for discussions with the Italian Foreign Minister. On Thursday morning we started the final ACP negotiating session, which went on with one short break on Thursday night until breakfast-time on Saturday morning. The willingness of my Community colleagues to remain available for meetings of the Council at all hours of the day or night (some of them played bridge while they waited), and the quite remarkable negotiating skill and judgement of the ACP negotiating team, which included among others Sridi Ramphal, later Commonwealth Secretary, enabled us to succeed with what was in fact a mammoth task.

The negotiations had to be interrupted occasionally to enable me to refer back to my colleagues. One such meeting was called for 2.30 on Friday afternoon. I waited in vain for a full attendance until 2.55; then I announced, 'With all the new-found authority of a grandfather of one-and-a-half hours' standing I call this meeting to order, even in the absence of the Danish delegation.' (I had rung home just before the meeting, and Joan had told me the news of the birth of a daughter, Doireann, to my son John's wife, Eithne.) This announcement was greeted with warm applause; to my knowledge Doireann remains the only baby whose birth has been so greeted by the Council of Ministers of the European Community.

I am not sure whether it was during this session or at another Council of Ministers later in the Presidency that I allowed myself to give vent to momentary irritation at the prolixity of someone speaking at length and more than once on behalf of the Italian delegation. I had been about to sum up the debate and move to a conclusion when I observed a hand raised once more. 'Not the bloody Italians again!' I groaned. The microphone was live and the interpreters obliged with multilingual translations. The meeting, Italians included, dissolved in laughter.

But to return to the final ACP negotiation: I had been advised that if it were to succeed I must ensure that the question of sugar was not introduced. Despite some agitation from Caribbean participants this was generally accepted. However, at 2.30 on the Saturday morning when I called a meeting of the Council of Ministers the Commissioner for Agriculture, Petrus Lardinois, who had not been involved in the discussions, arrived to find out how things were going, and proceeded to talk about sugar. At that point I lost my temper and, momentarily forgetting my commitment to preserve and enhance the Commission's role, I threw him out, to the entertainment and satisfaction of my Community colleagues. In his absence we narrowed down the outstanding issues, and by 8.30 a.m. had reached agreement, overrunning our 31 January deadline, but only by eight-and-a-half hours. I returned to Dublin, and bed, with a sense of exhilaration and relief.

Five weeks later we embarked for Lomé in Togo to sign the agreement. It was perhaps the most exotic moment of my political career, and it had its entertaining side. On arrival we had some time on our hands; I decided to explore the town. The oldest public building, my antiquarian enquiries showed, was the cathedral, built in 1904. (Togo had three colonial masters: Germany till 1914, Britain till 1919, and then France.) When I entered the cathedral the Stations of the Cross were in progress, and I waited to have a word with the priest afterwards.

That afternoon I was taken to see the port installations, and, while there, the bridge of my reading glasses snapped. I rushed back into the town to find an optician. The shop was closed, and I explained to a Togolese lounging against the wall why I needed to find the owner urgently: as President of the EC Council I had to read a speech at the following day's ceremony. He looked at me and said (I translate), 'But there are a number of speeches before yours: if you give them to him in the morning he'll have new ones for you before your turn comes.' I was impressed by his familiarity with the agenda for the signing ceremony, but unconvinced by his easy optimism about getting new glasses in time.

I went on to an official reception and, joining the receiving line, asked each person who arrived wearing glasses if I could try them on to see if I could read with them. I had no luck until the six-foot eight-inch (at least!) Prime Minister of Fiji arrived. He pointed out to me what in my near-panic I had failed to realise: that the glasses people wore when walking around were normally distance glasses, which would scarcely be of much use to me in my dilemma. 'Try my ambassador's,' he said. His ambassador produced glasses from his pocket. They worked.

The following day's ceremony was spectacular. In the auditorium, seating some three thousand people, each signature was greeted by a chant of welcome and a dance by two thousand Togolese women in long green dresses. When it came to my turn to speak I found that, while I could read the text with the Fijian Ambassador's glasses, they would not stay on my nose unless I held them. In the absence of a rostrum I had to hold my speech in my other hand, juggling with the pages. I felt that this somewhat inelegant performance required an explanation, which I offered, to the delight and hilarity of the hitherto staid audience.

When I went to Mass in the cathedral on the following day I had to await the end of the previous Mass. The closing announcements included an exhortation to attend the Stations of the Cross on Friday and thus follow the excellent example of the President of the EC. When I entered the church a Togolese woman sidled up to me in the pew and whispered that there were ten praesidia (branches) of the Irish lay Catholic organisation the Legion of Mary in Togo; before I had time to recover from this news I found myself the subject of the sermon, which extolled the essential equality of the human race, based on the fact that my eyes and those of the Fijian Ambassador required the same glasses. The extent to which Togolese television penetrated the interior of the country became clear to me, moreover, when at a barbecue in a forest up-country several days later elderly chieftains performing a ritual dance for our benefit called to me as they passed, 'Did you get your glasses fixed yet?'

Back in Dublin I soon found myself deep into preparations, physical and political, for the first meeting of the European Council, which, ironically in view of my opposition to the establishment of this institution, was to be held in Dublin.

We took considerable trouble with the preparations. The event was to be held in Dublin Castle. In contrast to the dispersed arrangements for the Paris summit, where the press facilities were several miles away from the conference venue, *we* located Premiers and press in the same premises; indeed the press room was directly underneath St Patrick's Hall, where the Council met— which led me to suggest frivolously that we arrange a hole in the floor beside my seat so that I could brief the press directly by dropping notes to them. St Patrick's Hall, where Presidents of Ireland are now inaugurated, is the great hall of the castle, where formerly the Knights of St Patrick (a British order created in the eighteenth century and now extinct) were inaugurated. Banners of the knights hang overhead, and I noticed that Giscard d'Estaing was to be seated under the sovereign's banner, the Royal Standard. My officials restrained me from suggesting to the photographers that they take an angled shot of the French President under a British monarch's standard; unfortunately, the photographers did not think of it themselves.

The press were enthusiastic about the telecommunications arrangements, which gave them instant contact with most of their capitals—something that in those days was far from universal, as I knew from visiting Paris and Rome, and indeed the diplomatic quarter of Washington. Amongst the many courteous letters we received from journalists after the meeting I recall particularly one from Mark Arnold Foster remarking that he had never previously been asked so politely to stop smoking: 'Would you be upset if I asked you if you would ever mind not smoking' contrasted favourably, he thought, with the harsh brevity of '*Nicht rauchen!*'

While the agenda for the European Council included energy, raw materials, relations with developing countries, the CSCE (due for signature in Helsinki four months later), current political problems, the world economic situation, and the economic and social position of the Community, this somewhat portentous list did not in fact involve much of substance. The meat of the sessions lay in the first items: the budgetary corrective mechanism and New Zealand— which was how the outstanding issues in the first British 'renegotiation' were described. Since Jim Callaghan's somewhat aggressive launch of the question twelve months earlier, British demands had been substantially narrowed down to these two issues, and it was fairly clear by this time that it would be possible to meet his government's political requirement for some concessions in advance of the rather belated referendum they intended to hold on EC membership two-and-a-half years after joining the Community.

Wilson sought to create a positive atmosphere at the outset by stressing in his opening remarks that if these problems were settled Britain would no longer be a reluctant partner in the Community but would play its part in its development and would have a vested interest in its cohesion. Later, in response to a direct question from Giscard d'Estaing about economic and monetary union, Callaghan answered somewhat evasively, but cleverly, by saying that Britain did not retract its commitment to EMU as expressed in the communiqué from the Paris summit, and that no-one else had gone any further than that.

I observed with some fascination the subsequent ritual dance of negotiation between the principal heads of government. The happy outcome was clearly pre-ordained, but before arriving at it honour had to be satisfied by various solutions being put forward and rejected. I was at first disturbed at the fact that the initial proposals from the French and Germans made no arithmetical sense; quite simply, they did not add up. When I pointed this out to the French, it was explained to me that this did not matter: the proposals in question were only 'fliers', not seriously intended, and would never have to face such a sophisti-cated mathematical test. I subsided, amused at the games the major countries play with one another.

When this dance came to its happy end, a formula was found within the financial limits that Helmut Schmidt had laid down at the outset as the maxi-mum his cabinet would accept. And another formula was found to serve as a resolution of the New Zealand butter issue. We then passed on to less substantial matters.

The meeting, over which Liam Cosgrave presided with dignity, was judged a success—and indeed was afterwards contrasted with the immediately fol-lowing European Councils, which did not have such a meaty issue as British renegotiation into which heads of government could get their teeth. I naturally did nothing to disturb this assessment, although privately I believed that the outstanding elements of the British renegotiation could, and would, have been settled by Foreign Ministers if the European Council had not existed.

On this occasion the after-dinner discussion, when, in accordance with what was to become a normal procedure, the Foreign Ministers joined the heads of government for coffee, was about the CSCE negotiations. Wilson, Schmidt and Giscard d'Estaing all showed a wish to bring these negotiations to a conclusion that summer, in case Brezhnev should retire and be replaced by a leader less committed to even a limited process of détente. Moreover, all three expressed suspicion that a proposal just received from Moscow for an end-of-June confer-ence might be the result of a secret agreement between Kissinger and Gromyko. As on many subsequent occasions, I was struck by the fact that the discussion on such matters by heads of government seemed to be informed by relatively few hard facts and to be, frankly, somewhat amateurish; but perhaps on relaxed occasions like these, without papers, it could hardly have been otherwise.

The next meeting in Ireland during our Presidency was to be the first of the series of six-monthly informal weekend meetings of Foreign Ministers, based on the Gymnich precedent. Remembering Gymnich, I decided to make it really informal by inviting the Ministers' wives, most of whom had not met each other. Finding a suitable location posed a problem, as the only Govern-ment-owned house adapted for entertaining, Barrettstown Castle in Co. Kildare, was too small for our purposes. Benjamin and Miranda Iveagh generously offered us the use of their home, Farmleigh, at Castleknock, near Dublin. It was eminently appropriate in location, accommodation, and privacy. Miranda Iveagh joined with Joan in hosting the occasion. Our preparations were meticulous, including seating arrangements for the meals in order to ensure that people had different neighbours on each occasion and that these neighbours would always have a common language—a problem of mathematical complexity. An expedition to Co. Wicklow was arranged for the wives on the Sunday, from which they returned in very good form, having found common ground in singing the tune called in different languages 'Tannenbaum', 'Mon Beau Sapin', and 'The Red Flag'! Jean Sauvagnargues, who had been accompanying Giscard d'Estaing on a visit to Algeria, arrived late, having stopped off in Paris to pick up his wife. Miranda Iveagh greeted them on arrival and showed them to their room. When they came down to dinner, Sauvagnargues, indicating Miranda, enquired: '*Qui est cette dame là?*' Joan replied that she was our hostess, Lady Iveagh. Sauvagnargues exclaimed: '*Mais elle n'est pas respectable!*'—meaning 'But she is too young and pretty to be the chatelaine of such a house': a classic example, I have always thought, of the danger of literal translations from French into English. So, at least, Joan and I recall this exchange.

In Sauvagnargues's absence we had talked with Leo Tindemans, the Belgian Prime Minister, about his work on a report on European union that the Paris summit four months earlier had commissioned him to produce, and this was followed after a short break by a discussion on how the working of the Community as now constituted might be improved.

Among the matters considered the following day was the question of Portugal, where after the April 1974 revolution the election campaign for a constituent Assembly was in its final stages. Despite German, Danish and Benelux pressure, no agreement was reached on possible pre-election EC action that might encourage the emergence of a democratic regime. Sauvagnargues was strongly opposed to any such move, pointing out that the Portuguese, having recently been a colonial power, were very sensitive to anything that might smack of colonialism on the part of Europe.

After the Portuguese election results had been announced it was agreed, however, that I should go to Portugal in early June as President of the Council to see what the EC could do to encourage a democratic evolution in that country, where the Armed Forces Movement set up during the April 1974 revolution remained in control.

Although I have no record of this, it is my recollection that I had raised the question of Portugal with Kissinger in February and that he had been sceptical about any initiative at that time. However that may be, I certainly broached the subject with him in Paris at the end of May, when I attended meetings of the International Energy Agency and the OECD. He was quite negative, expressing deep pessimism about the Portuguese situation; he seemed to feel fatalistically that Portugal was likely to emerge from its postrevolutionary trauma as, at best, a non-aligned country like Algeria or, at worst, a Soviet satellite, and that nothing could be done about it. However, without enthusiasm, he said we were welcome to make the attempt.

As Joan and I left Paris for Lisbon the omens were not too good. The Portuguese left-wing press had been featuring scare reports about a NATO fleet assembling in the area, and there was evident hostility towards western Europe among the extreme left, who, although the Communists had won less than a quarter of the Assembly seats in the election, seemed still to be the dominant element in the Armed Forces Movement.

My first engagement in Lisbon was to host a dinner at the Irish Embassy for the Foreign Minister, Antunes, and other Ministers. I asked Antunes to come early so that we could have a private discussion before the others arrived. I started by reiterating what I had said to him during a brief encounter on arrival at the airport: that there was general good will in the Community towards Portugal and no desire to interfere with the country's choice of economic system—but there *was* strong concern for the preservation of freedom and a democratic system there. Antunes responded by saying that he and the moderates (who, he claimed, were increasingly in control in the Armed Forces Movement) were concerned to prevent any Communist domination. They wanted to ensure the preservation of the rights of man and of individual freedom while finding a third way, by implication neither communist nor social-democratic, towards socialism. There had been very positive developments in the Armed Forces Movement during the previous fortnight. Freedom of the press would be guaranteed. Elections had started in the trade unions, and the Communists were losing out. Within weeks the trade union organisation, Inter-sindical, would cease to be Communist-controlled.

From my point of view the principal purpose of this preliminary discussion was to enable me to sound out how, in the talks about to begin, I could avoid the danger that Sauvagnargues had pointed out at Farmleigh—of which, as an Irishman, I was very well aware—while at the same time getting across the message that the Community would aid only a democratic Portugal. Accordingly, I now put the question to him directly: How could I phrase this condition clearly but sensitively? Without hesitation he replied: '*Il faut dire qu'une aide communautaire sera dans l'optique d'un développement démocratique en Portugal.*' That was what I needed. I stuck to this formula rigorously for the next couple of days—although I later found that the Socialist leader, Mario Soares, would have preferred more explicit conditionality. Antunes spoke at that point favourably of the idea of an agreement with the Community and hoped that impending discussions between himself and Giscard d'Estaing would go well. I encouraged him to visit Italy also during the next few weeks, as I felt he would find the Italians sympathetic. He went on to say that he felt that Kissinger seemed to have a rather closed mind on Portugal, although he felt he had made some progress with him; I refrained from comment on this.

Next day I met President Costa Gomes. Antunes had described him as 'a sensible man, with considerable wisdom,' although I was later to hear him called an opportunist. The President told me of his intention that action be taken to deal with the excessive level of Communist control in the media, possibly tackling the problem in the state radio and television service by putting a military officer in charge of it.

Prime Minister Gonçalves was another matter altogether. He gave me a prolonged but unimpressive lecture on the aims and objectives of the Armed Forces Movement, which was to provide the basic dynamism for Portugal's 'third way' to 'democratic socialism'. This, he claimed, would involve the political parties as a kind of 'sounding board'. While he refrained from repeating to me his public references to 'capitalist plots' against Portugal, he was reluctant to accept that the Communists posed any kind of danger. It emerged that he was quite unaware of the fact that members of his government had made concrete proposals to me for Community aid. 'Surely that cannot be correct?' he asked one of his Ministers present. The Minister confirmed what I had said.

In my official discussions with members of the government it became clear that Antunes and Lopes, the Foreign Trade Minister, placed great importance on Portugal's future relationship with the Community. Both they and the Industry and Technology Minister, Cravinho, emphasised the urgent need for substantial EEC credits by the end of July if the emerging democratic system were to survive. My response was to point out that in the absence until very recently of any concrete proposals from the Portuguese government, the Community had been able to take no decisions—but that a willingness existed to help Portugal 'in the perspective of a democratic development', assisting it to move towards a pluralist democratic system with full freedom of expression.

In the margin of the meeting one Minister made a special request to me. Their exports of port to Germany and France, to the value of £160 million, were at risk. There had been several droughts over three years, and, not having enough grapes to make brandy to fortify the port, they had imported brandy from Yugoslavia. Now the Germans were saying that the fortifying spirit could not have been genuine brandy, because their chemical tests had shown that the port was insufficiently radioactive. The spirit must have been made synthetically, the Germans argued, rather than from grapes exposed to the atmosphere, which contained some radioactivity. Consequently this port did not meet the German, nor apparently the French, customs definition of port wine. Could I ask these two countries to treat the question as still open by continuing their tests until the consignments of port had been delivered? I promised to ask Sauvagnargues and Genscher on my return to take whatever steps might be necessary to allow this inadequately radioactive port to be let into their countries. I did so on my return, and as I heard no more about it I presumed that my representations had succeeded.

Also in the margin of these official discussions I was asked by one Minister if I found out who the members of the Armed Forces Movement were to tell him: he would like to know who *was* running the country!

Among a number of political leaders not in government whom I met was the Socialist, Mario Soares, who first enquired cautiously about my political bona fides. Was I a social-democrat? Reassured that I belonged to the social-democratic end of the Christian democrat spectrum, he spoke freely about the way in which fear was starting to grow again in Portugal a year after the peaceful revolution against Salazar's dictatorship: fear of being bugged, fear of losing one's job, and so on. Opportunists were jumping on the extreme left-wing bandwagon; an internal coup had just taken over the centre PPD party.

I was struck by the fact that Antunes and himself, with a good deal in common and in key positions in the Armed Forces Movement and Socialist Party, respectively, did not seem to be in touch with one another. I suggested to Soares that such contact might be fruitful, and made the same point to Antunes on my departure. Soares and I agreed to keep in touch, and six weeks later a Portuguese Socialist politician came to see me at my home. He had been asked to contact me by Soares, who was anxious to convey on behalf of the Socialist Party that, despite the apparent dominance of the extreme left in a very fluid situation, the EC should not react by giving an unconditionally negative answer to Portuguese requests. A hard line in negotiations would have no good effect, but a very firm pro-pluralist position could helpfully be adopted in dealings with the regime. Europe was now in a very strong position, as the left in the Armed Forces Movement had been told by the Soviet Union that Portugal was a western European country whose problems had to be settled in that context: no Cuba in Portugal. Meanwhile the Socialists had established a firm alliance with the Church, and would also support Antunes 'au bout'. The opposition would provide a democratic alternative to the regime.

All this I passed on to my colleagues in the Community, who took due note of it. Four months later the crunch came in dramatic circumstances, and a fully democratic system emerged, with Mario Soares as Prime Minister.

*

In the latter part of our Presidency I also undertook a series of visits in the Middle East. In mid-May I went to Jordan, Syria, Lebanon, and Egypt, and some weeks later to Israel and Turkey. I also attended a meeting of an EC-Greece parliamentary body in Athens at the end of June under the Greek association agreement.

A week before leaving for the Middle East I had signed an EC-Israel supplementary agreement that had been discussed at Farmleigh several weeks earlier. Some adverse reaction to this from the Arab countries was to be expected, but the storm that burst was much more severe than anything that had been anticipated, and I had to face some hard questioning during my visit. In each of the capitals we visited I found that the EC-Israel agreement was in fact a very contentious issue, which had apparently been aggravated by what the Arabs felt was Israeli triumphalism.

Our visit to Lebanon took place under strange circumstances. On Thursday 22 May we drove from Damascus to Beirut. The journey seemed uneventful, although I noticed that at the border our Lebanese hosts evinced no enthusiasm for a suggestion that we try to fit in en route a visit to Ba'albek. Beirut appeared quiet, the streets surprisingly empty, as I drove from our hotel to meet the Foreign Minister and President Franjieh, and in the afternoon to a meeting with the EEC Ambassadors. In the evening I gave a reception. I was aware that fighting between the Phalangists and the Palestinians had broken out two days earlier when we had spent a night in Beirut en route to Amman, but the fact that we were in the midst of what turned out later to have been effectively the start of the Lebanese Civil War was nevertheless not immediately apparent. Joan and I were indeed somewhat taken aback on the morning after our arrival from Damascus to hear on the BBC World Service that 1,500 shells had fallen on Beirut during the night. The lapping of the waves on the shore in front of the Hotel Vendome had apparently drowned out the noise of this bombardment a mile and a half away.

When the time came to leave we reached the airport, however, without difficulty and flew to Cairo. En route I was told that the preoccupation of our hosts on the way from the border to Beirut the previous morning had reflected the fact that a member of the welcoming party had been injured in an ambush while driving up to the border to meet us. Later I learnt that during that week a hundred people had died and three hundred had been injured in the Lebanese capital.

In Cairo I told Mahmud Riad, Secretary-General of the Arab League, that the agreement between the EC and Israel did not apply to the occupied territories. He asked me was I speaking as President of the Council; I said that I had no authority to speak for the Council, as I was visiting the Middle East as Minister for Foreign Affairs of Ireland, but in that capacity I could state my Government's position on the agreement, and I believed that no other government would disagree with what I had said. He replied that an oral assurance on behalf of Ireland would not satisfy the Arab League. I agreed to commit the assurance to writing, and did so on the spot, in a text stressing that 'the area of application of the new agreement' did not include 'any of the territories occupied by Israel since 1967.'

He thanked me for my text but said that it would have to be confirmed as being the position of the Community. I remarked that it would be time-consuming and cumbersome to put this issue back into the Community decision-making procedure. 'Aren't you meeting your fellow-Ministers at a Political Co-operation meeting in Dublin on Monday?' he asked. I agreed that I was. 'Then this is what I propose,' he said. 'I'll put this piece of paper in my safe and show it to no-one. If at your meeting on Monday you tell them that you've given it to me and that you regard it as the view of the Community, and if they don't tell you to go to hell, send me a wire to that effect and I'll tell my Arab League colleagues that it's all right.' This somewhat informal approach to resolving the crisis appealed to me, and I agreed to his proposal.

On Monday I reported to my colleagues at our meeting in the Bermingham Tower of Dublin Castle. Most of them were delighted at the solution agreed between Mahmud Riad and myself. An exception was Roy Hattersley, standing in for Jim Callaghan. He said that I had in fact purported to act for the Community, because in the Presidency I could not divorce that role from my position as Irish Foreign Minister. I responded briskly, remarking that it was fifty-three years too late for a British Minister in Dublin Castle to be telling a member of an Irish Government what he could or could not do. I went on to ask him whether he was seriously suggesting that in two years' time, when Britain held the Presidency, its Foreign Secretary would be inhibited by his Community role from any bilateral action on Britain's own account? And I said I was perfectly happy to wire Riad to tell him that Britain had told me, in his words, 'to go to hell.' Hattersley subsided. After the meeting I gave Riad the 'all clear', the Arab League dropped its objections, and the Euro-Arab dia-logue resumed—unhappily, however, leading to no significant positive results.

A fortnight later we left again for the Middle East, to visit Israel and Turkey. The visit to Israel was bound to be somewhat difficult, because, to a greater extent than other Community countries except France and Italy, we had been sympathetic to the Palestinians' claim to a homeland. In the event, the visit proved beneficial, because I was in a position to give the Israelis a very full picture of what we had learnt during our visits to the nearby Arab countries, which they appreciated. Shortly afterwards I was able to do much the same in relation to another matter by passing information to the Greek government about Turkish views regarding a Cyprus peace line, as the Turkish Foreign Minister had clearly hoped I would do when he had explained his ideas to me in Ankara with the aid of a large relief map of the island.

Joan and I had already visited Turkey informally that April to attend a meeting of the Bilderberg group—an annual conference of leading figures in Europe and North America—at Çeşme, on the Turkish coast opposite Chíos. There I met a number of people whom I was later to come to know much better—among them Margaret Thatcher, recently elected as leader of the oppo-sition at Westminster, whom I had first met in London a month earlier. Andrew Knight and I had tea with her during an afternoon break. I was particularly interested in her views, because it seemed likely that at some point in the years ahead we would find ourselves on opposite sides of the table as representatives of our two countries, with their long history of conflict and mistrust, and perhaps tackling a still unresolved Northern Ireland problem.

She spoke about the undesirability of the kind of artificial polarisation that she felt had emerged in the economic debates at our conference. On the other hand, she had learnt a good deal from the discussions—for example the inadequacy of the money supply approach, because so much had to be done by way of supportive action to make the money supply work. If inflation were very high an incomes policy was necessary, but there should be a statutory policy only for a very short time. She favoured a political consensus so long as it was of people who agreed on a free society and a mixed economy. When inflation was low politicians would not give it priority, but if it were high priorities had to shift, and then it was no use saying that public expenditure could not be cut. As a spending Minister she knew the unpopularity that came from making such cuts.

Some of these views did not correspond to the picture that Knight and I had formed of the new opposition leader. Consequently we quizzed her vigorously and expressed some incredulity when she insisted that her aim was to create a centre force in British politics, thus attracting social-democrats from Labour. This latter point is not recorded in my contemporary note of her remarks, but my recollection of it was confirmed some time later by Knight when he and I were recalling our astonishment on that occasion—justified as we felt it had been by later events. He told me then that she had said much the same in a discussion at İzmır Airport with the Labour MP Dick Mabon.

The six months of the Presidency had been an exciting period and, I felt, a fruitful one. Ireland's position in the Community had been firmly established; we were seen by our partners as a positive force and not, as could easily have been the case, only as a *demandeur*, taking substantial material benefits from our partners through the Community budget without putting anything back. Our Presidency was in fact generally judged to have been unusually successful, and was indeed in later years frequently referred to in such terms: successful at the level of concrete results and also at the technical level in terms of practical efficiency. Our Ministers had chaired their Councils successfully, and the civil servants from all departments had risen to the challenge magnificently.

It was important that our EC partners be convinced that our membership was an asset to the Community, for, as we had foreseen when we had joined, Ireland had quickly become the largest net beneficiary in financial terms in relation to its GNP. This followed from its position as a northern European country, benefiting from the orientation of the Common Agricultural Policy in favour of products such as meat, milk, and grain, but with a much lower level of income per head than the rest of northern Europe, as a result of which it has also been a major beneficiary from the Regional and Social Funds.

The importance for Ireland of the CAP and of regional and social policy is self-evident: even small adjustments in these policies can have disproportionate effects on the Irish economy. While most of the issues involved are dealt with by sectoral Ministers in their specialist Councils, during my term of office as Minister for Foreign Affairs major aspects of regional policy and fishery policy, involving important Irish interests, fell to be dealt with by the General Council of Foreign Ministers. Another question that our Council had to deal with, which I had not foreseen, concerned the number and proportion of seats that each country was to have in a directly elected European Parliament. I had wrongly assumed that our representation would be the same as in the existing Assembly, the members of which were nominated by the national parliaments.

The first of these three issues to come up for decision was the distribution of the Regional Fund. In mid-July 1973 we heard that George Thomson, the British commissioner in charge of regional policy, had proposed to the Commission a Regional Fund of 3,000 million units of account for the three-year period from 1974 to 1976, with a 3.9 per cent share for Ireland. That would involve an average annual figure of £16 million for Ireland—as against the £100 million annual figure in 1973 money terms that we had identified as our need. Italy, the other country with problems of underdevelopment, was to get 33 per cent of the fund. The remaining 63.1 per cent was to be allocated to the countries that (apart from Northern Ireland as part of the United Kingdom) did not have such problems. Britain and France were to share equally half of the total fund.

This came as a great shock. There was, I felt, no precedent for a policy distortion of this magnitude in favour of a commissioner's home country, and the inclusion of France as well as Britain as a major beneficiary would—and was, I felt, designed to—ensure support from that country also for this extraordinary proposal, which we learnt had been so calculated as to secure for Britain a return of 25 per cent of its contribution to the EC budget.

On 26 July the Commission's decision on Thomson's proposals was announced. The size of the fund now proposed was one-fifth smaller than he had suggested. No reference was made to quotas; instead 'criteria' were proposed for allocating the fund—criteria that we believed were designed to justify ultimately the distribution of the fund along the precise lines we knew were contemplated by Thomson.

I felt the situation was so disturbing that I should visit the capitals of our partners to express my concern and to seek a fairer distribution. In a hectic round of meetings I left no doubt about the strength of our feelings. I took care to ensure that the approach of Italy, the other country that particularly needed regional aid, would be in harmony with ours. The Italians proved happy with my suggestions, and I later put it to them that Italy and Ireland might advocate that 25 per cent of the fund be hived off and allocated exclusively between the parts of the Community with the lowest GDP per head and highest emigration and unemployment rates, namely southern Italy, Ireland, and Northern Ireland, in the proportions 13.5 : 5 : 1.5. (This was one of a number of occasions during my period in office when we endeavoured to secure for Northern Ireland better arrangements than the British government was proposing.) I thought we might at best get agreement to a special allocation of 20 per cent, the net effect of which would be to raise Italy's share of the total fund from 33 to 41 per cent and our share from 3.9 to 8.1 per cent.

It was mid-October before the issue came before the Council. When my turn came I addressed my colleagues vigorously. I said that the Commission had failed without explanation to observe a guideline it had adopted five months earlier, to the effect that the fund should be concentrated 'very largely in those regions which are most in need in relation to the Community as a whole.' So far from designating the regions most in need, they had proposed that the fund be made available to assist areas comprising over half the geographical extent of the Community and containing one-third of its population. Within these areas the range of GDP per head varied by a factor of 3 or 4 to 1—but the Commission had not made any proposal to relate the volume of aid to the widely varying relative intensity of need within the designated area. Despite the fact that no quotas were formally proposed it was widely known that a share of 3.9 per cent was envisaged for Ireland, and this seemed to have been confirmed, perhaps unintentionally, by the President of the Commission when he had defended its proposals on the grounds that they would give Ireland a 3.5 or 4 times larger share than its population.

I went on to say that on the Commission's own admission the whole of our state qualified for participation in the fund, which meant that, unlike any other Community member, there was no developed part of the country the resources of which could be drawn upon to support the rest. Ireland was thus uniquely dependent on Community aid for regional development.

Finally, because of the large shares allocated to better-off states, three-quarters of the proposed fund would return to the countries that had contributed the money, and the average annual amount actually transferring between states would be only £100 million, i.e. about the scale of regional aid objectively needed by Ireland alone.

In my remarks to the Council I did not refer to the map that had emerged from the Commission showing the area to be covered by the fund, but off the record I pointed out to the press that, as well as Ireland and southern Italy, this area included *all* of Scotland (Thomson's home country) and Wales, the northern and south-western parts of England, half of France and Denmark, and significant parts of Germany and the Benelux countries.

My address to the Council was referred to by the *Financial Times* as 'impassioned' and 'refreshing' and by other papers as 'most vigorous' and 'forthright'. It had its effect. Two days later Thomson met the Irish journalists in Brussels and under pressure admitted that the criteria had been 'drawn up on a political basis, and on a very substantial map indeed, on the basis that each member country is entitled to feel it is getting some treatment for its special problems out of the Fund.' (The *Daily Telegraph* had put the point even more graphically by referring to his proposal as offering 'a clawback of the Danegeld', which it saw Britain as paying to the EC budget.)

The journalists gained from Thomson's remarks the impression that the Irish share might be increased. And so it was, to 6 per cent, over a year later—for the negotiations dragged on until the end of 1974. At the end of November in that year, shortly before the Paris summit, I received a phone call from George Thomson. The Commission was about to start this final discussion on a proposal of his that would give us 6 per cent of a greatly reduced fund of 1,400 million units of account. We should immediately take direct diplomatic action in Bonn, and also in Paris and London. The Italians and ourselves should adopt a very strong line if we wanted to achieve any improvement on the percentages now being proposed.

Following this somewhat surprising initiative on the commissioner's part we took further action in these capitals. Unfortunately the amount of the fund was reduced further at this stage by the Germans to 1,300 million units of account, despite a commitment by Genscher to me that they would accept the Commission's new figure; he was overruled in Bonn. To balance this—exactly— we secured at the Paris summit an increase in our share to 6.5 per cent.

A happy ending? Yes and no. For the argument over the fund had dragged on throughout a period of fourteen months, the aftermath of the first oil crisis, which had weakened the European economies seriously and had led to severe cuts in public expenditure throughout the Community. As a result, and particularly because of German pressure, the size of the fund had been reduced during this period from the Commission's proposal of 2,250 to 1,300 million units of account. Consequently the absolute amount secured by Ireland was not in fact raised by the increase in our share from 3.9 to 6.6 per cent. But everyone else got much *less* than had been originally envisaged, so that the battle I had aggressively fought turned out in the event to have been a good defensive action that at least protected us from the financial pressures on the fund during the years following the oil crisis.

The next issue affecting Irish interests that arose in the General Council related to the representation of member-states in the European Parliament. This problem derived from the decision of the Paris summit to initiate direct elections to the Parliament, such elections to take place, on an Irish proposal, 'in or after 1978'. Implementation of this decision had been left in abeyance until after the British referendum on UK membership of the Community. The next European Council, held in Brussels in mid-July 1975, decided that the Foreign Ministers should proceed with the matter and report back before Christmas.

When the Foreign Ministers picked up the subject at Lucca in October 1975, they merely agreed that they would meet a Parliamentary delegation before putting their own proposals to the European Council. No-one pursued Callaghan's statement that it did not matter what the European Parliament said: Westminster would decide what *it* would accept. At the Rome European Council two months later Wilson opened the discussion on direct elections much more positively, saying that the matter should be settled early in 1976. However, a taste of difficulties to come emerged when Giscard d'Estaing said that membership of the directly elected Parliament should be proportional to member-states' populations, subject only to a minimum level of representation for the smaller states.

The existing Parliament, the members of which were appointed by national parliaments, involved a weighted system of representation, with 36 seats for each of the larger states, the populations of which were around 60 million, 14 seats for the Netherlands and Belgium, with 14 and 9 million people respectively, and 10 seats for Denmark and Ireland, with their populations of 4.5 and 3.5 million. This gave Ireland just over 5 per cent of the seats for a population that was about 1.25 per cent of that of the Community of Nine. We were naturally anxious as far as possible to maintain this disproportion in a directly elected Parliament, and Giscard d'Estaing's proposal for proportionality, even when qualified with a reference to 'minimum representation for smaller countries', was not acceptable from our viewpoint. Liam Cosgrave made this clear. Den Uyl and Rumor offered support. Tindemans said that he supported '*avec acharnement*' the Parliament's own proposal for a semi-proportional system, which would give us about 3 per cent.

Most of the discussion tended to concentrate on other aspects of direct elections, such as the dual mandate and the proposal that the election take place on a single day in May or June 1978—a proposal strongly resisted by Denmark, which was still hoping to be allowed to elect its members as a by-product of its national general election, and by Britain also, which doubted the possibility of holding a poll by 1978.

Wilson both puzzled and amused other members by saying that in fixing the date we should have regard not only to church opposition in Britain to Sunday elections but also to 'religious festivals and spring holidays'. 'What was he getting at?' one of my Continental colleagues asked me afterwards. 'We didn't think Britain was such a very religious country.' Recalling my experience in Aer Lingus when I had had to make provision for seasonal fluctuations in holiday air traffic between Lancashire and Ireland, I explained that Wilson was probably concerned that an election in May or June should not coincide with Whitsun (the religious festival in question) or local 'wakes weeks', when a number of his constituents in Huyton and neighbouring areas might be on holidays.

Sabbatarianism being a factor in the Netherlands as well as Britain, den Uyl shared Wilson's concern about Sunday elections. But I noticed that Callaghan had nodded when den Uyl said that the important thing was that the votes be counted, rather than cast, on a single day.

When the European Council next met in Luxembourg on 1 April 1976 it returned to this question. Most countries wanted Sunday as election day, but Callaghan, now Prime Minister, wanted Thursday—thus implying a four-day spread for the election results. Why had it to be on Thursday in Britain? the French President asked. Liam Cosgrave remarked ironically that the British position was really quite open: it could be any day as long as it was Thursday. Jim Callaghan's response to Giscard d'Estaing was majestic in its simplicity, demonstrating, I felt, the delightful conservatism of the British Labour Party: 'Because elections in Britain have always been on Thursday.' I moved rapidly to defuse the situation by remarking that as the British were clearly a very incurious people who were quite prepared to wait for the result, the boxes in Britain might remain closed until Sunday night; and Giscard d'Estaing, despite an earlier expression of concern about the results in some countries getting out in advance of the count through exit polls, accepted this.

On the major question—for us—of the number of seats, Giscard d'Estaing repeated his wish for representation proportional to population, but suggested that direct elections might initially take place on the basis of the number of seats held by each country in the existing Parliament. Liam Cosgrave accepted this with alacrity, and a number of others said they could live with it. The Danes, however, objected, and the Italians kicked for touch, claiming they needed more time to consult. Jim Callaghan then declared his opposition, arguing that on this basis Northern Ireland's share of the United Kingdom's 36 directly elected seats would be only 1 as against 10 for the Republic; there would be a similar contrast, he added, between Scotland and Denmark. Eventually the discussion was abandoned and left over to the next meeting of the European Council.

Some weeks later I took advantage of an opportunity to raise this matter at a breakfast meeting at the Irish embassy in London with Michael Palliser, recently moved from the post of British Permanent Representative in Brussels to head the Foreign Office in London. He argued the British case for an enlarged Parliament with a bigger proportion of seats for the UK on the grounds of the danger that might otherwise be posed to the integrity of the UK by gross underrepresentation of Scotland, in particular, in the European Parliament. If this could be avoided he believed there was a fair chance of the United Kingdom surviving.

I pointed out to him that the new French willingness to maintain for the time being the status quo on seats in the Parliament, and a German variant involving a doubling of the existing representation of each country with some minor modifications, together risked leaving Britain isolated if it persisted with the idea of a change in the ratio of representation of different countries in order to reduce the disparity between Scotland on the one hand and Ireland and Denmark on the other. At a time when it was important for Britain to appear positive in Europe, this could be damaging to Britain's long-term interests. The Under-Secretary seemed to see merit in this argument and said that he would consider it seriously and put it to his political masters; nevertheless I doubted that my line of argument would work at the political level.

I was confirmed in the view I had put to Michael Palliser as a result of a phone conversation two days later with Gaston Thorn's chef de cabinet, from which I learnt that the French and the Luxembourg Presidency were getting in touch with the Italians to persuade them to withdraw their objections to the French status quo proposal, with the specific objective of isolating Britain in the hope of forcing a solution. I warned that this might not work, in view of Britain's concern about the Scottish situation, a concern that did not disappear even when a few days later Winifred Ewing told the House of Commons that, much as she would like to see the disparity in Scottish representation vis-à-vis Ireland and Denmark removed, the British government should not allow quibbles about numbers to hold up direct elections.

When the Foreign Ministers met informally in Luxembourg six weeks later, Gaston Thorn in the chair tried to revive the French proposal in a modified form. Tony Crosland, who had replaced Jim Callaghan as Foreign Secretary when the latter had become Prime Minister in March, immediately played his Scottish and Welsh cards: the status quo would leave these two parts of the United Kingdom grossly underrepresented vis-à-vis Denmark and Ireland. After further discussion the status quo proposal failed to secure acceptance, but it became fairly certain that Ireland would get 13 seats in a Parliament of about 355. I thought that this might be pushed up to 15, and we grounded our claim for this number of seats on the argument that under our multi-seat PR system it would be difficult to devise meaningful regional constituencies with fewer than 15 seats.

Discussion continued at other meetings, and while we had not yet reached agreement when the European Council met again in mid-July, there seemed by then to be acceptance that we should have the 15 seats that we felt we needed. But this had been won at the price of an inflation of the Parliament's total size from the proposed figure of 355 to 410, and not even this inflation of numbers satisfied Britain or Denmark, both of which still wanted additional representation.

There was, however, a further problem. It appeared that Britain proposed to allocate to Northern Ireland only 2 of the 72 seats now suggested for the United Kingdom. The voting strength of the two communities in Northern Ireland was such that both of these seats might be won by Unionists, leaving the nationalist minority unrepresented. The undesirability of such an outcome was so evident that it seemed appropriate for us, since we had effectively achieved our domestic objective of 15 seats, to switch our efforts to ensuring a third seat for Northern Ireland.

Accordingly, even though extra seats over and above 72 for the UK (and consequently also for the three other large countries, which insisted on equal representation with the United Kingdom) would further reduce our *proportion* of the total, Cosgrave gave his support early on in the meeting to Britain's request for six more seats, subject to this increase being used to correct the inadequate representation of Northern Ireland. The British were happy with our support, but were not prepared to allocate any of the six extra seats to Northern Ireland.

Further wrangling followed. Then Callaghan and Crosland came to us to say that they were going to propose 82 seats for the larger countries, which would enable them to give an extra seat to Northern Ireland, as well as extra seats to Scotland and Wales, bringing these to 10 and 5 seats respectively. We told them we would go along with this. In the end, at Giscard d'Estaing's urging in a top-of-the-table 'huddle', Callaghan said he would settle for 81 seats by dropping an extra seat claimed for England. So it was agreed. But in the event, interestingly enough, Scotland and Wales never got their extra seats. Although the need to make greater provision for Scotland and Wales had been the basis of the British argument for more seats, it was to England that the additional seats were allocated. Scotland's proposed 10 was reduced to 8, and

Wales's 5 became 4; while England got 66 instead of the 63 implicit in what Callaghan and Crosland had said to us.

Thus through our efforts to secure two more seats for our state and one more for Northern Ireland, the size of the European Parliament in advance of the enlargement to include Greek, Spanish and Portuguese members was increased by 67 seats, from the 355 proposed by the Parliament's rapporteur to 422. I made a personal resolution to write after the first European election to the 64 members of the European Parliament who would not have secured seats but for our efforts in order to let them know how greatly indebted they were to Ireland, but, like many good resolutions, this one fell by the wayside in 1979. As for our ploy of trying to secure, by proposing a 1978 election, that it would in fact coincide with the Irish local elections of 1979, that worked perfectly. Ironically, however, having secured this happy coincidence of European and local elections, this combination was abandoned by my Government five years later when, despite my telling the two parties in the Coalition that a postponement of local elections to 1985 would lose us more seats than if they were held on schedule in 1984 simultaneously with the European elections, they insisted on disregarding my advice.

The third matter that came up in the General Council involving a significant Irish interest during my term as Foreign Minister was the revision in 1976 of the Common Fisheries Policy. Prior to the enlargement of the Community in 1973, the original six members had made fishing rights an EC area of competence. As a result, unless modifications were adopted the EC as a whole would have enjoyed fishing rights up to every member-country's shoreline. This was serious for Ireland, where inshore fishing was important.

But the Community now faced the need to negotiate with Iceland and Norway, which were moving to create a 200-mile zone off their coasts, within which other countries would not be permitted to fish without agreement. In response to this an EC 200-mile zone was being considered. This would give Ireland protection against non-EC trawlers but not against boats of its Community partners. What would help would be a 50-mile national zone within this 200-mile Community zone, restricted to smaller vessels.

Ireland enjoyed exceptional bargaining power, since the approval of *all* member-countries was required for a mandate to negotiate access for Community fishermen to Icelandic and Norwegian waters, in which Ireland had no direct concern. Britain, on the other hand, was awkwardly circumstanced. It would obviously benefit from a national zone for its inshore fishermen, but its large trawlers also needed to fish in distant waters, so it could not afford, as we could, to frustrate attempts to reach agreement with Norway and Iceland by threatening to use its veto if it were denied concessions regarding its own coastal area. Its best chance, its only chance indeed, was to 'piggy-back' on Ireland's negotiating strength by seeking for itself whatever coastal concessions the Irish might acquire while concentrating its own negotiating weight on benefiting as much as possible from the talks with Norway and Iceland. The diplomatic manoeuvrings that followed were complex—and, when seen with detachment, more than a little entertaining.

Our officials advised me against seeking unrealistically large concessions for Ireland that might prove unattainable. Should my efforts fail, I was told, my political reputation could suffer. Several years later I received the same advice as Taoiseach in a precisely parallel situation regarding milk quotas. It is right that officials should advise caution in such cases; politicians would certainly not thank them if they were allowed to fall into political traps without warning by launching overambitious and ultimately unsuccessful high-profile campaigns on the international stage. Officials also know how strongly their counterparts in other administrations resist attempts to secure precedent-setting concessions of an exceptional nature—just as Irish officials have been trained to resist pressure for exceptional treatment domestically of particular issues that might create precedents leading to an uncontrollable expansion of public spending.

However, the buck stops with the politician, not the civil servant. I felt we had to take a risk in this instance; too much was at stake for us to play safe. Moreover—and this is a vitally important factor in such matters—the case that we could make was objectively a strong one: our fishing industry was grossly underdeveloped vis-à-vis those of other member-states. And so far as our partners were concerned the cost of concessions that would be of great value to us would be marginal. Accordingly, we staked our claim to a 50-mile coastal band under national rather than Community control.

After some months of fruitless discussion in the General Council the issue came before the European Council in Brussels in July 1976. Jim Callaghan launched the debate, adverting at once to the worldwide trend towards the extension of exclusive fishing zones to 200 miles. He proposed a declaration of intent by the Community to extend its zones in 1977. The UK as the country contributing 55 to 60 per cent of the new fish stocks deriving from enlargement of the Community had, he said, circulated proposals upon which they did not expect decisions at this meeting, but they looked for a sympathetic reaction from the European Council.

Liam Cosgrave followed. Ireland would be making a major contribution to the area of exclusive fishing rights accruing to the Community as a result of the creation of 200-mile zones: 23 per cent of the total Community zone would consist of Irish waters. Despite the underdevelopment of Ireland's fishing industry there was only one other member-state in which this sector provided a larger share of GNP and employment. It was a vital national interest for Ireland to preserve and protect the fish stocks off its coast from destruction by fleets of large vessels. This was the basis for Ireland's decision to seek a 50-mile coastal band under its own control within what would be a Community 200-mile zone. His government was prepared to discuss with other Community governments arrangements to enable fishermen on traditional-type vessels to fish in the outer part of the proposed Irish-controlled band.

In the subsequent exchange of views the Irish proposal was not adverted to. The inconclusive discussion left it to the Council of Ministers a week or so later to declare its intention of introducing a 200-mile Community fishery zone.

In the Commission's proposals to cater for these diverse interests, published towards the end of September 1976, the only concessions to Irish and British interests were provision for a 12-mile inshore band, which would, however, be subject to 'historic' rights for traditional fishermen, together with an unspecific 'special priority' for Ireland, northern Britain and Greenland in the distribution of Community total allowable catches.

I made a fairly uncompromising response to the Commission proposal, describing it as 'unacceptable to the Irish Government' and saying that it reflected only the interests of the original six member-states; it was 'clearly inappropriate to the needs and interests of the enlarged Community.'

As the weeks passed the situation became tense. The Germans in particular became impatient. Eventually in desperation they threatened that if agreement were not reached on a mandate to negotiate with Iceland and Norway they would go ahead with such negotiations bilaterally—which would be contrary to Community law. I was under no illusion that the Commission would easily capitulate on the key ideological issue of Community control of fishing rights, but faced with this German threat they would, I believed, have to propose *some* concession to us in order to break the deadlock.

The crucial meeting of the Council was fixed for Saturday 30 October in the Hague. Earlier in that week I got a call from Finn Gundelach, the Commissioner responsible for fishery policy. Could he see me on Wednesday? I agreed.

When we met he proposed that on top of the general provision for northern Britain, Ireland and Greenland (known as the 'Hague Preferences') there would be a special regime for Ireland. The Common Fisheries Policy would be applied so as 'to secure the continued and progressive development of the Irish fishing industry on the basis of the Irish Government's . . . programme for the development of coastal fisheries.' This programme was something that I had persuaded our Fisheries Department to cobble together so as to lend credibility to our expressed concern for the development of the industry in the context of the new 200-mile Community zone. It set out the objective of developing the Irish catch from 75,000 tons in 1975 to 150,000 in 1979, with further increases thereafter. Gundelach's proposal would thus guarantee that whereas the other countries' catches would be constrained by catch limitations in order to preserve stocks, we would be able to double our catch within three years and to increase it further after 1979.

In addition he proposed that, because we would be responsible for protecting 23 per cent of the Community's waters, the Community would finance 75 per cent of the cost of building two modern fishery protection vessels for the Naval Service.

I believed I could 'sell' Gundelach's proposal to our fishermen, with whom I had kept in the closest touch throughout the whole negotiation, bringing their representatives up to our delegation room on the thirteenth floor of the Charlemagne Building in Brussels where the Council meetings are held and even persuading them on one occasion to attack me for allegedly weakening in the negotiation, with a view to strengthening my hand with the Commission and the Council.

Accordingly, I went to the Hague on the evening of Friday 29 October with a light heart. During the day, however, a message had come from Tony Crosland proposing a meeting of the British and Irish delegations after dinner; courtesy required that we meet for what I knew would be a round of fruitless arm-twisting by the British. Crosland greeted me at the British embassy and proposed that we walk around the drawing-room while our officials settled in. He then tried to put me on the defensive by saying I should content myself with a verbal rather than written reprimand to our Ambassador in London. I stopped in my tracks and asked him what on earth he was talking about. 'This disgraceful business of his attempt to interfere with Parliament,' he responded. I still looked blank. 'You are probably unaware', he went on, 'that he approached the opposition to press the government in Parliament about an answer to be given to a parliamentary question on power-sharing in Northern Ireland, which he told them the Irish Government knew would be unsatisfactory. The opposition protested to us about the fact that he seemed to have fore-knowledge of the answer.'

'Oh, that!' I responded, enlightened at last. 'He did that on my instruction; I can hardly reprimand him on that account.' And I suggested we join the officials for the meeting.

We sat together on a couch, with the officials on chairs in a circle around us. He opened by saying that the British government had noted the concessions proposed for Ireland in the Commission's fishery policy document. Britain wished to secure similar concessions and felt that the best approach would be for us to propose that what had been conceded to us should extend also to the UK. I burst out laughing at his effrontery. 'If I did that I'd be out of a job by eleven o'clock on Monday morning,' I responded. At this he became quite cross. It would be intolerable, he said, that Irish fishermen should have such advantages and that Scottish fishermen, who were similarly placed—I noted that he was careful not to mention his own constituency of Grimsby—should not have the same treatment. The relationship between Ireland and Britain would be fundamentally affected if I would not co-operate in this matter; the British people would not forget our unhelpfulness. I should remember that we had an interest in Northern Ireland. I riposted that England had often been described in Ireland as 'our ancient enemy' but that I was beginning to think that perhaps Scotland was being groomed to fill the bill. A Scottish member of the European Commission had proposed a regional policy that had seemed to us to sacrifice Ireland's legitimate interests to Scotland's needs; our share of seats in the European Parliament had been reduced from almost 5 per cent to 3.65 per cent, partly because of British objections to Ireland having too many more seats than Scotland; and now we were being asked to put at risk for Scotland's sake what had been secured for Ireland in the Commission's revised proposals for fish catches and fishery protection.

My semi-humorous remarks about Scotland were not well received. Crosland thrust into my hand a typed sheet that contained the text of the Commission's proposals for Ireland, with an underlined 'and the United Kingdom' added wherever 'Ireland' appeared. I was to propose its adoption at the Council meeting next morning, he said. I took it from him, telling him once again that he was wasting his time. I thought that it would be a memento of the occasion, and anyway I wanted to show it to Finn Gundelach.

Back in the hotel I went up to Gundelach's room; my Dutch colleague, Laurens Brinkhorst, joined me on the way up, curious as to what had happened at my meeting with Crosland. They were both highly entertained by the British suggestion, and Gundelach was thus well prepared when, after my departure, the British Deputy Permanent Representative arrived at his door to deliver their demarche. Gundelach told me next day that he had recommended to the British official that Crosland be advised not to press such a non-credible proposal.

Next morning Crosland briefly mentioned at the start of our meeting that Britain should get the same terms as Ireland. When Denmark, Germany and Italy chimed in to say that they too had special claims, a 'stand-off' ensued between these countries, and agreement was eventually reached that the special regime should apply to Ireland only. We still maintained our claim to a 50-mile zone, however, despite German objections of a juridical nature.

The Commission's proposals were eventually adopted. The Irish Fishermen's Organisation paid a welcome tribute to my efforts, remarking that I had had to overcome immense obstacles to achieve this result. Today the Irish fish catch is at three times its 1975 level and the Naval Service boasts a purpose-built fishery protection vessel paid for as to 75 per cent from the Community budget, in recognition of our responsibility for protecting a large area of the Community's waters. (There were to have been two vessels but, as so often happens in such cases, prices escalated, partly because we insisted on building in Ireland, and only one vessel was in fact built.)

The fish saga did not end in 1976; the battle over access to fishing around our coasts had still to be fought. Under the decisions taken at the Hague we retained the right, in the absence of agreement on Community conservation action, to initiate national conservation measures of a non-discriminatory kind. In February 1977 we made orders banning fishing near our shores by large and powerful vessels, in the interest of conservation. The Commission objected to this action as discriminatory, on the grounds that we had hardly any boats in this category.

During the discussions in Brussels that followed the announcement of our controversial decision I unintentionally sparked off a row in Government. Paddy Donegan had recently been appointed Minister for Fisheries, now to be

Palliser welcomed my views as being close to his own and those of the Foreign Office. He added that it could be very useful for me to put this viewpoint forward to the new Foreign Secretary, Tony Crosland, who might take them seriously from me, although he would be inclined to suspect Foreign Office advice along these traditional lines. Perhaps I could find an opportunity to talk informally to Crosland at the forthcoming Luxembourg meeting of Foreign Ministers? I said that I would try to do so, or perhaps might use that occasion to set up an appointment with him in London shortly afterwards.

In the event many messages went backwards and forwards between Crosland and myself before this meeting was arranged. Months later I received a message: 'Thursday, 8 o'clock, Carlton House Gardens. With or without civil servants.' I replied immediately, 'Agreed. Without.' Ten minutes later he responded, 'With.' What led to this change of mind I never discovered.

At an appropriate moment during the dinner I broached, circumspectly, the subject of British foreign policy. Ireland's primary foreign policy objective had, I said, traditionally been the achievement of independence from Britain and full sovereignty. After 1922 the government, of which my father had been a member, had pursued this objective through multilateral diplomatic activity within the Commonwealth, culminating in the Statute of Westminster in 1931. Subsequently de Valera had taken matters further through his new Constitution, and in 1949 a republic had been declared. This, however, had not given us economic independence of Britain; that had been achieved through entry to the Community, within which we were now on an equal footing with our neighbour.

The problem of Northern Ireland remained, but inside the Community itself our relationship with Britain was now quite different. As had been the case with the Benelux countries for centuries, our interest lay in ensuring that a balance of power was maintained within the Community between the three major states; it was contrary to our interest that any one, or even two, of these should be dominant. The delay in Britain's entry to the Community and the subsequent British renegotiation that had been settled in Dublin the previous year had left something of a power vacuum, with France and Germany still taking the lead and tending to dominate Community affairs. A more active British role would protect our interests, not because we had any particular preference for Britain as against France and Germany but because we needed a better balance between the three powers than had so far existed.

At that point I stopped, and invited Crosland to comment, hoping in this way to engage a constructive dialogue on British foreign policy. I failed. He looked across at Michael Butler, the British Political Director, who subsequently became Permanent Representative in Brussels, and said, 'Michael, would you like to respond to that?' I had no more success than the Foreign Office in attempting to persuade Crosland to address himself to the issue of Britain's role in Europe.

Tony Crosland's sudden death a couple of months later, less than a year after his appointment, makes it impossible to judge how he would have turned out as Foreign Secretary in the longer run. After what seemed to me to have been an uncertain start the application of his undoubted intelligence to his office might in time have enabled him to become a major figure on the European stage, but he seemed to me at the time to have difficulty in adjusting from domestic to foreign affairs and to have little natural understanding of the European Community; when his Minister of State, David Owen, replaced him at Council meetings the relationship with our Continental colleagues always seemed more relaxed.

A decade later Susan Crosland came to interview me as Taoiseach. I was delighted to meet her, but disconcerted at her first question: 'Dr FitzGerald, what criteria do you and your wife apply in deciding what Ministers and civil servants you receive in your bedroom?' Clearly, to be able to pose such a question she had done her homework.

# CHAPTER SEVEN

# LAST TRAIN FROM LENINGRAD

In the summer of 1976 I intimated that I would like to take up an invitation issued three years earlier to visit the Soviet Union. Some time later Ambassador Kaplin asked to see me. I had prepared myself suitably. When the formalities had been gone through, Kaplin asked where I would like to go outside Moscow, where I would be arriving on a Monday evening.

'Leningrad,' I replied.

'Anywhere else?' he asked.

'It will be very cold in December,' I responded.

'Somewhere farther south?' he ventured.

'Yes,' I replied.

'One of our republics in the Caucasus?' he suggested.

'Yes,' I said again.

'Which?' he asked.

'Georgia,' I replied. 'We should be finished our business in Moscow by Thursday lunchtime, and if we take the 15.00 flight to Tbilisi we will have Thursday evening and Friday there, after which, if we leave by the 06.25 to Leningrad, we can have most of Saturday and all of Sunday there. We shall have to take the 23.55 train to Moscow on Sunday night, because the first flight from Leningrad to Moscow does not get in in time for the flight I shall have to catch to get back to Amsterdam for a meeting in the Hague on Monday evening.'

Diplomats are trained not to show any emotion, including surprise. He did not bat an eyelid, but noted down my suggestions. However, my plan, based on scheduled Aeroflot flights inside the Soviet Union, was not adopted; a special plane was laid on for the Moscow–Tbilisi–Leningrad part of the journey.

The discussions in Moscow with President Podgorny and with Gromyko—I did not meet Brezhnev—were fairly stilted and formal. Behind the rhetoric and well-tried formulas, so carefully designed to obscure meaning, I thought I detected two points of possible significance in my discussion with Gromyko. The first was his apparent disillusionment with the Arab countries and his unqualified commitment to Israel's right to existence; the second was his ready acceptance of the rights of the white minority as well as the African majority, not merely in South Africa but also, he volunteered spontaneously, in Namibia and Rhodesia (soon to be Zimbabwe).

At the end of our discussions I handed him a list of human rights cases I had been asked to raise. He accepted them without demur—or commitment.

At the luncheon that he and his wife offered in honour of Joan and myself I saw the interpreter approach him with some papers after the formal speeches: telegrams that had come in during the meal, I presumed. But he looked up from them and addressed me across the table in his accented English: 'I see that Joyce and Yeats and Shaw are all Irishmen. Why do you allow the English to steal your great writers?' My impression, formed at our first meeting, that he did not like the English was confirmed.

We enjoyed our visit to Georgia: the scenery, the antiquities, and the people. On the way from there to Leningrad we were in the front cabin of the aircraft, our hosts behind. As we crossed the Caucasus, with a marvellous view from the Sea of Azov to the Caspian, the interpreter, who had come into our cabin, saw our interest in the view and lent us a map. When the descent began, one of our officials, knowing that most Soviet maps were supposed to be deliberately flawed, but presuming that those in the aircraft must be accurate, slipped the map quietly into his briefcase; but the interpreter, who was standing in the door of the cabin, was alert. 'I'm afraid we need that,' he remarked, putting down his hand and withdrawing it.

Our brief stay in Leningrad ended with a dinner given by the Leningrad Soviet—presumably descended in apostolic succession from the body that had launched the Bolshevik Revolution. In my speech I referred to Tsar Peter the Great; he might not, I suggested, in the strictest sense of the word have been a socialist, but he had been a *great planner*. Huge applause; after what we had seen and heard in Leningrad during those two days I had known that this line would go down well. I then concluded my remarks by congratulating my hosts on Russian conservatism: the train we were taking to Moscow in an hour or so left at the same time—23.55—as it had in 1914. (It still does.) Audience un-amused. But, I went on, I also wanted to congratulate them on Soviet progress: it now got to Moscow five-and-a-half hours earlier! I sat down to loud applause.

Like so many other visitors, we could not but like what we saw of the people, and we looked forward to the time when they would have a chance to express themselves freely and find a way of participating more fully in the running of their own affairs. We were put off particularly by the rigidity of what seemed to be a hereditary caste system that had grown up as a result of the way in which untrammelled power had corrupted their society. The contempt with which members of this ruling élite spoke of what they described as 'the common working people' was particularly offensive to our democratic sensitivities; it seemed as if the attitudes of the rulers of Tsarist Russia had been transferred holus-bolus to their successors two generations later, in defiance of what had been happening to society elsewhere in the world.

Relationships with the other superpower, the United States, were, of course, qualitatively different. However, in my experience many European countries tended to be less than frank in their communications with the US government, owing to fear of offending such an important ally. Because Ireland is not a member of the western alliance we may perhaps have been less inhibited, although of course in other ways we too depended—and depend—upon American good will. Nevertheless it still seemed to me that there was little to be gained, and perhaps something to be lost, by emulating the reticence of some of our European Community partners in our dealings with the United States.

Thus it was that when I met Kissinger again in Washington, in October 1975, I took this opportunity to challenge him about the recent agreement with General Franco's government renewing US bases in Spain. I pointed out first of all that, unlike our Community partners, we had not withdrawn our Ambassador from Spain following the recent executions of Basques convicted of killing policemen, because we felt that the withdrawal of ambassadors was bound to be counterproductive, since their inevitable return after a short period would be presented as a victory for the regime.

Having said all that—and I felt that this independent Irish position on that question strengthened my hand in criticising US policy—I went on to suggest that the signature of the bases agreement with the Franco regime in what were clearly its closing stages (Franco was known to be dying) could have counter-productive consequences as Spain moved back to democracy, just as had happened in Greece after the overthrow of the Colonels, with whose regime the United States had appeared to be identified.

Kissinger's reaction was satisfyingly heated. 'What did we do in Greece?' he exclaimed. It was a rhetorical question: I was given no opportunity to answer it as he went on to talk about 'European countries taking a free ride and making mock-heroic decisions so long as they don't have to pay for them'; they had been 'hypocritical in the extreme', he added. Why should the execution of 'convicted cop-killers' be turned into a moral issue? While he could understand that the Franco regime was anathema to Europe, he felt that Europeans were living in the past so far as Spain was concerned, with their mythic memories of the Civil War as a struggle of democracy against fascism.

I managed to intervene at this point to remind him of my opening remarks: our Government had not followed its partners in reacting in this way, and his comments about European attitudes to Spain since the Civil War were not all that relevant to Ireland, where a much more divided view had existed about that struggle. My comments related solely to the *realpolitik* of the situation:

the unwisdom of the United States following a course of action that might be damaging to its longer-term interest in establishing a positive relationship with a future democratic Spain.

At that he calmed down and described the efforts the United States was making within Spain to establish good relations with democratic forces. If the bases agreement had expired without formal renewal, their bases could have been dependent solely on oral agreement—a risk that they could not justify. On Greece he said that America's policy had been 'passive'. He added that if they had not been so preoccupied with Vietnam they might have paid more attention to Greece.

I closed this part of the discussion by remarking that however much the United States might see European attitudes as based on myths arising from the Spanish Civil War, the emotions behind these attitudes were a political fact the United States had to reckon with. We then passed on to Portugal; but my last comment on the Spanish issue must have made some impact, for an hour later, as I was leaving, I heard him mutter to himself as he turned away, 'A myth, if widely believed, is a reality to be reckoned with.'

On Portugal I said that while the situation there was dangerous—it was only some weeks later that the breakthrough to democracy was finally achieved, with a successful challenge to the left wing of the Armed Forces Movement— nevertheless I had always been, and remained, fairly confident about the out-come. The strength of popular Portuguese feeling in favour of democratic evolution could be relied upon, and it had been, I felt, quite simply psychologically impossible for the Portuguese army to evolve within the short space of a year or two from being the spearhead of a revolution against dictatorship into the kind of repressive force that could withstand popular attitudes. Kissinger conceded that this judgement had proved correct. Discussion of EEC aid to Portugal, upon which the Community had decided earlier that week, revealed that the corresponding US aid offer had been held up within the State Department; Kissinger, visibly irritated by this delay, ordered that it be got out that evening.

Other topics discussed on this occasion included the impending north-south consumer-producer conference (on the oil crisis), the danger of US protectionism, Cyprus, and Northern Ireland.

On this as on most visits to the United States I travelled to various cities to speak at meetings on Northern Ireland as well as to deliver academic addresses on foreign policy. The Northern Ireland meetings were often stormy, as groups of IRA supporters sought to disrupt them, not merely by external picketing but in some cases by attending in strength and trying to shout me down.

One in particular, in the Biltmore Hotel in New York in 1974, remains in my mind. Three groups of IRA supporters in different parts of the hall drowned out my remarks, which I insisted on completing but which no-one can have heard. The State Department security people present were visibly nervous. Having failed to persuade me to leave after my address, they kept urging me to end my question-time. After a while, as the IRA supporters started a series of mini-rushes towards the platform, I saw Joan being reluctantly led out by a woman security officer. But only after irate members of the audience showed signs of throwing punches at the disrupters did I finally terminate the meeting and leave. I did not, after all, want the event to end with my invited guests being charged with assault on IRA sympathisers.

In the car to which I was led by the security people a bemused New York policeman sat beside me in the back seat. 'Jeeze,' he said, 'I t'ought de IRA was de good guys—ain't dey fighting de British? But when I went to de old country last summer, everyone tole me dey were [expletive deleted]. I don't understand it all any more.'

During my frequent encounters with these bands of protesters I noticed that they usually included a few vociferous recent immigrants from Northern Ireland, while the rest seemed to be second or third-generation Irish who had inherited parental or grandparental memories of a colonial war and who, with their curious frozen-in-aspic concept of Irish nationalism, saw democratically elected Irish Governments, whatever their composition, as quislings. I frankly found this hard to take. While it probably did not matter that I was dismissive of the IRA demonstrators, my impatience with the simplistic and ill-informed attitudes of many leaders of Irish-American organisations who were not directly involved with the IRA was, perhaps, at times too apparent—as indeed Michael Lillis, our information officer in the United States, tried to point out to me. I saw his point: our diplomats had the unenviable task of trying to per-suade these people gently away from their one-dimensional view of the Northern Ireland issue. But even when intellectually convinced by the wisdom of this advice, I did not always succeed in putting it into practice.

Nevertheless the process of challenging the IRA myth in the United States, started by Jack Lynch and his Minister for Justice, Des O'Malley, in 1972, made considerable progress during our term of office. There is reason to believe that the flow of funds from Noraid to the IRA diminished over this period, and by 1977 we had succeeded in rallying the leading Irish-American politicians to give vocal leadership to our cause in the United States.

The official visit by Liam Cosgrave to the United States in March 1976 was an important stage in this process. It was one of the first European official or state visits of that bicentennial year and, coinciding with St Patrick's Day, it received considerable publicity, which helped our cause. Almost fifty years had passed since his father, as President of the Executive Council of the Irish Free State, accompanied by my father, then Minister for Defence, had made the first Irish official visit to that country, and this appearance of a second-generation Irish leadership added spice to the bicentennial occasion.

Cosgrave's speech to a joint session of Congress was the highlight of the visit, which had begun at Williamsburg. The speech had, however, posed a problem. Shortly before our departure I had visited his office to discuss a draft. It was much too long, he said. 'Cut it in half.' In vain I tried to explain that Congress had allocated half an hour for the address and that failure to fill this 'spot' might cause problems—even, perhaps, offence. He would have none of it. The idea that he could offend anyone by too short a speech simply made no sense to him.

In despair I called in to the office of the Assistant Secretary to the Government, Dermot Nally, with whom I enjoyed a good rapport. I asked him what we were to do about the Congress speech. He went through the text carefully, deleted a couple of less important paragraphs, and proposed that the margins be narrowed and that the spacing between the lines be reduced. Presented in this way, the speech went back to Cosgrave, the number of pages virtually halved. He accepted it without further demur—whether because he actually thought we had halved its length or because on second thoughts he had decided to accept the need for a half-hour speech, I do not know. In any event he had the last laugh on us when in actual delivery he added a 'punch-line' plug for Irish whiskey, which I am sure we should have advised against had we been asked. We would have been wrong: the punch-line was a hit.

The political discussions on this occasion were not substantive, but a year later, when I visited Washington in mid-March to make contact with the new Carter administration, I had a meeting with the Secretary of State, Cyrus Vance, in the course of which I welcomed the emphasis the administration was placing on human rights. This, I said, would help to make clearer than ever the distinction between the United States and the Soviet Union. We had been concerned at the manner in which the Soviet Union had misused our case against Britain before the Court of Human Rights about the maltreatment of detainees when internment had been introduced in Northern Ireland five years previously. It was necessary to emphasise that, unlike Britain and ourselves, the Soviet Union was not subject to the checks and balances of an international human rights code and, unlike the United States and ourselves, it did not have the check of an independent Supreme Court enforcing a constitutional code of human rights domestically.

I noted with interest in the course of our discussion on the Middle East that Vance agreed that the Arabs as well as the Israelis were entitled to defensible boundaries; he volunteered that the Arabs would probably be entitled to ask for some kind of defensive positions on Israeli territory, just as the Israelis were concerned to have similar defensive positions in a West Bank Palestinian homeland.

I also took the opportunity to brief him on the concern we and the other smaller Community states felt at the fact that at the Rambouillet and Puerto Rico world economic summits the European Community institutions, which alone had a competence to speak for the nine Community states on matters such as trade, had not been represented as such. We would be fighting at the Rome European Council in ten days' time to secure such representation at the proposed world economic summit in London in May. Vance immediately asserted that the United States was very strongly in favour of such representation and had urged it from the outset—that was one of the reasons why Vice-President Mondale had visited Brussels first during his recent European visit—and they would continue to press the case for it.

This expression of strong US support for Community representation at the forthcoming world summit may, perhaps, help to explain the collapse of Anglo-French hostility to the idea between the time of the Council of Ministers meeting a week before my Washington discussions—when the French Minister had actually walked out in protest against the matter being pressed—and the Rome European Council ten days later, at which, as I have already described, Commission representation was agreed without further demur.

In the course of this visit to Washington I called on President Carter. Having presented him with a seasonal bowl of shamrock, I went on to tell him that our Government was concerned at newspaper reports—I showed him cuttings from two such diverse sources as the *Daily Telegraph* and the *Irish Press*—of White House statements on behalf of the President that were supportive of the IRA and had been issued through a spokeswoman, Marilyn Haft. The President was taken aback. 'Who's Marilyn Haft?' he asked, and, turning to Zbig Brzezinski, 'Is she one of yours, Zbig?' Brzezinski hastily disclaimed any knowledge of Miss Haft. 'Go find out have we a Marilyn Haft here,' the President told Bob Hunter. We dealt with other matters until Hunter returned. 'She's one of Zbig's,' he told the President laconically. Brzezinski was suitably contrite. It was explained to me that Marilyn Haft was one of a group of junior aides drafted in to deal with people who wanted to make representations to the White House—part of the new Democratic administration's policy of open government. Their job was to deal sympathetically with the public. Miss Haft had apparently interpreted this role overenthusiastically when approached on the issue of Northern Ireland; it was not clear that she knew what the IRA was.

My first contact with the Holy See had been at Helsinki in July 1973, when I had had a long discussion with the Papal Secretary of State, Archbishop Casaroli. I had explained to him the concern of our Government to establish a positive relationship with unionists as well as nationalists in Northern Ireland and my own belief that this constructive process might be aided if some features of our state that they found unattractive could be modified: these included the legal ban on contraception and the constitutional ban on divorce. But, I added, the most negative feature of all from the point of view of Northern Protestants seemed to be the Roman Catholic church's position on mixed marriages. I also mentioned the absence of integrated education, which helped to reinforce divisions within Northern Ireland itself. He appeared interested in these points, and even, I thought at the time, encouraging. It was agreed that I should put my views in writing and send a document on the subject to him prior to a further meeting in the autumn.

On my return home I prepared a memorandum for transmission to Casaroli, sending it first to the Taoiseach, whose views on these issues I knew to be much more conservative than mine. There was no negative reaction from him, and after account had been taken of some helpful comments from our Ambassador to the Holy See, the memorandum in its final form was handed to Casaroli on 14 August.

When I met him in Rome some weeks later, Casaroli gave me his interim response to my memorandum. He said that certain points that touched on doctrinal matters had been referred to the Sacred Congregation for the Doctrine of the Faith, and he was considering the remainder carefully himself. He had already received comments from the Nuncio, Mgr Alibrandi, to whom I had spoken about the issues I raised. Apparently the Nuncio had told him that Irish unity would not come soon. As the changes I proposed would not bring about unity, should we be upsetting people in our state by making such changes now?

I agreed that unity would not come soon but stressed that we needed an interim stage of appropriate reforms if we were ever to shift the opinions of a sufficiently large minority of unionists to bring about a majority within Northern Ireland in favour of unity. I emphasised the psychological blockage of Northern unionists, who were afraid of being swallowed up by the Catholic South. They feared the possible loss in a united Ireland of their present right to divorce through the imposition on them of the ban on divorce in our Constitution. Moreover, our laws made a criminal offence out of the sale of contraceptives to unmarried people, which Protestants regarded as a right. And on mixed education, public opinion polls had shown that two-thirds of Northern Catholics as well as a majority of Protestants favoured it in principle.

But the most important area of all was that of mixed marriages, where the problem was church, not state, law. While since Vatican II there had been considerable progress in this area at the pastoral level, the halving of the Protestant population of our state within half a century, due primarily to this factor, had had a disproportionate impact on Northern Protestant opinion, which wrongly attributed this massive demographic change to more sinister causes, namely repression leading to a form of forced emigration. This was a unique aspect of the Irish mixed marriage phenomenon that did not exist elsewhere and that justified, I suggested, a special church regime for mixed marriages in Ireland.

Casaroli kicked for touch at this point, suggesting discussions with the Nuncio, Cardinal Conway, and some of the bishops. A decade later I smiled to myself when I heard Bishop Cassidy at the New Ireland Forum kicking that ball back to Rome, saying that the Irish bishops had considered appealing to the Holy See for a derogation from the requirement that the Catholic partner promise orally to do his or her best to have the children brought up as Catholics, but that they had not gone ahead with this, as they felt there was not even a slight chance that Rome would accede to such an appeal. Two Government departments seeking to shift the bureaucratic onus to each other could not have been more skilful.

Casaroli did, however, go so far as to say that he was now of the opinion, having heard my case, that the Nuncio had given him the wrong slant; his— Casaroli's—comprehension of the complexities of the problem had been changed by our discussion. I wondered—not for the last time—just what the Nuncio had said to him.

Nothing more was heard of my initiative. However, around February 1977 in Strasbourg I happened to meet Archbishop Benelli, who at that time seemed to have the role of Prime Minister, while Casaroli was effectively Foreign Minister, of the Holy See. He suggested that I speak to the Pope—Paul VI—about Northern Ireland. A couple of weeks later I took him at his word, seeking an interview with the Pope after the Rome European Council of 25–26 March. Eventually, but only at the last moment, an audience was arranged.

The row about our unilateral fishery measures was in full spate at this point, and just as I was about to leave our embassy I was called to the phone. By the time the call ended we were very tight indeed for time, and as we drove through Trastevere at breakneck speed I was reminded that the last person who had been late for a papal audience was Idi Amin! Arriving there we moved rapidly through the corridors, reaching the papal apartments just in time. As I waited in the open doorway of the Pope's study for the signal to enter, I could hear someone talking continuously, as if giving a prolonged briefing. When I entered, there was no-one else there. I realised then as I sat at the desk opposite him that he had been reading aloud to himself the address in French that he was to make to me. It lasted some six or seven minutes. The theme was uncompromising. Ireland was a Catholic country—perhaps the only one left. It should stay that way. Laws should not be changed in a way that would make it less Catholic.

As he spoke on I began to wonder how on earth to respond to this quite long statement. Given his age and frailty, and the respect due to him, as well as the short period of my brief audience that would remain when he eventually finished, I could hardly launch into an argumentative response to all the points he was making. Accordingly, I replied to his address very simply by saying that an appallingly tragic situation existed in Northern Ireland to which we in our state were trying to respond in a positive and Christian way.

Before I could go any further he intervened. He knew how tragic the situation was there, he said, but it could not be a reason to change any of the laws that kept us a Catholic state. At that I more or less gave up. I left the audience somewhat shell-shocked. The tone and content of his remarks suggested that he had been told I was a dangerous liberal bent on destroying Catholicism in Ireland: someone who had to be admonished in no uncertain terms, and whose expressed concerns about the Northern Ireland tragedy should not be taken seriously.

A discussion with Casaroli on the same visit to Rome was as polished and smooth as on the previous occasion. He asked me whether my Government really wanted a united Ireland? I answered that this indeed was our aspiration, but one that we wished to come about only with the free consent of a majority in the North. I added, perhaps a little gratuitously, that the form of unity might be federal or confederal rather than necessarily involve a centralised unitary state. Quick as a flash he pounced: 'But in a federal state you could have divorce in one part and not in another.'

A meeting with Benelli proved as curious in its own way as my audience with the Pope. He explained that Casaroli would have spoken to me from a religious point of view. He, however, saw things politically and would speak to me as a politician. Would it not be important to pursue policies that would not lose us the Catholic vote? With as straight a face as I could I responded that I believed that the Taoiseach was indeed concerned not to lose the Catholic vote—which was 96 per cent of the total. He seemed reassured! As we went down in the lift after the meeting one of the officials accompanying me remarked that he sounded like a man thinking of standing for the Dáil himself.

All in all, it was a depressing experience. I had presented the problem in terms of the need to create conditions that might favour peace and reconciliation, which was how I saw it. I had not expected my suggestions to be welcomed, but I had thought that some discussion of the problem on the basis of a shared Christian concern might be possible and that what I hoped was the evident sincerity of my commitment might provide an antidote to some of the advice the Holy See had been receiving from Ireland. Instead, I had been faced with a combination of what appeared to me to be diplomatic evasion and arguments based on criteria of power rather than charity.

There was to be another twist to the relationship between Ireland and the Holy See before our Government's term came to an end. It had been clear throughout our period in office that the Holy See was being briefed from Ireland by conservative forces in the church opposed to my more liberal stance, which was influenced in part at least by my concern about Northern Ireland; perhaps that was to be expected. But there had also been disturbing signs of attempts to persuade the Holy See that our handling of the IRA threat was in some way to be deplored.

In one respect it could be alleged that we were vulnerable to criticism: there had been allegations of police brutality connected with the questioning of suspects—allegations to which I shall return in a later chapter. But the communication we now received from the Holy See raised a quite different issue: it concerned IRA hunger-strikes in two prisons.

Irish Government policy on hunger-strikes for decades past has been directed towards minimising the risk of death from such demonstrations, both by trying to prevent the circumstances from arising that would precipitate hunger-strikes and by making clear the Government's refusal to be blackmailed by hunger-strikes into changing its settled policy of prison management. This approach by successive governments has been so successful that since 1946 no hunger-strike in the Irish state has been pursued to a fatal conclusion. By contrast, in the 1970s and early 1980s the British government, with a less clear-cut approach, lost two prisoners through hunger-strikes in Britain and ten in Northern Ireland. Irish Governments are convinced that their approach has not only been more effective but, in the long run, more humane.

The decision of the Holy See to respond to pressure from some Irish church sources and, we believed, from the Nuncio, by presenting a note to the

Irish Government about the hunger-strikes in April 1977, just after these strikes had ended, thus evoked a strong reaction from our Government and, in particular, from the Taoiseach. No more loyal son of the church was to be found in Ireland, but Liam Cosgrave was not prepared to take lessons from anyone on how to deal with the IRA.

His reaction could have been foreseen by anyone who knew anything about him, and was foreseen by our Ambassador, to whom Benelli handed a note on the subject. The Ambassador turned it around on the desk so that it faced Benelli again—a traditional hint that a protest is not acceptable and would be better not pressed. Benelli ignored the hint, turning it back again. The Ambassador then warned him about the Taoiseach's probable reaction.

As it happened, the Government was already perturbed over a public statement on the strikes and on prison conditions in the state made by Bishop Daly of Derry just before the strikes had ended. There had also, I think, been a direct approach from the Nuncio, which had been rejected. Bishop Daly's statement was considered by the Government in my absence abroad on 26 April, at which point the existence of Benelli's note had not come to its attention. As a message on the following day to me from the Taoiseach about this Government meeting made clear, there was concern and resentment among Ministers at the bishop's public intervention, which it was feared might even have had fatal results if it had encouraged the hunger-strikers to continue a protest that we believed had in fact just ended because of the way the Government had handled the issue. But a conversation I had with Liam Cosgrave on the Saturday after my return—with both of us still unaware of the Benelli note—led to the Government's proposal being dropped. When, during my absence in Iceland the following week, the Government learnt that its proposed protest had not only been abandoned on my suggestion but had also been pre-empted by Rome, there was an explosion. A note from the Taoiseach was drafted, the text of which my officials in Iveagh House phoned to me in Reykjavík; they wanted to know what they should do with it.

Liam Cosgrave's note certainly pulled no punches. The Holy See was told uncompromisingly that the hunger-strike had been organised by persons convicted of murder and other crimes committed in the course of a campaign in which almost two thousand Irish people had been killed and nearly ten thousand injured. Government policy on the strike had been frequently and unequivocally stated by the Taoiseach and other Ministers; it was based on the rule of law. And there was a sting in the tail: the Government, the note said, wished to make known its concern at the timing and content of the Holy See's demarche—which, it was pointed out, had been given to our Ambassador when the hunger-strike had been over for some days.

I could see why my officials had decided to phone me for instructions, but I could not conceivably tell them not to deliver the note, especially after I had been responsible for the failure to implement the Government's earlier decision. Instead in my Reykjavík hotel I prepared an aide-mémoire for simultaneous presentation in explanation of the strength of the Taoiseach's and Government's reactions. In this aide-mémoire I said that the Government had been particularly disturbed that in the wording of its note the Holy See had used language that seemed to accept propaganda statements by convicted criminals engaged in a campaign to discredit the Government. The Government was all the more concerned because it had believed that its commitment to policies of moderation and Christian reconciliation in the difficult circumstances created by the Northern Ireland crisis were appreciated by the Holy See. It had hoped that my recent visit, during which I had explained our policies in relation to Northern Ireland and the whole problem of violence in Ireland, would have dispelled any misunderstanding that might have existed. (I thought I was entitled to this reminder of my fruitless efforts to persuade them to help us with our efforts to promote conditions for reconciliation.)

A final explanatory comment of mine to the effect that the Government could not but wonder about the reliability and impartiality of the sources of information upon which the Holy See had drawn in preparing their demarche was, at the suggestion of the Ambassador to the Holy See, incorporated in the note itself, as was a reference to annexed statements by the Minister for Justice on the hunger-strike.

Benelli's reaction when our Ambassador presented the Taoiseach's response was defensive on the issue of the reliability of his sources. He added that it had not been the intention of the Holy See to intervene but merely to bring to our attention letters that they had been receiving. I think that the strength of our reaction and the fact that the Taoiseach was involved, and not just me, had its effect.

The episode, taken together with my experience in the Vatican some six weeks earlier, illustrated the difficulties of an Irish Government's relationship with the Holy See—difficulties that I have to say seemed to be aggravated by the activities of the Nuncio, Mgr Alibrandi, who was left for almost twenty years in Ireland despite clear indications by the Irish Government of its unhappiness with his interventions in affairs of this kind, in which he appeared to some of us at times to confuse Catholicism with extreme republicanism.

At the Conference I had called in April 1973 I had been impressed by the commitment of the department to development co-operation for Third World aid. In my foreign policy speech in the Dáil on 9 May of that year I was able to announce that the Government proposed to increase the annual level of assistance to developing countries in absolute terms and as a percentage of GNP in a planned manner over a period of years. Shortly afterwards I secured agreement to the allocation of £100,000 in the current year to finance the establishment of an Interim Agency for Personal Service in Developing Countries, which was designed to mobilise skills available in Ireland for voluntary work in these countries. Later this agency was established as a permanent independent body, and since then thousands of Irish volunteers have served under its auspices in Third World countries.

In November 1973 I brought to the Government a memorandum on aid to developing countries, which proposed the adoption and communication to the Community of a specific target for the expansion of our development aid, 'aiming at an annual increase of the order of .05% of GNP taking one year with another over a five-year period.' The memorandum came up for discussion at the end of a cabinet meeting when, exceptionally, only seven Ministers remained. Despite strong opposition from the Minister for Finance—the heady optimism of our early months in Government had been punctured several weeks earlier by the Yom Kippur War and the oil crisis—the memorandum was finally agreed by four votes to three, the balance being swung by one Minister who said, 'If we're Christians at all, we must agree to this.' Given the economic crisis into which the world had been plunged six months earlier our commitment was a brave undertaking. In the event it was not wholly fulfilled; the extraordinary financial difficulties that Ireland with other countries faced in the aftermath of the oil crisis made it impossible to sustain the full momentum of expansion envisaged. Nevertheless, despite the crisis the level of our development aid did increase between 1972 and 1977 from less than £1 million to over £7 million, and over this period the share of GNP devoted to it increased three-and-a-half times, which certainly compared favourably with other countries, many of which cut their aid programmes during this period.

Some part of this increase would have been necessary in any event in order to cater for increased multilateral commitments to UN agencies and through the European Community, but we envisaged that this expansion of multilateral aid would, although rapid, be a good deal slower than the growth of our total allocation. The residual, which at the time we envisaged as growing rapidly, would fund a new Bilateral Aid Programme, including the activities of the new Agency for Personal Service Overseas. Nevertheless in absolute terms the amounts available for this purpose would remain small for some time to come, and we decided to concentrate our aid on five countries initially: Tanzania, Lesotho, and Sudan, which were among the poorest countries in the world; Zambia, which we had already helped at its request with training for its army and civil service in the 1960s; and India. We later decided to confine our efforts to the four African countries, as the aid we could provide would be an infinitesimal drop in the bucket so far as India was concerned.

In July 1974 I had to attend for twenty-four hours an EEC-ACP conference in Jamaica. Returning by Air Jamaica to New York I found myself sitting beside two Africans. They were from Lesotho: a Minister and a Permanent Secretary. We got talking, and I told them of our plans, saying that if they were in Europe later in the year they should come to see us, as we might be able to offer them some modest help through our new Bilateral Aid Programme. Several months later representatives from Lesotho arrived in Dublin to take up this offer, and since then that country has been a major beneficiary of Irish aid.

Most EC countries have separate Ministers or Secretaries of State for Development Assistance, and by 1975 it was clear to me that I needed such help. I asked Liam Cosgrave in April if a Junior Minister could be appointed. He offered me the late Professor John Kelly, the Chief Whip; and although John's whipping responsibilities would obviously limit the amount of time he could give to the job, I was happy to have the help of such an outstanding junior Minister. A distinguished academic lawyer and constitutional expert, he was also the wittiest and most entertaining speaker in the Dáil, with a quirky humour and unrivalled turn of phrase. Our political viewpoints were somewhat different— insofar as he could be defined, he was a radical conservative—but we had a good, although not close, personal relationship, and I knew that I could not do better than have the use of whatever portion of his time he could give to the job. In addition to development co-operation I also delegated to him full responsibility for cultural affairs, the Legal Section of the department, the Council of Europe, consular affairs, and passports.

Shortly after his appointment we discussed the administrative arrangements for development co-operation with representatives of APSO and later, in February 1976, called a meeting to discuss these structures in greater depth with all interested parties, including a recent arrival on the scene: DEVCO, the Development Co-operation Organisation, which had been established at the initiative of Brendan O'Regan of the Shannon Free Airport Development Company to mobilise the resources of state bodies for Third World development.

APSO, DEVCO and the voluntary agencies generally favoured the devolution of the development co-operation functions of the department to a new state agency to be established for this purpose. My department was strongly opposed—indeed it wanted to reabsorb APSO into the department as part of an executive office under an Assistant Secretary. John and I thought the idea of a development agency had merit, however, and we asked the department to produce a paper that, regardless of the departmental view, would present the pros and cons fairly as part of a wider document to be published as a White Paper.

For the first and only time the department failed to do the job I asked it to do. Its draft referred to the idea of a state-sponsored body with what I can only describe as studied distaste. John and I felt that we had no alternative but to write the White Paper ourselves, so that the case in favour of such an agency would be properly stated, but we did not find the time to complete the task before the Government changed in June 1977. Within a couple of years after that the concept of an independent development agency had been conclusively buried by an interdepartmental committee of civil servants, who, whatever their departmental differences, were prepared to unite against the threat of an independent agency taking over any part of their work.

In fairness I should perhaps add that a strong case exists against such an agency as well as in favour of it, and even if John and I had been able to present the proposed White Paper to the Government it is far from certain that our case would have convinced our colleagues.

The 1977 general election took place on Thursday 16 June. By lunchtime the following day it was clear that Fianna Fáil had had an overwhelming victory. There is an interval of up to three weeks after an election before the new Dáil meets to elect a Taoiseach; in this instance the date for the assembly of the Dáil had been fixed for 5 July. But on the Wednesday after the election, in circumstances that I have described elsewhere, Liam Cosgrave announced his resignation as leader of Fine Gael. When I left a meeting of the Council of Ministers in Luxembourg four days later I already knew that I was likely to become leader of the party and thus, if and when we returned to Government, Taoiseach rather than Minister for Foreign Affairs.

The Ministerial Council meeting in Luxembourg was therefore an emotional occasion for me. During the previous four-and-a-quarter years I had attended some seventy Council of Ministers meetings in Brussels and Luxembourg—as well as over twenty EC Ministerial meetings in other capitals. These gatherings of Foreign Ministers were occasions at which I had felt at home and where I believed I had been able to contribute to the future of both Ireland and Europe. Now it seemed that this would be the last Ministerial Council I would be able to attend.

As often before, I was accompanied by Justin Keating, the Labour Minister for Industry and Commerce, with whom I had struck up a warm friendship after he had entered the Dáil in 1969 and especially when we had campaigned together all over Ireland—on opposite sides—in the EEC referendum of 1972. He had attended many meetings of the General Council of Ministers in his capacity as Minister responsible for foreign trade, which had, of course, become a Community competence under the Treaty of Rome. I believe that, despite his theoretical opposition to the European Community, he shared my sadness at the end of this particular era.

We said our farewells. Then Joan and I travelled to London for my final European Council meeting as Foreign Minister. Liam Cosgrave had asked me to invite Jack Lynch, who would become Taoiseach a few days later, to accompany us to the London meeting, but Jack Lynch had declined, saying that he thought this would be an awkward arrangement, and anyway he was busy forming his cabinet.

The London European Council itself was dull, but it was a social occasion of some brilliance, for it coincided with the Queen's Silver Jubilee celebration, and we were invited to dinner in Buckingham Palace rather than to the usual luncheon given to European Councils by heads of state. Moreover, it had been arranged that after dinner there would be a tattoo by the massed bands of the Brigade of Guards on the floodlit lawn at the back of the palace.

Although Joan was not feeling her best it was nevertheless an enjoyable evening. When, after we had assembled, the royal party appeared in the ante-room—somewhat unexpectedly, as Schmidt and Genscher had not yet arrived—we formed ourselves into a rough-and-ready line, introducing ourselves as they came to each of us. By chance Joan was ahead of me in the line and she was taken aback when, as the Queen passed on from her to me, Prince Philip asked her as he shook hands, 'Do you always put yourself in front of your husband?'

Fortunately, whether through tact or otherwise, she failed to make the obvious reply.

After dinner we walked from the dining-room to the balconies to watch the tattoo, and Prince Charles fell in beside me. He asked a series of highly relevant questions about Northern Ireland. The tattoo itself was impressive. As the floodlit flags of the Nine were lowered one after another at the end Joan thought of Ian Paisley, and we wondered what he would have felt had he— improbably—seen the honour paid in this place to the Irish Tricolour. I thought also of my father, who once told me how, when he had attended his first function there as Minister for External Affairs in 1923, he had had to make diplomatic excuses to King George and Queen Mary for the absence of his anti-Treaty wife.

After the tattoo the Queen Mother asked me to sit down and talk to her in the gallery from which some of us had been watching the display. There Joan found us some time later, alone in the vast room, and there the Queen found the three of us when she came looking for her mother to join in the farewells. Helmut Schmidt wanted to leave before Giscard d'Estaing, who, as the only head of state present among the guests, should have been allowed to go first. Schmidt had already upstaged Giscard, and shown discourtesy to his hostess by arriving late, and the Queen's lighthearted comments to her mother in our presence on this latest *faux pas* disguised an evident annoyance at his behaviour.

As Joan and I descended the great staircase beside Jim Callaghan, he asked if the Queen had found me; apparently she had been looking for me to discuss Northern Ireland. 'I must have got the wrong Queen,' I replied.

It is in the nature of autobiography to be self-centred, and the account I have given in this and previous chapters of my period as Minister for Foreign Affairs inevitably fails to place these events adequately in their context—and in particular in the context of the Department of Foreign Affairs, within which I was working. I could not conceivably have had any measure of success as a Minister without the remarkable back-up that I got from my department. At the very least such successes as I had would have been overshadowed by accompanying failures if my enthusiasms had not been restrained and channelled by wise officials; and many of these successes might not have been achieved at all but for the groundwork undertaken by the civil servants.

The quality of officials in the Department of Foreign Affairs is generally high, although of course there are some weak links—in some cases because of faulty initial selection but more often, I suspect, because the strains of a series of postings, mostly abroad, have taken their toll, leading occasionally to a mediocre performance at the end of what may in its earlier phase have been a brilliant start to a career.

In my experience the high calibre of the staff was attested by the almost universally high quality of reporting and drafting and the unfailing accuracy of the material presented to me as Minister—something which, from my experience as Taoiseach, I know not to be universally true elsewhere in the public service, although standards in this respect are generally high among Irish bureaucrats. The advice offered to me by the department—which I did not always accept—was excellent, invariably showing subtlety and insight.

The energy, enthusiasm and commitment of the staff was outstanding. Morale was high at that time because of the challenge of our entry to the Community and, for a number of officials, the challenge also of working for peace in Northern Ireland against the malevolent efforts of the IRA and loyalist paramilitaries and the often uncomprehending and misguided approach of some— although by no means all—British Ministers and civil servants. In human terms the rapid expansion of the department—which during my relatively brief period in office grew by two-fifths to a strength of almost two hundred diplomats, while the number of missions abroad increased by almost half—provided unique opportunities for promotion. Three-fifths of the ambassadors in post when I left office had been promoted to that rank during my term, which meant that effectively all officials of Counsellor rank had become Ambassadors, or Assistant Secretaries at home. The same was true of the forty-odd Third Secretaries who were on the strength when I became Minister: almost all were promoted. Of course, the relatively large influx of staff during this period—over sixty new entrants, almost half of them in 1974 alone—created subsequent promotional blockages, which have inevitably affected morale in more recent years, but that problem had not begun to arise during my time as Minister.

I have already referred to Hugh McCann, Secretary of the department for the first year of my period as Minister and subsequently a distinguished Ambassador to France. As his successor I appointed Paul Keating, a cousin of my friend and fellow-Minister Justin Keating, who was a brilliant diplomat still just short of fifty and who had been Political Director for some time previously, that is, the official in charge of the political as distinct from economic aspects of foreign policy. Paul had a subtle mind, a quick and puckish sense of humour, and a pungent style. Even today I could identify at once a paper of which he was author. He combined a refreshing sense of irony that was in no way destructive with a very deeply ingrained idealism. His interests lay primarily in the area for which he had held high responsibility: the political side of foreign policy; he did not have an intense interest either in the European Community or in Northern Ireland, but my own enthusiasm in these two areas of policy and the exceptional quality of Paul's deputies compensated for the imbalance of interests on his part. He did not want to be Secretary for too long, however, and I sent him to London as Ambassador early in 1977. Later he was moved to New York as Ambassador to the United Nations, but died tragically there of a sudden illness shortly after his arrival.

Joan's relationship with the department was more intimate than has perhaps normally been the case, although all Ministers' wives in Foreign Affairs are required by the nature of the job to play a larger role than in other departments. Once she had got over her fear of flying she accompanied me on many journeys, getting to know our diplomatic staff overseas and their wives, while at home she threw herself into the official entertaining, applying her skills and energies to all the problems that such work entails. She was notably considerate of and supportive of the staff and their spouses, who we both felt had a particularly hard time. Especially, but not only, when serving abroad, spouses are expected to represent a state that imposes on them a demanding role with few parallels elsewhere in the public service—one which, however, is not compensated or even officially recognised. And their family lives are totally disrupted every three or four years, when they have to uproot themselves, moving to a different country. In truth Joan identified with the department as much as I did, just as she had done in UCD while I had been teaching there. From her point of view as well as mine, the years in Foreign Affairs were the high point of our joint career.

# CHAPTER EIGHT

# SUNNINGDALE:
# THE FIRST MILESTONE

At the outset of this chapter I should explain that in the Irish system of government the practice has been that the primary responsibility for matters relating to Northern Ireland rests with the Taoiseach rather than with a departmental Minister. The role of the Minister for Foreign Affairs is a supporting one: he and his department provide advice to the Taoiseach and implement policy under his general direction. My involvement with Northern Ireland between 1973 and 1977 must be seen against this background. Naturally the Government as a whole has collective responsibility for this, as for all other aspects of policy, and when issues of importance have to be decided they are discussed in cabinet—in my experience very fully—and the ultimate decisions are taken there. Nevertheless, even in cabinets that are 'democratic' (i.e. in which most issues are decided by a majority decision, which the Taoiseach of the day does not attempt to override) Northern Ireland issues tend to be treated somewhat differently. If, as is normally the case, the Taoiseach and the Minister for Foreign Affairs are agreed on the line that should be followed, other Ministers tend to be reluctant to reject—although they certainly feel free to question—the course of action proposed. If the Taoiseach does not have full confidence in his Minister for Foreign Affairs in relation to the sensitive issue of Northern Ireland, or if for other reasons there are tensions between them, the system of policy formulation and operation in relation to Northern Ireland may be seriously weakened. This can also happen if the Department of the Taoiseach develops within itself a second centre of policy formulation or even of operational contacts. Happily, in the 1973–77 Government and, I believe, in the two Governments that I later led, these errors were avoided, and the system worked well. Indeed the tensions that had previously existed between Liam Cosgrave and myself completely evaporated in Government, and the differences in our attitudes to Northern Ireland that had caused problems in opposition also disappeared. Relations between our departments at official level were also good; Dermot Nally, the recently appointed Assistant Secretary to the Government, who handled Northern Ireland affairs for the Taoiseach, and the officials in Foreign Affairs established a good working partnership, as did the Government press officer, Muiris Mac Conghail, with the department's information officer, Noel Dorr.

In the 1973–77 Government a new element was added to this complex equation, however, in the form of Conor Cruise O'Brien, Minister for Posts and Telegraphs and de facto Minister for Information, for at the very outset Cosgrave had delegated to him operational control of the Government Information Service, to which (at Joan's suggestion, when Conor asked us for advice at a parliamentary press gallery dinner a few days after the formation of the Government) he had appointed Muiris Mac Conghail, the brilliant and—for the best of reasons—controversial television producer.

I do not need to introduce Conor Cruise O'Brien. But it is relevant to recall here that a quarter of a century earlier, as an official of the Department of Foreign Affairs, he had been an exponent of the prevailing sterile anti-partition propaganda line that I had rejected all my life. I recall a meal to which he invited me in Jammet's restaurant in the 1950s to meet a young British Conservative MP, Norman St John Stevas. If on that occasion he expected me to support the official line on partition, I am sure I must have disappointed him.

By 1973 Conor had swung to a very different position: he had become highly sensitive to Unionist concerns, not, as some of his many enemies contend, because he agreed with their views but because he believed, with reason, that insensitivity towards the genuine fears of unionists was dangerously counter-productive. In propounding this position with what has seemed to me at times to be the fervour of a convert he has since courageously challenged cherished nationalist myths.

Where I found—and still find—myself in disagreement with him is in relation to his single-minded concentration on one of two dangers in Northern Ireland and what I regard as his unwillingness to take adequate account of the other danger, namely, that *exclusive* attention to legitimate unionist concerns may dangerously exacerbate tensions on the nationalist side, thus abandoning mainstream moderate nationalism to the IRA. In that way too there is a serious risk of provoking violence.

It was therefore on issues of judgement and prudence, not of principle, that we differed—but perhaps also in one other respect: I could always see *his* point of view; I am less certain that he was equally able to see mine.

But to return to 1973: some years earlier Conor had swung the Labour Party away from the temptations of 'republicanism' (as the more extreme form of nationalism is so often, if misleadingly, described), and Labour's leader, Brendan Corish, respected his judgement in this area. When the Government was formed in March 1973 Conor consequently carried over into the Coalition cabinet his Labour Party role of spokesman on Northern Ireland, and established with Liam Cosgrave a convention that as Brendan Corish's adviser on the North he should be actively involved in everything to do with Northern Ireland.

While I genuinely welcomed his involvement as a balance against more traditional nationalist sentiments within the cabinet—my views were in many ways much closer to his than were those of most other members, perhaps even of *any* other member—this undoubtedly created some problems. While, like myself, he had come to know the SDLP leaders well in opposition, because of their Labour links, seeing even more of them perhaps than I had, a number of them were unhappy with what they regarded as his overpreoccupation with Unionist fears. His insistence on being present at all meetings between them and members of the Government was not always helpful. I do not recall that I ever consciously sought to exclude him from such discussions; but when Declan Costello and I met John Hume and Paddy Devlin informally on one occasion in October 1973, and failed to alert Conor and invite him to join us, he sent me a reprimand in his inimitable style, ending by pointing out that a comment of mine in the Government that his information on the North was not as up to date and adequate as it might be, while no doubt true, must surely mean that he should be enabled to correct this defect—which would not be easy if he were excluded from these 'important and presumably enlightening talks'. And he ended with a typical Conorism: '"We must not discourage these comrades," as Joe Stalin said when he sent the Soviet intellectuals to dig the White Sea Canal.'

But whatever difficulties or tensions his insistent involvement may have caused, I have to add that any objective historian of the period will be forced to conclude that he was more nearly right than I and the rest of us were in the run-up to Sunningdale and in his judgement of the conference itself. I am less sure about the years that followed, for I am tempted to feel that the legitimate conviction that he had been right on that occasion may have encouraged him in a delusion of near-infallibility thereafter! However that may be, his presence in that Government helped to promote a balance in our assessment of the complex Northern Ireland issue that previous Governments, and some subsequent ones, more uniformly traditionally nationalist in their composition, lacked. Given his later unpopularity even with more moderate nationalists and the strength of feelings aroused by some of his later stands—for example his opposition to the Anglo-Irish Agreement—this point needs to be made at the outset of my account of what might be described as the Sunningdale period.

The issues that preoccupied us in our relations with the British government concerning Northern Ireland in 1973 were complex enough. There were several sources of serious tension: the Littlejohn affair, the Strasbourg case, and the (to say the least) uneven behaviour of the British army in Northern Ireland, as well as differences concerning the implementation of the policy outlined in the British White Paper published a few days after the formation of our Government, a policy that in its general outline we strongly endorsed. Subsequently there was our involvement in the Sunningdale conference and its frustrating follow-up: the disastrous Ulster workers' strike, and the period of uncertainty that followed when British policy on Northern Ireland seemed dangerously unclear. Through-out the whole of this period there were tensions arising from cross-Border incidents with the British army, and in the latter part of the period tensions relating to the British handling of the Frank Stagg hunger-strike and funeral and the renewed abuse of interrogation methods in Northern Ireland.

This is not an easy tale to disentangle. Before attempting to do so, let me set the scene in terms of the policy of the Irish Government and the policy or policies of the British Cabinet as perceived by us.

There was, I think, more consistency of *policy* on the Irish side, which is not to say that our *judgement* was necessarily always right. We sought a resolution of the internal political problem in Northern Ireland through a system of joint devolved government within which the Unionists would naturally be in a majority, as well as the ending of discrimination against the Catholic nationalist minority and some kind of North-South link that, without prejudice to the Union, would meet the concern of Northern nationalists to have some focus for their Irish loyalties pending the possible emergence in the longer term of consent to political unity by a majority in Northern Ireland. The implementation of such policies would, we believed, offer the best hope of isolating the IRA politically. Such policies, if they had been pursued with vigour and consistency and been combined with determined but sensitively directed security measures and with a clear policy on the part of both governments of refusing to negotiate with paramilitaries or to give in to blackmail (for example from hunger-strikes in support of political objectives), might within a reasonable time-scale have marginalised the IRA and forced it to abandon its campaign of violence.

Naturally I cannot give a first-hand account of British policy, but as observed by us from outside it did not appear to be coherent or consistent. We were, of course, fortunate enough to come into office at a moment when, after four years of uncertain handling of the situation, the British government of the day had come to the same conclusion as we had done much earlier about the shape of the political structure that needed to be set up in Northern Ireland and between North and South. Moreover, as was to be true again in the 1984–85 period, on the occasions when a British government and its advisers apply the whole of their minds to a problem of this kind, the result, both conceptually and in its detail, can be impressive, partly because the British administration can mobilise remarkable resources of talent for such an initiative.

The trouble is that the new policy line of 1972–73 was not maintained in the face of pressures from unionist extremists and, as far as we could see, also from the British army, which, both at the level of its tactics on the ground and at the level of the 'advice' it offered the British government during the Ulster workers' strike in May 1974, seemed effectively to undermine the thrust of that government's policy.

Moreover, by their handling of the IRA successive British governments of both parties in Britain at various stages convinced the leaders of that organisation that continued violence would eventually lead to a 'British withdrawal', thus further undermining Britain's own objectives. It is not my purpose here to urge this or any other view of British policy; but in order to understand the actions of the Government of which I was a member it is necessary to know that this is how we *perceived* the British position.

The immediate issue before us after taking office was the British White Paper, to the formulation of which we had sought to contribute on the day after our installation. On the whole we found it satisfactory, and I had the opportunity a fortnight after its publication to discuss initial Northern reactions to it with the Secretary of State, Willie Whitelaw, in London, and to seek clarification on aspects of the document at a further meeting in London two months later.

Our first meeting, on 4 April, was devoted mainly to a general *tour d'horizon*. Between this and the next meeting I paid my first Ministerial visit to Northern Ireland. I undertook a tour of the troubled areas with some young people I had met at a conference in the Corrymeela Reconciliation Centre after Christmas 1972. We travelled in a van through the various 'ghettos' of north and west Belfast. I could see how much local knowledge was required to get around these areas: we speeded up at certain points but slowed down at others, depending on whether the various paramilitaries and the British army were prone to shoot at fast-moving vehicles or to attempt to halt slow-moving ones. After a quick meal with some of the Passionist priests at Holy Cross in the Ardoyne, we met a number of local people from the nationalist community: members of a Relief Committee of the Ardoyne People's Assembly and of the Farrington Gardens Rebuilding Scheme.

I then moved across the sectarian divide to meet members of community groups in the loyalist Sandy Row area, some of them, I heard afterwards, people of extreme views. The meeting, which went on until nearly 11.30 p.m., gave me a fascinating insight into the way in which working-class Protestants viewed the Republic. They alleged discrimination against Protestants in the South. I asked for examples. Three firms in the Republic, they claimed, had notices up saying *No Protestant need apply*. Two of the firms they named were Guinness and Jacobs; the third a shoe polish firm which, I believed, had gone out of business years before. They were taken aback when I burst out laughing. Guinness and Jacobs, I told them, were firms in which the management until quite recently had been overwhelmingly Protestant. I heard after the meeting that they had been sufficiently impressed by my hilarity to have discussed sending someone to Dublin to check up on their information.

Most of my second meeting with Willie Whitelaw on 9 June was at a fairly technical level on the subject of the Northern Ireland Constitution Bill. I was amused to note that despite Ted Heath's comments on the judicial review of human rights, and although Whitelaw did not himself advert to the point, the Bill provided that any legislation passed by the Northern Ireland Assembly would be void to the extent that it contained any discriminatory element—the decision on whether this was or was not the case would, of course, have to be made by the courts.

After discussing the Bill I raised the question of the imbalance in the Northern Ireland civil service, and especially in its higher ranks, between Protestants and Catholics. Without some element of positive discrimination, it did not seem to me that that could be remedied in less than thirty or thirty-five years. This point was not challenged, but there was such an evident reluctance to embark on a programme of this kind that I did not take very seriously Willie Whitelaw's offer to examine my point and see what could be done.

I also expressed concern at the failure to incorporate in the legislation the European Convention of Human Rights, a possibility that we felt had been foreshadowed in the White Paper.

On the police I said that changes must be made; these should involve changing the name as well as the uniform of the RUC, and breaking it into a number of local forces on the British model. Whitelaw replied that he would be considering further the whole question of police reform. However, tragically in my view, nothing was ever done about this. I felt then and still feel that, however difficult and even risky such a radical transition might have been, failure to attempt such a reform in 1973 almost inevitably condemned Northern Ireland to continuing violence and insecurity. True, the RUC subsequently became a highly professional force, the great majority of the members of which operated to high standards, although some of them were responsible for such aberrations as the Castlereagh interrogation centre as well as the 'shoot to kill' cases of 1982 and subsequent 'cover-ups'. But without the kind of radical changes I then proposed, the police could not within any foreseeable future become an acceptable force in the areas that had suffered most intensely from the old RUC, in particular the nationalist 'ghetto' areas of Belfast and Derry. This is certainly one of the major lost opportunities of the prolonged Northern Ireland tragedy.

I then raised with Whitelaw a recent border incident that I had had to take up with the British Ambassador on several occasions. This illustrated graphically the problem of patrolling such a very eccentric border, and is worth recounting for that reason. A British army patrol had approached a house that was diagonally bisected by the border in a salient of the Republic almost totally surrounded by Northern Ireland save for 150 yards of unbridged river. The front door, on the *north* side, was in the Republic; the back door, on the *south* side, was in Northern Ireland. Soldiers from the jeep, who wished to question the owner of the house about a car bomb attack, went to the back door in Northern Ireland. Getting no reply there, they went around to the front door in the Republic and tried to get in that way. The soldiers in the jeep, becoming worried about their prolonged absence, drove across the border to the front of the house, where they picked up their colleagues—and then drove on into the Republic instead of back up the road to Northern Ireland. They got lost and eventually stopped a garda in the town of Clones to ask their way back to the North.

When I had raised this matter with the British Ambassador, Sir Arthur Galsworthy, he had brought me a denial that the soldiers had ever been near the house and a claim that they were on a road-block patrol, which was clearly nonsense, as they had only one weak torch with them. I had told him to go and enquire further; he returned, somewhat deflated, to say that they had in fact gone to the house, but only to the back door in Northern Ireland. I had suggested he return again and make further enquiries. On his third visit he admitted that they had gone round to the front, but, as I recall it, denied they had knocked on the door. I had excused him from a fourth clarification, suggesting, however, that he would understand if in future I had difficulty in accepting denials of border incidents from British army sources or in ordering the early release, on the basis of explanations about 'map-reading errors', of British soldiers found on our side of the border, for in this case there had been repeated attempts to mislead me. The actual event itself was relatively trivial (although the man whose house they had tried to get into in order to arrest him might not see it in that light). But the incident was symptomatic of the problems that we experienced with security forces in Northern Ireland, which clearly could not be relied upon to be frank with our police, and I felt it useful to alert Whitelaw to this aspect of the cross-border problem.

He and I concluded our discussion with an exchange of views on the political situation in Northern Ireland. He was clearly concerned lest his government's attempts to encourage the emergence of a power-sharing government in Northern Ireland might fail because of SDLP or Alliance unwillingness to serve under Faulkner as chief executive, or, on the other hand, because of a failure by official Unionists, despite their loyalty pledge to Faulkner, to follow him into a power-sharing arrangement. Whitelaw proposed to encourage the Unionists to accept power-sharing by telling them that if there was not a proper working Executive by 30 March 1974 he would dissolve the Assembly and that in that event 'people in the United Kingdom will want their Government to look again at their policy in the North.' I expressed doubts about the wisdom of vague threats of this kind, which could easily rebound; he accepted that I had a point, but his frustration with Unionist attitudes clearly made him reluctant to give up any weapon that might concentrate their minds on power-sharing.

On 12 June the Government had approved proposals submitted by me some weeks earlier for discussions between the Interdepartmental Unit on Northern Ireland (known familiarly as the IDU) and Government departments on the possible functions and structures of a Council of Ireland as envisaged in the British White Paper, and for the establishment by the Attorney General of a committee to examine the constitutional and legal aspects of such a council. At that meeting also I had suggested to the Taoiseach that in the run-up to the Assembly elections on 28 June it might be desirable for us to make a constructive input into the situation in Northern Ireland by way of a speech setting out our position. A week later I sent him some suggestions for such an address. He accepted the proposal, and the bulk of my draft was in fact incorporated in a speech he delivered on 21 June. He dropped several passages, however. One of these stated our willingness to re-examine our Constitution and laws so as to identify what changes were necessary to demonstrate that we had learnt from past errors and that we were determined not to tolerate anything that gave offence to the religious minority within the state. The other concerned the revival of an all-party committee on the Constitution that had been established by Jack Lynch eighteen months earlier but had lapsed with the general election, with terms of reference requiring it to report as soon as possible on changes in our Constitution that might seem desirable.

When the Taoiseach and the Prime Minister met on 2 July they agreed that an Executive based on a coalition between the Faulkner Unionists, the SDLP and Alliance would be acceptable, and that it might be formed once the Northern Ireland Constitution Bill had been passed, probably at the end of the month. On discrimination in the civil service Ted Heath was willing to redress the imbalance at senior level if it could be done discreetly (i.e. without imposing early retirement), but he had no proposal to make on police reform. On the Council of Ireland he foresaw the need for much preliminary work at official level between the two governments, and he asked about recognition of Northern Ireland by the Republic. On the last point Cosgrave kicked for touch, saying that it would be unwise to get bogged down in legalities, but adding that the Constitutional Committee, to which I had suggested he should refer in his speech, was being reconvened to continue its work on these matters.

Meanwhile I had been monitoring the deliberations of the Interdepartmental Unit, which at that point was considering what functions might be devolved to a Council of Ireland. By mid-June my officials had reported that the going was hard; other departments were notably reluctant to concede parts of their responsibilities to this proposed North-South body, which they seemed to see as some kind of external threat to the institutions of the state. As I had always suspected, partition had struck very deep roots in the South! However, after the exercise of some ingenuity and considerable firmness I was able by 30 July to submit to the Government a comprehensive memorandum on a possible structure for a council with a wide range of executive functions as well as provision for the harmonisation of certain other activities that would continue to be discharged by the Northern and Southern administrations. This memorandum was approved by the Government on 5 September, and a copy of the proposals for the Council of Ireland was transmitted to the British government on the following day.

Meanwhile during August the Littlejohn affair had hit the headlines. Shortly before we came into office, two brothers named Littlejohn had claimed during extradition proceedings in England that British Intelligence had requested them to carry out the Dublin bank robbery with which they were charged. The greater part of this extradition proceeding had been held *in camera* in January 1973, and even the public part of the hearing had been withheld by the British press and the BBC, although it had been published in our papers. The brothers had said that the robbery had been part of a plan to provoke the Irish authorities to introduce internment. Although the British government had denied the allegation, it had admitted to our Ambassador that the Littlejohns had in fact been in touch with the Intelligence Service. Papers on the subject that had been shown to the then Taoiseach, Jack Lynch, were ultimately filed in the Department of Foreign Affairs. Now in August 1973 a controversy sprang up as the Littlejohns came to be tried in Ireland. Jack Lynch denied that he had been aware of the papers on the subject, and he was very vocally supported by Colm Condon, who had been his Attorney General. When Hugh McCann contacted Lynch at my request, the former Taoiseach immediately accepted his reminder of the events of January, and issued a statement apologising for his lapse of memory, adding—unnecessarily, I felt—that it had been a serious lapse and that he would have to consider whether he should continue as leader of the opposition. Ironically, when I in turn asked Hugh McCann if I could see the documents, he exclaimed in surprise, 'Oh, Minister, don't you remember I showed them to you in May?' My sympathy for Jack Lynch went up immeasurably. In fact the entire confusion had arisen from the distraction of the general election and a visit to the United States that Lynch had had to make at the same time. Under the pressure of events, everybody involved had forgotten what had happened, apart from the vigilant Hugh McCann.

Most unfairly—for, as I have just demonstrated, it is all too easy to forget an episode in the busy life of a Government member—Jack Lynch's reputation suffered thereafter, and a degree of fun was poked at him for having forgotten what he had known about this curious incident in Anglo-Irish relations.

On the day after this comedy of errors reached its climax I wrote to Liam Cosgrave suggesting that we take advantage of our strong moral position vis-à-vis the discomfited British government by not merely conveying to them our feelings about these events but seeking some redress. Anglo-Irish relations had been damaged by the affair, which I described as 'the employment of crooks with a clear expectation that they would engage in criminal activities, the British Government being content with a conventional warning that such activities would not be stood over.' The situation had been aggravated by the fact that no regret had so far been expressed; instead a bland statement had been issued that no damage had been done to Anglo-Irish relations and that the Irish Government had not been disturbed by these events. This had seriously damaged our position at home.

Some indication of my frame of mind at that time may be gathered from my remark in this letter that we had seen virtually no quid pro quo for the uniformly constructive and friendly approach to Britain which, since our Government had been formed in March, we had undertaken at considerable political risk to ourselves. This approach had included public acceptance of the need for the British army in the North, acknowledgement of the good intentions of the British government, and the postponement of the Strasbourg case from July to October in order to facilitate political developments in Northern Ireland. Now, I proposed, we should take this opportunity to demand what the British had hitherto failed to concede: reform of the Northern Ireland civil service and police along the lines we had earlier proposed; release of some forty to fifty detainees who had severed their connections with the IRA and whose return to their families could have a valuable influence on others who had not yet made this break; and a 'substantial and perceptible change in the manner in which the British army is carrying out its duties in Northern Ireland.' Some regiments had been harassing the nationalist population in a manner that was undermining the good work of more disciplined units with superior leadership.

My proposal was not adopted in that form, but a note was sent to the British government in somewhat less aggressive terms proposing simultaneous action on police and civil service reform, the setting up of a Council of Ireland, and the establishment of the power-sharing Executive in Northern Ireland. This note dealt also with the Strasbourg case.

On the same day that I wrote my letter to Liam Cosgrave I paid a further visit to Belfast, where I called to the offices of three newspapers, lunching first with members of the editorial staff and political writers of the *Belfast Telegraph*. I then met the Minority Rights Group and later the Central Citizens' Defence Committee. The latter meeting provided an opportunity to explain our decision to postpone the Strasbourg case. The discussion with them then turned to the problems raised by the manner in which the British army carried out its duties. The failure of the army to concentrate on preventing people being intimidated out of their homes was criticised: some 60,000 had by then been forced to move, a figure that eventually reached 100,000, of whom 85,000 were Catholics. While the original briefing document for soldiers serving in Northern Ireland, which included such material as a bloodcurdling but fictitious 'Fenian oath' designed to prejudice soldiers against the nationalist community, had been replaced, the new briefing document was unreadable, with the result that the committee believed the first version continued to be influential. There were divided views on the desirability of the British army withdrawing from various areas. Some members of the committee took exception to my having received John Taylor in Dublin, which gave me the opportunity to explain my policy of contacts with unionists. In fact, after this meeting I went straight to north Belfast to meet Protestants from the Shankill Road area—a meeting that took a somewhat similar shape to my previous encounter with Protestants from Sandy Row.

A fortnight later, Cosgrave and Corish met the SDLP leadership to clarify common ground in advance of a summit between the Taoiseach and the Prime Minister, which took place at Baldonnell military airport, Dublin, on 17 September. That summit did not go well. The central issue was whether the Executive should be formed before or after the conference to be held between the two governments and the Northern Ireland parties to agree on a Council of Ireland. Heath wanted the Executive established first so that it could join as such in the conference and thereby obviate the need to invite the extreme Unionists and other parties dedicated to wrecking the new structure of government for the

North. He also feared that if the SDLP secured the Council of Ireland first, they might lose interest in creating an Executive.

Cosgrave explained the corresponding fear on the SDLP side that, once they got an Executive, the unionists would stall over the Council. The encounter was a dialogue of the deaf and, although the heads of government returned to the subject ten or eleven times during their nine-hour meeting, they made no progress. A suggestion by Hugh McCann, who accompanied Cosgrave, that an Executive might be agreed but not launched before the conference was dismissed by Heath as 'not realistic'. Yet this in fact proved in time to be the way in which the dilemma was eventually resolved.

No progress was made on other issues of concern to us: reforming the police and civil service in Northern Ireland to give fair representation to the minority at the higher levels; restraining the behaviour of the more aggressive units of the British army in Northern Ireland; or releasing prisoners who had severed their links with the IRA. Ted Heath's response on the last issue illustrated a feature of the British government's approach with which I was to become familiar: a bureaucratic concern for adhering to existing procedures, however counterproductive these might be in achieving the aims of British policy.

As sometimes happens when a meeting of this kind has been unsuccessful, an early attempt was made to get the show on the road again. Several weeks later, at a meeting of officials in London on 5 October, a more positive British view in relation to the conference and the Council of Ireland emerged, with a clear implication that a postponement of the actual formation of an Executive until after the holding of a conference to discuss the Council of Ireland was no longer out of the question. It also emerged that our proposals of 6 September for the working of the Council contained much that was now acceptable to the British—including the proposition that, subject to the agreement of the Faulkner Unionists, the Council should have executive functions. In the meantime the Faulkner Unionists, SDLP and Alliance had reached agreement on the social and economic policies to be pursued by an Executive if and when established.

By 23 October I was able to report to the Government that the conference might now take place sooner than expected—possibly towards the end of November. I also reported that John Hume had told Seán Donlon a few days earlier that Brian Faulkner would like to hear at first hand an outline of our proposals on the Council of Ireland. Three days later Dermot Nally and Seán Donlon met him at his home in Co. Down and told him what we had in mind, stressing the principle of reassuring the Northern majority by (*a*) giving equal representation to North and South on the Council's Ministerial body, despite the fact that the South has twice the North's population, (*b*) providing that all decisions be taken by unanimity, and (*c*) giving to the representatives of the Northern majority a determining voice in the timing and method by which the Council would evolve.

Faulkner agreed to the devolution of executive functions to the Council, subject to a check back with the two governments for approval before final decisions were taken, and he favoured the institutionalisation of security co-operation, but he opposed a parliamentary tier for the Council as likely to provide a forum for wreckers. More generally, he said he was pleased with the interparty talks on the formation of a Northern Ireland Executive, and in particular with the positive approach of the SDLP.

Despite objections from Faulkner to such a visit, I felt I could not at that stage cancel a trip to Belfast arranged for 31 October, when I was to meet the SDLP and Alliance parties informally as well as to appear on a BBC television programme. I did, however, cancel another visit that I was to make for a different purpose three days earlier.

Because they were detained at a negotiating meeting with the Unionist and Alliance parties, the SDLP leaders arrived only towards the end of my meeting with their party. They reported that they had had a stormy session, at which they had had to resist strong pressure to discuss the Council of Ireland—something they were not prepared to do in the absence of the Irish Government. They were not going to be 'picked off' on this issue and be talked into an agreed position on the Council, with the obvious objective of presenting us with a fait accompli at the conference.

The Alliance Party, in turn, told me of their frustrations. They had not expected agreement to be reached on the Council of Ireland by the 'Executive parties' but understood that it had been agreed that their respective positions would be discussed at this session. They claimed that the SDLP had 'gone back on their word' and that 'out of the blue' they had wrecked the session. When they calmed down, however, they went on to stress the weakness of Faulkner's position and his feeling that he needed to go to the conference as Chief Member of the Executive and not just as a party leader. They believed he saw the Council of Ireland almost exclusively as a means of institutionalising security co-operation—a view they did not share.

They went on to say that when they had met Whitelaw earlier that evening he had expressed considerable irritation at my visit and had shown a degree of personal hostility towards me. The Alliance leaders added that they were in no doubt whatever that my judgement in persisting with the visit had been correct; but their account of a negative attitude on Whitelaw's part received some confirmation from another source shortly afterwards. Three days after my visit the Dublin political correspondents were invited to Belfast to meet the Secretary of State. A very senior British civil servant referred to Conor Cruise O'Brien and myself in Whitelaw's presence as 'third-rate academics', one of whom had been in charge of a 'second-class' colonial area—a reference to Conor's role some thirteen years earlier as UN Administrator in Katanga. Whitelaw had looked at the journalist to whom these remarks were addressed, showing no inclination to demur at them. The senior civil servant had gone on to ask rhetorically, 'Do you think seriously that the British government is going to put money into this f— Council of Ireland?' Whitelaw had backed this up quite emotionally, apparently because he feared that the British government would be expected to spend money through the Council of Ireland for Ireland as a whole. 'Britain is not a milch cow,' he had added, saying that there would be no diversion of money to Northern Ireland through the EC Regional Fund.

As to the concerns Faulkner and Whitelaw had expressed about my visit, I felt reasonably vindicated when my BBC interview evoked a very substantial and remarkably positive response from the unionist community—including immediate congratulatory phone calls from two leading Unionist politicians. When I next met Whitelaw in London on 8 November he immediately withdrew his criticism of my visit in view of what he described as my 'magnificent and most helpful' performance in the BBC interview. I began to wonder if I should examine my conscience about my television appearance.

We then discussed the progress being made in the interparty talks in Northern Ireland. Faulkner might be able to concede something on the mechanics of the Council of Ireland, according to Whitelaw, and even on the parliamentary tier, but he still wanted the Executive to be formed before the conference. Neither the SDLP nor Alliance would accept that, I responded, as they were each determined to present their own views on the Council and not a pre-agreed Executive compromise on the matter—but it would be reasonable for Faulkner to seek consensus on the number of members each party would have in the Executive. Whitelaw accepted these points and hinted that the question of timing as between the conference and the formation of the Executive would be resolved, probably, I thought, in the way Hugh McCann had suggested, namely by announcing agreement on the formation of the Executive before the conference but not setting it up until afterwards.

On the thorny issue of the relationship between policing and the Council of Ireland, Whitelaw said that the police forces, North and South, should stay under their respective governments, which changed the emphasis of comments he had made in an interview some weeks earlier when he seemed to favour a Council role in policing. I responded that, without prejudice to the authority of the governments, it should be possible to fit the Council of Ireland in some way into the hierarchy of police control or direction. This could help the minority with the problem they had in identifying with the RUC, which would be important in view of the fact that apparently the name of the force was not going to be changed—one of only two issues on which, I added, Whitelaw had made mistakes during his difficult eighteen months in the job, the other being his decision to meet the IRA in Chelsea a year earlier. Whitelaw said that he had got himself on a hook in relation to the IRA at too early a stage, adding that he would probably have been forced onto it later in any event. But had he changed the 'Ark of the Covenant' of the RUC name, he would immediately have been faced with three hundred resignations of his best policemen.

I took the opportunity to hand over a paper on policing and common law enforcement that I had brought with me, which set out various ideas we had worked out. While not proposing the placing of the Gardaí under the Council of Ireland, this nevertheless suggested several roles in policing for the Council.

The discussion then moved on to conditions in Long Kesh, sectarian murders, intimidation (which Whitelaw said was even worse in Protestant than in Catholic areas), and financing of the Council of Ireland, on which I said somewhat pointedly—echoing his reported comments to our journalists on the matter— that we did not regard the UK as a 'milch cow for the whole of Ireland'. When I raised once again the need to redress the balance in top civil service appointments, Whitelaw undertook to do what he could in respect of prestige or outside appointments. The senior British civil servant present intervened to say that my public references to the problem had slowed down reform. I ignored this gratuitous comment.

Meanwhile our preparations for the conference were continuing apace, with weekly discussions in the cabinet on memoranda submitted by me about the institutional structure and financing of the Council and on our approach to the delicate question of our acceptance of the status of Northern Ireland. These proposals envisaged a permanent core of Ministerial members on the Council with others attending when matters in their area of responsibility were discussed. Further evolution of the Council was to be subject to a double veto, at Ministerial and parliamentary level, which, it was felt, should be reassuring for the Unionists.

On financing I favoured an own-resources system similar to that of the EEC, with contributions levied at rates that would secure a balance between receipts and spending in the Republic, any shortfall on the Northern Ireland side to be made up as hitherto by the British government. As I mentioned earlier, we had already prepared a list of functions that we thought could be handled more efficiently by the Council of Ireland than by two separate administrations.

The whole structure as we had drawn it up was designed to respond in a balanced way to the different aspirations of nationalists and unionists. On the one hand it would be open-ended, with the capacity in principle to evolve towards an all-Ireland political institution, thus responding to the nationalist aspiration; on the other hand, both its initial functions and any extension of its role were to be subject to unionist agreement.

A week later, on 16 November, Cosgrave received a formal communication from Heath notifying us of the progress that had been made towards agreeing the shape of the proposed Northern Ireland Executive. It would have eleven members: six Unionists, four SDLP, and one Alliance, with Brian Faulkner as Chief Executive Member and Gerry Fitt as Deputy Chief Executive Member. The announcement on 19 November would reaffirm publicly British acceptance of a North-South Council of Ireland involving no British participation, with an advisory parliamentary tier in addition to a Ministerial Council, which would have some executive functions.

Heath also notified British acceptance of the idea of a common law enforcement area, which we had seen as a means of getting around the constitutional difficulties that had hitherto prevented the courts from endorsing extradition of 'political' offenders.

On the crucial question of which would come first, formation of the Executive or the tripartite conference to discuss the Council of Ireland, Heath said that it was absurd that with so much now agreed, success should be frustrated by an essentially procedural point, adding, however, that the British government was considering this and might be able to draw upon some of the ideas we had put forward at Baldonnell: in other words, Hugh McCann's compromise.

On 30 November I held my last meeting with Willie Whitelaw; immediately afterwards he was replaced by Francis Pym, thus depriving him, very harshly I thought, of the opportunity to attend the conference to which his efforts over twenty-one months had contributed so much. At our meeting he referred to the fact that Paisley had refused to attend the separate consultations offered to parties in Northern Ireland not participating in the Executive, and had therefore not been invited to Sunningdale. He had solid support in Parliament for not inviting Paisley to the conference, and he intended to stand firm. He added that there had been an idea of allowing him to attend, speak, and depart. I said that if it were felt necessary to have him there we would not stand in the way. In fact we had been quietly encouraging the idea of participation by anti-Faulkner Unionists with a view to mitigating their hostility to the proposed agreement.

There was a long discussion on the relationship between policing and the Council; we wanted the police authority to be appointed by the Council, but Whitelaw was doubtful at first about this, although by the end of the discussion he seemed to have come around to it.

Finally we discussed the proposed declaration by our Government on the status of Northern Ireland. Unionists, Whitelaw said, were expecting some further commitment by us. Aware that the formula I favoured had at that stage been watered down in Government, I avoided a direct reply and raised instead the question of a parallel declaration by Britain that if a majority of the people of Northern Ireland wished to join a united Ireland, the British government would support and facilitate such a decision. In response Whitelaw referred to something Ted Heath had said in his 1972 Mansion House speech about Britain not standing in the way of unity by consent. I countered with a reference to the much more positive wording of the 1920 Act giving Home Rule to Northern Ireland.

Whitelaw switched the discussion back to our proposed declaration, which, he said, could be the key to unlocking numerous doors and to encouraging Faulkner to favour an effective Council of Ireland. I batted the ball back, asking if Whitelaw had anything to add on a British declaration. He said he would look at this again; and on that note the last pre-Sunningdale Anglo-Irish encounter ended.

On the following Monday we met the SDLP to brief them on our final negotiating position, and two days later we were on our way to Sunningdale. At 3.30 p.m. on Wednesday 5 December I took off from Dublin Airport on the first of two flights carrying the forty-odd members of the Irish delegation to the conference, which was to start at 10.30 on the following morning and was provisionally planned to conclude at lunchtime on Saturday 8 December. In the event it overran its schedule by more than twenty-four hours.

Sunningdale Park in Berkshire is a civil service college. The conference itself was to take place in the principal block, Northcote House, and the participants—other than Liam Cosgrave, who was to stay at the Irish embassy, and the members of the British Cabinet—were accommodated in residences on the estate some five hundred yards away.

Northcote House, a 1930s mansion that we were told had been built by a newspaper baron for his mistress, is constructed around a mock 'great hall'. From the balcony that surrounds the hall at first-floor level and off which the offices of the Irish and British delegations were housed, the floor below was like a stage set; from our vantage point we could observe the entrances and exits of other participants, and speculate why, and concerning what, A was talking to B, or C sedulously avoiding D. The heavy armchairs were usually occupied by anonymous figures who never seemed to move and who were, we speculated, British civil servants attending in case—as never happened so far as I could see—some special problem should require their particular expertise. On couches around the fireplace sat—or in some instances lay—politicians awaiting their next call to action. In corners of the hall knotty problems were the subject of intense discussion amongst active participants. The impermanent air of this stage-set atmosphere lent a degree of unreality to our proceedings, which contrasted with the seriousness of the issues that we were tackling together.

The conference was a unique occasion. Never before had the political leaders of the British and Irish states and of the two communities in Northern Ireland been gathered together in one place. Some 120 people attended, including a dozen members of the Irish and British cabinets and a score of politicians representing the Ulster Unionist, Alliance and SDLP parties in Northern Ireland.

On Thursday morning we met a number of our colleagues at breakfast. I was with Brian Faulkner when Liam Cosgrave arrived and joined our table. They had already met in the hunting field, I gathered, and within minutes they were chatting away about mutual acquaintances. They were quickly on good terms, strolling around the grounds together during breaks in the meetings.

We still did not know what were to be the arrangements for chairing the sessions; we had proposed Gaston Thorn, Luxembourg's Foreign Minister, but the British had demurred at this, and we were not prepared for Liam Cosgrave to sit under the chairmanship of a British Secretary of State. It was not clear how much of the conference Ted Heath would be attending. In the event these two issues solved themselves and each other; the Prime Minister took the chair at the outset that morning, reasonably enough as the host, and it gradually became clear that he intended to be present at all plenary sessions. He presided over the initial meeting so successfully—and fairly—that the issue of chairmanship simply evaporated.

The extent of Ted Heath's commitment to the Sunningdale negotiation became clear several days later when the Italian Prime Minister of the day, Mariano

Rumor, paid an official visit to Britain, staying at Chequers. By that time our conference was overrunning its allotted timetable, but rather than abandon it at that point in order to meet his official guest he told his people at Chequers to give Rumor tea and send him for a siesta, subsequently making a hasty helicopter trip to Chequers to meet him during an interval between plenary sessions.

In his opening speech Ted Heath pointed out that the conference would have to determine its own agenda; our task was to prepare an agreed 'package' covering all the main issues before the parties came together in an Executive— a far cry from his position at Baldonnell less than three months earlier. The main issues, he said, were the structure of a North-South Council of Ireland, with participation by parliamentary representatives, which would take decisions by unanimity; law and order, including detention without trial; a common law enforcement area and extradition; policing, which must be by the RUC; and 'the vital issue of the territorial status of Northern Ireland'. The conclusions of the conference would be incorporated in a communiqué, and then, following appointment of the power-sharing Executive and devolution of powers to it, a formal conference would be held to ratify the agreements reached at Sunningdale.

Some matters were quickly agreed. Ministerial Council decisions were to be unanimous; extension of the Council's functions was to be determined by a majority vote in the Council Assembly; the Council was to have an independent Secretariat headed by a Secretary-General; there was to be equal representation of both parts of the island in the consultative Assembly (a significant concession by us in the light of the two-to-one population ratio in the Republic's favour); and the Ministerial Council was to consist of five members each from North and South.

Unfortunately, due to a misunderstanding, the provisional agreement reached on the last point was conveyed to journalists that evening by our Government press officer, Muiris Mac Conghail. This was quite contrary to the decision of the conference that all agreements were tentative until a whole 'package' had been worked out and that accordingly nothing should be conveyed to the press until the conference had concluded. All hell broke out the following morning when this 'leak' became known; confidence amongst the participants was shaken, and the agreement on the composition of the Ministerial Council was formally withdrawn, throwing this issue—itself of relatively little intrinsic importance—back into the melting-pot.

Meanwhile, on the functions of the Council it was agreed that in addition to harmonising laws between North and South, as proposed by Paddy Devlin, the Council would from the beginning have certain executive functions in sectors where there was at present North-South duplication, such as tourist promotion, electricity generation, and agricultural and industrial research. I was one of those who pressed this matter, and when a working group was formed to list the executive functions that should be devolved to the Council I was appointed the 'lead' member on behalf of the Irish Government.

Both Faulkner and the Alliance leader, Oliver Napier, stressed the need to settle the status issue as a precondition to establishing the Council of Ireland. Faulkner raised the question of amending the Irish Constitution to delete articles 2 and 3 with their reference to the whole island as 'the national territory'. Conor Cruise O'Brien responded that a simple proposal to delete them would certainly be rejected by the people in the referendum that would have to be held to alter the Constitution; the Irish Government should not be pushed on the issue, he said. Faulkner recognised the difficulties but wanted an acknowledgement by the Republic of the right of the people of Northern Ireland to order their own affairs and to remain part of the United Kingdom as long as a majority of them so wished. Another working group was therefore set up to draft reciprocal declarations that would be made by the two governments.

On law and order, Declan Costello explained our concept of a common law enforcement area comprising the whole island, with a court consisting of an equal number of judges from North and South to be appointed by the Council of Ireland. This court would try persons accused of scheduled offences in the jurisdiction where they were arrested. The Government had approved this proposal as a means of circumventing the difficulties created by our High Court, which had rejected extradition for 'political offences' on constitutional grounds. The court's judgement had seemed to us so conclusive that we had decided against an appeal to the Supreme Court. This may seem surprising in view of the interpretation of a 'political offence' arrived at by the Supreme Court in 1982, but I have to say that I still doubt that an appeal would have succeeded in 1973: changes in the composition of the Supreme Court in the intervening years may well have shifted the balance on the question from what I would now judge to have been a somewhat theoretical 'liberal' stance to one concerned more with the practical matter of protecting people on the island of Ireland from violence, just as later, in 1990, the balance seemed to shift at least momentarily back towards the libertarian line.

Be that as it may, our acceptance of the High Court judgement, which determined the attitude of successive Irish Governments for years thereafter, was certainly not motivated by any political consideration on our part. If our courts had been able to extradite to Northern Ireland on the basis of fair criteria we would have had no qualms about this, and would have had no problem about ignoring the inevitable protests from IRA sympathisers.

Given what appeared to us to be the impossibility of adopting proposals on extradition, and given the seemingly favourable reaction to our suggestion of a common law enforcement area when mentioned to the British government before the conference, we found the negative attitude of the Alliance Party and the British Attorney General, Sir Peter Rawlinson, on these issues hard to take. Between them they raised endless obstacles to our proposal, which we were then convinced could resolve once and for all this problem of fugitive offenders. They sought instead a way out by suggesting changes to the extradition law that, on the basis of the decision against us in the High Court, were quite impracticable. If the Unionists had been the objectors we would have had sympathy with them in view of their evident political need for clear progress on the issue. The less vulnerable political position of the Alliance Party, however, and what looked to us like a deliberate unwillingness on the part of Rawlinson to understand the constitutional issues involved, ensured that the objections we faced from these quarters were badly received on our side. The discussion ended for the time being when I referred to the problems posed by our written Constitution, of the provisions of which Rawlinson had shown no sign that he was aware. Ted Heath then said that the problem should be tackled by a legal advisory panel, but warned against overoptimism about the time-scale for implementing any decision, which on their side, he said, would probably take a minimum of nine months to get through Westminster.

We moved on to the issue of policing. The Minister for Justice, Pat Cooney, elaborated on our idea of police authorities functioning in each part of the country under the Council of Ireland. If the Council were to be given responsibility for the two police authorities, he added, it would have to be an effective decision-making body, or else safeguards would be needed to ensure effective policing in the event of deadlock. This somewhat negative formulation may have reflected his own and his department's reticence about the proposals he had been mandated to put forward; the police authority for the Republic agreed at Sunningdale was to prove slow in taking shape during the early months of 1974, and despite my protests at the time it was dropped by the Department of Justice with alacrity after the effective disappearance of the Council of Ireland concept following the Ulster workers' strike.

Brian Faulkner was quick to turn this argument around; since the Ministerial Council had to be unanimous, he contended, the police would be placed in an impossible position if the police authorities were subject to it and if it failed to achieve unanimity. He went on to emphasise that the power of a government depended on its ability to provide policing; if the Council had power to hire and fire the police authorities, and to call for reports from them, would this not derogate from an essential power of government? Roy Bradford added that if the police seemed to be controlled from the Republic their acceptability in Belfast might be reduced rather than enhanced. The SDLP representatives, on the other hand, spoke of their concern to secure identification of the people with the police as a prerequisite to freedom from violence, adding that in the absence of a change in the name 'RUC' this could be done only by linking the police with the Council of Ireland. Policing, in the end, was also referred to a working group of the conference.

The arrangements for participation in the various working groups had been left vague; it seemed to be expected that mine, on the executive functions of the Council, would comprise representatives of the Irish Government and the Unionists only. I was unhappy about this, and after dinner I tried but failed to make contact with Paddy Devlin, who I understood to be the SDLP representative concerned with executive functions. The British government had not nominated anyone to this working group. I suggested to Ken Bloomfield, the former Assistant Secretary to the Stormont government, who was currently listed on the strength of the Northern Ireland Office, that he should attend on behalf of the British government, which, with some amusement at the role I was thrusting upon him, he accepted.

Next morning I made further fruitless efforts to contact Paddy Devlin, both before and after breakfast. Eventually, shortly after ten o'clock, our group assembled without SDLP representation. We made rapid progress, reaching agreement on a significant list of matters suitable for executive action by the Council of Ireland. Then the door opened suddenly and Paddy Devlin appeared. What were we doing, meeting in the absence of the SDLP? he demanded. I explained that I had repeatedly tried to contact him about the meeting. What had we agreed? With some pride I showed him the list of functions that might be devolved to the Council. 'Out of the question,' he asserted after a quick glance at the piece of paper on which I had noted the results of our meeting. He was not going to have his friends—gesturing towards the somewhat bemused Unionists—hung from lamp-posts on their return to Belfast, as they assuredly would be if the list of executive functions we had agreed were published. And he attacked the list vigorously—combining some items and eliminating others—so that it was reduced to half its original length. Further compression at a later stage reduced the resultant thirteen items to the eight that finally appeared in the Sunningdale communiqué.

By the time we met again briefly in plenary session at 6.00 p.m. that Friday evening a more or less agreed draft was available, which covered a large part of the areas under consideration. However, among the matters still to be agreed at that point were the 'status' declarations by the two governments, the financing of the Council, human rights, and policing. The common law enforcement area and extradition were also outstanding, with the British Attorney General still referring to the proposed new all-Ireland tribunal as 'that botched-up court', the work of which, he insisted, could best be done by the existing 'local' courts. The Alliance Party were continuing to support him, with less strong backing from the Unionists.

Meanwhile the declarations on the status of Northern Ireland still posed a possible constitutional problem for us, because in the draft text the British declaration preceded ours, and this statement could thus be held legally to govern the meaning of the word 'status' in our declaration, thus putting at risk the constitutionality of the agreement in our state. An attempt to resolve this by reversing the order of the British and Irish declarations failed in the face of Unionist opposition. The dilemma was resolved, however, during Friday night. Some time after 2 a.m. I dropped in to the office used by Francis Pym, a couple of doors along the gallery from our Ministerial office, for a chat with a couple of senior Northern Ireland Office officials who were using it at the time. I assumed Pym was in bed, but at one stage his head popped around the door. Seeing us he immediately said 'Sorry,' and withdrew—which, considering we were sitting in *his* office, was distinctly odd. The officials seemed quite unmoved by this incident, however. (It should perhaps be added that, because of his very recent appointment and unfamiliarity with the issues, Pym was like a fish out of water at Sunningdale, tending to buttonhole other participants to ask anxiously: 'What's happening?')

My conversation with the British officials turned to the deadlock over the presentation of the 'status' declarations. Suddenly I had a brainwave. 'Why not put them side by side?' I exclaimed, and I added, humorously employing schoolboy slang, 'Bags the left-hand side,' in other words the prime position reading from left to right, which should avoid any suggestion of the British interpretation of 'status' governing its meaning in the Irish declaration. They agreed.

Argument continued on the financing document, the common law enforcement proposal, human rights, and the relationship between policing and the Council of Ireland. By 11.15 p.m. agreement had been reached on the text dealing with the financing of the Council; Patrick Jenkin, Financial Secretary to the Treasury, had arrived during the evening and had overruled his officials' objections to some aspects of the proposals.

Progress was also reported at this stage on other matters—except for policing, which by this time was emerging as the principal obstacle to agreement. Work was to continue during the night, although policing was left until 9.15 the following (Saturday) morning, in the hope that single-minded concentration after a night's sleep would enable those concerned to make a breakthrough in time to conclude the conference by lunch that day, as originally planned. Some felt that such an on-time conclusion was important because of the tense security situation in Northern Ireland; others urged that our decisions not be rushed, lest failure to achieve a properly worked-out agreement should eventually precipitate further violence.

Next morning the Irish delegation reviewed the position at 10 a.m. We were told that agreement had effectively been reached during the night on a text covering extradition and common law enforcement but that the Alliance Party had 'reneged' on it. Final agreement seemed likely on the manner of presenting the 'status' declarations. But there was no progress to report on policing or human rights. We met again at 11.30. Extradition remained a problem, but Declan Costello hoped that a technical proposal of his that would enable trials for murders in Northern Ireland to take place in the Republic without the need for prior legislation might break the deadlock: he had discovered a provision in a United Kingdom Act of 1861, still valid in our state, that would make it possible to introduce such a procedure by order rather than by an Act.

The issue of policing seemed irretrievably stuck, however, with the SDLP requiring a major role for the Council, the Unionists resisting it and demanding transfer of policing to the power-sharing Executive, and the British refusing to contemplate transfer of control either to the Executive or to the Council.

At 1.30 the SDLP delegation came to see us about the deadlock. John Hume's strongly held view was that if the SDLP could not support policing wholeheartedly they should not be in government at all, and that the political reality was that they could support it only by having the police associated with the Council. I agreed with him.

During the afternoon, as we awaited developments, we watched racing on television, Liam Cosgrave and Pat Cooney being racing enthusiasts. The rest of us were amused to see the expression on Cosgrave's face when, in the middle of a race, he was told that Heath was anxious to have a word with him. I think, but cannot be certain, that he watched the end of the race before responding to this request.

At six o'clock the working group on policing broke up to consult their principals. Unless the Executive had real policing powers, Faulkner believed he would not be able to 'sell' the overall agreement to unionist opinion. The SDLP saw no way of overcoming nationalist alienation from the police unless the RUC were seen in some way to be responsible to the Council of Ireland, in which the Government of the Republic would have a key role. The British government, while failing then as later to appreciate the overwhelming psychological importance of securing moral authority for the police in the eyes of the nationalist community, absolutely refused to repeat what they privately saw as the fatal error of putting security control into the hands of a provincial assembly. These differences were to delay the conclusion of the Sunningdale conference by some thirty hours.

*Our* position on policing was clear. Despite qualms in some quarters, a Government decision favouring in principle 'a common form of policing for the island' had been made during the preparations for the conference, and this had been communicated to the British government. This evolution of the Irish stance had followed the fatal British decision to retain the name 'RUC' and not to make changes at the top of that force—measures that alone, in our view, could have made it an acceptable Northern Ireland police force so far as the nationalist minority was concerned and thus have secured an early defeat of the IRA before they struck deeper roots in that community. Once the British government had adopted its position on this issue, we believed that only some kind of common policing for the island as a whole, involving the RUC and the Gardaí, could achieve this objective, although the proposal for such a common system was put forward with deep reluctance by many on our side in view of the dangers to the security of our own state that our involvement in such an arrangement might entail.

The British government's reaction to this had been conclusively negative, however. They had seen no possibility of committing themselves to the creation at any time in the future of a common form of policing for the whole of Ireland. The most we could hope for at this conference, therefore, as a way of securing nationalist acceptance of policing in Northern Ireland was an arrangement under which police authorities, North and South, would both be responsible to an effective Council of Ireland. We therefore supported the SDLP position, leaving it to them, however, to determine what variations in an arrangement of this kind could be agreed without endangering the impact of such a limited link on the acceptability of the RUC in nationalist areas.

I should add that our policy on policing, which subsequent events seem to me to have validated, took full account of the fact that by mid-1973 the RUC was a substantially reformed force. The majority of its members—although, as would later transpire, not all—have since that time been dedicated and professional policemen. Our concern was with the limited but vitally important additional steps that needed to be taken if policing was to command the assent of the whole community and thus bring about the defeat of the IRA. We were in no way unaware of the traumatic effects that changes in the name and senior personnel of the force would have had on the unionist community. But whereas the British saw these effects as an absolute impediment to making further changes, we believed that the importance of defeating the IRA transcended all other considerations, and saw clearly, as British governments have always had difficulty in seeing, that the key to this lay in the achievement of acceptable policing, whatever the risks.

During the coffee and tea breaks Ted Heath would stand beside the refreshment area, sometimes alone, his status and his shyness combining to leave him somewhat isolated. Once or twice I had taken the opportunity to go over to him and exchange a few words. Now I decided to use the opportunity of a tea break to test his sentiment on this crucial issue. I found him implacably opposed to any devolution of authority over security. Without ever referring to the massacre in Derry in January 1972 or to any other specific incident, he made it clear that neither he nor Parliament would be prepared to agree to such a devolution of security functions, involving ultimately, as in his view it must, de facto local control once again of the back-up role of the British army. It seemed to me as I talked to him that there should nevertheless be room here for some kind of compromise, at least in relation to normal policing as distinct from security. But he showed no willingness to make a distinction of this kind on any of several occasions when I took it up with him informally.

In the face of this deadlock it was decided that the best that could be done before Saturday drew to a close was to hold a plenary session to consolidate the agreement that had by that time been reached on the remaining issues, in the hope that this would concentrate the minds of those involved in these policing discussions and give them an added incentive to reach agreement on some compromise later in the night. This plenary meeting concluded at 11.20 p.m.

A prolonged confrontation between Ted Heath, Brian Faulkner and John Hume (who had effectively taken over the leadership of the SDLP delegation, at any rate on this issue) then began in Ted Heath's room, diagonally across the well of the great hall from our delegation office. We stood by, awaiting a signal that would require us to consider, and hopefully agree, a compromise on this vital question. We believed that any solution to this problem to which John Hume could agree would be acceptable to us, for this was essentially an internal Northern Ireland matter, albeit one with obvious direct implications for the British government as the sovereign power, and some potential implications for us also.

As the night wore on, the scene in the hall below provided us with some entertainment. Politicians and officials sat or lay around in varying degrees of somnolence. Gerry Fitt was unambiguously asleep on a couch; indeed, I seem to recall him performing the impressively athletic feat of sleeping perched along the top edge of a couch, but my memory of this may have been enhanced by time. We judged that one British civil servant, equally fast asleep in a huge leather armchair, would gradually slip forward until he would eventually be lying flat on the carpet in front of the chair, and we took bets among ourselves on the time at which this logical outcome would be achieved; I think the final stage was accomplished around 4 a.m.

Much of the time was spent, of course, in our delegation office sitting around the fire with the Assistant Government Secretary, Dermot Nally, behind us. At about 4 a.m. he asked us if we would like to play a game. He distributed pieces of paper and told us to give marks to each of the two governments, to the Unionists and to the SDLP on the basis of what each had secured from the conference so far under the main headings: Council of Ireland functions, law enforcement, human rights, and so on. The Alliance Party were omitted, I think on the basis that they had a less demanding constituency to satisfy than any of the other four delegations. The marks were then given to me to add up: I could identify only Conor Cruise O'Brien's writing as well as my own. Out of, I think, a possible 3,200 marks, it was our collective judgement that the UK government had thus far secured 1,835, the Irish Government 1,755, the SDLP 1,580, and the Unionists only 1,205. The game achieved its purpose by identifying which delegation most needed to gain something from the issue of policing, still to be settled. Reflecting his consistent view, Conor had given the Unionists a much lower mark for achievement than any other delegation, and only one amongst us had given them anything other than the lowest, or joint lowest, mark.

It was against this background that we received a very agitated SDLP delegation of John Hume and Austin Currie just before 6 a.m. They said that the Unionists had decided to wreck the conference by demands that were in contravention of the Constitution Act. We were all, they said, in real trouble, all the more so because the Unionists, who late the previous night had raised difficulties on sabbatarian grounds about continuing beyond midnight on Saturday night, were now saying that an adjourned session could not resume before 12.15 a.m. on Monday morning! I asked a Scottish Presbyterian Counsellor from the Foreign Office when in his view the Sabbath began; his reply, although humorous in intent, to the effect that it began when one got up after going to bed, boded ill for an early resumption if we adjourned, as was now absolutely necessary in view of the evident exhaustion of so many of the key participants. I was downstairs in the SDLP room discussing this dilemma when Peter McLachlan, at that stage a Unionist adviser, came in. 'We're meeting again at two,' he said. '2 a.m.?' I asked—meaning on Monday morning. 'No,' he said, '2 p.m.' We breathed a collective sigh of relief, and at about 8.30 a.m. we went to bed for four hours or so.

When I woke at about 12.30 p.m. my mind was as clear as it had been fogged when I had retired earlier. No doubt I had been reflecting subconsciously in my sleep on the result of our 'game' in the middle of the night. I dressed, walked back to Northcote House, found a typewriter, and hammered out the following:

Put emotion on one side.

Who should give in a negotiation of this kind when it is at the crunch? The parties who have gained most to the parties who have gained least. On any objective assessment the Irish Government and the SDLP have gained most and the Unionists least.

Which direction should give in in any negotiation at the crunch? By *adding* something to the package that will help a party rather than by taking something away that will damage another.

Who will have best balance, e.g., gain/loss, from a breakdown at this point? The Unionists, who will avoid the immediate and terrible political risks of being destroyed.

What type of concession is most likely to reduce violence post-talks? One to the Unionists, which could reduce danger of loyalist violence—and above all save Catholic lives.

What is involved in a concession to the Unionists? Merely putting into words what all are agreed would and should happen eventually—devolution of power over normal policing back to Executive.

To this I appended a possible draft statement on policing, which I felt could provide a basis for compromise:

The British government envisages that, without prejudice to the question of security, control of normal policing should in due course be vested in the new Executive. This is not possible at the present time. When security conditions permit, and when such a course of action would no longer create a danger of political instability within the system of government of Northern Ireland, it is, therefore, the intention of the British government to transfer normal police powers to the Executive. The position in this respect will be reviewed in six months' time and annually thereafter.

This done, I watched for Paddy Devlin along the path from the residences. As he approached the hall door I swung it open and said, 'Paddy, I want you to read this.' 'Come down to our room,' he replied. I did so. He read my analysis and my draft, and said, 'Right, I'll try to persuade John.'

The Heath-Faulkner-Hume session resumed at 3 p.m. I was on the gallery near Ted Heath's room when the door opened two hours later and John emerged, smiling, followed by Brian Faulkner and Ted Heath, also smiling. As John passed me he said something like 'We've settled,' and gave the thumbs-up sign to those on the floor below. There was a cheer. I slipped into a delegation room and rang Joan. She was thus the first outside Sunningdale to know that we had reached agreement, although my emotion was such that I had difficulty in telling her the news.

What had finally been agreed on policing was this. On the one hand the British government grudgingly agreed to meet Brian Faulkner's requirement by conceding that 'as soon as the security problems were resolved and the new institutions were seen to be working effectively, they would wish to discuss the devolution of responsibility for normal policing and how this might be achieved with the Northern Ireland Executive and the Police.'

On the other hand an attempt was made to meet the SDLP's requirements by providing that the two governments would co-operate 'under the auspices of the Council of Ireland' through their respective police authorities. The members of the police authority in the Republic were to be appointed by the Irish Government after consultation with the Ministerial Council of the Council of Ireland, and appointments of the members of the Northern Ireland Police Authority were to be made by the British government after consultation with the Northern Ireland power-sharing Executive, which, in turn, would consult the Ministerial Council of the Council of Ireland.

It was thin enough as a means of securing the loyalty of the minority to the police, but it was the most that could be extracted from a very reluctant British government, and the most that SDLP and Unionists could concede to each other. From the SDLP's point of view it was a far cry from the proposal in the draft that had been under consideration as recently as Thursday afternoon. That draft had included tentative provision for a Standing Joint Police Authorities Committee with equal membership from both authorities. This joint standing committee would have been constituted under the aegis of the Council of Ireland and would have reported to the Ministerial Council on all matters within the purview of the two authorities, one-third of the membership of each of which was to have been appointed by the relevant government on the nomination of the Council of Ireland.

It took some time to put the text of the agreement, including the new policing clauses, into a shape appropriate for signature, but at 8.20 our delegation met and formally endorsed it. Five minutes later the final plenary session took place to hear concluding statements, after which the agreement was signed. There followed our farewells to fellow-participants, which were quite emotional;

then the press conferences and the flight home. The mood on the aircraft was euphoric, as it also was at Dublin Airport.

There was nothing inevitable about the collapse six months later of the carefully constructed edifice of which Sunningdale was intended to be the copingstone. Nevertheless, it is fair to reflect on whether this collapse might have been more readily avoided if the outcome of Sunningdale had been somewhat different.

Two reflections occur to me at this remove.

First, the issue that held up for thirty hours the conclusion of the conference proved almost irrelevant to the outcome. The agreement on policing that Brian Faulkner had eventually extracted from Ted Heath and John Hume, and to which I had endeavoured towards the end to contribute, never seemed to feature in the heated debates within Unionism that followed Sunningdale, nor did it do so in the discussion of the agreement within the nationalist camp. Both sides at the conference seem to have exaggerated the importance of the formulae for policing that they put forward, although I think the SDLP at least would argue that a stronger commitment on the role of the Council of Ireland might have helped to weaken the IRA in the post-Sunningdale period. For my own part I still wonder whether even in the stronger form envisaged by the SDLP, involvement in policing by the Council could have had enough impact on the ground to secure full acceptability of the police in nationalist areas.

Second, in retrospect I believe that all of us—Brian Faulkner included—underestimated the significance of the status issue. We, the Irish Government representatives, were handicapped by our concern lest any formulation we agreed be struck down as unconstitutional by our courts. And the constitutional action taken by former Minister Kevin Boland against the agreement after its signature, together with the terms of the judgements in the High Court and Supreme Court dismissing that action, show that we were right to be so concerned.

It is true that, once this action had been finally disposed of three months later, we felt able in the light of the terms of the Supreme Court judgement to improve on Sunningdale by stating the factual position of Northern Ireland as being 'within the United Kingdom'. We were able to declare at that point that 'the Government accepts this and solemnly reaffirms that the factual position of Northern Ireland within the United Kingdom cannot be changed except by a decision of a majority of the people of Northern Ireland.' At the time some said that had we felt able to state our stance in these terms at Sunningdale, Faulkner's post-Sunningdale position would have been strengthened, and I am sure this is true, although whether, as has also been suggested, he would have been able on this basis to overcome hard-line Unionist opposition to the agreement appears to me to be more arguable. Certainly there was little evidence that our eventual 'clarification' made any great impact when we finally felt able to produce it without prejudice to a successful outcome to the Boland case.

In the light of events at that time, as well as after the later Anglo-Irish Agreement, I believe that the sting will not be taken out of Unionist hostility to any North-South arrangement, however modest, until and unless circumstances arise that make possible a reformulation of articles 2 and 3 of the Constitution along lines that would substitute for the controversial concept of the whole island being the 'national territory' an aspiration to political unity of the people of the whole island to be achieved with the free consent of a majority of the people of Northern Ireland.

At the time we ruled out, with no serious discussion that I recall, the possibility of amending the Constitution along these lines in the immediate aftermath of Sunningdale. Should we have given such a move more serious consideration? There is a case to answer. Sunningdale—like the Anglo-Irish Agreement twelve years later—proved much more popular with public opinion in the Republic than those of us in Government had foreseen. This may have reflected the fact that Fine Gael and Labour tend for historical reasons to feel more vulnerable than they need on the 'national issue' and therefore tend to underestimate the potential groundswell in the aftermath of successful negotiations in favour of 'moderate' stances on Northern Ireland—especially stances that offer a prospect of reducing or ending violence there.

Certainly the chances of successfully launching a campaign to amend the relevant articles of the Constitution were better in December 1973 than we had believed possible before Sunningdale. A moderate nationalist supporter of Fianna Fáil who was deeply concerned about Northern Ireland, and who was also quite close to Jack Lynch, reminded me years later that even *before* Sunningdale he had told me that we should 'go for' a constitutional referendum immediately after the conference, and had given it as his view then that Fianna Fáil would not have opposed the move; but the Fianna Fáil reaction in the Dáil when the agreement came to be discussed did not suggest that there would have been much chance of that.

So much for that side of the argument. On the other side it has to be said that the stakes were very high. If we had tried and failed to amend articles 2 and 3, we would thereby have destroyed the Sunningdale settlement, which the British government, the three Northern Ireland parties that were proposing to participate in the power-sharing Executive and we ourselves had done so much to achieve. It must be recalled, moreover, that while it may well be the case that Jack Lynch would have *wished* to facilitate such a constitutional move, his position in his party was not then such as to give us confidence that his viewpoint would carry the day. His victory over more extreme elements in Fianna Fáil three-and-a-half years earlier, when the Arms Crisis had broken, had been as much a matter of luck as anything else. Charles Haughey was still within the fold, smarting from his removal from office in May 1973 and beginning already to build up the grass-roots support that enabled him to succeed Lynch as leader six years later. Finally, Lynch had lost a general election only ten months earlier and was correspondingly vulnerable—all the more so since the embarrassment of the Littlejohn affair.

Against this background a decision to propose a constitutional amendment immediately after Sunningdale could easily have had the effect of destroying the consensus between Government and opposition on the agreement itself, a consensus that we rightly believed Jack Lynch to be anxious to establish, and it might indeed have brought him down and replaced him with someone else who, whatever his own convictions, would have been likely in the circumstances to have been a prisoner of extreme elements in his own party. In other words, a constitutional referendum in the aftermath of Sunningdale carried with it a risk not alone of destroying the agreement but of undermining the consensus within our democratic system, upon which at that time—less than two years after the riots that had accompanied and led to the burning of the British embassy—the peace of our own state arguably depended.

And to what purpose? As a gamble to consolidate the achievement of a power-sharing arrangement in Northern Ireland that we then felt was likely to succeed without further intervention on our part.

I recite the two sides of the argument on the issue in order to place events in their historical perspective, lest my own feeling, with hindsight, that it might have been worth attempting the gamble of a constitutional referendum on articles 2 and 3 be given undue weight.

# CHAPTER NINE

# ULSTER WORKERS
# WILL FIGHT

On the Tuesday after our return from Sunningdale Richie Ryan instructed his officials to contact the Minister for Finance in Belfast with a view to proceeding immediately with studies not merely of the financing of the Council of Ireland, which was within his sphere of responsibility, but also of the executive functions of the Council, which was not. My department was told of this but was not invited to a joint meeting on this initiative between the Departments of Finance and the Public Service, following which meetings were arranged by these two departments later that day with other 'line' departments. The Northern Ireland Ministry of Finance was then phoned in order to initiate discussions.

The next we in the Department of Foreign Affairs knew was a message on the following day to the effect that a meeting had been arranged for Tuesday 18 December, to discuss four 'priority functions' proposed by the Secretary of the Department of Finance. Our department immediately protested at this attempt by the Department of Finance to secure in collaboration with 'minimalist' Northern Ireland civil servants what they had attempted but failed to achieve in conjunction with other departments during the discussions in the Interdepartmental Unit before Sunningdale, namely a narrowing down of the potential role of the Council of Ireland. The Finance answer was that this priority list to be discussed with the Northern Ireland civil servants had been agreed at the previous day's meeting—from which our department had been carefully excluded.

In view of the fact that the responsibility for dealing with the functions of the Council had been allocated by the Government to the Departments of Foreign Affairs and the Public Service, with the Department of Finance having only a consultative role in these matters, this was a quite extraordinary performance.

This was a small problem, however, compared with the difficulties that Brian Faulkner faced following his return from Sunningdale; difficulties that were seriously aggravated by several developments on our side of the border.

The first of these developments passed almost unnoticed at the time in the Republic, but had a considerable impact in Northern Ireland. It was an answer that Liam Cosgrave gave to a question on Irish unity in an interview with the *Sunday Press* of 16 December, when he had said: 'There is no question of changing our Constitution with regard to our claim of sovereignty over all of Ireland.' Ian Paisley and Austin Ardill quoted this in the Assembly debate of 19 December as evidence that the Irish Government's solemn declaration in the agreement on the status of Northern Ireland was worthless, using this to rally unionist opinion against Faulkner.

The second event, with serious implications in turning unionist opinion against the agreement, was the announcement by Kevin Boland—the former Fianna Fáil Minister who had resigned from Jack Lynch's Government in May 1970 in protest against the sacking of Neil Blaney and Charles Haughey—that he was initiating an action to have the agreement declared unconstitutional.

This had two damaging effects. First, from the moment the action was initiated we felt inhibited by the sub judice rule from defending the agreement against unionist attacks by pointing to, and elaborating on, our declaration that the status of Northern Ireland could be changed only with the consent of a majority in the area.

But worse was to come, namely our actual defence to the action, which was submitted on 2 January. The lawyers advised that if we were to ensure that the carefully drafted 'status' formula in the agreement would stand up to the constitutional scrutiny to which it would now be subjected, we must be able to deny and disprove *all* the claims made by Boland. This involved being able to deny that the two declarations by the Irish and British governments were part of an intergovernmental *agreement*, or that our declaration acknowledged that Northern Ireland was part of the United Kingdom, or that it purported to limit the national territory to a portion of the island of Ireland. We also had to deny that it purported to prejudice the right of the Irish parliament and Government to exercise jurisdiction over the whole of the national territory, or to preclude the courts set up under the Constitution from exercising jurisdiction over the whole island of Ireland. And we had to be able to assert that our declaration at the conference merely enunciated the *policy* of the Irish Government as to the manner in which a united Ireland could come about.

Legally we had an impeccable defence—and it succeeded. Politically, in its impact on unionist opinion, it was totally disastrous. The subtle legal arguments used to defend the agreement were not merely lost on unionists: they totally destroyed the value of the declaration, undermining Faulkner's already shaky position and leaving a legacy of distrust that contributed to, without being in any way the prime cause of, unionist rejection of the Anglo-Irish Agreement twelve years later. If when we had been preparing for Sunningdale we had realised fully what our careful drafting of the 'status' declaration implied from the point of view of a defence against constitutional challenge we might perhaps have given more serious consideration to a constitutional referendum.

Finally, a shortsighted attempt on our part to help to consolidate the new Executive by arresting a substantial number of IRA suspects backfired badly when the great majority had to be released shortly afterwards because charges against them could not be sustained. On the positive side, however, the Attorney General's idea of making murder an extraterritorial offence under the terms of an 1861 Act was given effect by an order made by the Government on 20 December. Thereafter a murder in Northern Ireland was a crime amenable to courts in our state.

On 5 January Dermot Nally was told on the phone by Brian Faulkner that the situation he now faced was such that he must ask that no North-South meetings of Ministers take place for the time being, and that he could not for the moment meet Liam Cosgrave, as had been envisaged. Faulkner had had to resign from the leadership of the Ulster Unionist Party following the previous day's meeting of the 820-member Unionist Council called by his opponents. At that meeting he and the Sunningdale settlement were rejected by a margin of fifty-three votes, the hostile majority including all of the Orange Order, who voted *en bloc*. He later told Cosgrave that he believed he could have won if he had had a further month in which to 'sell' the settlement to the Unionist Party. All the party staff, save one typist, stayed with him, and at that point he retained the support of half of the most senior members of the party and half of the Unionist Associations. He could rely on at least eighteen Assembly members of the party, also about half of the total. At that stage the division in the party was in fact a very even one at all levels.

A meeting between Cosgrave and Faulkner took place at Baldonnell military airport on 16 January. Faulkner made no bones about why an initially favourable reaction amongst unionists—to the tune of 60 per cent or more, he believed—had turned sour so quickly: he cited Liam Cosgrave's *Sunday Press* interview, the Boland case, our statement of defence in this suit, and finally the release of the great bulk of the IRA suspects we had arrested. He said that he now had no credibility at all in his community and that unless the question of the status of Northern Ireland was satisfactorily cleared up and 'firm action' taken on terrorism it would be politically impossible for him to attend a second formal stage of the Sunningdale conference and for the Executive to have much of a future.

Cosgrave explained in reply the rationale of our defence to the Boland action—which was in fact decided in our favour in the High Court while their meeting was going on. It seemed fairly clear that Faulkner had not understood the nature of our defence, and the meeting was useful in that the clarification satisfied him, although I doubt whether he felt able to convey all the legal subtleties of our position to other Unionists after his return to the North. Cosgrave went on to give details of the recently announced expansion of the

Garda force and of the record of convictions of IRA suspects by the Special Criminal Court. Faulkner was sufficiently reassured by all this to give the go-ahead for the delayed meeting of Ministers, which it was agreed would take place before 6 February.

On the following day I met Francis Pym in London; this was my only bilateral meeting with him during his brief tenure of the post of Northern Ireland Secretary. Faulkner had already told him that he had been very pleased with the previous day's Cosgrave meeting. I urged on him the importance of not delaying unduly the formal second-stage Sunningdale conference, because it was vital that the people of Northern Ireland should see the agreement working before a referendum that it was proposed to hold in the North that summer.

I then raised the question of a cessation of the forcible feeding of the Price sisters, who were on hunger-strike; Pym said he would raise this with the Home Secretary. I also took up with him the increasing harassment of the nationalist population in west Belfast by British troops, as well as the recrudescence of an unacceptable form of interrogation of suspects in two RUC stations. We were seeking assurances that these interrogation methods would be abandoned, that uniformed RUC men with identifiable numbers be present at future interrogations, and that detailed rosters be kept of soldiers on duty on these occasions. I also raised the question of the release of detainees.

At the end of the meeting we returned again to political issues. The performance of the Executive during its first couple of weeks had been impressive, and Pym paid tribute to the sense of responsibility of the SDLP members; they had refused to be provoked by the speeches of some Unionist Executive members who were behaving 'nervously'.

A meeting in London on the same day with Merlyn Rees, the Labour spokesman on Northern Ireland, who within seven weeks was to be Northern Ireland Secretary, yielded little of interest apart from his expression of dissatisfaction with the Tory government's failure to tackle the UDA and other extreme loyalists—an aspect of government policy at which he said Labour would wish to take a very close look if an early election brought them back to power. I was to recall this remark with a sense of irony four months later when Rees and his government so spectacularly failed to tackle the extreme loyalists who organised the Ulster workers' strike.

An interministerial meeting took place at Hillsborough on 1 February. We arrived by helicopter, as I was to do again a dozen years later for the signature of the Anglo-Irish Agreement. We 'fielded' our Sunningdale team: the Taoiseach, Tánaiste, myself, and four other Ministers, as well as the Attorney General. Their team was led by Brian Faulkner and Gerry Fitt, and included also the Alliance leader, Oliver Napier; two other Unionists; and two other SDLP Ministers, John Hume and Paddy Devlin.

Faulkner's opening statement contained no surprises. He himself was convinced about the value of the Council of Ireland, but it would not work or last without majority unionist support, and this required an unambiguous public affirmation by the Taoiseach of the right of the people of Northern Ireland to self-determination, the implementation of the forthcoming recommendations of the Common Law Enforcement Commission, and satisfactory security co-operation.

Cosgrave went over the ground of our legal defence against the Boland action again and explained our problem about making any further statement until the judicial process was exhausted; Boland had another eight days in which to lodge an appeal to the Supreme Court. He rejected the idea that the second-stage formal conference had to await the report of the Common Law Enforcement Commission. The Sunningdale communiqué had made the position on this quite clear. I pointed out that the delays in this matter were not of our making; we had put forward our proposals for a common law enforcement area in November, hoping this concept could be adopted at Sunningdale, but the British Attorney General had unfortunately insisted that the idea be referred to a commission, thus causing a delay of many months. A long argument ensued during which Conor Cruise O'Brien said that by agreeing to give the unambiguous assurance on the status of Northern Ireland that the Unionists were demanding we were already putting our political necks on the line and that the difficulties thus created would be aggravated unless there was visible progress on the Council of Ireland. We had to ensure that in facilitating the Unionists we did not erode our own support, he added.

The discussion drifted on to a somewhat recriminatory debate on cross-border security, in the course of which Gerry Fitt expressed deep concern over indications of a coming together of the men of violence on both sides of the community divide in the North, and Pat Cooney complained bitterly about the 'no-go' area north of the border where there was no RUC presence—a phenomenon that had no parallel in the Republic. For my part I sought the assistance of the Executive in getting action from the British to deal with misbehaviour by the British army; there had been no response from the British government to the complaints I had made to Pym three weeks earlier.

Finally we got down to the Council of Ireland. Faulkner launched the discussion on this with warnings about giving the Council too much power too soon. Discussion followed on possible areas for executive action by the Council on the basis of lists produced by both sides. An agreed joint list emerged, which was remitted to joint working parties of officials with instructions to report back within three weeks on what aspects of these activities should become executive functions of the Council, how these functions should be discharged, and the date from which a transfer of executive responsibilities could be contemplated in each instance. A co-ordinating steering group for this activity was proposed by Faulkner, and agreed.

On the question of when the formal conference should be held, Faulkner agreed that it should not be allowed to drag on, because as long as it did so it would be a festering sore. However, they must see a complete acceptable package first. It seemed to me that we were still some distance away from this conference, which certainly could not now take place before March.

A few days later Faulkner wrote to Cosgrave about a matter that, he said, he had intended to raise at the conference but that had not been reached because of pressure of business. The establishment of the parliamentary tier at the outset of the Council's life would, he said, endanger the whole process, by giving the impression of an all-Ireland government and parliament in embryo. Cosgrave replied that the concept of this Consultative Assembly pre-dated Sunningdale, and its postponement now could cause a dangerous and perhaps fatal loss of credibility in relation to the Sunningdale package.

By this time, however, the dialogue between Dublin and Belfast was over-shadowed by the UK general election, called by Ted Heath as a response to the challenge to his government by the coalminers. The election could not have come at a worse time for Brian Faulkner and his supporters. The Heath government, with its commitment to Sunningdale, was replaced by an insecure Labour government under Harold Wilson, and in Northern Ireland anti-Faulkner Unionists swept the board in the eleven constituencies held by Unionist MPs, thus fatally weakening Faulkner's moral authority. We had been unable to help in time with a clear statement on the status of Northern Ireland, because the judgement of the Supreme Court, to which the Boland case had been appealed, was not available until ten days after the election.

A couple of days after the change of government and Merlyn Rees's appointment as Northern Ireland Secretary, I met him in London. He assured me that the new government's commitment to the Sunningdale agreement was absolute: they would not move at all from the basic position of the pre-vious government. But, he said, the Faulkner Unionists were deeply gloomy and inclined to push ratification of the agreement miles into the future, with some of them, including Roy Bradford, suggesting that they would have to look in other directions. This was not the first time that Roy Bradford's name had come up in discussions with the British, as well as with members of the different Northern Ireland parties, as a weak link in the Faulkner camp. How-ever, Rees said, Faulkner himself realised that the SDLP would not stay in a power-sharing Executive unless the Council of Ireland were established, and he would stick by the commitment.

Rees's suggestions as to what might be done to help the Faulkner Unionists included an early declaration by us on the 'status' of Northern Ireland (to which I told him we were committed as soon as our hands were 'untied' by the Supreme Court verdict in the Boland case), a 'PR exercise' on cross-border security—as if the counterproductive effect of such moves had not been sufficiently demonstrated with the arrest in December and subsequent release of IRA suspects—and early action on the Law Enforcement Commission's report, which, however, was not now due before mid-April. I made it clear that we wanted to ratify Sunningdale by Easter.

Discussion later turned to other matters, including a recent incident when a unit of the British army had crossed into the Republic and threatened to shoot gardaí who intercepted them.

Within ten days the vindication of the agreement by the Supreme Court left us free to make the promised declaration on the status of Northern Ireland. Both Oliver Napier and Frank Cooper, Permanent Secretary of the Northern Ireland Office, told us that this declaration had achieved its objective and that 'status' was no longer an issue, although Rees had some difficulty in persuading Brian Faulkner to accept it gracefully and not to raise fresh issues. Soon afterwards we sent to Faulkner copies of our proposed version of the agreement to be signed at the ratification of Sunningdale when the formal meeting for that purpose was eventually held, and Cosgrave wrote to Faulkner suggesting 10 April as the date for the meeting.

It was around this time that we began to be concerned about the attitude of the new Labour government towards the Provisional IRA. We had never forgotten Harold Wilson's action as leader of the opposition in going behind the backs of the Irish Government and opposition by using them as a 'cover' for meeting the IRA in Dublin in 1971, a meeting that had also involved Merlyn Rees. Subsequently there had been the meeting between Whitelaw as Secretary of State for Northern Ireland and the IRA in Chelsea in 1972. Now we had reason to believe that there had been an approach of some kind by the IRA to the Labour Party before the general election, and Frank Cooper, in an informal discussion with Seán Donlon, John Hume, and Austin Currie, had spoken openly of expecting a further approach from the IRA in the next few weeks; this would be a natural development, he said, because of their contacts with Rees in opposition. We knew too that Faulkner feared that the new British government might talk to the IRA.

Significantly, when Rees met the Northern Ireland Executive five days later he told them—to their horror—that he would be announcing in the House of Commons on 4 April the legalisation of Sinn Féin and the UVF, hitherto banned organisations in Northern Ireland. To Faulkner's plea not to leave the Executive 'completely naked' and not to undermine the SDLP, Merlyn Rees replied that he wished to bring within the political arena as many shades of opinion as possible.

At the Executive meeting following this disturbing indication of the Labour government's thinking, Faulkner made a further attempt to water down Sunningdale, proposing that the ratification should exclude the Council of Ireland provisions and that the Ministerial Council should be established with the sole task of studying its structure and future development. Then, after six months' study, the proposals as they had emerged from this process should be the subject of referenda to be held on the same day North and South. The SDLP were unhappy with a proposal that would not alone push the Council of Ireland into a vague future but would encourage the paramilitaries on both sides to maintain their violence for a prolonged period in pursuit of their common objective of sabotaging Sunningdale and the Council.

On 5 April we had our first meeting with the new British government, including Harold Wilson. On our side Brendan Corish, the Tánaiste, and I accompanied Liam Cosgrave; Harold Wilson had with him Jim Callaghan, as Foreign Secretary, and Merlyn Rees.

In a tete-à-tete with Wilson, Cosgrave led off by saying that now that we had provided the clarification of the 'status' issue, no requirement for holding the formal ratification conference remained unfulfilled, and any further delay would help only those opposed to the agreement. He had to be cautious, however, in referring to the police authority, which the Minister for Justice, Pat Cooney, and his officials seemed to see as an intrusive body coming between them and the Garda Síochána. The British and the Unionists were well aware of this, and I was much concerned that our negotiating position would be weakened by the evidence that on our side, in one area of government at least, an element in the Sunningdale package was viewed with less than enthusiasm. Wilson in fact remarked on this occasion that it was important to increase identification by the minority with policing, which was why they were reforming the Northern Ireland Police Authority—a delicate reference that was clearly designed to indicate his awareness of our vulnerability on this police authority issue.

The two premiers then moved straight into the usual debate on cross-border security and fugitive offenders—*plus les gouvernements britanniques changaient, plus c'était la meme chose!* Wilson had clearly been fed, and had swallowed—or, for tactical reasons, had pretended to swallow—the same diet of cross-border security propaganda as his predecessors.

Cosgrave pointed out that of 108 murders in the previous six months only eighteen had been in border areas, and twelve of these had been in or near the 'no-go' Crossmaglen area, where the RUC did not operate. He added that as a result of the action Declan Costello had taken in December, murderers in Northern Ireland could now be prosecuted in our courts.

The subsequent general discussion between the two delegations followed no pattern. We went round and round various issues in a thoroughly disorganised way. The three British participants had clearly not got their act together, and much of the discussion was in reality a debate between them, in which Rees, who had clearly lost confidence in his capacity to carry Sunningdale through to a successful conclusion, argued for delay and dilution against a tough and determined Callaghan and a Wilson who was trying, not with complete success, to appear decisive and in command.

On the question of cross-border security measures I explained the difference between the role of the Irish army in giving support to the civil power, i.e. the Garda Síochána, and that of the British army, which had direct responsibility for security in border areas. I went on to express our concern at the lack of co-ordination between the British army and the RUC, which contrasted with the effective liaison across the border between the RUC and the Gardaí. Rees remarked defensively that the recent shooting of two British soldiers by the

RUC was due to an administrative accident and not to an operational mix-up—a subtle distinction that we accepted with straight faces.

Wilson commented that the real trouble in the North had begun following the change of government in mid-1970; action had been taken then—the Falls Road curfew—that would not have been taken if the government had not changed. I was to recall this comment seven weeks later when the Executive fell, because in our view—and in Ted Heath's also, as he made clear later on—action had not been taken by the Labour government that would have been taken if the Heath government had been returned in the election called in February 1974.

I then proposed that we agree a timetable for the ratification of Sunningdale, which, I suggested, should follow the publication of the Law Enforcement Commission report, expected on 11 April; that we announce in Dublin and Westminster reciprocal extraterritorial legislation for the trial in either part of Ireland of those accused of terrorist offences; and that we also announce a Ministerial meeting on security between Merlyn Rees and Pat Cooney.

Rees responded by trying to raise several further issues, but Cosgrave became impatient with his stalling and said that we had made an agreement and everyone should carry it out. Jim Callaghan seemed to share our impatience. Faulkner, he said, had to go on or he would be finished; 'you can't go around Aintree twice.' Harold Wilson, ignoring this somewhat inaccurate reference to a racecourse in the vicinity of his constituency, then joined in, saying that they could not have an attempt to renegotiate Sunningdale; the SDLP would be unable to take this. He reverted to the need to maintain bipartisanship at Westminster in view of the negative public attitude in Britain to involvement in Northern Ireland. He claimed that Ted Heath had been 'playing hooky' by offering the Conservative whip to the eleven anti-Faulkner Unionists—adding, however, that Willie Whitelaw and Francis Pym seemed to have put a stop to that. Labour, he said, remained firm on the bipartisan approach. If because of a breakdown of the Executive they had to return to direct rule, all hope would then be destroyed; the issue of British soldiers serving in the North could then bring about an 'agonising reappraisal'.

A discussion on border security ensued, in the course of which the divergence between Callaghan and Rees again emerged. Callaghan accepted that the violence was basically indigenous and that responsibility for dealing with it must therefore be placed on people in the North, while Merlyn Rees tried to tie it into the Republic, on the grounds that those responsible for the bombing were supported from the South and that unionists believed all the violence came from the South. I retorted that it was up to the British government to demolish this myth, and I pointed to the problem posed by 'no-go' areas in Armagh, to which Rees defensively replied that there were differences in method between the RUC and the army, and the police could not patrol there as they would all be killed.

Eventually Wilson accepted the three-stage process I had suggested. When I proposed that we should now fix the date for the formal ratification conference, he said this date was beginning to emerge, and Cosgrave agreed, suggesting an early-May conference. At that Merlyn Rees again intervened urging 'caution', and on this negative note we concluded.

All in all it was an unimpressive occasion, to which, perhaps unsurprisingly, Merlyn Rees makes no reference in his memoirs. In retrospect both ourselves and Harold Wilson and Jim Callaghan were probably unrealistic, having failed to appreciate the scale of the growing crisis inside unionism in Northern Ireland. Rees was clearly much more aware of this crisis; but he had failed to devise an appropriate approach to the problem, and his suggestions, which were not supported by his colleagues, bore little relation to Faulkner's actual concerns as expressed to us around this time. Also, while we probably accepted too readily Wilson's and Callaghan's support for our position, we were disturbed by what Wilson had to say about Heath, and we were unhappy with his talk of an 'agonising reappraisal' if the Executive fell.

Meanwhile Faulkner had written to Cosgrave to say that early ratification of Sunningdale was not in the realm of practical politics. He wanted the Irish Government to propose that the Council of Ireland should be established with functions only in relation to policing and human rights, and he wanted the executive functions of the Council to be deferred in favour of intergovernmental co-operation, subject to review by the Council. He also wanted the Consultative Assembly to be dropped, at least for the present.

This was a tall order, not least because the other two parties in the Executive were working on totally different lines. Thus the Alliance Party believed that the Sunningdale agreement could and should be implemented gradually. They suggested starting with an early North-South interministerial meeting that would agree on an immediate transfer to the Ministerial Council of executive decision-making in respect of several matters, such as Carlingford Lough and cross-border economic planning in the north-west, and would continue with similar meetings at which further transfers would be effected at intervals of a few months. By degrees other aspects of the agreement would be implemented, and formal ratification would follow at the end of this process.

The SDLP, for their part, knew of the difficulties facing Faulkner but remained unaware of the proposals he had put to us, and were still working on the assumption of early ratification. On 12 April Faulkner had, it is true, written to Fitt along lines similar to his communication to Cosgrave. But Fitt does not appear to have told his colleagues about this letter. The first Paddy Devlin, his closest ally in the party at that time, knew about it was when at a meeting with us some ten days later, attended only by Devlin and Fitt, the latter produced the Faulkner letter.

Thus the precondition for action along the lines Faulkner had proposed to us—prior agreement on his proposal in the Executive—had not even begun to be fulfilled several weeks later; each of the three parties in the Executive was still proceeding along quite different lines. And with the British government still assuming ratification by early June at the latest, we were tempted to think that the Faulkner approach to Cosgrave had only been a bargaining move.

On 25 April I flew to London to meet Rees in order to discuss how the Law Enforcement Commission report, which was finally ready for publication, should be handled. I told him that if we could agree on early publication of the report we would introduce legislation in the Dáil on the following Tuesday for the extraterritorial handling of terrorist cases: the 'second-best' solution to the fugitive offenders problem in the light of the constitutional obstacles to extradition that had been identified by the two Irish Supreme Court judges on the commission. If the two governments were agreed on this form of legislation we would not be worried by the British legislation being delayed after ours; the important thing was for *us* to move as rapidly as possible to fulfil *our* commitment.

Despite the clear view concerning the constitutional invalidity of extradition in the case of political offenders that had been expressed by our two Supreme Court judges who were members of the Law Enforcement Commission, the British officials present on this occasion tried to argue the case for extradition. They attempted to deny that at our meeting on 5 April agreement had been reached on the introduction of legislation to implement the extraterritorial solution, if, as we had then expected, the commission found it to be the only feasible solution. Rees had to intervene to assure me that there was no question of the British government wanting to backpedal on this. Even then one particularly persistent official tried to continue with his argument and had to be headed off.

The argument then switched to the timetable for action, with the British officials producing endless reasons for postponing both publication of the report for three weeks and also the proposed security meeting between Rees and Cooney. Nevertheless it was finally agreed that implementation of the report and the holding of the security meeting would help the setting of a date for ratification of Sunningdale.

Even after this meeting the British officials persisted in reverting to the extradition issue, alleging that despite the report of the Law Enforcement Commission our objections were politically motivated.

On the following Sunday Declan Costello and I saw Oliver Napier, who told us that Brian Faulkner had agreed with proposals that the Alliance Party had put to us on the previous Wednesday, involving a meeting of Ministers from North and South within a fortnight, followed by the transfer of a couple of executive functions, before mid-July, with formal ratification at a later stage. However, when the matter of the functions of the Council was raised at an Executive meeting two days later the Unionist reaction was so negative that the SDLP became very pessimistic about their capacity to remain in the Executive beyond the end of May.

The situation was deteriorating rapidly. As May began, the campaign by British officials on extradition continued, and despite the assurances to me as late as 25 April that the British were working towards ratification by early June at the latest, briefings were given both by the NIO in Belfast and by the British embassy in Dublin to the effect that ratification was to be postponed for six months. Faulkner had also postponed further discussion of the issue at the Executive until the following week. On top of all this, on 2 May Rees, without consulting us, released the report of the Law Enforcement Commission to the members of the Executive, on the strength of an alleged claim by Roy Bradford, which had no foundation, that we had given copies to the SDLP. Within an hour or two, leaks about the report were flowing from Belfast. I rang Merlyn Rees late that afternoon, and finally made contact with him later that night, to express the Government's grave concern at this sequence of events.

On the following day our Government reviewed the situation. We approved a letter to Brian Faulkner that pressed him to establish what kind of consensus could be reached among the parties in the Executive on the proposals he had been putting to us, stressing our concern to be as helpful as possible. Our approach gave heart to the Executive, and at a meeting on 7 May of the Northern Ireland Administration (i.e. the Executive plus the four junior Ministers) the mood favoured holding the formal ratification conference within three to four weeks. A final decision on this was held back, however, until a subcommittee reported on agreed positions regarding four contentious issues: the functions of the Council, the Consultative Assembly, the Secretariat, and the location of its headquarters.

Simultaneously the SDLP were discussing with the NIO the ending of internment and were optimistic that the formal conference might be marked by the release of all those interned before direct rule was imposed in March 1972. They expected that the formal conference would also clear appointments to the two police authorities, which would enable the SDLP shortly afterwards to call publicly on nationalists to back the RUC. The SDLP were concerned, however, at British statements to them that we would not be ready to set up our police authority within this time-scale.

The SDLP recognised the need to offer Faulkner concessions on the Council of Ireland, and they would therefore propose that initially the Council, while taking only certain executive decisions and deciding on harmonisation, should not have direct executive responsibility; that the Consultative Assembly would come into existence only when a majority in both the Dáil and the Northern Ireland Assembly nominated members to it, which would not be until after the summer recess; and that the Unionists be given a veto for the time being on the setting up of a headquarters for the Council and of a Secretariat.

These remarkable and heartening developments came just as I left for a brief five-day visit to the United States. They were discussed on Wednesday afternoon by the available Ministers who had been involved in the Sunningdale conference; it was agreed that we should place no obstacles in the way of any compromise or agreement along these lines amongst the parties in the Executive. On the other hand, depressingly, when Dermot Nally raised the question of the introduction of the police authority legislation, Pat Cooney demurred at an early announcement, on the double grounds that we were not yet ready with a Bill for second-stage debate and that he did not wish to pre-empt consultations with the Garda representative bodies.

On the following Saturday, 11 May, while I was still away, Conor Cruise O'Brien, Declan Costello and Richie Ryan met John Hume and Paddy Devlin at short notice at their request. The SDLP's news was now as depressing as the news in mid-week had been encouraging. The group of Ministers from the Executive discussing the four outstanding issues was deadlocked. The Unionist proposals put to them were largely unacceptable: they envisaged the implementation of executive functions only by unanimous decision of the Council, which would mean that the Unionist members—or indeed any one of them—could sabotage the Council's entire work. The Unionists also proposed that the introduction of legislation to transfer functions to the Council for the establishment of the Consultative Assembly and for the establishment of a permanent headquarters should take place only after a referendum in Northern Ireland on a decision of the Northern Ireland Assembly following a general election. Meanwhile unrest within the SDLP at the delay in implementing the Sunningdale agreement was now eroding any margin of manoeuvre the SDLP Ministers might have had on some of the outstanding issues.

Thus by the time Joan and I arrived back in Dublin at the weekend the Government had passed through the full cycle from euphoria to renewed depression. On Monday 13 May Rees came to Dublin for a meeting with Declan Costello and myself. The principal topics were the handling of the report of the Law Enforcement Commission and the arrangements for the proposed meeting on security between Rees and Cooney. The British seemed to have an almost inexhaustible capacity to go over the same ground again and again on these two issues. However, this time the meeting was less contentious than previously. We indicated our intention of introducing the extraterritoriality Bill on 28 May.

There followed a long but largely inconclusive discussion between us on the ratification of Sunningdale. At one point Merlyn Rees enquired why Sunningdale had ended with an agreed communiqué rather than a formal agreement—a somewhat surprising question from a Secretary of State two-and-a-half months in office. I explained patiently that we had reluctantly agreed to this against our better judgement because the British government had pressed us to accept this procedure in order to facilitate the Unionists, who were concerned that the agreement should be signed by a formally constituted Executive.

In the course of the discussion I explained that we could accept a 'phasing in' of the Council of Ireland, with some elements coming into place later than others, and that we understood the problem about naming a specific date for a particular stage of implementation, as this would encourage the men of violence to maintain their activities until then. But we could not accept that implementation would be left to the Unionists to decide, as in that event it would never happen. I asked Merlyn Rees if he had any solution to this dilemma.

It was clear that he had not; he contented himself with stressing the dangers deriving from a breakdown of the Executive, which, among other things, could seriously affect public opinion in Britain and increase pressure for a British withdrawal—a subject that seemed to preoccupy him. This comment was presumably intended to encourage us to be flexible on the implementation of the agreement.

There the matter ended for the moment. The only concrete result from this meeting was the introduction—for a brief period at least—of a significant presence of military police in the Whiteabbey area after I had raised with Rees the intimidation of Catholics from their homes in the greater Newtown Abbey area, accompanied by sectarian murders, in respect of which the RUC had been reported to us to be unhelpful.

On the following morning, Tuesday 14 May, Joan and I had to leave Dublin for Brussels, accompanying President Erskine Childers on an official visit to Belgium. The morning papers that we read on the plane reported a threat by loyalist workers to cut off supplies of electricity if the Assembly failed that afternoon to support an anti-Sunningdale motion. This announcement had been made by a body calling itself the 'Ulster Workers' Council' at a meeting of a 'study group' of the United Ulster Unionist Council, attended by representatives of the UDA and the UVF and presided over by Ian Paisley. (The UUUC comprised the Unionist political parties and paramilitary organisations.)

That evening the Assembly rejected the anti-Sunningdale motion by 44 votes to 28, and the strike was declared. On the following morning most of industry was closed down as a result of a 40 per cent reduction in electricity supplies. Stanley Orme, the Minister of State at the Northern Ireland Office, met an Ulster Workers' Council delegation that included three political leaders—Ian Paisley, Bill Craig, and John Laird of the official Unionist Party—together with leaders of the paramilitary organisations, the UVF and UDA. Three armed 'observers' were also present. When I read of this meeting in Brussels on the following day I was depressed by this further evidence of the willingness of British governments to deal with paramilitaries, with whom 'democratic' Unionist politicians were now openly involved in an attempt to bring down an elected government.

By the time we returned to Dublin the position had gravely deteriorated. Large-scale intimidation had enforced the strike, which at the outset had far from full support from law-abiding Unionists and had in fact been denounced by at least one courageous anti-Faulkner Unionist Assembly member.

Moreover, on Friday 17 May bombs set off in Dublin by loyalist paramilitaries—the people with whom leaders of the Unionist political parties had been co-operating in the UWC and with whom Stan Orme had been talking two days earlier—had killed 28 people instantly and injured 137 others, several of whom subsequently died. At the time of writing this remains the highest death toll from any terrorist outrage in either part of Ireland or in Britain in twenty years of violence.

On Sunday after my return I decided to call in the British Ambassador, Sir Arthur Galsworthy, on the following day to ask him for his government's evaluation of the situation. He told me that the Executive was to meet that morning, its members being collected by helicopter. They were to make a further effort to reach a consensus on how to proceed with the Council of Ireland—a process in which Merlyn Rees and his Permanent Secretary were now involved. I made it clear that, while we were in general willing to be guided by an Executive consensus, there were limits to the modifications we would accept in regard to the Council of Ireland.

The Ambassador went on to tell me that although, in accordance with an announcement about troop reductions in Northern Ireland by the Labour government after it had taken up office, one battalion of troops had already been sent back to Britain, the second battalion that it had been proposed to withdraw was now to remain and a further battalion in Great Britain was on stand-by to be sent to Northern Ireland. He added that military technicians were available to take the place of striking workers if necessary. However, the British government believed that the trade union movement should be given a chance to do what it could; it was desirable to have the UWC strike broken by the trade unions rather than the army.

I asked if this meant that his government was going to wait several days before taking strong action against the blocking of roads, the hijacking of vehicles and the burning of buses that had begun that morning. We had been in agreement with the approach by the British government to the strike itself—namely standing firm but avoiding confrontation—but there was now a totally new situation, which called for urgent and effective action. The Ambassador replied that they would be taking action as soon as possible on road blocks etc. I responded to this reassurance—which soon turned out to be quite groundless—by saying that if the strike were mastered there would be an important opportunity for a political advance and that therefore it would be better to delay decisions in the Executive about modifications of the Council of Ireland proposal. The SDLP were clear about our views on this.

I also suggested that the statement on the Law Enforcement Commission report that it had been planned to make on Thursday might be postponed, because in present circumstances its impact would be lost and Brian Faulkner would thus be deprived of a useful card that could be better played at a later point. However, as so often happened in relation to Northern Ireland, I was told that this consideration would have to take second place to the exigencies of the British parliamentary timetable: the statement had to be made in Parliament, and Parliament was about to break for the Whitsun recess. Realising of course that this adjournment was a sacred ritual that something as unimportant as a threat to democratic government in part of the United Kingdom could not be allowed to disrupt, I restrained myself, with difficulty, from telling the Ambassador what I thought about this argument for early publication.

Most of the rest of our discussion was about the terms of the statement to be issued by the British government on the report of the Law Enforcement Commission. I handed him our comments on the British draft, which to our concern had included what we regarded as a gratuitous statement that the British government regretted that extradition was not 'acceptable' to us. This carried the implication that our position on the matter was due to lack of political will, despite the fact that the British government knew perfectly well from the views expressed by the Irish members of the Commission—who included two Supreme Court judges—that the obstacle to extradition at that time was constitutional, not political.

On the following day, Tuesday, I reported to the Government on my meeting with Ambassador Galsworthy, and in London Merlyn Rees reported to Harold Wilson and other Ministers concerned with Northern Ireland. A statement was issued after the Downing Street meeting saying that the government would continue to maintain essential services in Northern Ireland, and would not be intimidated or blackmailed into departing from the Constitution Act and proceeding with the Sunningdale agreement. It added that the access roads to Belfast were open, although 'some' roads were blocked and some Protestant paramilitary organisations were creating hazards for free travel as well as intimidating those who wished to lead normal lives. The security forces had been increased in numbers 'to deal with this situation'.

But the security forces were not dealing with the situation. As the newspapers reported, some barricades were removed voluntarily on Tuesday, but none were removed by the security forces, and most remained in place during the day. The British army was described as 'unwilling to clash' with the strikers, and failed even to ensure access for a number of workers seeking to join the tiny demonstration that was the result of the British government's somewhat pathetic proposal to allow the official trade union movement, led by Len Murray, the General Secretary of the British Trade Union Congress, to attempt to break the strike.

That Tuesday afternoon the Executive, deeply divided on whether to concede on the Council of Ireland, were nevertheless united in presenting what was in effect an ultimatum to the British government: was that government going to take action or was it going to allow anarchy to take over?

In response to this united call by the Executive the army belatedly moved early on Wednesday morning to take down some barricades; but there was still no sign of action to restore the electricity supply, which was being kept at a much reduced level by the loyalist power workers, whose highly dangerous domination of the major power stations had never been challenged by either the Tory or Labour governments during the two years since direct rule had been introduced.

In mid-morning we received a phone call from John Hume about the Executive discussions that had been taking place on the Council of Ireland. He told us that proposals for a 'climb-down' to conciliate loyalist opinion and help to keep the Unionist members in the Executive had just been turned down by the SDLP Assembly party by 11 votes to 8. This proposed 'climb-down' went far beyond anything that we had understood to be on the cards and met neither of two requirements that we believed to be essential, namely some executive functions to be allocated to the Council from the outset, and no prior step by way of Assembly vote, election or referendum to be required as a precondition of the parliamentary tier coming into existence. (The 'climb-down' would have involved a general election before the creation of a parliamentary tier.)

As we met in a hastily called cabinet meeting to consider this dramatic development, events were moving rapidly in Belfast. There was a threat that direct rule would be reintroduced 'within the hour'. Stan Orme met the SDLP at lunchtime, and a further meeting of the SDLP Assembly party was then called with a view to reversing the earlier decision. When they met a new vote was put, despite the fact that some of those present complained that they were being intimidated into voting for a proposal they had not even seen in writing. In the face of a threat of the immediate collapse of the Executive if they failed to reverse their earlier decision, a number of members then switched their votes in favour of a Council of Ireland climb-down, thus producing a majority in favour of the proposal.

The Executive then reassembled, and at 4.30 p.m. the proposal was formally agreed by its members.

Outpaced by events, our Government met again. However, we had no alternative but to put the best face on the debacle. At 8.45 p.m. Liam Cosgrave made a statement to the Dáil accepting the fait accompli.

On the following day Liam Cosgrave sent a message to Harold Wilson asking that immediate action be taken to deal with the strike and to restore normal government and order in Northern Ireland. He also proposed that the formal Sunningdale conference be now held at a very early date and that the Council of Ireland also hold its first meeting quickly. In his memoirs Merlyn Rees describes this proposal as 'breathtaking'; we for our part regarded as breathtaking the abdication of responsibility for law and order in Northern Ireland by the British government in favour of an illegal body, the membership of which included an organisation that had just murdered thirty-one people in our capital city (three more had died during the intervening period).

When our Ambassador, Dónal O'Sullivan, saw Wilson to deliver this message, the Prime Minister tried to convince him that the climb-down on the Council of Ireland had not been a victory for the UWC, because a week earlier the Executive had been 'almost' agreed on the modification of the Sunningdale agreement. To say the least, this was straining the facts. On the action to be taken to end the strike, Wilson appeared confused. First he said that the technicians flown in from Britain at the start of the strike with a view to restoring power supplies could not keep the power stations going without the co-operation of middle and lower management, which was not forthcoming because of intimidation. But he then added that on the basis of new advice the British government could well adopt a different attitude next day. Later in the discussion he volunteered that it might be necessary to put the technicians in quickly and that he would talk to his experts about it. He also claimed that the troops had 'taken a very strong line' about the barricades and that this problem was 'considerably' reduced. This in no way corresponded to our information about the situation on the ground.

Whilst this was happening the Law Enforcement Commission report was published, in order to satisfy the British Parliament's desire to see it before it broke up for its Whitsun holiday. As we had predicted, the report published in these circumstances made no impact whatsoever, and offered no benefit to Brian Faulkner.

It was around this stage of the strike that I rang Merlyn Rees to discuss the situation with him. When I got through he asked me if I had a scrambler on my phone. I said that I had, but that I doubted if it would work on an outside call to the North. 'Try it,' he urged. I did, and it worked. He told me then that the switchboard at Stormont Castle was insecure, being manned by people some of whom were working for the UWC. His evident acceptance of this as a fact of life told me something about the extent to which he felt himself to have no grip on the situation in Northern Ireland.

Next day, Friday, Harold Wilson met the leaders of the Executive at Chequers, and the British Cabinet discussed the crisis at considerable length, the discussion ending at about 8.45 p.m. Gerry Fitt, who got word to us during the discussions, was optimistic, but what followed was the anti-climax of Harold Wilson's disastrous broadcast on Saturday night in the course of which he alienated both communities in Northern Ireland with his reference to people in Northern Ireland as 'spongers' on the British exchequer. In the midst of this appalling crisis he momentarily succeeded in uniting both communities in Northern Ireland in hostility to that insult, while at the same time making it plain, by what he did not say, that no serious attempt would be made either to restore order or to restore electricity supplies. The taking over of petrol distribution by the army early on Monday morning was all that ever emerged from Friday's meetings in London.

On Sunday Paddy Devlin and Ivan Cooper came to Dublin to discuss the situation with us. Paddy arrived at our house, and as we welcomed him in the hall he took off his jacket, revealing a gun in a holster, of which he divested himself. He handed it to Joan, whom he asked to look after it for him. She placed it gingerly in a neighbouring room, and told Mark to stay away from it. When the two Ministers later sought to return to the North they were stopped at a loyalist paramilitary road-block on the main road and forced to turn back. Disconcerted by this development, they returned to Dublin and asked us to seek assistance from the British authorities to enable them to return to their posts as Ministers in the Northern Ireland Executive. My recollection is that the British were unhelpful, showing their disapproval of the two Ministers' visit to Dublin by simply denying that they had met any road-block on the way back—the official story, of course, was that main roads were being kept clear— and suggesting that the story had simply been invented.

*The Fine Gael Social Democrats: with Tom O'Higgins and Jim Dooge at the 1970 Ard-Fheis.*

*With Young Fine Gael about 1978.*

US Visits. With
Henry Kissinger
in 1975 asking for
Student Visas after
the Walter Lippman
Memorial Service
in Washington
Cathedral.
And with
President Cater
in 1977 during a
St Patrick's Day
visit.

*Signing the Lomé Agreement in 1975* (above), *and* (below), *with François-Xavier Ortoli, President of the European Commission, on the way back to Brussels.*

*The first European Council in Dublin 1975, with Commission President Ortoli, Liam Cosgrave and Commissioner Haferkamp.*

*Meeting King Juan Carlos in Madrid, 1980.*

*The Pope and the Opposition in 1979, with Joan and Frank Cluskey,*
*Leader of the Labour Party.*

*Laying a wreath in Moscow.*

*Pony-trekking politicians: The Christian Democrats in Killarney in 1979.*

*Looking a gift bullock in the mouth during the 1981 General Election.*

*The lighter side of electioneering in 1981.*

*With Charles Haughey, Taoiseach, at Radio Telefís Éireann during the 1981 election campaign.*

The morale of the Executive, both unionist and nationalist members, was shattered by what they saw as their betrayal by a British government that seemed to them—and to us—to be fearful of its own army, the unwillingness of which to act was made plain by leaks to the press from their headquarters in Lisburn. Years later a member of that British Cabinet confirmed to me that fear of the army failing to carry out orders was a significant factor in the way events turned out. What I had not been aware of until I had this conversation was that similar fears had apparently prevented Harold Wilson's previous Labour government from acting to end UDI in Rhodesia, and that memories of this were apparently present in the minds of some at least of the members of the Cabinet when the issue of restoring order in Northern Ireland was discussed.

During those last few days we became increasingly concerned with the manner in which BBC Belfast broadcasts were dominated by the views of those challenging the British government's authority. Threats and warnings of impending chaos, not just by the strikers but by spokesmen for public bodies, were transmitted repeatedly in what seemed to us a blatant attempt to force that government to cave in to the revolt. I was present when Conor Cruise O'Brien rang a very senior person at the BBC in London to ask if the BBC authorities there knew of the role being played by the BBC in Belfast. My recollection is that Conor was told the authorities in London were unaware of this, as they did not monitor BBC Belfast.

On this issue at least the British government shared our view, as Merlyn Rees records. His account of the attempted justification of the BBC's action subsequently given in a lecture by their Northern Ireland controller is illuminating, and should be alarming to anyone concerned for the preservation of democratic government.

The end came on Tuesday 28 May. The failure of the British government to give adequate support to the Executive that it had caused to be established by a democratic process, and its incapacity to maintain essential services, led to a complete collapse of self-confidence amongst the pro-Assembly Unionists.

At this time Faulkner felt obliged as a result of pressure from his Unionist colleagues to propose the appointment of a mediator to negotiate with the political-cum-paramilitary leadership of the UWC. This was more even than the British government was prepared to concede at that point. Faulkner, together with his Unionist colleagues, then resigned, following which Merlyn Rees announced that there was no longer any statutory basis for the Executive, and reinstalled direct rule.

Irish nationalists, North and South, believed at the time that had the British army been willing to take prompt action against road blocks, barricades and overt intimidation when these features first made their appearance, the strike could have been broken. Nationalists also believed that it had been totally irresponsible and indefensible to have allowed, through tolerating discrimination in public employment, a situation to develop and to persist that put control of power supplies into the hands of extremists from one section of the community.

The aftermath of the collapse of the Executive was a period of deep uncertainty about the future of British policy in Northern Ireland, and consequently about the future security of our state. We had to face the fact that in the part of Ireland under United Kingdom sovereignty a British government had been unwilling or unable to control events. The future existence of the Northern Ireland nationalist community was now potentially at risk, and with it the peace of the island as a whole. If, as now seemed momentarily conceivable in the light of the collapse of British authority in the face of the UWC strike, the British were at some point to abandon their responsibilities in Northern Ireland and to permit the emergence there of a fascist-type political entity run by extremist unionist politicians and loyalist paramilitaries, the peace of all Ireland could be threatened. Such a possibility had not previously entered our heads; now for a while we felt that we had to take it seriously, especially in view of the statement by NIO officials on a visit to Dublin on 5 June to the effect that withdrawal was not *at that time* being considered by British Ministers as an option (my emphasis). In the year that followed, much of our efforts were directed towards examining how we should handle such a situation were it to arise. At the same time our diplomatic efforts were directed towards ensuring that it did not occur.

Our first post-strike contact with the British government came several weeks after it ended. On 14 June our Ambassador, the new Assistant Secretary for Anglo-Irish Relations, Seán Donlon, and myself joined Merlyn Rees and several of his officials for an informal dinner at the Reform Club. Merlyn Rees opened the discussion with a very defensive—and correspondingly illuminating—account of the strike. He said that there had been no possibility of defeating it militarily; the loyalty of the army had never been in doubt; reports of the role of the Northern Ireland civil service had been greatly exaggerated; there had been no question of bypassing the Executive, which, however, except for Brian Faulkner and John Hume (whose efforts he described as 'magnificent'), had virtually ceased to govern. I contented myself with comments on the failure of successive British governments to tackle the problem of the domination of electricity supply by extremist elements from one community, and on the behaviour of BBC Belfast—which he made no attempt to defend.

Merlyn Rees went on to say that in order to satisfy Parliament, from which he would have to seek certain legislation in July, he was thinking of announcing in the House of Commons that an autumn election would be held in Northern Ireland for a constituent assembly with clearly defined terms of reference. I argued strongly against a July announcement, which I feared would launch all sides into a pre-election situation at a time when the two communities were at their most polarised. The interests of Northern Ireland should not be sacrificed—once again, I nearly said—to the whims of Westminster. When I added that no such announcement should be made without consultation with moderate opinion in Northern Ireland Merlyn Rees responded dismissively— and revealingly—that much of the trouble in Northern Ireland in the previous five years had derived from taking advice too often from moderates. The only other event of note on this occasion was that our Ambassador understood one British senior official to say that the island of Ireland was heading in the direction of a Marxist socialist republic.

A fortnight later, on 1 July, I made a visit to Northern Ireland to meet a range of politicians, both Unionist and Nationalist. In addition to calling on John Taylor at his home in Armagh I lunched with Brian Faulkner, and met Oliver Napier and Bob Cooper of the Alliance Party and Gerry Fitt and Paddy Devlin of the SDLP. I also had a meeting with leaders of the official Unionist Party: Harry West, Rev. Martin Smyth, and John Laird.

Two things stick in my mind about this latter meeting. I recall arguing the case that Northern Ireland's interests within the European Community would be better looked after as part of an Irish rather than a British state. Harry West conceded my point, at least so far as agriculture was concerned—but added that unionists nevertheless wanted to remain in the UK.

At the end of several hours of amicable discussion the Unionist leaders told me they felt obliged to issue a statement asserting that I had no right to be in Belfast, as I had not, in accordance with international practice, asked permission from the British government to visit Northern Ireland. At that I burst out laughing. I pointed out that I had never yet as a Minister asked any government for 'permission' to visit a country. Did they seriously think that when I went for example to Paris or Brussels or Luxembourg that I sought permission first?

The Unionist leaders were clearly disconcerted by this reaction, and apologised for the fact that it was too late to correct their statement, as it had already been issued. We parted on good terms, and I heard no more of this matter. On subsequent visits during the next seven years both as Minister for Foreign Affairs and later as leader of the opposition I met Unionist leaders without fuss, and was indeed entertained to lunch by them on occasion. I think I established a certain rapport with a number of them.

In addition to meeting Unionist leaders in the North, I invited some of them to Dublin. On several occasions individuals came to dinner at my home, but I also ensured that invitations went to Unionists—as well, of course, as to representatives of all other constitutional parties in both parts of the country—for official dinners given by me for distinguished visitors from abroad, and for the traditional St Patrick's Day dinner that the Minister for Foreign Affairs then gave for the diplomatic corps. Several of them attended these functions.

There were other, less orthodox contacts, by accident rather than design. I recall one occasion several years later when I was leader of the opposition and was visiting Belfast together with Paddy Harte, our spokesman on Northern Ireland, whose contacts, unlike mine, ranged right across the spectrum to include Ian Paisley, with whom he once had a marathon eight-hour discussion. At the end of a long day of talks with the main parties other than the DUP I ended up three-quarters of an hour late for an appointment in east Belfast with Ernest Baird, the leader of a small breakaway Unionist Party. We stopped outside his chemist's shop, which seemed to be bolted and barred. As we got out to see if he was there, a car pulled up in the middle of the road with a screech of brakes. A head appeared out of the driver's window. 'How'ya, Paddy?' a voice shouted. 'And is it Garret yourself? As commander of the UDA in this area I welcome you to east Belfast. Are you looking for Ernest?' I said we were, and he offered to track him down for me—which he did, in a hotel some distance away.

Apart from whatever unannounced UDA presence there may have been amongst community groups that I had met on several occasions from loyalist areas, this unscheduled encounter was in fact the only occasion when I had any contact with a member of a paramilitary organisation, in accordance with our policy of never meeting members of organisations engaged in violence. On one occasion, however, when with Paddy Harte I was meeting Unionist politicians in the Europa Hotel and found myself short of money to buy them a drink, Paddy, without telling me at the time what he was up to, borrowed ten pounds from Andy Tyrie of the UDA, whom he had seen elsewhere in the hotel.

In July 1974, in the aftermath of the Ulster workers' strike, we were, however, apprised of the views of the UDA leadership as they wished their position to be represented to us. The scenario they presented, involving negotiated independence leading 'inevitably' to a united Ireland, seemed designed to encourage us to accept the emergence by agreement of an independent Northern Ireland, in which the UDA rather than the Unionist parties would have a key role. However, immediately afterwards there was a rapid escalation of UDA violence in Belfast, including massive intimidation of the minority in the Rathcoole area in the months that followed, which contrasted sharply with the prospect earlier held out to us by the UDA of eight months of peace to allow for talks with the SDLP. Nevertheless, it is always useful to know what an opponent wants you to think his position to be.

In early July the British government announced that an election would be held for a Convention in which the Northern Ireland parties would be invited to work out a devolved governmental system for themselves. On 15 July the Bill to establish this Convention passed the Commons, and two days later, with the Bill in the Lords, Stan Orme came to Dublin for discussions with me. In these talks I was able to establish that it was the intention not to hold the Convention elections before November at the earliest, and possibly not until the spring of 1975, namely well after the British general election that the Labour government was expected to call in order to secure a clear majority. This conformed to our preference: it allowed time for the SDLP to recover from the shock of the debacle in May, and gave time also for possible cracks to appear in the loyalist monolith that had been created by the success of the Ulster workers' strike.

Stan Orme told me that the British government had concluded that permanent direct rule or power-sharing on a new basis were the only feasible options in the North. They had chosen the latter. I said it was absolutely vital that the

British government spell out more clearly the terms of reference of the Convention, defining unambiguously concepts like 'power-sharing' and 'Irish dimension'. In response he assured me that any proposal not acceptable to the minority community would not be agreed by the British government.

I also raised with him the familiar problem of the counterproductive behaviour of elements of the British army in Northern Ireland. As on previous occasions, much of the problem seemed to stem from the wide differences in the behaviour and discipline of different regiments of the army: a well-disciplined regiment that carried out its duties intelligently was all too often followed in an area by a regiment with quite different standards. This often undid all the good work of its predecessor. A particular problem at this time was the behaviour of a regiment currently in the Creggan area of Derry, which had harassed thousands of people in the previous few weeks, thereby acting as an effective recruiting agent for the IRA. Stan Orme was aware of the problem and was trying, he told me, to find a solution. He had no more success than other British Ministers in Northern Ireland, none of whom seemed able to influence the current behaviour of British army regiments there.

I also raised the question of a prisoners' resettlement committee that had recently been established and which had a strong IRA orientation. We wanted a stronger involvement in it of constitutional nationalists, but Stan Orme defended its composition on the grounds that the members had to be 'acceptable to the communities in Northern Ireland', which for this purpose were apparently defined as the Provisional and Official IRA and the Protestant paramilitaries. The SDLP, which represented the vast majority of Northern nationalists, was excluded by him from this definition. I protested vigorously against this extraordinary and to our minds quite perverse approach, but could not shake Stan Orme's conviction that it was better to keep the SDLP out of this operation, a policy that I believed had the effect of simply building up the credibility of the paramilitaries. As so often, I was beating my head against a stone wall; all British governments have tended to show the same insensitivity to issues of this kind, preferring often to take the line of least resistance, either in relation to the IRA or other paramilitaries or at other times swinging to the opposite extreme in response to vocal public opinion in Britain. We never succeeded in convincing them of the long-term damage done in different ways through each of these mutually contradictory approaches, which together built up support for the terrorists in the two communities. It will indeed be interesting to see to what extent historians eventually apportion to actions of this kind by successive British governments responsibility for the survival in particular of the IRA as a terrorist organisation in Northern Ireland throughout the 1970s and 1980s.

Finally I noted that Stan Orme seemed to be hoping for IRA agreement to a cease-fire. Remembering how two years earlier another British government had entered into negotiations with the IRA during a cease-fire, I could only feel considerable concern at this.

Meanwhile it was increasingly clear that the nationalist people of Northern Ireland were in a state of shock following the Ulster workers' strike. They feared that the British government, having failed to tackle that challenge to its authority, might be unwilling or unable to frustrate a possible attempt by loyalists to establish an independent Northern Ireland state. There was widespread concern about what was described as a 'doomsday' situation that might follow such a coup. In July the Catholic Church authorities set up diocesan Relief Advisory Services to handle possible emergency situations that might arise, whether from a renewed Ulster workers' strike affecting this time essential food supplies to nationalist areas, from possible local pogroms, or from full-scale civil war. This action reflected concern lest in emergencies of one kind or another the IRA might seek to gain credibility amongst nationalists by taking a leading role in such relief activities; in previous crises nationalist relief activities had been thus infiltrated by the IRA.

These fears of a doomsday situation made nationalist opinion sensitive to contacts between the Irish Government and Unionists; it was not easy for people living in such conditions of uncertainty to appreciate the rationale of our attempts to stave off these very dangers by building bridges to such elements in the Unionist community as we could make contact with.

Perhaps underestimating the fears of the minority, in the aftermath of the UWC strike I had initially given priority to these Unionist contacts. A hostile public reaction by Paddy Devlin in a public statement to the fact that I had met Unionist as well Nationalist politicians in Belfast on 1 July was a salutary reminder of the need to demonstrate with equal urgency our concern for the nationalist community as well as to pursue, and be seen to pursue, our close collaboration with the SDLP in working towards common ends.

I should perhaps add that nationalist concern about the emphasis of our policy had been exacerbated by a speech by Conor Cruise O'Brien on the day before my visit to Belfast—a speech that had evoked a congratulatory statement from the official Unionist Party. As was to happen on a number of occasions during the life of the 1973–77 Government, Conor's single-minded concern about unionist reactions and his relative insensitivity to the danger of a swing in nationalist support from the SDLP to the IRA had helped to unbalance our policy as perceived by nationalists.

Up to this stage his point of view in Government had, I felt, provided a constructive balance vis-à-vis more traditional nationalist attitudes amongst Ministers, and I had on the whole welcomed his involvement in the Government's handling of the Northern Ireland issue. From this point onwards, however, I began to judge his public interventions more negatively, and he reciprocated by taking an increasingly negative view of the policy mix that I favoured in these difficult circumstances.

The danger of nationalist alienation from our Government became very clear when the SDLP leadership met a group of Ministers in Dublin on 2 August. In the absence of Liam Cosgrave the meeting, which I had arranged, was chaired by the Tánaiste, Brendan Corish. Conor Cruise O'Brien was also away at the time, on holidays in Kerry, and, not wishing to disturb his holiday but anxious to ensure equitable representation of the Labour Party at the meeting, I had asked Justin Keating to attend. When Conor heard of this meeting he upbraided me for not asking him to travel to Dublin to be present at it, which he interpreted as an attempt not only to exclude him but also to interfere in the internal affairs of the Labour Party by substituting Justin for himself. I only then realised that these two Labour Ministers had been in deep disagreement with one another over Northern Ireland since before the formation of the Government.

While this action of mine, taken without any intention of deliberately excluding Conor, did not help my relationship with him on Northern Ireland—we remained good friends in all other respects—it probably saved this meeting with the SDLP from disaster, for that party was by now dangerously alienated. Its representatives seemed convinced we had turned away from them, thus leaving the Northern Ireland minority a prey to the IRA. John Hume told us of the 'deep anger' amongst Northern nationalists. Gerry Fitt went on to refer to 'some Irish politicians' who he claimed had been saying that they did not want anything further to do with the Northern situation. Paddy Devlin was more specific: Conor Cruise O'Brien had implied to the press that the SDLP were coming too frequently to Dublin and were frightening the loyalists. Austin Currie added that Paddy Devlin's feelings about Conor Cruise O'Brien's attitude was shared by every member of the SDLP from the grass roots up. Devlin also repeated his criticism of my contacts with the Unionists on 1 July; the meeting with Gerry Fitt and himself had been only an afterthought, he suggested. I had to explain that the short notice of that meeting with them had, in fact, been due to security reasons.

We then got on to the substance of their concerns, and I think that I succeeded in explaining our complex strategy in terms that made sense to them. Our failure to do this earlier had clearly been a bad mistake. By the end of the meeting John Hume was commenting that the discussion had established that our objectives and theirs were identical, and that only the means to be employed were under discussion.

A meeting with the British government was clearly desirable to secure some assurances from them that might assuage the fears of the nationalist minority, as expressed to us by the SDLP. I had argued for such a meeting on a number of grounds. There had been threats of a loyalist 'Third Force', which was apparently to be a paramilitary body on a much larger scale than the UDA or UVF, and with 'respectable' support from well outside the ghetto areas of Belfast. According to some sources—including the Alliance Party—the British army's behaviour in nationalist areas had become much less restrained since the Ulster workers' strike. Even more serious was a growing danger that Northern Ireland might become a political football after the forthcoming British general election: the Unionists were convinced that in the event of a further indecisive result, which seemed a strong possibility, they could re-forge their historic alliance with the Tory party.

Accordingly, it was agreed in Government on 20 August that Liam Cosgrave should seek a meeting with Harold Wilson. There was agreement on the importance of getting the British at this meeting to recommit themselves firmly to the principle of power-sharing as the only acceptable form of devolved government in Northern Ireland. It was felt that strong and explicit British commitment on this point might remove a reticence that had developed within the SDLP about participating in the elections for the Convention, abstention from which would, in the Government's view, weaken seriously the moral strength of the nationalist position.

The meeting with the British government took place on the evening of 11 September. Wilson and Rees had already met the SDLP on the previous day and had assured them that power-sharing in government remained a precondition of devolution in Northern Ireland and that the British government also favoured an, unspecified, Irish dimension. We were glad that this had been done in direct contact between them, and as our main concern had been about the continued commitment of the British government on these two issues, the meeting with Wilson and his colleagues was in these circumstances relatively relaxed.

In the opening tete-à-tete between Cosgrave and Wilson, the Taoiseach confirmed that we were going ahead with the legislation for a common law enforcement area, but he stressed our anxiety about operations by the British army, which were tending to throw the Northern minority into the arms of the IRA. Wilson in turn referred to the assurances he had given to the SDLP. Although it appears that when the danger of a political vacuum had been mentioned he had replied, 'Please God the vacuum will continue; we don't want Northern Ireland as an election issue . . .' he had gone on to reassure the SDLP that any attempt to set up a constitution otherwise than by law would not be accepted by the British government or Parliament, and that any attempt to establish a constitution that did not incorporate the principle of power-sharing in government together with an Irish dimension would also be completely unacceptable.

During the subsequent discussion between the two delegations the activities of the British army in Northern Ireland occupied a good deal of time, but as usual no satisfactory response was elicited on this issue. A defensive action from Merlyn Rees seemed to imply unhelpfully that the level of army activity was at least partly a function of keeping the Unionists happy. The assurances given to the SDLP and ourselves on power-sharing in government and, more vaguely, on the Irish dimension seemed, however, reasonably encouraging. Nevertheless—as soon became clear—this did not in the event greatly reassure the nationalist community, which remained preoccupied with fears of a doomsday situation arising from possible loyalist paramilitary action, and which was notably unenthusiastic about being left indefinitely in a political vacuum—

however comforting that might be for British politicians principally preoccupied with an impending second general election following the relatively inconclusive outcome of that held in the previous February.

Two days after our meeting with the British government I went to Derry to meet the SDLP organisation in the city and county at John Hume's request. Early on in the evening I was faced with the question whether in the event of a 'doomsday' situation in the North the Irish Government would intervene. I had given thought as to how I should reply to this question if, as I expected, it were asked.

I told the audience that before I answered I wanted them to reflect for two minutes on what the consequences for them might be if I said either yes or no and if my reply subsequently became known to loyalist paramilitaries. After a two-minute interval I asked them if they now wanted me to answer this question. There was a unanimous chorus of 'No.' They had understood without further prompting from me that if I had answered in the negative and this had become known to loyalist paramilitaries, it could have been an encouragement to them to attack the minority, and if I had replied positively and this response had become known to loyalist paramilitaries, it could have been a provocation to them to do so.

This meeting was, I believe, at least momentarily useful in steadying the nerve of the SDLP in and near Derry at a very difficult time for them. My visit also provided an opportunity to meet members of other parties in the Derry area, including not only the Faulkner Unionists (now the Unionist Party of Northern Ireland) and the Alliance Party but also some Official Unionists. Under the local power-sharing arrangement introduced in Derry by the SDLP, which had a dominant position on the reformed city council, the Mayor at that time was an Official Unionist, Jack Allen. He extended to me the courtesy of an official reception—the first, I believe, ever to have been accorded by a Unionist Mayor of Derry City Council to a Minister from the Republic, or indeed to a Roman Catholic visitor.

The October general election came and went. Frank Maguire, a nationalist independent, won Fermanagh-South Tyrone from the Unionists. With a majority of only three at Westminster, Labour was now condemned to a measure of dependence on the Liberals for what might be a full term in office. That they might also seek a 'reinsurance' in the form of a deal with the Unionists in return for additional Northern Ireland seats at Westminster was not foreseen by us at the time, and did not in fact happen for several years.

Whatever temporary effects the British government's pre-election reassurances to the SDLP and ourselves may have had at the time, these soon disappeared after the election. A wave of loyalist sectarian assassinations in Belfast, concentrated in the northern part of the city and its suburbs, intensified the fears of the minority throughout the province. They saw a striking contrast between the absence of searching or even patrolling in loyalist areas and the saturation of minority areas of the city by troops searching houses and arresting young people. Our own officials visiting Belfast were able to confirm this picture and to report that no attempt was being made to screen people entering nationalist areas from nearby loyalist ghettos. At the same time the minority in their then state of mind may not have given sufficient credit to the RUC in this matter; at the end of October an NIO civil servant claimed to us that the RUC had arrested ten people for fifteen of these murders.

However that may have been, the climate of fear and despair amongst the minority was deeper than at any previous time, bringing with it the danger of a sharp growth in support for the IRA, which, in the absence of action by the security forces, was increasingly being seen by many in threatened areas as the only possible protection against the loyalist paramilitary murder campaign.

On the political front the SDLP concluded—correctly—from their contacts with Unionist politicians that there was little chance of a successful outcome to the proposed Convention. Moreover, what they saw as the failure of the security forces to tackle the greatly intensified loyalist sectarian murder campaign soon persuaded most of the SDLP, including John Hume, that the British were preparing to withdraw from Northern Ireland and to negotiate with the loyalists the establishment of an independent Northern Ireland. That this might not be totally excluded if the Convention failed, as it seemed virtually certain to do, seemed to be confirmed to our officials by a senior NIO civil servant in Belfast, who, while himself opposing such a withdrawal, referred to its attraction for British politicians. At the same time this official felt that Merlyn Rees himself had exaggerated the desire for withdrawal amongst the British electorate, possibly because of the strength of feeling on the issue in his own constituency.

Against this generally discouraging background a further meeting with the British government was arranged for 1 November. The Tánaiste, Brendan Corish, and I accompanied Liam Cosgrave, and Merlyn Rees was present with Harold Wilson. In the preliminary tete-à-tete on this occasion Liam Cosgrave raised again our concerns about the Convention. The substitution in the Queen's Speech of the phrase 'in the direction of affairs' for 'in government' as part of the definition of power-sharing had re-aroused our suspicions, which were by no means allayed by Harold Wilson's airy assurance to Liam Cosgrave that they were only saying the same thing over again, using a different form of words. He added that before the election the Conservatives had been toying with the idea of watering down power-sharing in government 'until I rumbled it'; then they had denied any intention of shifting ground on the issue. They would certainly not do so under Whitelaw, who would 'vomit at the thought'.

During the general discussion Cosgrave asked point blank what steps were being taken to deal with a repetition of the strike. Wilson said he did not know. When I pressed the point, adding that the implicit threat by loyalist power workers to abuse their control of the power stations had been known for five years, Rees hastily tried to change the subject to the British government's proposals for the Convention, adding, however, that discussion on power-sharing would not cause another strike: it was the Irish dimension that had 'knocked everything' last May. I pointed out that the last strike had been specifically directed at bringing down the power-sharing Executive, and that if a similar strike took place again it could be accompanied this time by attempts to seal off minority areas; the loyalists were now completely convinced that the British government would not intervene and confront them.

Wilson again attempted to dodge the issue by saying that Westminster would not restore the Stormont system. I responded that we feared that the minority in the ghetto areas in Belfast could be starved out in the event of another strike and that nothing the Prime Minister had said had convinced us that the British government would cope with this. Rees insisted that if the minority community were under threat, steps would be taken to protect them; there would be no question of letting them be killed or starved.

Cosgrave pointed out that in the Rathcoole area of north Belfast almost five hundred Catholic families had now been intimidated out of their homes, without *any* British response—to which Rees, apparently oblivious of any contradiction with his previous response, replied calmly that these things could and had happened, and that Glengormley and the small Catholic areas in east Belfast were under similar threat; but in a strike situation the British army would have as a prime objective the protection of the minority.

I refrained from asking why the British army could not protect the minority under peaceful conditions if, as Rees suggested, it could do so when overstretched during a strike; instead I asked how loyalist paramilitaries could be persuaded that the British government would ever take action against them when, despite what had happened and was happening, no such action was now being taken? Merlyn Rees asked what action could they take against sectarian assassinations. I replied that for a start the army could act in the same way in both loyalist and nationalist areas; so long as security action appeared uneven, the nationalist minority feared they would not be protected and the loyalist majority operated on the assumption that they could get away with anything.

This suggestion that the army should act impartially, evoked from Merlyn Rees a statement that this would involve a radical reappraisal of policy. When Brendan Corish asked what was being achieved by the army harassing and brutalising Catholics in minority areas, Merlyn Rees did not challenge this description of what was happening but simply replied that it was stopping soldiers being shot.

We were obviously wasting our time. After a further brief joust between Rees and myself, Corish raised the Frank Stagg hunger-strike issue, and I asked whether the search procedures for Stagg's visitors could not be carried out in a less unpleasant manner and whether his wife might be allowed to visit him immediately in view of the latest news of his condition. Merlyn Rees said he would refer my requests to the Home Secretary, Roy Jenkins.

It was a depressed and frankly furious Irish party that left Downing Street that day; but an unexpected opportunity for a further discussion between Cosgrave and Wilson occurred shortly after this following the funeral of Erskine

Childers, who only eighteen months after his election as President dropped dead when he had just delivered an address to the College of Physicians. He had taken his duties as President very seriously, and, moving to this office from the position of Tánaiste in the previous Fianna Fáil Government, had experienced difficulty in coming to terms with the constraints of office as a constitutional president.

Some weeks after his election I had had personal experience of his frustration. After the presentation of credentials by an ambassador, an occasion when it was my duty as Minister for Foreign Affairs to be in attendance on the President, he had asked if he could have a word with me in his office. We had always had a good personal relationship, which transcended our different political allegiances. He told me then that he was faced with an impossible situation. During his campaign for election as President he had promised to establish a 'think-tank' to look ahead to the longer-term needs of the country, but he had now been told by the Taoiseach that he could not carry out this commitment. As he could not dishonour his promise to the electorate, he felt that he must resign.

Summoning up such resources of tact and diplomacy as I possessed I set about dissuading him from such a dramatic course of action. At first I had little success. Then I thought of an analogy that I felt might influence him. 'President,' I said, 'could you envisage what the attitude of a British government would be if the Queen established a think-tank in Buckingham Palace to plan the evolution of Britain? The Queen is above politics, but until several months ago you were the Tánaiste of a Fianna Fáil Government, now in opposition. Surely you can see that this would create an even greater problem than in the case of the Queen?' The analogy worked. He accepted my point, and the threatened crisis was resolved.

His sudden death in office eighteen months later was the first such event in Ireland, and involved a state funeral with representation from many countries throughout the world, including the King of the Belgians, the Grand Duke of Luxembourg, Crown Princess Beatrix of the Netherlands (as she then was), Earl Mountbatten and Harold Wilson, and a US delegation led by the Chief Justice.

The opportunity for a further Cosgrave-Wilson discussion came just before the Prime Minister's departure. In this encounter Wilson reasserted the importance that he and his colleagues attached to agreement on an acceptable form of devolved government emanating from the Convention. He could not see direct rule as a permanent feature, and said that the consequence for Northern Ireland of 'getting the British out' would be extremely serious.

On the chairmanship of the Convention, elections to which were to be held in March, Wilson mentioned that they were thinking of the Lord Chief Justice of Northern Ireland, Sir Robert Lowry—a name that Cosgrave felt would be well received. The Taoiseach went on to raise again our concerns about the loyalist sectarian assassination campaign, the provocative behaviour of the British army, and internment, without evoking much response from Wilson on any of these issues.

On the day after the funeral we had a further meeting with the SDLP, attended by the Taoiseach, Tánaiste, and myself, three other Ministers, and the Attorney General. The Secretary of the NIO, Frank Cooper, had, they said, been 'floating' proposals involving a two-thirds remission of sentences, an amnesty for those surrendering illegally held arms, and a withdrawal of British troops to barracks in certain areas, linked to a cease-fire before Christmas. Cooper was asking what would happen if troops were withdrawn from, say, the Bogside and south Armagh: would the IRA take over these areas? Could these soundings conceivably be a prelude to a British withdrawal from Northern Ireland as a whole?

At the same time the SDLP were concerned that the IRA might have taken a definite decision that only a civil war, involving the South, could enable them to achieve their aims, combined with an all-out bombing campaign in Britain designed to provoke what they hoped might be an irresistible demand in Britain for the withdrawal of the British army.

Shortly before this, Mary Holland had interviewed Dáithí Ó Conaill on London Weekend Television. While there was not much new in what he said about Northern Ireland, his remarks about our state were, perhaps, more revealing of IRA thinking than usual. The IRA's objective was to see the 'Southern establishment go by the board.' Having said that he visualised an Algerian-type situation, with the unionists in the role of the French settlers, he went on to say that in a 'doomsday situation' with Catholics being massacred by a loyalist army the people of the South could 'create an army' to intervene in the North. 'In such a situation the first casualties will be the politicians: the likes of the Cosgraves, the Lynches, the O'Briens, who'd be shown up for what they are . . . Significant sections of the Irish army would not stand by irrespective of what orders came from the politicians.'

John Hume believed that a British withdrawal scenario with consequences for the island as a whole could be pre-empted by a commitment by the two governments to work together to establish new agreed institutions, together with a British undertaking to remain in Northern Ireland until these were established. In the meantime others on the SDLP side wanted us to prepare contingency plans for a withdrawal and to discuss them with the British. We refused, however, as this would give the British the excuse they might perhaps want to get out of Northern Ireland, and it was our clear policy to avoid this at all costs. Pat Cooney summed up the dilemma succinctly: the SDLP regarded as a certainty, or near-certainty, what for the Government was so far only an unspoken thought, namely that despite their assurances and attitude up to now, the British might in fact withdraw from the North.

Given the difference between our appreciation of the situation and that of the SDLP, the meeting ended inconclusively. We were quite simply not prepared to take the risk involved in overtly raising with the British the possibility of their withdrawal, especially as, although we recognised the danger of such a development, on balance we thought it improbable.

The Birmingham pub bombings, which occurred on 21 November, killing 19 people and injuring 182, had an immense impact on opinion in Britain, where a clear distinction between the IRA and the rest of the Irish people had not yet emerged, as it later did in the 1980s. Nor was the British government of that period as sensitive as British governments later became to the need to emphasise this distinction. The fall-out from these bombings in relation to the Irish community in Britain was huge, including the arrest of the Birmingham Six. Within less than a week the Prevention of Terrorism legislation was published. Draconian though its provisions were, we at least succeeded in persuading the British government not to introduce passport requirements for travel between Ireland and Britain.

Our suspicion that, against this background, the Labour government might be prepared to consider some watered-down form of power-sharing in order to conciliate the Unionists was reinforced some weeks later by a conversation that our Ambassador had with Stan Orme on the occasion of the long-planned security conference in London between the Minister for Justice, Pat Cooney, and Merlyn Rees. Orme stressed the undesirability of the SDLP being 'oversticky' in its demands. He added that any institutionalised form of an Irish dimension was now out, saying that our Government should bring this home to the SDLP; a reference to the Irish dimension in the Queen's Speech had already been described to us by a British official as 'the quintessence of watering down'.

Shortly after this, on 19 December, I met Rees at the NIO in London at his suggestion. The Gardaí had just broken up a meeting on 10 December at Feakle, Co. Clare, between the IRA and a group of Protestant clergymen from Northern Ireland who had put forward proposals for a cessation of the violence in the North. The response of the IRA to the clergymen, although generally negative, had included a proposal for a cease-fire from 22 December to 2 January. While Merlyn Rees denied that the British were directly involved in talks with the IRA, our official note of my meeting with him recorded that the tone of the discussion gave rise to some doubts about this. It later transpired that some time previously Rees had authorised a contact with Provisional Sinn Féin but that the first he actually heard of the proposed Feakle talks appeared to have been from one of the intermediaries involved.

I told the Northern Ireland Secretary of our concern at the apparent downplaying of the Irish dimension by the British government, and I was disturbed to hear from him that in the forthcoming Green Paper on Northern Ireland he proposed to set out forms of power-sharing that existed in countries like the Netherlands, Belgium, Switzerland—and Lebanon! At this stage no particular system should be ruled out, he added. I felt that the mention of such inappropriate models could be highly dangerous.

The discussion at our meeting was devoted largely to cross-border security issues. In answer to the usual complaints from the British side about communications problems, I asked if they could give any instance where they had been dissatisfied with the reaction of the Gardaí, or, in appropriate cases, the Irish army, to requests for assistance. There was no reply to this. With regard to complaints by Merlyn Rees of alleged quantities of arms and explosives coming into Northern Ireland from the Republic, I responded that allegations to this effect were being made by the British to newspapermen, Council of Europe delegates, and others, but in the whole of 1974 we could trace no specific information having being passed to us by them about such finds, save for one case involving explosives that had proved a false lead. In the previous seven weeks five specific requests to the British as to whom on our side had allegedly been given such information had moreover elicited no reply. This statement of mine produced no specific information either.

I then proposed that, if they could give us no information about arms or explosives, they should desist from their propaganda campaign, which, as at other times during the 1970s and early 1980s, appeared to us to be a smoke-screen designed to divert attention away from the performance of the security forces in Northern Ireland. I took the opportunity, moreover, of protesting against incidents where the British army had entered the Republic and had hijacked cars or fired on the Gardaí or the Irish army.

Jumping ahead for a moment, we discovered some time later that throughout 1973 and 1974 the British army had in fact been making finds in Northern Ireland of explosive wrappers from Frangex explosives stored at Enfield, Co. Meath, but had told us nothing of these discoveries, either at diplomatic or security level. Statistical data on explosives finds furnished by the British authorities in March 1974 had omitted any reference to identification of the origin of these explosives, and other messages and discussions had related solely to explosives manufactured with fertilisers. It was hard to resist the conclusion that the British army had preferred to use these discoveries as a basis for a propaganda campaign against us rather than to give us information that could have helped us to stop the flow of explosives in 1973. In the meantime we had ourselves discovered a leakage of explosives from a store in Enfield and had arrested and tried six soldiers in early 1975 in connection with this, but we could have acted much earlier, and many lives might have been saved, if the British had given us details of the information in their possession at the time when they had made these discoveries instead of using them for black propaganda about our state.

When I took this scandal up with Stan Orme some weeks after this December meeting his response was that he was not interested in looking back before the accession to power of the Labour government in March 1974, a reply that did not explain why his own Government had neglected to give us this information for nine months, and that in any event seemed to me to show an extraordinary attitude to security.

But to return to my London visit on 19 December: I also met Jim Callaghan on EC matters, and I used the occasion to press on him my concern that

Merlyn Rees had started to talk about 'voluntary' power-sharing, and also seemed to be weakening on the Irish dimension. He asked his private secretary to ensure that he saw the draft of the forthcoming Green Paper on Northern Ireland during the Christmas break.

I made the same points when I met Ted Heath in the House of Commons. He said that he understood my concern: he had himself noted the absence of any reference to an 'Irish dimension' in recent Commons debates, and it would be foolish of the Government to consider voluntary power-sharing in the Northern Ireland context.

On the next day the IRA announced a cease-fire to run from 22 December to 2 January 'to give the British government an opportunity to consider proposals for a permanent cease-fire.' The cease-fire was accompanied by contacts between the NIO and Provisional Sinn Féin, about which the SDLP and ourselves were, as ever, suspicious, and on 2 January the cease-fire was extended by the IRA for another fortnight. A week later an NIO official came to Dublin to brief us on the statement that Merlyn Rees was to make in the House of Commons on 14 January.

By this time we were also deeply concerned lest the British government water down power-sharing to a degree that would threaten the restoration of Unionist power on lines not greatly dissimilar to Stormont, thus pushing the nationalist population in desperation towards the IRA. Before leaving for the United States for my 8 January meeting with Henry Kissinger in my new capacity as President of the EC Council of Ministers, I drafted a strong letter to Harold Wilson for Liam Cosgrave's signature. It was considerably modified before being transmitted, but it evoked the response we sought. In reply Wilson assured Cosgrave that there was no change in British policy and that to be acceptable to them any proposals from the Convention must include some form of power-sharing in government. He added that the examples of power-sharing in other countries that we knew they proposed to mention in their forthcoming discussion document would be accompanied by the clarification that many of these arrangements, while useful in any system, would not of themselves ensure the active sharing in government that the British government considered essential.

This came as a relief to us; we had feared that the inclusion of such references in the discussion document might have been intended to give a green light to Unionists for forms of power-sharing that would fall short of participation in government. All in all we felt that our efforts over the preceding months, when there had been every sign—especially at official level—of a backing away from the commitment to power-sharing, had been well worth while in heading off a dangerous trend in British policy.

On the day on which Liam Cosgrave had written to seek this assurance I had been meeting Henry Kissinger in Washington. I did not raise with him our concerns about British policy in relation to Northern Ireland during the formal discussions, but afterwards when travelling in his car with his wife,

Nancy, and himself to a memorial service for Walter Lippmann I told him privately of our worries. I said that I knew of his non-interventionist stance so far as Irish affairs were concerned and was not seeking any action by the United States at that time; but in the event—unlikely, I hoped—of a shift in British policy towards withdrawal from Northern Ireland in advance of an agreed political solution we would then seek US assistance in persuading Britain not to embark on a course of action that could be so fraught with dangers not just to Northern Ireland but to the whole of Ireland, and con-ceivably even—given the involvement of Libya, for example, with the IRA, and Cuba's long-distance role in Angola—to the wider peace of north-western Europe. He agreed that he would be open to an approach from us in the event of such a grave development.

While I had been in Washington, disturbing rumours had been circulating about the British government's contacts with Sinn Féin regarding the contin-uation of the cease-fire. During a visit to Belfast to meet Unionist politicians a Department of Foreign Affairs official passing through a hotel lobby was intro-duced to Séamus Loughran, the Belfast organiser of Sinn Féin, who was involved in the cease-fire talks. Our policy precluded contact by officials with the IRA or Sinn Féin, but in the circumstances the official felt it appropriate to listen to Loughran, who told him that the British government and Sinn Féin were planning negotiations abroad and were currently trying to agree on three 'negotiators' on each side. Sinn Féin wanted our Government to make a number of gestures to assist the cease-fire, including, if the negotiations came to anything, free passes for key people, such as Dáithí Ó Conaill, Chief of Staff of the IRA, Séamus Twomey, commander of the Belfast Brigade, and Kevin Mallon, IRA commander in the border area.

As may be imagined, we ignored these proposals, but the encounter increased our concern about the British contacts with the IRA through Sinn Féin. We noted that when Merlyn Rees made his statement to the House of Commons on 14 January it was only in the course of his replies to subsequent questions that he said there would be no negotiations with the IRA—a point that one might have thought was of sufficient importance to have been included in the statement itself, especially as Merlyn Rees has since said that he had gone over it again and again, 'more than any Budget speech.'

The cease-fire ended on 16 January, but three days later Merlyn Rees issued a statement in which he said that his officials had met members of Provisional Sinn Féin, 'not to negotiate but to explain very carefully and very fully the Government position as it has been publicly stated.' The next day the British Ambassador told us of further contacts, naming Provisional Sinn Féin person-alities involved, and on 23 January he said that there had been a second meeting, 'but little had taken place, because the Sinn Féin people had had little to say.'

On 4 February I saw Galsworthy myself. He told me that 'a third meeting' had taken place on 1 and 2 February but gave the impression, as my officials recorded, that it was neither significant nor conclusive. In the House of

Commons on the following day Merlyn Rees delivered what he has since described as the most important speech he ever made on Northern Ireland, which in his words enabled his officials to 'return to the talks able to emphasise that British government policy was as set out in Parliament.'

Four days later the Provisionals announced a further cease-fire, and within forty-eight hours Robert Fisk published in the *Times* details of what he described as twelve points alleged to have been agreed to by the British in the course of these contacts. We immediately raised this with the NIO in London, who were suddenly unforthcoming on the number of meetings held and on the Sinn Féin personalities involved. They said they were 'at a loss' to explain where the twelve points had come from, but agreed to give us a further full briefing in due course. In his autobiography Merlyn Rees says that these twelve points had in fact been presented by the Provisionals on 21 January, at a time when—according to what the Ambassador had been instructed to tell us—'little had taken place, because the Sinn Féin people had had little to say.'

It can readily be understood that against this background we were sceptical of British attempts to rubbish the twelve points, all the more so because in his Commons statement on the day of the Fisk story Merlyn Rees had made no reference to them, and it was only in response to a question from Julian Amery that he committed himself to the very limited denial: 'There have been no *signed* documents' (my emphasis).

The 'full briefing' promised to us was given by the British Ambassador on 14 February. He said that there had been two further meetings with Sinn Féin after his meeting with me on 4 February but that they had dealt only with incident centres and with Rees's Commons statement of 11 February. He denied knowledge of any participants in these talks other than the three mentioned to us earlier. Our scepticism must have been evident.

A week later, the British government having had considerable time to reflect, the Ambassador asked to see Liam Cosgrave personally. He told him 'as a matter of utmost secrecy' that contrary to what he had said a week earlier the Sinn Féin representation had in the 'later stages' been broadened to include 'one or two others', including Ruairí Ó Brádaigh. The talks had been inconclusive until 'suddenly the Sinn Féin representatives produced a 12-point document.' Sinn Féin had then been told that if they continued the cease-fire the army would end its screening and house and identity checks, its strength would gradually be reduced to peacetime levels, and it would be withdrawn to barracks. The number of detainees would be reduced, with a view to ending detention, but there could be no question of an amnesty or immunity from arrest or granting the Provisionals any role in policing. Carrying firearms would be permitted only in accordance with law, which 'generally' required an RUC permit. This was clearly nearer to the truth than what we had been told before Bob Fisk had run his story, but just how 'clean' the British had now come with us we could not be sure.

Quite apart from the damage done to the Anglo-Irish relationship by the blatant attempt to mislead us about what had transpired in the talks with the Provisionals, we were concerned that the cease-fire might have been primarily designed by the IRA to give them a breathing space before restarting the violence on an even more extensive scale. But our main concern was that the Labour government might ultimately do some kind of political deal with the IRA.

Following the publication at the end of January 1975 of the Gardiner Report on internment, Merlyn Rees had set about gradually releasing the internees—a process that was certainly facilitated by the existence of the cease-fire, and which may, indeed, have been a major consideration on the British side in arranging the cease-fire in the first instance and in encouraging its continuance throughout most of the year.

In mid-February I paid a further visit to Northern Ireland, during which I lectured in Queen's University on the Irish Presidency of the European Community, which had begun seven weeks previously. In my lecture I mentioned that during this six months Dublin would be the francophone capital of the Community—for we were determined, as the first English-speaking country to hold the Presidency, not to weaken the hitherto exclusive role of French as the working language of Political Co-operation at official level, a decision that had a very positive effect on subsequent Franco-Irish relations. I was amused to be told by a member of the audience, Professor Con O'Leary, that I was reversing what Garrett Mór FitzGerald, Earl of Kildare, had done in 1487 as Lord Deputy after Henry VII's usurpation of the throne, when he had sought to win favour with the new King by substituting English for Norman-French as the official language of Ireland for legal purposes. (Incidentally, our decision to retain French as the working language forced the British to follow suit in 1977; later on we were told by a Foreign Office official that some of the tension between Tony Crosland and his Permanent Secretary, Michael Palliser, had derived from Palliser's insistence that they must follow our precedent—which was described as 'an unwarranted break with the tradition of Palmerston, who established the practice at the Foreign Office of transacting all business and communications in English.')

Early in March I was in London again, and I availed myself of the opportunity to call on the newly elected leader of the Conservative Party, Margaret Thatcher, at the House of Commons.

When I arrived Willie Whitelaw took me aside. He wanted to assure me of his commitment to the principle that there could be no devolution without power-sharing in government; if his new leader went back on this, he would resign as deputy leader. He would also oppose any deal with loyalist groups in Northern Ireland, and believed that his position in the party was still such that he could prevent any such deals. I thanked him for what he said, which, however, did not reassure me as to Margaret Thatcher's likely attitude towards Northern Ireland.

He did not remain for the meeting, at which the new leader was accompanied by Airey Neave and an official from Conservative Central Office. As was to be my practice at future meetings with her in the Commons or over breakfast at the embassy while I was Minister for Foreign Affairs, I opened the discussion with some comments on the current position in the European Community. I calculated that, if I could be useful to her by way of such briefings, she would be willing to see me in the future and thus give me the opportunity to get across to her from time to time our position on Northern Ireland.

Looking forward to the British renegotiation being concluded in Dublin at the first European Council meeting in five days' time, she expressed the hope that a 'one and indivisible' British government would come out and campaign for continued British membership. It was, she said, an appalling aspect of the whole affair that Britain had lost respect and support by so blatantly dishonouring an international treaty obligation. This comment on the 1974–75 renegotiation was to come back to me some years later when she herself initiated the second renegotiation of British accession.

When we turned to the subject of Northern Ireland she and Airey Neave listened without much comment. I said that while the cease-fire was welcome, the circumstances in which it had come about, involving discussions with the IRA through intermediaries, gave cause for worry—as did the 'incident centres', which could, we feared, develop a policing role. The minority were extremely unlikely to accept IRA policing, and the prospect of UDR policing particularly unnerved them. We had found the British government's attitude to loyalist violence, especially during the Ulster workers' strike, most unhelpful, and would like to see it confronted.

Airey Neave wondered if the opposition should call for the abolition of the incident centres, but I said that once they had been established, however unwisely, their abolition would certainly threaten the cease-fire. The mistake had been in talking to the IRA in the first instance—something that successive Irish Governments had always refused to do—instead of undermining them by stepping up the release of internees.

I added that we were generally pessimistic about the Convention, in which the loyalists would have an absolute majority and which would, we believed, remain opposed to power-sharing. I went on to describe the contacts we had established with all constitutional parties in the North, which I believed were helpful in easing Unionist fears of the Republic and in keeping us sensitive to Unionist preoccupations. This had a drawback from the point of view of our domestic opinion, but in prevailing circumstances it was the best way that we could contribute to the situation.

Finally I stressed the importance of boosting the position of the SDLP as far as possible; their morale was currently low because of the impact upon their position of British dealings with the IRA. Airey Neave said he hoped to visit Northern Ireland soon and would make a special point of spending time with the SDLP. And there we left it.

As it happened, some weeks later Margaret Thatcher's path and mine crossed again in more relaxed surroundings when, as I have related earlier, we found ourselves together at a Bilderberg meeting in Turkey. Our informal contacts there helped to strengthen the relationship I had endeavoured to establish on constructive foundations in her room at the House of Commons.

# CHAPTER TEN

# COLLAPSE OF THE CONVENTION

In mid-April 1975 Harold Wilson arranged a further briefing by the British Ambassador on his government's contacts with Provisional Sinn Féin. The Ambassador said that there had been two more meetings at Laneside, the NIO office, on the initiative of the British authorities, but that no written documents had been handed over or exchanged, apart from published material that amazingly, he said, Sinn Féin either had not got or had not read or understood. The British had refused immunity or safe conduct for people guilty of criminal offences. There had been no negotiation whatsoever on the political future of Northern Ireland. He added, however, that when the Sinn Féin representatives had 'harped on' the question of a British withdrawal—a reference that made it clear that withdrawal had been raised frequently during the discussions—'the reply had always been on the extreme complexity of the problems of Northern Ireland and a reference to the Northern extremists,' with a query why Sinn Féin did not talk to them.

The contorted obscurity and evasiveness of this reported response, which could even be read as involving an implication that if the two groups of paramilitaries could get together the British might then consider withdrawal, were thoroughly disturbing from our point of view. A couple of days after the Ambassador's briefing Merlyn Rees came to Dublin, and we had an informal discussion at the British embassy. He was not very optimistic about the Convention, and feared that if it failed, pressure in Britain for a withdrawal from Northern Ireland might mount. On the other hand he did not feel that such a failure was likely to precipitate a repetition of the Ulster workers' strike. Under pressure he admitted that if there were another strike the power stations would still present problems; in such circumstances, he added depressingly, 'you don't control the situation and you can't hope to control it.'

On the campaign of sectarian murders—there had been 339 so far, for three-quarters of which loyalist paramilitaries were believed to have been responsible—I pointed out that only 12 convictions had been secured. And I pressed for an effective and visible security presence in danger areas.

Rees told me that he hoped to have all internees released by October, and he described as 'unfortunate' the public criticism of the cease-fire by the GOC, Sir Frank King. (At a meeting that he apparently did not know was attended by a journalist Sir Frank had said, 'If the cease-fire had not been agreed the campaign would have been over in two months.') I told him, as I had told Margaret Thatcher some weeks earlier, that we would have preferred the release of all detainees to British talks with the IRA.

I was particularly concerned about one aspect of Merlyn Rees's attitude to the Convention. He was unhappy, he said, about what he felt to be the excessively generous pay and allowances for its members, especially when compared with those of British MPs. The salary of Convention members was to be £2,500 a year, as against the figure of about £4,500 for Westminster MPs at that time. I argued the contrary case strongly, pointing to the importance of enabling good people to stay in politics in Northern Ireland under conditions that were immensely worse than those prevailing in our state or in Britain; politicians in the North were, after all, potential targets for assassination.

A year later Merlyn Rees's blind spot on this issue led him to cease paying Convention members their miserable allowance entirely and to close down the Stormont building as soon as the Convention had finally failed to reach agreement. It was with visible reluctance that when the Convention was in session he had allowed its members to make representations on behalf of their constituents, and he made it clear that he was determined that these politicians should play no role of this kind once they had ceased to perform their deliberative function. He insisted that Ministers should thereafter receive representations only from Westminster MPs.

His British background seemed to inhibit him from understanding the value of facilitating personal contacts between politicians from the two communities, for which the bar and restaurant at Stormont uniquely provided a discreet forum. Moreover, because, understandably, politicians of neither community were inclined to drop in to the NIO's fortified headquarters for a casual drink or cup of coffee, the closure of the Stormont building to politicians also deprived the British government after March 1976 of its only point of informal contact with non-Westminster politicians in Northern Ireland, who were, almost by definition, the only politicians likely to have an interest in devolution.

Another point I noted during our discussion in the British embassy was Merlyn Rees's dismissive attitude towards Airey Neave, whom he described as knowing nothing about Northern Ireland and showing no ability to learn about it quickly. He thought that Neave's only interest was in trying to arrange a link-up between Unionist MPs and the Conservative Party, and he expressed the hope that I might succeed in giving Neave a broader picture. It later became clear that some of his officials shared his view of the opposition spokesman on Northern Ireland.

Reflecting on our discussion, I was worried by what he had said about his government's inability to deal with another loyalist strike. I therefore suggested to Liam Cosgrave that he write again to Harold Wilson on the subject, and this letter was sent early in May. It asked that Wilson would look again at the problem in relation to essential services such as electricity with a view to ensuring that no group of workers could in future abuse their position by frustrating the implementation of the British government's policy on Northern Ireland. Wilson's reply a fortnight later accepted that in the event of a failure by the Convention to reach an agreed solution to the problem of devolution in Northern Ireland they could not exclude a renewed threat to essential services, and he added, unhelpfully, 'As your message implies, the responsibility for deciding how to deal with such a situation lies with us, and I can assure you that it is being taken into account in our planning.'

The composition of the Convention elected at the beginning of May 1975 was much as we had expected: the UUUC, as the alliance of anti-power-sharing Unionist parties was known, won 47 of the 78 seats; the SDLP had 17; the Alliance Party 8; and the Faulknerite Unionists 5.

On the RTE radio news programme on the Sunday following the election Conor Cruise O'Brien was interviewed. In reply to a question about power-sharing at Ministerial level he replied: 'I think it's not on. In fact I think there isn't going to be a power-sharing Executive.' Earlier in the interview he had already said that he saw no possibility of agreement in this Convention on an institutionalised 'Irish dimension', and he had also agreed with the interviewer that these had been the two main planks of the Government's and the SDLP's policy.

As it happened, Seán Donlon was with John Hume as he listened to this interview, which provoked a stream of telephone calls to John from other SDLP members. John Hume then asked Seán to return to Dublin at once to deliver a message to the Taoiseach. The message began by recalling that despite grave doubts the SDLP had taken the political and physical risk of standing for the Convention—at our urging, he might have said but did not—and they feared that if they withdrew from it at this stage the IRA could emerge as the leading influence in the nationalist community. Because of the danger of violence, both the SDLP and the UUUC had very responsibly decided to restrict their comments on the results so as to ensure that if the Convention failed it would do so in a way calculated to minimise the reaction on the streets in Northern Ireland.

He went on to say that the SDLP found it unacceptable that a spokesman for the Dublin Government should without consultation with them have announced on the heels of the election results that the policies to which that Government and the SDLP were committed were unattainable. The participation of the SDLP in the Convention was now extremely difficult; their credibility in the eyes of the minority community would be drastically reduced if they participated in a Convention on an electoral mandate based on policies said to be unattainable by a Minister in the Dublin Government. John Hume added that if the Taoiseach had any message for the SDLP arising from the results of the Convention election they would appreciate receiving it as soon as possible, preferably before the Convention met.

This protest was the more effective for being worded with such studied moderation; no doubt Seán Donlon's presence had contributed to its tone. It carried, nevertheless, a strong implication that unless something were done to redress the impact of Conor's interview the SDLP might find it impossible to take part in the Convention and that we would then have to take the consequences for our state as well as Northern Ireland of the resultant boost to the IRA.

I immediately drafted a statement that the Taoiseach could make in the Dáil on Tuesday. With a few amendments this was approved by the Government, and Liam Cosgrave made the statement in the Dáil that afternoon. It reiterated that the Government's policy was based on the need for a power-sharing Executive in the North, and it stressed that the Government would continue to keep in close touch with the Northern political parties—in particular with the SDLP, without whose approval, as the party that had repeatedly secured the confidence of the vast bulk of the minority, no effective system could be put into operation in Northern Ireland.

The rift was healed, but scars remained; the already uneasy relationship between the SDLP and Conor Cruise O'Brien never recovered from this unfortunate episode.

A fortnight later, when Joan and I were passing through Lebanon en route to Jordan, I was told that the early stages of the Convention were going badly. Having made little progress, it eventually adjourned on 26 June for six weeks; but it had been decided that during this recess there would be private talks between the parties. Later the recess was extended until early September.

While these informal talks were in progress Liam Cosgrave and I were in Helsinki for the conclusion and signature of the CSCE (Conference on Security and Co-operation in Europe) agreement. We took the opportunity to brief other governments on the Northern Ireland situation. It was a measure of our continuing concern about what might happen if the Convention were to fail that we laid stress in these discussions on the danger of an escalation of violence; this, we said, would carry with it 'a very real risk of massacre and/or expulsion of exposed minorities,' and would threaten the peace of the whole island. The continued containment of violence in Northern Ireland by the sovereign UK government was therefore essential both for us and to prevent the creation of a dangerous vacuum in that part of north-western Europe.

At about this time we heard that IRA men were being allowed to move around Northern Ireland unmolested, carrying side-arms. In particular we were disturbed to be told that Séamus Twomey, who had escaped from prison in the Republic (and whom Merlyn Rees in his book describes first as 'Belfast Brigade Commander of the IRA' and later as being 'correctly' identified by the British army as 'Chief of Staff of the IRA', but 'no longer a wanted man'!), was being left to go about freely. It was reported that Twomey had been identified by a British army patrol near the Springfield Road but had not been arrested. When asked about this in the House of Commons by Jim Molyneaux some weeks later, Rees confirmed that a patrol had seen someone like Twomey but that they had been unable to get a positive identification without reinforcements, and that by the time reinforcements arrived 'the man had left in a taxi.' He added that he did not know where Molyneaux got his information about Twomey being Chief of Staff of the IRA or whether he had any evidence that would lead to a criminal prosecution in Northern Ireland. And he denied that people wanted for criminal offences enjoyed immunity.

To say that this reply, and especially the second part of it, raised eyebrows in Dublin would be to understate our reaction. Our Ambassador was instructed to present a written request for an assurance that Twomey, whom the British knew was wanted in the Republic for his prison escape, was being actively sought in Northern Ireland and that if the RUC became aware of his whereabouts they would communicate this through police channels so that extradition proceedings could be initiated. We received, belatedly, the assurance we sought.

The whole of this year was indeed dominated by uncertainty about British policy regarding the security and political aspects of the Northern crisis—an uncertainty so general and pervasive as to raise the question whether it might not have been deliberately encouraged by the British government. That was indeed the view that I put forward in mid-July when I had the opportunity to address an audience at the Royal Institute of International Affairs in London. In my remarks there I suggested that during the period after the loyalist strike British policy-makers may have felt they had two options. The first was to make it absolutely clear that there could be no self-government in Northern Ireland except on a power-sharing basis, which might have induced a shift in attitude on the Unionist side on the basis that 70 per cent of power was better than 0 per cent; the second was to seek to create uncertainty about its intentions in order to frighten genuine unionists into accepting power-sharing lest they put the union with Britain at risk by intransigence. I went on to add that it was widely believed in Ireland that the British were pursuing the second option, because the 'credibility gap' in Northern Ireland about their intentions was so wide on both sides of the community divide that success with the first option would have been very difficult.

In retrospect I feel, however, that in my analysis of the British position at that time I may well have fallen into the trap about which I have often warned others: that is, believing that a British government was actually pursuing any thought-out strategy when its actions in creating uncertainty may in fact have been the product of confusion and muddle, at least at the political level. In this instance the situation may have been further complicated because of the temporarily dominant role of civil servants in the NIO, openly contemptuous of their political masters in their discussions with our officials and with some members of the press, and possibly pursuing somewhat different objectives from those of their Ministers.

Having indicated in my remarks how the uncertainty regarding British intentions had encouraged some loyalists to talk about 'negotiated independence' for a new state of 'Ulster', to which both communities could give their allegiance, I concluded by saying that it was because of the inherent instability and other dangers inevitable in an independent Northern Ireland that the policy of our Government had consistently favoured self-government within the United Kingdom, leaving the question of the ultimate status of the area to a future when a decision on the long-term question could be taken in conditions of peace and rationality.

This indeed reflected our settled view, which had been reaffirmed by the Government nine months earlier after a study in depth of all alternative possibilities that had been carried out after the loyalist strike. In making this study we had, as I have just mentioned, the advantage of contacts with a wide range of politicians in Northern Ireland, drawn from all parties. Some I met myself, on visits to Belfast or in Dublin or London; other contacts were developed by officials of the Department of Foreign Affairs in the course of visits to Northern Ireland, which, following my appointment as Minister, had been extended to cover the Unionist part of the political spectrum. And some political contacts beyond the range possible for these officials were maintained by Paddy Harte, the Fine Gael TD for Donegal, who has devoted so much time and energy to the problems of Northern Ireland.

We were at that time, I believe, closer to the Unionist political scene than at any moment before, or perhaps since. Of course it was not always easy to be sure whether some of those we were in touch with were 'selling us a line' or whether they were actually bringing us genuinely into their confidence. The views expressed to us and the information we obtained had to be very carefully sifted before we could be reasonably certain that it offered us a solid basis for our policies. Nevertheless it is, I believe, fair to say that during much of 1975 and 1976 we were not alone able to work constructively with the SDLP and with Unionists who favoured a genuine power-sharing structure but also maintained useful and friendly contacts with more negative and traditional Unionist politicians. And I believe, that for a period at least, a greater degree of trust and confidence existed between many of the leaders of both communities in the North and our Government than existed between any of these politicians and the British government at that time. Moreover, as our mistrust of British policy began to diminish with the weakening of their contacts with the Provisionals it became possible for me to communicate some of what we knew about Unionist thinking to the British government, which, especially after the ending of the Convention in March 1976, had tended to lose touch with the politicians in Northern Ireland.

But that was for the future. For the moment there was no possibility of my passing on personally to Rees any information about Northern political attitudes that might come my way, for he had decided that he would not meet me—

indeed, that there should be no meetings between the two governments so long as the Convention was sitting, lest any such meeting should alarm the UUUC (with a number of the leaders of which we seemed to be in closer contact than he was) or should make them suspicious of Dublin interference. By thus leaning over backwards to keep the UUUC happy he was, in fact, contributing to the growth of suspicion and misunderstanding between our two governments, especially as we were thus deprived of any opportunity to explain to him personally the nature of our concerns.

I was glad therefore when an opportunity arose for an informal contact with another member of the British government in relaxed circumstances that might, I hoped, enable us to break through Merlyn Rees's 'wall of silence'. I must first explain the background to this encounter.

In August 1975 we holidayed in west Cork. Belatedly, during July, we had picked quite arbitrarily on Schull, where the local auctioneer had found us a beautiful house, with its own beach and a pier from which one could swim, the only disadvantage of the house being its collection of Burmese antiques, to the survival of which holidaying children might be a hazard.

During the month of August over a score of friends stayed with us, and several dozen others visited us; but in the context of this chapter the most significant visitors were Jim and Audrey Callaghan, who were holidaying with their daughter and son-in-law, Margaret and Peter Jay, at their house in nearby Glandore. We had two meetings with the Callaghans: one a dinner engagement at the Jays' together with Jack and Máirín Lynch, and the other a lunch at our house a few days later, with Brendan and Phyllis Corish. Jack and Máirín Lynch, to whose house we had been invited earlier in the month for their traditional August party, were to have been with us on the second occasion also, but he had to go unexpectedly to Dublin to pay a last visit to Éamon de Valera, who was dying.

In preparation for these two social occasions I asked my department to prepare suggestions for points I should make if the opportunity arose, and I arranged for Conor Cruise O'Brien, with whom I had discussed the proposed Callaghan meeting, to make an input to this briefing. (He and his wife, Máire, and their two children had also been among our visitors there.)

The after-dinner discussion on the first occasion was led off by Callaghan, who asked how Lynch and myself saw Northern Ireland three to five years hence. Jack Lynch responded that he saw little hope of success at the Convention, now in recess, and a very uncertain situation thereafter in view of the strength of the paramilitaries—an assessment with which I concurred. Asked by Jim Callaghan what I thought the British government should do, I dodged the question by propounding my earlier thesis that since the loyalist strike the British government had seemed to us to have been deliberately creating uncertainty with a view to inducing realism amongst Northern politicians. Callaghan commented that he had disagreed with the handling of the strike: the British government should not have given in to the strikers but should have sat it out.

I went on to stress the gravity of the problem that would be created for us should there be a failure on the part of the British government to control the situation and to protect the minority. It would not be within our power to resolve the crisis that would then arise, and such a failure could threaten democratic government in our state. When Callaghan suggested that this was too pessimistic a view I pointed to the situation that had arisen after the massacre at Derry in early 1972, when the Government of the day had not been able to prevent the burning of the British embassy in Dublin. Jack Lynch supported me, pointing to the problems that he had also faced in 1969. I emphasised the danger of a political vacuum in Ireland in which extra-European powers, such as the Soviet Union, China, or Libya, might be tempted to meddle.

Among other points I raised was the imbalance of armed forces in Ireland at that time. When I said that our army was only 12,500 strong and could not be increased to a level that would afford us security without such an action appearing provocative to Unionists, Jim Callaghan challenged this, saying that we could raise it to 20,000 without having this effect. When I pointed out that such an increase would require the calling up of reserves or the introduction of conscription, he did not further contest the point. I went on to say that British army strength in the North had been sharply reduced. On the other hand the replacement for the 8,000 B Specials—the UDR and RUC Reserve, whose strength had now grown to 14,000—could not be relied on, since in a 'dooms-day' situation they would be likely to support the 20,000 to 25,000-strong loyalist paramilitaries. Even on the assumption that the RUC remained neutral until it saw who won, there was now a dangerous imbalance in the strength of the armed forces in the island. Callaghan did not challenge this, and said that it had been a mistake to allow the new forces established in Northern Ireland to exceed 4,000.

Repartition was raised by Callaghan: I said that it would be unworkable and unacceptable, leading to an unstable situation like that in Cyprus, or in Palestine, which could last for thirty or fifty years, placing the security of Britain as well as Ireland at risk throughout such a period.

On the question of a British declaration of intent to withdraw from Northern Ireland after a period, Jack Lynch said that in the present unstable and emotional atmosphere such a declaration would be highly dangerous—a view with which I wholeheartedly concurred.

In my report of this discussion I commented that Jim Callaghan seemed genuinely convinced of the importance of Britain staying in Northern Ireland and making a stand against the loyalist paramilitaries, and that I thought we had significantly reinforced his view about the danger to Britain as well as Ireland of Britain not fulfilling its responsibilities there, but that as a last resort he might be prepared to consider repartition combined with an exchange of populations.

When Callaghan came to lunch with us three days later he was very taken with the house we had rented, and as we walked down to the pier together he wondered whether it might be for sale. While Harold Wilson had told Jim

Callaghan that he would give him three months' notice if he intended to retire so that Callaghan might prepare to succeed him, Callaghan did not think Wilson would take this step in the foreseeable future, and accordingly, as he was older than Wilson, he was contemplating retiring, possibly in 1976. The house we were in was the kind of place he would love to be able to stay in after retiring. Barely six months later he replaced Wilson as Prime Minister.

When we reverted to discussing Northern Ireland, Callaghan said that in a 'doomsday' situation Harold Wilson would be 'all right', but there would be a number of people on the Labour benches in favour of disengagement, and a number of Tories who would support the loyalists.

I said that the Anglo-Irish relationship had been less close since the Ulster workers' strike. He asked if this was because his government had failed to act; I replied that this was in part the reason but that the problem derived also from continuing uncertainty about British policy, aggravated by the discussions taking place between them and Sinn Féin. We did not feel that we had been brought fully into the confidence of the British government. There was now reason to believe that in the course of these discussions officials had allowed the IRA to suppose that a declaration of intent to withdraw would be considered by Britain if and when the Convention talks broke down.

Jim Callaghan doubted whether British officials would have acted in this way. They sometimes acted beyond their authority, but this was a rare event. He went on to ask whether Merlyn Rees—who was, he said, a close friend of his—had been made aware of our feeling of uncertainty and of not being in the full confidence of the British government. Had we spoken to Merlyn Rees as bluntly as we had spoken to him? I said that we had not, adding diplomatically that Rees was, we knew, under very great pressure. I thought it better at that stage not to press the point about Rees's refusal to meet us during the life of the Convention.

My caution was immediately rewarded. Did I think, Callaghan asked, that a joint meeting between Merlyn Rees, himself and myself would be a good thing? That could be very valuable, I responded, with an inward sign of relief; we had made the breakthrough, or so at least I hoped. He would try to arrange such a meeting, he said.

About ten days later, when Callaghan and I met again in New York at a UN special session, he was still keen on a joint meeting. But a week after that I had a further discussion with him in Venice, in the margin of a European Political Co-operation meeting, at which it became clear that Rees had taken his proposal amiss. Such a reaction had always been a strong possibility, of course, and I had had some warning of what was to come, because an NIO official had told our Ambassador in London on the day before my Venice meeting with Callaghan that the 'request' for a meeting with the two Secretaries of State together was 'a bit strange', and that Rees might not agree to it. The comment suggested that Callaghan might have decided it was more tactful in his relations with Rees to turn *his* suggestion for such a joint meeting into a request from me—with predictable consequences.

It quickly emerged that Jim Callaghan had found no takers for the idea of a joint meeting between the two Secretaries of State and myself. In fact it became clear that he had not merely met resistance to such a meeting but had been told to head off the idea of *any* meeting while the Convention continued. The possibility of restoring some kind of trust and confidence between the two governments, never mind developing a common strategy towards the post-Convention situation, had been aborted by Merlyn Rees's determination to avoid any contact with us.

Despite his claim not to have talked 'seriously' to Rees since Schull, it was obvious that Callaghan had now been fully briefed by him. For he went on to say that he had checked on the matter raised by me on several occasions in Schull, namely whether the British government had been allowing an impression to arise that it might contemplate a 'pull-out' from Northern Ireland. In words clearly chosen with great care, he continued that Merlyn Rees had told him that he was quite clear that there had been 'no such statement' by Sir Frank Cooper, the Secretary of the Northern Ireland Office, or anyone else. Callaghan wanted to assure me that such a 'proposal' had not come before the Cabinet—and he was in a privileged position to know this—nor had it been before any 'official committee', nor had there been any such statement to anyone. This was as categorical a denial as he could make, he added, for he wanted to remove any lingering doubts about the British government's attitude—'to date'. The last two words were stressed, but were accompanied by the slightly humorous smile that was often a feature of his delivery, as if to say that the British government's conscience was clear so far but that the future was never wholly predictable. That at any rate was the impression of the official accompanying me on that occasion.

And, of course, the carefully worded denial had not been categorical. For I had never said that there had been a *statement* to Provisional Sinn Féin about a possible British declaration of intent to withdraw, only that British officials might have allowed the IRA to derive such an impression and to continue to believe that such a declaration might be made in the event of a breakdown of the Convention.

On 22 September the *Daily Telegraph* published a story to the effect that a document found on Dáithí Ó Conaill (reportedly Chief of Staff of the IRA at that point) when he was arrested by the Gardaí had been a copy of an agreement between the British government and the IRA on eventual withdrawal. This story, which we were in a position to deny, gave me an excuse to ring Merlyn Rees to explain that as soon as we had seen the story I had contacted the Minister for Justice and the Taoiseach with a view to getting a denial out in time for the lunchtime news. I went on to say that I hoped that there had been no misunderstanding about what I had said to Jim Callaghan in Schull. He accepted my explanation of our position, and then took up the question of a meeting between us, saying that this was precluded by their concern that the Convention proceed without any interference from outside. I rejected this argument and said I felt it was undesirable that such a long period should elapse between our meetings, as this led to misunderstandings and difficulties arising between our two governments.

I was indeed most disturbed to find during this conversation that he now wanted to postpone a meeting, not merely until after the Convention had reported but until after he had presented its report to Parliament. My suspicion that he might be using the Convention as an excuse to put off any meeting for as long as possible in order to avoid a fuller discussion of his government's relations with Provisional Sinn Féin and the IRA was strengthened.

Meanwhile a suggestion by Bill Craig for a 'voluntary coalition' had been rejected by the UUUC on 8 September, following a sudden shift in Ian Paisley's position. Paisley had taken serious fright in the face of grass-roots dissent within his church at his conciliatory approach. One account we were given by a leading Unionist suggested that two days after a meeting at which Paisley had characterised as 'the only way forward' the voluntary coalition proposals, he had been challenged on this at his Martyrs' Memorial Church by a group of his Free Presbyterian clergy, particularly from the Armagh area, and that they had headed him off the idea. And once Paisley had backed off the voluntary coalition idea the official Unionists never found sufficient courage, despite the views of leaders like Harry West, to maintain support for it.

Then in late October an attempt by Paddy Harte to 'travel' the idea of a direct approach by the UUUC to Dublin to discuss extradition, security, and articles 2 and 3 of the Constitution, which was initially well received, by Paisley amongst others, came to nothing.

On 7 November the UUUC majority in the Convention endorsed an uncompromising report rejecting power-sharing and proposing a return to majority rule; but meanwhile, in mid-October, with the Convention close to its conclusion and the cease-fire also for all practical purposes at an end—that was the British assessment—Merlyn Rees finally agreed to meet me for breakfast in our embassy in London on 5 November, a time that fitted in with a visit I was making to Brussels for a Council meeting.

We began by looking at issues of cross-border security co-operation. Rees seemed at first to be moving towards proposing a direct army-to-army contact, to take place perhaps in London, in relation to areas like south Armagh where, he said, the RUC was not operational. But on reflection he backed off this idea, because he did not want to give the RUC any impression that the army had exclusive control of certain areas. Instead, after some discussion he came round to the idea that what was needed, at least in the first instance, was for the British army and the RUC to examine together the problems in areas like south Armagh, which tied in with our assessment at that time that a major internal co-ordination problem existed between these two forces in certain places.

We then turned to the political situation in Northern Ireland. Seán Donlon and I gave our impressions of how matters stood at that time. We believed that a number of Unionists were ready to move from entrenched positions provided they could be shown conclusively that majority rule was not on. The rejection of the impending UUUC Convention report would, I said, need to be put in a way that was not unnecessarily offensive to Unionists but that was nevertheless extremely firm. It would be better to err on the side of hardness than in the other direction.

Merlyn Rees agreed. Moreover, in addition to having talks with the leaders of the various parties he was going to meet individual members informally. The problem as he saw it was how to incorporate the voluntary coalition idea into legislation. I said that it would have to be up to the parties to work out an agreement for any voluntary coalition, and if they overcame this hurdle the legislation should not present insuperable difficulties.

On the whole this part of the discussion was reassuring. We seemed to be on much the same wavelength in relation to how the British should react to the Convention report, although, of course, in the event our hopes and theirs about an eventual UUUC acceptance of the idea of a voluntary coalition came to nothing—partly at least, we believed, because of the delay by the British government in responding to the report. But so did the fears we had earlier entertained about a possible violent reaction amongst loyalists to the rejection of their majority rule proposals.

Nothing was said about British contacts with the IRA through Sinn Féin. By this time the effective breakdown of the cease-fire had rendered our fears irrelevant, and I felt there was no point in going back over old ground.

This meeting marked the end of the period of serious tension between our two governments that had followed the Ulster workers' strike. Many other problems arose, of course, during the remaining eighteen months of our administration, some of which momentarily revived tensions that had marked the Anglo-Irish relationship during 1974 and 1975. But on the whole greater harmony prevailed thereafter.

Following the final presentation of the Convention UUUC report, Merlyn Rees spent six weeks reflecting on it and meeting the Northern Ireland political parties before recommending to the Cabinet a reconvening of the Convention in mid-January for a limited period. If the tension of the period up to the autumn of 1975 had continued, it might indeed have been necessary thus to let the Unionists down lightly in relation to their report, in order to avoid a violent reaction to the British government's refusal to accept the UUUC proposals for a return to majority rule. But the psychological climate had been fundamentally changed by the August-September discussions amongst the parties on voluntary power-sharing, and we believed that by November the need was for speedy action to try to revive this proposal rather than for cautious action to avoid an explosion that was no longer really likely. But despite Rees's own relative optimism in early November about the voluntary power-sharing option, no such change of tactics was attempted by the British government.

Meanwhile bipartisanship in the Dáil and the unity of the SDLP were coming under strain. In October 1975 Michael O'Kennedy broke ranks with a speech shifting the emphasis of Fianna Fáil policy in opposition towards the

'British withdrawal' line, and, despite an effort by Jack Lynch to pull the party back from this stance, it was clear that Fianna Fáil's solidarity with our Government on Northern Ireland policy, which had been a feature of the Sunningdale period, was now under severe strain as a result of pressures within Fianna Fáil— perhaps the same pressures that also brought Charles Haughey back onto their front bench after a five-year period in the cold following the Arms Crisis.

This shift in Fianna Fáil found a parallel within the SDLP, where two of the founder-members had begun the process that was to lead them to drift away from the party and from politics. Paddy Devlin made no secret of the fact that he and Ivan Cooper were privately in touch with Fianna Fáil people—other than Lynch and Brugha 'who were only getting the Hume line,' including Charles Haughey and Ray MacSharry. Paddy Devlin himself had started working for the Irish Transport and General Workers' Union, where he was reporting to the republican-oriented Dublin union leader, Micky Mullen.

Within the SDLP mainstream there had also been a marked hardening of attitudes following the failure of the 'voluntary coalition' talks in October, although John Hume had now come to accept that direct rule was the least of all evils if and when the Convention finally failed.

In early January 1976 our concentration on the political aspect of the problem was interrupted by a security crisis. Loyalist paramilitaries murdered five Catholics in Armagh, and in swift and appalling retaliation on 5 January a minibus carrying twelve workers was intercepted, the solitary Catholic ordered out, and the eleven Protestant workers shot, only one of whom survived.

Two days later, on the eve of a security meeting in London between Pat Cooney and Merlyn Rees, the British government announced the sending of the Spearhead Battalion to *south* Armagh and the introduction of the SAS into Northern Ireland. We noted that the public statement by the British did not conform to the assurance volunteered to Liam Cosgrave by Harold Wilson on 6 January, that 'both in what we do and what we say we shall be concerned with the whole of Armagh and the "murder triangle", viz. with loyalist paramilitaries as well as the IRA.'

After being reconvened, as Merlyn Rees had recommended to his Cabinet, the Convention finally collapsed in mid-February 1976. Shortly afterwards I met Rees briefly for a working lunch in Dublin before a rugby international. He told me that in announcing the end of the Convention to the House of Commons he would indicate that there would be no change in the existing pattern of direct rule. There had been discussion of a possible referendum in Northern Ireland on power-sharing as a way to break the deadlock. (All polls in Northern Ireland through the 1970s had shown overwhelming support in *both* communities for power-sharing itself, combined, however, with overwhelming support amongst unionist voters for anti-power-sharing *parties*.) But while Rees accepted that at the outset there might be as much as 70 per cent popular support for power-sharing, he believed that this figure might fall to a bare majority by the time the vote came to be taken, and such a result could then be effectively reversed by a subsequent election in which the same voters would support the Unionist parties that opposed power-sharing.

There was obviously much truth in this, and it would have been unwise to assume that the official Unionists would accept a popular vote for power-sharing and agree to implement it, although some at least of their leaders might wish to do so. Accordingly I did not press the issue further, although it clearly held some attractions.

Merlyn Rees went on to discuss possible variations on direct rule that might be considered in July when the legislation came up for review. He was not keen on an advisory body but was looking at the idea of establishing a kind of greater county council, with administrative functions only. He added that there would be no increase in Westminster representation for Northern Ireland; this could not happen in any event in advance of the 1979 constituency redistribution, he said.

It was agreed that these matters would be discussed by the Taoiseach and Prime Minister when they met on 5 March. I was not present at that meeting in London, at which Liam Cosgrave was accompanied by the Tánaiste, Brendan Corish. At the outset Harold Wilson told them that when the Convention was wound up the British government would keep its head down—proposing no new initiative, including no referendum—because even if they got a favourable result from a referendum they would be unable to implement it through the structures in Northern Ireland. He made it clear that the Convention members would no longer have any status: the British government would in future deal only with Westminster MPs and party leaders, plus whomsoever a party leader might bring with him. Cosgrave pointed out that if the Convention members were marginalised in this way the SDLP could disintegrate, thus creating a dangerous vacuum as far as the minority were concerned. Merlyn Rees's response was that he was tired of dealing with broken taps in houses, and while he would deal with anyone Gerry Fitt brought along to a meeting, he would not provide money for these politicians; there must be a stop to the continual demands of people to be met—they were pouring into Stormont.

Liam Cosgrave neatly changed tack, remarking that if contact with constitutional parties were to be abandoned it would be important not to talk to paramilitaries. Merlyn Rees, caught on the hop, said that most of the rumours on this subject were utter rubbish, although Andy Tyrie of the UDA came to an official's house occasionally, as they were personally acquainted.

Cosgrave persisted, saying that discussions with paramilitary groups weakened the authority of elected politicians, but Rees was unyielding, insisting that such contacts were much too valuable to be broken off. Wilson claimed that they had known of the impending loyalist strike because of such contacts. (He did not explain what good that had done them.)

The discussion later turned to the Strasbourg case concerning the maltreatment of detainees in 1971. Wilson recalled that the events at issue had happened under a different government and that at the time he had attacked what was going on, condemning the 'methods of barbarism' used, and had been as a result the subject of 'the dirtiest cartoon he had ever experienced', which was referred to the Press Council. How committed were we to 'pushing it'? Cosgrave replied cautiously that we had not yet discussed the matter in the Government. Wilson responded by saying that he would do 'whatever was proper', by way of statement in the House of Commons or an exchange of letters. There the matter was left for the time being; but in the event the British never felt able to make proposals for a friendly settlement of the matter, preferring to stand on the action they had already taken, which turned out to be quite insufficient to prevent a recurrence of brutality in interrogations at Castlereagh Barracks several years later.

Cosgrave and Corish then returned to the embassy, where Margaret Thatcher and Airey Neave came to meet them. I was now present, having meanwhile arrived in London. The conversation turned to the prospects for direct rule following the final breakdown of the Convention talks. Margaret Thatcher thought it would be important that some alternative be in prospect so as not to leave the field to the paramilitaries, and went on to tease out the possibility of some kind of administrative council as a forum for political activity. Without something of the kind, she argued, politicians might find it hard to keep going—financially as well as politically; but we discouraged this suggestion, as we knew the SDLP was disinclined to participate in a body without real power.

Less than ten days later Harold Wilson resigned, and was succeeded by Jim Callaghan on 5 April. For the time being Merlyn Rees continued as Northern Ireland Secretary. We remained concerned about the contacts between the British government and Sinn Féin. Later Rees was to explain that these talks had ended early in the year, but we were not told this at the time. On the contrary, when he came to Dublin to meet Pat Cooney and myself at the end of May he defended the meetings with Sinn Féin, on the grounds that he found it useful to know what they were thinking. When I argued that nevertheless— in view of the fact that the talks were the only thing that gave the IRA credibility, encouraging their belief that the British would eventually negotiate a withdrawal from Northern Ireland—the balance of advantage must be with breaking off the contacts, he replied stubbornly, 'If it is considered necessary it will happen again.'

He persisted in arguing that the talks were necessary in order to convince the IRA that there would *not* be a British pull-out: the exact opposite of the effect we saw them as having on his interlocutors. Nevertheless, within two months both sides announced the cessation of these contacts; perhaps our persistence eventually paid off.

Among the other matters discussed between us at the end of May was the Criminal Law (Jurisdiction) Act, now about to come into force, which I told him I hoped would be used to put away any IRA men in our state against whom there was evidence in Northern Ireland or Britain. The Act was so used, but only rarely, apparently because, despite the incessant political and media clamour in Northern Ireland and in Britain about members of the IRA 'hiding out' in the Republic, there were in fact hardly any such cases in respect of which evidence—as distinct from suspicion—existed. In that connection I was able to point out to Merlyn Rees that only 3 per cent of all incidents in Northern Ireland in recent times had been connected with the border, a figure that he did not contest.

I raised another problem with him: the recruitment into the RUC Reserve and UDR of people involved in paramilitary activities. Merlyn Rees had to admit that this was a real problem, which they were 'trying to solve'. They came 'under pressure' when they rejected recruits because of such paramilitary involvement. I found this admission a bit hair-raising; it might have been thought that the exclusion of such people from the security forces would have been automatic and that 'pressure' to admit them would have been absolutely resisted.

Shortly after this we had the opportunity to hear an authoritative official Unionist Party view on our security performance. Unqualified admiration was expressed; if only the British had the same 'will to win' the problem could be solved quickly—an overoptimistic assessment, I felt. The OUP speaker added that many IRA men on the run were finding it easier to hide out in Northern Ireland than in the Republic. This encomium augured well for my contacts with Unionists when I went to the North again shortly afterwards.

On that trip I met leading members of the SDLP and Alliance Party and of several Unionist parties. The official Unionists were remarkably optimistic about the outcome of post-Convention talks with the SDLP, of which we had been informed towards the end of April and which had become public knowledge only in June. They looked forward to a possible recall of the Convention in September if agreement were reached, as they hoped would be the case. But shortly after the return of Rev. Martin Smyth from the United States in September—his absence had led to a break in the talks—the OUP without prior warning to the SDLP announced that the discussions were being discontinued. In subsequent statements the two parties' positions on an Executive appeared to be as far apart as ever.

This ended the long series of informal talks between parties that had accompanied and followed the election of the Convention in May 1975. These talks had never been given much credence by the British, who in the end were proved right in their scepticism. It was disturbing, however, to hear NIO officials speculate in early September about independence as the eventual solution. One official became quite irritable with his Irish opposite number's unwillingness to accept that this was the way things would go in Northern Ireland.

Anglo-Irish relations had for several reasons been going through a difficult period during 1976. Early in the year a serious problem had arisen in connection with the funeral of Frank Stagg. Our Government was very conscious of what had happened in 1974 when Michael Gaughan had died in Parkhurst Prison following a 65-day hunger strike in support of a claim for political status. His funeral in both Britain and Ireland was the occasion for demonstrations of support by IRA adherents that caused concern in both islands. Following that funeral a fellow-hunger-striker, Frank Stagg, had been ordered by the IRA to take food. But after a further hunger-strike later that year he had embarked on a third, and he died in prison on 12 February 1976.

The IRA wanted to repeat the propaganda exercise of the Gaughan funeral, despite the fact that Frank Stagg's widow, who lived in England, desired a private funeral. She was threatened by the IRA with being shot through the head if she pressed her view. We were told that the authorities in Britain had refused to accord her a police guard on her home and had entered into a deal under which it was agreed to ignore her right to her husband's remains and to hand them over to the IRA to bring to Ireland in return for agreement by the IRA to confine their demonstrations to our island. They proposed to parade the coffin through Dublin and various other towns before bringing it to Ballina, Co. Mayo, for interment.

His widow approached us on the matter. I was appalled at the British actions, whoever had authorised them, and I sent an immediate message to Roy Jenkins that unless he assured me within three hours that Mrs Stagg's wishes would be respected and the deal with the IRA repudiated I would call a press conference to expose this macabre plot between authorities in Britain and the IRA.

I got an immediate response. The body was brought to London Airport, where it was handed over to us, and we arranged for the aircraft bringing it back to Ireland to be diverted from Dublin to Shannon. Meanwhile Mrs Stagg flew to Dublin from Birmingham on a flight on which IRA supporters, including other relatives of Frank Stagg, were also travelling. At Dublin Airport she was met and brought to a different hotel from that in which the others were staying, where she was provided with Garda protection. At six o'clock the following morning she was brought to Garda headquarters, where Pat Cooney and I met her. We were appalled to hear that, despite the precautions taken, her room had been invaded during the night and for three hours she had been subjected to intimidation designed to 'persuade' her to hand over the remains to the IRA— intimidation that with great courage she had resisted.

We told her that we would respect her wishes and that in view of the pressure she was under we would understand if she decided to release her husband's body to the IRA, although we would not allow them to bring it to Dublin or on a tour of the country. She said she wanted her husband's body to be brought to Ballina under escort for a funeral Mass there, after which, if the IRA wanted to take charge of the interment locally, she would not resist this. We accepted this; but when the IRA heard that they were not to be allowed to bring the body on a tour of the country, they refused to accept this proposal and took no part in the funeral. But although we took the precaution of placing a concrete slab over the grave to prevent desecration, and guarded the grave for a period after the funeral, the IRA later exhumed the coffin and reburied it in a 'republican plot'.

From this dreadful episode I retain the memory of a remarkably courageous and dignified woman, who was supported throughout by her husband's brother, Emmet Stagg, later to be elected as a left-wing Labour TD.

In May came the episode of the SAS intruders, which began for me with two phone calls in one night from Pat Cooney. Two groups of armed men in civilian clothes had been arrested one after the other by Gardaí near the border in Co. Louth. They claimed to be British soldiers who had strayed unintentionally into the Republic. In the frequent cases of accidental border crossing by members of the security forces it was normal to send them back. Some time previously, however, a man had been kidnapped in this area, taken into Northern Ireland, and murdered. The Gardaí wanted a forensic test carried out on the latest intruders' firearms to see whether any of them might have been used on that occasion, and they wished to hold them overnight for this purpose. In the circumstances, I agreed.

The following morning Pat Cooney told me that the test on the guns had proved negative. I immediately organised a meeting of Pat, Declan Costello (the Attorney General) and myself with the Taoiseach in his office in Leinster House. It was decided that the soldiers—they had now been clearly identified as such—should be released forthwith. Pat Cooney rang the Garda Commissioner, only to be told that the men had been charged with possession of firearms with intent to endanger life, on the instructions of the Director of Public Prosecutions, who unknown to us had earlier ordered the Gardaí to notify him immediately of any people found with arms in border areas with a view to taking prompt action in such cases.

It was now past midday. The DPP was contacted but, very much his own man, stood on his rights as an independent law officer—which, under recent legislation we had introduced, he had just been constituted.

I had to inform the British of this and seek their assurance that the men—members of the SAS, whom Harold Wilson had sent to Northern Ireland to head off parliamentary pressure for tougher security measures in Co. Armagh after the sectarian murders there earlier that year—would, if released on bail, return to face trial. The British reacted with fury. They could not envisage a law officer acting independently in this way (an incomprehension we would meet again), and they insisted that the DPP's determination to press the charges despite our contrary view was a politically motivated act by our Government. Indeed, Jim Callaghan rang Liam Cosgrave to demand the men's release. But in the end they had to agree to send the men back for trial, which they did some months later. In the event the soldiers were found guilty only on a lesser charge of illegal possession of firearms, were fined £100 each, and released.

Early in July I had attended, as I had done most years since its establishment, the annual conference of the British-Irish Association in Britain. There I met the newly appointed British Ambassador to Ireland, Christopher Ewart-Biggs. I found him charming and unconventional, and we would, I felt, be able to establish a good personal relationship.

He was to pay his first official visit to me at 10 a.m. on 21 July. Just as I had finished clearing my desk to receive him, I was told there had been an explosion near his residence. Soon word arrived that he and a secretary had been killed by a bomb detonated under his car. The Permanent Secretary to the Northern Ireland Office, Brian Cubbon, and the driver had been seriously injured. Merlyn Rees would have been in the car as well but for a vote in the House of Commons the previous night that had unexpectedly detained him.

I was filled with horror at the atrocity, with shame that Irishmen had murdered the envoy of a neighbouring country, and with shock at our failure to protect him. In contact with the British embassy I was told that his widow, whom I had also met at the British-Irish conference, had heard the news of the explosion in London on her car radio and was shortly leaving for Dublin on a special flight. As soon as I heard the expected time of her arrival, Joan and I drove to Baldonnell to meet her, and because the British embassy staff were slightly delayed we were in fact the only people there when she and Mrs Cubbon stepped off the plane.

During the days that followed we did what we could to comfort her and her children. And at the memorial service in St Patrick's Cathedral, Dublin, it fell to me to express the horror and shame of the Irish people. It was one of the most difficult moments I had experienced; I am not good at controlling my emotions on such occasions, but fortunately I succeeded, although I do not think anyone could have been in doubt as to how deeply I felt this tragedy. (The text of my address at the service, to the preparation of which I had given much thought and time, is in Appendix Two.)

The reaction of Jane Ewart-Biggs was—and has ever since been—a noble demonstration of Christian charity. She might so forgivably have turned against Ireland and everything Irish; instead she took to her heart the country that had deprived her of her husband, and has worked ever since for reconciliation amongst Irish people and between Ireland and Britain. Our two countries are deeply in her debt.

The third issue that during these months tested the Anglo-Irish relationship was the case we had taken to the European Commission on Human Rights at Strasbourg regarding the brutalisation of many of those interned in 1971. We had hoped a friendly settlement might have been reached, but the British government had not felt able to respond in a manner that we could accept. As I have already mentioned, our reticence in this matter found some justification a couple of years later when there was a recurrence of organised brutality in the course of interrogations at Castlereagh Barracks.

To minimise tension between the two countries it was agreed that neither side would brief the press in advance of the publication of the report of the European Commission on Human Rights on 2 September and the announcement of our decision on the next step in the case. To my fury and that of the Government this agreement was breached on our side a week or so earlier, in circumstances that were never clarified. Naturally enough the British felt justified in retaliating. Their briefing to their press very successfully diverted attention from the finding of the report: that the combined use of five inter-rogation techniques, developed by the British army in Aden and introduced by them to the RUC's Special Branch, constituted 'not only inhuman and degrading treatment but also torture.'

In particular we were accused of bringing the matter unnecessarily before the European Court of Human Rights. The fact was—as I pointed out unavailingly to the British media—that once the friendly settlement procedure had failed we were *required* by the Strasbourg procedures to bring the Commission's report either before the Committee of Ministers of the Council of Europe or before the European Court of Human Rights. We chose the latter in order to avoid unnecessary damage to Anglo-Irish relationships through a politicisation of our differences in the Committee of Ministers of the Council. The British knew, of course, why we had chosen this course, and some at least on the British side appreciated our motivation; but this did not prevent the misrepresentation of our position by the British government to the press, a misrepresentation that, as the editorials in the British papers showed, proved highly successful.

A week or so later at a Political Co-operation meeting in the Hague—Tony Crosland's first meeting as Foreign Secretary—I found myself at lunch beside a 'D. Owen MP', who, given the nature of the occasion, I knew must be a Min-ister, although for some reason I had not noted his appointment to the Foreign Office in the previous day's reshuffle. As he sat down and introduced himself, Owen asked me how I felt about the British reaction to the Strasbourg report. He seemed to take in a relaxed and non-partisan way the points I had to make. During the following nine months, when our paths ran in parallel until the defeat of our Government in June 1977, we established a good working relationship.

The reshuffle that brought David Owen to the Foreign Office as Minister of State also saw the replacement of Merlyn Rees by Roy Mason as Secretary of State for Northern Ireland. My first meeting with Mason was in London a fortnight later, just before I left for New York for what was to be my last UN session as Minister for Foreign Affairs.

Mason told me of his contacts in the North since his appointment, laying stress on the steps he was taking on the economic front. On the political side he summed up his stance as favouring 'strong, decisive direct government' for as far as one could see ahead. The aim was 'devolved government on acceptable terms as soon as political conditions allowed,' which he clearly envisaged as being in the fairly distant future.

We went on to discuss the SDLP's new and more aggressively nationalist stance. That party had, I said, been seriously demoralised by the manner in which its talks with the official Unionists had been terminated unilaterally and abruptly. It now seemed that people like John Hume and Austin Currie, who had always held fast against those in the party who favoured a 'declaration of intent' to withdraw by Britain, might have lost the will to resist pressures from the more hard-line wing owing to their disillusionment with the Unionists.

This, I went on to say, was for us a very serious development, which, following the slippage in Fianna Fáil's position a year earlier, threatened the whole policy of 'no reunification without consent' that Fine Gael had initiated in 1969 and that for a number of years past had had the support both of the SDLP and of Fianna Fáil.

All this could have grave implications for our Government and could lead to Fianna Fáil's return to office in circumstances that might have serious consequences for North-South and Anglo-Irish relations.

Roy Mason said that it would be a pity if there were to be major political difficulties for the Irish Government at that stage; our policy over the last three years had been 'stout and good'. But, although he expressed willingness to try to persuade the Tories of the need to dispel Unionist illusions about the possibility of devolution without power-sharing, I had the impression that Mason was not deeply interested in the political situation and was preoccupied with security co-operation. While he at least told us without equivocation that no contacts were taking place or were planned with Sinn Féin, he was not able to go beyond reiterating Merlyn Rees's unsatisfactory statement that he would take account of our views on the desirability of announcing the cessation of these contacts.

For my part I was able to tell him that our contacts with Libya through Arab leaders seemed to have produced some results, in the form of a recent Qadhafi interview with *Newsweek* in which he had said that he now understood our position on subversive organisations.

An exchange on the Strasbourg case led nowhere.

Meanwhile I was continuing my efforts to reinforce British support for power-sharing in government. We had become increasingly concerned about what appeared to be a drift away from this commitment by the Conservative spokesman on Northern Ireland, Airey Neave. It was agreed that I should see Margaret Thatcher to raise the matter bluntly with her. The first opportunity was on my way back from the United Nations, when I had an appointment with the Foreign Secretary to discuss the EC fishery policy; and, as it happened, the date of this appointment—14 October—coincided with a visit to Northern Ireland by Airey Neave, who would not therefore be there to hear my criticism of his record.

The Tory party conference had taken place during the previous week. During a debate on Northern Ireland Rev. Martin Smyth had called for the implementation of the majority Convention report, and in his reply to the debate Neave had not only once again failed to advert to the Tories' power-sharing commitment but had seemed to commend Smyth's remarks, saying that he had spoken 'not from theory but from practice and from the very heart.'

This had been too much for the SDLP. At the weekend their Executive had met and prepared a scorching response, which had been published by them three days before my meeting with Neave's leader. They made it clear that they refused to meet him while Conservative Party policy was 'unclear, as a consequence of speeches made by yourself and others at the recent Conference of your Party.' And they went on to pose a series of questions, including a specific query whether the Conservative Party accepted that any future devolved government in a deeply divided Northern Ireland must be a partnership involving both sections of the community in executive office, and to declare that a devolved government based on sectarian majority rule was unworkable.

Neave had replied, avoiding the first point and dodging the second with a reference to the need for a devolved government to have 'the widest possible support'. The SDLP had then retorted with a demand for straight answers.

These public exchanges made my meeting with Margaret Thatcher both more necessary and also potentially more difficult.

When I arrived in her room in the House of Commons she herself was not there. Willie Whitelaw and Reggie Maudling were waiting for me, and I had to head off discussion until she arrived. I then started by suggesting that in view of the SDLP letter it might be better if our meeting were kept private, lest it be connected in the public mind with the controversy that had just been making the headlines. It was immediately clear that, while Whitelaw knew of the row and tried to pooh-pooh it, neither Margaret Thatcher nor Maudling had heard anything about it. Recovering from my astonishment at this, I reviewed the commitment of the Irish Government and of two successive British governments to the principle of power-sharing in a devolved government in Northern Ireland, adding that a new situation had now arisen. As a result there was a real danger that the SDLP would call for a declaration of intent by Britain to withdraw from Northern Ireland. Given the shift in Fianna Fáil policy forced on Jack Lynch, a movement by the SDLP to such a position would endanger the joint policy of the two states, and firm action was now needed to save the situation.

'What action?' asked Margaret Thatcher and Whitelaw.

The minimum needed, I replied, was for the British government and opposition to reassert in unequivocal terms their adherence to the policy of no devolution without power-sharing. This would steady the SDLP and at the same time weaken the more intransigent elements on the Unionist side by removing their belief that a change of government in Britain would give them back majority rule.

'How could anyone think that this could happen?' enquired my two interlocutors (Maudling remained silent throughout our discussion). Their policy had not changed one iota, they claimed. I replied that speeches by their spokesman on Northern Ireland, Airey Neave, had consistently either omitted any reference to power-sharing or had seemed to modify or water down the commitment.

They demurred at this. I had anticipated this reaction, and before going to see them had asked my officials to reduce the 6,000-word brief they had given me into a short summary, listing all Neave's recorded statements since his appointment as shadow spokesman, none of which contained any positive reference to power-sharing in government and a number of which had been dismissive of the concept. When I presented this document to Margaret Thatcher I could see that it was most unwelcome to her, but there had been no other way in which I could prove my point conclusively.

I went on to tell her and her colleagues that in my personal contacts with a Unionist leader during the previous year he had repeatedly insisted that he was confident that the Conservative policy would change and that they would restore majority rule, and in my most recent encounter with him I felt that he now believed what earlier he had merely hoped. It was our clear impression that this, amongst other factors, had influenced the official Unionist Party decision to terminate their talks with the SDLP.

After further discussion I was satisfied that the reality of Unionist beliefs about Tory policy was now beginning to impinge on my listeners, even though they were careful not to admit it. 'What should be done?' I was again asked. I replied that if the British government, which we believed was now convinced of the seriousness of the problem, took an opportunity to clarify *their* position, it was essential that this should be unambiguously and immediately endorsed by the Conservative opposition. It would be helpful if this could be followed by a major speech by Margaret Thatcher herself on Northern Ireland.

She replied that she had hitherto avoided talking about political aspects of Northern Ireland; she was impressed by the fear felt by people living there and had accordingly confined herself to security matters. She did not exclude making such a speech, but she could not, of course, commit herself to any course of action until she had had an opportunity to talk to Airey Neave. I said that I fully understood this.

I then moved the discussion on to other aspects of Northern Ireland policy, and especially security policy, in respect of which I said humorously that it would help if we were not praised more than twice a week by British politicians; she said she could arrange to keep it down to once a week.

More seriously I adverted to the dangers of the British army adopting a higher and more aggressive profile in the North after a Tory victory—something that had happened immediately after the Tories had come to power in the summer of 1970, even though I was sure this was not something that new government had wished. Even a change of Northern Ireland Secretary within the same government had recently seemed to have such an effect. It was not helpful, for example, for housewives to watch soldiers burning down a community centre and then to hear denials from the army on the following day that this had happened, or for thirteen-year-old boys or pregnant women to be killed or injured by rubber bullets.

Margaret Thatcher then asked me why politicians in Northern Ireland could not reach agreement with each other. As I tried to explain the depth of the differences between them it became clear that she was labouring under the illusion that the majority Convention report had involved a proposal for emergency power-sharing over a five-year period. I endeavoured to put her right on this. At the end of our discussion I renewed my earlier invitation to her to visit

Dublin, but from the tone of her response I knew she had no intention of coming in the near future.

I left torn between dismay at the fact that even after eighteen months of party leadership she was still so poorly briefed on Northern Ireland and a measure of hope that I might have made sufficient impact to reverse the drift in Conservative policy under Neave's spokesmanship. I had: shortly afterwards Neave wrote to the OUP leader, Harry West, reaffirming Conservative support for power-sharing.

The opportunity for a public clarification of both Labour and Conservative policy arose almost immediately. A parliamentary question was put down on the subject; we learnt that Roy Mason's proposed reply was worded in an unsatisfactory manner. Liam Cosgrave asked Jim Callaghan on 27 October to have it strengthened, and I asked our Ambassador in London to approach Willie Whitelaw in order to ensure opposition support for an unambiguous statement. Our efforts were successful; to Roy Mason's annoyance an explanatory sentence was added setting out that power-sharing 'means a system which will command widespread support throughout the community and in which both the majority and the minority will participate,' and the reply on 28 October was endorsed by a reluctant, and we later heard angry, Airey Neave, who was furious that on top of our complaint about him to Margaret Thatcher we had approached Willie Whitelaw rather than him about the Conservative reaction to the parliamentary question.

This result was achieved at some cost, however. Mason was clearly annoyed at our success in persuading Callaghan to require the addition of the clarifying statement, even though in discussions with us several months later he actually took credit for having flushed out Airey Neave and for forcing him to support power-sharing in government! At the same time our representations to Whitelaw provoked a protest from Margaret Thatcher to Callaghan about the draft answer to an opposition question being made known to another government before the reply was given in the House of Commons, a protest Tony Crosland confronted me with in the Hague a couple of days later.

We had used up much of our credit both with the government and opposition in Britain in an attempt to steady the nerve of the SDLP—an attempt that visibly failed to secure its objective. For by the time the SDLP Conference was held in November, eleven of seventeen Convention members had declared themselves in favour of a British withdrawal. There was much criticism of our Government; and a motion instructing the party's Executive to undertake an immediate study of negotiated independence with the participation of all levels of the party machinery was passed at the Conference by 147 votes to 51, in the absence of Gerry Fitt and John Hume, who had become so disillusioned with what was happening that they had left the hall. The assessment given to our Government when it came to review the situation two months later was that the influence of Provisional IRA thinking on the SDLP was now a major threat and that the danger of a split in the party during 1977 loomed on the horizon.

On the other hand, on the Unionist side our efforts to ensure that the British stood by their commitment to allow devolution only on the basis of power-sharing in government seemed to be bearing some fruit. A reassessment within the OUP of its position resulted in a speech by Jim Molyneaux in a devolution debate in the House of Commons suggesting that administrative devolution rather than legislative devolution might offer a way ahead, as 'it is essentially legislative and not administrative devolution which raised the dilemma between the irreconcilable ultimate objectives in Ulster and rendered insistence on majority rule as essential to one side as it was unacceptable to the other.'

Harold Wilson privately encouraged the SDLP to have a close look at this proposal, and Gerry Fitt and John Hume saw it as a suitable basis for a further round of interparty talks. Although Harry West reacted unfavourably to this idea at first, Rev. Martin Smyth subsequently endorsed it. Nevertheless, in view of the history of all previous attempts at a compromise solution to the devolution problem, we were not very optimistic about its prospects. In the Government in January 1977 it was agreed that while giving all possible support to further OUP-SDLP talks we should begin to consider how we would react if following a failure of these talks the SDLP began to disintegrate, with a majority committed to a British declaration of intent to withdraw. In the meantime we should keep in touch with the 'dissident' elements in the SDLP as well as with the embattled leadership.

By the end of January 1977 the Molyneaux initiative was dead, however, as a result of a backlash among his fellow-members of the OUP. When the SDLP then met Roy Mason, political progress was clearly no longer on the agenda. The SDLP raised various grievances, to which Mason offered no response. Nevertheless the tone of the meeting was good. Mason was at pains to sound as positive and sympathetic as possible, even at the expense of giving an account of the events of the end of October in which he featured as a stout defender of power-sharing in government rather than someone whose reluctance to be specific had had to be overridden by the Prime Minister, on our insistence. John Hume subsequently described the encounter as much more successful than he had expected in influencing the 'wild men' of the party. The process of pulling the SDLP back from their drift towards more extreme policies was under way, and was helped by a meeting the SDLP had with Airey Neave in early February, when he reassured them that there was no question of the Tories abandoning their support for power-sharing. They were also heartened by the fact that in the House of Commons on 10 February Roy Mason firmly placed the blame for lack of political movement on Unionist intransigence—the first time this had been said so unequivocally.

The collapse of the Molyneaux initiative confirmed the British in their distaste for ill-prepared approaches of this kind, as they told us themselves, and it probably influenced Roy Mason to eschew further attempts at political progress during his term of office.

Nevertheless by April informal contacts had been established between John Hume and Martin Smyth, and while we were not very hopeful of anything coming of these we were concerned that the simultaneous contacts between the integrationist Westminster Unionist MPs and the British government about the further development of regional or local government should not sabotage tentative discussions about devolution with Unionists in Northern Ireland. These secret talks with Unionist MPs at Westminster had arisen from the instability of the British government's parliamentary position, and now raised a new hazard. In the early spring of 1977 I had been warned by a senior British official that Michael Foot and Merlyn Rees had made approaches to the Westminster Unionist MPs for their support as an alternative or 'back-up' to the support they were receiving from the Liberals under the 'Lib-Lab Pact'. In early April this was confirmed to us by a Unionist source; there had been an exchange of draft letters, to be signed by Jim Callaghan if the deal had come off. Reference was made to Enoch Powell's views on the underrepresentation of Northern Ireland in the House of Commons—a decision justified in 1920 by the establishment of a Home Rule Parliament in Belfast—and this matter was to be remitted to a Speaker's conference. Moreover, the British government proposed to commit itself to 'consultations on the widest possible basis' and would 'endeavour to establish an upper tier of normal regional government', which, Jim Molyneaux was assured, would not be subject to an SDLP veto. In return the Unionists were to support the Labour government in Parliament.

This first attempt at a deal behind the backs of our Government, the SDLP and possibly also Roy Mason failed, because the Unionists demanded further concessions in relation to security that involved increased powers for the police; but such a deal was hammered out later on, as eventually became public knowledge.

By this time our primary concern was with the attempt by an umbrella group of paramilitaries—the 'Ulster Unionist Action Council', comprising the UDA, UVF, Red Hand, Down Orange Welfare, and the new Ulster Service Corps— to organise a major confrontation with the British government on the pattern of the loyalist workers' strike just three years before. We had had early information about this from a Unionist source. The legitimate Unionist parties were coming under pressure from the UUAC, and some politicians had swung behind the strike, but the British government was clearly much better prepared for this than it had been three years earlier. The SDLP was sufficiently happy with the British determination to face down the threat for John Hume to express his satisfaction with their contingency measures following a meeting with Roy Mason on 26 April.

When the strike came it failed ignominiously. Bus and oil tanker services continued to operate, and adequate power was maintained at the Ballylumford power station, as we had learnt in advance would be the case, since the workers there would not join a strike in which Ian Paisley had chosen to take a leading role. The strike was dealt with efficiently by the RUC with a minimal need for army intervention; in particular the arrest of Paisley was deftly managed. During the strike we received a call from a senior Unionist thanking us for our carefully maintained silence throughout this period.

Another political matter had been concerning us around this time. There was an evident reluctance on the part of the British government to implement the agreement we had reached about seats for Northern Ireland in the European Parliament in a manner that would provide the minority, about 38 per cent of the electorate, with the possibility of representation by one of the three MEPs to be elected for the area. The British did not want to extend the PR system (which had been used for non-Westminster elections in Northern Ireland since the reforms of some years before) for the European election in the North, lest this be seen as a precedent for the remainder of the United Kingdom. Eventually, however, we won this battle, to the annoyance of some, but not all, Unionists—as was clear from our contacts with them.

A week before what turned out to be my final meeting with Roy Mason I had a discussion in Dublin with Frank Judd, Minister of State at the Foreign Office, on European Community matters. Afterwards the talk turned informally to Northern Ireland. I said that the problems posed by the trial of the SAS cross-border intruders and the Strasbourg case were now effectively behind us (the final verdict from the European Court was due quite soon), and the manner in which Anglo-Irish relations had withstood the tensions created in these cases underlined the strength of the basic relationship. If there was any difference now between our two governments it was on the need for the British once and for all to abjure contacts with the IRA; the contacts that had taken place had had the effect merely of prolonging the violence by deluding the IRA into believing that a British government would eventually negotiate a settlement with them. Judd agreed, stressing his government's satisfaction with the outcome of the SAS case but regretting that the Strasbourg case had seemed to play into the hands of the Soviet Union. I pointed out that when I was in the United States recently I had taken pains to emphasise the significance of the British government's acceptance of the Strasbourg court's jurisdiction. Finally I expressed concern at the British failure to make use of the provisions of the Criminal Law (Jurisdiction) Act save in a single case, while continuing to refer to IRA suspects in Ireland as 'wanted' men.

When I met Roy Mason in London a week later he was much more interested in security matters than in politics. He was proposing to increase the RUC establishment, to re-equip them, and to give the RUC Reserve 'more interesting work', in the form of participation in mobile patrols. The strength of the UDR and, in particular, the number of full-time members was to be increased, and another resident battalion of the army was to be formed. Finally, while the number of SAS men was not being increased, their activities throughout Northern Ireland were to be intensified.

I welcomed the increase in RUC numbers but expressed our continuing concern about the UDR; there had already been eight convictions of UDR men in the current year for offences involving serious violence, and the courts had expressed disquiet about the screening of recruits to the force. Mason countered by saying that they had behaved well when called up during the recent strike and that convictions for violence were declining. I said that we would like to see the RUC presence strengthened in border areas. Garda-RUC co-operation on the border was working very well and had contributed significantly to the reduction of IRA activity, with only ten incidents originating in our state reported by the British authorities so far in the current year.

On the political front I remarked that while the Unionist attitude to the SDLP was now negative, SDLP morale was greatly improved following the collapse of the attempt to repeat the 1974 loyalist strike, and for the moment at least the problems in that party that had preoccupied us so much had been got over. And I concluded by saying that Northern Ireland was not likely to be a significant issue in our forthcoming general election; we would not make it so, and the opposition was unlikely to do so. This forecast proved accurate.

On that note my direct involvement in the Northern Ireland problem ended for the time being. I summed up my feelings about this period of my life in my first speech in Dáil Éireann as Fine Gael leader on 6 July: 'My greatest pride is a remark by a Northern politician that our Government had won more respect from both sections in the North than any previous Government had won from either.'

# CHAPTER ELEVEN

# MEETING THE CHALLENGES OF COALITION

The National Coalition of 1973 came into office with a clearly defined economic and social programme, the product of the negotiation that had taken place between Fine Gael and the Labour Party immediately after the dissolution of the Dáil on 31 January. This important innovation in Irish politics had arisen from the perceived need to fight the election on a common platform. A fairly clear-cut set of fourteen policy points had been agreed, which in fact were substantially implemented during the following four years, despite the catastrophic effects on our economy, as on those of so many other countries, of the oil crisis that followed the Yom Kippur War of October 1973.

But before discussing the policies pursued by this National Coalition Government I must say something about its members.

The new Taoiseach, Liam Cosgrave, had survived by a hair's breadth the crisis in Fine Gael the previous December, when he had momentarily found himself one of a minority of two in the party supporting the Fianna Fáil Government's Offences Against the State (Amendment) Act. The dissolution of the Dáil by Jack Lynch two months later had been intended as a surprise move to take advantage of the presumed disarray in Fine Gael following this debacle. It proved to be a disastrous miscalculation—not merely because it threw Fine Gael and the Labour Party together but also because it rallied Fine Gael itself under Liam Cosgrave's leadership. There was an instant dissolution of the tensions in the party that had developed over several years as a result of personality differences and ideological divergences. For those not involved in politics the apparent transformation of relationships within the party must at the time have been suspect, but politics has its own peculiar chemistry, including combinative reactions as dramatic as those in physical chemistry that enable gases like oxygen and hydrogen to combine to form water.

Such a reaction required a two-way process: the 'dissidents' had to be prepared to submerge their previous unhappiness with Liam Cosgrave's leadership, and their ability genuinely to do so depended on their leader in turn demonstrating a new trust and confidence in them. He did so, and it worked. For my part—and my differences with him had been deeper than most—I found it as easy to work with him in Government as I had found it difficult in opposition, and I hope that he found the same. Only once in the four-and-a-quarter years that we served together in this administration did any strain arise between us, and that was the result of an accident that was no-one's fault. The transformation in our working relationship was all the more striking in view of the fact that traditionally the relationship between a prime minister and a foreign minister is prone to tension. This is so because this particular relationship involves a greater measure of responsibility-sharing by a head of government than with any other department head, for every prime minister must necessarily be involved directly in many aspects of foreign policy. And the potential for conflict is inherently greater than normal in the Irish situation, where traditionally, and for good reason, the policy responsibility in relation to Northern Ireland, and therefore Anglo-Irish relations, remains with the head of the Government, the role of the Minister for Foreign Affairs and of his department in this area being effectively to tender advice and to operate the policies decided upon.

The potential for tension in this particular relationship made it all the more surprising, on the surface at least, that Liam Cosgrave should have appointed me Minister for Foreign Affairs, for our disagreements in the immediately preceding years had come to be centred on aspects of Northern Ireland policy. I can only speculate why, against this background, I was appointed to this post. Several factors may have been at work. First, given that we had joined the European Community only ten weeks earlier and that the successful development of our relations within this new context was clearly going to be of great importance, my enthusiasm for, and the extent of my knowledge of, the Community, about which I had been lecturing at UCD throughout the previous fourteen years, must have been in my favour. On Northern Ireland itself he may perhaps have felt that at least I had the merit of being deeply concerned about the tragic situation there, and that, with Richie Ryan now preoccupied with his Finance portfolio, the stresses that had arisen in the past from my interference in what had been Richie's responsibility would abate and I would have the wisdom to accept the traditional primacy of the Taoiseach's role in this critical area.

More negatively, there seems to be reason to believe also that he had qualms about the possible impact of my radicalism on the Finance portfolio, where I had been shadow Minister since 1971, and that he may have seen a straight switch between Richie Ryan's shadow role and my own as a means of solving this problem in a way that both Richie and I would find acceptable. He may also have hoped that it would fully resolve the problem of my relationship with Richie over Northern Ireland.

Finally, he could also have been influenced incidentally by memories of his father's Cumann na nGaedheal government of the 1920s, in which my father had served as Minister for External Affairs until 1927; in this connection it may be significant that Declan Costello, who had returned to politics in this election after a period of withdrawal for a combination of health and political reasons, was simultaneously appointed to the post of Attorney General, which *his* father, John A. Costello, had held under W. T. Cosgrave in the latter period of that first government.

Since that time some people have cynically suggested that he may also have felt that as Minister for Foreign Affairs I would be absent for much of the time. I doubt this, however, because apart from anything else, up to that time almost the only significant absence of this Minister had been for the autumn session of the United Nations, and the extent of the external involvement of a Minister for Foreign Affairs in EC business had not yet become apparent in March 1973.

Another remarkable appointment was that of Pat Cooney as Minister for Justice, for three months earlier Pat Cooney, together with Tom O'Higgins, Jim Dooge, and myself, had led the opposition to the Offences Against the State (Amendment) Bill that had almost cost Liam Cosgrave the leadership of the party. Pat Cooney's description of that Bill as comparable only to repressive legislation in South Africa, and his stance at that time on liberal issues such as contraception, can scarcely have recommended him to his leader for this portfolio. True, in the years that followed Pat Cooney moved to the right, but that was hardly predictable in March 1973.

The allocation of the portfolios between the two parties was governed by considerations that are easier to explain. Some ministries were clearly seen by Liam Cosgrave as natural briefs of Fine Gael as the leading party in the Government: Finance, for obvious reasons; Justice and Defence, as fundamental to public order; Education, because of the sensitivity of relationships with the Catholic Church; Agriculture, because of the party's strong rural base and the traditional farmer hostility to Labour; and Foreign Affairs, which could not credibly have been allocated to the Labour Party less than a year after that party had been leading the referendum campaign against EEC membership. Given a choice of the remaining departments it was natural that the Labour Party should have opted for the two social ministries—Health (including Social Welfare) and Labour—and for the other major economic department, Industry and Commerce, as well as for Local Government, where an opportunity existed for a Labour Party Minister to emulate a predecessor in the 1948–51 Coalition Government who had expanded the public housing programme rapidly from a low postwar base. The Labour Party's fifth choice of portfolio was Posts and Telegraphs, which included responsibility for radio and television.

The remaining three portfolios—Transport and Power, the Gaeltacht, and Lands—fell to Fine Gael, which also held the Attorney Generalship and, naturally, the post of Government Chief Whip.

Liam Cosgrave's decision to offer the Labour Party a fifth ministry when its parliamentary strength entitled it to only four seats in the Government was inspired. By proposing this, perhaps before Labour could even raise the issue, he ensured a smooth start to this new Coalition—the first to comprise these two parties only—and, together with his visible commitment to treating his Labour Party colleagues with respect and consideration, this initial move secured their willing loyalty throughout the life of the Government.

In the event Labour's weight in the Government was even greater than this one-to-two ratio of cabinet seats would suggest. In the first place, Brendan Corish's decision to delegate full authority over his Social Welfare department to Frank Cluskey, his Parliamentary Secretary, virtually gave them a sixth Government seat, as Frank had to be present whenever Social Welfare matters were discussed—which, given our extensive programme of social reform, was very frequently—and Liam Cosgrave's respect for Frank Cluskey's political judgement led him sometimes to suggest that he remain on afterwards to join in discussion of other matters. Second, at the very start of the new Government Conor Cruise O'Brien persuaded Liam Cosgrave to give him responsibility for the Government Information Service, which had hitherto always answered directly to the Taoiseach of the day through its—uniquely—politically appointed head. Third, the combination of the exceptional intellectual calibre of some of the Labour Party Ministers and the weight of the portfolios they collectively commanded gave them a higher profile than numbers alone would account for.

This does not mean that the Government leaned ideologically to the left, however. Jimmy Tully of Labour was instinctively to the right of most Fine Gael members, and Conor Cruise O'Brien's concern for law and order tended to pull the Government to the right as well. Liam Cosgrave's own conservatism, the respect in which the Labour Party Ministers held him, and the pragmatic manner in which we addressed our agenda as a Government all combined to ensure a balanced approach to most problems and to minimise ideological tensions.

The determination of all concerned to ensure the solidarity of the Government was evident in the way we tackled our business. The Labour Party sought to avoid becoming isolated on potentially contentious issues, and if there were any danger of this happening at least one Fine Gael Minister joined them in the relevant vote—frequently myself (usually by conviction) or in my absence some other Fine Gael Minister (sometimes as a matter of political prudence).

Liam Cosgrave proved to be an effective chairman of the Government. This was helped by the fact that he was older than most members (although Conor Cruise O'Brien was his senior by four years). Because of the length of time Fianna Fáil had been in office, he and Brendan Corish were the only ones amongst us who had previous Government experience. Moreover, although he could relax and become a warm personality on informal occasions when he found the company congenial, he had an instinct for the exercise of authority combined with a reticence and a certain remoteness that did not encourage overfamiliarity, with the result that where he clearly had a strongly held view most Ministers were reluctant to challenge him. In opposition, without the extra authority of office, these attributes had not been sufficient to protect him from challenges over issues on which his conservatism tended to isolate him; in Government they proved effective in safeguarding his authority.

Given the disparate personalities involved, remarkably few tensions developed in the Government. The main problem was within the Labour wing of the cabinet. It centred on Justin Keating, who, it eventually transpired, was the object of suspicion or hostility on the part of three of his Labour Party colleagues. In opposition Conor Cruise O'Brien and he had quarrelled over Northern Ireland; Michael O'Leary feared that he might become his rival for the succession to Brendan Corish as next leader of the Labour Party; and Jimmy Tully disliked his intellectualism—although why this led Jimmy to align himself with Conor against Justin I never fully understood.

I had come to know Justin well during the EEC referendum campaign, as we had travelled the country together, putting the arguments respectively for and against membership. As Minister for Industry and Commerce he asserted the traditional claim of his department to handle foreign trade issues—a claim that Foreign Affairs had contested unsuccessfully since the early days of the state. As a result, from the outset he accompanied me to meetings of the Council of Foreign Ministers whenever, as was frequently the case, the Community's foreign trade competence was under discussion.

Rather than contest his right to attend these meetings, an argument that I would inevitably have lost, I accepted his participation at EEC level and concentrated my defensive efforts on repelling, on the whole successfully, attempts by his civil servants to carve out new areas of external responsibility for their department in order to compensate for the transfer of foreign trade from national to Community control. The strength of our personal relationship as it had developed during the referendum period enabled us to work well together at meetings of the Council and to settle, at intervals of six months or so, the regular accumulation of demarcation disputes between our two departments.

It was only in 1975 that I became belatedly aware of the fact that his three Labour Party colleagues believed that, instead of being tolerantly accepted, Justin's attendance at Council meetings in Brussels and Luxembourg had been contrived by me as part of a plot to promote his candidacy for leadership of the Labour Party. I knew (although clearly his Labour fellow-Ministers did not) that Justin had in fact decided not to contest the leadership but instead to seek appointment as the next Irish Commissioner in Brussels when the current incumbent—the first Irish appointee, Paddy Hillery—came to the end of his term. By the time I found out the suspicions these three Labour Ministers entertained about me it was too late to convince them that they had got the wrong end of the stick.

Meanwhile I had come to the conclusion that Justin Keating was in fact the best available Irish candidate for the Commissionership, for it soon became evident that the only other member of the Government interested in the post was Dick Burke, the Fine Gael Minister for Education, who did not seem to me to have the same intellectual capacity as his Labour Party colleague.

This landed me in a further problem with my Fine Gael colleagues. Unknown to me, Dick had sought and secured from them before the end of 1975 agreement to support his candidature for the post of Commissioner if, as was the case, I was not a candidate myself. My support for Justin Keating's nomination in the course of 1976 may well have irritated some of his Labour Party colleagues, who may have felt their hand being forced with a view to making an issue of his appointment, which in the interest of the solidarity of the Government they might have preferred not to do. And it certainly annoyed a number of Fine Gael Ministers, who regarded my stance as disloyal to my party. In the event Dick Burke's nomination was agreed by nine votes to six, and he served as Commissioner from 1977 to 1980 and again, on Fianna Fáil's nomination, from 1982 to 1984.

The spring and summer of 1973 were a honeymoon period for our Government. We inherited an economy that had been growing on a scale without precedent. A disturbing factor however was wage inflation, which, at 20 per cent by mid-1973, was far beyond what the increasing cost of imports would justify and which was pushing up consumer prices at an accelerating rate: inflation rose from 8 to 12 per cent within six months. This we would have to tackle.

But net emigration had been replaced for the first time in recorded history by net immigration; young Irish people in the 25–39 age bracket were returning from Britain with skills acquired there so as to take up employment in the new industries being established throughout the country by foreign investors, and were bringing with them their young children, who unexpectedly swelled the numbers in our primary schools. This bright picture was further cheered by the new inflow of financial resources accruing to us through the EC budget, modestly estimated at £30 million in that year, which we had decided to allocate to improvements in the social welfare system.

No-one could have foreseen, in Ireland any more than elsewhere, that before the year was out all this would be threatened by the oil crisis sparked off by the Yom Kippur War in early October.

Despite my heavy commitments in the Department of Foreign Affairs—during the part of 1973 when I was in Government I spent the equivalent of two months on fifteen journeys outside Ireland, and I was also deeply involved in the preparations for the Sunningdale conference—I nevertheless participated fully in the work of implementing our many policy reforms at home. I served on three cabinet bodies that in the early years of that Government had an unusually large role in policy-making: the Economic, Social and Education Subcommittees.

During 1973 the Economic Subcommittee was mainly engaged in assessing the economic prospects, with special reference to likely price trends, as a guide for possible Government action on incomes—in view of the inflation explosion this had to be a priority—and in implementing the proposals for capital tax reform that I had managed to get inserted at a late stage into the National Coalition election programme. The Social Subcommittee was concerned with our social reforms, the details of which I had incorporated in a speech I had prepared for Liam Cosgrave at short notice in the course of the election campaign. The Education Subcommittee was—much less successfully—engaged on an attempted reform of the structures in higher education.

The deliberations of the Economic Subcommittee on the proposal to substitute an annual wealth tax for the traditional estate and legacy duties were of particular concern to me. I had first put forward such a reform as part of my contribution to the Just Society policies in 1964–65 before joining the party, and, as I have recorded earlier, had been disappointed, and indeed disconcerted, by the rejection of my proposal by the Policy Committee of the party under Liam Cosgrave's chairmanship. Given that what I suggested could affect adversely at most 1 per cent of the electorate—the richest 1 per cent—and would alleviate the burden of estate duties on many others, as well as being broadly redistributive in favour of the great majority of taxpayers, I could not understand the rejection of my proposal on the grounds that it would be 'unpopular'.

I had made a further attempt to get the idea accepted at a two-day policy meeting of the Fine Gael front bench in 1969, but with equally little success. It was only when I returned to Leinster House after getting myself nominated as a Fine Gael candidate in Dublin South-East after the election was called at the end of January 1973 that I had successfully inserted the proposal into what became known as the fourteen points of the National Coalition programme, then at a final draft stage. I had hammered out a sentence on the subject on my typewriter in the office I shared on the third floor, and, Richie Ryan having approved it, it had been adopted by the Fine Gael and Labour Party negotiators. It read: 'With a view to relieving the heavy and unjust burden on house purchasers and farmers, the National Coalition Government will abolish estate duties on property passing on death to widows and their children and replace them with taxation confined to the really wealthy and to property passing on death outside the immediate family.'

The members of the Economic Subcommittee appointed on 17 April were the Minister for Finance, Richie Ryan, who naturally chaired it; Justin Keating and Michael O'Leary from the Labour Party; and Mark Clinton (Agriculture) and Peter Barry (Transport and Power), as well as myself, for Fine Gael.

It soon became evident that the Department of Finance was vehemently opposed to this reform of capital taxation. Ten days after our appointment to the committee the department submitted a memorandum to the Government that argued in effect for the abandonment of the election commitment on wealth tax, and followed this up with another salvo four weeks later. It put forward a series of difficulties about the wealth tax proposal, and submitted an alternative involving a gift tax and a capital gains tax combined with the retention of estate duties in the form of an inheritance tax—in other words, anything and everything except an annual wealth tax.

After some of us had made it clear what we thought of these extraordinary attempts to reverse Government policy, Richie withdrew the department's memoranda, on the basis that we would consider all aspects of wealth tax.

On 18 June the members of the committee first met civil servants from the Department of Finance, the Revenue Commissioners, the Valuation Office, and the Department of Industry and Commerce. At a second meeting a month later the Department of Finance put forward a series of questions that sought once again to reopen its proposal for retaining 'some form of inheritance tax'. This further attempt to challenge the Government's decision to *replace* inheritance taxes on property within the family with an annual tax on capital provoked a strong Ministerial reaction, and it was decided that, insofar as a combination of wealth tax with other taxes was concerned, we must remain faithful to the Government's commitment to abolish estate duties.

Four months of work on our proposals followed. Then, on 17 November, the indefatigable Department of Finance submitted yet another document to the committee, suggesting that the option it had put forward on 27 April—which involved retaining an inheritance tax and *not* introducing an annual wealth tax—be further considered. We rejected this fourth attempt to sabotage our policy, and continued with our work. The Department of Finance was not, however, prepared to give up: at our meeting on 20 December it made a fifth attempt, resubmitting its November proposal in a new form, describing it as 'an alternative system of capital taxation embodying a modified system of estate duty and gift tax, the present legacy/succession duties and a capital gains tax.' At the same time it produced a draft document called 'Economic Implications of Proposed Changes in Capital Taxation'. We had asked for a document to provide the necessary economic argument in favour of our policy; in effect what we received confined itself to arguments *against* the Government's proposals. When I pointed this out at a meeting of the subcommittee, the departmental response was to ask sardonically, '*Are* there any arguments in favour of the Government's proposals?'

This piece of sarcasm was the last straw. The committee decided to bring the issue to the Government, by means of an interim report that was to comprise both a history of the work of the subcommittee and what was politely described as 'the contribution made to its work by the Department of Finance', together with an analysis of the arguments for and against the abolition of estate duty and its replacement with a wealth tax. I set about preparing a draft of this report during the Christmas break, including an account of the arguments on both sides of the case—after our experience I was not prepared to leave that task to the Department of Finance—and an appendix showing the way in which the comparisons of yields from the existing capital tax system and the proposed new system had been prepared by the officials. (The officials had persisted at meeting after meeting, despite protests from me, in using two different sets of data, so that they were not comparing like with like, as a result of which the relative yields of the two systems were distorted by some millions of pounds in favour of the existing system.)

I sent my report and its appendices to Richie Ryan on 2 January. Throughout the prolonged battle with his officials he had presided over our discussions in an unbiased manner and had been careful not to reveal his own view of the issues. Now, however, he reacted sharply to my draft, complaining that it was discourteous and disingenuous for a Minister to report on the workings of a committee that was the primary responsibility of a colleague, and describing my memorandum as 'tendentious' and containing 'misstatements of fact and unfair imputations'.

What had upset him specifically, because of its impact on his relations with his officials, was a remark in my report that he had told the Government that the Finance memoranda of 27 April and 25 May had not been approved by him, together with an assertion that these memoranda had been 'rejected' by the Government. This was in fact the only specific criticism he made of my draft. He proposed that we thrash out our differences in the subcommittee.

I was not prepared to accept this approach. Accordingly, I modified the draft to meet the particular points he had raised, and, with the agreement of our four colleagues on the committee, handed it out at a Government meeting two days later, which was in clear breach of cabinet procedure: this requires that memoranda with financial implications be submitted to the Department of Finance for comments before being circulated to the Government.

Three days later Richie submitted a counter-memorandum protesting against my actions and making further criticisms of my draft, which did not, however, challenge the validity of almost any of the facts that I have set out above.

The upshot was that the Government confirmed its decision, and a White Paper along the lines of its policy was prepared and published three months later. However, the proposals that eventually emerged in legislation involved a higher threshold (£100,000 in 1974 money terms, or perhaps £500,000 today) and a lower rate of wealth tax (1 per cent) than we had envisaged, with the result that during our years in Government the proceeds of the new capital tax system were less than the yield from the old estate duties.

But when the Government changed in 1977, Fianna Fáil abolished the wealth tax in response to what struck me as a most unscrupulous campaign by some among the wealthy people affected by it. This campaign had been designed to arouse irrational fears amongst people of quite modest means who were in no danger of even being found liable to pay wealth tax. The deeply ironic result was that the net effect of all my efforts over a decade to substitute a more effective method of limiting the accumulation of wealth in too few hands, which would at the same time bear more equitably on those paying it, achieved the exact opposite result: a much *lighter* burden of capital tax than hitherto.

When we returned to Government in 1981 in a new coalition with the Labour Party, the weight of 'popular' opinion amongst the middle classes against a reintroduction of wealth tax inhibited my party from responding to continuous pressure from Labour to restore the system that we had succeeded in introducing in 1974 against so many obstacles.

How typical was this affair of relations between Government and civil service? I would say that it was untypical. Civil servants rightly conceive it to be their duty to advise Ministers fully of the possible adverse consequences of a proposed political decision; they would be failing in their duty were they to do otherwise. It is also humanly understandable that they should often tend to feel that the status quo, the product largely of their own and their predecessors' efforts, has a certain merit and deserves to be preserved unless very cogent arguments are put forward for altering it. Some resistance to change is thus to be expected from the civil service, each department of which tends to have its own attachment to policies developed in the past—for example the commitment of the Department of Industry and Commerce to the policy of industrial protection, developed in the 1930s, which inhibited it from playing a positive role in the movement to free trade in the 1960s. But normally both the process of warning about the dangers inherent in any change and the emotional attachment to traditional policies are kept within reasonable bounds and are not pushed beyond a certain point, which a Minister will recognise and appreciate.

However, the opposition to our proposal to replace estate duties with an annual wealth tax went well beyond the normal pattern of civil service resistance to change. It may be that the Finance officials sensed some uncertainty on their Minister's part about the wisdom of this reform, although Richie Ryan had supported the proposal when I originally suggested it during the preparation of our fourteen-point programme—and after the scheme was announced in the spring of 1974 he defended it with such vigour that conservative critics of the reform most unfairly christened him 'Red Richie'. But even if the Finance officials felt during the second half of 1973 that they had shaken their Minister's convictions on the desirability of the change, in my view their tactics of challenging the Government's decision over and over again, and of presenting non-comparable sets of figures that suggested a loss of revenue that would not have occurred at the tax rates then proposed, went beyond reasonable limits. If they believed that revenue would be lost because the thresholds and tax rates would be watered down, as in the event happened, or that the wealth tax would be repealed by a subsequent Government, as also happened, they did not to my recollection advance these arguments in support of their case.

All in all the episode should be seen as an untypical response, demonstrating the distance civil servants *can* go in challenging Government policy rather than the distance they normally *do* go in warning Governments of the consequences of their actions.

I should add, however, that a factor influencing the civil service approach to this issue may well have been the extent to which during the latter part of the previous sixteen years of Fianna Fáil government they had become accustomed to exercising power without much interference from most Ministers. A new Government coming into office with fresh policies of its own and a determination to implement them may well have come as an unexpected and unwelcome shock to a system in which policy had come to evolve through the interaction of politicians and civil servants in a relationship that had obviously become a relatively 'cosy' one. It is worth recording that while the wealth tax battle was unique in the manner in which it was fought, Ministers in other departments found resistance to our policy initiatives in various areas during 1973; but this seemed to die down when the civil service became accustomed to working with a new, reforming Government.

By the time the Economic Subcommittee had completed its work on the reform of capital taxation, Ireland—together with the rest of the industrialised and developing world—was facing into a major economic crisis deriving from the fivefold increase in oil prices engineered by the Arab oil-producing countries as their response to Israel's victory in the Yom Kippur War. As energy prices rocketed, price inflation accelerated sharply, undermining our attempts to restrain pay increases. There was, indeed, a rapid escalation of already substantial pay claims, which led to a further sharp rise in inflation.

Government spending was thus pushed up as the cost of the goods and services consumed by the public authorities rose sharply; and transfer payments such as social welfare benefits had to be raised very substantially to minimise hardship. While inflation increased revenue from some taxes it lowered the *real* yield from income taxes, as the purchasing power of incomes fell. Even with reductions in the real level of some forms of public spending, borrowing rose sharply as we, like other non-oil-producing countries, sought to finance our unbalanced budget by borrowing a small share of the additional billions of dollars being transferred to the oil producers through the price system. In all this we as a Government were at a particular disadvantage, because of the fact that we had inherited an exceptionally high and rapidly rising inflation rate when we had come into office just eight months before the oil crisis hit us.

By the end of 1974, however, externally generated inflation was starting to abate. As a result, in the first half of 1975 the import price index, which had jumped by a massive 40 per cent in the course of 1974, was rising at an annualised rate of only 7 per cent. Unfortunately the correspondingly massive imported inflation of the previous year had induced a parallel escalation in the rate of domestic pay increases. The already grossly excessive annual pay increases of about 17 per cent that we had inherited had become an annual rate of increase of 30 per cent by early 1975.

Moreover, an inept negotiation between employers and unions, which, under an arrangement negotiated by our predecessors, we as a Government were tied into by virtue of being an employer, produced a national agreement that, if the Government took no action to keep the cost of living down, could yield a 26 per cent pay increase within the twelve months to November 1975. And if we *did* take such action it would lead to pay rising faster than prices, thus increasing effective demand at a time when demand needed to be curbed rather than expanded.

It seemed to us in Government that the most urgent task facing us was to halt this spiralling cycle of price and pay increases. We got little help from the civil service in tackling this, however, because the Department of Finance was so mesmerised by the evident need to reduce public spending that it seemed unprepared to address any other issue. Its preoccupation with controlling public spending was understandable: it had continued to rise quite rapidly at a time when, as in many other countries, real resources were being squeezed by the massive transfer of purchasing power to the OPEC countries as a result of the huge rise in oil prices; but it should not have excluded tackling all other problems, as appeared to us to be the case.

In mid-May, on the eve of my departure to the Middle East, I produced a set of proposals designed to hold price increases below 4 per cent in the following two quarters and below 23 per cent for the year to November—which would at least minimise pay increases under the national agreement. My proposals involved the temporary elimination of VAT on clothing, textiles, footwear, furniture and some other household goods on 1 August, with further VAT cuts to follow before November if this proved necessary in order to achieve my objective. This, and other moves to stimulate employment in house building, and more generally by offering incentives to firms to employ additional workers, was to be financed by a once-off 15 per cent surcharge on income tax and a reduction in aid to building societies and in private housing grants, which I suggested should be replaced with a temporary state mortgage scheme related to new housing starts in the months ahead. I also opposed an early revaluation of the currency, which had been suggested as a means of reducing inflation, while accepting that at a later stage it might form part of an anti-inflation package involving a pay pause at the end of the current pay agreement.

These proposals and similar suggestions from colleagues on the Economic Subcommittee, which we estimated would, taken together, reduce the consumer price index by 2 per cent, were promptly shot down by Finance in a memorandum that among other things rejected our assertion that the main positive action the Government could take was to reduce the consumer price index and encourage employment, reiterating instead the department's belief that the main thrust of Government action should be to reduce current expenditure. The trouble with this was that it ignored the fact that under the terms of this national pay agreement, by which we were bound as an employer, spending on public service pay and unemployment benefit and assistance would rocket if we failed to minimise inflation. On the other hand our proposals would not have achieved sufficiently dramatic reductions in the cost of living to make it possible to seek a renegotiation of this disastrous pay agreement. Something far more radical was needed.

Happily help was at hand. The National Economic and Social Council, comprising representatives of employers, trade unions and farmers as well as senior civil servants and some independent members appointed by the Government, was currently preparing a report on the causes and consequences of inflation in Ireland. A member of the Government obtained a copy of the draft of a crucial section of the report, and this became the basis of a much more radical approach to the prices-pay spiral.

This draft said bluntly that unless the Government could persuade employers and unions to change the national pay agreement, national output would decline, inflation would rise to 25 per cent, and the Government would have virtually no pay options open to it. If on the other hand the pay agreement could be changed, a policy package could be devised that would reduce inflation, improve employment prospects, and leave those with below-average pay rates better off—all this at no net cost to the exchequer. The package they proposed included many of the suggestions I and other members of the Economic Subcommittee had put forward, but was much more drastic. It included, for example, the subsidisation of sugar as well as subsidies to reduce electricity and gas prices and transport fares. Because these measures were estimated to cut the consumer price index by over 4 per cent they could provide a basis for a deal involving the cancellation of the next quarterly pay increase and the elimination of the 4 per cent minimum for pay increases in subsequent quarters.

Encouraged by this document, the very existence of which within a body such as the NESC suggested some willingness by unions to accept a modification of the pay agreement, the Economic Subcommittee returned to the attack, and we carried the day. On 26 June the Government announced a package of measures, including food subsidies, which actually reduced the cost of living slightly in the current quarter, in contrast to average quarterly increases of over 7 per cent during the first half of the year. This tactic worked: the unions accepted a renegotiation of the pay agreement; and although inflation was temporarily at a high level in the early part of 1976 it wound down rapidly thereafter, dropping from 24 per cent in the twelve months ending May 1975 to 6.5 per cent three years later, before starting to rise again as a result of the inflationary measures introduced by Fianna Fáil after their return to office. This breakthrough in 1975 owed little to the Department of Finance, however; the 'mini-budget' of 26 June 1975 was, almost uniquely, the work of the Government itself, aided by the social partners within the NESC.

A price, of course, had to be paid for this achievement. The food subsidies we introduced were not phased out in the late 1970s as they should have been. With poetic injustice it thus fell to us to remove them during the life of the 1982–87 Coalition, at the cost of considerable unpopularity, through raising food prices at a time when, in order to reduce the massive rate of borrowing we had inherited from the 1977–81 Fianna Fáil administration, we were also forced to raise taxes and cut public spending.

My membership of a second Government subcommittee, that dealing with social affairs, enabled me to play a full part in the massive programme of social reform that this Government introduced. The measures implemented by us included all those I had set out in the speech I had drafted for Liam Cosgrave during the election campaign, together with others proposed principally but not exclusively by the Parliamentary Secretary for Social Welfare, Frank Cluskey. The initial measures were in fact put to the Government in a memorandum personally typed by me in Brendan Corish's office in the Department of Social Welfare, where I worked on this programme with Brendan and Frank.

Our social reforms increased significantly the purchasing power of social benefits, and especially children's allowances, which were also extended to the age of eighteen for those not in employment and were made payable to mothers rather than fathers. They also involved the introduction of schemes to cover new categories of beneficiary: unmarried mothers, prisoners' wives, single women over fifty-seven years of age, and old-age pensioners' dependants. Moreover, the pension age was reduced from seventy to sixty-six, where it has since remained stuck.

Other measures of social importance included a 50 per cent increase in the public housing programme, together with a reform of the differential rent system for such housing and a liberalisation of tenant purchase arrangements. The less well off also benefited significantly from the implementation of our commitment to abolish VAT on food.

That these and other social reforms were introduced during a term of office six-sevenths of which coincided with the worst economic crisis the world had seen for decades testifies to the commitment of both our parties to social-democratic objectives. There were of course, both in politics and amongst the public, some who felt that by persisting with these reforms after 1973 we were attempting to do too much and that the social-democratic swing in policy throughout our term of office was inappropriate to a period of crisis. Some expenditure taxes had to be increased to pay for these reforms, and there was of course extensive borrowing—as in all other industrialised countries during this period. But the other side of the coin was that income tax rates were simultaneously reduced, the top rate from 80 to 60 per cent and the lowest rate from 35 to 20 per cent; the rate of company tax was also cut; and domestic rates were halved.

A favourable factor throughout this period was the continued high level of industrial investment; manufactured exports expanded more rapidly than in any other industrialised country, and our high industrial growth during these four years was exceeded only by Spain and Italy.

Our reform programme extended outside the social and economic spheres. Legislation was also introduced to secure equal rights for women, and other legislation gave workers the right to participate in membership of the boards of the principal state enterprises. Adoption legislation was liberalised, among other things by removing the ban on adoptions by couples of different religions. Parents were given a role on new management bodies established in primary and local authority second-level schools. A Law Reform Commission was also established.

Another policy change adopted by Fine Gael in the 1960s and included in the Coalition's fourteen-point programme in 1973 was the removal of the Irish language requirement for the award of the Leaving Certificate and for entry to the public service. The founders of the state had been conscious of the debt they had owed to the late nineteenth and early twentieth-century language revival movement, which, although itself apolitical, had been the meeting-place in which many of those who had launched the revolutionary movement for Irish independence had found each other—as, indeed, my own parents had done in London. Inspired by the sense of a debt to be discharged and by a personal commitment to the language, the first Cumann na nGaedheal government made Irish an essential requirement for entry to the public service and, from 1928, for the Intermediate Certificate.

In 1934 Fianna Fáil extended this requirement to the Leaving Certificate: a failure in Irish in this examination deprived children of the right to any certificate of their achievement in school, regardless of how well they performed in any other subject. Inevitably within a few years, as I can recall from my own secondary school experience in the late 1930s and early 1940s, 'compulsory Irish' became profoundly unpopular, but the issue was not addressed politically until the 1960s. As long as the first-generation political leadership remained in office— Éamon de Valera and Richard Mulcahy leading Fianna Fáil and Fine Gael, respectively, until 1959—the Irish language requirement was effectively excluded from the agenda of political debate. James Dillon, who succeeded General Mulcahy as leader of Fine Gael in 1959, raised the issue in the 1961 general election, but it was not until I put forward specific proposals in 1967 that Fine Gael formally committed itself to eliminating a requirement that, whatever the motivation for its introduction almost half a century earlier, had proved profoundly counterproductive in its impact on public esteem for the language.

The removal of the Irish language requirement for public service entry took several years to implement, but I got agreement to earlier action in relation to the exceptionally large intake of twenty-nine third secretaries into the Department of Foreign Affairs in 1974, with the result that no fewer than seven of this number came from Northern Ireland, drawn from both communities there. Few if any of these would have been able to qualify for entry to the foreign service but for the exemption from Irish.

The Education Subcommittee was less successful than the other two Government subcommittees of which I was a member. Our main task was to help Dick Burke, the Minister for Education, to formulate a solution to the problem of university structures, which had been a controversial issue during the previous five years, following the decision of an earlier Minister, the late Donagh O'Malley, to break up the NUI and to merge its Dublin college, UCD, with Trinity College. This committee included two other academics, Conor Cruise O'Brien and Justin Keating. Our efforts produced no tangible result; three academics was perhaps too many!

An issue that particularly concerned me in the early period of this Government was the revision of constituency boundaries. In the late 1960s a constituency revision had been carried out by Kevin Boland, Minister for Local

Government before his 1970 resignation in protest against Jack Lynch's sacking of Neil Blaney and Charles Haughey over the arms importation affair. In the Dublin region, where Fianna Fáil was weak, with around 40 per cent of the vote, he had concentrated four-seat constituencies, giving his party typically half the seats with its two-fifths of the votes. In the west, where Fianna Fáil was then stronger, with over 45 per cent of the vote in many areas, he had concentrated three-seat constituencies; even with somewhat less than half the votes, his party could usually secure two out of the three seats in such constituencies. The result of this gerrymander was that Fianna Fáil tended to secure a total number of seats disproportionate to its national vote—about 5 to 6 per cent more seats than votes overall.

I was opposed to the artificial distortion of the electoral system, which I regarded as disreputable, and I was concerned lest our Government be tempted to undertake a tit-for-tat reverse gerrymander. Accordingly, immediately after the election of the Government I prepared a memorandum that I sent to Liam Cosgrave and Jimmy Tully, proposing an independent constituency commission. I included a detailed analysis of the contemporary political geography of the state, demonstrating that in the current situation a commission operating on the basis of straightforward terms of reference would have little choice but to recommend a redistribution that in practice, as luck would have it, would tend to favour Fine Gael and the Labour Party over Fianna Fáil. A gerrymander was thus superfluous.

The logic of my memorandum (from which, as I recall, I was careful to omit any arguments of principle that might have justified its dismissal on the grounds of political naïveté!) was ignored. Four years later our defeat in June 1977 was all the more overwhelming because what came to be known as the 'Tullymander' rebounded against us: Jimmy Tully's calculations had been too finely judged altogether, and a shift in the voting pattern that he had not foreseen led to our losing more seats than was necessary.

Two years after the Tullymander a memo was submitted from the Department of Finance proposing the cancellation of the 1976 census as an economy measure. Because of the scale of population changes in the postwar period brought about by large-scale emigration, censuses had since the war been held at five-year rather than ten-year intervals. By 1975 there was considerable indirect evidence that net emigration had been replaced since the late 1960s by net immigration. It was important to have this confirmed and to establish the pattern of immigration for planning purposes; to the extent that Irish people now coming home were bringing families with them, this had implications for housing and primary education facilities. There could scarcely have been a worse moment to cancel a census.

The Government nevertheless decided to consider this memorandum in the absence of the Minister for Finance, who was away, I believe, in Brussels. Despite the strong arguments I and several others adduced in favour of going ahead with the census, it was decided to adopt the Finance recommendation;

and it became clear during the discussion that for some members of the Government part at least of the motivation for this decision was a concern lest publication of data from such a census should raise the question of a further constituency revision that might undo the Tullymander.

Next day, when Richie Ryan heard what had been decided he exploded, telling me that he had allowed the memorandum to go to the Government only to demonstrate what daft ideas for economies his department was producing. It was too late to go back on the decision, however, and an alternative that Richie considered, involving a sample census, proved too complex and expensive.

When Fianna Fáil returned to power in 1977 it revived the census proposal, with the result that censuses were carried out in 1979 and also again in 1981. The 1979 census was used as the basis for a constituency revision undertaken for the first time by an independent commission with neutral terms of reference. Because the 1970s had been a period of rapid population growth, and because it was decided to maintain Dáil representation at the maximum level permitted by the Constitution (1 seat per 20,000 population), this revision increased the size of the Dáil by eighteen seats, from 148 to 166. This was of enormous assistance to me as leader of Fine Gael at that time, because it enabled me to encourage many Fine Gael deputies in that Dáil to accept the addition of strong candidates to the ticket in their often enlarged constituencies, on the basis that, with extra seats available, they would need to be both lazy and stupid to lose out to other Fine Gael candidates. I was thus the eventual, if inadvertent, beneficiary of the census postponement decision that I had myself stoutly resisted.

But to return to 1973: after six months in Government some of us felt that we should review our progress, and it was decided to hold an informal 'political' meeting of the Government away from our usual environment. I suggested that we hold it in Iveagh House, and that was readily agreed. When my officials heard of this proposal they pointed out that department funds could not properly be used for the entertainment of the Government. Accordingly I had to purchase the food and drink myself, levying the cost on my fellow-Ministers. This was readily accepted in principle, but it took me the best part of a year to recover ten pounds a head from every member of the Government.

The session was found to be very useful, and it was agreed that we would repeat the exercise every six months. In the event we failed to keep this good resolution: the pressure of events after the oil crisis proved too great. In retrospect I feel this was a pity, for at normal Government meetings urgent business inevitably takes precedence over more long-term considerations. Later, as Taoiseach, I ensured that we held a number of 'think-ins' of this kind, either at Barrettstown Castle, Co. Kildare, which had been presented to the Government for occasions of this kind, or, once, at a Dublin hotel.

An episode during this period in Government that caused a considerable stir was the defeat in July 1974 of our Bill to liberalise the law on contraception. When this matter came before us in the spring of 1974 Liam Cosgrave, who was known for his religious conservatism, stayed silent during the discussion on the terms of the Bill. This was not strictly a Government Bill but one introduced by the Minister for Justice, Pat Cooney, on his own account, a distinction that I am afraid was far too subtle for many people to grasp. Three times at this meeting Conor Cruise O'Brien endeavoured to extract from the Taoiseach a reaction to the proposed Bill, but each time he failed. We left the meeting no wiser about his attitude. The final drafting of the Bill and its insertion into the parliamentary calendar took some time, and it was several months later, in July 1974, that the second stage debate was held in the Dáil. Fianna Fáil opposed the Bill, in accordance with its consistent policy of supporting the conservative standpoint of the Catholic Church on such issues, and eventually a vote was called.

Curiously, despite Liam Cosgrave's silence, even when repeatedly questioned by Conor Cruise O'Brien at the Government meeting months earlier, his stance was not worrying us at this stage. Somehow we had managed to convince ourselves that he would support the Bill when the time came, the interval since the discussion in Government having insensibly eroded earlier doubts. The Chief Whip, the late John Kelly, clearly had no qualms on the matter and was busy persuading the small number of anti-contraception Government TDs that they should vote for it, as, according to him, Liam Cosgrave was doing. What we did not realise was that John Kelly had no direct assurance from Liam Cosgrave but was, it seems, relying on an impression of his attitude gleaned from his private office, where the Taoiseach's position had apparently been misunderstood.

TDs had already begun passing through the lobbies when John discovered his error. Appalled at having misled some conservatively minded deputies into voting for the Bill on a false premise, he immediately urged the Taoiseach to vote without delay—for, unaware of John Kelly's activities, Liam Cosgrave had loyally intended to wait until the end before casting his vote so as not to influence other members of the party. Once urged by John, he voted immediately against the Bill, and some who had not yet passed through the lobbies decided to follow him. By then, having voted, I was back on the front bench, and, seeing what was happening, I said to Pat Cooney, 'Wouldn't it be funny if he defeated the Government?'—not realising yet that this was what in fact had happened.

Naturally the defeat of our Bill in these extraordinary circumstances caused a sensation and damaged the standing of the Government. Our insistence that it was not a Government Bill binding all Government Ministers in collective responsibility was regarded as sophistry, and we were accused of having thrown this crucial constitutional doctrine overboard.

Inevitably my absence abroad meant that I missed quite a number of Government meetings and as a result on several occasions was unaware of significant decisions that had been taken, since the practice was to circulate decisions only to those actually responsible for their implementation. In order to avoid possible embarrassment—I recall creating such embarrassment on one occasion by indignantly denying in public that a particular decision on university policy had been taken that in fact involved a reversal of an earlier decision of which I *was* aware—I arranged after a while to get copies of all decisions.

Despite my frequent absences, when any matter of particular concern to me was due for decision I usually managed to ensure that I was present, or occasionally to have the decision postponed; and the meetings of the Government subcommittees of which I was a member—Economic, Social, Education, and also, when matters of external concern arose, the Security Committee—could usually be arranged to coincide with my periods at home.

As I became increasingly involved in my portfolio I found, however, that I often did not have time to study fully the extensive memoranda before the Government on issues of economic importance on which I felt I should contribute, and even where I *was* able to study them I often did not have time to undertake my own research into the issues at stake. I was not, therefore, contributing as fully as I might have done to Government discussion of these matters.

At the same time I was very conscious of the assistance some Labour Party Ministers were receiving from economic advisers, some former students of mine with whom I had a good relationship. In the spring of 1975 I suggested to some of my Fine Gael colleagues that we should make similar appointments. There was no general enthusiasm for the idea, but I got agreement that I could go ahead on my own. In June 1975 therefore I appointed Brendan Dowling, another of my former students, as my economic adviser to help me to contribute more effectively to Government discussion on domestic issues. Given the quality of advice available to me within my own department I did not need assistance in relation to foreign affairs. The department was naturally content with this arrangement. However, I was amused to find after a while that my officials, off their own bat and without mentioning it to me, sometimes sought Brendan's help also on economic issues of concern to the department.

An example of the way such advisers can help make things happen that might not otherwise take place arose later that year. There was a poor potato crop, as a result of which prices rose sharply and, at a time when we were struggling to master inflation, the consumer price index was consequently in danger of being forced up by an additional 1 per cent on this account. I got agreement in Government to the appointment of a working group comprising Brendan Dowling and Willy Scally (Justin Keating's adviser), together with officials from Agriculture and Finance, with a view to examining the possibility of removing restrictions on the import of potatoes in order to bring prices down. The Department of Agriculture appeared to be so mortally offended at even the suggestion of allowing potatoes to be imported that they did not attend. With their case thus gone by default, and with Finance concerned about inflation, the two advisers succeeded within the space of a single working week in getting the necessary decision taken. The threat of significant imports, together with actual import of a mere 50 tons, halved prices literally overnight. If the normal departmental processes had been employed the authorisation of imports would probably have been effected around the time of the next potato glut.

Security matters absorbed a good deal of our time in Government. Within a fortnight of our coming into office the *Claudia* was intercepted by the Naval Service off the Waterford coast, as a result of good intelligence work by the British. Its arms cargo was seized, and several of those involved, including Joe Cahill, a senior IRA man, were arrested and convicted of the attempted import of arms.

In the autumn we were told that members of the Government were under threat of kidnapping by a subversive group. Until then our protection had been limited to the carrying of a gun by our official Garda drivers; my understanding of their instructions was that when we left our cars they were not to accompany us but were to remain with the car, so it seemed that the guns were for the protection of the state cars rather than the Ministers! Now for a time we were accompanied by two armed detectives in an escort car whose job was to guard *us*.

At an informal discussion in Government of the kidnapping threat we recognised that, even if the armed escorts discouraged efforts to kidnap Ministers, our families would remain vulnerable. We agreed that if any member of our families were kidnapped the Minister in question would opt out from discussion of the matter and that, regardless of the threats that might be made against the person kidnapped, no concession should be made to the kidnappers. I had already at a much earlier stage had a similar discussion with the Foreign Affairs staff visiting Northern Ireland, and they had similarly asked that no concessions be made if any of them were kidnapped in the North; all they sought was somewhat better compensation arrangements than those provided for their families by the ordinary civil service scheme, which seemed to me eminently reasonable.

When shortly after this we had to fight a by-election in the border constituency of Cavan-Monaghan to fill the seat vacated as a result of Erskine Childers's election to the Presidency, the Gardaí insisted that for security reasons members of the Government stay in the same small hotel. In the event the by-election was entirely peaceful. Some months later, however, in mid-March 1974, a Presbyterian Fine Gael senator, Billy Fox, was murdered in this area by the Provisional IRA while he was visiting his fiancée. When he arrived at her parents' house one night a raid was in progress by a dozen Provisionals, the sectarian character of which was demonstrated when they threw family Bibles into the fire; he was chased into a field and shot down when cornered. The Provisionals immediately tried to throw a smoke-screen over their actions by accusing the UDA of the atrocity and sending a wreath to Billy Fox's funeral, as well as issuing a statement alleging that he was well disposed towards them. Unknown to them, however, several of the murderers had been intercepted after the killing, and as a result all twelve of the gang were arrested, convicted, and given long sentences.

A year later the kidnap threat was carried out but, possibly because of the protection afforded to the members of the Government, the victim was a Dutch businessman, Tiede Herrema, rather than a Minister. Joan and I were in Chicago when we heard the news, and I immediately phoned my Dutch counterpart, Max van der Stoel, but in his absence abroad spoke to the Minister of State, Laurens Brinkhorst. I assured him that we would do all in our power to track down the kidnappers and to release Herrema. Neither then nor later did the Dutch propose to us that we should negotiate with the kidnappers or accede to their demands.

When the Gardaí eventually tracked down the kidnappers and their victim to a house in Monasterevin, some thirty miles from Dublin, and laid siege to the house, I rang van der Stoel to tell him the news. He immediately asked if we could arrange for a psychologist or psychiatrist to assist the Gardaí in the siege. I agreed to contact the Department of Justice on this point, but they had anticipated me, and I was able to ring my colleague back within twenty minutes to tell him so.

Several weeks later after a debate in UCD I went into the bar in the nearby Montrose Hotel to have a drink with some students. As I went to order drinks a man beside me said, 'He's out.' I looked blankly at him, and seeing my puzzlement he added, 'Herrema, he's out; they've freed him.'

I dashed to a phone, rang Joan, told her I was going to the Dutch embassy residence in Dundrum, where I was sure he would be brought, and suggested that she drive up in her car and meet me there. There followed a chapter of confusion when we found nobody at home in the embassy and, after a Garda car bringing the Herremas arrived, had to trespass on the hospitality of neighbours across the road, where Joan and I and Tiede Herrema were eventually joined by Mrs Herrema and the Ambassador and his wife. We then retired to the embassy, where we remained until the early hours, listening to Tiede Herrema's account of his experiences after he had had a bath and a meal. I arranged for him to give RTE an exclusive interview, which was retransmitted throughout the world.

The murder of the British Ambassador, Christopher Ewart-Biggs, in July 1976 provoked widespread demands for tougher action against the IRA. The Irish political system may be somewhat better equipped than that of Britain to resist pressures to respond to the latest atrocity, but it is not immune to such influences. On this occasion we succumbed to public pressures; worse still we did so belatedly. Instead of acting immediately by recalling the Dáil to enact supplementary legislation at once, we allowed the process of preparing the legislation to take a leisurely course over the following two months, so that by the time it reached the Dáil after an abbreviated summer recess public opinion had reverted to its normal condition, concerned to balance the need to tackle the IRA effectively against the need to protect individual rights, and, on reflection, suspicious of measures that seemed to be prompted by an emotional reaction to a particular atrocity.

The debate on these measures was, I believe, damaging to our Government, reinforcing the unhappiness of a public that was already critical of the economic measures we had had to take during the previous two years in response to the first oil crisis. There was, moreover, public concern at this time about reports by investigative reporters in the *Irish Times* of Garda brutality in the interrogation of suspects by what was described as the 'Heavy Gang'. I was distressed by these reports, which appeared to me to warrant investigation. Several of my colleagues shared my anxiety. Having reflected on the matter during our holiday in France in August, I decided to raise it in the Government and, if necessary, to force the issue to a conclusion by threatening resignation. In the event I was deflected from my purpose by a consensus in the Government that we would be sending very conflicting signals to public opinion if at the same time as enacting legislation that, among other things, extended to seven days the maximum period for which suspects could be held under the Offences Against the State (Amendment) Act, we instituted an inquiry into the interrogation of suspects held by the Gardaí. I allowed myself to be persuaded to leave this sensitive issue over for several months, and my recollection is that I raised it again in November and/or January, but to no effect; I have no record of this, however.

In mid-February 1977 I was asked by two responsible members of the Garda Síochána if I could see them privately to discuss a matter of concern to the force. Although they were members of a different representative body from that which I had served as consultant between 1962 and 1973, I knew them from that period and accordingly agreed to meet them. They told me that there was widespread worry among the Garda force about these allegations of brutality. Many of the allegations were false, they said, concocted by subversives to undermine the Gardaí and in the hope of avoiding conviction for offences of which they were guilty. In cases that had come to trial up to that point, brutality had not been employed by gardaí, despite allegations to this effect. But in some pending cases it was believed by some in the force that confessions had been extracted by improper methods, and Garda morale would be seriously damaged if these cases went ahead and some gardaí were persuaded to perjure themselves in the process. I told them I would do what I could to get action to deal with the matter.

My problem was how to proceed. From earlier contacts with Pat Cooney, the Minister for Justice, I knew that he was unsympathetic to such allegations, and while at one level the fact that I now had a basis for my concern from within the force should add credibility to a further attempt by me to raise the matter with him, at another level any reference by me to contacts of mine within the Gardaí would naturally irritate him; I was already aware of his sensitivity to my former involvement with the representative body.

At the same time my persistent but unsuccessful attempts to raise the 'Heavy Gang' issue in Government had made it less likely that I could take the issue up again at that level with any hope of a positive result; if I disclosed to the Government as a whole that I had been in touch with members of the Garda

Síochána I would almost certainly get a very negative reaction from Ministers who would have resented a similar involvement by me in their own areas of responsibility.

I finally decided that the best approach would be to Liam Cosgrave directly, but given his intense preoccupation with law and order and his protectiveness vis-à-vis the Defence Forces and Garda it would have to be very carefully judged; indeed it would have to be designed to meet some of his own security preoccupations in a very direct manner as well as addressing the problem of averting any future Garda misconduct.

At this point I fell ill with gastric and throat infections, complicated by general exhaustion, and was told that I would have to rest for a fortnight. Before retiring to my bed I hammered out on my typewriter a letter to Liam Cosgrave. In it I proposed three measures:

> First, to institute a review of the 'right to silence', which could, I suggested, be a factor that might tempt a minority of guards to use strong-arm tactics to get a statement—any kind of a statement—out of a suspect.

> Second, to trade off representation of guards (e.g. by a barrister) in internal disciplinary inquiries unconnected with brutality to prisoners (a Garda demand at that time) for agreement to the participation of an outsider in inquiries into complaints by the public against members of the force.

> And third, to introduce a rule that all arrests under certain types of legislation would have to be notified to the court within six or twelve hours, so that an officer of the court could be sent at any time thereafter to be admitted instantly to see the prisoner.

I added that he should not underestimate the concern of the Gardaí with the situation as it existed. We needed to help them discreetly. And I concluded that I hoped the matter could be kept open until my return from my sick-bed, but that if it did come up for discussion before then would he let me know, so that, doctor or no doctor, I could come instantly.

That was the letter I wrote in February. At the present distance in time I cannot be sure—in view of my doubts about the wisdom of pressing the issue when, despite my concluding paragraph, I might not be in a position to follow it up in person in the near future—whether I sent it then or later, but a letter in these terms was certainly sent. However, the election was called before I could pursue the matter further. After the Government changed there were reports of a 'shake-up' in the Gardaí by the new Fianna Fáil Minister for Justice, and thereafter complaints of ill-treatment of suspects ceased to be an issue.

Why did I not pursue the matter to a conclusion at some point during the nine months from September 1976 to June 1977, if necessary by resigning on the issue, as I had at one stage contemplated? I cannot now answer that with any certainty. I suppose I must have convinced myself that I should remain on in the Government in the hope of getting action at some stage; it is easy to convince oneself that it is not yet time to take the ultimate step of resigning on an issue of principle when the issue has not been brought to a conclusion.

But to revert once more to the legislation provoked by the Ambassador's murder: in mid-October 1976 it passed both houses and was sent to the President, Cearbhall Ó Dálaigh. Before describing what followed I should first explain the circumstances in which Cearbhall Ó Dálaigh had become President. He had been a distinguished jurist and had served as Chief Justice for eleven years before his appointment as the Irish member of the EEC court in 1972. He was held in high regard by artists and writers for his cultural interests. In his youth he had held republican views; when he was appointed to the Supreme Court I sent him for his entertainment the police file, found amongst my father's papers, on a public meeting he had addressed in 1931 (with, among others, Cyril Cusack) denouncing my father's proposal to establish an officer training corps of the army in UCD, where he was then a student. He enjoyed this reminder of his radical past. I had come to know him quite well in the late 1960s, when he used to call to collect his wife, Máirín, a distinguished Gaelic scholar, after caucus meetings of the opposition group on the UCD Governing Body in my house.

After Erskine Childers's funeral the Government had had to consider possible names to be put forward to the opposition in the hope of securing agreement on a successor and thus avoiding the trouble and expense of a nationwide election for an office that is mainly, albeit not exclusively, honorary in character. Our first choice had been Erskine Childers's widow, Rita Childers, but two other names were added as possible alternatives: Cearbhall Ó Dálaigh and Dónal Keenan, president of the GAA. When Liam Cosgrave consulted Jack Lynch on the matter he too favoured Rita Childers, but he warned that his chance of securing his party's support for her depended on complete secrecy being maintained.

That evening the Minister for the Gaeltacht, Tom O'Donnell, had to attend a public function in Skibbereen, Co. Cork. A journalist asked him what he thought of Rita Childers as a candidate, a local council having passed a resolution in her favour. Misunderstanding the basis of the question, and thinking that agreement between Fianna Fáil and the Government on her nomination must have been reached, and announced, he endorsed her in terms that implied Government support. Jack Lynch was furious at what he naturally saw as a leak, and his support and that of his party shifted to our second choice, Cearbhall Ó Dálaigh, who was selected and inaugurated shortly afterwards.

Although he was generally popular, President Ó Dálaigh did not seem entirely happy in the job and did not adjust easily to his new position. It was believed that he and his wife might have regretted taking on the responsibility, although this was never confirmed. Some believed that this might have been a contributory factor to his resignation in October 1976, but if so it can only have been a subordinate consideration.

Under the Constitution, if the President has doubts about the constitutionality of a Bill he may instead of signing it refer it to the Supreme Court, having first heard the views of the members of the Council of State. This power is usually exercised when such doubts have been expressed in the Oireachtas during the debates on a Bill. In the case of the September 1976 anti-subversive legislation such doubts were expressed, not unreasonably in view of the length of time proposed for detention before a person was charged, which seemed to be at or near the margin of what could be considered reasonable given the provisions of the Constitution on the liberty of the person. Since reasonable doubts existed, it seemed wise to me (and I think to some other members of the Government) to have it tested then instead of having it found defective at a later stage when challenged by someone in detention.

Paddy Donegan, the Minister for Defence, held a contrary view, however, and held it strongly. He attended a ceremony in Columb Barracks, Mullingar, where he made impromptu remarks in the course of which he attacked the President's referral of the new Bill to the Supreme Court in confused terms:

'It was amazing that when the President sent the Emergency Powers Bill to the Supreme Court he did not send the powers of the army, he did not send the seven years' maximum penalty for membership [of the IRA], he did not send the ten years' maximum penalty for inciting people to join the IRA to the Supreme Court. In my opinion he is a thundering disgrace. The fact is that the army must stand behind the state.' The words 'thundering disgrace', as reported by the only journalist present, may have been a euphemism for the words actually spoken.

The other Minister present, Pat Cooney, rang the Taoiseach at once to report what had happened. As soon as Paddy Donegan realised fully the implications of what he had said, especially in view of the fact that the President ex officio is titular commander-in-chief of the Defence Forces, he offered his resignation. Liam Cosgrave rejected the resignation, however, and Paddy instead sought an appointment with the President to apologise. This request was not granted, and on the following day, when the matter came before the Government at a meeting in Liam's room in Leinster House, we were faced with a letter from the President protesting at the Minister's remarks.

I had been away and I arrived after the meeting had begun. Liam had, as I understood it, just read out the letter. I asked to see it, and may have been the only Minister who had the opportunity of poring over the text. The letter did not directly threaten resignation but took the form partly of a series of rhetorical questions. Having said that the relationship between President and Minister had been 'irreparably breached', the President went on to ask whether the sequence of remarks by the Minister could be construed otherwise than as an insinuation that the President did not stand behind the state: had the Minister any conception of his responsibilities as a Minister, and in particular as Minister for Defence?

Most members of the Government, ignoring the words 'irreparably breached', were inclined to draw some comfort from the absence of an unambiguous threat of resignation. With the advantage of having actually read the text I was much less sanguine. I did not, however, feel in a good position to challenge strongly the optimistic view formed before my arrival—not least because to have done so would in effect have been to demand Paddy Donegan's resignation, and as my relationship with him had for many years been one of some distance, I felt ill-placed to be the one person pressing the issue. I contented myself therefore with voicing a measure of pessimism about the more generally accepted interpretation, without attempting to take the matter further.

Two days later I had to attend the President on the presentation of credentials by an ambassador. I found him in strikingly good form. As we parted I expressed my personal distress at what had happened, and he responded warmly. Struck by his good humour, and wrongly thinking it reflected satisfaction with the letter of apology that the Minister had in the meantime addressed to him, I rang Liam Cosgrave to tell him I was more optimistic about the outcome in view of the mood in which I had found the President. The Taoiseach, however, had meanwhile made a statement to the Dáil regretting that the Minister's remarks had slighted the President but denying that he had attacked our institutions: 'He made what he and I regarded as serious comment on what the President did in a disrespectful way,' said the Taoiseach, asserting that the extent of the Minister's apology demonstrated the extent of his regret. Even ignoring the weakness of the syntax, which could have been perversely read as suggesting that it was the President who had been disrespectful, it was a somewhat halfhearted apology, and Liam Cosgrave's statement that he as well as Paddy Donegan regarded the latter's remarks as 'serious comment', however disrespectfully expressed, was unwise to the point of provocation.

The following afternoon at 4.25 I received a call from the Taoiseach asking me to come to his office at once. I was there within three minutes, as were several other Ministers whom he had summoned. He told us he had been informed that a dispatch-rider was on his way from the Park with a message from the President, which he feared might contain his resignation. I suggested that he phone Paddy Donegan, who was at home, and belatedly accept his resignation, so that before the message arrived from Áras an Uachtaráin he could inform the President that the Minister had resigned. He did so, and Paddy immediately agreed. But the President had laid his plans with care. He had left Áras an Uachtaráin at 2.30 for an engagement on the south side of the city, from which, at that very moment, he was departing to go with his wife to his own house in Co. Wicklow. His resignation, which arrived a few minutes later, was irretrievable, and the damage done to the Government was immense. Liam Cosgrave had been fatally betrayed by his own excessive loyalty to one of his Ministers.

Feeling that a President with political experience was desirable (although it was far from clear that Cearbhall Ó Dálaigh's lack of such experience had been a factor in his precipitate departure), the members of the Government came rapidly to a unanimous decision to propose to Fianna Fáil the name of Paddy Hillery, former Fianna Fáil Minister for Education, Labour, and Foreign

Affairs, who would shortly be ending his term as Irish member of the European Commission. This proposal could not, we felt, be turned down by the opposition, and we would thus avoid an expensive Presidential election, which in the unhappy circumstances in which we found ourselves we would certainly have lost, whoever might be our candidate. Our suggestion for an agreed candidate was accepted, and in December 1976 President Hillery was inaugurated, and served for two terms until 1990.

What came to be seen as the excessively drastic anti-subversive legislation of September–October 1976 and the fiasco of the Presidential resignation arising from Paddy Donegan's remarks undoubtedly damaged the public image of the Government as it completed three-and-a-half years of its maximum five-year term—thus approaching the point at which people's minds were starting to turn towards the next election. The 'Heavy Gang' stories and the Government's failure to investigate them added to this negative image; as did an unfortunate incident involving Conor Cruise O'Brien and the *Irish Press*.

In the course of an interview in 1976 with Bernard Nossiter, the distinguished London correspondent of the *Washington Post*, Conor, in what he believed to be an off-the-record comment, illustrated a criticism he had made of the *Irish Press*'s treatment of the IRA by pulling open a drawer in his desk and showing Nossiter a sheaf of cuttings from that paper. Nossiter gained the impression he was collecting these in order to take some unspecified action against the *Press*. When Nossiter's account of the interview appeared it looked to some people as if the Government intended through its anti-terrorist legislation of autumn 1976 to threaten the freedom of the media, and this added to the negative image already generated by the other recent events.

Conor Cruise O'Brien had some time previously introduced a Bill to narrow the terms of the order intended to keep the IRA and their supporters off the air and to transfer from the Government to the Dáil the power to sack the RTE Authority, a power that had been used by the Fianna Fáil Government several years earlier to remove an Authority that it felt had not enforced this order with sufficient vigour. Conor felt, with some justice, that vagueness in the wording of the order had contributed to the earlier disagreement between the Government and the Authority. His action in making the wording more specific was clearly in easement of the situation, as was his legislative change to prevent a future Government from removing an Authority without Dáil approval. But the fact that these actions, which left the ban on the IRA and other subversives in place, were taken by someone who had in the past been seen as a 'liberal', together with the vigour and clarity with which he defended the principle of the ban, had made him the target of libertarian criticism—to such an extent indeed that a myth developed, which still exists in some circles, that he was the original author of this prohibition of IRA appearances on radio or television. When the Nossiter story broke, all this was remembered against Conor.

Of the ban itself it is sufficient to say that there are two sides to the argument about it. On its efficacy against subversives there can clearly be legitimate differences of opinion by people opposed to the IRA—leaving on one side the inevitable attacks on it by the IRA itself and its fellow-travellers. The case customarily made against it is, however, far from compelling. The claim, frequently made, that if free expression were allowed, the potential damage from the publicising of extreme views would be countered by skilled journalistic handling, including interviews with IRA spokesmen, has no obvious foundation. To take an example of a person expressing extreme views (which, however, fall short of incitement to violence), Ian Paisley, I have yet to see *any* interviewer in a quarter of a century 'cutting him down to size', and the same was in my view true of at least some interviews with the IRA or Sinn Féin spokesmen before they were banned on RTE. Moreover, as RTE is the public broadcasting service of a state that many unionists have traditionally seen as hostile, the Irish Government can be argued to have a special duty to restrain expressions of support for the IRA on its air waves that could further inflame the prejudices and fears of extreme unionists who over the years have been responsible for the murder of many hundreds of innocent nationalists.

I do not suggest that these arguments are irrefutable; but neither are the more theoretical arguments against a ban on the IRA having access to the air waves. And the case for the ban has convinced successive Irish Governments under four Taoisigh during two decades to maintain the order, despite its unpopularity with liberal opinion and the media, and notwithstanding the many anomalies to which it has given rise.

By New Year 1977 media speculation on a general election had begun. As is so often the case, this speculation in a mysterious way generated its own reality by stimulating uncertainty within the Government. There were no very evident reasons to hold an election before the summer, and one very strong reason to postpone it: the recovery of the economy then under way in the aftermath of the oil crisis, which the Government had handled skilfully and effectively at least from mid-1975 onwards. Recovery from a crisis of this magnitude, however, requires a period of several years to bring to fruition. And public recognition, whether of crises or of booms in the economy, tends to lag behind events by a further year to eighteen months.

By mid-1977 it was clear that we had brought the economy back to rapid growth, with, by the standards of the time, a relatively low and falling level of inflation and an end to foreign borrowing. It should have been equally clear that full public recognition of this fact would be delayed by at best a further six to nine months—possibly a year. If ever there was a case for a Government remaining in office until as near as possible to the end of its term, this was it.

But when, as the summer of 1977 approached, we came to discuss this in Government such arguments, advanced by Richie Ryan and myself, secured the support of only four other Ministers: mainly, as I recall, urban-based Ministers. The remaining six Ministers present (two were absent) expressed a preference for an immediate summer election. As far as I can recall, their case was defensive: that if an election were left over to the autumn something might go wrong, such as the harvest. This reflected, I believed, a drop in morale as a result of the bad press we had been receiving, for reasons mentioned earlier, and the prolonged speculation about an election that had begun at the start of the year.

When we had taken the head count with its tied result, I remarked to Liam Cosgrave, 'It seems that the decision is back to you, Taoiseach,' fairly confident that, left to himself with no pressure either way, he would, with his customary caution, decide to postpone a dissolution. To my surprise, he decided on a June election; I do not know why, beyond noting that the completion by the Government of four-and-a-quarter years in office, longer than any other Government since the war, represented for him a target attained, proving that coalitions can survive as long as, or longer than, single-party Governments.

Our two parties were utterly unprepared. Fine Gael's organisation had run down during our time in office; party morale was low, for much the same reasons as Government morale was low; and we had no clear idea of where as a party we should be going next. The amount that we had achieved in terms of social and other reforms and in overcoming the oil crisis successfully was certainly impressive, and gave us, for what it was worth (very little, I am afraid, in view of the shortness of the public memory), a record on which to stand with some pride. But we seemed to have difficulty in putting together a convincing programme for the years ahead.

By contrast our opponents had no inhibitions about what they were prepared to promise: a programme of tax cuts and public spending that at any time would have been disastrous if implemented but which was doubly so at a time when the economy was already expanding at an almost record rate of about 6 per cent.

It soon became clear that this explosion of opposition promises was politically superfluous: Fianna Fáil would have won the election if they had promised nothing, for the people were tired of us. These extravagant commitments, which severely damaged the economy for a period of at least fifteen years, proved to have been to no political purpose.

All this came about in part because of the slow development of sophistication in the Irish political system. Although an opinion poll had been held as early as 1961, although a major polling exercise had been carried out by the Labour Party in 1969, and although a number of polls on party support had been undertaken during the years from 1970 onwards, most politicians had continued to reject these tests of the state of public opinion as 'unreliable'. Liam Cosgrave was known to be particularly dismissive of polls, preferring rather oddly to be guided on public opinion by individual letters he received from time to time, extracts of which he sometimes read to us in Government. The thought that we should commission an opinion poll before deciding to hold a June election had struck me and, I believe, one or two other Ministers, but we were inhibited from suggesting it by the dismissive reaction we believed we would have met from most of our colleagues, including the Taoiseach. Our inhibitions were akin to those we might have felt about proposing that we consult an astrologer.

However, no sooner had the decision to dissolve the Dáil been taken, and the members of the Government had dispersed to their constituencies, than the ad hoc election committee, comprising some Dublin Ministers and a couple of aides, took the decision we had hesitated to propose to our colleagues in the Government. We commissioned the Market Research Bureau of Ireland to carry out a rapid nationwide poll with a sample of six hundred. The result arrived a few days later: 59 per cent of those who expressed a view intended to vote Fianna Fáil. The margin shown by these private polls of ours narrowed during the campaign, to 51 per cent, but the public perception nevertheless remained one of a probable Coalition victory, largely because the newspapers did not publish party strength figures from polls they commissioned, apparently because they did not believe the figures that emerged. In the event the unpublished polls proved correct. Fianna Fáil secured 51 per cent of the votes and a twenty-seat majority.

# CHAPTER TWELVE

# LEADING THE OPPOSITION

In the immediate aftermath of the June 1977 election there was some speculation that the leaders of the two defeated parties, Fine Gael and Labour, might resign. The speculation tended to concentrate on Brendan Corish, who was known to be reluctant to continue, rather than on Liam Cosgrave; and on the whole it was felt that nothing dramatic was likely to happen in either case in the immediate future. Those of us who felt we knew Liam Cosgrave thought it unlikely that he would opt out of political life at such an early age; he was only fifty-seven.

A party meeting to review the national results was called for the Thursday after the election. Liam Cosgrave chose this occasion to announce his resignation as leader. He paid tribute to his Fine Gael colleagues in Government, mentioning only one by name, myself. Given our difficult relationship in the past and the fact that I was obviously going to be a candidate for the succession, this caused some comment, but may not have been significant.

When he finished speaking there were moves from a dazed parliamentary party to persuade him to change his mind; Paddy Donegan led this rearguard action. It did not take off: almost everyone knew that Liam Cosgrave was not the man to use a resignation offer as a ploy to get himself drafted back into the leadership. Once he had decided to go he was not going to be shifted from his decision, and he made this bluntly clear in his inimitable, uncompromising manner. There followed valedictory speeches. Then he proposed that the election of his successor take place in eight days' time, on Friday 1 July. He clearly did not wish a repetition of the procedure by which he had himself been proposed without warning to a party meeting that had endorsed him without time for reflection.

When the meeting ended, at around five o'clock, I was due to leave for the annual OECD meeting in Paris. Joan was in the car outside, with our luggage, ready to leave for the airport. I went down to her and told her what had happened; we must abandon the Paris visit and I would join her later at home.

I then had discussions with some of the other possible candidates for the leadership with a view to agreeing a tentative modus operandi. Richie Ryan was at a meeting in Washington and was then due to travel to Luxembourg; he was not expected back in Ireland until the following Tuesday. It was agreed that any of us who decided to contest the leadership should not canvass for support until Tuesday; otherwise, if Richie were a candidate—as then seemed likely—he would be at a disadvantage vis-à-vis those of us at home. Other possible candidates at that time seemed to be Peter Barry, Tom Fitzpatrick, and Mark Clinton. Shortly afterwards John Kelly indicated that he would be available but would not seek the position. This offer was not pursued: there were already more than enough candidates in the field, and although until his unexpected and untimely death in early 1991 he was extraordinarily popular and greatly admired both inside and outside the party, his individualist temperament did not attract support for him as a leader of the party.

Returning home I rang Richie in Washington; he had already heard the news of Liam's resignation. I told him of our 'no canvassing' agreement, but urged him to return as soon as possible; it would be hard to hold this line for long so far as our respective supporters were concerned. He said he could not get out of his Luxembourg commitment but would travel there via Ireland. Joan and I then took advantage of an invitation to dine with Mary and Nick Robinson in Roundwood, Co. Wicklow, which we had earlier turned down because of our Paris commitment.

Next day the papers reported that I was the favourite in the Fine Gael leadership stakes. A group of TDs came to see me to tell me that they supported my candidature and that from initial soundings they believed I would have majority support. I was grateful for their initiative but told them that, as had been agreed amongst the potential candidates, I would not be approaching anyone before Tuesday, and I asked them—without, as it turned out, much success—to limit themselves to soundings, as distinct from seeking support for me.

At the weekend Richie Ryan passed through Ireland en route from Washington to Luxembourg, staying only briefly in Dublin and then stopping in Cork to meet Peter Barry.

I remained in daily amicable contact with Peter Barry during this period. I recall one discussion in the course of which he said that he thought that I would be a better leader than he in opposition but that he might be better able to cope with Government. By Monday he had emerged as the only other candidate in the field, subject to Richie Ryan's still unknown intentions. He believed that in any event I would win but that in order to avoid what had happened in 1965 it was important to have a contest.

On Tuesday I methodically phoned the members of the party. One phone call sticks in my mind particularly: John Boland, then a senator, cross-examined me for almost half an hour on my intentions as leader. We had never been close, and he can hardly have thought that this somewhat aggressive approach would endear him to me. In fact I was impressed, and decided he should be on my front bench if I were chosen as leader.

That night I rang Peter Barry to compare notes. The total electorate—the Fine Gael members of the new Dáil and those Fine Gael members of the old Seanad who had not been elected to the Dáil in the recent election—was 62. I reckoned that I had the support of something like 43, leaving Peter with just under 20. He on the other hand believed he had 25 supporters, and was slightly upset that our figures did not tally. I told him that if only half a dozen members of the party—less than 10 per cent—had allowed *both* of us to believe they were supporters, that showed a very high level of political honesty!

Given that there had been ample time for reflection by the party, he felt that my support was now large enough to make a contest unnecessary after all: my authority would be undisputed even if on Friday I were chosen without a vote; so he announced his withdrawal. And on Richie's return from Luxembourg it emerged that he too was unlikely to stand.

On Friday the party met and on the proposition of Peter Barry I was chosen as leader without a contest. Simultaneously the Labour Party was also meeting to elect a leader, for Brendan Corish had resigned on the previous Sunday. The Labour TDs (only Fine Gael accords a say to senators in such matters) elected Frank Cluskey as leader by 9 votes to 7 for Michael O'Leary.

After my election I paid tribute to the generous and considerate way in which Liam Cosgrave had led his Government. And I told the party that if my performance commended itself to them I would serve for a decade. (In the event I remained leader for nine-and-three-quarter years: close enough!) In case there should be any doubt on the matter, in view of my pre-1973 record of multiple careers, I added that I would be a full-time leader. Finally I told them that I would appoint my front bench in September, and in the meantime the eight Fine Gael ex-Ministers re-elected to the Dáil would constitute an ad hoc front bench.

Later I met the press. Foreshadowing the changes I envisaged in our party's role, but also anxious to reassure more traditional supporters, I said that if a new emphasis were needed to preserve or improve our society, this must be explored, but a consensus must be sought and secured in order to avoid a polarisation of the generations. I saw this as a potential danger of the 1980s, given that at the next election, due in 1981 or 1982, one-third of the electorate would be under thirty-two and that our older population was very conservative. The energies of this young electorate—much larger in relation to the population as a whole than in any other industrialised country—must, I said, be constructively channelled. There was a need also for a reintroduction of idealism and of a sense of the overall interest of society as against the dominance of sectoral interests, fighting with each other for scarce resources.

I went on to assert that Fine Gael was the party best equipped to tackle these tasks, using its established capacity for self-renewal. It could, and should, combine its traditional concern for personal independence and freedom with concern for those who under the social conditions of our society were unable to provide for themselves.

Having thus reasserted the social-democratic principles of the Just Society policies of the 1960s, I went on to stress the importance of not weakening the coalition option with Labour, so that at all times an alternative Government would be available, and to assert also that the friendship and contacts between our two parties would endure—a sentiment that was given visible form in the next day's papers, which published photographs of Frank Cluskey and myself together after our respective elections.

I took the opportunity moreover of a television interview following the press conference to appeal directly to people to join our party.

Next day I wrote a message to the party organisation, emphasising my determination to strengthen the links between the constituencies and the party, which had inevitably been weakened during our period in Government. I told them that I proposed to visit all the constituencies at weekends during the winter and spring ahead, for business rather than social purposes, in order to have serious discussions with the local organisations, and also to hold public meetings in every area. (This was a new concept in Irish politics, with which I had experimented when in opposition in the early 1970s.) And I asked our activists to welcome new members who might join in response to my television appeal.

That done, I had to turn my attention briefly back to Government affairs—for we were still in Government, and Liam Cosgrave was still Taoiseach. During this period the Government had been making appointments to fill various vacancies in the judiciary and on the boards of state enterprises. I was unhappy with this procedure; it seemed to me that, without prejudice to the quality of the appointments, if a Government had failed to fill such vacancies before or during an election campaign it should refrain from making good this failure after it had clearly lost the confidence of the electorate at the polls. This view was not popular with some of my colleagues; nevertheless I resolved that in any Government that I led this practice would not be followed.

On Tuesday 5 July the new Dáil assembled and elected Jack Lynch as Taoiseach by 82 votes to 61.

At an early stage in the life of the new Government I arranged with Jack Lynch an increase in the state allowance to the parties and a new transport allowance for opposition leaders. My own financial needs as a full-time leader were met by a decision of the ad hoc front bench at its first meeting to recommend to the party trustees that I be paid an allowance equivalent to that received by a Minister.

The advent of the summer recess enabled me to concentrate on my preparations for reorganising the party. The general secretary, Commandant Jim Sanfey, had decided to retire, enabling me to broaden the scope of the job by recruiting a national organiser who would also carry out the functions of general secretary. From 1966 to his tragic death in a car accident in February 1970

Gerry Sweetman, a man of exceptional energy, had combined his parliamentary duties with the role of national organiser. Thereafter the post had in effect been vacant, and the party had suffered accordingly. I was convinced that we needed a national organiser from outside the parliamentary party, as well as a full-time press and public relations officer; and with the approval of the ad hoc front bench I advertised these two posts.

The successful applicant for the post of national organiser was Peter Prendergast, who in 1973 had been selected as a candidate in my constituency and had stood again in the recent election, unsuccessfully on both occasions. Ted Nealon, the television presenter and commentator, had, to my great pleasure, applied for the PRO position and was appointed.

They were a formidable pair, who worked well together, Ted Nealon in Leinster House and Peter Prendergast in our head office in nearby Hume Street.

Ted benefited from being already a national figure. The party was delighted that he had thrown in his lot with us, and he was greeted with enthusiasm throughout our organisation. Highly regarded in journalistic circles, he had easy access to the media, where his established reputation as a political commentator was a major asset.

Peter had been a member at different times both of the National Council, comprising representatives of constituencies, and the National Executive, the body responsible for party organisation. As a result he was widely known to Fine Gael people throughout the country. This had disadvantages as well as advantages, for he had made enemies as well as friends, and while he had the confidence of some key people in almost every constituency, others were more negative towards him. However, it is more important for a party organiser to be widely feared than universally liked, and the important thing was that he already knew intimately our organisation at local level—and knew whom he could, or could not, trust.

At no point in the past had our party organisation ever matched the professionalism of Fianna Fáil, and in opposition in the 1930s and 1940s it had declined rather than developed. Peter Prendergast's ambition was, by hook or by crook, to remedy this defect. Under his skilful, subtle—some would say machiavellian—guidance Fine Gael was to reach and surpass in sheer professionalism its hitherto dominant rival. Such an achievement was not attained without trauma.

When Peter and I sat down to review what had to be done we found ourselves in immediate and instinctive agreement. During my years in the party I had observed, as he had, the disastrous effects in many constituencies of the dominance of the local deputy over the organisation in his area. In the Irish multi-seat constituency system deputies feel threatened just as much, and often more, by possible rivals from within their own party as by their political opponents. Many of ours had been unable to resist the temptation to use their position as the only Fine Gael deputy in a constituency to dominate their local organisation and, consciously or otherwise, to discourage or prevent the emergence of a strong second candidate, who might perhaps win a seat but who, alternatively, might in the attempt to do so succeed only in displacing the sitting TD.

Extracting the branches in each constituency from under the thumb of the local TDs was only one of our urgent needs. A replacement had also to be found for our poky head office in Hume Street, which contrasted so badly with the relatively impressive Fianna Fáil building in Upper Mount Street. And, far more vital, the base of the party's support had to be broadened. I determined to attract as big a proportion as possible of the younger generation, whose voting strength was currently being greatly increased by the upsurge in the birth rate of the 1960s and the lowering of the voting age to eighteen in 1972. At the same time I believed that we should try to unleash the political potential of women, whose consciousness of their own worth and rights had been aroused by the non-political—even at times anti-political—feminist movement of the early 1970s. Such objectives as these demanded radical change, and radical change required a new approach to decision-making within the party. My tour of the constituencies would provide the opportunity for rallying support behind my ideas, which hopefully would result in approval for a revised party constitution at my first ard-fheis.

On 14 September, before embarking on the tour, I announced my front bench. My plan had been to appoint Mark Clinton as deputy leader. He was a senior and respected party member who had been a very popular Minister for Agriculture from 1973 to 1977 and came from the more conservative wing of the party. He turned down my suggestion firmly, on grounds of age: he was sixty-two. (Two years later he was elected to the European Parliament, where he served with distinction for a full decade.)

In these circumstances I appointed Peter Barry, from the centre of the party, who in July had emerged as my main rival for the leadership. He filled the key portfolio of Economic Affairs, including Finance and the Public Service. Almost all the available former Ministers were included, with Richie Ryan in Foreign Affairs and Pat Cooney, defeated in the Dáil election and now in the Seanad, as leader of that house. Alexis FitzGerald was his deputy. John Bruton held the Agriculture shadow portfolio, John Kelly that of Industry and Commerce. Two new deputies, Jim Mitchell and Jim O'Keeffe, were given responsibility for Labour and for Law Reform and Human Rights, respectively, which I separated out from the security-dominated Justice portfolio. While I retained overall responsibility for Northern Ireland affairs, Paddy Harte took responsibility under me for this area, and for the security side of Justice.

These appointments made, I set out on my tour of constituencies. I decided that each visit should normally comprise a meeting with the constituency organisation to elicit their views on organisational matters and to encourage them to think radically about these issues; a meeting with the local Fine Gael councillors, who seemed to me to be fairly loosely linked to the party at national level; and a public meeting, which I would address for perhaps half an hour about my vision of Ireland's future, followed by a question-and-answer session for about an hour and a half. As our efforts to interest more young people in politics began to bear fruit, I later added a separate meeting for this group. I excluded attendance at social functions, which in the Irish political system do not start till 11 p.m. or later and often continue till 3 or 4 a.m., during which time one is expected to talk seriously to everyone against blaring music on the dance floor. I hate loud noise, and find such occasions physically exhausting—something that inevitably becomes evident to my hosts.

Following this pattern I visited about half the constituencies between September and December 1977. I was well, indeed enthusiastically, received. Following our sweeping defeat a new leader was bound to be a source of hope, and my more relaxed and open style by comparison with that of my predecessor suited the mood of the late 1970s. By Christmas it was clear that my assessment of the need for radical organisational change was quite widely shared—although not, of course, by many TDs, some of whom were beginning to rumble what I was at. The process of reform in which I was engaged was helped by the fact that, in contrast to myself, Peter Prendergast knew a vast number of members of our organisation locally and could quickly identify those open to change—and those who were likely to oppose the necessary reforms.

The scale and consistency of support for the kind of changes I had in mind was, however, such that by Christmas I decided to take a short-cut. Rather than waiting for the end of my constituency visits before putting forward a draft new constitution, I decided to launch it in February as a basis for discussion during the second half of my tour.

The most important single change I proposed in our constitution was in the method of electing the National Executive. Hitherto this body had tended to represent the interests of TDs rather than the party as a whole, because the National Council—a body representative of constituency organisations, many of which were in effect controlled by a local TD—elected twelve members and the parliamentary party a further eight. Even the national officer posts—four vice-presidents and two honorary secretaries—had until the early 1970s normally been held by prominent TDs, whose nominations for election by the ard-fheis had until the early 1970s rarely been contested.

My new constitution proposed to transfer to the ard-fheis the power to elect most of those hitherto chosen by the National Council. The general membership represented at the ard-fheis would tend to be more interested in the future of Fine Gael than in the fate of individual TDs.

As I had anticipated, the party members found this proposal so attractive that when the new constitution came before the ard-fheis in May, that body voted to increase its representation from my modest suggestion of eight to twelve. Some three dozen other amendments to my initial draft, some proposed by me as a result of comments made during the second part of my tour but most put forward by the ard-fheis itself, were adopted, with the result that the members of Fine Gael could legitimately feel that the final document was *their* constitution as well as mine.

Among important new features accepted by the ard-fheis was a provision for a Young Fine Gael organisation, independent of but of course linked to the senior party, which was given substantial voting strength at constituency level, despite the qualms of many older members. Women members of the party, incidentally, turned down my offer to establish a Fine Gael women's organisation, preferring at that time to rely on the momentum of the national women's movement and on my own support and encouragement. To overcome the excessive rural bias in our structure I made provision for weighting branch representation by reference to the electorate in a branch area; and to encourage new talent to come forward at organisational level I introduced a maximum of three years for tenure of officership. And I introduced new posts of constituency organiser and public relations officer.

The ard-fheis also approved a provision that within two months of any general election that did not result in the party taking office the parliamentary party would hold a vote by secret ballot on the leadership. This was designed to reduce tension in the party after an electoral defeat by ensuring that TDs and senators could vote secretly against the leader without having to challenge him or her overtly.

Meanwhile Peter Prendergast and I had found suitable premises for our head office. As chance would have it, the building was just opposite Fianna Fáil's headquarters in Upper Mount Street. Having checked that our house was fractionally higher (and that we would therefore be able to look down on Fianna Fáil!) I went ahead with the purchase for a sum of £250,000, about twice what the recent general election had cost the party at national level. To finance this ambitious move we launched a 'Buy a brick' campaign throughout the party organisation, which raised the greater part, although not all, of the purchase price.

The ard-fheis in May was a huge success. Fianna Fáil had recently moved its ard-fheis from the traditional venue of both parties—the Round Room of the Mansion House in Dublin—to the Great Hall of the Royal Dublin Society, which easily accommodated four thousand people. We had never had more than about half this number at our ard-fheiseanna, so that to follow Fianna Fáil successfully to this venue would be an immense challenge. The time to take it on was now, when the excitement of radical changes, the debate on the new party constitution and proposed policy debates on a wide range of topics, some controversial, would be likely to attract large numbers.

We took the gamble. It paid off. The hall was packed for my first presidential address: there were, I thought, about five thousand people there. Moreover, and more significant perhaps, the attendance at other times was substantial, and the experiment of arranging simultaneous debates in different halls succeeded on this occasion, although it did not prove possible to maintain this conference structure in the years that followed.

My concentration on party organisation and domestic policy matters during this period did not preclude a continued close involvement with Northern Ireland. At the end of October 1977 I had paid a first visit to Belfast as leader of the opposition, meeting members of all parties other than the DUP. I was sufficiently encouraged by these contacts to write to Jim Callaghan, Roy Mason and Margaret Thatcher about what seemed to me to be a tentative consensus *in principle* on the idea of a devolution of executive and legislative authority, subject to withholding the transfer of executive power and the final word on legislation until a widely representative executive emerged; but from the replies I received I had not got the impression that this information about potential common ground was received with much enthusiasm by Roy Mason.

On a subsequent visit to Northern Ireland, in June 1978, I discussed other approaches to power-sharing with political contacts, and also met the current leaders of the Presbyterian Church. The Presbyterians told me that the mal-treatment of prisoners under interrogation, which they said had ceased in the autumn of 1977 as a result of representations by the churches, had recently begun again. A group of loyalist paramilitaries had recently been beaten up in Castlereagh as part of an interrogation procedure. They asked me to do what I could to have this stopped.

Shortly afterwards I went to London with Paddy Harte to meet Margaret Thatcher as well as Roy Mason. I explained to Margaret Thatcher our concern about this report from the Presbyterian leaders, adding that British army tactics vis-à-vis the nationalist community were also proving counterproductive in the context of our joint concern to isolate and defeat the IRA. The opposition leader's reaction was quite negative. She embarked on a prolonged lecture about law and order, in the course of which she seemed to imply that it was 'bad form' for me to have raised the brutality issue in view of the 1976–77 'Heavy Gang' allegations about the Gardaí. When I met Jack Lynch some time later to discuss Northern Ireland affairs I described her attitude on this occasion as 'unyielding and unsympathetic'.

Our subsequent lunch with Roy Mason was less abrasive, and ranged much more widely, but I did not feel that we made much impact on the Castlereagh issue. Had there been a more receptive approach to our representations at that time Britain might have been spared the subsequent embarrassment of the Bennett Inquiry and Report.

I also raised with Jack Lynch at this time the importance of our diplomatic representation in the United States. As a counsellor in our Washington embassy, Michael Lillis had established a relationship with the political leaders on Capitol Hill that had no parallel amongst other EC missions. This was of major importance in relation to Northern Ireland, but it would also be extremely valuable during our next EC Presidency in the second half of the following year. At the time of the change of Government a year earlier I had suggested to the new Taoiseach that the retention of Seán Donlon for a year or so as Assistant Secretary in the Anglo-Irish Division of Foreign Affairs could be very valuable to him, but I now felt that Seán was by far the best-equipped person to exploit to the full, as Ambassador to Washington, the spectacular opening that Michael Lillis had achieved. Jack Lynch said that he was inclined to agree: Seán was needed either in Washington or in London, and in the event he appointed him to Washington shortly afterwards. The combination of Seán Donlon and Michael Lillis in that posting was to prove extraordinarily beneficial, as will be seen.

Throughout these years from 1977 to 1979 I kept in close touch with Jack Lynch as Taoiseach on Northern Ireland affairs. While there were, inevitably, some differences in emphasis between our approaches, we were much closer in our views than he was to the 'rhetorical republicans' in his own party, some of whom had forced on him in 1975 a shift towards the 'British withdrawal' theme, from which he was clearly most anxious to pull back. I knew that so long as he was in charge any information I passed on as a result of my contacts in Northern Ireland or with British politicians would be used for constructive purposes, and accordingly I kept the Department of Foreign Affairs, and, where appropriate, Jack himself, fully informed of anything I learnt on these matters.

In mid-February 1978 I had secured the support of my front bench for a public commitment to publish a Fine Gael 'White Paper' on Northern Ireland and for the appointment of a steering committee to assist me with this task. The front bench members involved were Peter Barry, Paddy Harte, Richie Ryan, and Jim O'Keeffe, because of their front bench positions, as well as John Kelly and Alexis FitzGerald, because of their special knowledge of the problem; Mark Clinton was also asked, and agreed, to join. Work on this policy document went on throughout the following twelve months.

The 'White Paper' based itself firmly on the principle of 'no reunification without consent', which had been fundamental to the policy the party had adopted in 1969. It set out the benefits Northern Ireland might secure through a political association with our state. These might include:
— The sharing of facilities now provided separately in sectors such as industry, tourism, and export promotion abroad.
— The possible creation of an all-Ireland anti-terrorism force, the operations of which would not be constrained by the border.
— The involvement of Northern Ireland in the economic dynamism that had been a feature of the Republic since 1959 (during this period manufacturing output had grown two-and-half times as fast in the Republic as in the North).
— More effective representation of Northern Ireland's interests abroad, and in particular in the European Community, where the often divergent interests of Great Britain tended necessarily to take precedence in the formulation and operation of UK policy.

The 'White Paper' went on to argue that independence was not a realistic option for Northern Ireland, and it presented an analysis of various political models, leading to the conclusion that amongst possible alternatives the best from Northern Ireland's point of view would be a confederal arrangement. Each part of the island would retain control of its own affairs, save for security, foreign policy (including representation in the EC), and monetary policy, as well as aspects of fiscal policy inextricably related to monetary policy. As the Republic would not be in a position to continue the subsidies currently received from the UK government, provision would be needed within such a confederal structure for a continuance of these subsidies for a number of years, and US and EC aid for Northern Ireland would also be desirable, and might, it was suggested, be available.

The document emphasised the need for Northern Ireland and the Republic to be on a basis of complete equality within this structure, despite the two-to-one population ratio in favour of the Republic. It also stressed the need to ensure that in this new situation the long-standing relationship that existed between Northern Ireland and Great Britain be respected. An element in this could be the retention of two heads of state of the confederation, to both of whom and by both of whom ambassadors could be accredited.

The steering committee and the parliamentary party approved the 'White Paper', with only one amendment, which I had rather expected: a specific reference to the monarchy in the context of the suggestion for the possible retention of two heads of state was omitted. This did not matter, as the very concept of two heads of state opened up this possibility.

The document was very favourably received. Fianna Fáil described it in a statement issued on Jack Lynch's instructions as 'well researched and worthy of careful attention'. Even amongst Unionists the reaction was not totally negative. Harry West said that 'although it was of no interest, the OUP would be willing to have talks on the document,' and on television Martin Smyth took a similar line. Ernest Baird of the VUPP, a Unionist splinter-group, said that 'it would be less than fair to dismiss it out of hand.' The *Irish Times* described it as 'a message of love, hope and fellowship.'

A week later I returned to Belfast and spoke about our proposals to a meeting of the East Belfast Branch of the SDLP and also in a neutral forum, the non-political Irish Association, where David Trimble gave a Unionist reaction.

In the course of the British general election of that year an American Congressional delegation, led by the Speaker, Tip O'Neill, visited Britain and Ireland. The Speaker in particular was unimpressed with British politicians' approach to Northern Ireland. When the delegation arrived in the Republic a dinner was given for them by Jack Lynch in Dublin Castle. Tip O'Neill made an impressive and indeed moving speech, which showed sympathy and understanding for the unionist as well as nationalist community in Northern Ireland. His irritation with his recent British interlocutors showed through, however, in a reference he made to the North becoming a political football in Britain.

This isolated remark provoked a political and media storm in Britain; politicians and newspapers attacked Speaker O'Neill and other Congressional leaders of Irish extraction in terms that seemed to suggest that they were IRA sympathisers. In view of the solid support these leaders had given to us in the propaganda war we had been waging against the IRA in the United States, this was unjust to the point of absurdity. I was so incensed that I could not sleep that night, and eventually got up and hammered out a furious letter to the *Daily Telegraph*, of which the Speaker was subsequently very appreciative. His attitude to Margaret Thatcher, however, was soured by this episode.

In June, after the British election that brought the Tories to power under Margaret Thatcher, I was able to present our Northern Ireland policy document to an audience at the Royal Institute of International Affairs in London, taking the opportunity to meet the Labour Party leaders, now in opposition, starting with David Owen, then shadow Minister for Energy. He told me that when he and Jim Callaghan had met Ted Kennedy some time previously with Peter Jay, Callaghan's son-in-law and Britain's Ambassador to Washington, Callaghan had frankly admitted that his government had no policy on Northern Ireland. Jay, who had spent two years trying to assure Ted Kennedy and other members of Congress that the British government had such a policy, had been shaken by this admission, he said.

In my subsequent discussion with Jim Callaghan it quickly became evident that he too was very concerned about the attitude of Congressional leaders. I explained to him diplomatically that the Americans had been unfavourably impressed by their discussions in London, suggesting that Callaghan might not have appreciated how strongly they felt about the Northern Ireland tragedy and how upset they had been to find that Peter Jay's account of British policy-making on Northern Ireland, which they had believed, had been lacking in foundation. Callaghan responded irritably that if the Speaker was as naïve as that he should not have the job he held. For the future he recognised that the Labour Party would have to adopt a somewhat more positive position, but he added emphatically, twice, that they could not be led by the nose by the SDLP: Labour policy would not be settled by Gerry Fitt or Kevin Macnamara—whom he seemed to regard as an Irish politician who had nothing to do with the British Labour Party.

A few weeks later Jack Lynch arranged for me to have a brief discussion with the British Foreign Secretary, Peter Carrington, when he visited Dublin. After speaking favourably of Fine Gael's Northern Ireland policy document, he added that if the Northern Ireland question were not resolved within a year or two it would have a very serious effect on Anglo-American relations as well as on British relations with the Irish Government.

Ten days after meeting Carrington I met the new Secretary of State for Northern Ireland, Humphrey Atkins, in London, with the new Permanent Secretary of the Northern Ireland Office, Ken Stowe, who had just been transferred from the Cabinet Office. Atkins was concerned to demonstrate his commitment to the replacement of direct rule with a power-sharing devolved government in the North. Given this commitment and the fact that it was our first encounter, I did not go into the issues in detail with him. I was amused, however, to be asked by Stowe on one point, 'How do you think we could get around the Prime Minister on that matter, Dr FitzGerald?' Already, within weeks of the formation of the Thatcher government, I was hearing the theme that was to be repeated so often thereafter by British Ministers and civil servants.

Later that day at the British-Irish Association conference I had a much fuller discussion with the Minister of State, Hugh Rossi, and I raised with him the failure of his government following the Bennett Inquiry to remove those implicated in acts of brutality at Castlereagh. I pointed out that if Roy Mason and Margaret Thatcher had listened to me a year earlier the need for the Bennett Inquiry could have been avoided. Rossi promised to take this matter up, but no such action seems to have been taken.

In August came the appalling murder in Sligo of Lord Mountbatten and the son of a friend of his from Northern Ireland. Two of those involved were subsequently charged and convicted of the offence on forensic evidence. In September, with Jack Lynch and Frank Cluskey, I attended the memorial service in Westminster Abbey.

Three months later Humphrey Atkins published his White Paper on Northern Ireland policy. It was ill-judged, in that it went too far towards the Unionist position by specifically excluding from the terms of reference for a proposed conference of the Northern Ireland parties any discussion of an 'Irish dimension'—something to which the SDLP, in political isolation since the end of the Convention almost four years previously, and under political pressure within its own community, had recommitted itself. As a result Gerry Fitt, who had apparently told the British that he could 'deliver' his party to such a restricted conference, resigned the leadership.

John Hume was the obvious successor. In the interval before his election I discussed with him the problem posed by the White Paper, seeking a way out of the impasse. On 25 November I asked the British Ambassador to let Peter Carrington—with whom I felt more comfortable than with Humphrey Atkins—know that if after John was elected leader he were invited by Margaret Thatcher to meet her, and if she should propose to him that the 'Irish dimension' could be added to the agenda for discussion *after* devolution, John would take the risk of Ian Paisley walking out after the discussion on devolution had ended. Unhappily nothing came of this initiative, to which only John Hume and I were privy. The conference met without the SDLP, and was a failure.

On a later visit to Northern Ireland in early 1981 Joan and I stayed with Lord Brookeborough in Fermanagh, and with him I visited a number of the Protestant farmers who had lost relatives or friends in the course of the IRA's murderous campaign in this border area. On the same occasion I spoke at Portora Royal School to pupils from the secondary schools in Enniskillen. Before the meeting the late Dowager Duchess of Westminster, who had lived there for decades, confided to me that 'these people' (the unionists attending the reception) 'are not British at all; I thought they were when I came here first, but they aren't; *they're all Irish.*'

While I was working on Northern Ireland policy in 1978 and 1979 we also published a number of policy statements on issues on which members of the front bench had ideas that they wanted to advance—on local government, local radio, and urban affairs; but before attempting a more general policy review I wanted us to address amongst ourselves in a non-political way the problems of the Irish state. In mid-1979 I presented to some of my colleagues the results of my reflections in a very detailed document of some 25,000 words. This was in no way a draft manifesto; on the contrary, it concentrated on raising difficult problems without regard to the 'politics' involved. Not because it contains anything very original but because it set out the approach that I sought to adopt during the remainder of my political career, I summarise it here.

Rejecting the 'materialistic nihilism' of capitalism and the 'suffocating uniformity' of extreme socialism, I suggested that the only concept that might hold the key to a coherent and satisfying approach to the needs of Irish society was that of human development. At the same time I recognised that this would leave room for disagreement on particular issues, because one person's rights frequently became another's obligations or duties. But the advancement of human development should be attempted in a way that would safeguard the more basic human rights and also 'high culture', the preservation and encouragement of which required a skewed distribution of resources in its favour.

The main points to be built in to such an approach were presented as:
— Increasing the volume of material resources in order to fulfil needs for human development.
— Distributing these resources to the best effect.
— Seeking this objective by a judicious admixture of widening educational opportunities and creating conditions that would minimise stresses on the human personality, whether deriving from inadequate material resources, pressures from public authorities, or private commercial interests, or from a materialist atmosphere arousing expectations that in a world of limited resources were bound to be incompletely fulfilled.

The paper went on to consider how resources could be released to deal with the consequences of the developing labour surplus, for example by reductions in certain types of public spending and by tackling 'circular transfers'. (These include the payment of children's allowances to well-off people; subsidies for higher education that reduce fees primarily for the benefit of those able to pay the rest of the cost, using up resources that could have been used to provide generous grants to students from less well-off homes; and the subsidising of services to better-off as well as less fortunate people in rural areas—all of which pushed up the level of tax to be paid by the same people, to their great resentment.)

I drew particular attention to the problem of employment in the decades ahead, pointing out that against the background of the recent rise in the birth rate—it peaked at around 74,000 early in the following year—it was highly unlikely that any conceivable combination of investment, entrepreneurship, foreign investment and expansion of external markets could make possible an expansion of employment in the 1980s and 1990s on the scale that would then be necessary, as this would require, I then believed, a sustained annual growth rate of 6 to 8 per cent. Given that public service employment was very high already and that the burden it imposed on the economy needed to be reduced, the public sector could clearly not provide the answer to this problem.

This thesis was put forward for consideration by our party at the very time when the incumbent Government was pursuing a precisely opposite course: increasing the volume of public spending by over 50 per cent and, in 1980 alone, increasing the numbers in the public sector by 6 per cent and average pay rates in that sector by almost 30 per cent.

A specific proposal put forward in this paper to alleviate the impact of un-employment on young people was a provision to ensure that they got an opportunity of employment for a period or periods at least—something to which I gave effect during my second term as Taoiseach. At the same time I argued the need to apply revenues that might be released by the abolition of some circular transfers to the expansion of the educational sector, rejecting force-fully the contention that we were overqualifying many of our young people in relation to available employment opportunities. The need for special measures to reduce the drop-out rate from second-level education, including student grants for some, was also argued, as well as the need to meet as far as possible the desire of some parents for interdenominational or non-denominational education.

Among the housing reforms envisaged were the substitution of a system of fair rent tribunals for rent control, and the introduction of a new type of house mort-gage involving repayments based on a share of income—a system that we intro-duced through a new Housing Finance Agency when we were in Government.

After a section on the environment (directed towards protection of our architectural heritage and the need to tackle the burden of compensation payments to frustrated developers, rather than wider issues of pollution) the paper went on to address the problem of the excessively narrow concept of 'Irishness' then prevalent and the need for 'a pluralism that would give a status and validity in the national context to the Anglo-Irish and the Ulster Scots equal to that which we give to those with Gaelic Catholic origins.'

On church-state relations reference was made to the 'powerful campaign of pressure mounted by lay and clerical sources, including organisations like the Knights of St Columbanus, in opposition to the reform of the law on contra-ception,' which contrasted so strikingly with the Catholic hierarchy's June 1976 formal rejection of any church role in pressing politicians to implement Catholic teaching in legislation. I referred to the fact that this campaign had been 'powerful enough in its impact on Fianna Fáil at any rate to ensure the enshrining (in a law on contraception, enacted by Charles Haughey as Minister for Health) of Catholic theology in the form of a reference to "natural family planning"—something which five years earlier many people would have regarded as unlikely to occur again.' In this church-state context I also referred to 'another disturbing development . . . the public references by Cardinal Ó Fiaich to British withdrawal and to 'our boys' in Long Kesh, which no political party or leader has felt strong enough to challenge.' I added that in the light of these events 'the problem of Church-State relations in the Republic remains a serious one,' which was 'also a serious obstacle to progress in resolving the Northern Ireland problem.'

Finally I turned to the need for political reform, pointing out that a rural Minister was normally in Dublin for only four days, that is, from Monday lunchtime to Friday lunchtime. With Tuesday and Friday morning Government meetings, and Dáil attendance required from Tuesday lunchtime to Wednesday night, and often also on Thursday, 'conditions are inimical to serious work because of interruptions by divisions, visits, delegations, opening functions, travel abroad and Parliamentary Party meetings, apart from the lack of ready access to papers and personnel' in Leinster House. All this made necessary as a minimum the introduction of a 'cabinet' system for each Minister, on the Continental model—drawing on a temporary basis upon academic life, research institutes, industry, agriculture, trade unions, and the like, for a range of expertise appropriate to each case.

I also made suggestions for a greater use of Government committees and for reform in the Oireachtas and the civil service, including the appointment of an ombudsman.

Such then were some of the issues preoccupying me half way through my initial period as leader of the opposition. On the basis of this analysis, preparation of our manifesto proceeded for the next general election—although inevitably the document finally presented to the electorate highlighted only the more 'saleable' elements of my proposals for reform.

We now faced our first electoral test: the European and local elections of mid-1979. How well placed were we for these contests? In the aftermath of the 1977 election and up to February 1979 the opinion polls had reflected the bandwagon effect of Jack Lynch's enormous popularity, with Fianna Fáil faring better than it had done in the election itself. A subsequent fall-off still left it well ahead, but I was satisfied that the large number of 'don't knows' among the people questioned meant that the gap between the parties was much narrower than it seemed. The two elections more than confirmed this interpretation. In the European election our vote was only 1.5 per cent lower than that of Fianna Fáil, and in the local elections it was less than 4 per cent lower—as against the 20 percentage points that had divided our two parties in June 1977.

These elections were in fact a disaster for Fianna Fáil—and for Jack Lynch. In the European election, in a campaign that was fought mainly on domestic rather than European issues, that party won only 5 of the 15 seats. Fine Gael won 4 seats, as, by a fluke of the PR system, did the Labour Party with less than half our vote.

In the local elections Fine Gael made very significant gains indeed: an increase of 10 per cent, securing 310 seats in the county and city elections as against Fianna Fáil's 347.

These results owed a good deal to the unpopularity of Fianna Fáil at this time because of a prolonged national postal strike and a refuse disposal strike in Dublin. But our local election gains, a particularly welcome feature of which was a 60 per cent increase in the number of Fine Gael women councillors, also reflected the remarkable organisational work Peter Prendergast had put in during the previous twenty-one months in every part of the country, and in particular his skill in identifying and securing the adoption of suitable candidates. Ten of these new local authority candidates were elected to the Dáil two years later, as were two candidates who had been unsuccessful in the European election: Nuala Fennell and Alan Dukes.

Five months later Fianna Fáil was unlucky enough to have to face two by-elections in Cork. Its vote plummeted from 59 per cent in Cork City—Jack Lynch's own constituency—and 48 per cent in Cork North-East to 36 per cent in each case. The two seats fell to Fine Gael. By the time the votes were counted the Taoiseach had arrived in the United States on an official visit (in connection with which I sent him a message of solidarity) and was at a clear disadvantage in dealing with this debacle from such a distance.

Within Fianna Fáil Charles Haughey had been working his way back following his dismissal from the Government and subsequent trial in 1970. Restored to the front bench in 1975, he became Minister for Health and Social Welfare in 1977. He was now poised to challenge for the leadership when Jack Lynch retired, as he was thinking of doing early in 1980.

The other candidate for the succession was George Colley. A schoolfellow of Haughey's, Colley had already contested the party leadership with him in 1966, when the latter had withdrawn, leaving Colley to fight a losing battle against Lynch. Now the struggle between the two schoolfellows was to recommence.

The story that reached us in Fine Gael at this point was that Colley had persuaded Lynch—who strongly favoured him as successor—to resign two months earlier than he had intended, because Colley believed that at that moment the advantage lay with him. We were told he had been led to this view because three TDs believed to be Haughey supporters had let it be understood—mendaciously as it turned out—that they had now switched to Colley.

Jack Lynch's resignation, announced at the party meeting on Wednesday 5 December, sparked off a bitter struggle between the two candidates. The election of the new leader was fixed for two days later, Friday 7 December. On the Thursday afternoon several Fine Gael TDs reported to me that a number of their Fianna Fáil colleagues had told them that they were being intimidated by Haughey supporters, who had warned them that the ballot would not in practice be secret. Could we do anything to ensure a genuine secret ballot, they had asked? In response to these somewhat surprising requests I arranged for a message on the point to be passed to a person involved in arranging the election.

By chance that evening I met the person in question, who told me that the matter was in hand: booths of some kind had been arranged at each end of the party room, where deputies could vote in complete privacy.

The result of the vote was a majority of six for Charles Haughey. Around Christmas I met a member of the Fianna Fáil parliamentary party who told me—and confirmed the statement to me ten years later—that despite the polling booth arrangement some deputies had not felt that the privacy of the ballot had been ensured, because the voting papers when marked at either end of the room had to be deposited in a box near the centre of the room. Some deputies claimed they had been told that unless as they walked back to deposit their votes in the box they showed them to members of the Haughey camp they would be assumed to have voted for Colley and would subsequently be treated accordingly.

After the election there were rumours of a split in Fianna Fáil. The tension was eventually relieved by a report that George Colley had given a kind of conditional loyalty to the new leader, on the basis that he would have the final say in the appointment of the two security Ministers, Defence and Justice. That such an arrangement was felt to be necessary by the Colley half of the party was not very reassuring for the rest of the country.

Possibly because of the rumours of a split that might prevent Charles Haughey's election by the Dáil on Tuesday 11 December, but also, I think, to allow time to consult my front bench, I did not start to prepare my speech for this debate until late on the Monday night. I found it a very difficult task. Charles Haughey and I had known each other since the autumn of 1943, when we had met while studying several first arts and commerce subjects together in UCD; and although there were deep differences of personality and outlook, our personal relationship had always been friendly, although not close. In 1961 he had tried to involve me in Fianna Fáil. In the summer of 1968 we had met on the steps of Government Buildings, and he had confided to me his health worries at that time: a virus infection that he had suffered from in 1967 that had now returned, leaving him without enough energy even to go on a holiday. This encounter antedated by some months the car accident to which some have attributed the start of his health problems. In autumn 1970, after the Arms Crisis, we had met one day on Leinster Lawn, and I was struck by the warmth with which he responded to my greeting; I got the impression that because of recent events he had expected me to pass by without acknowledging him. Later, at the time of the Public Accounts Committee inquiry into that affair, I was accused by some people of 'going easy' in my examination of him as a witness because of our long relationship. In fact this was unfair; I was testing the ground for a much tougher grilling on a subsequent occasion, which never took place, because his brother, Jock, whom we had asked to give evidence, successfully challenged in the Supreme Court our power to compel the attendance of witnesses, and the committee's inquiry was unexpectedly cut short as a result.

The long relationship between us could not, however, be allowed to inhibit me from stating in the Dáil before his election as Taoiseach the reasons why at that moment I and so many others in all parties regarded him as unsuitable to be head of the Government. This, we felt, had to be put firmly on the record. Thereafter if, as seemed certain, he were chosen as Taoiseach he would have to be accorded the respect due to his office. The task was not made any easier by the knowledge that what I had to say would, because of its necessarily personal character, be badly received even by many who would be much more scathing privately than I intended to be about the Taoiseach-designate.

I opened my remarks in the Dáil next day by explaining that because of the inhibitions that would necessarily limit what members of the Government party opposed to Charles Haughey could say publicly, I knew that I would have to speak for them as well as for the opposition. (A number of Fianna Fáil members later thanked me privately for having done so.) Then, having explained the background of my long relationship with Charles Haughey and having acknowledged his talents—the political skills and competence he had shown in the departments in which he had served as Minister, which were important qualities in a Taoiseach—I said that these were not enough. All his six predecessors—three of his party and three of mine—had been united by a common bond: they had come into public life to serve their country, and even their severest enemies had never accused any of them of taking up politics for any motive other than the highest. All had thus commanded the trust of those close to them. Charles Haughey came to the job, I went on to say, with a flawed pedigree, because he differed from all his predecessors in that his motives had been and were widely impugned, most notably, although not exclusively, by people close to him within his own party. Having observed his actions for many years these people had made their human interim judgement on him, and they attributed to him an overwhelming ambition not simply to serve the state but to dominate it, and even to own it.

The phrase 'flawed pedigree', an oratorical embellishment that must have owed something to the hour of the night at which I had drafted my remarks, achieved lasting fame, being described almost invariably since then as 'that infamous comment'. Although the contrast between him and his predecessors that I had been making was justifiable, as a politician I should of course have recognised the danger of using a colourful phrase that could easily be distorted by being taken totally out of the specific context of a comparison between Charles Haughey's and his predecessors' repute amongst their peers.

The second point I made was that he clearly did not command the genuine confidence of even one-third of the Dáil, although formally he would secure a majority of votes. Many of those who would vote for him, including a clear majority of those who had served with him in Government, were withholding their consent in the interior forum, consoling themselves with the hope that they might not have long to serve under a man they did not respect. I named many of the Ministers who were known to have voted against him and to be bitterly opposed to his leadership, expressing the hope that no-one would feel slighted at the omission of his or her honourable name from my list. Of those who had supported him not all were people ambitious for office, I said; some were inspired rather by a narrow and dangerous nationalism: a patriotism that excluded from the nation as they conceived it one million Irish men and women. They did not believe in seeking unity by consent but craved unity by constraint.

I went on to say that Charles Haughey as Taoiseach would be an uncovenanted bonus for Fine Gael: a precipitating factor that would bring to our support many good and patriotic people who had previously voted Fianna Fáil.

Given the Taoiseach-designate's political skill and energy, why, I asked rhetorically, would the Dáil be taking a chance by electing him to this office? First, I said, because a question mark remained over a man who, having been found not guilty of importing arms for the IRA, had chosen to seek the plaudits of the crowd outside the court for a fellow-accused who represented that organisation, and because for nine long years thereafter, until his election as leader, he had refused to utter one word of condemnation of the IRA, on the extraordinary grounds that he was not responsible for Northern Ireland policy in the Government.

Secondly, this long-practised deliberate ambiguity would make him, as Taoiseach, an obstacle to the achievement of Irish unity by agreement. Moreover, as Minister for Health he had brought in a Bill on contraception the language of which was denominational and therefore damaging to the cause of Irish unity. Finally, he had failed to articulate any idealism that might inspire the younger generation.

In conclusion I made it clear that in speaking as I had done I had deliberately chosen to reject advice tendered to me to refrain from such a course and was prepared to take any criticism that might come as a result.

The criticism came, hot and heavy. Although most other opposition speeches in the debate took a similar line—Noel Browne was particularly trenchant—condemnation was directed primarily at me as the lead speaker. I could see that I had unnerved some of my party colleagues. It will be for historians to judge whether placing my view bluntly on the record at that point was counterproductive or whether it may have contributed to my opponent's failure to secure an overall majority at any of the five subsequent general elections.

The Government that was announced after this debate lacked four of Jack Lynch's Ministers, including unsurprisingly Jim Gibbons, whose evidence on oath at the Arms Trial with that of three others was seen by the judge as directly contradicting the testimony of the new Taoiseach. I mention this here because this conflict of testimony remained at the root of the bitterness that divided Charles Haughey's first Government and later precipitated three known attempts to remove him as leader, as well as an earlier attempt in November 1980 that has not hitherto been recorded.

In that month we put down a motion taking note of an article in *Magill* on the Arms Trial, seeking clarification of matters raised by it. Shortly afterwards I was approached on behalf of George Colley by a mutual friend with the suggestion that we amend our motion so as to include a more direct reference to the clash of sworn testimony at the Arms Trial, in such a form that the motion would have to be rejected by the Taoiseach. If we did this George Colley and a number of others would abstain, and the motion would be carried. Those concerned felt that such an amendment would provide the last possible opportunity to show their feelings; if it were not provided many of them might leave politics altogether. Because the issue was not one of collective responsibility but involved a personal matter, they took the view that they could abstain on it without breach of the whip, or that a whip could not properly be applied.

While the prospect of winning such a vote naturally interested me, I saw many difficulties, which I put to the intermediary. On 19 November I met George Colley at a party and he confirmed the proposal, saying that about twenty members would abstain.

On 21 November I put the issues involved to my friend Alexis FitzGerald. The first and most obvious was the question of what guarantee we could have that if we put down the proposed amendment to our motion (which because of its nature would be criticised as highly personal) there would in fact be a significant number of abstentions. Would there be enough—at least twenty would be needed—to secure passage of the motion? Given the reference that had been made to the inapplicability of the whip, those concerned would seem to envisage the possible survival of the Government, which did not seem realistic; but if the Government fell would there then be an alternative Government that could be formed from the existing Dáil, or, if an election were called, how would the Fianna Fáil dissidents be likely to act in such a contest?

There followed further contacts through Alexis FitzGerald, but when I put the matter to the test by inviting George Colley to draft the amendment himself—which seemed to me the best way of ensuring that the abstentions would in fact occur—he backed away from the proposal. I felt that my caution had been justified, and I turned my attention back to the immediate preparations for the general election that, although not statutorily due until mid-1982, seemed certain to be called at some point during the twelve months ahead.

By now, towards the end of 1980, I was well placed to take on this task, for difficulties that I had faced within my party had been overcome. In the parliamentary party (as distinct from the party organisation throughout the country) concern about the impact that the strengthening of our panels of candidates would have on the electoral prospects of existing TDs had been accompanied by unhappiness at the substantial shift in the party's policies that I had effected. A minority was actively opposed to the new liberal and social-democratic thrust; others who had no strong personal views feared that the new policy emphasis would lose the party more support than it would generate. (Politicians know whence their existing support comes, but find it hard to envisage additional votes being secured from new sources; not losing votes thus tends to loom much larger than gaining them.)

These concerns, aggravated by worries about media reactions to my Haughey speech, had created strains between the parliamentary party and myself that by mid-1980 seemed to me to have become quite acute. At a special party meeting I told my colleagues bluntly that I was not happy with the situation. I felt that I was seen by some at least as being a useful vote-getter, but only so long as I refrained from voicing what I believed Fine Gael stood for. I could not, I said, be an effective leader of a party if I had to be looking over my shoulder, not knowing where I stood. If I knew the party was fully behind me in what I was doing I would get on with the job with renewed vigour; if not, now was the time to face the problem and draw the obvious conclusion.

This had the desired effect. While I knew that some remained unenthusiastic, or secretly hostile, the overt grumbling was stilled. My relationship with Fine Gael TDs at this time was incidentally helped by the fact that the independent Constituency Commission established by Jack Lynch had proposed that the size of the Dáil be increased from 148 to 166 seats, as a result of the dramatic population rise that had been revealed when the postponed census had eventually been held in April 1979. These recommendations were adopted, and this meant, as I pointed out to the Fine Gael parliamentary party, that if we did no more at the next election than recover the votes we had lost in 1977 our Dáil membership would go up by 14; unless a TD positively neglected his or her constituency, none accordingly need fear losing a seat either to a Fine Gael colleague or to Fianna Fáil.

During this period my involvement with the European Community had continued through the Christian Democrat movement, in which Fine Gael was on the left wing with the Benelux parties and with some of the French and Italians. The German Christian Democrats, by contrast, tended to see themselves as conservative and had to be headed off from forming an alliance with, among others, the British Tories.

The proposal in 1978 to establish a European Monetary System with an exchange rate mechanism together with the British decision to keep sterling outside the ERM posed a dilemma for the Irish Government, in the resolution of which I was able to play some part. Ireland was by this time less dependent on the United Kingdom than before we joined the Community, but in 1978 47 per cent of our exports were still sold in the British market. An Irish currency linked in the ERM to the Deutschmark, when almost half our exports were still being bought by the UK in sterling and barely 30 per cent were sold to ERM countries, would be very delicately balanced.

At the negotiations in Brussels the Irish representatives sought, reasonably enough, to secure some financial support from the Community to assist the transition from one currency link to another. They seem to have misjudged their negotiating strength. As a result, at a crucial European Council meeting a decision to establish the ERM was taken with Ireland sidelined, its representatives having refused the 'best offer' made. Jack Lynch returned home at the weekend in a state of evident confusion, with Martin O'Donoghue, the

Economics Minister, and himself offering conflicting accounts of what this offer had been.

This was humiliating and potentially disastrous for Ireland. After careful reflection, but consulting no-one, I decided to see if I could help to find a solution. It was Saturday, but I rang the French Ambassador and arranged to see him. I told him that I wanted to get a message through to Giscard d'Estaing to ask him to arrange in conjunction with Helmut Schmidt some face-saving additional offer to help our Government off the hook on which it had impaled itself. Knowing that the Secretary-General of the Quai d'Orsay, Jean-Marie Soutou, had ready access to the President, I asked the Ambassador to track him down for me. He found he was spending the weekend in a cottage somewhere in France, and on the phone I put my suggestion to him. He said he would pass my message on to the President, and that he thought that in view of my position as opposition leader it would carry particular weight. During the following week an offer of additional bilateral aid came from France and Germany, which enabled the Government to announce that we would join the ERM after all. Much later I told Jack Lynch what I had done and asked him if he thought it had influenced the outcome; he said he believed it had.

My range of international contacts continued to broaden. In 1980 Joan and I made a journey to the Middle East with an Italian journalist and a former Japanese ambassador, to prepare a report on the problems of the region for the Trilateral Commission, of which I was a member, which comprises politicians, academics, journalists, businessmen and trade unionists from Europe, North America, and Japan. I also wrote a book on development co-operation for UNCTAD and gave lectures in the United States, in various European cities, and in Hong Kong, where the reporter who interviewed me for the *South China Morning Post* was suitably disconcerted when I asked her to tell her editor I was still waiting for the £78 they owed me since they had terminated my weekly column on Irish affairs without notice twenty years earlier.

But the task that absorbed even more of my spare time in these early years of party leadership, keeping me sane by distracting my mind in leisure moments from the cares of politics, was analysing the geographical pattern of the decline in the use of Irish between 1770 and 1870. I found the data I wanted in the nineteenth-century censuses of population, and each weekend as I was driven around the country on my constituency visits I propped up the old census volumes on the dashboard of the passenger seat and embarked on the hundreds of thousands of calculations required to produce a comprehensive picture of what had happened to the language during this period. I completed my first draft in the autumn of 1979, but it was some years before I was able, while Taoiseach, to publish the results of my work, as a Royal Irish Academy paper, illustrated by detailed maps prepared by my brother Fergus.

At the end of September 1979 the Pope visited Ireland. Joan and I returned from a French holiday just before the visit began. At London airport we encountered Lord Longford, whom I had first met around 1933 when, as

Frank Pakenham, he had come to see my father in the course of writing a book on the Anglo-Irish Treaty of 1921. He enquired anxiously whether there would be room at the site at Knock in Co. Mayo, where the Pope was to say Mass, for him to use a folding chair he was carrying. Not wishing to disturb his faith in my omniscience, I assured him all would be well. I never heard whether he got to sit down.

After the impressive Mass in the Phoenix Park we were able to get home for a rest before going to the Nunciature to meet the Pope. While waiting with Joan and the Labour Party leader, Frank Cluskey, it struck me somewhat belatedly that the occasion of this visit should be used to raise with the Pope the need to modify the operation in Ireland of the Catholic Church's mixed marriage code. I crossed the corridor to the room in which the members of the Government were awaiting the Pope's arrival and spoke to Jack Lynch about this matter—unaware that our discussion was being televised, thus arousing some public curiosity, as I afterwards learnt. He told me he had had exactly the same idea, and that President Hillery was also going to raise the matter if he had a chance. In the event, however, the Pope was so far behind schedule that all these encounters were too rushed to enable any of us to raise this issue.

I visited the United States several times during these years, lecturing and maintaining my political contacts. One in particular of these American visits I recall vividly. It was in January 1980, just after Charles Haughey had become Taoiseach. Seán Donlon, Ambassador to the United States, invited me to stay in the embassy residence, as I had done in various capitals since becoming leader of the opposition. Jack Lynch had always insisted that every courtesy be extended to me in that position; one Minister who had objected to the treatment accorded respectively to him and to me by embassy officials when our arrivals coincided at an airport received short shrift from his Taoiseach.

I thanked Seán but told him that it would be wiser for Joan and me to stay elsewhere on this occasion. He objected strenuously, ringing me back later to say that he had asked for and been given Ministerial authority for his invitation. I still refused, saying that when we met I would explain why. A day or two later he rang again, crestfallen, to say that the authority had been withdrawn, on a direction from higher up.

The visit itself, I believe, proved a particularly useful one from an Irish point of view. Amongst the engagements arranged for me was a meeting at the State Department with officials from various American agencies. Never while in office as Minister had I met so many people at this level: some forty people from well over a dozen different parts of the administration. Their questions were nearly all about the new Taoiseach, and his likely attitude to Northern Ireland and to Britain. I told them that I believed he would take a constructive line on Northern Ireland and would seek a better relationship with Britain. There was some surprise, perhaps a little incredulity, but also some acceptance that such an analysis coming from me was worthy of a certain amount of credit.

In what I said at that meeting I did not, of course, foresee in any detail the actual approach that Charles Haughey was to adopt in his negotiations with Britain some months later; nor, on the other hand, did I foresee the clumsiness with which he was to handle the remarkable relationship that had been built up with the US Congress and administration during the previous couple of years. By the nature of things I was involved only marginally in these events, but I followed them very closely at the time, and they were to have an effect on the tactics I was myself to pursue in Government shortly afterwards. Let me therefore recount them as they appeared from my perspective.

First it must be said that by the time Charles Haughey became Taoiseach the situation in Northern Ireland was sunk into stalemate and, following the murder of Lord Mountbatten, the tide of the Anglo-Irish relationship was at one of its periodic low ebbs. By contrast, Ireland's relationship with the United States was at its flood tide, closer than at any time before or since.

Improving the relationship with Britain posed a major challenge to a political leader who was popularly seen as anti-British and was still identified in the public mind with the events of the Arms Crisis in 1970. His instinct must have told him to face this challenge imaginatively. Coming from him, an attempt to put that relationship on a new plane would have the advantage of surprising and perhaps heartening the new Conservative government of Margaret Thatcher. It was, however, a 'high risk' policy, the more so because his own supporters, deluded by their own traditional rhetoric into a simplistic belief that Irish unity was attainable in the short term, would be unlikely to be satisfied with the kind of results that such an initiative might produce—results that might have been seen as major progress if achieved by a Fine Gael-Labour Government. In order to gain room for manoeuvre vis-à-vis these supporters he needed to be able to send them a 'hard-line' signal that would satisfy their emotions, while behind the scenes he got on with his diplomatic encounter with the Thatcher government.

There was, however, no room for a hard-line gesture to his backbenchers on any matter of substance related to Northern Ireland; that would destroy the possibility of a negotiation with Britain, which had to be his primary target. Perhaps, then, he could provide his followers with the short-term satisfaction they sought by throwing them a morsel in a quite different and, as he may have seen it, subordinate theatre: the United States. Fianna Fáil supporters had for long been assiduously courted by extremist 'republican' elements in America—elements that both the Fianna Fáil Government under Jack Lynch up to 1973 and from 1977 to 1979 and our National Coalition Government from 1973 to 1977 had sought to marginalise, because of the sympathy shown by them to the IRA.

Quite apart from the expectations of his supporters within Fianna Fáil, he may have been under pressure from Neil Blaney—so the media were suggesting. It was implied that with an election in his sights he was concerned at the growing support the polls showed to be accruing to me, and hoped to offset it by securing the votes of Neil Blaney's supporters. For in December 1979 Blaney had visited the United States and had made a speech very critical of the Lynch Government's policy towards the Irish-American lobby, a speech that the press reported as having been accompanied by a memorandum from Neil Blaney to the new Taoiseach on the subject.

If considerations of this kind influenced Charles Haughey at this early stage in his career as Taoiseach, it was a highly dangerous diversion. For, at the very time when the new Taoiseach's ambitious plans for a major Anglo-Irish negotiation would require all the support they could get from the United States, an approach designed to mollify the 'hard-line republicans' there (if that is what it was) risked destroying a powerful card that skilful diplomacy had brought into play for the first time since 1921: US support for the policy of the Irish Government in relation to Northern Ireland.

To explain how the United States had come once again to be an important factor in the Anglo-Irish equation I must go back a few years. During most of my period as Minister for Foreign Affairs our diplomatic efforts in the United States had been defensive and directed primarily towards limiting the damage that Irish-American elements could do to our interests by their support for the IRA. Since at least 1972, when Jack Lynch and Desmond O'Malley had confronted this issue, successive Irish Governments had been struggling in conjunction with the SDLP to win as much as we could of Irish-America back from its tendency to sympathise with the IRA as an atavistic expression of inherited anti-British feeling. Together with John Hume we had achieved a good deal in this field by 1976, successfully countering pro-IRA influence in Congress and starting to reduce the flow of contributions to the IRA front organisation Noraid, some of whose members were engaged in the purchase and dispatch of arms and explosives to the IRA.

In undertaking this work the SDLP and ourselves were at times inhibited by the counterproductive impact on the Irish community in the United States, and especially on Irish-American members of Congress, of the extensive British propaganda effort there. Much of this British effort was inevitably directed towards trying to explain away aspects of British rule in Northern Ireland that were not readily defensible, and which Irish Governments spent much of their time trying to get changed, such as British army harassment, directed almost exclusively against the nationalist community, and maltreatment of suspects. This had been condemned in the mid-1970s by the European Commission and Court of Human Rights and further exposed in the Bennett Report in 1979. And from time to time the British diplomatic service abroad, which tended to be much more aggressive towards Ireland than was often the case with the Foreign Office itself, launched unjustified attacks on the seriousness of our commitment against the IRA, which had to be countered. The credibility in the United States of Irish Governments espousing moderate policies and seeking to undermine support for the IRA required that we face there, just as we had to do at home and in Strasbourg, thorny issues of this kind.

Thus our diplomatic service was often fighting defensively on two fronts in the United States, which made it difficult to take effective initiatives of a positive kind. Moreover, so far as the US government itself was concerned, while Henry Kissinger had always been friendly and helpful he was determined not to involve himself in the Irish issue—a determination he himself attributed to the advice of his Irish wife, Nancy—and the State Department was traditionally strongly Anglophile.

Nevertheless, by the end of the Ford administration in January 1977 we had built up with John Hume's assistance strong support for our position in Congress. Tip O'Neill, Ted Kennedy and Pat Moynihan, supported outside Congress by Governor Hugh Carey of New York (collectively known as 'the Four Horsemen'), were holding a firm line against the IRA-sympathising Ad Hoc Committee on Irish Affairs, chaired by Congressman Mario Biaggi, not to speak of Seán MacManus's Irish National Caucus and the IRA organisation Noraid.

With the transfer to Washington in 1976 of Michael Lillis, the counsellor who had been serving for the previous two years as our information officer in the United States, based in New York, a new phase in Irish-American relations had begun. Michael brought our contacts with the Irish Congressional leadership to a stage of intimacy never hitherto achieved, the results of which were demonstrated in the joint statement of the 'Four Horsemen' on St Patrick's Day 1977, which launched the Friends of Ireland movement in Congress. He successfully countered an attempt by Biaggi and the Irish National Caucus to win Jimmy Carter's support during the later stages of his election campaign and persuaded the White House to adopt the Carter initiative, which was launched in July 1977, just after Jack Lynch took over from Liam Cosgrave. This initiative promised substantial US aid to Northern Ireland in the event of progress being made towards a political solution there. (This 'cheque' was cashed eight years later under a different administration with the establishment of the International Fund for Northern Ireland to back up the Anglo-Irish Agreement of that year.)

As second counsellor in the Irish embassy Michael Lillis had shown how, with John Hume's help, we could move from what had hitherto been essentially a defensive position, fighting against IRA propaganda and also frequently against the British information service, to one in which we held the initiative and could influence Congress and even the administration in our interest. To secure the full benefits of this breakthrough the level of activity needed to be raised to an even higher plane; this was the background to my suggestion to Jack Lynch in June 1978 that Seán Donlon, although then well under forty, be moved from his position as head of the Anglo-Irish Division of the Department of Foreign Affairs to be Ambassador to the United States. Like Michael Lillis, Seán had the unique combination of qualities required for the Washington post: the intellectual capacity and diplomatic skill needed to deal with the White House, National Security Council and State Department at an appropriate level, and the personal and human qualities needed to penetrate and command the attention of Congress. Like Michael, he also had a particularly good relationship with John Hume, who worked very closely with him in this task.

By 1979 Seán Donlon's efforts had yielded such results that in its first contacts with the Carter administration the new Thatcher government found itself under immediate pressure from the President, the Secretary of State, Cyrus Vance, and the Defence Secretary, Harold Brown, to find a solution to the Northern Ireland problem.

But the remarkable success of Michael Lillis and Seán Donlon on Capitol Hill and with the administration had infuriated the Irish 'republican' lobby in the United States, who had been effectively marginalised by their efforts. These groups looked to the new leader of Fianna Fáil and head of the Irish Government—whose progression from dismissed Minister accused of importing arms for the IRA to Taoiseach they had followed with enthusiasm—to vindicate their cause by getting rid of the ambassador who had so effectively opposed their efforts.

So it was that at the end of June 1980 Seán Donlon was called back to Dublin and told that he was being moved to the post of Permanent Representative to the United Nations in New York. On Friday 4 July he returned to the United States, stopping in New York for the weekend to prepare the ground for his new posting. But the *Daily Telegraph* correspondent in Washington got word of the proposed move, and his story was picked up by the Irish Sunday papers that weekend. By Wednesday 9 July our papers were reporting the fury of the 'Four Horsemen' at this proposed move. They were said to be scathing in their criticism of the proposed removal of Ambassador Donlon, which a Government spokesman had in the interval sought to justify as a 'peripheral matter . . . removing a pawn to gain a knight' (that is, Neil Blaney). O'Neill, Kennedy, Moynihan and Carey were reported to be 'deeply hurt'; they had 'received no thanks for their efforts in the past,' which were not even 'tolerated'. Despite the Four Horsemen's success in getting the goal of Irish unity inserted in the Democratic election programme, the Irish Government had 'decided to align itself with other forces in the U.S.' In particular they resented the apparent support of the Government for Congressman Biaggi, whom they saw as 'an instrument of Noraid and its offshoot, the Irish National Caucus.'

Before this storm the Haughey reed broke. On the following day it was announced that the report of Seán Donlon's transfer was 'totally without foundation' and that the diplomat Noel Dorr was being appointed to the UN post. The papers reported however that other postings that had to be altered as a result of this last-minute change of plan were now held up, because of the need to seek agreement from governments—which of course was unnecessary in the case of the UN post.

At this point Frank Cluskey and I demanded that the Taoiseach also dissociate himself from the Irish National Caucus and Noraid, a call supported by John Hume, whose normal anxiety to maintain good relations with the Government took second place on this occasion to his concern to retain the powerful support he had helped to build up in the US Congress. In order that all shades of suspicion be removed and this unfortunate affair be closed, said John Hume, 'it is necessary that it be made absolutely clear that the activity of the Biaggi Committee enjoyed no support whatsoever from any substantial section of opinion.'

Very foolishly from his own point of view, the Taoiseach, smarting from the rebuff he had suffered in relation to Seán Donlon, ignored this demand, and the situation was not improved by the Minister for Finance, Michael O'Kennedy, who, while condemning 'any organisation associated with the pursuit of violent methods to deal with the Northern Ireland problem,' replied ambivalently to the question whether this referred to Congressman Biaggi's committee, the Irish National Caucus or Noraid by saying, 'That is open to interpretation.'

Accordingly, on 21 July in a letter to the Taoiseach, the publication of which I postponed to give him an opportunity to make a public statement on the matter, I asked him formally whether he maintained the position of all Governments during the previous decade in relation to these organisations. The Taoiseach responded with a letter saying that he would be speaking at the weekend about the matter, adding, however, that I should consider whether the course I was 'now pursuing in this crucial policy area is in the best interests of the peace and reconciliation which we all seek.'

My letter achieved its purpose, however: at the end of that week the Taoiseach provided belatedly the necessary clear repudiation of the groups in question, condemning Noraid and adding that this organisation's links with the Irish National Caucus cast grave suspicions on that organisation. The caucus's leader, Seán MacManus, responded that the Taoiseach's statement was a 'response to threats and blackmail' from me, and that I had 'once again dictated policy to Mr Haughey'—a statement that I did not feel it necessary to deny.

This unfortunate affair had come in the middle of the negotiations that had been opened in the late spring between Charles Haughey's Government and that of Margaret Thatcher. One day in May 1980 the Taoiseach had asked me to come to see him in his room. He raised with me a parliamentary matter that hardly seemed to warrant a special meeting. Then he said: 'You know I'm meeting Margaret Thatcher next Tuesday?' 'I knew you were meeting her soon,' I replied, 'but I didn't know the day.' He started to say something, stopped, hesitated, and with an obvious change of gear said lamely, 'Well, if you think of anything I should say to her, let me know.' Politely I said I would, but it did not seem to me appropriate to take up this invitation.

Following an official briefing in Dublin, the *Sunday Times* had reported that the Taoiseach intended during his meeting with Margaret Thatcher to propose 'Anglo-Irish co-operation on defence and foreign policy'. I was not therefore too surprised some time later to be told that at a meeting to prepare for the London summit he had speculated on the possibility of consulting Frank Cluskey and myself about proposing to the British Prime Minister some form of bilateral defence agreement, but that on reflection he had decided that the Labour Party's commitment to military neutrality made it impractical to consult Frank Cluskey on the issue. This, I thought, might explain what had happened at our meeting: he might have intended to raise this defence proposal with me but had last-minute second thoughts.

Although no record seems to exist of the tete-à-tete between the British Prime Minister and himself on the occasion of this first meeting between them, the defence issue may have been raised by him on this occasion.

Apparent confirmation of this exists in three respects. First, at his press conference after this bilateral meeting the Taoiseach flatly rejected the idea of Irish membership of the Commonwealth, but, pointedly I thought, did *not* reject in similar blunt terms a defence agreement. Second, ten months later, in the course of a Dáil debate on defence and neutrality, his Government voted *against* a statement that there had been no such proposal. Finally, at about the same time the British Prime Minister rejected publicly the idea of such a bilateral arrangement, adding that if Ireland wanted to join in defence it should do so through multilateral arrangements, i.e. through membership of NATO.

A second Anglo-Irish summit meeting of 1980 took place in Dublin on Monday 8 December, at a time when the first H-block hunger-strike was at its peak. The communiqué on that occasion included reference to 'institutional arrangements' and to 'the totality of the relationship' between Ireland and Britain.

In his press conference after this summit meeting the Taoiseach said that in joint studies that the two governments had agreed to undertake on the relationship between the two states in the context of this 'historic breakthrough', he did not set 'any limits on the arrangements that might be agreed.' A Government spokesman put a gloss on this by talking of the possibility of 'federal, confederal or other innovative structures'. Only Commonwealth membeship was, once again, ruled out. But asked about the reference to confederation in particular, Mrs Thatcher in her press conference was totally dismissive: 'absolutely no possibility,' she responded, and the Northern Ireland Secretary said that constitutional changes were ruled out.

Despite the British Prime Minister's obvious discomfort when questioned in Parliament on this issue and attacked by Ian Paisley in particular about the Irish Government's claims in relation to the constitutional position of Northern Ireland, these warning notes were not heeded by the Fianna Fáil Government.

True, pressed by me and others in the Dáil on the issue the Taoiseach became visibly more cautious; tongue in cheek, I thanked him for clarifying the fact that the constitutional position of Northern Ireland was not at issue, to which he responded that he did not accept what I said. On the following day, however, the Minister for Foreign Affairs, Brian Lenihan, reiterated that 'all options are open,' that 'everything is on the table,' and that the next meeting between the Taoiseach and Prime Minister could be a decision-making one.

The Haughey-Thatcher relationship never recovered from this. Indeed, thereafter on Irish affairs the British Prime Minister became extremely wary of her own advisers as well as of Irish Taoisigh, a problem I had to reckon with in due course. At the time, however, this aftermath of the second Haughey-Thatcher summit meeting was obscured by the ending of the first H-Block hunger-strike a week after the Dublin meeting.

Thus concluded Charles Haughey's Northern Ireland initiative, on which he had placed great hopes. In retrospect it can be seen that these hopes had been illusory: they had been built on sand. It became even more clear to me later when I became Taoiseach that there had never been any possibility that a constitutional change in the position of Northern Ireland could have emerged from these negotiations. However, by his fostering the illusion that something of the kind might be on the cards, Unionist fears had been fanned to a dangerous level, which made rational discussions with them about devolution much more difficult thereafter and may have contributed to their later unreasoning hostility towards the Anglo-Irish Agreement of 1985.

For its part the SDLP, whose hopes had been unreasonably raised by these events, found itself ill-placed after this debacle to cope with the tensions created by the subsequent 1981 hunger-strike. In accordance with its policy of working with the Government of the day while maintaining its own identity and policy stance, it had gone along with Charles Haughey's initiative. At the same time, faced with pressure from Haughey to espouse the demand for a British withdrawal, John Hume had cleverly sought to avoid this issue. He had tried to maintain the SDLP policy of 'unity by consent' by developing a subtle distinction between this latter principle and the British guarantee of the union, the removal of which he called for. This call for the removal of the 'British guarantee' was, however, vulnerable to Fianna Fáil pressure to expand it into the 'British withdrawal' demand it was intended to pre-empt.

Moreover, the distinction between, on the one hand, Britain dropping its guarantee of Northern Ireland's position within the United Kingdom until and unless a majority there favoured Irish unity, and, on the other hand, seeking Irish unity without requiring such consent was too subtle for the Unionists—and, I have to add, for Fine Gael, which viewed this shift in SDLP policy with alarm. However, my own personal relationship with John Hume and some other SDLP figures helped to bridge the policy conflict thus created with Fine Gael.

I knew that the superficial alignment between the Fianna Fáil and SDLP stances worried John, just as he had been disturbed when we were in office by equivalent Fianna Fáil paranoia about the SDLP's relationship at that time with Fine Gael and, to a lesser extent, the Labour Party. Late in 1980 I suggested to a member of the SDLP who spoke to me about John's concern on this score that if he wanted to reassure Fine Gael (although I did not myself feel this was necessary) all he had to do was tip off the 'Backchat' column in the *Sunday Independent* about his holiday with Joan and myself in the south of France that summer. When this idea was put to John shortly afterwards he immediately rejected it; but within a fortnight the story appeared in 'Backchat'— and it was not I who leaked it.

Throughout these years in opposition we had been very critical of Fianna Fáil's handling of the economy and of the Government finances. Despite the enormous problems created for Ireland, as for so many other countries, by the first oil crisis in 1973, the National Coalition Government had left the economy in very good shape four years later, a fact generously recognised by the incoming Taoiseach, Jack Lynch, in the end-of-year adjournment debate six months after the June 1977 change of Government. On that occasion he recorded that in 1977 our growth rate, at 5 per cent, had been 'near the top of the league internationally'; investment had been dynamic; exports had risen at three times the average rate for industrialised countries; and there had been an average rise of 7,000 in manufacturing employment during the year. The volume of agricultural output was up 9 per cent, he added; and he summed up the whole picture by saying that 'this is the kind of foundation on which we can build.' He could have added that inflation, which had momentarily attained 25 per cent at the height of the oil crisis, was down to an annual rate of 6.75 per cent in the second half of 1977.

The abolition of road tax and of rates on domestic dwellings by Fianna Fáil reduced the buoyancy of tax, the proceeds of which in 1978 rose as a result by only half the rate of increase of current expenditure. This led to a doubling in that year of the current budget deficit, which we had reduced to the point where the temporary foreign borrowing that, like so many other industrialised countries, we had had to undertake during the oil crisis years had by 1977 virtually been eliminated.

By the end of 1977, however, the EC Commission was already warning of the dangers inherent in overstimulation of demand in Ireland, which, 'although it would bring about a temporary improvement in the employment situation . . . would ultimately necessitate undesirable measures to curb activity.' This advice was ignored, then and later. The volume of current exchequer spending had been increased by no less than 20 per cent by 1979, despite which the economic growth rate fell sharply in that year.

Thus by the time Charles Haughey succeeded Jack Lynch as Taoiseach in December 1979 the rate of exchequer borrowing had doubled, and the national debt was more than two-thirds higher than when Fianna Fáil had taken over from us two-and-a-half years earlier. Thereafter the situation deteriorated at an accelerating rate. Far from any corrective action being taken, the position was further aggravated by a campaign undertaken by Charles Haughey's new Government to increase the number of public servants, regardless of need; and pay claims were settled with such abandon that average pay rates in the public service rose by almost 30 per cent in 1980. The planned current deficit in that year was exceeded by no less that 60 per cent, and exchequer borrowing rose by a further 50 per cent.

Against this background the 1981 budget presentation was treated with a scepticism that in the event proved to be fully warranted. Exchequer spending was officially forecast to rise by no more than one-sixth—the rate that inflation had now attained—and a marginal fall in the current budget deficit to just over £500 million was projected. We believed the deficit would exceed by a considerable margin the published estimate, which we thought had been deliberately held at unrealistic levels, unattainable on the basis of the policy decisions taken (or, rather, not taken) by the Government with respect to spending programmes. We were right.

All in all, the Fianna Fáil Governments led by Jack Lynch and Charles Haughey between them increased the volume of current public spending by almost half, more than doubled in real terms the annual level of borrowing, and almost trebled the national debt. As well as this the rate of inflation almost trebled, and the Central Bank rediscount rate virtually doubled.

In early 1981 the accelerating speed at which this deterioration was taking place was not, however, known to the public—or to us in opposition. The presentation of the financial returns to financial journalists during this period was later to be the subject of severe criticism. The undermining of confidence in the public administration in this sector was, with that of security, the aspect of the events of this period that most concerned me in 1981 and 1982. I gave corresponding attention to restoring this public confidence when I became Taoiseach.

In preparing our manifesto for the election that we believed would be called in the first half of 1981 we had to face the reality of this appalling financial crisis—as far as we knew it. While we believed that the economic reforms we proposed could stimulate enough additional buoyancy to eliminate a current budget deficit of, perhaps, £300 million, we were under no illusion that a deficit of £800 million (the figure we then believed it would reach, not knowing how much worse the situation had in fact become) could be absorbed in this way. We made this explicit in our manifesto, and proposed to eliminate the soaring deficit over a period of four or five years, giving preference in this process to reductions in public expenditure as against tax increases.

We also proposed a number of complex financial reforms that in fact were not to be carried through, partly because of the brevity of our period in Government after the 1981 election and partly because of the further rapid deterioration in the financial situation that had occurred during the final months of Charles Haughey's first Government. But happily other proposals in our manifesto *were* implemented by one or other of the Governments I led, such as, for example, the establishment of a Youth Employment Agency; tax allowances for elderly tenants of rented accommodation; the provision through a new Housing Finance Agency of housing loans with repayments limited to a fixed share of income; the abolition of the concept of 'illegitimacy'; and the establishment of an independent Examinations and Curriculum Board to take over important functions from the Department of Education—although this board was later abolished by Fianna Fáil.

Meanwhile we had prepared our election campaign in great detail, with a precise day-by-day programme for the early part of the campaign, including the timing of the launch of our manifesto and arrangements for my tour of the country, which was to begin with a lightning trip to the main centres by special train—an innovation in Irish electoral history.

The success of Fianna Fáil in the Donegal by-election of December 1980—the first electoral test to be faced by Charles Haughey since his election as Taoiseach twelve months earlier—had provided a salutary shock for Fine Gael, and in particular for myself. Clearly it brought a general election much nearer, possibly in the new year, and that election would not be easily won. To meet this situation I put in place a Strategy Committee comprising both front-benchers and non-Oireachtas members, the latter element of which would, together with several senators, become our election committee the moment the Dáil was dissolved and TDs had to return to their constituencies. My experience before becoming leader had convinced me that deputies trying to get themselves re-elected could not run a general election campaign effectively. What we needed were people from outside the party structure with a wide range of management and public relations skills who would have learnt to work with the party leadership in the run-up to the election and who, given this experience, could then take on this task in conjunction with a small number of senators and others with political experience, and with the professionals, Peter Prendergast and Ted Nealon.

This new form of election organisation proved its worth when the election was called in May, and in the two further elections that took place at nine-month intervals thereafter. Indeed I believe this structure was one of the most successful organisational systems devised by a political party in independent Ireland.

The director of elections was Seán O'Leary, a Cork accountant and barrister who had himself been a Dáil candidate and whose qualities of warmth and vitality, political gut instinct, natural authority, toughness and *joie de vivre*, together with his excellent relationship with our national organiser, Peter Prendergast, equipped him ideally for this task. Derry Hussey, Gemma Hussey's businessman husband, provided a key element of calm, stability and order as chairman of the team. The late Alexis FitzGerald and a former senator, Jim Dooge, each with a third of a century of accumulated political wisdom, looked after policy issues and guided the work of a scriptwriting team of young professional people.

Ted Nealon had organised a team of experts who brought first-rate marketing skills to bear on this campaign. He was not available for the campaign itself, however, because of his nomination as a candidate for Sligo-Leitrim, which he has since represented in the Dáil, and his place was taken at short notice by Liam Hourican, the former RTE journalist who had played a distinguished role as correspondent in Belfast at an important juncture in the 1970s and who had recently completed a term in Dick Burke's cabinet in Brussels. After the election I appointed him Government Press Officer.

A perennial problem with election financing is ensuring that no matter what the political pressure during the campaign, expenditure is not allowed to out-run revenue. In our case this was ensured by combining the responsibilities of fund-raising and expenditure authorisation in one person: Seán Murray, a hard-nosed accountant who had the combination of dynamism and toughness necessary to undertake this dual responsibility. He brought us through these three elections of the early 1980s in most difficult circumstances, balancing the books each time.

By the time the 1981 election was called this team was well prepared for the task ahead, and during the campaign needed only minimal guidance from frontbenchers seeking re-election—although, of course, I kept in touch with them myself day by day, and when in Dublin joined their meetings, as did some of my colleagues.

Because of the tragic fire in the Stardust ballroom in the Taoiseach's own North Dublin constituency in February, in which forty-eight young people lost their lives and scores of others were maimed, the election was postponed until May. Well signalled in advance, the dissolution was announced on the evening of Wednesday 20 May. The Taoiseach stated that he was seeking a clear mandate because of the grave situation in Northern Ireland, where the renewal of the 1980 hunger-strike had already led to two deaths. Two more of the hunger-strikers died within hours of the dissolution of the Dáil.

The latest public opinion polls, published some weeks earlier, had shown support for Fine Gael and the Labour Party exceeding that for Fianna Fáil by about ten points; but the natural tendency of public opinion to rally to a Government at a time of crisis made it unlikely that this advantage would be maintained—a fact of which Fianna Fáil may have been aware from their own research, and which was confirmed a few days later when a post-dissolution poll showed Fianna Fáil with 52 per cent support, 9 points ahead of the combination of Fine Gael and Labour. What had happened was that a significant part of the support had swung from the opposition to the Government or had moved to a sceptical 'don't know' position. Moreover, Charles Haughey was at this point marginally more popular than I was, reversing my earlier ten-point advantage over him. We were thus starting the campaign from behind.

Thirty-six hours after the dissolution, however, I launched our programme, which immediately became the focal point of the campaign and provided a basis for a co-operative relationship with the Labour Party. Michael O'Leary for that party immediately characterised the general thrust of our programme as 'acceptable'.

On Saturday Joan and I started a two-day countrywide tour by special train. This electoral innovation, organised by a member of our election committee, Joe Jennings, who worked in CIE, was a well-kept secret. It secured us good initial publicity, both at national and regional level. In two days we visited nine provincial cities or towns—I with one arm in a sling as a result of a domestic accident. I made speeches or gave press conferences, and accepted a proposal for a television debate with the Taoiseach.

As the days passed, Fianna Fáil was increasingly being drawn into criticising—and thus further publicising—our programme, in the process losing credibility by alleging that its implementation would cost £800 million.

By the second weekend it was clear that we were pulling in the floating voters, a fact confirmed by the pollsters, who early in the following week showed both Fine Gael and myself closing the gap with Fianna Fáil and its leader. Many of the 'don't knows' were now rallying to the opposition, and particularly to Fine Gael. At this point the Government party went on the defensive by withdrawing its agreement to a head-to-head confrontation on television between its leader and myself. Fianna Fáil demanded that the Labour Party leader, Frank Cluskey, be included in that television debate.

At the same time the press reports of the leaders' tours suggested that Charles Haughey was more at home in this kind of environment and that I was less than comfortable with crowds and the trappings of populism. In part this was a stereotyping exercise—woolly-headed academic versus practised professional—but there was an element of truth in it, for I have always been chary of all forms of populism and have perhaps been inordinately fastidious about the kind of artificial adulation of the leader that seems to be an inseparable element of party set-pieces, including party conferences and election meetings. Moreover, while usually comfortable addressing non-political audiences I have never been happy making political speeches at outdoor meetings, to audiences whose attention to my remarks I cannot help feeling to be governed by considerations of loyalty or courtesy rather than by any actual interest in my necessarily partisan observations on such occasions.

But I was very often deeply moved by the enthusiasm of so many of our party workers engaged in the patriotic work of electioneering and in other less dramatic tasks to be performed between elections; their efforts, and, of course, those of activists of other parties, which ensure the alternation of governments so vital to the preservation of democracy from corruption and the abuse of power, deserve far more recognition than they ever receive from the general public. And I could not fail to be heartened by the warmth of so many ordinary Irish people, uninvolved in politics, who frequently feel moved to express their appreciation of those who take part in the democratic process. Without the reward of such enthusiasm and such sporadic public gratitude the political process would often seem thankless.

During this first general election campaign that I undertook as leader the journalists accompanying me were, initially at least, more conscious of my reticences than of my positive reactions; in particular they missed my exhilaration at the youth of the people who thronged to our meetings, many of them young parents with their children and babies, and at the warmth of the welcome they gave to my reforming ideas.

It was indeed a blissful dawn to what turned out to be a most gloomy decade. I could not but be cheered by finding that at least for that brief moment there was a genuine appetite for social reform and for more liberal and pluralist attitudes. Many of the new generation that had grown up in the

1960s and 1970s clearly wanted to turn their backs on the sterile, inward-looking form of nationalism that had dominated postrevolutionary Ireland for so long. Above all, when the sun shone, as it did for at least part of the time during what turned out to be a rather showery early summer, there was a mood of gaiety and warmth, and an evident belief that politics *could* be constructive. Somehow this had not come across in the media during the first half of the campaign. However, as the tide visibly turned I was reported to be 'good-humoured and relaxed'—albeit 'polite to the point of self-effacement'.

I had said that I would make one speech on Northern Ireland during the campaign, to state our position without making it an election issue—a practice I followed in subsequent campaigns.

On Thursday 5 June I told an audience in Roscommon that in Government I would place more emphasis on relations with Unionists in Northern Ireland; Charles Haughey, I felt, in his diplomatic efforts during the previous year had placed inordinate reliance on relations with the British government.

The tour was, of course, physically exhausting; at one point Joan remarked, as one journalist recorded, that she had never seen me so weary in my life. However, physical tiredness is a short-lived phenomenon, from which I recovered easily, especially as I had wisely insisted on building into the process of electioneering at least one rest period during the day. Even forty-five minutes lying down was enough to enable me to go full speed ahead again afterwards.

I should add that on this and other such campaigns the fact that Joan, despite her severe arthritis, accompanied me, bringing her cheerfulness and wit to bear on our enterprise, made a huge difference to my morale and, I believe, to that of the rest of the team also. At the same time the clear-sighted objectivity of her comments, especially on my own performance, helped to keep my feet on the ground.

As more and more floating voters were coming our way, three days from the end of the campaign the polls were suggesting a very close outcome indeed between Fine Gael-Labour and Fianna Fáil, and the bookmakers' odds shifted in our favour. It was at this stage that an RTE compromise was finally arrived at to get around Charles Haughey's reluctance to undertake a face-to-face confrontation with me on television. It involved each of the three party leaders being interviewed by a group of political correspondents—a clumsy arrangement that I was not at all comfortable with. This must have been evident. The Taoiseach was adjudged to have been more relaxed, and I 'hesitant and slightly nervous'.

Polling was on Thursday 11 June. As the reports of the party 'tallymen' watching the checking of the ballot papers came in during Friday morning, it was clear that the result was likely to be indecisive. And so it turned out. By late Saturday afternoon it was clear that neither Fianna Fáil, with 78 seats, nor Fine Gael plus the Labour Party, with 80 seats between them (65 Fine Gael and 15 Labour), had a majority. Two abstentionist IRA candidates had been elected in border constituencies, and there were six independents or representatives of small parties who were going to hold the balance of power.

Nevertheless, while the absence of a clear majority for a possible alternative Fine Gael-Labour Government was disappointing, it seemed likely that I would be elected Taoiseach when the Dáil met in three weeks' time. And by any standard the scale of our achievement was impressive. We had increased Fine Gael's share of the vote by one-fifth, to the highest level attained in over half a century, taking virtually all those votes from Fianna Fáil. We had increased our Dáil representation by over half, from 43 to 65, in effect winning all eighteen additional Dáil seats and four others besides, so that Fianna Fáil, which had also lost two seats to IRA candidates, had six fewer seats than in the previous, much smaller Dáil. Only one of our former deputies who had contested the election had lost his seat. Over half the Fine Gael deputies elected had not been members of the previous Dáil: an unprecedented influx of new blood into our political system. Many were in their twenties or thirties; and six were women, as against one in 1977. (Five other women were later elected to the Seanad in the Fine Gael interest, thus increasing overnight the number of Fine Gael women in the Oireachtas from two to eleven.)

One of the casualties of the campaign, however, was the Labour Party leader, Frank Cluskey, with whom I had worked closely for the previous four years. Six days after the election the Labour parliamentary party met and chose Michael O'Leary as its new leader. During the days that followed he rejected advances from Charles Haughey, despite pressure from elements within his own party, especially in Dublin. He and I then embarked on talks at the home of a mutual friend, Gay Hogan. We were later joined by our deputy leaders, Peter Barry for Fine Gael and Jimmy Tully for Labour.

Michael and I had been friends for years. However, as leader of Fine Gael I had had to give priority to maintaining a good relationship with Frank Cluskey as Labour Party leader, and considering the tension that existed between him and Michael O'Leary I had had to keep my distance from Michael to some extent during the years from 1977 to 1981. Joan, however, not being subject to the same political inhibitions, had kept in touch with him during this period. Michael and I were now faced with the task of devising together a joint programme for Government that our respective parties could accept. For this purpose the very comprehensive Fine Gael policy document provided a framework, the essential elements of which could be developed or supplemented along lines that could reflect specific Labour Party concerns.

The idea of presenting our joint programme in the context of a four-year national plan to be drawn up in consultation with various sectors was helpful to the Labour Party, as was the concept of a National Planning Board, which in any event I favoured. The Fine Gael proposal for a Public Enterprise Board was transmuted into a National Development Corporation. A new commitment was given to capital taxation, involving as an objective the restoration of the yield from these taxes to the 1972/73 level, which seemed reasonable. The Fine Gael commitment to the re-establishment and funding of a National Poverty Committee that Fianna Fáil had abolished was placed within a framework involving an anti-poverty plan. A proposal for a national income-related pension scheme contained in a Green Paper published by Frank Cluskey when he had been a Minister of State in the 1973–77 National Coalition was reintroduced.

The social-democratic orientation of the Fine Gael programme facilitated the marrying of our two parties' objectives, because Fine Gael policy contained nothing with which the Labour Party disagreed. At the same time, as few in Labour had actually read our programme and as most Labour Party members had been conditioned to assume that Fine Gael was a right-wing party, the inclusion of large parts of the Fine Gael document in the joint programme was seen by many in the Labour Party, quite erroneously, to be a victory for Labour over Fine Gael.

By Saturday 27 June the joint programme was agreed, as was the allocation to the Labour Party of four of the fifteen Government posts, together with three junior Ministerial appointments. As in the 1973–77 Coalition, this gave Labour more than its share of portfolios in proportion to its Dáil seats.

The joint programme was to be put to our respective parties on the following Sunday. In our case this involved our parliamentary party, but in the case of the Labour Party a special conference of over 1,200 delegates was held in the Gaiety Theatre, Dublin—hence the name 'Gaiety Programme' by which the joint policy somewhat incongruously came to be known. I had no qualms about what my own party's decision would be, but the Labour Party's special conference was very far from being a foregone conclusion. In the event, the document was adopted by both parties—in the case of Labour by a less than overwhelming majority of 737 votes to 487.

The first business of the new Dáil when it met on the afternoon of Tuesday 30 June would be the election of the Ceann Comhairle. Neither Fianna Fáil nor Fine Gael-Labour was prepared to forfeit a vote in such a delicately balanced situation by nominating a party member for this position. One of the independents, John O'Connell, was a former Labour Party member of some standing who currently had a Fianna Fáil, or at any rate Haughey, orientation. Although Labour was somewhat reluctant, we proposed him for the post, and he was elected.

As two of the eight independents were IRA abstentionists, that left five. Neil Blaney supported Charles Haughey, thus giving the latter a total of 79 votes when he was proposed as Taoiseach. Three of the others—two left-wing independents, Noel Browne and Jim Kemmy, and a single representative of the Workers' Party, Joe Sherlock—voted with the Labour Party and ourselves, thus defeating the former Taoiseach by a margin of four votes. I was then elected by 81 votes to 78, Jim Kemmy alone of the independents joining with the Fine Gael and Labour members for this purpose.

# CHAPTER THIRTEEN

# REVOLVING-DOOR TAOISEACH

Immediately after my election by the Dáil as Taoiseach, the Secretary to the Government, Dermot Nally, with whom I had worked closely when he had been Assistant Secretary during the 1973–77 Government, accompanied me to Áras an Uachtaráin to receive my seal of office from President Hillery. During the journey he told me that the financial situation of the state was far worse than we had realised; next morning I would have to meet the Finance officials with my new Minister for Finance to consider emergency action.

On returning to Leinster House I summoned my Government nominees and, meeting them individually, offered them their portfolios. I saw them individually (rather than collectively, as Liam Cosgrave had done), so that I might have the opportunity of a private word with each. I was concerned in particular to ensure that none of them was a member of any organisation of which membership was not a matter of public knowledge. In our state, as distinct from the United Kingdom (where my grandfather had been, as I understood it, a high-ranking Freemason and the representative in the UK of the Grand Lodge of Alabama), it was highly unlikely that Freemasonry played any role in politics; but there are comparable Roman Catholic organisations, membership of which is similarly not a matter of public knowledge, and I believed that Ministers should not be members of any such organisation, because no-one should ever feel they had reason to fear that their legitimate interests or the common good might be adversely affected because any member of a Government led by me owed private allegiance to such a body.

I then announced my Government to the Dáil. Michael O'Leary as Labour Party leader was, of course, Tánaiste. Unwisely in my view he also took on responsibility for Energy, as well as for the industrial side of Industry and

Commerce. This was far too heavy a load for a newly elected leader of the Labour Party, who would have his work cut out to rally the support of the 40 per cent of his party who had opposed participation in Government. Moreover, the splitting of a department in which responsibility for industry and for trade had been combined since the foundation of the state was disruptive, and John Kelly, whom I asked to take charge of Commerce and also Tourism, was understandably unhappy at this division of responsibility.

The other Labour Party portfolios were the Department of Labour, placed in the steady hands of Liam Kavanagh; Health and Social Welfare, a double load that was, I think, a burden for Eileen Desmond, whose own health was not robust; and Defence, which went to the party's deputy leader, Jimmy Tully. (Jimmy's career as Minister for Defence almost came to an abrupt end some months later during a visit to Egypt in connection with our UN peace-keeping involvement, when he found himself on the reviewing platform with President Sadat at the moment of the president's assassination, and lost some of his teeth to a ricochet bullet.) On the whole this did not seem to me to be a particularly successful choice of portfolios from the Labour Party's point of view.

When I offered the Fine Gael deputy leader, Peter Barry, a choice of portfolios he opted for Environment, which includes local government. For the key Finance appointment, which was clearly going to be of crucial importance, I selected 34-year-old John Bruton, who had been an honours student of mine in the late 1960s and a junior Minister in the 1973–77 Government. He was young for the job by any standards, but was a very serious and principled politician as well as being imaginative and innovative, and also both generous and strong-willed. Two survivors from the 1973–77 Government, Tom Fitzpatrick and Pat Cooney, I appointed to Fisheries and Forestry and to Transport and Posts and Telegraphs, respectively.

New to office as Minister for Justice, but with the experience of a Dáil term behind him, was 34-year-old Jim Mitchell. He had shown his mettle—and his extraordinary generosity of spirit—over the previous decade, when on several occasions, once successfully, he had pressed Declan Costello to re-enter the Dáil as a representative of his local area of Ballyfermot in west Dublin, at the expense of his (Jim's) own candidature. I believed he would be sound on security and liberal on law reform. What I did not allow for was his unbounded enthusiasm, which prompted him to arrive in our bedroom at all hours of the night to brief me on urgent security matters. But Joan and I soon became accustomed to these incursions.

To the Education post I nominated 34-year-old John Boland, whose political intuition and ability to see around corners outweighed in my view his abrasiveness of manner. And Paddy O'Toole, a gentle westerner and Irish-speaker, became Minister for the Gaeltacht.

That left Agriculture and Foreign Affairs. To the former I appointed 36-year-old Alan Dukes, like John Bruton a student of mine from the 1960s, who had been adviser to the Irish Farmers' Association in Dublin and Brussels.

Later he had become a member of the cabinet of Dick Burke, then the Irish member of the European Commission in Brussels, until I persuaded him to stand for election, first for the European Parliament in 1979 and then for the Dáil. I was of course aware that some past appointments of deputies to the Government on their first day in the Dáil were regarded as unfortunate; but I needed someone in the Agriculture portfolio who would have the confidence of the farming community while never becoming a prisoner of their sectional interest; and Alan, despite his lack of political experience, seemed—and indeed proved—ideally suited for this role.

Because of my personal experience of Foreign Affairs and my recognition of its key importance in view of the crisis in Northern Ireland and our involvement in the European Community, I had been very exercised about who to put into that department. Joan had come up with the answer. She suggested that Jim Dooge was the one man to whom I would certainly be willing to delegate responsibility in this sensitive area; and she wisely identified the risk that, at this critical juncture, with anyone else I would be tempted to adopt an unduly 'hands on' approach. A scientist of world reputation in the field of hydraulics, and with political experience extending back to an early stint in local government in the 1940s, followed by a return to politics in 1961 in the Seanad, where he had been both Cathaoirleach and Leas-Chathaoirleach, Jim Dooge had one of the wisest political heads in the country. The only problem was that he had left politics in 1977 for a second time in order to concentrate on his academic career. I was, however, entitled under the Constitution to appoint up to two Ministers from the Seanad—although this provision had only once been employed in the almost half-century of the Constitution's existence, and most people had probably forgotten that it existed. However, by using in Jim Dooge's favour one of my eleven nominations to the Seanad I could have him constitutionally qualified for the Foreign Affairs portfolio within two months; and in the interim John Kelly could act formally as Foreign Minister. It was with some difficulty, however, that I persuaded Jim Dooge to enter politics for the third time in his life in order to give me the support I felt I needed in this key area.

Another innovation was the appointment of Senator Alexis FitzGerald as special adviser to the Government, with the provision that, like the Attorney General, he would attend cabinet meetings. I had known Alexis—who had been one of Joan's lecturers in UCD—for a third of a century. He was the founder and senior partner of one of Dublin's largest and most highly regarded firms of solicitors, and was also an economist and in later life a student of theology. He had acted informally as adviser to his father-in-law, John A. Costello, the head of the Coalition Governments of 1948–51 and 1954–57. In that capacity Alexis, together with his close friend Paddy Lynch (a civil servant in the Department of the Taoiseach who, in the interval between those two Governments, joined the Economics Department in UCD, where he had a most distinguished career), had been responsible for the initiatives in late 1956 that started the reorientation of the inward-looking postrevolutionary Irish economy to the world outside. This was the process that was later brought to fruition through the efforts of T. K. Whitaker's First Programme for Economic Expansion in the years after 1958.

In the Seanad, where he had served since 1969, Alexis's talents had been deployed to such effect that even when he was in opposition his objective criticism of legislation was taken extremely seriously by Ministers and their civil servants—even to the point of halting the proceedings on occasion in order to get his help in re-drafting! I did not think that I could reasonably appoint two members of the Seanad to Ministerial office—that would have been too big a mouthful for my Dáil colleagues to swallow—but by this alternative arrangement I hoped to be able to avail myself fully of his legal skills, economic expertise, business experience, and immense political wisdom.

His appointment to this novel position nevertheless caused a stir. Some of the Labour members of the Government feared that he would in effect be a twelfth Fine Gael Minister. Charles Haughey described his appointment as 'cronyism', as if I had in some way conferred a benefit on Alexis, whereas in fact he was giving up his Seanad seat and his leading role in his firm for an underpaid and undefined appointment of uncertain (and, as it turned out, very brief) duration.

Finally, as Attorney General I appointed Peter Sutherland, a barrister in his mid-thirties whose energy and enthusiasm was already a byword and who accepted without hesitation an appointment that cut his earnings to a small fraction of their previous level.

With four key departments and the Attorney Generalship placed in the hands of men in their mid-thirties, with another key Ministerial position allocated to someone who was not then a member of either house, and with the creation of this new post of special adviser, it is fair to say that my Government caused something of a sensation. This was all the more the case because I had omitted former Ministers who by virtue of their seniority—traditionally a dominant consideration in Government-making—had been expected by many in the party and in the media to be included. But I wanted my Government to break new ground by bringing in fresh and younger faces rather than to be a virtual replica of the Cosgrave Government of the mid-1970s.

As it turned out the feature of my Government that seemed to stir up most controversy was quite a different aspect, which in a country other than Ireland would not even have been noticed: the geographical distribution of the Ministers. Perhaps because the establishment of elected local authorities preceded the institution of a national parliament by a quarter of a century, national politics have some curiously parochial features. Many people outside Dublin seem to see each Government not as a government of the state but as a kind of federal superparliament in which their particular county needs to be represented in order to secure its interests vis-à-vis the rest of the country—and in particular vis-à-vis Dublin, which is still widely perceived in rural Ireland as if it were even today a centre of alien colonial rule.

Because six members of my Government represented Dublin constituencies and four more had been elected in constituencies bordering Dublin—and above all because only one was from the west—I came under immediate attack, both within my own party and more widely. At no stage was it suggested that more competent candidates were available: the issue of competence seemed to be almost universally regarded as totally irrelevant.

I was more amused than irritated at this reaction. There were far more serious matters to attend to: the financial crisis at home and the hunger-strike in Northern Ireland, which together totally dominated our hectic first month in Government.

To tackle these two problems I would be drawing on the skills of the Departments of Finance and Foreign Affairs. I would need, however, a personal 'cabinet' to assist me with this and my other tasks of government. In the latter part of my period in opposition I had strengthened my office by the appointment of a young graduate, Katherine Meenan, as my personal aide, with particular responsibility for our relations with the Christian democratic movement in Europe, of which we were part, but also to assist in handling relations with members of our parliamentary party. She came with me into Government to continue this work. I asked the Central Bank to second Patrick Honohan, a brilliant theoretical economist with a practical bent and a delightful sense of humour, whose good personal relationship with many of the Finance officials made him particularly suitable for this position. As Government Press Officer I appointed Liam Hourican, the former RTE correspondent who had also served in Dick Burke's cabinet in Brussels and who had stepped into Ted Nealon's shoes during the election campaign. And CIE seconded to me Joe Jennings (who had been responsible for the launch of my campaign by special train) to head the Government Information Service.

With a view to ensuring effective liaison with Foreign Affairs I appointed Michael Lillis as my diplomatic adviser. His performance in the United States as information officer and later as counsellor at the Washington embassy had impressed me enormously, and more recently he had acquired European experience in Dick Burke's cabinet. Moreover, he had a rapport—if occasionally of a combative nature!—with our Ambassador in the United States, Seán Donlon, whom I intended to bring back as Secretary of the Department of Foreign Affairs.

As private secretary I appointed Declan Kelly from Foreign Affairs, who had been my assistant private secretary in that department. Since then he had served as private secretary to two other Ministers for Foreign Affairs and to two Ministers of State in that department, one Fine Gael and three Fianna Fáil. This appointment caused a storm in the Department of the Taoiseach. Whereas in Foreign Affairs the private office was vacated when a new Minister was appointed—even if he be from the same party—to enable the Minister to choose his own private office staff, in the Department of the Taoiseach the tradition was totally different: the practice had hitherto been that the private secretary and the staff of the private office remained, even when there was a change of administration. I had been quite unaware of this.

My decision came as a bombshell to my new department, and was the subject of strong protests on behalf of the staff. Even though the terms in which this reaction was expressed appeared inappropriate to me, I could understand the feelings of those concerned when I realised how far I was departing from precedent. Nevertheless I held to my decision; and indeed when I returned to office at the end of 1982 I reappointed Declan Kelly, who had in the meantime served as private secretary to yet another Fianna Fáil Minister for Foreign Affairs, and he remained in this position until 1985.

Quite apart from Declan Kelly's own outstanding personal qualities of discretion and judgement I believe that, given the potential tension between a private secretary, whose task it is to look after his political master's interests, and the Secretary of the department, who may have a different and, as he would see it, more long-term view (compare the television programme 'Yes, Minister'), there is a good case in principle for Ministers being free to draw private secretaries from other departments. In fairness, however, I should say that I am not personally aware of cases where tension of this kind has caused problems in the Irish system of Government.

However that may be, the team thus assembled (which, partly by virtue of his physical location on the floor below my office, included the Attorney General, Peter Sutherland) proved to be a 'happy ship'.

The Department of the Taoiseach itself posed some problems. During the Haughey administration from 1979 to 1981 the short-lived Department of Economic Planning and Development, established by Jack Lynch in 1977, was abolished and its functions merged with the Department of the Taoiseach, which thus overnight grew from a small and compact cabinet secretariat to a full-blown department with a staff of two hundred and with two departmental Secretaries: the Secretary to the Government, Dermot Nally, and the Secretary of the department, Noel Whelan, who was succeeded in 1982 by Pádraic Ó hUiginn. I was never happy with the resultant dual structure, which seemed to me to be top-heavy, although both parts of the department had some able staff.

From the moment of my appointment I found myself deeply involved with the new Minister for Finance, John Bruton, in tackling the disastrous financial crisis. The exchequer borrowing level, which, after peaking in 1975 as a result of the oil crisis, had been reduced by the National Coalition Government to a little over 10 per cent of GNP in 1977, had jumped to 13 per cent in 1978, and had then drifted upwards to 14 per cent in 1979 and almost 15 per cent in 1980. The 1981 budget had purported to reduce it to 13 per cent of GNP, but when John Bruton and I met the Finance officials on the morning of 1 July they told us that current spending had been running almost one-sixth ahead of the budgeted level—in addition to which a number of the state enterprises that had been allowed to run into a loss-making phase were demanding substantial capital injections, for which no provision had been made. Unless emergency action were taken, exchequer borrowing was likely to reach 20 per cent of GNP in the current year and almost 21 per cent in 1982. Furthermore—something we could not reveal to the public at that time without prejudicing our ability to borrow the huge sums that would still be needed while we were getting things under control—the Central Bank had turned down in mid-April a request from the Department of Finance for a loan of £350 million.

How had such a drastic deterioration, involving in 1990 money terms an expenditure overrun of £1,200 million, occurred in five short months since the budget? Questions were raised in our minds, and in those of economic commentators, whether the spending estimates on which the budget had been based had in fact reflected, in accordance with the practice followed since the foundation of the state, the actual cost of implementing the policies of the Government of the day, as assessed by the experts in the Department of Finance. We soon discovered that the estimates that had been agreed by the Haughey Government in late 1980 had subsequently been arbitrarily cut by £115 million—sums of £5 or £10 million being cut from individual departmental votes without any policy decisions being taken that would justify these adjustments. In addition, £100 million of capital expenditure had quite unrealistically been presented as coming from the private sector, although no arrangements to this effect had ever been made.

Two days later John Bruton circulated to the members of the Government a memorandum proposing an immediate meeting of Ministers to curtail excess spending and to consider other financial measures, involving additional indirect taxes, which would inevitably increase the cost of living. Not only the current deficit and borrowing level now facing us but also the external payments deficit was now twice as high as in Belgium and Italy, the other EC countries with the worst financial problems.

As we were already over half way through the financial year 1981, the main thrust of the supplementary budget presented to and passed by the Dáil on 21 July was necessarily directed towards bringing the situation for the following year under control. Nevertheless the expenditure cuts and tax increases that we introduced were designed to reduce the threatened 1981 borrowing level by £336 million, from 20 to 16.5 per cent of GNP. In the event the borrowing outturn for the year was kept below 17 per cent of GNP, which was a good start to the process of bringing our finances under control. So far as 1982 was concerned, the decisions we took in these three weeks reduced the likely borrowing level by over one-fifth, from the threatened level of almost 21 per cent of GNP.

During these three traumatic weeks of July, however, I had to give much of my attention to the evolution of the hunger-strike crisis. Our position on this was that, in accordance with the traditional policy of Irish Governments on such strikes within their own jurisdiction, we would not press the British government to concede to paramilitary prisoners the political status demanded by the IRA. We had, however, noted proposals made by the Commission for Justice and Peace of the Roman Catholic hierarchy on 3 June. The commission had suggested the extension to male prisoners in the Maze Prison of the arrangements for the use of their own clothes that applied to women prisoners in Armagh Jail, as well as greater freedom of association, not involving military-type activities, and orientation of work towards cultural and educational activities. Even though these proposals did not meet their five demands, the prisoners had expressed appreciation of the commission's proposals; this sounded hopeful.

Immediately before the Dáil reassembled Charles Haughey had called in the British Ambassador and had issued a statement saying that the time to find a solution to prevent further deaths was now. The British government had responded to this with a long statement saying that there was scope for development in the prison regime but that this process of improvement could not proceed further under the duress of a hunger-strike.

The IRA reaction, allegedly on behalf of the prisoners, had been to describe this response as 'arrogant'. Nevertheless the Commission for Justice and Peace saw the British statement as encouraging—as did we—and sought further clarification. Our information from the prison was that, despite the IRA statement purporting to speak for them, the prisoners wanted the commission to continue its involvement. We were also aware that the relatives of the prisoners on hunger-strike were becoming increasingly restive at the IRA's intransigent approach.

On 1 July Michael O'Leary and I communicated our view on these points to the British Ambassador and urged that the NIO meet the commission again and allow the commission to meet the prisoners. We also warned against any policy of brinkmanship, which—especially in view of the nearness to death of one hunger-striker, Joe McDonnell—could harden attitudes, including in particular the attitudes of the relatives, who had the power to influence developments. That night I rang Margaret Thatcher to make these points directly to her.

At this point the relatives of the hunger-strikers asked to see me. Despite the fact that I believe it generally undesirable in an issue of this kind to become involved in potentially emotional situations with the relatives of those concerned, I agreed to see them, in view of their crucial role and the fact that almost all of them were known to want a settlement—as indeed, it seemed, did most of the prisoners at that point. This meeting on 3 July was, as I had expected, intensely distressing, but it enabled me to see for myself that while there were those among them who took a straight IRA line, most of them were indeed primarily concerned to end the hunger-strike.

Both that day and the next the Minister of State at the NIO, Michael Allison, met the commission again. He gave the impression that he wanted to be more conciliatory, but referred to 'the lady behind the veil', namely the Prime Minister. As we had proposed, he cleared a visit by the Commission for Justice and Peace to the prisoners, who then issued a statement that, as we had thought likely, was much more conciliatory than the one published by the IRA on their behalf three days earlier. They said they were *not* looking for any special privileges as against other prisoners, and that the British government could meet their requirements without any sacrifice of principle. It looked as if the commission would now be able to resolve the dispute with Michael Allison, who seemed close to accepting their proposals.

Several days were to elapse before we learnt what happened next. Following the conciliatory statement by the prisoners, direct contact had been made with the IRA by an agent of the British government, through an intermediary. Disastrously, his proposals, while close to what the prisoners and Allison, through the commission, were near to agreeing, went further in one respect. Not unnaturally the IRA preferred this somewhat wider offer, and above all the opportunity to be directly involved in discussions with the British government. They were then allowed by the British authorities to send Danny Morrison secretly into the prison for discussions with the hunger-strikers and with the IRA leader there, Brendan McFarlane. This visit was later described by the IRA as a test of the authority of the British government representative in touch with them to bypass the NIO.

The commission, unaware of all this, was preparing its document, which was to be the basis for an agreement involving the ending of the hunger-strike. On Monday 6 July at 3.30 p.m., according to the account given to me shortly after these events, Gerry Adams phoned the commission seeking a meeting, revealing that the British government had made contact with him. An hour and a half later two members of the commission met Adams and Morrison, who told them that this contact was 'London-based' and had been in touch with them 'last time round', i.e. during the 1980 hunger-strike. Adams demanded that the commission phone the NIO to cancel their meeting.

Members of the commission, furious at this development, then met Allison and four of his officials. They asked him if he had been in communication with the hunger-strikers or with those with authority over them. He said that no member of his office had been in contact, and, when pressed, repeated this line. They then discussed the Commission's own proposals.

When the commission contacted us immediately after this meeting they told us nothing about the London contact with Adams and Morrison—understandably, given that this was a telephone call—which in any event still did not loom large in their eyes at that point beside the agreement they believed they had reached, which indeed seemed to them to have settled the dispute and to be about to end the hunger-strike. The commission had produced to Allison the statement on which they had been working, which they described as 'a true summary of the essential points of prison reform that had emerged.' They told Allison that this statement was considered by the hunger-strikers to be 'the formation [*sic*] of a resolution of the hunger strike,' provided that they received 'satisfactory clarification of detail and confirmation by an NIO official to the prisoners personally of the commitment of the British Government to act according to the spirit and the letter' of the statement. Although there was a difference of opinion on whether certain of the concessions were 'illustrative' or not, this does not seem to have been a problem for the British at the time, since Allison went out to make a phone call and then came back to say that he had approval. He proposed that an NIO official would see the prisoners with the governor by mid-morning the following day, Tuesday. When we received this information Dermot Nally phoned the British Ambassador to urge that this confirmatory visit take place as soon as possible.

Late that night, however, the commission was phoned by Danny Morrison seeking a meeting, which they refused; but half an hour later he arrived at the hotel, saying that the Sinn Féin-IRA contacts with the British were continuing through the night and that he needed to see the actual commission proposals. This request was refused, although he was given the general gist of them.

Twelve hours later, on Tuesday afternoon, Gerry Adams rang to say that the British had now made an offer but that it was not enough. Three members of the commission then met Adams and Morrison, who produced their version of the offer that they said had been made to them. The commission saw this as almost a replica of their own proposals but with an additional provision about access to Open University courses.

Meanwhile the commission had spent an agonising day, for while London had been negotiating with the IRA, Allison and the NIO had prevaricated about the prison visit, repeatedly promising that the official was about to go to the prison. But at ten o'clock that night Allison phoned to say that the official would not now be going to the prison until the following morning—adding, however, that this delay would be to the prisoners' benefit.

At 8.30 p.m., however, Morrison and a companion had come without warning to the hotel where the commission had its base. Their attitude was threatening. Morrison said their contact had been put in jeopardy as a result of the commission revealing its existence at its meeting with Allison; the officials present with Allison had not known of the contact. Despite this onslaught the commission refused to keep Morrison informed of their actions.

Just before 5.00 a.m. that night Joe McDonnell died. At 6.30 the governor, in the presence of an NIO official, read a statement to the prisoners that differed markedly from the one prepared by the commission and, in their view, approved by Allison thirty-six hours earlier. Fifteen minutes later Adams rang the commission to say that at 5.30 a.m. the contact with London had been terminated without explanation.

When we heard the news of Joe McDonnell's death and of the last-minute hardening of the British position we were shattered. We had been quite unprepared for this volte-face, for we, of course, had known nothing whatever of the disastrous British approach to Adams and Morrison. Nor had we known of the IRA's attempts—regardless of the threat this posed to the lives of the prisoners, and especially to that of Joe McDonnell—to raise the ante by seeking concessions beyond what the prisoners had said they could accept. We had believed that the IRA had been in effect bypassed by the commission's direct contact with the prisoners at the weekend, which we had helped to arrange.

That afternoon the Commission for Justice and Peace issued a statement setting out the discussions they had had with Allison leading to the agreement reached on Monday evening. I then issued a statement recalling that I had repeatedly said that a solution could be reached through a flexibility of approach that need not sacrifice any principle. While the onus to show this flexibility rested with both sides, the greater responsibility must, as always, rest on those with the greater power.

I have given a full account of these events (some of them unknown to us at the time they took place) because in retrospect I think that the shock of learning that a solution seemed to have been sabotaged by yet another and, as it seemed to us, astonishingly ham-fisted approach on behalf of the British government to the IRA influenced the extent and intensity of the efforts I deployed in the weeks that followed, in the hope—vain, as it turned out—of bringing that government back to the point it had apparently reached on Monday 6 July.

During these weeks in July and early August I may also have been influenced more than I realised at the time by the frustration I felt at having to deal thereafter with the British government while I had, in a sense, one hand tied behind my back. For I would naturally have liked to confront them with—and would have liked even more to be able to make public—my knowledge of the furtive contacts on their behalf with the IRA, which seemed to have proved fatal to the resolution of the problem. But careful reflection led me to conclude that any revelation to the British of our knowledge of these activities would be likely to render a solution *less* rather than *more* likely. Disclosure of this knowledge could have driven the British government, and the Prime Minister in particular, into a state of embarrassed intransigence. This might have been accompanied by denials, which—if we had refused to accept them, as in honesty we would have had to do—would have made impossible the development of any kind of reasonable relationship between that government and ourselves. The fact moreover that our information, while absolutely convincing in its detail, was necessarily second-hand (it was what a member of the commission told us Adams and Morrison had said to them) reinforced the need for caution.

My frustration became all the more intense when a week later the IRA, with which an organ of the British government had chosen to deal behind our backs, launched a demonstration on our streets that threatened public order in our own state. Foreseeing the emergence of such a threat, I had written on 10 July to Margaret Thatcher telling her that a rising tide of sympathy for the hunger-strikers was threatening the stability of the Republic and that we were convinced by the account of the Commission for Justice and Peace of what had transpired in regard to a settlement at its meeting with Allison on Monday.

I urged her, in order to avoid a serious and progressive deterioration in bilateral relations, to accept as the foundation of a solution the detailed description of a possible future prison regime set out by the commission; and I added that the ending of the hunger-strike would deprive the IRA of its most potent weapon and would restore a climate in which our efforts could again be directed to more positive and constructive endeavours in pursuance of the process initiated by her and my predecessor in December 1980, to the continuance of which I attached great importance.

Simultaneously Jim Dooge, accompanied by John Kelly, who was for the moment formally acting as Minister for Foreign Affairs, met Humphrey Atkins and Ian Gilmour for two hours in London. I was interested in Atkins's explanation of the delay of almost twenty hours in sending an official to the prison on 7–8 July. Allison, he said, was a first-class Minister but had not sufficient authority to take the final decisions in such matters, which rested on the Secretary of State 'and on my colleagues'. He himself had had to be in London, and the difficulties of communication could not, he said, have been overcome more quickly.

The report of this meeting recorded that the Irish Ministers had been 'insistent and frank', and described the British as 'non-committal and defensive' but possibly shaken by the intensity of the discussion and by the extent of the information at our disposal—even though, of course, the British did not know that by now we knew of their contacts with the IRA.

Three days later, after the death of a further hunger-striker, Martin Hurson, on Monday 13 July, I issued a statement calling on the British government to respond to the arguments put forward by our Ministers in London.

During a telephone conversation with John Hume on the following Friday, Atkins told him that as a result of my letter to the Prime Minister and the Ministerial meeting in London 'the whole matter is under reconsideration,' a remark that temporarily raised our hopes. Nevertheless it seemed desirable to exert whatever pressure we could at this crucial point. Accordingly I wrote to President Reagan to ask him, in view of the increased support accruing to the IRA as a result of the situation, which was threatening our security, to use his influence with the British Prime Minister to secure the implementation of what I described as 'an already existing understanding' mediated by the Commission for Justice and Peace. Our Ambassador, Seán Donlon, had the opportunity of discussing Northern Ireland directly with the President for almost an hour when seated beside him at dinner in the Irish embassy that evening. The President wanted to know 'what we could do' to help resolve the Northern Ireland problem, but, Seán Donlon reported, he did not show a great deal of close understanding of the problem, which he seemed to think would be eased if church leaders on both sides would only co-operate more closely and if eastern European interests ceased their machinations. This was too much for Seán, who told him bluntly but courteously that the problem was being aggravated by unhelpful activities in the United States rather than by anyone in eastern Europe.

Arising from my letter about the hunger-strike, the President said to Seán that several days previously he had conveyed to Margaret Thatcher the concern of Tip O'Neill and Ted Kennedy in relation to the matter—which would not, I felt, have had much impact on her if, as seemed to be the case, he had not indicated that he himself shared this concern. He added, not very encouragingly, that he had a difficulty as he did not wish to aid prisoners detained for terrorism. He did not, however, rule out an intervention on his part.

Seán was not very encouraged by his contacts that day with the White House 'triumvirate'. Mike Deaver, to whom he handed my message, was not negative, but said the issue was problematic because it involved prisoners' rights. Jim Baker remarked that they were considering how to deal with queries, especially from the British press, about my letter. Later, at a reception that preceded the dinner at which he had his discussion with the President, Ed Meese took Seán Donlon aside for forty minutes to discuss my letter. Meese had been Reagan's head of correctional facilities during his Governorship of California, and Seán found this discussion less useful than those with Deaver and Baker.

Seán's easy access to the key policy-makers, and informally to the President, which many far larger countries would envy, reflected the extraordinary success of our diplomatic efforts in Washington during the previous five years. On this occasion, however, we were asking the Americans to jeopardise their relationship with Britain on an issue they did not fully understand and on which, because convicted terrorists were concerned, they were not instinctively sympathetic.

Meanwhile on 15 July I had finally received Margaret Thatcher's reply to my letter. She repudiated any suggestion of bad faith on the British side in relation to the account given by the Commission for Justice and Peace of their meeting with Michael Allison on Monday 8 July, and asked me to accept that he, and through him the British government, had acted honourably throughout. She went on to say that the commission had 'over-estimated the possibility of persuading the hunger strikers to accept the Commission's compromise proposals.' (The only evidence produced for this statement was not anything the prisoners had said at the time but the latest IRA statement issued in their name after the breakdown of the talks.) And, responding to remarks in my letter about the problems of ensuring security co-operation in these circumstances, she remarked that the British reaction to any suggestion of less than full co-operation in security matters would be 'sharp and bitter'. But she added that the British government was taking up an offer by the International Red Cross to visit and report on prisons in Northern Ireland.

Three days later the IRA-dominated H-Block Committee organised a demonstration and march to the British embassy in Dublin. There were five thousand people in the march, many of them from Northern Ireland. They repeatedly attacked gardaí along the route with stones, and many carried pick-axe handles. In Ballsbridge five hundred of the two thousand gardaí on duty were deployed behind barriers blocking the main road leading to the embassy.

A delegation was allowed through, three of whom forced their way into the embassy when the door was opened to receive their letter of protest, and were later removed by gardaí. Meanwhile the main body of marchers charged the barriers behind which the gardaí were massed, hurling missiles at them, and using eight-foot poles as lances. The ringleaders from Northern Ireland, experienced in such riots, shouted orders to aim for the gardaí's legs, which were unprotected by their short shields. In several cases gardaí's trousers were set on fire. For twenty-five minutes the gardaí sustained this assault without responding, suffering over a hundred injuries requiring hospital treatment. At one point the line nearly broke under this sustained assault. Fortunately it held; for if the mob had swept through and on to the embassy they would eventually have faced the last line of defence, a unit of the army. That was a confrontation we were most anxious to avoid. Eventually the gardaí moved to disperse the mob with a baton charge. Within five minutes the demonstration was over; but on their way back to the city the marchers broke scores of windows and stoned gardaí along the route. Houses near the scene of the riot suffered severely, many of them having been ransacked for missiles to throw at the gardaí. On the following day Joan, on her own initiative, visited the area to sympathise with the occupants.

These events were reviewed by the Government during the following week. Although naturally concerned about the possible consequences of a conflict between soldiers and the mob, we eventually concluded that we had no choice but to maintain an army presence at the embassy, for a further march was threatened for the following Saturday. However, on my suggestion arrangements were made to take pressure off the gardaí manning the barrier by having a second group available to take the mob in the flank and rear on the next occasion. This tactic proved successful; the second march was in any event on a much smaller scale.

Meanwhile relations between the British government and ourselves became more tense, especially when Margaret Thatcher in a letter to the 'Four Horsemen' in the United States (Speaker Tip O'Neill, Senators Ted Kennedy and Pat Moynihan, and Governor Hugh Carey) misrepresented our position by suggesting that we were in agreement with the latest British handling of the prison situation. She based this on a press report, the inaccuracy of which we had specifically drawn to the attention of the British government two days earlier. Something approaching an apology, to the effect that the Prime Minister had been 'entirely unaware' that she was in any way misrepresenting our position and that she recognised that there were 'differences of appreciation' between us, was received at the end of the month. Privately we had already learnt from the British Ambassador that the letter to the 'Four Horsemen' had been drafted by the Northern Ireland Office without the knowledge of the Foreign Office, which would certainly have omitted the misstatement of our position.

By this time it was clear that there was considerable anxiety in London at official level about the unfortunate turn Anglo-Irish relations had taken as a result of the way the hunger-strike had been handled; and a meeting between the two cabinet secretaries, Dermot Nally and Sir Robert Armstrong, helped to ensure that despite the tensions thus created work continued to go ahead in preparation for the meeting between Margaret Thatcher and myself that must take place in due course when the hunger-strike ended.

Towards the end of July one of the hunger-strikers was taken off his fast by his mother when he became unconscious. This has been described as 'with hindsight . . . the beginning of the end,' although four more were to die in the first three weeks of August. My meetings with the relatives came to an end on 6 August when some of them attempted to 'sit in' in the Government ante-room, where I had met them on such occasions, after a stormy discussion during which I had once again refused to take the kind of action some of them had been pressing on me.

The period of intensive diplomatic activity ended around this time. In less than six weeks there had been no fewer than twenty-five exchanges between the Irish and British governments, fifteen of them at Prime Minister or Ministerial level. There was simply nothing to be gained by pressing the British government any further; we should just have to live with the consequences of the way they had handled the situation, although clearly it would take years rather than months for the ground thus lost to the IRA by the SDLP and ourselves to be recovered.

The hunger-strike ended on 3 October, after the new Secretary of State, Jim Prior, had visited the prison and when those still fasting realised that their relatives would, as in an earlier case, intervene to save their lives when they reached the stage of unconsciousness.

By early August I had in fact come under increasing pressure from a number of sources to wind down the confrontation with the British government. In the light of hindsight this note of caution had some justification. However, given the damage done by the continuation of the hunger-strike—and, I have to add, the human tragedy of these deaths, which I felt deeply despite my abhorrence of the violence these men had been involved in before being sent to jail—I was happier to have done too much rather than too little in attempting to bring it to an end, with whatever lack of success. Moreover, the scale of the efforts made on our side may in some degree have modified the potentially destabilising impact of this whole episode on domestic opinion, which would certainly have been aggravated had we shown a lack of compassion and concern.

I convened a Northern Ireland review conference in Iveagh House on 24 and 25 August, to be attended by Michael O'Leary, Jim Dooge, Peter Sutherland, Alexis FitzGerald, Dermot Nally, our Ambassadors in London and Washington, our Permanent Representative at the United Nations, and relevant officials from my department and Foreign Affairs.

After two days of discussion it was decided amongst other things to give priority to developing our contacts with leading Unionists, including if at all possible Ian Paisley, with a view to seeing how they could, for example, be involved in structures flowing from the joint studies process. I had always felt that a solution to the Northern Ireland problem should be sought primarily in conjunction with the constitutional political parties in the North rather than through the British government. I was later to come to the view that if failure to make progress with the Unionists threatened the viability of constitutional nationalism in the North this policy orientation could not be indefinitely sustained in the absence of a response from them; but in August 1981, when the impact of the still-continuing hunger-strike on the balance of forces within Northern nationalism was not yet fully evident, I was not ready to make this jump.

At this conference we were all very conscious of the threat to the stability of our state posed by a paramilitary organisation like the IRA that contested the state's legitimacy. Moreover, although the IRA did not recognise our Constitution, the provisions in that Constitution that were interpreted as involving a claim to the territory of Northern Ireland (articles 2 and 3) seemed unhelpful to the cause of peace and stability in Ireland. I welcomed therefore the support that emerged at this conference for a review of the Constitution by the Attorney General.

Of course in relation to any constitutional changes there would always be problems about timing, as the report on our discussions recorded. Those present at this conference recognised that, bearing in mind the thrust of the legislative changes introduced in our state since 1922, which had tended to encourage the perpetuation of partition, it was not certain that our people actually *wanted* a non-sectarian state. What appeared to us to be desirable might not, it was felt, necessarily be politically feasible. For if a constitutional initiative were undertaken on articles 2 and 3 and failed, the existing situation might be considerably worsened; and a successful constitutional change without a bipartisan approach—of which there was little prospect—would be very difficult. Only with proper attention to timing, the elaboration of a package and the vigorous selling of that package to the people could significant progress be made.

Nevertheless, in the light of the gravity of the situation in Northern Ireland it was agreed that the matter should be seriously considered forthwith. And it was felt that if the approach to constitutional change were broad enough, involving the development of a more pluralist society in our state, we could perhaps capture and then hold the republican ground that the IRA had attempted to usurp.

The conclusions of this conference were presented to the Government in a memorandum a month later. Meanwhile I had been reflecting on how best to launch such a constitutional initiative with any prospect of success. I was sceptical of securing support for, or acquiescence in, such a move from the leader of the opposition. It was already clear that he had a preference for opportunist rather than constructive opposition; also, given his insecurity within his own party, where he was relying for support primarily on 'hawkish' elements with a penchant for extreme nationalist rhetoric, he was most unlikely to feel able to, or perhaps even want to, support the kind of initiative we were contemplating. That being so, our best hope might be to launch our ideas for constitutional reform unilaterally—but in an imaginative way that might bypass the party political process.

While I was mulling over how best to make this move I gave an interview to the *Cork Examiner*, in the course of which I was asked questions about the Constitution. I agreed that articles 2 and 3 were unhelpful, as were some other articles that, originating in the 1930s, seemed to me to be sectarian in character. Two days later Peter Sutherland, speaking as Attorney General to a group of Irish-American lawyers and later on radio, referred to the Constitution's many merits but also made reference to articles that might not appeal to all Irish people and might usefully be looked at again.

In subsequent interviews George Colley was disappointingly negative, and Brian Lenihan was hostile; indeed he ended his comments by announcing that Fianna Fáil would 'lead a crusade against the abolition or modification of these articles.' He went on: 'We will get support from nationally minded people of this country, and we will win.'

These exchanges were discussed at an off-the-record luncheon I held with political correspondents. Listening to them I became convinced that now the debate had started it must at once be given a strong lead if it was not to be snuffed out immediately by Fianna Fáil intransigence. If that party was going back on what it had joined in advocating fourteen years earlier in the report of the 1967 Constitutional Commission, clearly we had to go on our own in proposing an even more fundamental reappraisal of the Constitution in the interest of peace in Ireland and the removal of obstacles to Irish unity.

At this point I was asked to undertake a Sunday radio interview on our first three months in power. It struck me that this would provide an opportunity to present the case for constitutional change directly to the people, in a far more effective way than would be possible through press reports of a Dáil debate or even in a necessarily static and formal Ministerial broadcast. This, of course, had its drawbacks too: in an interview it would not be possible to choose my words with deliberation, and I would have to respond to whatever questions my remarks might evoke. But I would at least be able to present my views with the enthusiasm I felt and to convey the force of my commitment to a different kind of Ireland from that in which I had grown up.

Accordingly, before going on the air I told the interviewer, Gerry Barry, that if he gave me an appropriate opening I would have something significant to say on this subject. As a result, two-thirds of the way through a long interview, after extensive questioning on the economy, our tax reform plans, and the H-Block hunger-strike, Barry asked me about constitutional reform. In reply I said that one of the things that had brought me into politics had been the fact that our state as it had evolved over the decades was not the non-sectarian state that the national movement for independence had sought to establish, one in which Catholic, Protestant and Dissenter would feel equally at home; it had rather become a state imbued with the ethos of the majority in our part of the island. Initially partitioned by the British, our island had been further partitioned by constitutions and laws alien to the whole people of Ireland. With my family background—my mother from a Northern Presbyterian family, my father a Southern Catholic—I could not accept this.

Challenged by the interviewer on how I was going to put these matters to the test, I picked up a phrase used by Brian Lenihan two days earlier, turning it around the other way: 'What I want to do, if I may, is to take a phrase from somebody the other night on television: I want to lead a crusade, a republican crusade to make this a genuine republic.' If I could do that, I went on to say, 'I believe we would have a basis on which many Protestants in the North would be willing to consider a relationship with us. If I were a Northern Protestant today, I cannot see how I could be attracted to getting involved with a state that is itself sectarian—not in the acutely sectarian way that Northern Ireland was . . . [but] the fact is our laws and our Constitution, our practices, our attitudes reflect those of a majority ethos and are not acceptable to Protestants in Northern Ireland.'

I was not going to rush into a referendum, I went on to say, but I would try to lead our people towards the objective of a pluralist society, and if I felt there was sufficient support and that a referendum might be successful, not just on articles 2 and 3 but on a Constitution, I would do so. I did not know whether I could succeed or not, and if eventually it transpired that the Irish people did not want such a state but wanted to remain a 26-county state with a majority ethos, I would accept defeat and leave politics if necessary.

I have no doubt that many of my colleagues in Government felt that my broadcast was more quixotic than wise, although in general they were too polite to say so. What was remarkable, however, was the surge of enthusiasm this interview evoked among a large section of Irish people—almost certainly still a minority, but a large one. For the first time this section of our people found inspiration in a political credo that responded to their deeply felt frustration at the narrow and exclusive rhetoric with which politicians who addressed the issue of nationalism had traditionally presented their views.

The hackneyed argument—beloved particularly of the political left—that Fianna Fáil and Fine Gael were indistinguishable, overnight lost all its force as Fianna Fáil flatly rejected my concept in language hallowed by decades of traditional rhetoric—as, incidentally, did Ian Paisley in the North. My remarks had caused 'deep dismay among all those of us in every part of Ireland who cherish the ideal of unity,' said Charles Haughey. 'The Unionist people are not going to be fooled by that,' said Paisley. I had 'presented the enemies of unity with a gold mine of propaganda,' said Haughey. I had not got 'a pup's chance of succeeding,' said Paisley.

According to Fianna Fáil it would be a waste of time to talk about changing the Constitution so as to make it acceptable to unionists. The views of unionists should be taken into account, but not to the exclusion of the view of the 'vast majority of the people of Ireland'; a reflection of a Catholic ethos in our legislation was 'quite natural and what you would expect'; this was a 'red herring' debate, designed to get away from the economic issues—as if we had any interest in distracting people from the disastrous economic situation that Fianna Fáil had left behind them.

But this partitionist rhetoric was for the moment at least almost drowned out in the media by the vocal response of those who agreed with me—not on a party political basis but from a much broader spectrum of society in the state, from the Church of Ireland, and in Northern Ireland from spokesmen for the SDLP and the Alliance Party, as well as from Bill Craig. In an effort to belittle the initiative James Molyneaux was reduced to expressing fears that the stability of our state might be threatened by what I had done.

As part of the process of provoking a rethink of traditional Irish nationalism, I had been anxious to face our public opinion with an authentic unionist voice that would challenge the cosy illusions of many Southerners about the possibility of persuading Northern unionists to join one day with the kind of state we had become during sixty years of independence. The problem was that the leaders of the OUP and DUP were clearly unwilling to beard the nationalist lion in his Dublin den; moreover, perhaps because of the political pressures on people in leading positions in Unionist parties, their presentation of the unionist case tended to be couched in terms that carried little credibility with moderate nationalists in the South.

What was needed was a more cerebral expression of the deep-seated convictions of the unionist community. Accordingly I had asked Michael Lillis in early September to go to the North and try to find some person or group who would perform this educational task. He reported success in mid-September, and on 8 October with full publicity a group led by two barristers, Bob McCartney and Peter Smith, presented the unionist case to me in Government Buildings, and later that day to the leader of the opposition.

In their presentation they explained why unionists found objectionable not only articles 2 and 3 of the Constitution but other clauses also. Bob McCartney said that the process of transforming the Republic from something bordering on a theocracy into a pluralist society would be a long and difficult journey, but that if there was to be hope that the two traditions in Ireland might ultimately meet upon the same road then the first steps, however faltering, must now be taken; the alternative to this course was to underwrite partition on a permanent basis. And, they added, Northern Ireland too must emerge from the shackles of its history and assume its own identity.

This presentation of the unionist case in Dublin was helpful to what I was trying to achieve, and I made specific reference to it in the speech I delivered in the Seanad on the following day, in the course of which I set out in detail and in a considered way what I had presented in a necessarily less coherent form on radio ten days earlier. The Seanad proved an effective forum for a debate on the issues I had raised. In my speech there I invoked both Seán

Lemass, who had complained about the straitjacket of the Constitution in relation to the North in particular and had said that it should be changed every twenty-five years, and also Jack Lynch, who had said that we should try to accommodate in the Constitution and in our laws the views of people who legitimately saw aspects of the Constitution as infringements of their civil rights and as giving offence to their liberty of conscience. But the Fianna Fáil senators, or to be precise the small number who spoke, had had their marching orders from Lemass's successor, Charles Haughey, and, albeit with evident discomfort, they stuck to their brief. From the Government and independent benches there came strong support, however.

Following this debate the Government asked the Attorney General, Peter Sutherland, to undertake a review of the Constitution, a task that, with the aid of an expert committee, we thought might take about six months. That process was of course terminated when the Government changed following our defeat on the budget three months later.

When my second Government was formed, in December 1982, this process could have been restarted, but I chose to give priority at that time to the establishment of the New Ireland Forum as a prelude to the negotiation of an agreement on Northern Ireland with the British government. The success of the Forum depended on co-operation by Fianna Fáil, which would clearly not have been forthcoming if I had pursued a general constitutional reform against their bitter opposition. And the best being the enemy of the good, I had to set aside the broader objective for the time being, although in certain circumstances it might prove possible to tackle articles 2 and 3 as part of my new approach, and later on in Government to hold a referendum on divorce. But by the time the fruits of the Forum's work emerged, in the form of the Anglo-Irish Agreement in November 1985—fourteen months later than I had hoped at the outset—it was too late in the life of our Government to restart a general constitutional review process, and in any event the sharp swing to the right in religious as well as political affairs that had marked the first half of the 1980s had created an environment that was much more hostile than that of 1981 to the refashioning of the Constitution on pluralist lines.

To that extent my constitutional initiative was stillborn. But nevertheless it represents a time-bomb ticking away at the heart of the narrow and exclusive form of Catholic nationalism to which Fianna Fáil traditionally tied its fortunes. Fine Gael, by contrast—together with the Labour Party and the Progressive Democrats—has secured a vantage point on the high ground, for the future certainly lies with those who favour a pluralist society in Ireland. In the struggle yet to be fought to determine a basic Irish philosophy and identity, those who seek to hang on to a divisive form of single-ethos nationalism are ultimately on the losing side. The battle lines were drawn on 27 September 1981, and even though the subsequent uneasy truce may prevail for some time to come, the vision I propounded then is not dead but sleeping.

But to return to the autumn of 1981: I went to some lengths to prepare the ground carefully for my impending summit meeting with Margaret Thatcher. Contacts between Jim Dooge and Peter Carrington as well as between Dermot Nally and Robert Armstrong were undertaken to go over the possible agenda. I had a meeting myself with Robert Armstrong, which marked the beginning of a fruitful relationship with a man for whose ability, diplomatic skill and constructive approach to Anglo-Irish relations and to the Northern Ireland problem I came to have deep respect. In the course of our discussion he said, with reference to the possible involvement of Northern Unionists in future discussions, that the important thing was not to allow whatever was set up to be destroyed, as earlier hopes had been. I responded that that was all very well but I thought it important that representatives of Northern Ireland should be brought into the new Anglo-Irish process from the beginning— without, of course, conferring a right of veto on them.

The new Northern Ireland Secretary, Jim Prior, also came to Dublin, where Michael O'Leary and I had private discussions with him. He gave it as his opinion that the Prime Minister would be influenced by what she believed would have been the attitude of Airey Neave. Echoing the words Airey Neave had used when I had last met him shortly before his murder by the IRA, Prior added, 'She is really a unionist at heart.'

The summit meeting took place in London ten days later, on 6 November. It began with a restricted session confined to Margaret Thatcher, Jim Prior, Michael O'Leary, and myself, with the two cabinet secretaries taking notes. At the outset Margaret Thatcher thanked me for having visited in hospital a member of the Irish Guards who had been injured in an IRA bomb attack. There followed a discussion on current security problems, during which Margaret Thatcher described cross-border co-operation as 'absolutely mar-vellous'. And we went on to discuss the SDLP's stand against the IRA. Margaret Thatcher agreed with me that they were a moderate party in comparison with the Unionists, adding that they were very courageous.

Before leaving with Jim Prior for a separate meeting that he was to chair, Michael O'Leary said that he wanted Margaret Thatcher to know that my constitutional 'crusade' had the full support of the Labour Party. She pursued this theme further, asking among other things whether the word 'secular' should be used to describe the kind of state I was aspiring to. I headed her off this term, which in Ireland has a connotation of excluding religion rather than building on common ground shared by the different denominations, and suggested that 'pluralist' would be a more appropriate description. I defined my objective as achieving a Constitution that would reflect the ethos of all the people of Ireland and remove from the present document its 'confessional aspects'. With regard to articles 2 and 3 I felt that the Constitution should reflect the aspiration to unity but should not express this aspiration in legalistic terms and should declare that the aspiration was to be pursued only by peaceful means.

After the departure of Jim Prior and Michael O'Leary, Margaret Thatcher and I turned to the issue of publishing the joint studies on matters other than security that had been undertaken at civil service level since the Haughey-Thatcher summit meeting of the previous December. This was agreed, although Margaret Thatcher had some qualms—unjustified, as it turned out—about how they would be received by unionist opinion. She made it clear that she still felt bruised by the way the December 1980 summit meeting with my predecessor had been used; she had suffered from 'previous insinuations'—suggestions that all kinds of agreement were being reached behind people's backs—and from the bandying about of the words 'institutional' and 'constitutional'.

I had already discussed with Robert Armstrong the possibility of an Anglo-Irish Council with a parliamentary tier. She felt it important that this should be let come out in the joint studies before taking it further; there was, she said, a danger that by pressing ahead too rapidly with this we could go one step too far and find ourselves taking two steps backwards.

She went on to say that she could not possibly accept a reference in the draft communiqué to the idea of an all-Ireland court—which was particularly attractive to us—because she had not discussed this with the Lord Chancellor. When it was pointed out that possible advantages had been seen in this proposal in the 1974 report signed by, among others, the Lord Chief Justice of Northern Ireland she agreed that, as long as we were not proposing that the court be set up now, the Attorneys General would be free to pursue the matter, which in the communiqué was covered by a reference to 'possible new institutional structures' and to 'further improvements' in the legislation with respect to fugitive offenders to be considered by the Attorneys General.

When we resumed in plenary session after lunch the Prime Minister recorded an agreement during the tete-à-tete to the name 'Anglo-Irish Intergovernmental Council' for the body that had been envisaged in the joint studies, and to the publication of these studies.

There ensued a long argument on the issue of a possible reference in the communiqué to the British government 'supporting' Irish unity if a majority in Northern Ireland were to give their consent to it. Margaret Thatcher argued against this and in favour of the word 'accept', on the analogy of her willingness to 'accept' a Labour government if they won an election, although she would not 'support' it. The gap between us on this issue was eventually bridged by the addition of a clause saying that in the event of a Northern Ireland majority accepting Irish unity the British government 'would support legislation in the British Parliament giving effect to it.'

The British Ministers welcomed our decision to extend the franchise at our general elections to British citizens resident in the Republic, and we secured agreement to the next summit meeting taking place in Dublin 'in the Spring of next year'—which, of course, never happened, for reasons beyond my control.

I also secured acceptance of my proposal that a parliamentary tier of the Intergovernmental Council could comprise members drawn from the Irish and

British parliaments, from the European Parliament, and from any elected assembly that might be established in Northern Ireland. The reference to the European Parliament ensured an SDLP presence in this body if it were established before a Northern Ireland assembly came into being, since at that time there was no SDLP member at Westminster. But the Prime Minister's insistence that it would be for the parliaments concerned to consider at an appropriate time whether there should be such a body put the proposal on what in Ireland is called 'the long finger'; although just how long it would be—over eight years—I did not foresee at that time.

It had been a useful meeting. I felt that it had gone a long way towards restoring a relationship that had suffered severely from the manner in which the previous summit meeting had been presented on the Irish side, and from the tensions created by the hunger-strike.

The Anglo-Irish Council announced by the summit meeting was formally established at an official-level meeting in Dublin on 20 January 1982, which agreed a memorandum of understanding. During this meeting difficulties of co-ordination on the British side, due to the different roles of the Foreign Office and the Northern Ireland Office, emerged clearly, and our officials accepted that because of these difficulties the cabinet offices should have the co-ordinating role. This development proved of enormous importance for the future development of Anglo-Irish relations. It was also agreed that the Presidency of the Council would alternate between the two states, and that summit meetings would take place once or twice a year. In the event the change of Government shortly afterwards and the subsequent clash over EC sanctions against Argentina in May 1982 prevented this regular pattern of heads of government meetings from becoming established.

A curious feature of this whole affair was that a concept that had originally been envisaged as a price that had to be paid by the Irish Government in order to promote Unionist confidence so as to get a dialogue going with them had subtly been turned on its head, so that at the end of the day the Anglo-Irish Council emerged rather as an Irish achievement at the expense of the Unionists, leading to strong Unionist protests. This arose largely because our media, and indeed the Fianna Fáil opposition, presented the new arrangement not as a concession but as a gain for our Government—one that was, however, seen by some as having been somewhat spoiled by what was held to have been a failure on our part to get immediate action on the parliamentary tier. The SDLP in particular found this inversion of the real situation disturbing.

A month after the summit meeting the British Ambassador expressed to Seán Donlon his concern at what he saw as a weakening of the SDLP, and wondered whether what he saw as a worrying political vacuum might not be filled by Cardinal Ó Fiaich and the Northern members of the Catholic hierarchy! This was not the only time that we detected a curious, and to say the least anachronistic, British concern to elevate the Catholic bishops in Northern Ireland into political representatives of the Northern minority. Seán Donlon pointed out firmly to the Ambassador that both prominent Fianna Fáil spokesmen and myself had quite recently made it clear that the people of our state looked to the SDLP for leadership of the nationalist community in the North; trying to substitute the Cardinal for John Hume would get the British nowhere.

On 18 January we held our second internal Northern Ireland policy review conference. In a discussion on security it was suggested that the High Court decisions against extradition of people charged with what were described as political offences might perhaps be usefully challenged in the Supreme Court. This was in fact subsequently done by Peter Sutherland, and as a result the blockage that had held up extradition of such people was in effect removed in the early 1980s. This facilitated extradition in political cases for the remainder of the decade, until at the end of the 1980s what seemed to be a shift in the Supreme Court's attitude made extradition once again more difficult in some instances.

At this meeting Peter Sutherland also developed his concept of a joint court with a common judicial membership North and South, proposing that it operate as a Special Criminal Court in each jurisdiction—an arrangement that would get over constitutional obstacles to an all-Ireland court. He had already had a preliminary technical discussion with his English opposite number on this matter.

The meeting then turned to matters of interest to Northern nationalists that might be brought up through the Anglo-Irish Intergovernmental Council, including human rights issues, cultural matters, support for Northern Ireland interests in the EC and elsewhere, and cross-border security. A border security zone, an idea that the British were prone to put forward from time to time, was dismissed; apart from any other consideration it was seen as merely creating two borders for the IRA to escape across instead of one. On the constitutional review I made it clear that I would like to have the committee's report by October.

Jim Dooge met Jim Prior and Lord Gowrie, then a Minister in the Northern Ireland Office, in London on 29 January, the first Ministerial meeting of the Intergovernmental Council, which took place in the immediate shadow of the general election called after our defeat on the budget. While that election campaign was in progress we heard from the parties in Northern Ireland—SDLP, Alliance, and official Unionists—about the discussions they were having with Jim Prior on an impending British initiative in relation to devolved government. These reports suggested that Prior had dropped strong hints, in the form of an apparent afterthought at the end of the discussions, that he might be thinking of establishing an 'unboycottable' Executive drawn from both sections of the community and separate from the proposed Assembly—on the American model of separation of powers. This idea seemed interesting and, lest he drop it prematurely and follow more traditional lines, I asked Jim Dooge to suggest that no decision be taken until our Government, or another elected in its place, had a chance to make its views known. That, I think, was the last communication at official level between my first administration and the British government. Most regrettably, in my view, this concept of devolution did not feature in the proposals the British government later published, or thereafter.

I must now return to the domestic scene after the supplementary budget of 21 July 1981. I had been determined to expedite work on our 'Programme for Government', and accordingly I prepared personally some scores of queries to Ministers about action to be taken in relation to these issues. These queries were sent out from my office on 14 August, with a request for replies by 15 September. On 9 September I dispatched follow-up letters reminding them of these queries and explaining that I wanted six or eight reforming Bills ready to be taken in the Seanad in early October, before the Dáil resumed; this, I hoped, would establish our identity as a reforming Government. Such a flow of legislation would also, I felt, give the Seanad a higher profile, for its debates are much more fully reported when the Dáil is not in session, and this would provide an opportunity for our new Seanad members, many of them people of ability, to display their talents.

In the event only one reforming measure was ready in time, and even this was not enacted before our Government fell: a Bill to abolish capital punishment in those instances in which it still applied in theory, namely the murder of a policeman or a prison officer or of a foreign head of state. The slow emergence of legislation from the administrative system proved to be a problem for this and subsequent Governments. This hold-up occurs at several levels. First of all, despite the substantial size of the civil service (which was, however, fairly drastically cut in the 1980s), far too few civil servants are actually available to draft legislation. At one stage I asked in desperation for a list of all departmental civil servants with legal qualifications, and I received 120 names. But for one reason or another almost none of those who were engaged on duties other than the preparation of legislation seemed to be both available for this work at departmental level and capable of doing it, so this trawl produced no result. Secondly, both in the Parliamentary Draftsman's office and in the Attorney General's office there was a severe shortage of staff, causing a further bottleneck; remedying this proved extremely difficult in view of the embargo on recruitment that we had imposed as part of the July measures, any breach of which in one area would have provoked an avalanche of pressure for additional posts in many other departments.

I have to add that, especially in the early period in Government, we also suffered from a marked reluctance on the part of some civil servants to contemplate changes in existing policies, about which they had become very defensive, and from a tempo of activity at administrative level very far removed from that of a businessman or a politician. I had an inkling of the slow reaction some Ministers were likely to experience from their civil servants in responding to my requests for speedy action when I read the note from my private office to the Secretary of my department accompanying my batch of September letters: 'I don't think we can attribute too much importance to these letters,' he wrote, 'and the real difficulty that I would see is in convincing various Departments as to just how important they are.'

The replies I received from Ministers usually enclosed copies of the notes submitted by their officials. Some of them were revealing; I cite one instance.

Among the issues I had raised was the possibility of a sliding scale for state funding of the purchase of sites for primary schools in order to give a free choice of type of school to local communities. A problem in this connection was that, while the churches were able to draw on their general resources to finance the purchase of sites on which the state would build new de facto denominational schools for them, parents seeking to establish a multi-denominational or non-denominational school from scratch had no such resources, and as a result such projects often fell at this very first hurdle. The civil servant who dealt with this query of mine concluded her recital of all the obstacles in the way of the establishment of such schools with this acid comment: 'All in all the establishment of schools outside the denominational structure could give rise to many problems and *I* [my emphasis] see no good reason for giving the promoters special encouragement over and above the normal grants for the provision of school buildings'! It was easy to see who she thought should decide public policy, and it certainly was not the elected Government.

My concern to remedy the long delays experienced by patients at hospital clinics evoked a similarly discouraging civil service response: 'This system seems to work satisfactorily,' I was told, in defiance of the accumulated knowledge of practising politicians. As for extending the clinic hours in order to convenience patients, 'the workers' unions might not be favourable to a situation in which their members would have to work what they would consider to be unsocial hours.'

In fairness, negative reactions of the kind mentioned above were the exceptions. A more common cause of delay in implementing the Government's decisions was the genuine need to overcome various constitutional problems and the need to consult various interested parties before proceeding—a process, however, that can involve very long delays if any of those concerned drag their feet. In many cases there were of course also problems of cost, which were difficult to overcome at a time when we were having to cut spending in so many areas; and of course in some cases genuine and convincing arguments were put forward in favour of the view that the advantages in a particular policy change that we had seen when in opposition would be outweighed by disadvantages to which we had not sufficiently adverted.

Despite all these reasons, good and bad alike, for not carrying through parts of our programme or for delays in implementing it, during the brief seven months from June 1981 to January 1982 we made a good deal of progress outside the legislative area.

A major initiative that was pushed through speedily was the establishment of the Youth Employment Agency, with representatives of young people on its board and with substantial finance deriving from a new 1 per cent levy on incomes supplemented by EC aid from the Social Fund. In the years thereafter the training and work experience programmes thus initiated cushioned for many young people the impact of the deflation of the economy that we were forced to carry through. Relative to Ireland's size, this youth programme was one of the most extensive in Europe.

Another important initiative was the introduction of a new system of mortgages for people on low incomes seeking to buy a house, with repayments based on a fixed percentage of income through the life of the mortgage. This type of finance, provided by a Housing Finance Agency that I had been planning personally in opposition, gave the purchasers security against the impact of oscillations in interest rates.

A Combat Poverty Agency was also established; and in the field of education a Curriculum and Examinations Board was set up informally to start the process of making these aspects of second-level education independent of the Department of Education. This was done despite the shocked—and revealing—comment by the department that this would raise the question of what say the Minister would have in regard to what was or was not to be done in the schools.

Another significant reform we introduced during this brief period in Government, one that was inevitably fairly costly, was a radical revision of the higher education grants scheme. Since its introduction in the late 1960s this scheme had been drastically eroded by inflation. In our July budget we increased the income thresholds by half and the grants by two-thirds, thus giving a major new impetus to higher education in the early 1980s. Between 1980 and 1986, despite the economic crisis, enrolments in third-level education rose by 40 per cent.

A further reform we sought to introduce was a radical extension of the hitherto very limited committee system in the Oireachtas. We proposed four new committees, to deal with women's rights, youth affairs, development co-operation, and aspects of marriage breakdown. The Youth Affairs Committee that I proposed was an unusual initiative in that it was to comprise representatives of young people as well as Oireachtas members. The response from the opposition was notably discouraging; Fianna Fáil in Government had tended to be unenthusiastic about enhancing the role of the Oireachtas through an expansion of the committee system, and it seemed that a hope of returning soon to Government was leading them even in opposition to maintain this negative attitude.

I sent details of the proposed terms of reference of these committees to Charles Haughey at the end of November. I received a positive response on the Committee for Development Co-operation, but he announced that his party would not participate in the proposed Committee on Marriage Breakdown, on the grounds that I had pre-empted the work of the committee by saying that I wished divorce to be introduced 'in the lifetime of this Dáil'. I challenged him to verify this statement, which he was unable to do. Instead he announced that he was setting up a committee of his own on this subject.

Having heard nothing from him on the other two committees, I mentioned in a speech in mid-December my intention to set up a committee on women's affairs, and this evoked a response by a Fianna Fáil spokesman to the effect that they would consider participating in such a committee. Eventually in mid-January Charles Haughey agreed to the three committees other than that on marriage breakdown; but the Government fell before they could be established.

In early January 1982 Joan and I took a brief break in the Canary Islands, which came to a sudden end when on the evening of Friday 8 January I heard from home that a heavy snowfall was bringing the country to a standstill. Next morning I rang Michael O'Leary at home. He confirmed that the position was critical; nothing was moving. I suggested that he establish an Emergency Committee to co-ordinate measures to meet the crisis; meanwhile I would try to get home as quickly as possible. Only Shannon Airport was open, but I discovered that the Government jet had actually been diverted there and would be available to collect me on the following day. It could not reach Tenerife, however, and the best solution would thus be for Joan and me to get to some European airport by scheduled service and to pick up the jet there. I discovered that there were seats on a flight to Toulouse the following morning (Sunday), and I arranged that we would rendezvous with the Government aircraft there. From Shannon an Air Corps helicopter flew us to Dublin.

I found that Michael O'Leary had been doing his best to co-ordinate the crisis measures required to deal with the situation. He had not found it easy. His attempt to rally the administrators at Government Buildings on the previous day had evoked a less than enthusiastic response. When he had arrived there—falling on the ice-covered steps, which no-one had attempted to clear—he found no-one there at first except my diplomatic adviser, Michael Lillis, and had not found it easy to persuade others that something more closely co-ordinated was needed than making phone calls from their homes.

Far from receiving any public gratitude for his efforts, his role of crisis co-ordinator brought down on his head the unreasoning resentment of a public that seemed to have lost any appetite for self-help in a crisis of this kind, such as had occurred three times in my lifetime: in 1933, 1947, and 1963. The public expectation seemed to be that 'the Government' would arrive at once to clear not only the roads but also the paths to their houses and the front steps as well. The one moment of light relief during that extraordinary week came when the Secretary of the Department of Health reported that a Dublin prostitute had asked for a delivery of contraceptives by helicopter.

Before coming to the January 1982 budget, on which our Government fell, something should be said of my only direct involvement in European Community affairs during this brief administration.

In the latter part of 1981 the Common Agricultural Policy was coming under increasing pressure within the European Community because of the cost of financing food surpluses, particularly the surplus of milk. I had foreseen this danger during my period as Minister for Foreign Affairs in the mid-1970s, and I had argued fruitlessly in the Ministerial EC Committee of that period against Irish support for excessive increases in Community farm prices, which I saw as damaging to Ireland's long-term agricultural interests. Because farm prices in Ireland had been so low before we joined the Community—a consequence of the impact of Britain's cheap food policy on an agricultural economy that for historical reasons was almost totally dependent on the British market— very substantial farm price increases had to take place in Ireland in any event as part of our adjustment to the Community system, even if the Community farm price level itself did not increase significantly. Rapid increases in Community farm prices were liable not alone to create unsustainable surpluses but also, in conjunction with the accession adjustments to Irish prices, might tempt our farmers into unwise overinvestment, especially in land—as actually happened at the end of the 1970s, with very damaging effects on Irish farmers' finances into the 1980s. But even more important perhaps in the long term was the fact— which I particularly stressed in these committee discussions—that if we pressed for and, with support from some other countries, secured a stabilisation of the Community common price level during this period when our farmers would be benefiting very substantially from the accession price rises, higher-cost Community farmers in countries like Germany would be squeezed out. Then, taking advantage of our comparative cost advantage in climatic terms, our market share, especially in the case of milk, should rise significantly.

These economic arguments had carried little weight with my colleagues, however, as against the political attraction of maximising farm price increases in the short term. It could of course be argued that in any event the stance of a small country such as Ireland on EC farm price levels was unlikely to have been significant. However that might be, by the early 1980s the day of reckoning was approaching. Farm price increases were by then being held well below the high inflation rates of the period after the second oil crisis, and the consequent sharp drop in real farm incomes had led to a collapse of the astronomically high Irish farm land prices of the late 1970s. The depressed state of the industry was being further threatened by intense pressure— from Britain in particular—to cut the high cost of the CAP by restraints on production.

This was one of the major issues discussed at the European Council meeting of 26 and 27 November 1981 in London. I argued against artificial limitations on farm output, pointing out that the share of the Community budget devoted to the CAP had fallen sharply in the course of that year to little more than half the total budget, and that the real income of farmers had dropped. I argued that production targets or quotas were contrary to the market principles of the Community, and I stated our 'total opposition' to a proposed milk superlevy. The Council failed to agree on the agricultural issue, which was remitted back to Ministerial level.

When I returned home I decided that the situation in relation to agriculture was sufficiently threatening to require personal contact with François Mitterrand, the new President of France, the country that was our natural ally on many agricultural issues.

I had met Mitterrand once before, although I did not think he would have remembered the occasion. It was on a beach near Saint-Tropez in August 1976 when Joan and I were on holiday in the Var with friends. As we found our way onto the beach I had seen my French colleague Jean Sauvagnargues and his wife sitting on the beach with another couple; the other man, I thought, looked vaguely familiar. Joan and I went across to them, and Sauvagnargues introduced us to his companions. The vague familiarity was accounted for by the fact that the man was François Mitterrand, leader of the Socialist opposition.

If he had remembered that occasion he would have been singularly unimpressed with my aquatic skills. With two teenage girls in our party I was trying, with notable lack of success, to master the technique of the sailboard; Sauvagnargues, seeing my ineffective efforts, shouted bilingual instructions to me, which I failed to grasp because they depended upon knowing the front of the sailboard from the back. (Incidentally, I often wondered afterwards whether the replacement of Sauvagnargues as Foreign Minister a couple of weeks later had arisen from someone else having seen him on the beach with the leader of the opposition.)

The lunch to which Mitterrand invited me was to be attended by Edith Cresson, his Minister for Agriculture. She arrived somewhat late. While we waited for her, Mitterrand and I found ourselves talking about the Catholic intellectual tradition in France, speculating about why there seemed to have been a gap between the period of Lamennais and Lacordaire in the first half of the nineteenth century and that of my father's friends, Gilson and Maritain, in the twentieth. I learnt later that this random conversation had helped to establish a good relationship between us; on the strength of it he described me to another member of the European Council as '*un homme cultivé*'!

When Edith Cresson arrived we all went in to lunch. Political matters were first on the agenda. Mitterrand spoke of his recent visit to Portugal, and of the real danger of a Soviet take-over that had existed at one stage. In this context there was some discussion of my visit to that country in June 1975 as President of the Council of Ministers, which had helped to stabilise the situation there. We moved on to Poland; Mitterrand felt that Jaruzelski's decision to impose martial law had prevented worse happening, in the form of Soviet intervention. We spoke also about the Middle East, where a current issue was Israel's decision to annex the Golan Heights.

I moved the discussion as soon as possible to agricultural questions in the Community. The main purpose of the visit from my point of view was to convince Mitterrand of the objective merit of the Irish case for the maintenance of Community policies that would enable our farm sector to benefit from its comparative advantage, in dairy products especially. I explained how until we joined the Community Irish agriculture had suffered from the neocolonial relationship of independent Ireland with a Britain that had pursued a cheap food policy since the middle of the nineteenth century. I said that it would take at least twenty-five years for Irish farm production to respond to the opportunities offered by Community membership by reaching the level of output appropriate to its natural advantages, a level that it had been prevented from attaining for well over a century because of the unremunerative prices available in its only market. Artificial restraint on farm production would halt this process, because it would prevent Ireland from securing the benefits of EC membership, for which it had been paying a high price since 1973 in opening its hitherto protected market to EC industrial goods at a cost of some 40 per cent of jobs in traditional industries. We did not of course rule out action to tackle farm surpluses as they arose, but we could not accept a permanent artificial limitation of our agricultural production, as this would destroy the part of the Community achievement that was of most importance to Ireland.

Edith Cresson immediately came in to support my thesis, and Mitterrand asked her to develop her thinking on the matter. This she did with vigour and eloquence, explaining why the interests of France and Ireland were closely aligned on this issue. She criticised American attacks on the Community support system as hypocritical: their butter price, for example, was artificially maintained at 18 per cent above the European level. Under pressure from Mitterrand on the overproduction issue she criticised vehemently both the Commission, whose work she described as 'lamentable' and in many ways anti-Community, and the 'English' Presidency of the Council, under which, she said, other countries' defence of the CAP 'was not even written down.' Under present arrangements the Dutch, Danes and Germans were the main beneficiaries of the CAP—and most German farmers, she said, worked only half-time.

Mitterrand drew this part of the discussion to a close by saying that it was in no-one's interest to wreck the CAP, from which all benefited, but this should not be used to prevent progress on everything. Edith Cresson was clearly unhappy with this response; and when the President left the room for a few minutes after the formal toast to me she turned to me and said, 'You must continue the discussion on agriculture. He does not understand agriculture. The Socialists do not understand agriculture. The government does not understand agriculture.' I had in fact intended to pass on to the subject of Northern Ireland when we moved to the ante-room for coffee, but in the face of this impassioned plea I had no alternative but to revert to agriculture again when the President returned. This led Mitterrand to sum up the French position for me in more detail. France was ready to make concessions—but there were conditions. The UK could not demand '*juste retour*' from the budget—namely to get as much out of it as it put in; the Dutch could not insist on treating their 'milk factories' in the same way as genuine farms; and the problem of Mediterranean products must be treated equitably. This summary did not seem to me to commit France specifically against limitations on production, which we saw as the main danger. When I pressed this point further both the President and Edith Cresson agreed, but they seemed to me more concerned about the issue of the proposed limitation on the proportion of the budget to be spent on the CAP than about the possibility of production limitations.

I had to turn at this stage to the Northern Ireland question, explaining our policy. I said that we saw three essential conditions: any solution must be peaceful; any change in the status of Northern Ireland must be subject to the consent of a majority there, freely given; and it was necessary to try to win the confidence of the unionist majority. The unionists were very suspicious, feeling that the British might leave before a political solution was reached; we were trying to deal with this by constructive contacts with the British government with a view to creating a framework within which the unionists could feel secure, but there had always been problems with the UK, which tended to act insensitively. The situation was potentially dangerous, not only for Ireland but for Europe, and a peaceful solution must be found. Mitterrand asked about the IRA; I replied that their aim—which they tended to expound more freely abroad than at home—was to establish a military dictatorship over the island. But while they had little support in Ireland, as elections and polls demonstrated, they had the capacity to continue the present level of violence almost indefinitely. We hoped that a solution could be found in conjunction with Britain and with the help of our friends abroad, such as France and the United States.

At this point Mitterrand asked me to join him in his office upstairs to continue the discussion *à deux*. During this final half-hour discussion I secured his agreement to the withdrawal of a French objection to the use of Community funds to support housing construction in Northern Ireland. Then and later I was impressed by his calm and self-contained demeanour, the elegance of his style of speech, and the consideration he always showed towards me and towards issues involving Ireland.

A day or two later we received some encouraging feedback from the Élysée about this meeting. The President had been pleased with my 'precise explanations', which had been useful, as information reaching the Élysée was not always of the same immediacy. And there I left the production limitation issue, which, however, I was to face in a more immediate form when I returned to Government a year later.

Much of our time in Government in the closing months of 1981 had necessarily been devoted to the preparation of the January 1982 budget. Further progress had to be made towards reduction of the budget deficit—which we had committed ourselves to eliminate over a four-year period—and towards the reduction of borrowing from the quite unsustainable level we had inherited.

But we were also committed to a radical change in the tax system in the interests of equity. Our proposals at the time of the June elections had envisaged the substitution of tax credits for tax allowances (which I saw as inequitable, because they benefited disproportionately people with larger incomes); the payment of half the tax credit to a spouse working in the home; and, associated with this, an income supplement of up to £500 a year for low-income families. In addition to this we had proposed to reduce the standard tax rate from 35 to 25 per cent (a rate that already existed as a lower tax rate for an initial transfer of income).

The loss of income tax revenue as a result of these radical changes was to be made good by corresponding increases in indirect taxes. Rightly or wrongly, we had reached the conclusion that since 1975, when anti-tax marches had begun to be organised by the trade unions, the high level of income tax on workers had become just as big an incentive to pay claims as price increases had been in the past, and that the substitution of indirect for direct taxes as part of a scheme whose total impact would be progressive would not further increase inflationary pressures. Our programme envisaged that as part of the move towards equity all forms of income would in future be taxed, including short-term social welfare benefits, the exemption of which from tax reduced the incentive to work and, contrary to popular belief, tended to benefit almost exclusively people with quite substantial incomes who had other sources of livelihood. Brendan Dowling, who had been my economic adviser in Foreign Affairs, and I had devised this package of reforms in late 1980.

In the changed circumstances of 1982 we had no choice but to accept a modification of our scheme that would involve its introduction by stages. In particular the move to a 25 per cent standard tax rate was postponed. We went ahead with our other reforms, however, substantially in the form we had proposed in our election programme, although with some adjustments to overcome short-term administrative problems. Thus, the difficulty of identifying, from the data available to the tax authorities, spouses working at home who had no incomes of their own made it necessary to invite such spouses to apply for the tax credit of £500 a year or £9.60 a week. As a result the take-up rate from this scheme proved somewhat disappointing, and Fianna Fáil abandoned the scheme when it came to power.

Another adjustment was needed in the case of our proposal to tax short-term social welfare benefits. This required close liaison between the Revenue Commissioners and the Department of Social Welfare. The latter department was strongly resistant, on the ideological grounds that it was not its function to assist in tax collection. When we challenged this we were told (somewhat triumphantly, I felt) that in any event our proposal could not be implemented, because the computers in the two departments were incompatible and it would take a long time to put right the administrative blunder that had led to this situation. We countered this by suggesting that as an interim measure a fixed proportion of the pay-related element in social welfare benefits could at least be deducted and corrective adjustments made subsequently by the Revenue Commissioners.

I remember vividly the dénouement of this particular trial of strength between Government and civil service. We were having a late-night session of the Government when we were told that even this simple temporary way around the problem was technically impossible. Fortunately one amongst us, Jim Mitchell, was an expert on this matter, being a computer analyst. We sent for the relevant official, and Jim Mitchell went out to tangle with him. I recall, as we awaited his return, Alexis FitzGerald remarking that the traditional view that the expertise in government lay within the civil service was being stood on its head. Jim Mitchell won the battle at about 2 a.m., and it was decided to take this first step towards greater equity in the tax and social welfare system, although in the event, because of the fall of our Government, this decision was not implemented.

Finally, considerable progress was made towards two other objectives of my tax reform programme. I had always been unhappy with the inequity involved in lower-income families benefiting only from children's allowances while those on higher incomes also had the advantage of child tax allowances, which were worth most to those with the highest incomes, who paid the top tax rate. I had proposed the abolition of the child tax allowance and the substitution of an enhanced system of child benefit. For technical reasons, connected with the postponement of the move towards a 25 per cent standard tax rate, we could not in this budget go the whole way towards my objective without creating some inequitable anomalies, but we halved the child allowance in the tax code and introduced child benefit at rates from 25 to 90 per cent higher than the existing children's allowances.

The other largely implemented reform was my proposal to treat widows, widowers and single parents in the same way as married people in the tax code.

All in all, and considering the financial crisis we faced, the reforms actually announced in our budget were far-reaching. Moreover, we made provision for a 25 per cent increase in social welfare benefits from April, the size of this increase being designed to ensure that social welfare beneficiaries would be better off even after a proposed cut in food subsidies, which in fact was only partially implemented. Because of the rapid decline in inflation during 1982 and early 1983 (following a successful negotiation with the trade unions in which Liam Kavanagh, the Minister for Labour, played a crucial role) the eventual effect of this measure was to increase the average purchasing power of social benefits by about 8 per cent during the year beginning April 1982—a remarkable redistributive exercise at a period when for much of the time the purchasing power of earnings was falling at a rate of about 7 per cent.

Of course all these reforms had to be paid for. Even though three-quarters of the cost of the benefit increases to the Social Insurance Fund was to be borne by employers and workers—an added burden whose significance did not strike home to the public until the increased deductions were levied in April— the total cost to the exchequer of the reforms was £210 million, over two-thirds of which was accounted for by the social welfare improvements. Because we had also to continue the process of reducing the current deficit and the level of exchequer borrowing, initiated in our supplementary budget six months earlier, the total gap to be bridged in the budget was half as large as this again, amounting to 3 per cent of GNP. Part of this, however, was to be met by a budget cut in the food subsidies additional to the spending reductions already effected partly in July 1981 and partly during the pruning of the estimates of public spending in preparation for this 1982 budget.

The sheer scale of the overall budgetary changes proposed was by any standards remarkable. We were of course attempting to carry through simultaneously two major operations: an exercise in what came to be known popularly as 'financial rectitude', involving a drastic deflation of the economy, and also a major redistributive reform programme. This was a most ambitious undertaking; it is, indeed, hard to think of a precedent for it in any other country. In the event, because we attempted too much, it failed—if only by a very small margin. Paradoxically, however, it was not defeated by resistance from conservative forces, as might logically have been the case, but ultimately by the vote of one left-wing independent deputy.

We knew of course that both the cuts in food subsidies and the increases in some indirect taxes would be sensitive areas for the two socialist independents who supported us, Noel Browne and Jim Kemmy. We might, I suppose, have minimised or even perhaps eliminated the risk of losing their support by proposing a somewhat less ambitious reform programme, either on the tax or social welfare side, but, rightly or wrongly, I was reluctant to compromise our reform programme for what seemed such a perverse reason: a fear of losing *left-wing* support. Logically, I felt, these two socialist independents must when the crunch came support such a redistributive budget, and this view was shared by most of my colleagues in Government, including the Labour Party members.

I could not of course discuss our budget proposals with the socialist independents, but I did meet them to hear what they had to say. I cannot recall our discussion in detail, but I was satisfied at the time that their position was accurately summed up in a statement Jim Kemmy issued on 15 January. He said then that he would support the budget only in the event of 'the continuation of food subsidies', and on VAT he said that 'as a general principle' he would oppose 'any major shift from direct to indirect taxation; in particular, there should be no increase in the lower rate of VAT.'

Without touching the food subsidies or VAT we could find £265 million. But we needed £380 million to achieve our budgetary targets and to carry through our reform programme, so £115 million had to be found in what had been now clearly signalled to us as danger areas. Jim Kemmy's statement had not, however, mentioned as objectionable an extension of VAT to clothing, which was zero-rated; moreover, on an optimistic linguistic interpretation of his reference to food subsidies he had not seemed to require that they be maintained in full.

These considerations led us to modify our proposed budget by leaving untouched the subsidies on bread, flour, and margarine, while raising the greater part of the required £115 million, first by reducing the butter subsidy and by substituting for the general milk subsidy a more generous school milk subsidy, which could be financed mainly with EC funds, and second by extending VAT at the lower rate to clothing and footwear. No corresponding reduction of proposed social welfare benefit increases was undertaken, however. This left us still short of a significant sum. It seemed to us we could secure this only by increasing the 15 per cent VAT rate to 18 per cent, hoping that Jim Kemmy and Noel Browne would wear this, despite the former's warning.

The budget speech was a long one, followed, in accordance with tradition, by an extempore response by the Fianna Fáil shadow Minister for Finance, Michael O'Kennedy. Then there was a brief suspension of the sitting, after which the budget resolutions were to be voted on, starting with the one that increased the tax on beer. This was a relatively non-contentious issue, but it was one that could of course be used by the Dáil to reject the budget symbolically; if we were defeated on this or any other budget resolution we would have lost the confidence of the Dáil.

During the suspension of the session some of the independents came to see me in my room. One was Seán Loftus, a right-wing Catholic with a penchant for issues such as the preservation of Dublin Bay from development and the annexation of Rockall, the isolated rock in the Atlantic Ocean north-west of Ireland. I did not get the impression that he had serious difficulties with the budget; indeed at our meeting he said very little. When I showed the two socialist independents how the overall effect of the budget on social welfare beneficiaries was positive, Noel Browne indicated that he was prepared to support us, taking account of its overall redistributive thrust. But Jim Kemmy was deeply unhappy. Unlike Noel Browne, he did not seem to be willing to see the budget as a whole but focused rather on particular parts of it, or on the omission from it of provisions that he had hoped to see in it.

One of these omissions was an increase in capital tax. As a Government we were committed to increasing capital tax, which, since Fianna Fáil had abolished the wealth tax that we had substituted for death duties in 1974, was almost non-existent. But the only part of this commitment we had been able to come up with during our brief six months in office had been a levy on the banks, which Jim Kemmy dismissed as inadequate. Also, the apparent ambiguity of his earlier reference to food subsidies now resolved itself into a rejection of *any* reduction in the subsidies, even when compensated several times over by substantial real increases in social welfare.

However, even if Jim Kemmy voted against us with two other independents we could, we thought, survive with the support of Noel Browne and Seán Loftus.

When the Dáil reconvened to debate the resolution on the beer tax it appeared, however, that for reasons that were far from clear Seán Loftus, at the best of times a somewhat mercurial figure, was now a quite uncertain quantity. This was surprising, for if he brought down the Government he seemed most unlikely to hold his seat—which, with the aid of a large number of Fine Gael votes, he had won at our expense by a margin of less than four hundred votes. Consequently, as he had not seemed to have any strong views about the budget we had believed that he would continue to support us. But with his vote now in doubt, Jim Kemmy's became crucial. When, after a brief debate on the beer tax, the Ceann Comhairle called a division I mounted the steep steps to the voting lobby, and as I passed Jim Kemmy I bent down to urge him to reconsider his vote. This was perhaps an incautious action, which was inevitably observed and subsequently wildly commented upon.

When the rest of us had voted, the independents rose and mounted the step up from their back row to the voting lobby. Noel Browne turned our way; Jim Kemmy moved into the Fianna Fáil lobby; Seán Loftus hesitated, then drifted, still somewhat uncertainly, towards the Fianna Fáil side, where he naturally was received with enthusiasm.

As the Fianna Fáil whip bounded down the steps with the result in his hand— 82 to 81, a one-vote defeat for the Government—I experienced a moment of total exhilaration: *this was it*. We were going into battle on a budget that we could defend with conviction and enthusiasm, both on social and financial grounds. We would be able to contrast our vigorous tackling of the financial crisis and the honesty with which we had prepared the budget against Fianna Fáil's appalling four-year record of extravagance and the dishonest budget they had produced a year earlier, in which spending figures had been arbitrarily slashed without any policy decisions being taken to implement these nominal cuts.

We might not win the election now about to be called but at worst we would lose only a couple of seats, I believed, and could prevent Fianna Fáil from securing the overall majority they sought. By contrast, had we won the vote in the Dáil our Government would have fallen within months with the explosion of a time-bomb in the budget that no-one, it seemed, had yet noticed: a 3.5 per cent increase in social insurance contributions, to be shared equally between employers and workers. This increase was to hit pay packets in April, and in an election at or shortly after that point we could, I thought, have lost all the seats we had gained in June 1981. (Fianna Fáil four months later was to lose the crucial Dublin West by-election, largely, in my opinion, because of public fury over this measure, which it retained in its March budget.) Of course despite this belief I had hoped—as any politician would—to have won the budget vote. However logical it might have been to have sought to precipitate an early election before the detonation of this unnoticed time-bomb, it is not in the nature of a politician to act in that way.

I have to say that I did not detect the same enthusiasm amongst my colleagues as we left the chamber. Nevertheless when immediately afterwards a parliamentary party meeting was convened, the emotion of the moment displayed itself very positively. John Bruton and I received a standing ovation, and the meeting adjourned shortly afterwards in a fighting mood.

I also met the press. I told them truthfully that I was 'happy and exhilarated', although I don't think they believed me. My buoyant mood betrayed me, however, when I came to answer a question about why we had not exempted children's clothing and footwear from our extension of VAT to clothing generally—an issue that I had just been discussing with Department of Finance officials in the light of some early criticism of this aspect of our budget. I allowed my sense of humour to overcome my judgement, disclosing that I had been told by the officials that in Britain just such a distinction had given rise to intense public dissatisfaction, because children with large feet had to buy adults' shoes, which carried the tax! The press, in a much more serious mood than I was, wrote this down solemnly as the actual reasons that had led us to reject an exemption for children, whereas the financial considerations I have just outlined had led us to conclude that we needed the money that would come from an undifferentiated tax on clothing and footwear.

This was subsequently used against me mercilessly; and although up to that point this question of children's clothing and footwear had not, I believe, been a significant factor in the defeat of the budget a short time earlier, the issue really took off from the moment I gave this answer—so much so, indeed, that the February 1982 election is now firmly embedded in popular mythology as the election caused by our Government's decision to impose VAT on children's shoes.

My next duty was to go to the President to seek a dissolution. For reasons that were not clear to me at the time, my departure to Áras an Uachtaráin was delayed. Even when I was allowed to go to my car, which for some reason was in the crowded forecourt of Leinster House rather than, as was normally the case, in the discreet North Lane at the rear, beside Government Buildings, there was a further delay. This became embarrassing as the excited crowd—not all of them supporters, I felt—peered in the window and even hung onto the roof. Finally I asked one of my private office staff to tell the Secretary to the Government, Dermot Nally, for whom I was waiting, that I had gone ahead and would await him some distance short of the gates of Áras an Uachtaráin.

There we eventually effected our rendezvous, at about 10 p.m. Dermot Nally explained to me that the Secretary to the President, whose presence at Áras an Uachtaráin was essential, had been at the Peacock Theatre and that my assistant private secretary had had to seek him out there, trying to identify him in the dark without interrupting the play, and that there had been papers to prepare.

When we arrived at Áras an Uachtaráin I was ushered in to a disturbed and indeed quite angry President Hillery. During the delay the Áras had apparently been besieged with phone calls from members of the Fianna Fáil front bench— seven calls from them in all, I was told later—proposing that he exercise his prerogative by refusing me the dissolution I was seeking and calling on Charles Haughey to form a Government. Haughey had himself told the press that he was available for consultation if the President so wished. These repeated phone calls—a misrecollection of which was to contribute nine years later to the defeat of the Fianna Fáil candidate for the Presidency, Brian Lenihan, by Mary Robinson—were regarded by the President as unwarranted attempts at political interference with his office. Indeed he was so upset by what had happened that he kept me there for three-quarters of an hour, thus leading many back in Leinster House to speculate that he might in fact be exercising his prerogative, the inappropriateness of which in current circumstances he was so vigorously propounding to me.

A curious twist to the story of Fianna Fáil's abortive attempt to prevent a dissolution emerged when I got back to my office after eleven o'clock. One of my private office staff told me that he had been puzzled by a phone call from the Independent Fianna Fáil TD Neil Blaney urging, as I recall it, that I go to the Áras at once. This did not seem to make any sense—until I realised that what must have happened was that Neil Blaney had got through by mistake to my office, thinking he was ringing Charles Haughey.

By the time I returned to Leinster House our 1981 election committee had reassembled on its own initiative and was well advanced with its election preparations, a heartening reaction, which confirmed my confidence that we were well placed to run a very powerful campaign. On my way home after that meeting I was pleased to see Fine Gael posters, left over from the June election, already up on lamp-posts.

For Finbarr Fitzpatrick, who had just been appointed national organiser, it was a sudden immersion in a new and demanding job. Although it had not been intended that he take up office until several weeks later, he was there that night, and fought a great campaign during the following three weeks.

How well placed were we in the public opinion polls at this point? The most recent poll had been six weeks earlier, when the figures (with the vote at the June election in parentheses) had been Fianna Fáil 46 per cent (45 per cent), Fine Gael 39 per cent (36 per cent), Labour 10 per cent (10 per cent), others 5 per cent (8 per cent). Clearly up to December at least we had gained some ground since the June election, and, allowing for the probable reversion to Fianna Fáil since the hunger-strike of most of the 2.5 per cent who had voted for IRA candidates, Fianna Fáil had not gained any. Even allowing for some temporary loss of ground since, because of disgruntlement over the snow episode, we were therefore still quite well positioned electorally as well as morally.

Another pointer to the way the election might go was the unusually emphatic reaction of the *Irish Times*, which in its editorial the following morning told its readers that if they placed any value on the virtues of tenacity and honesty, and on their own future, they should return our Government with a thumping majority.

Fianna Fáil's initial reaction to this unexpected opportunity to get back into Government was uncertain and unconvincing. Charles Haughey was obviously reluctant to abandon the populist high-spending approach that his party had pursued since 1977. He held out the bait of filling five thousand vacancies in the civil service; and when pressed about what cuts in spending he would propose he seemed unable to think of anything more than saving £500,000 by abolishing special advisers to Ministers and by 'renegotiating borrowing'! At the same time he made a bid for the right-wing Catholic and 'republican' votes by reiterating his commitment to introducing a constitutional ban on abortion, and suggesting that he would consider allowing Sinn Féin public representatives to have access to television. He also accused us of being 'hypnotised' by the borrowing problem. Altogether it was an undistinguished start to the Fianna Fáil campaign. Meanwhile we for our part moved to mend our stand on the children's clothing and footwear issue, announcing at the weekend a Government decision not to impose VAT on these items, on the grounds of 'preventing a trivialisation of the issues'. Better late than never; this ceased to be an issue in the campaign from that point, although the furore about it immediately after the budget may have contributed to a small but nevertheless significant shift against us in the first post-budget poll, published ten days after the fall of the Government. A heartening sidelight from the polls however was the revelation a few days later that an opinion survey in Northern Ireland had shown the vast majority of nationalists and almost 95 per cent of unionists preferring me to Charles Haughey.

By the time this poll was taken the campaign was well launched, and it seemed that we might be able to prevent any further deterioration in our position. Our election meetings were enthusiastic affairs, with our supporters happy to see us holding the high moral ground of financial responsibility and with Fianna Fáil apparently floundering. I was particularly pleased with a meeting in my own college, UCD, where I received a standing ovation from seven hundred students.

Meanwhile we had forced Charles Haughey to accept the validity of our budget deficit and borrowing figures. We then offered him the facilities of the Department of Finance to cost any alternative proposals he might have for a budget framed within these parameters, and a fortnight into the campaign this offer was taken up.

On Friday 12 February Fianna Fáil finally produced its 'alternative budget'. It proposed dropping our tax on clothing and footwear, but not modifying the food subsidy decision. The cost of these and several other minor adjustments was to be met by an additional tax on banking and insurance; by bringing forward the date of payment of corporation tax; and by applying VAT on imports at the point of import instead of on sales. The latter two proposals would bring £81 million of 1983 revenue back into 1982, a once-off gain that avoided the whole issue of the need to continue the process of reducing the current budget deficit and exchequer borrowing that we had started. The remaining gap was to be bridged by additional revenue buoyancy deriving from this relaxation of budgetary discipline. At the same time £30 million of the £90 million we had allocated as the absolute minimum required to prevent the collapse of some state enterprises that had accumulated large deficits between 1977 and 1981 was to be diverted to an expansion of investment in construction activity. Two days later this £30 million had become £100 million in Charles Haughey's election speeches, but without any further proposals for financing it.

Despite the irresponsibility of producing 'once-off' revenue windfalls as a means of reducing the budget deficit, this 'alternative budget' may have had some impact on the electorate, for a poll taken on 11–13 February, the great bulk of the sampling for which was done before the Fianna Fáil proposals had appeared, had shown us at that point catching up on Fianna Fáil. Its support had dropped to 44 per cent while ours was shown as rising from 39 per cent to a record of 41 per cent; moreover, 54 per cent saw me as the best Taoiseach from the country's point of view, as against 40 per cent for Charles Haughey. If such a swing towards us did in fact occur in the first fortnight of the campaign, then given the actual outcome there must have been a counterswing of equal magnitude towards Fianna Fáil in the last few days, for which the 'alternative budget' could provide an explanation.

On Tuesday 16 February Charles Haughey and I came face to face on television for the first time. Knowing how much hangs on an occasion like this, and conscious of how one misplaced word can prove disastrous in such a gladiatorial contest, I was tense, and probably showed it more than he did. I hit hard at the outset, asserting that in his 1981 budget a year earlier expenditure had been notionally slashed by well over £100 million without any actual policy decisions being taken to achieve this result, and that shortly afterwards the Central Bank had refused his Government an overdraft of £350 million; in each case, as the viewers could see, I had documentary proof in front of me. He was rattled by these accusations, which he nevertheless denied flatly— although under press questioning on the following day he hedged about the Central Bank overdraft issue, saying he would not have known about it.

A 'spot' survey carried out later that night put my performance ahead of his by margins of over three to one in credibility, honesty, and reliability, and by a very large margin also in relation to leadership. But he was felt to have been almost equally ahead of me in confidence and debating prowess.

As I was completing a tour of my constituency on polling day, news came that Charles Haughey's friend and election agent, Pat O'Connor, a solicitor, was to be charged with the offence of voting twice, in two different polling stations at which he had been doubly registered. The charge later failed on technical grounds: it could not be proved that he had voted on the second ballot paper. Nevertheless, although the charge failed, the episode set the scene for the extraordinary Government that was to come to power under Charles Haughey several weeks later.

As the votes were counted on 19 February it soon became clear that we had held our ground fully vis-à-vis Fianna Fáil; both parties had gained a percentage point at the expense of Labour and independents, with Fianna Fáil securing a further 1 per cent as a result of the return to it of votes lost to IRA candidates the previous June.

Inevitably there were some gains and losses of seats, but only in one-third of the constituencies. Apart from the two seats Fianna Fáil recovered from the IRA abstentionist TDs, they had a net gain of one seat, winning four and losing three; we gained three but lost five; there was no change in the Labour Party's representation; and the Workers' Party won two seats in addition to the one they already held. Fianna Fáil was still in a minority, but it now had three more seats than Labour and ourselves, whereas in the previous Dáil they were two seats behind us. Clearly the odds had shifted in favour of Fianna Fáil forming a minority government this time round; but nothing was certain.

On the Monday after the election came word of a move in Fianna Fáil to unseat Charles Haughey. Two days later Des O'Malley declared himself as the challenger, but on the next day the challenge collapsed. The forty-odd deputies who had initially indicated support for Des O'Malley dwindled under intense pressure to half that number, with the result that, on the surprise proposal of Martin O'Donoghue, a close ally of Des O'Malley, the matter did not come to a vote.

That night as Taoiseach I attended and addressed the annual conference dinner of the Confederation of Irish Industry. Afterwards I was invited to join members of the confederation's executive for a postprandial drink; the conversation quickly turned to the political stalemate. Although many of those present— probably the great majority—were traditional supporters of Fianna Fáil, they were virtually unanimous in their fear of a Haughey-led Government dependent on the Workers' Party. Quite bluntly, they said that such a Government could be highly dangerous. In his ambition for power Charles Haughey would, they felt, be quite unscrupulous in his relations with the Workers' Party. At that time this party was still called 'Sinn Féin the Workers' Party' and was closely identified with the official IRA, which even within the previous year had been engaged in bank robberies in our state. They were, moreover, a socialist party on the Soviet model, having close links with the Soviet Union and some communist states in eastern Europe as well as North Korea. On security grounds as well as on ideological ones I was urged to make every effort to prevent the emergence of a Haughey Government dependent on this kind of support. If there had to be a minority Government dependent on the support of the Workers' Party or other left-wing independents, which seemed almost inevitable given the composition of the new Dáil, then for the country's sake I, whom they could trust, should lead it rather than Charles Haughey, whom most of them seemed to see not as the leader of the party of which many were traditionally supporters but as a dangerous and unpredictable maverick.

This spontaneous and overwhelming vote of confidence from the leaders of the business community in favour of a renewal of our Coalition with the Labour Party, even if supported by left-wing independents and perhaps dependent also on the Workers' Party, could not but make me think more seriously than I had done hitherto about the possibility of trying to ensure my re-election as Taoiseach. The arithmetic, however, was against this. Charles Haughey needed only two more votes to secure a majority; I would need five. But perhaps it was worth trying. Thus it was that, against my own judgement and instinct, I allowed myself to be drawn into a competition for marginal Dáil votes in adverse circumstances.

While I related better than Charles Haughey to social-democrats in the Labour Party and to people like Jim Kemmy (despite his vote against our

*With President Hillery receiving the Seal of Office in June 1981 (above), and at the Council of State in December 1981 discussing the constitutionality of a Bill (below).*

*In London with Jim Prior, Michael O'Leary and Margaret Thatcher at Downing Street during the Anglo-Irish Summit in November 1981.*

*At Buckingham Palace during the meeting of the European Council in December 1981* (From left to right) *Prime Minister Marc Eyskens of Belgium, Prime Minister Andreas Papandreou of Greece, Prime Minister Giovanni Spadolini of Italy, Prime Minister Anker Jorgensen of Denmark, President of the European Commission, Gaston Thorn, President Mitterrand of France, Prime Minister Pierre Werner of Luxembourg, Queen Elizabeth, Chancellor Schmidt of Germany, the Princess of Wales, the Prince of Wales, myself, Prime Minister A.A.M. van Agt of the Netherlands, Prime Minister Margaret Thatcher of Britain, and the Duke of Edinburgh.*

HOME – AT LAST

*Returning Home: as Foreign Minister in 1975 (above),
and as Taoiseach from Tenerife to the snow crisis in 1982, (below).*

*With Jack Lynch at the Mass marking the opening of the new Dáil in November 1982.*

*Informal Cabinet Meeting at Barrettstown in July 1983.*

*With Peter Barry, Tanaiste.* (above) *and* (below) *In session* (from my right), *Peter Barry (Foreign Affairs), Sean Barrett (Chief Whip), Peter Sutherland (Attorney-General), Pat Cooney (Defence), John Bruton (Industry & Energy), Jim Mitchell (Communications), Austin Deasy (Agriculture), Paddy O'Toole (Gaeltacht, Fisheries and Forestry), Michael Noonan (Justice), John Boland (Public Service), Liam Kavanagh (Labour), Alan Dukes (Finance), Gemma Hussey (Education), Frank Cluskey (Trade, Commerce and Tourism), Barry Desmond (Health and Social Welfare), Dick Spring (Trade and Environment).*

*At the White House during an official visit in 1984. In the back row Ambassador Patrick McKernan, Cabinet Secretary Dermot Nally, Secretary of the Department of Foreign Affairs Sean Donlon, Secretary of State George Schultz, Ambassador Margaret Heckler (partially, but deliberately, obscured on orders from above!) and Vice-President George Bush.*

*With Brian Mulroney, Prime Minister of Canada in 1985.*

*Joan and Mark with
Nancy Reagan at the
White House in 1984.*

DEKUN INC.

*Speakers at the Tip O'Neill Retirement Dinner in Washington 1986.*

*Sporting Occasions:*

*Receiving a baseball from the New York 'Rose of Tralee' contestant in 1981.*

*With Mark at a Rugby International in Lansdowne Road 1984. The Attorney-General Peter Sutherland and Tom O'Higgins, Judge of the European Court, are behind us.*

Government), this proved of little relevance to my dealings with the Workers' Party of 1982, or with the newly elected independent socialist, Tony Gregory, from the north inner city. The Workers' Party was, I think, primarily concerned with keeping its rival, the Labour Party, out of office, while Tony Gregory clearly felt more comfortable dealing with his fellow-northsider Charles Haughey than with me.

Tony Gregory was concerned to extract for his deprived constituency—perhaps the most disadvantaged in the country—the maximum possible package of special measures. The genuine needs of the area made me sympathetic to his aspirations, and, as it happened, I had already three months earlier taken an initiative in relation to the acquisition and development, in part for social purposes, of a major site in the constituency: the Custom House Dock. I was thus in a position to produce to Tony Gregory the tentative plans we had already prepared for this area. But his requirements went far beyond the limited package I felt I could properly offer, and I was not surprised when he gave his support to Charles Haughey.

Part of this post-electoral exercise in seeking Dáil support for a new Coalition included a further look at our budgetary proposals. It was when we came in Government to re-examine the budget that I discovered something quite extraordinary, and frankly shocking. We were told that an additional £23 million non-tax revenue was now available. I demanded to know where it had come from, and why we had not been informed of this when we had been preparing our budget. It then emerged that it represented profit from the sale by Bord Gáis to the ESB of quantities of gas the Government had authorised for 1981 and 1982, and that a further allocation now proposed would bring this figure to £27 million. Unbelievably, the £23 million revenue flowing from decisions that had been taken by our Government had been omitted from the total of non-tax revenue presented to us by the Department of Finance. When I demanded an explanation, it transpired that before our budget a Finance official had gone to the Department of Energy to get information on the matter but had not been given it.

It was too late to investigate this affair or to take any disciplinary action that might be called for; but the sense of having been badly let down was acute amongst the members of the Government, for had we known of this additional revenue we would certainly have introduced a somewhat different budget, in all probability dropping either the tax on clothing or the increase in the standard rate of VAT from 15 to 18 per cent. There was a real possibility that but for this piece of extraordinary incompetence our Government might not have fallen.

Our revised budget proposals involved principally the substitution of a higher top VAT rate and further excise duty increases, together with the extra £27 million now available from Bord Gáis, for our original imposition of VAT on clothing and footwear and for the reduction in food subsidies. This alternative budget received short shrift from the Workers' Party and Tony Gregory and, as was to be expected, from Neil Blaney. I soon regretted I had ever

embarked on the course of seeking such unlikely support at the cost of modifying the budget proposals on which we had fought the election, although the
actual performance of the Fianna Fáil Government that now came to office
proved even more alarming in some respects than anything I had foreseen
when deciding to make the abortive effort to keep them out of office.

When the Dáil met, John O'Connell, a former Labour Party deputy elected
as an independent in 1981 after a constituency row with his leader, Frank
Cluskey, was re-elected as Ceann Comhairle. I was persuaded to go to him to
suggest that he withdraw his name, not, as he has since suggested, to prevent
the constitutional formation of a Government, thus forcing another election—
his withdrawal could not have had this effect—but to weaken Fianna Fáil's
majority by forcing them to find a Ceann Comhairle amongst their own members
or independent supporters. Not surprisingly, he rejected this suggestion, and
later joined Fianna Fáil.

Although the Administrative Council of the Labour Party had decided that
Labour should not join us in a coalition, they had also decided that I should
be supported for Taoiseach. It was Michael O'Leary who proposed me for the
post, a nice gesture in the circumstances. Peter Barry seconded.

The Workers' Party announced their support for Charles Haughey, on the
grounds that Fianna Fáil's economic and industrial policy was what the country
needed, that our Coalition had shown a 'lack of coherence', and, rather oddly
I thought, that 'continuity of Government' was desirable.

Neil Blaney based his support for Fianna Fáil on Charles Haughey's 'commitment and conviction' in relation to job creation and on the 'good and
receptive hearing' Haughey had given him on the issue of Britain leaving the
North. He had not had quite the same reaction from me, he added.

Jim Kemmy, whose vote on the budget some weeks earlier had helped
to defeat us, announced that he would support me, because the Fianna Fáil
'Brits out' line was bunkum and nonsense and because of the importance of
this decision to the long-term interests of the people.

But the speech that astonished everyone, and horrified very many, even in
Fianna Fáil, was that of Tony Gregory. He listed the written deal he had made
with the new Taoiseach, which he had had witnessed by the General Secretary
of the Irish Transport and General Workers' Union. He later estimated the cost
at £150 million, and independent assessments at the time suggested it would
cost £80 million in 1982 alone. It included, amongst a long list of 'goodies',
housing and environmental works schemes in Dublin to the tune of over £25
million; the nationalisation of Clondalkin Paper Mills, currently threatened
with closure; a £3 million community school for the inner city; and a new
National Community Development Agency.

The vote on my nomination was 79 to 86, and Charles Haughey was duly
elected. A few hours later the new Fianna Fáil Government was announced.
George Colley was not included; Haughey would not appoint him as Tánaiste,

and he preferred not to participate on any other basis. He was replaced in that office by the new Minister for Finance, Ray MacSharry.

At 11.00 a.m. on 24 March, two weeks after the formation of the new Fianna Fáil Government, I was due to face a vote of confidence by the parliamentary party, in accordance with a requirement I had introduced into the Fine Gael constitution, and at 3.30 p.m. the same day Ray MacSharry was due to introduce his revision of our January budget.

On the previous evening Michael Lillis, my diplomatic adviser in the recently defeated Government, who in 1980 had served for a period in Dick Burke's cabinet in Brussels, rang to ask if he could see me. When he arrived he told me that Dick Burke had asked him to inform me in the strictest confidence that Charles Haughey proposed to reappoint him to the Commissionership; his earlier appointee, Michael O'Kennedy, had returned to contest the recent election and was now a member of the Dáil, thus leaving a vacancy in Brussels. It seemed to me that Haughey's ploy was to precipitate a by-election in Dick's constituency of Dublin West, with the object of winning that seat and thus ending his dependence on the Workers' Party and Tony Gregory for a Dáil majority. But I gathered from Michael Lillis that Dick Burke did not see it that way.

This confidential approach faced me with an unenviable dilemma, about which I expressed myself forcibly to Michael Lillis. If I respected the confidence I would have to remain silent on the matter at our party meeting on the following morning, which would be grossly unfair to my fellow-TDs and which they could reasonably resent deeply afterwards; and if I told them of this proposal Dick Burke and Charles Haughey would be entitled to denounce me for dishonourably breaching a confidence. I was trapped, and was furious at being placed in this position.

On the proposal itself I was also in a dilemma. I knew that Dick Burke felt he had had a raw deal from me, both when I had failed to support him for the Commissionership in 1976 and when I had omitted him from my Government in the previous June. Against this background he could be tempted to attribute a rejection by me of his reappointment as Commissioner to personal antipathy towards him on my part. And if I now objected to his reappointment as Commissioner this would not, I believed, prevent him from accepting the nomination, and accordingly it would make no difference to the political outcome—but it *would* leave me open to a charge, which I was sure would be levelled against me, of being motivated in my objection by personal hostility towards him.

In the face of all these considerations I finally told Michael Lillis—with grave qualms about whether in so doing I was acting rightly—that I would not stand in Dick Burke's way, commenting somewhat bitterly that in binding me to confidence he seemed to expect me to act surprised when the announcement was made in the Dáil.

After a bad night, as I agonised over whether I had done the right thing, I took my place on the front bench just before 10.30 next morning. Jim Mitchell approached me to say that according to Maurice Manning a journalist had just reported rumours in Brussels that Dick Burke was to be reappointed as Commissioner. I asked him to check this, and after the order of business I walked across to our party room in a state of inner turmoil.

With some difficulty I persuaded our party chairman, Kieran Crotty, to put the vote of confidence as required by our constitution; he was concerned that some members of the party might vote against me, but I told him that that was the purpose of the exercise. I expected at least a dozen votes to be cast against me; in the event there were only five, with sixty-two in favour.

At that point, before I could raise the Dick Burke issue, as I now felt I had to do, word came that the appointment had been announced in Brussels. (Someone had come out from the Commission meeting and had leaked the news to the press.) All hell broke loose. Jim Mitchell, who with his usual generosity had accepted Dick Burke as a fellow-candidate in Dublin West in the recent election and had worked extraordinarily hard to get him elected as a third Fine Gael TD in this five-seat constituency, was predictably furious at Dick's acceptance of the nomination. Faced with this violent reaction, Dick Burke agreed after an adjournment not to accept the post. He was emotionally shattered, and for a long time we walked up and down the forecourt of the Dáil. It was clear that he had been totally taken aback by the hostility of his colleagues at the meeting. My gentler reaction, reported to him the previous night, may have left him unprepared for the ferocity of his colleagues with their sense of betrayal. Finally, at his request I accompanied him to his office upstairs in Leinster House to help him break to his wife his decision to reject Charles Haughey's offer. She was understandably deeply upset at this development. It was a difficult encounter.

Three days later I was surprised to learn that he had changed his mind and was accepting the job. Having received his assurance three days earlier that he would turn down the offer, the parliamentary party was shocked at this development. I was blamed for not having taken a tougher line with him from the outset. The situation was not greatly helped by his announcement that he had asked Charles Haughey not to contest the resultant by-election in Dublin West, especially when Haughey issued a statement denying that such a request had been made.

Liam Hourican and Michael Lillis went with Dick Burke to Brussels as his chef de cabinet and deputy chef de cabinet, respectively. In their bitterness about the affair some of my colleagues took this amiss, most unfairly in my view. I was glad that they were there to help Dick pick up the threads again in Brussels.

Meanwhile, immediately after the dramatic party meeting at which news of Dick Burke's reappointment had broken, we had listened to Ray MacSharry's revised version of our January budget. He increased spending by £70 million above our proposed level—some of this being required to pay for the new

Taoiseach's deal with Tony Gregory—and reduced revenue by eliminating our VAT imposition on clothing and footwear. The resultant gap was filled by a combination of bringing forward no less than £170 million of VAT and corporation tax receipts from 1983 to the current year and assuming an additional £45 million of revenue buoyancy. This unstable edifice—which largely collapsed during the course of the year—proved to be the last, and politically most counterproductive, gasp of Fianna Fáil creative accountancy, which Ray MacSharry himself made an attempt to redress from July onwards. Despite his belated efforts, the outcome of this budget left my second Government facing a far worse financial situation at the end of the year than would have been the case if the Bruton budget had survived on 26 January.

Jim Mitchell now set about finding a candidate for the Dublin West by-election. Eventually he put forward the name of a businessman called Liam Skelly who had been born in the constituency and was now living in another part of it. None of us had heard of him previously, but we backed Jim's judgement. I appointed John Boland as director of elections, and he went to work with ruthless energy.

It was a great campaign. I think Charles Haughey hoped that the fact that the Fianna Fáil candidate was Eileen Lemass, his own sister-in-law and daughter-in-law of Seán Lemass, would help to swing the vote in favour of Fianna Fáil. He must also have hoped that his Government's announcement at the outset of the campaign that, following the sinking of the *Belgrano*, it was going to withdraw from EC sanctions against Argentina would win votes from those who favoured 'Brit-bashing'. However, if this was part of his calculation it did not come off, for neither in working-class nor middle-class parts of the constituency did it produce many echoes.

But the clinching factor in the election was, I believe, the time-bomb effect of the sharp increase in PRSI contributions in our January budget—an increase that had been retained by Fianna Fáil in its March budget and that began to affect take-home pay during April. Taking advantage of this, the Workers' Party mounted a campaign that doubled its support. When its candidate was then eliminated his votes broke over two-to-one in our favour, giving Liam Skelly on the last count a margin of 5 per cent over Eileen Lemass.

This by-election was one of the most significant in recent times. It severely damaged Fianna Fáil morale, and weakened Charles Haughey's position in the party, which was already under challenge. His attempted 'stroke' with Dick Burke had backfired, with the result that we still held three of the five seats in Dublin West as well as the Commissionership—even if many in our party refused to look on Dick Burke as Fine Gael! The Workers' Party learnt that its support for Fianna Fáil was extremely unpopular with the voters, and this encouraged it to 'ditch' the Fianna Fáil Government at the first suitable opportunity six months later.

In the meantime the morale of our party was sharply raised. The disappointment that had naturally followed our loss of office three months earlier was replaced by a growing conviction that we would be back in Government before long.

Meanwhile in early June I announced my new shadow cabinet, appointing a very large number of deputies to the front bench or as junior spokespersons. To the Education portfolio I named Michael Noonan, who had proved an effective debater from the back benches during our brief period in Government. Gemma Hussey, who had just been elected to the Dáil (she had been the Fine Gael leader in the Seanad during the previous nine months), became shadow Minister for the Arts, Culture, and Broadcasting. And I appointed Austin Deasy, my most outspoken critic in the party, shadow Minister for Foreign Affairs. All three were to become members of my next Government.

Of the members of the 1981–82 Government only the late John Kelly was omitted. At the end of April he had announced that he would prefer to remain on the back benches, in order 'to be free to speak on certain matters'—specifically, it appeared, to question the desirability of a further coalition with the Labour Party. He favoured a 'grand coalition' of Fine Gael and Fianna Fáil—an idea that evoked little enthusiasm elsewhere. Such a coalition, with 85 per cent of the seats in the Dáil, would in my view carry great dangers, because of the potential corrupting influence of such a huge and invincible majority upon the parties involved in it; for these parties, once joined in such an alliance, might eventually have been tempted to remain in office almost indefinitely.

Meanwhile Anglo-Irish relations had deteriorated sharply, first as a result of Charles Haughey's hostile reaction to the British White Paper on Northern Ireland, published on 6 April, and then as a consequence of his sudden change of stance on EC sanctions against Argentina a month later. This White Paper had indeed been a disappointment, but the principle of power-sharing at Executive level was at any rate preserved, and it seemed to me that it was not for us in Dublin to sabotage this honest, if somewhat unimaginative, attempt to get the political process in Northern Ireland restarted. Accordingly I issued a statement describing it as the first attempt in many years to tackle the fundamental problem of bringing about devolved government in Northern Ireland on a basis that would secure the interests of both sections of the community there, adding that I felt that detailed reaction should come in the first instance from the parties in Northern Ireland.

The Taoiseach, however, described the White Paper as an 'unworkable mistake', which was faced with 'inevitable failure'. It ignored, he added, the 'broader dimension of the problem', i.e. the issue of the relationship of the North with our state. And the SDLP clearly felt that they had little alternative but to echo his term 'unworkable', for they could not afford to seem less nationalist than a Dublin Government.

Five days earlier Argentina had invaded the Falklands, and as I had watched British television during the course of that Friday evening I had become more and more depressed. As I said to Joan that night, Enoch Powell would soon be drawing fake analogies between Northern Ireland and the Falklands, which could defer progress in Northern Ireland indefinitely. Within twenty-four hours my foreboding on that point proved justified: I heard him in the House of Commons making the very speech I had predicted the night before.

At the EC Foreign Ministers' meeting a week later the Fianna Fáil Government's reaction seemed uncertain. There appeared to be a reluctance to join in sanctions against Argentina, although such sanctions seemed to me to be a reasonable joint reaction to aggression. A failure even to agree on sanctions at least for a period would deprive our partners and ourselves of any credible leverage with which to influence British policy in a moderate direction. However, several days later the Irish Government and others who had been hesitant rallied to the majority view.

My relief at this outcome was short-lived, however. On 2 May the *Belgrano* was sunk, with appalling loss of life and in circumstances that evoked strong reactions in Ireland and elsewhere. That night Paddy Power, the Minister for Defence, pre-empted the Government's as yet unformulated reaction by denouncing the British as the 'aggressors' in this conflict—which, whatever one might think of the jingoistic character of some British reactions to the Argentine invasion or of the sinking of the *Belgrano*, was palpable nonsense.

Next day a Government statement announced that Ireland was abandoning sanctions against Argentina—something that in fact we had no power to do at that point, as such a decision could be taken only by the Council of Ministers that had imposed them. The damage to Anglo-Irish relations through this ill-conceived and, in the form in which it was announced, illegal decision would clearly be immense. It was difficult to see how in the light of this *acte gratuit* it would ever be possible to make any progress towards a peaceful settlement in Northern Ireland in conjunction with a British government led by Margaret Thatcher.

The Government statement included an announcement that it was calling for an immediate meeting of the UN Security Council—a peculiarly ill-judged initiative at that moment, which, as I pointed out at once in a counterstatement, could interfere seriously with peace moves being made by the Secretary-General. I also said that the unilateral announcement of the ending of Irish sanctions could undermine efforts by the Community countries as a group to influence the British government towards a peaceful solution.

The Irish position at the United Nations was partially retrieved by our Permanent Representative, Noel Dorr, who, with his Minister's agreement, reinterpreted the call for an 'immediate meeting of the Security Council' to mean 'calling immediately' for such a meeting. On the sanctions issue in the EC the Government had to climb down and to wait a fortnight for the temporary EC sanctions decision to run out before taking the formal step of not joining in their renewal. Italy took the same position at that point, but without any apparent ill effects on Anglo-Italian relations, partly because Italy was seen to have a genuine interest in Argentina and partly because we had drawn on ourselves the brunt of British anger by our unilateral announcement two weeks earlier.

During the weeks since leaving office I had been reflecting on the situation in Northern Ireland. It was becoming increasingly clear that the British handling of the previous year's hunger-strike had led to a sharp deterioration in the political situation in the North, involving not merely greater polarisation of unionist-nationalist tensions but also a radicalisation of much of nationalist opinion. If Sinn Féin contested the Assembly elections foreshadowed by the April White Paper it could now for the first time hope to win a significant share of the nationalist vote. This might in turn precipitate a further swing in the direction of that party, and the hitherto unswerving commitment of the vast majority of the nationalist voters to constitutional parties, in particular the SDLP, might wither.

The SDLP was under pressure, not alone from Sinn Féin but also, I believed, in a different way from Fianna Fáil. Charles Haughey's contemptuous rejection of devolution seemed to be forcing the SDLP to place even greater emphasis on the 'Irish dimension': the role of the Irish state in relation to the North.

These developments could not be ignored. Whatever my own predisposition to seek progress by dialogue with the Unionists rather than by talking over their heads with the British, I could not in conscience persist with such a policy when it seemed to be leading us into a dangerous dead end; nor could I reasonably reject the need to combine some kind of 'Irish dimension' with our pro-devolution policy if, as now seemed likely, such a rejection would contribute to a further, possibly disastrous, radicalisation of Northern nationalist opinion and an erosion of the position of the SDLP in favour of Sinn Féin.

These issues were now emerging as potential threats to the security of the island, including that of the Republic. Were support for the IRA and Sinn Féin in Northern Ireland to grow to a level that might enable them to make a credible claim to majority support within the nationalist community, the IRA might then be emboldened by this to raise its threshold of violence to the point of risking outright civil war in the North, something from which it had always hitherto drawn back. In this way it could create a situation into which it would then attempt to drag the Irish state: the 'worst-case scenario' that had been the nightmare of successive Irish Governments since 1969.

I realised of course that in radically changing my approach in the way that now seemed necessary I risked losing the regard, and in some measure the support, of Unionists that, uniquely amongst Irish political leaders, my stance hitherto had won me. Unionists would not readily understand or accept an approach by me to Britain designed to create for Northern nationalists a focus of loyalty within Northern Ireland by giving our state a limited political role there. Indeed Unionists would be likely to misinterpret such a development as a kind of betrayal of the trust I had built up amongst them, and would probably end up seeing me as a sinister figure who had sought to lull them into believing that I was genuinely committed to the principle of unification only by consent while plotting all along to persuade Britain to impose on them a relationship with the Republic that they would inevitably misinterpret as part of a drive towards enforced political unity.

There would also be personal consequences. My ability to visit freely the part of Ireland outside Dublin in which alone I had relatives with whom I had had close ties since childhood would be affected. As Minister for Foreign Affairs and also as leader of the opposition from 1977 to 1981 I had continued to visit Northern Ireland quite frequently. If I took the course of action that I was now contemplating I would be unlikely thereafter to see much of Belfast until after my eventual retirement from office.

These reflections in the spring of 1982 on future Northern Ireland policy— some of which may anticipate the full development of my thinking about the North during the course of that year—were in part prompted by a proposal from the BBC, just before our Government fell, that I deliver the 1982 Dimbleby Lecture. This offered an opportunity to present to several million people in Britain a view on Northern Ireland that might conceivably influence British policy in a constructive direction.

The title I chose for the lecture was 'Irish Identities'. There were, I suggested in the broadcast, two principal identities in Ireland, deriving from our history, each in its different way fractured and confused. The Ulster Scots identity was confused as between British, Irish, and Ulster—or some combination of the three. Within Northern Ireland each community was moreover in some measure alienated from its roots: the unionists resentful of Britain's handling of the situation in the North, the nationalists dissatisfied with the attitudes of Southern nationalists towards them. For its part the Irish identity was confused as between a narrow, exclusive Catholic-Irish concept and a broader idea of a pluralism that would include the unionists of the North.

The resultant situation was complex and not susceptible of a simple solution. The division of the island had not brought peace; a repartition would only create fresh problems; integration with Britain was acceptable to neither Britain nor Ireland; an independent Northern Ireland was neither desired by its people nor acceptable to either sovereign state; enforced reunification would lead to massive uncontrollable violence.

In any event none of these 'simple' solutions went to the root of the problem: how to devise a political structure in Ireland and between Britain and Ireland that would adequately express and at the same time safeguard the senses of identity of the two traditions in Ireland. Any solution must maximise common ground between the two traditions, provide structures that respected their diversity, and be flexible enough to cope with changing attitudes over an extended period.

Amongst the concrete suggestions I made were that, without prejudice to any political issue, an all-Ireland policing and judicial system would help the British and ourselves to ensure that members of the IRA could not evade arrest and conviction by passing rapidly from one jurisdiction to another.

As to an eventual political solution, I commented that it would necessarily have to be complex and probably without international precedent, but that this should not worry us any more than it had worried those who had established the European Community. What we should be looking for was a structure, however novel, that would enable the people of Ireland to tackle together things that could not be as well done separately, such as security and the pursuit of their interests in the EC where these differed from those of Britain, while at the same time continuing to do separately those things best done that way, through different political structures appropriate to our respective domestic conditions. At the same time Ireland and Britain could move towards a form of common citizenship; each of our peoples already enjoyed some rights of citizenship in each other's territory.

Meanwhile we in our state should seek to create the kind of pluralist society that might have evolved if Ireland had not been divided sixty years earlier. And Northern unionists in their turn might consider giving expression to the willingness of the unionist majority, expressed repeatedly in half-a-dozen public opinion polls over the previous decade, to work with their nationalist fellow-citizens in devolved government. A move by us towards pluralism in our state, involving a response to Northern Unionist sensitivities, might also usefully be matched by a similar response by the British government to the sensitivities of Northern nationalists, designed to give practical recognition to their Irish identity.

I thus foreshadowed a number of the themes that were to be taken up in the New Ireland Forum in 1983–84 and in the Anglo-Irish negotiations of 1984–85, some with a measure of success, others abortively.

The lecture, delivered before an invited audience that included Jim Prior, was broadcast on 20 May, five days before the Dublin West by-election. In the closing days of the campaign I was struck by the reaction to it in the working-class Ballyfermot area where I was then canvassing. Many had watched it and expressed appreciation of its tone and content. In the general election six months later, however, some points in my lecture, in conjunction with a visit I made to London five weeks afterwards when I met Jim Prior and the Duke of Norfolk, were used against me in curious circumstances that I shall relate at the end of this chapter.

Meanwhile the Taoiseach, in the United States for a Fianna Fáil fundraising event, had denounced IRA violence but had failed to refer to Noraid—once again reminding everyone of his previous reluctance to tackle that issue during his first period in Government. And in early July the usual bilateral meeting of the Taoiseach of the day with the British Prime Minister during the course of a European Council had notably failed to materialise, a development that was widely interpreted as a post-Falklands snub by Margaret Thatcher. This further blow to Anglo-Irish relations was followed a week later by a revelation by Grey Gowrie, Minister of State in Northern Ireland, that the parliamentary body agreed in principle at my summit meeting with the Prime Minister eight months earlier had been 'postponed' as a result of British 'frustration' with my successor.

Five days after this disclosure the IRA launched two murderous attacks on members of the Brigade of Guards in London, and a week later the Foreign Office declared that there was no obligation to consult the Irish Government about Northern Ireland.

At the end of August the Taoiseach rejected a proposal I had put forward that the Dáil should move to establish the British-Irish parliamentary body— on the grounds that this body must be established by the two governments. And a fortnight later the British government announced that the idea of a meeting between the two governments had been shelved to give time for reflection.

It had been an appalling six months for Anglo-Irish relations.

Meanwhile in the North the Assembly elections at the end of October were contested for the first time by Sinn Féin. It secured 10 per cent of the total vote, representing over a quarter of the nationalist vote of about 38 per cent and over half the SDLP figure. It was not quite as bad as I had feared but was nevertheless very disturbing, for, having established this base, Sinn Féin seemed likely to build on it the next time an election gave it an opportunity to do so.

All this convinced me that it was now a matter of national importance that the Haughey Government be replaced, so that a fresh approach to the Northern Ireland crisis might be attempted. This conviction was strongly reinforced by a series of developments that in the later months of 1982 began to discredit not just Fianna Fáil but the whole process of government in Ireland.

When we were on holidays in France a murderer being tracked by the Gardaí was found to be staying in the apartment of the Attorney General Paddy Connolly in Dublin, whose Garda-chauffeured car had been used by the wanted man to go out to purchase a gun. The Attorney General was of course entirely innocent, being completely unaware of what his visitor had been engaged in. But, having made a statement to the Gardaí immediately after the man's arrest, the Attorney General had left at once for a prearranged holiday in the United States, despite a phone call from the Taoiseach to London Airport suggesting that he return. Having reached New York he then belatedly cancelled his holiday, returned home, and resigned his office.

These events reached the public initially in garbled form, causing great confusion. In the light of the political uncertainty thus created I decided to break off our holiday in the Dordogne, and after a hair-raising drive to the nearest main-line station we caught a train with literally no seconds to spare— it was moving as I boarded it—and flew home from Paris.

We returned to find a most confused situation. In his attempt to explain these extraordinary events Charles Haughey described them as involving a 'bizarre happening', an 'unprecedented situation'—grotesque and unbelievable.' Conor Cruise O'Brien used his talent with words to devise from the initials of the Taoiseach's adjectives the word 'GUBU', used thereafter to describe other remarkable events occurring during the life of this brief Government.

In his unscripted comments to the media on this occasion the Taoiseach unfortunately spoke of the arrested man in terms that implied that his guilt was established, thus making himself liable to an allegation of contempt of court as a result of these comments being broadcast in Britain. (The Irish media deleted his incautious words from their reports.) This, and his failure to insist on the Attorney General's immediate return from London, provided material for political criticism, of which I made full use.

Several weeks later there was another episode. A public outcry arose over a proposal by a Minister of State to make a three-week trip around the world to look at public parks, at a cost of £25,000. Taken aback by the reaction, the Taoiseach cancelled the trip.

Later that month there occurred a significant event that was to have repercussions on North-South security co-operation, and thus on Anglo-Irish relations, for several years to come. A garda who was a brother-in-law of Seán Doherty, the Minister for Justice, came before a court charged with assault. The case failed, because the key witness was prevented from attending through being detained for the day by the RUC. The Dowra Affair, as it came to be known (from the place where the controversial assault had occurred), raised the question of a possible cross-border police conspiracy to undermine the course of justice in our state. This affair, together with reports of attempts by the Minister for Justice to move a Garda sergeant in his home area who had reportedly been attempting to enforce the licensing laws, cast a considerable shadow over the integrity of law enforcement under this Fianna Fáil Government.

On 1 October Charles Haughey's party leadership was again challenged, this time by a motion of confidence put down by an independent-minded backbencher, Charlie MacCreevy. In the face of this challenge two Ministers, Des O'Malley and Martin O'Donoghue, refused to pledge party loyalty to the Taoiseach, and a couple of days later they resigned from the Government in protest against what they described as a lack of respect for the rights of members of the party. They revealed that they and their families had been subjected to a campaign of intimidation, including death threats, and both the mover of the no-confidence motion and Jim Gibbons, the former Minister whose evidence on oath in the 1970 Arms Trial had contradicted that of Charles Haughey, were assaulted in Leinster House itself by a mob of supporters of the Taoiseach. Against the protests of some courageous members of the party, the confidence vote in the leader was taken by roll-call instead of by secret ballot. In the face of this intimidatory tactic only twenty-two of Charles Haughey's opponents were prepared to challenge him publicly, and his leadership was reaffirmed by the votes of fifty members of the party.

In late October, just before the defeat of the Government that led to a general election, a further incident occurred involving the Minister for Justice. The press reported a threat of a strike by instructors at the Garda Training Depot in protest against an alleged attempt by the Minister to secure a pass in the final examination for a trainee from his constituency. The Minister was also reported to have given a party at the Training Depot for the trainee in question.

Meanwhile for some time I had been receiving even more disturbing reports from journalistic and, indirectly, from Garda sources about an abuse of the telephone interception system that existed as part of the state's security arrangements. I was told that it had been used to intercept telephone calls being made to two journalists believed to be in touch with members of the Government opposed to the Taoiseach. This subversion of the state security system for party political purposes had most serious implications for our democratic system of government. Gardaí who had no political alignment and wished only to serve the public interest were finding themselves faced with having to choose between going along with improper activities undertaken in the interest of one group within the governing party or exposing this subversion of the security system, at great risk to themselves and against all their instincts of loyalty to the Government of the day.

In our party only Jim Mitchell, Minister for Justice in our 1981–82 Government, and myself were aware of this situation. Given the gravity of the matter and its implications for national security, I felt I could not properly confide in other members of the front bench. I thus faced alone the difficult political decision of whether to endeavour to bring down the Government at once or—what I believed would be politically more advantageous to us—to wait until after the January budget. I knew that since the summer the Minister for Finance, Ray MacSharry, had persuaded a most reluctant Charles Haughey that the fresh financial crisis created by their imprudent stopgap March budget must belatedly be tackled, and it would probably be better from our point of view to defeat the Government after rather than before they had taken the kind of tough action so badly needed to curb the spending overrun and to supplement the revenue shortfall that was now emerging.

However, on balance it seemed to me that the possibility of gaining a political advantage through postponing the day of reckoning was outweighed by the urgency of removing an administration that, as it was operating, was undermining in a most dangerous way confidence in the structure of government. This conclusion was reinforced by the fortuitous temporary vulnerability of the Government as a result of the death of one of their TDs and the illness of another, which created an opportunity to defeat them that might not recur for some time.

I was also encouraged by the fact that recent polls had shown a major shift in public opinion in our favour: Fianna Fáil had dropped seven points to 39 per cent, and we had picked up much of their lost support. I was preferred as Taoiseach by 51 per cent, as against 31 per cent for Charles Haughey and 18 per cent undecided.

I believed, however, that we were vulnerable in two quite unrelated areas. First of all the Government had prepared a National Plan with expert assistance from outside the public service, with which it clearly hoped to rally public opinion, despite the fact that the plan was objectively open to considerable criticism—and even susceptible to having gentle fun poked at its studied vagueness in some important areas. For example, on one page a whole series of paragraphs began with the delightfully non-committal and studiedly non-decisive phrase 'It is envisaged that . . .'

The other area of possible vulnerability related to the pressure from anti-abortion groups for a reinforcement of our existing ban on abortion. This issue had been raised with the political parties at the end of April 1981, shortly before the June election was called. The point put to me when I had met a delegation from the Pro-Life Amendment Campaign on 30 April had been that in the light of the US Supreme Court judgement some years earlier that had declared anti-abortion legislation unconstitutional, we should take steps to ensure that no such decision could be made by our Supreme Court. It seemed highly improbable that our court would in any conceivable future make such a decision, but, influenced in part by my personal antipathy to abortion and conscious of the opposition of the vast majority of people in Ireland, North and South, Catholic and Protestant, to abortion—one of the few issues on which there was a united view—I agreed to support an amendment to the Constitution that would limit the court's functions in this matter. A month later I included a commitment to this effect in the Fine Gael election programme.

What I failed to appreciate at that time was the extraordinary difficulty of drafting a constitutional amendment that would have the desired effect, given, first, that any such amendment must constitutionally be interpreted by the Supreme Court itself, and second, the need to make continued provision for the termination of pregnancies in cases where the life of a mother was at risk.

Following my constitutional initiative in September 1981 I had been further pressed on this issue by the PLAC, and when I met them again in December I told them that a constitutional change in relation to abortion would be incorporated in the general constitutional review I had proposed. They were dissatisfied with this commitment, and I told them I would consider their representations and respond to them within two months; as it happened my Government fell seven weeks later.

With other party leaders I was pressed further on this issue during the campaign that followed. In response I told the PLAC that I had instructed the Attorney General to advise me about the best way of giving constitutional protection to the life of the child and that during the course of the next Dáil I would take such steps as might be necessary to provide this constitutional protection. Charles Haughey went one better by promising an amendment during 1982.

During the subsequent months in opposition I stuck to my view that such an amendment should be incorporated in my proposed general review of the Constitution. In the course of the summer I became aware of a whispering campaign against me, alleging that I was 'soft' on abortion. In mid-September I tackled this head on, denouncing this campaign and reiterating my deep conviction that abortion was wrong and should not be legalised. But, I insisted, any amendment must not be sectarian or denominational, by which I meant couched in terms designed to reflect the Roman Catholic position with its very specific provision for two exceptions only—ectopic pregnancies and cancer of the womb—based on the principle of 'double effect'. At our October 1982 ard-fheis I restated my position in favour of an amendment as an integral part of a constitutional review, saying, 'All life, whether of citizens or of people of other nationalities, whether born or unborn, should be protected by our Constitution.'

This was the position when at the end of October we tabled our motion of no confidence in the Government. On 2 November, two days before this motion was to be taken, Fianna Fáil published a proposed amendment to the Constitution dealing with the abortion issue. It read: 'The State acknowledges the right to life of the unborn and, with due regard to the equal right to life of the mother, guarantees in its laws to respect and, as far as practicable, by its laws to defend and vindicate that right.'

On the face of it this formula seemed to meet the criteria I had laid down: it was expressed in positive pro-life terms and it contained no apparent echoes of the specifically Catholic position. Moreover there had been press reports of consultations during October with Protestant Church leaders, which had involved showing them a draft, and it was suggested that this formula was acceptable to them. (It has since been confirmed that the draft was shown to and approved by the Church of Ireland Archbishop of Dublin.) Against this background and with an election looming within forty-eight hours I did not seriously consider rejecting the text. I was frankly greatly relieved that the draft—which was clearly produced at that moment as an election ploy—was one that in conscience I could accept.

It was not until much later that I realised that whatever consultations had taken place between the proponents of an amendment and the Fianna Fáil Government had in reality stood on its head the original proposal as I had understood it, for this amendment left several key issues ambiguous—and therefore to be determined by the very court about the possible future orientation of which the protagonists of an amendment had expressed such concern. The newly elected leader of the Labour Party, Dick Spring, deserves the credit for having identified the dangers of ambiguity in the proposed wording at the time of its announcement, and for having shown considerable political courage in refusing to be stampeded into accepting it. He had just been elected leader of the Labour Party in extraordinary circumstances. The party's annual conference had voted on 24 October, by 671 votes to 493, against involvement in a further coalition without prior approval by a special party conference. Michael O'Leary, who had opposed this restriction, took this as a vote of no confidence in himself. Four days later he resigned the leadership, and on 1 November Dick Spring was elected in his place.

Dick, a barrister and former international rugby player, was then only thirty-two—younger than my eldest son, John—and had been a member of the Dáil for less than eighteen months. On Michael O'Leary's proposal I had appointed him in the 1981–82 Government to be Minister of State in the Department of Justice in charge of Law Reform, an aspect of the work of the department that seemed to me to have been neglected for some time previously in favour of pressing security matters. Charles Haughey, in the first half of the 1960s, had been the last Minister who had had both an interest in law reform and the opportunity to give time to it without the distraction of major security problems.

Dick had been seriously injured in an accident involving two state cars late in 1981, which had left him with a permanent back problem, involving persistent and severe pain. In taking on in these circumstances the leadership of the Labour Party—not an easy task at the best of times—he showed remarkable courage, especially as a general election was at that moment looming up in a matter of days.

I think it was on the evening of Dick Spring's election that I answered a ring at my front door to find Michael O'Leary outside. He walked in and told me he wanted to join Fine Gael. I agreed to put his application before my party, and it was immediately accepted. I knew, of course, that his entry to Fine Gael would create some short-term problems with the Labour Party, but that could hardly be grounds for refusing him the Fine Gael whip. However, it was soon made clear to me both by my own party and by Labour that he would not be acceptable as a member of a coalition Government. It is one of the unattractive features of politics—not only in Ireland—that a person who crosses the floor to join another party is rarely persona grata thereafter with the party he has left, nor in many cases wholly acceptable, at least at first, to the party he has joined.

Two days later the minority Fianna Fáil Government was defeated in the Dáil by 82 votes to 80. They had discredited themselves with the public, and it was time for them to go. Carrying the knowledge of their phone-tapping activities, I was totally determined to put Fianna Fáil back into opposition, and was confident that we could do so. For I believed that, despite the inconclusive result of the Labour Party conference on the issue of coalition, Labour would support me rather than Charles Haughey for Taoiseach. And I was buoyed up by the poll published a week earlier, which for the first time ever showed Fine Gael level-pegging with Fianna Fáil, each having the support of 42 per cent of the electorate, with the Labour Party at 8 per cent.

Shortly after the dissolution we announced our election programme. It involved among other things pay restraint in the public sector; further redistributive measures, including the introduction of the family income supplement for low-paid workers (a scheme of ours that Fianna Fáil had cancelled on their return to office in March); greater contributions by private patients to the cost of the health services; the establishment of a National Development Corporation; and an end to political interference with the Gardaí.

Our prospects were improved next day by a Labour Party statement that they had an open mind about entering into a coalition arrangement. The bookmakers' odds were now one to three on a Government led by me, and the latest polls, while showing some slippage in our support, still left us with 40 per cent of the vote. With the Labour Party now at 10 per cent, our two parties were holding onto their joint 50 per cent of the vote.

Fianna Fáil then sought to recover ground by playing the 'green card'. Shortly before I was due to make my now traditional single election speech on Northern Ireland, Jim Prior had been reported as having said in the United States that I would be proposing an all-Ireland court and an all-Ireland police force. This scarcely showed great prescience, for he had been in the audience when I had made precisely this suggestion to several million people in the course of the BBC Dimbleby Lecture six months earlier; but Fianna Fáil, relying on the shortness of the public's memory, presented this statement of Jim Prior's as evidence of 'collusion' on my part with the British government; I was their 'puppet', saying what they told me to say. To accept this allegation would require a considerable suspension of disbelief, for the British government was not greatly given to proposing all-Ireland institutions; but my idea of an all-Ireland police force to tackle the paramilitary threat to the Irish people was skilfully transformed by Fianna Fáil into a plan to have Co. Kerry policed by the RUC.

An extra twist was given to this story by a revival of an earlier allegation that I had lobbied the Duke of Norfolk in support of Jim Prior's White Paper proposals on Northern Ireland, the duke being described as a member of the British intelligence services. (When I had met the duke at his request in July the only matter on which I had lobbied him was against the British government's exclusion of the candidature of Séamus Mallon, deputy leader of the SDLP, from the revived Northern Ireland Assembly because of his membership of our Seanad.)

On the following day I made my Northern Ireland speech. In it I regretted Jim Prior's failure to follow through on his January idea for an 'unboycottable' Northern Ireland Executive. His decision to abandon this idea in favour of yet another proposal for an Executive that the Unionists could boycott had contributed, I said, to the frustration amongst nationalists that had led almost three out of ten members of that community to support Sinn Féin in the recent Assembly elections.

In the circumstances, I went on to say, a 'complete and radical rethinking of British policy' was now needed quickly if the situation were not to drift to chaos. To achieve such a rethink we in our state would have to demonstrate our good will towards unionists as well as nationalists, a will to change our society in order to remove fears and suspicions on their part.

At the same time we must take effective measures against violence, and the best way to harness our joint resolve in this regard would be, as I had pointed out on several occasions, most notably in the Dimbleby Lecture, through the operation of a court and a police force common to both Northern Ireland and the Republic. These measures, as well as matching the subversives' capacity to create a single entity of terrorism on the island, could also end the now almost total alienation of young people in the Northern nationalist community from the forces of order.

Having thus foreshadowed what I had begun to envisage as some of the main theses of the new Anglo-Irish Agreement that I hoped to negotiate during my term of office, I went on to re-echo a proposal I had made in a speech on reconciliation in Pittsburgh six weeks earlier that there should be consultations by the Irish Government and other parties in the Dáil with all those in Northern Ireland who might be willing to talk to us—whether they sought, opposed or were indifferent to Irish unity. I thus brought directly into the political arena what later was named the 'New Ireland Forum'.

At the time these proposals were overshadowed—and their significance was lost for most people—as a result of the row that Fianna Fáil had sought to stir up over my reference to an all-Ireland court and an all-Ireland police force, a row that some in my party and elsewhere thought accounted for a loss of ground by us towards the end of the campaign. But if there was such a loss it did not amount to much, for our final share of the vote was only one point less than the result of the public opinion poll taken just after the campaign had begun.

The inevitable television debate ended the campaign. When I arrived at the studios it emerged that RTE was proposing that Charles Haughey and I be photographed shaking hands before the debate. This was too much like the preliminary to a prize fight, and I turned down this proposal, an action that one of my advisers suggested might have the additional advantage of disconcerting my opponent just before our encounter. With this consideration also in mind I delayed my entry to the studio until immediately before the broadcast was due to start.

During the first section of the debate, on the economy, I was well prepared for the Taoiseach's claims that his National Plan had been endorsed by the Central Bank, the Council of the Economic and Social Research Institute, and the European Commission in Brussels. I was able to refute each of these statements in turn and to document my refutation. I also led him into disclaiming responsibility for the disastrous economic decisions of the 1977–79 period, when he had been Minister for Health and Social Welfare, a disclaimer that enabled me to point to his evasion of collective responsibility as a member of that Government.

When we reached the subject of Northern Ireland he accused me of proposing a 'British-Irish force' to police Ireland—but was unable to sustain this allegation when I handed him my speech and asked him to point out where there was any reference to a 'British-Irish force'.

The debate was, I think, reasonably successful from my point of view. For once I succeeded in speaking relatively slowly—and in avoiding statistics. The encounter was in fact adjudged to have been at worst a draw, and the *Irish Independent* said that I had been the victor.

The result of the election was satisfying. Our vote was at its highest level ever: over 39 per cent. And we gained seven seats, which brought us within striking distance of Fianna Fáil for the first time in half a century, with 70 seats as against 75 for them. Together with the Labour Party we would have an overall majority of six in the Dáil; hopefully that should be enough to see us through what was bound to be a very difficult period, during which we would have to carry out a prolonged and painful deflation of the economy and rebuild the intergovernmental relationship with Britain, now at its lowest ebb for very many years.

But at the moment of victory these considerations were not uppermost in my mind. My principal feeling was one of satisfaction that I would have the chance to restore the credibility of the institutions of state, which had been so seriously undermined during this disastrous nine months. The GUBU period was at an end.

There followed the negotiation of a programme for Government with Dick Spring. For this purpose we held a series of meetings together with a couple of close colleagues. The press never traced the venue; it was in fact a small convent, with which someone on his side must have had a contact. Although Dick and I knew each other only slightly at that stage we soon established a rapport, based on our common commitment to social-democratic values and to integrity in public life. A common programme for Government was hammered out, and accepted by both our parties in advance of the first meeting of the new Dáil, at which I was elected Taoiseach for the second time, by 85 votes to 79.

# CHAPTER FOURTEEN

# SECOND TERM: PICKING UP THE PIECES

Before embarking on an account of my final term of office I should perhaps say something of how our personal lives had been affected by the changes in my political fortune.

Since my appointment as Minister in March 1973 our pattern of living had been significantly altered. During the years to 1973 I had been under great pressure as I tried to juggle my four careers of university lecturer, economic consultant, journalist, and front-bench opposition politician. For me the change to a single, if highly demanding, job as Minister for Foreign Affairs had been something of a relief; but for Joan the change had been traumatic: she had had to adjust to travelling by air after seventeen years of avoiding that form of transport, as well as to my frequent absences from home. However, once she had overcome the air travel barrier she had found a new role as participant in diplomatic activities.

My subsequent transformation from Minister for Foreign Affairs to leader of the opposition in 1977 had involved a further hiatus in her life. While at election time the wife of a party leader can play a significant role, this is much less the case between elections. Joan disliked my frequent absences during the years from 1977 to 1981 as I toured the forty-one constituencies, most of them twice; and while, as always, she identified with my new career, domestic politics on this scale was certainly less interesting for her than Foreign Affairs had been.

A new dimension had entered our lives since 1975, however. Doireann and Iseult, John and Eithne's two eldest children, had been born while I was Foreign Minister, and their sister Aoife arrived in 1980, in the latter part of my stint as leader of the opposition. The new and welcome role of grandmother helped Joan to adjust; for my part, ten years were to elapse, and several more grandchildren were to arrive, before I was able to give as much time as I would wish to being a grandfather.

We were both very distressed when in August 1981 our daughter, Mary, and her husband, Vincent Deane, had to emigrate to Tromsø in Norway, well north of the Arctic Circle, where the sun does not rise for two months in the winter. Mary had spent several years as a temporary lecturer in English in Maynooth, where she had been very happy; but despite the efforts of her professor, Fr Peter Connolly, she did not secure a permanent appointment, and after two further years of temporary lecturing in UCD she found herself unemployed in 1980. The only work she could find that year, in addition to some part-time lecturing, was designing furniture for a factory in Co. Donegal, which entailed travelling through Derry. In 1981, as the hunger-strike situation deteriorated, this became a hazardous journey for the daughter of such a prominent enemy of the IRA, and after a disturbing experience in Derry she had to abandon this work.

The only academic post available was a senior lecturership in English at Tromsø. She found that her students there were not much stimulated by English literature but were fascinated by Ireland; and when she went back to Norway after the 1981 Christmas holiday she took a library of books on contemporary Ireland, and inaugurated courses on Irish politics and economics. Joan and I visited Mary and Vincent at Easter 1982, when I took up an invitation to give a lecture there on Northern Ireland.

Her mother was determined that if Mary had to be an emigrant she should be a more accessible one, and by dint of pursuing every relevant advertisement in the *Times Higher Education Supplement* Joan eventually tracked down a post as head of the English Department at the Crewe-Alsager Higher Education College in Cheshire, a mere 150 miles from Dublin. There Mary remained for seven years, until a back problem forced her to retire on health grounds, and she returned to Ireland to start a new career in painting. Vincent, a scholar specialising in *Finnegans Wake*, was fortunately able to carry on his work wherever Mary happened to be.

During my years as Taoiseach, Mary's house in the Elizabethan market town of Sandbach in Cheshire became a place of refuge for Joan and myself. We stayed there frequently, enjoying the tranquillity of the Cheshire countryside and the freedom to move about among the uninquisitive Cheshire people. Until 1985, when the impending Anglo-Irish Agreement heightened my profile in Britain, I was not encumbered by security there, and was glad to be able to wander the town on foot or occasionally on Vincent's bicycle.

In December 1985, just after the signing of the agreement, we had the joy of acquiring two more granddaughters: Réachbha, born to Mary, and Ciara, born to Mark's wife, Derval O'Higgins. In 1975 Mark had fulfilled his ambition to enter an auctioneering firm as an apprentice. By 1982, at the age of twenty-five, he had become the managing director of the firm, Sherry FitzGerald, which before the end of the decade he had developed into one of Dublin's leading real estate agents. Throughout my period as Taoiseach he and Derval lived in a flat in our Palmerston Road home, where, on their marriage in 1983, they had replaced Mary and Vincent as co-owners of the house with Joan and myself. Thus it was only in 1988, after more than forty years of marriage, that for the first time Joan and I found ourselves without offspring in the house; but Mark, and shortly afterwards Mary, settled within a few hundred yards of us, and John's home is only four miles away, so we saw a lot of our children and grandchildren.

This expanding family enriched our lives, provided Joan with new interests as my involvement in politics became more demanding, and absorbed much of what time I had to spare from my responsibilities.

When we could we liked to spend some hours with our closer friends, almost all of them from outside politics—for, like many politicians, I endeavoured to keep my personal life separate from my political one. While I enjoyed the company of many of my political colleagues during the working day, I preferred in spare moments to relax with old friends. After becoming leader of the party, and later Taoiseach, it also became important to avoid being more friendly with some members of the party than with others, lest this create suspicions of favouritism. Some, although perhaps not all, of what has been seen as a certain detachment from personal relationships in my political life reflected this factor.

Turning back to politics, I must describe the political atmosphere in which we were operating, and the spirit in which we approached our task. Naturally enough, like any government anywhere in the world, we were concerned that our parties should emerge successfully from the endeavour, with a fair prospect of being re-elected to office. That was sufficient motivation for sticking together in the face of adversity—and we had no illusions about the amount of adversity we were going to face. But in our case this motivation was reinforced by three considerations that went well beyond the normal concerns of party politicians; and all these related to the dangers that we felt the country would face if Fianna Fáil were to return prematurely to power.

First, the experience of two Haughey Governments, and particularly that of 1982, raised in our minds serious concern about the future of the country if such a Government were to be re-elected in the near future with an overall majority. I had moved, some would argue too hastily, to bring down the second Haughey Government in November 1982 because of the urgency of restoring the non-political character of the Garda Síochána, and neither I nor my colleagues could easily contemplate allowing through any default of ours the circumstances to recur that had led to the GUBU events of 1982.

Second, while I recognised, as did some at least of my colleagues, that there had been a reversal of the disastrous financial approach of the Fianna Fáil Government in July 1982, when the Minister for Finance, Ray MacSharry, had asserted himself, it was not clear that Charles Haughey's conversion to prudent financial policies was genuine and irreversible. Ray MacSharry had disappeared from the Fianna Fáil front bench after the revelation that he had secretly tape-recorded a conversation with a colleague, Martin O'Donoghue; and our suspicions of Charles Haughey's own economic predilections were confirmed when in September 1983 he advocated a reflation of the economy at a time when exchequer borrowing was still, despite our initial measures, running at 14 per cent of GNP.

Third, in my mind at least (in the early stages of our Government it may have been less true of some of my colleagues), there was a belief that we might make some progress towards eliminating the risk of IRA political success in Northern Ireland and laying the foundations for future progress towards peace and stability there by concluding an agreement with the British government. Following the events of 1980, and more particularly Charles Haughey's actions in 1982 at the time of the Falklands war, this I felt would be politically impossible for a Fianna Fáil Government, at any rate as long as Margaret Thatcher remained British Prime Minister.

The combination of these considerations meant that it was vital not alone for our party but also for the national interest that Fine Gael and the Labour Party should maintain their unity in Government for the four years or so ahead. Against this background I simply had not got the option that as Taoiseach I might have had in other circumstances, of bringing the Government to an end by a dissolution in order to resolve differences that might arise between Fine Gael and Labour.

This carried implications for the manner in which the Government was to operate. Although for my own part I was prepared in respect of most domestic affairs to have decisions in Government taken by a majority vote, even if this meant (as it often did!) that I was myself left in a minority, such majority decisions could not without great risk be taken on a basis that would involve Fine Gael overruling Labour. Where the Labour Party Ministers as a group, as distinct from individual Ministers, saw a particular issue as one of vital importance to their party it had to be resolved by discussion, and where necessary compromise, rather than by a vote or by a ruling by me, either of which, if the decision went against Labour, would risk a split that could have disastrous consequences not just for one or other or both of our parties but, in our estimation, for the country itself.

The onus for getting the necessary decisions taken against this background fell primarily on me and required that I exercise my authority judiciously and in close concert with Dick Spring, who, it must be said, recognised fully his responsibility in maintaining the cohesion of the Government in the circumstances in which we found ourselves. In a sense what resulted was a threefold system of decision-making. In the area of Northern Ireland policy and in certain limited areas of particular concern to me, such as the volume of development aid, I operated rather as a chief than as chairman. Most matters of domestic policy however were determined by the Government by consensus, or where necessary by a vote. But in a third category of decisions, where such a vote could clearly have divided the Government along party lines on an issue that either party saw as vital, the calling of such a vote clearly had to give way to settlement by discussion; and discussion of this kind could often be extremely prolonged.

Such sensitive issues were relatively few in number, but because there was no clear-cut method of resolving them they tended to take up a lot of time. They included a small number of financial questions in each budget, and an even smaller number of other legislative matters on which the parties were divided (for example the terms of reference of a new National Development Corporation and a proposed Local Broadcasting Bill). It must be added, however, that as in any other government, decisions on departmental estimates, regardless of party, were also inclined to lead to prolonged discussion, because of Ministers' reluctance to vote down a colleague on some expenditure item of particular concern to him or her, lest they be voted down on a similar matter when their turn came. Perhaps in this area I allowed more latitude for discussion than was desirable in the interests of efficient government—so some of my colleagues clearly felt!—but some of these were sensitive issues for the Labour Party, and my Fine Gael Ministers might not have appreciated being overruled when this would not have been possible in cases involving Labour Party Ministers.

I was conscious at times of the frustration felt, by some of my Fine Gael colleagues in particular, with the length of time taken to resolve certain delicate questions; they were not always as conscious as I was of the danger of taking the easy path of calling a vote, which could precipitate serious problems between the parties.

There was another element in my own approach to Government that I should perhaps mention at this stage. From the outset it seemed to me that the scale of the financial problems we had inherited made it possible that no effort of ours could bring our economy back to a growth phase in time for this happy outcome to influence voters at the next election. My experience both as an economist and as a politician had led me to the conclusion that even when economic recovery has begun after a period of recession, at least eighteen months have to elapse before this begins to impinge on public consciousness. That meant that in order to be well placed to win the next election we would need to complete the adjustment within two-and-a-half years.

It is of course conceivable that had we taken much more severe measures at the outset, bringing the public finances under control more rapidly, we might have faced a more favourable political situation in 1987; I suspect that this may today be the 'conventional wisdom' on this issue—and, of course, it may be right. But the scale of deflation that would have been involved if we had sought to resolve the problem of public finances within two-and-a-half or three years would, I believe, have been of a severity unknown in western Europe or the United States since the war, and it is at least equally likely that the result of this would have been an even longer recession, with the economy simply unable to recover from such a tremendous shock.

I am content to leave that debate to economic historians; it is for them rather than for me to attempt to judge the merits of the approach we adopted. The political reality however was that from the outset a serious doubt existed whether, regardless of what course we adopted, our Government would be re-elected in 1987; and for me it became a primary aim of policy to work towards a situation in which if a change of Government took place in that year it would happen in circumstances in which our Fianna Fáil successors would be least likely to repeat the errors of that party's recent administrations.

So far as Northern Ireland policy was concerned the best way of thus ensuring the survival of whatever arrangements we might be able to put in place during our term of office was, I felt, to have these brought into effect as early as possible, so that there would be time for any initial Fianna Fáil Pavlovian opposition to them to be replaced by a more rational acceptance of our achievements as a basis for further progress by that party in Government. So far as economic policies were concerned there was less we could do to insure against a repetition of the Fianna Fáil blunders of 1977–82; but it seemed to me that if we could achieve a sufficient degree of progress with the public finances by 1987 for a Fianna Fáil Government coming to power at that time to be able to see a clear advantage in continuing on the same lines, there was a reasonable prospect that the difficult and unpopular task we were undertaking would not again, as in 1982, be undone.

The economic task ahead of our new Government was indeed formidable. In tackling the public finances we would be starting from a position notably worse than that which we had left behind a year earlier. This was so for two reasons. First, the level of economic activity in 1982, and thus of tax revenue, had been far lower than forecast at the start of the year by the Department of Finance. And second, as I mentioned earlier, Fianna Fáil in its post-election March budget had increased both current and capital spending above the level proposed by John Bruton, while at the same time eliminating a number of John's taxes. The resultant gap was temporarily filled by a once-off transfer of tax revenue back from the following year, 1983. As a result of these factors the opening borrowing requirement for 1983 was far higher than that which John, a year earlier, could reasonably have expected it to have been at this point on the basis of his budget.

Against this background it was clear that, despite two years of falling living standards and rising unemployment, further stringent and prolonged budgetary action would have to be taken, involving a continuing deflation of the economy that was bound to create tensions both within and between the parties in our new Government. Moreover, the common ground between Fine Gael and the Labour Party lay in the commitment of both parties to reforms in our social and legal systems, which, while in most cases not involving large expenditure, would almost inevitably involve the deployment of *some* additional resources. And such additional funds were clearly unlikely to be available on any significant scale during the lifetime of our administration. The fact that as a Government we would thus be inhibited from undertaking many of the initiatives that would reflect our joint aspirations would not be helpful to our cohesion.

In tackling the financial crisis left by Fianna Fáil we could expect no assistance from that party in opposition. I knew that they would oppose ruthlessly and opportunistically all the unpleasant measures that their past actions in Government would now force us to take. Furthermore, the steps that I saw as necessary to salvage the Anglo-Irish relationship would be unlikely to commend themselves to Charles Haughey, and, while I knew that he shared my concern about the threat posed by the growth of support for the IRA in Northern Ireland, it was far from certain that he would support the kind of political action that I contemplated with a view to tackling this problem. Anything we might achieve in this area—even if it exceeded what Fianna Fáil might have secured—would be attacked by that party as falling short of its rhetorical aspirations.

How well equipped was our new Government to tackle these daunting tasks? Its members could be said to be short on experience. Only one of the four Labour Party Ministers had previously served in Government, although Frank Cluskey had been present at many cabinet meetings between 1973 and 1977. And as a result of my decisions when forming my June 1981 Government, only two of the Fine Gael members, Peter Barry and Pat Cooney, had served in the 1973–77 Government, although five others had had their baptism of fire in 1981–82 and had come well out of that ordeal. Intellectual capacity and personal commitment would have to make up for shortage of experience.

What was somewhat unpredictable despite our 1981–82 experience was the interaction of the two sets of Coalition parliamentarians, especially if some of our respective backbenchers pulled us in opposite directions. Both of our parties had some mavericks, as well as quite a number of deputies with a limited stomach for the kind of rough ride that I knew we were in for.

Much would obviously depend upon the kind of relationship that would develop between the Fine Gael and Labour segments of the Government team. I had been heartened by my experience of negotiating the formation of the Government with Dick Spring, and I believed that at a personal level he and I could work well together. It was clear to me that he was a serious politician. We shared many of the same values; my own instinctive sympathy with the younger generation, derived from my years as a university teacher and from what I had learnt from my own children, would, I believed, help me to overcome the age gap between Dick and myself, although it might take some time for him to feel entirely comfortable with someone so much older.

When he and I had discussed portfolios he had decided that he himself would take Environment, which I thought rather heavy given his other responsibilities as Tánaiste and leader of his party. He proposed the Labour portfolio again for Liam Kavanagh, and we agreed on Health and Social Welfare for Barry Desmond, and Trade, Commerce and Tourism (the truncated department that had been the by-product of Michael O'Leary's choice of Industry as well as Energy in the 1981–82 Government) for Frank Cluskey.

Barry Desmond I had known for almost twenty years. As Minister of State in the Department of Finance in the 1981–82 Government he had found inadequate outlets for his frustrated energies, which had led to some friction with his Minister, John Bruton; but as a Minister in charge of two major departments he would find full scope for his capacity for work and his ability to command the most complex of briefs. Liam Kavanagh I had come to know well during the period of the 1981–82 Government, when his calmness, cool judgement and trade union experience had proved a great strength to us. The friendly working relationship I had established in the 1973–77 period with the fourth Labour Party Minister, Frank Cluskey, had continued throughout the period when we had been the leaders of two opposition parties. Joan and I had been particularly close to him when his wife, Eileen, had died. I looked forward to working with him again, not foreseeing the differences over Northern Ireland policy and the Dublin Gas issue that were to mark his brief period as a Minister before he resigned at the end of 1983.

Three of the Fine Gael Ministers in my previous Government were not available this time. John Kelly had opted out because of his unhappiness over a coalition with the Labour Party; Jim Dooge, sadly, did not feel able, for health reasons, to serve again; and Tom Fitzpatrick had accepted nomination as Ceann Comhairle. To replace them I selected Austin Deasy, my severest critic after the January election, whose independence of mind and sense of 'grass roots' feeling would, I felt, be valuable; Michael Noonan, whose parliamentary performance since his election to the Dáil eighteen months earlier had been impressive, both as a Government backbencher and later in opposition; and Gemma Hussey, who, although with limited Dáil experience, seemed to me to have the capacity to be an effective Minister in a reforming portfolio.

Peter Barry was one of the more 'nationalist' members of Fine Gael. I felt that he could play a very important role in maintaining a strong link with the SDLP during the difficult period ahead. It was at that time far from clear that the SDLP would accept my idea of a New Ireland Forum open to Unionists and to the Alliance Party, and tensions could also arise with the leadership of that party during the necessarily confidential negotiations with the British government that I hoped to initiate after the Forum had reported. Accordingly, to strengthen our links with the SDLP and Northern nationalists generally I asked Peter to take the Foreign Affairs portfolio, which included responsibility for implementing Government policy on Northern Ireland, the initiation of which is the Taoiseach's responsibility.

In allocating the remaining portfolios to other Fine Gael ex-Ministers, only one of whom had Government experience pre-dating 1981 and most of whom were likely to remain prominent in politics long after I would retire, I was concerned—perhaps excessively so—to ensure that during my leadership they would each have experience of more than one department.

Accordingly, except for Paddy O'Toole, whose command of Irish justified his retaining the Gaeltacht portfolio but to whom I allocated additional responsibility for Forestry and Fisheries, I switched all the others. I appointed Alan Dukes to Finance—like John Bruton he had an economics degree—and gave

John the major Industry and Energy portfolio, which involved responsibility both for industrial policy and for some of our ailing state enterprises. The other department responsible for a large number of state enterprises was Communications, to which I appointed Jim Mitchell, whose dynamism and determination would, I believed—correctly, as it turned out—make a major impact on many of these loss-making bodies.

I was particularly concerned about the need for public service reform, which I felt had been neglected because the Department of the Public Service had been combined with the Department of Finance under a single Minister. Given the state of the public finances, no Minister for Finance, however competent, was going to be able both to restore financial stability and at the same time bring about the necessary reforms in the public service. Accordingly, against the conventional wisdom, I decided to give the Department of the Public Service a separate Minister, at least for this administration; and John Boland seemed to have the necessary qualities for this demanding job. I knew that he would not allow himself to be bullied or cajoled by the civil service into backing off what needed to be done. He was, I have to say, most unenthusiastic about taking on the task, partly because he had hoped to return to Education and partly, I think, because up to that moment he had not given much thought to the need for public service reform.

To the other former Minister, Pat Cooney, I offered Defence; and I asked Austin Deasy to take Agriculture—much to his astonishment. He objected that he had no special knowledge of the area, but I told him that, in view of the pressure on the Common Agricultural Policy, what we needed in this department in the period immediately ahead was a tough negotiator and that I felt he had the requisite qualifications. Gemma Hussey was equally astonished to be offered Education; I believed, however, that she would tackle it with vigour and imagination, initiating reforms that were long overdue.

Finally I asked Michael Noonan to take the Justice portfolio. I judged that he had the combination of qualities needed to tackle sensitively and successfully the subversion of our security system for party purposes, of which I had become aware in recent weeks, and to restore the independence of the Garda Síochána by securing the force against the kind of political interference that had become a source of public concern during the previous nine months. He too was taken aback at the offer of this portfolio, more particularly when I told him that I had reason to believe there was substance in reports that had recently appeared in the press about the improper phone-tapping of two political journalists, Bruce Arnold and Geraldine Kennedy. The unravelling of this would be bound to involve him at the very outset in a painful confrontation with the top level of the Garda Síochána. I shall return later to this affair.

The interval before the formation of the Government had given me an opportunity to prepare a letter to each of the members of my cabinet setting out in some detail a number of matters relating to their duties and to the general running of the Government. Much of this had to do with working arrangements for the Government as a whole and relations between departments, but I took the opportunity to raise some other points. For example, I insisted that differences on points of *fact* between departments be reconciled before memoranda came to Government. In my previous administration it had seemed to me absurd that we appeared to be expected to reconcile such differences at the cabinet table. And I also insisted on the co-ordinating role of the Department of Foreign Affairs in relation to external policies; this was something that domestic departments often ignored, especially in the EC framework.

I took this opportunity to raise a number of other points with my new Ministers. I required those who had to travel outside the state for purposes other than EC Council meetings to inform my office and the Department of Foreign Affairs as soon as such a visit was mooted, and to keep that department posted on any changes of plan; on occasion, I added, our ambassadors in certain capitals had found themselves handling simultaneously as many as three quite separate Ministerial visits, one or more of them without notice.

On a further practical point, having discovered as Minister for Foreign Affairs how the concern of civil servants that their Ministers be well treated could lead to greater expenditure on visits abroad than Ministers themselves, if apprised of what was involved, might wish to incur, I suggested that the hiring of limousines be avoided unless for a stated reason they were essential, and that rooms rather than suites be booked in hotels unless it was the intention to hold an official meeting in the Minister's room, as is, in fact, often necessary on such occasions.

I also put in writing the view I had put verbally to Ministers in my previous Government before appointing them, that membership of any organisation in which participation was by policy not a matter of public knowledge would be incompatible with membership of the Government. Word of this must have leaked out, for one day in the Dáil I was asked by the backbencher Oliver Flanagan if I had imposed such a requirement in order to rule out participation in Government by members of the Knights of Columbanus, of which he was himself a declared member. I replied that as I had not seen the rules of that organisation I could not say whether this decision applied to it—which foxed him.

Other matters I dealt with in this letter of appointment were the arrangements for Ministers' private offices, the making of appointments by Ministers to the boards of state bodies, the roles of Ministers of State, and the briefing of the press after Government meetings.

I ensured a measure of control over the appointment of special advisers in Ministers' private offices—which in principle I favoured if they were people with relevant expertise—by requiring that prior to any such engagement I be informed of the reasons and of the expert qualification of the person concerned. At the same time I asked that until a study of past practices in relation to employment of civil servants to deal with Ministers' constituency correspondence (as distinct from correspondence with deputies and senators) had been completed in a few days' time, such work not be allocated to civil servants. This enabled me to ensure shortly afterwards that there would be no repetition in my administration of the excessive use of civil servants to deal with constituency matters that was reported to have been a feature of the Government we had just replaced. (It had been suggested that some Ministers in that Government had engaged a dozen and more civil servants on this kind of work. Indeed, when I became Taoiseach I had noted with some amusement the discreet disappearance of a 'General Section' of my department, comprising sixteen people, who I gathered had been looking after my predecessor's constituency work. In my case the personal secretary who, in accordance with custom, had accompanied me from opposition took care of this side of my activities.)

During my earlier term of office as Taoiseach I had come to realise that, although it was the practice for Ministers to inform their colleagues of intended appointments to the boards of state bodies for which they were responsible, and sometimes to invite comments on their proposed nominations, it was in fact difficult at such a late stage in the appointment process to influence their choices. Accordingly I laid down that each Minister was to notify me in advance of his or her intentions in relation to all such appointments once 'a preliminary view' had been arrived at about who should be nominated, so that I might 'have an opportunity to consult with him or her before any initiative is taken in the matter.' This arrangement enabled me to consult Dick Spring about proposed appointments—as I did in relation to everything of consequence coming to Government—before discussing the suggested names privately with the Minister concerned in advance of the relevant Government meeting. This process proved an effective deterrent to an excessive number of appointments based on political allegiance, overindulgence in which, often without adequate regard to the capacity of the individuals concerned, had in my view been in part responsible for the deterioration over the years in the performance of a number of state bodies, including some key enterprises.

It is my recollection that during the four-and-a-quarter years of the Government this procedure ensured that with only two exceptions no more than one 'political' appointment was made to any given state body, and that those thus appointed were people capable of contributing significantly to the success of the organisations concerned. Together with the contribution made to the work of state bodies by Ministers responsible for a number of them, such as Jim Mitchell and John Bruton, this approach helped to secure the recovery of many of the institutions concerned from the unhappy and in some instances disastrous situation prevailing in them when I took over the reins of Government.

I should incidentally add, lest what I have written give a contrary impression, that most of my Ministers were as concerned as I was to make effective appointments. One Minister indeed went so far as to spend two days interviewing individuals for a single vacancy on one board in order to make the best possible appointment, which I have to say seemed to me a case of excessive conscientiousness.

Some boards are appointed by the Government as a whole, and this responsibility was taken very seriously by our cabinet, especially in the case of the RTE Authority. One member of the outgoing Authority was an active supporter, indeed an adviser, of Fine Gael; he was also an extremely able participant in the work of the Authority. When the time came to appoint a new Authority I decided that he should be retained but that all the *new* appointments to the Authority would be non-political. The members of the Authority we eventually selected were chosen specifically by the cabinet collectively so as to secure a board that would stand up to pressure from *any* Government—our own included. However, only one of these was reappointed by our successors in 1989; there seemed to be clearly no inclination on their part to follow our example of ensuring a strong and politically independent Authority.

Another area of public appointments with which I was involved was that of judges. In the late 1970s Jack Lynch had broken away from the practice of making appointments of judges on a purely political basis, and I was determined that we should not revert to it. No vacancy in the Supreme Court occurred in our time, but we had to make a number of appointments to the High Court and Circuit Court, and in each case we sought to appoint on merit as best we could judge it. In a number of cases, however, our first or even second choice was not available; judges' salaries are far lower than the earnings of many senior barristers, some of whom cannot afford to accept a judicial appointment, especially while they still have children to educate. We were, for example, particularly anxious to maintain the tradition of having at least one Protestant judge in the High Court; but none of the senior Protestant barristers we approached was able to accept appointment when the occasion arose. We did, however, appoint the first Jewish High Court judge, Henry Barron.

The appointment of district justices poses a particular problem, because a very large number of lawyers seek these appointments. The great majority of those concerned will be unknown to most members of the Government. In the absence of any rational system of placing applicants in some kind of order of merit, appointments tend to be quite haphazard. One or other candidate may be known to a particular Minister, and in the absence of any other rationale his recommendation may carry the day. The wonder is not that some district justices are eccentric or unsatisfactory but that so many of them perform so well.

Towards the end of our period in office I proposed the introduction of a rational system designed to place the candidates for the District Court in order of merit, taking account of their qualifications and experience; but unfortunately the Government fell before we were able to give effect to this reform.

But to return to December 1982: I was concerned that all Ministers of State should have specific tasks formally delegated to them by their Ministers, something that in the past had often not been the case. Accordingly I decided in each instance the duties of the junior Minister, and asked that the formal assignment of these functions be made by the member of the Government concerned.

In addition to the Chief Whip, Seán Barrett, I appointed two other Ministers of State to my own department. I gave responsibility for Arts and Culture to Ted Nealon. For some decades past Government involvement in this area, including the appointment and financing of the Arts Council, had been the responsibility of the Taoiseach, and I knew that I would not have the time to give detailed attention to this area of activity. Ted proved an energetic and creative Minister.

I asked Nuala Fennell, one of the best-known amongst the group of mainly feminist women who had been elected in the Fine Gael interest to the Dáil in the contests of 1981–82, to undertake the co-ordination of women's affairs across various departments that handle issues affecting women's rights and interests. She tackled this assignment with energy and enthusiasm, but found it frustrating, because many of the civil servants and some of the Ministers upon whose areas of responsibility her co-ordinating function impinged were notably unwilling to allow her the freedom of action she needed. In some cases this reflected a measure of male chauvinism, but for the most part it was simply the instinctive response of Ministers and departments to any attempt at co-ordination that impinged upon their responsibilities. All in all she had a thankless task, and she found it particularly frustrating when some of her former colleagues in the women's movement criticised her for not doing things she would have loved to do, and might have been able to do had her efforts been better received in some key departments.

At Government meetings Dick Spring initially sat in the traditional Tánaiste's position, to the left of the Secretary to the Government, Dermot Nally, who was himself on my left. This is not in fact a good position for contact between Taoiseach and Tánaiste: while each can lean across behind or in front of the Government Secretary to speak to the other, there is no possibility of eye contact, which can facilitate sensitive handling of difficult situations. Accordingly some weeks later, when Dick returned from treatment in hospital for his back, with his agreement I moved him to a position at the centre of the long side of the oval table directly opposite myself. This new position put him on Alan Dukes's left, which also had possible advantages when difficult financial issues were being discussed. (Incidentally, I was always amused by the manner in which Ministers always sat in whatever place they chose by chance at their first Government meeting—sometimes forging surprising ad hoc alliances with the neighbours they found themselves beside.)

The first issue our new Government had to face was in fact the financial situation. Rightly or wrongly, we had set a five-year budget target in terms of a reduction in the current deficit. Arguably we might have been wiser, at least politically, to have done so in terms of the total borrowing requirement, for in the event it proved easier to cut capital spending than current spending.

As a Government new to office we had an evident temptation to take the toughest possible budgetary action at the outset, blaming it (with good reason in this instance!) on our predecessors. But in the light of the deeply depressing

Department of Finance projections for an undeflated economy such a course of action carried the risk of precipitating a collapse of economic activity. Might it not be wiser economically, whatever about the politics, to act with more restraint?

The difficulty was that the Department of Finance was by this time single-mindedly determined to cut the deficit by the maximum amount possible, almost regardless of any economic consequences. They seemed to feel that unless the current deficit were reduced to a figure close to £750 million in 1983, external confidence in our economy might wither, and our ability to borrow this sum, plus our capital needs, might thus be prejudiced. Alan Dukes, pitchforked into the Finance portfolio in the most adverse circumstances conceivable, was in no position to challenge this rather apocalyptic view of his officials.

In these difficult circumstances it seemed to me that we needed some kind of cross-check on the Department of Finance's assessment that in international financial markets we would not 'get away with' a current deficit significantly in excess of £750 million. Accordingly I decided to attempt an independent verification of this Finance view. I knew that, after his replacement as Secretary of State by Zbig Brzezinski in 1977, Henry Kissinger had set up a politico-economic consultancy service—of a fairly expensive kind. My personal relationship with him was such, however, that I knew if I asked him to check something for me he would do it without a fee. Early in January therefore I rang him and asked if he could check in New York financial markets how decisions on our part to achieve current budget deficits of either £750 million or £900 million would be viewed.

On the afternoon of Monday 10 January he rang me back. He said that the New York financial markets were more concerned that we should have a programme to which we would stick rather than a more ambitious one that would fall apart. The expectation—he could almost say prediction—in New York was that we would be going for 'the moderate programme', namely a current budget deficit of around 7 per cent of GNP (just over £900 million) and total exchequer borrowing of 12 per cent of GNP (about £1,600 million). There was no expectation that we would go for lower figures, and there was a feeling that with such a 'moderate' programme we would have a chance of 'making it'. This assessment had been based on contacts with the research departments of the leading New York banks.

He asked if we had any idea of going to the IMF. I told him that we had no such intention, and he responded that he strongly agreed with this; the feeling in New York was that at this stage we had the possibility of solving our own problems.

This conversation, which seemed to confirm my suspicion that Finance had been overstating its case, provided me with good grounds for rejecting its demand for a £750 million current deficit. The department, which presumably had not previously had its advice challenged by a cross-check of this kind, was, not surprisingly, furious. Within hours Alan Dukes—under pressure from his advisers, I assumed—came out publicly in favour of a £750 million deficit.

Dick Spring, with whom of course I had also been in continuous touch on these matters, and who was about to go into hospital for treatment for his back, wrote to me at once to protest formally at Alan's public statement, urging that there be no further comment on budgetary matters until decisions were taken by the Government. The matter was discussed that Tuesday afternoon, following which a statement was issued saying that the Government had not yet decided on the appropriate level of the current budget deficit and that there had been concern on the part of the Taoiseach and a number of Ministers of both parties lest the figure of £750 million, which the Minister for Finance had mentioned as a target to aim at, should be taken as reflecting a Government decision.

Having established our key parameter of a £900 million current deficit, we went to work to achieve it. It was a painful exercise, but with the aid of large tax increases, an increase in non-tax revenue and some cuts in proposed expenditure (which nevertheless left budgeted spending in 1983 above the 1982 level) we were able to meet the current deficit target while making provision for social welfare increases going beyond the forecast cost-of-living increase. Helped by a £200 million or 20 per cent cut in capital spending, these measures brought total exchequer borrowing down from 16.5 to 13.5 per cent of GNP—some seven points lower than the figure we had faced for 1982 when we had taken office eighteen hectic months before.

In December I had sent Alan Dukes a note of a number of proposals Dick Spring and I had discussed in the course of our negotiations on the formation of the Government. These were measures that Dick had recognised required further consideration and that were to be examined with a view to possible implementation 'unless they give rise to technical or administrative obstacles that cannot be overcome or would have adverse economic effects which in the [Finance] Department's view would make them seriously inadvisable.'

These proposals included an increase in the top income tax rate to 65 per cent; increases in taxes on luxuries, such as video recorders, cosmetics, and furs; and an increase in the ceiling for PRSI contributions—all of which in fact were introduced in this budget. Moreover, an income-related residential property tax was announced in the budget, and brought into effect by legislation later that year. Other measures on this list were introduced in later budgets during our term of office.

The income-related property tax was an idea of mine on which I had worked during 1982 with my daughter-in-law Eithne, a social economist who is a Labour Party county councillor and has since 1982 been a Dáil Labour candidate. While it could be argued that people with limited means who live in small dwellings should not have to pay local authority rates, it seemed absurd that since 1977 well-off people in larger houses also made no contribution to local services. There is an economic case against very high income tax rates even on large incomes: they certainly lead to large-scale avoidance and evasion by many wealthy people; but similar arguments do not apply to taxes on fixed property, in particular residential property, which by definition cannot be moved elsewhere. The impact of a residential property tax is, in my view, both economically and socially beneficial, because it discourages a wasteful use of residential accommodation, which is normally in short supply. By introducing such a tax, which was eventually fixed at a rate of 1.5 per cent but was limited to houses worth £60,000 or more in 1983 and whose occupiers had incomes of £20,000 or more, with indexation in subsequent years, I felt we would be raising some additional income in a way that would not be open to criticism either on economic or social grounds.

Naturally enough, when I had put this to Dick Spring during our post-election discussions he had been happy to accept my proposal, which came to be seen in due course as a 'Labour' tax, despite the fact that I never made any secret of the fact that it was my idea. I have to say that I was quite unimpressed by subsequent middle-class criticism of this tax, criticism that became more acute in the late 1980s, when house prices, which had for years lagged behind the cost of living, belatedly adjusted upwards into line with the trend of consumer prices.

While the Government had been engaged in the laborious and painful task of preparing this first budget, Michael Noonan had reported to an astonished cabinet the results of his inquiry into the telephone-tapping affair. During the debate on the appointment of the Government in mid-December it had been suggested to me that there could be a danger that relevant papers might be destroyed. As Michael Noonan and I had mounted the steps to the lobby to vote the Government into office, I had told him that he should go at once to his department to ensure the security of any documents relating to this matter. I need not have worried. The Secretary of the Department of Justice, for whom the independence of the Garda Síochána from political interference was fundamental to the security of the state, had taken all necessary steps to see that the relevant records were secure. Having established from these documents the facts known to the Department of Justice, Michael Noonan asked that the Secretary interview the Garda Commissioner about what had happened. Statements were then sought from the members of the Garda Síochána concerned, and these were received on 3 January.

Deputy Commissioner Ainsworth (who at the time of these events had been an Assistant Commissioner in charge of the Intelligence and Security Branch of the Garda Síochána) said in his statement that he had been telephoned in April by the then Minister for Justice, Seán Doherty, who had discussed with him leaks from Government departments and possibly from the cabinet to the press. Ainsworth had told him of his own suspicions that the media had contacts not alone in Government departments and in politics but also within the Garda Síochána. He had added that the way things were moving they would soon be into breaches of the Official Secrets Act and that the security of the state would be in danger on an international basis. Foreign papers and foreign powers were interested in happenings here because of the unstable position of the Government, which could fall at the wish of the Workers' Party, a party that had connections with the official IRA. He had told the Minister that a stable Government was necessary to ensure the safety of the state, especially since subversive groups were increasing rapidly in numbers and would eventually attempt to overthrow the Government regardless of who was in power.

Following this remarkable response to his Minister's reference to press leaks from the Government, Ainsworth was later called to his office and told by the Minister of his concern about leaks of sensitive information to political corre- spondents. Seán Doherty mentioned Bruce Arnold of the *Irish Independent* in particular, about whom Ainsworth told his Minister that he knew very little. Doherty then said that in the interest of the security of the state there should be an intercept on Bruce Arnold's telephone, to which Ainsworth said he had responded that he would not favour such a tap unless there were good reason for it. Nevertheless, Seán Doherty told Ainsworth that because of Bruce Arnold's articles in the papers his telephone should be intercepted. Accordingly Ainsworth tapped Bruce Arnold's phone from 12 May, but because Bruce Arnold was heard saying several weeks later, 'The less said on the phone the better,' he cancelled the intercept on 12 July, without consultation with his Minister.

Seán Doherty subsequently told Assistant Commissioner Ainsworth that Geraldine Kennedy of the *Sunday Tribune* was producing very sensitive infor- mation and that there were suspicions of unauthorised leaks from the cabinet. If this continued the security of the state could be endangered; an intercept on Geraldine Kennedy's phone might disclose where the leaks came from. Accord- ingly Ainsworth arranged that her phone be tapped. It subsequently transpired— although no explanation was ever forthcoming for this—that on 27 October, arising from a regular quarterly review of this intercept, it was certified that this tap was yielding results. But Ainsworth said that, again without consulting his Minister, he had cancelled the intercept on 16 November. No explanation was given for this decision either.

For his part the Commissioner said that on 10 May he had had discussions with Ainsworth about 'Government leaks and security matters'. In the light of these discussions he had been satisfied that the telephone taps proposed to him on that day, including one on the phone of Bruce Arnold, should be sought. However, until this controversy had arisen he had had no knowledge that a telephone tapped some time later had been regularly used by Geraldine Kennedy (whose phone, it was later discovered, had been tapped on the basis of a warrant made out mistakenly in the name of a previous subscriber), and he had never seen transcripts of these tapes.

The Commissioner said that Ainsworth had stated that the Minister had told him that the Government was very concerned about leaks of highly con- fidential Government matters and was very anxious to establish how the leaks were occurring. On 23 October, together with Ainsworth and another senior officer, he had been summoned by the Taoiseach, Charles Haughey, to a conference not attended by the Minister for Justice, Seán Doherty, who was absent on that day. The Taoiseach had enquired whether any progress had been made in discovering the source of Government leaks and what action was being taken to prevent Garda leaks. He was extremely concerned about these, and directed that they must be stopped.

Ainsworth added that after this meeting with the Taoiseach Seán Doherty asked him to reintroduce the tap on Bruce Arnold's phone, but that he had told the Minister that such a tap was useless because of Bruce Arnold's suspicions, and that this was also true of Geraldine Kennedy. The Minister, he said, did not pursue the matter further.

The only other point of interest in these statements was the concern felt by gardaí involved in listening to the tapes and in transcribing some of them. One stated that it had been openly said amongst them that they were being asked to do work of a purely political nature, and there was general relief when the intercept on Bruce Arnold was terminated. They had been pressed almost daily about whether anything was coming from the intercepts.

Finally it emerged that in both cases the proposed phone taps had been very properly queried by the relevant official in the Department of Justice when the request had been received there, but Assistant Commissioner Ainsworth had referred him back to the Minister on both occasions. The reason given to the official for the Bruce Arnold intercept was that he was 'anti-national', and the official advised the Minister to refuse this intercept, a recommendation that the Minister did not accept. In the case of Geraldine Kennedy the official was told that the Minister was aware of the detailed reason; the official was accordingly not in a position to make any recommendation on its sufficiency or otherwise, but he made a negative recommendation regarding the form of the accompanying certificate, which, contrary to precedent, mentioned 'national security'. The Minister had nevertheless accepted the recommendation that he had himself initiated.

A couple of days after these statements had been received, newspaper reports suggested that information had been turned up that required the investigation to be widened. As we were aware of no such development we issued a statement saying that these reports were wholly speculative and devoid of foundation. But less than two weeks later we had to make a further statement, for in the meantime we had heard that, faced with the recollection of a secretary who had typed the relevant transcript, Ainsworth had admitted that towards the end of October his Minister had rung him to ask him to deliver a tape recorder with a sensitive microphone to the Minister for Finance, Ray MacSharry, and that on the following day Seán Doherty had asked Ainsworth to have a tape of a conversation transcribed quickly, as he wanted it at Government. This was done, and two copies of the transcript were delivered to the Minister. The copy retained by Ainsworth, which he now handed over to the Department of Justice, was read only by Michael Noonan, Peter Sutherland, and officials of the Department of Justice. On my instructions no-one else, myself included, was allowed to hear it or see a transcript of it. But following this Martin O'Donoghue, who had been Minister for Education in the Haughey Government, was asked to identify the tape. It was of a conversation between Ray MacSharry and himself, which Martin O'Donoghue clearly did not know was being recorded. He asked for a copy of the transcript, which in the circumstances he seemed entitled to; and he then released it to the newspapers.

Meanwhile Michael Noonan reported to us that the investigation into the phone-tapping had been completed. On the advice of Peter Sutherland (who as senior counsel had acted for a previous Commissioner who had been dismissed by a Fianna Fáil Government), the procedure adopted was for Michael Noonan to see the two senior Garda officers separately to put to them the facts as they had been ascertained and were seen by the Government, and to ask them to reflect on their positions. Next day both Commissioner McLoughlin and Deputy Commissioner Ainsworth resigned, and on 20 January the Government issued statements announcing these resignations and setting out the facts about the telephone-tapping and the MacSharry-O'Donoghue affair.

On the following day Ray MacSharry resigned from the Fianna Fáil front bench, but Charles Haughey made it clear that despite these revelations he intended to fight on as leader of Fianna Fáil. He survived a challenge to his leadership, but his party was clearly deeply divided. Seán Doherty and Martin O'Donoghue (by this time in the Seanad) resigned the Fianna Fáil whip almost immediately afterwards.

Meanwhile our Government had its own problems. One of these was the constitutional amendment on abortion to which I had committed Fine Gael before we took office.

One evening towards the end of January as I was about to leave for home, Peter Sutherland came to my room and handed to me his formal legal opinion on the Fianna Fáil wording of this amendment. This opinion demonstrated that the Fianna Fáil amendment was ambiguous in ways that I had not appreciated. While it was possible that these ambiguities might never give rise to a problem if the wording were not tested in the courts, it was, I felt, morally impossible for us to propose to the people a formula that the Supreme Court at some time in the future might feel obliged to interpret in such a way as either to exclude the preservation of the life of the mother in certain cases or, at the opposite pole, actually to permit abortion in the early months of pregnancy, to which all members of the Government were opposed.

The first of these possible interpretations could arise from the part of the wording that referred to the mother and the child having an 'equal' right to life: Peter Sutherland advised that this wording not merely might but was likely to be interpreted by the Supreme Court as excluding the kind of intervention that takes place in hospitals in accordance with the existing law so as to save the life of a mother who has cancer of the womb or has an ectopic pregnancy. This was because if such operations were to be put to the test in the courts after the enactment of this amendment, a surgeon who had carried out such an operation with fatal consequences for the child could not reasonably be said to have upheld the right to life of the unborn child equally with that of the mother.

The alternative unacceptable interpretation was less likely, but still possible: the word 'unborn'—left hanging in the air without qualification or interpretation in Fianna Fáil's proposed amendment—was ambiguous. It was a noun that appeared in no dictionary and could refer either to that which comes into existence at fertilisation or at the time the foetus is implanted in the womb or, alternatively, only to a child *capable of being born*—for if it were not capable of being born the word 'unborn' could be argued to be inapplicable. If the court accepted the latter interpretation, then abortion up to the point where the foetus was viable might be permitted.

The Labour Party Ministers had already indicated that they would not support the Fianna Fáil amendment. Accordingly, before bringing the Attorney General's opinion formally before the Government I called a meeting of the Fine Gael Ministers in my room. The dilemma facing us was painful. We were under no illusion about the consequences of rejecting the amendment as it was phrased at this point: we would be accused by Fianna Fáil of going back on our pre-election commitment to support their wording and, unscrupulously, of being 'soft on abortion'. The damage to our party would be considerable, and it was far from certain that we could secure a majority either in the Dáil or in the country for an alternative wording, which Peter Sutherland warned us might in any event prove very difficult to draft. Yet my colleagues did not hesitate; the possibility that the Fianna Fáil wording could be interpreted in the ways Peter Sutherland had suggested was enough for them. Within twenty minutes we had reached a unanimous decision to withdraw our support for this dangerously ambiguous wording and to seek a safer alternative formulation.

The fact that, faced with a clear moral issue of this kind, none of my colleagues hesitated about taking a decision bound to arouse deep—and dangerous—controversy was, and remains today, for me a source of great pride. I am conscious also of the irony of the fact that it was this profoundly moral decision that precipitated one of the worst confrontations in Ireland between the state and the Catholic Church.

Immediately afterwards, on the morning of budget day (and my birthday), 9 February, the second stage debate on the Amendment Bill opened in the Dáil. Michael Noonan explained the background to the amendment, making it clear, however, that he had himself an open mind on its wording; there had been, he said, many other drafts before this particular one had been adopted by Fianna Fáil on the eve of the November 1982 general election. This comment alerted public opinion to the possibility of a change in the wording.

I was naturally anxious that the rationale of our decision to amend the wording be understood by public opinion. I knew that there were groups of extreme right-wing Catholics, deeply hostile to us because of our stance on issues like contraception and divorce, who would welcome any opportunity of denouncing our attitude on this issue. Our change of position on the wording would triumphantly be misrepresented by them as 'proof' that we were 'soft on abortion'; some of those involved would have neither the capacity nor the willingness to understand the moral basis of the decision we had taken. The hierarchy of the Catholic Church was, I knew, under constant pressure from these groups, whose members seemed to feel themselves rather than the bishops to be the true guardians of the faith. It was important therefore that the bishops should understand the reasons that had impelled us to review the wording of the proposed amendment before they came under pressure from the right-wing extremists to attack our decision.

Accordingly I had rung Bishop Cassidy of Clonfert, whose house in Ballina-sloe I would be passing on my way to a Young Fine Gael conference in Galway (at which this whole issue was passionately debated), to ask if I could have a word with him. When we met I told him of the decision we had been forced to take as a result of the moral imperative of concern for human life, and of my anxiety that our action when announced should not be misunderstood by the Catholic hierarchy. How could we best convey this directly to the bishops and keep in touch with them so that they would know what alternative wording we were likely to put forward? He expressed his understanding of our dilemma and said he would consult his colleagues and come back to me about a channel of communication.

As I continued my journey I reflected upon the irony that in a country that many outside observers have seen as one in which church and state are closely linked the relationship is in fact so remote that no established channel exists for contact at the institutional level, thus necessitating the kind of informal approach I had just initiated, based on my personal acquaintance with a bishop whose house I had happened to be passing. This reflection was given added point by the phone call I received from Bishop Cassidy shortly afterwards. The bishops, he told me, would not meet the Government but would appoint a representative to whom we could talk. I was astonished and deeply disturbed at this reaction. It was unprecedented for any group or organisation to refuse contact with the elected Government of the state. Was it possible that the hierarchy, or some influential group within it, was planning to exploit the moral problem we faced in order to engineer a confrontation, or, at best, was seeking to avoid facing, as we had done unhesitatingly, the moral issue posed by the ambiguity of the draft amendment? Or was their unwillingness to meet us due to fear of a reaction to such a meeting from the right-wing lay Catholic lobby, from which I knew some bishops felt themselves to be under pressure? I had heard rumours that some of them feared, or had even experienced, denunciation to Rome by some of these extremists.

Whatever the reason, this refusal boded ill; it would make it difficult to convey to the Catholic hierarchy, individually and collectively, as personal contact would have enabled us to do, our sincerity in facing this problem. And there was always the danger of misunderstandings arising where communication had to be carried on through an intermediary. These fears proved fully justified.

As far as the public was concerned the matter rested there for over a month. Meanwhile, however, Peter Sutherland and Michael Noonan were wrestling with the task of finding an alternative to the Fianna Fáil wording that they could in conscience recommend to the Oireachtas and to the electorate. It soon became clear that there was no way in which both the Oireachtas and the Supreme Court could be excluded simultaneously from having a future role in the matter. Any wording designed to tie the hands of the Oireachtas would have to be fairly specific in order to deal with the complexities of the problem, and the intricacies of that very precise wording would then necessarily be subject to interpretation by the Supreme Court. On the other hand, if a wording were employed that sought to preclude the Supreme Court from intervening to rule a law against abortion to be unconstitutional, as the United States Supreme Court had done, such a provision would necessarily leave the issue to the Oireachtas.

Michael Noonan and the Department of Justice favoured an attempt to resolve the problem by making changes in the Fianna Fáil wording designed to eliminate the two ambiguities I have referred to. These amendments involved substituting for the ambiguous word 'unborn' a reference to life beginning with the commencement of pregnancy. This would have the advantage of being in keeping with the wording of the Offences Against the Person Act, 1861, the British statute that was still the ordinary law of Ireland making abortion illegal, for this Act referred to the 'termination of pregnancy'. Second, it was proposed to include a qualifying phrase specifically designed to ensure the protection of the life of the mother in all cases.

These proposed modifications of the wording were put by Michael Noonan to representatives of the various churches, to see whether agreement could be reached on them. This evoked from the Protestant churches and the Jewish community a reluctant and unenthusiastic acceptance; but when Michael Noonan met the Catholic hierarchy's nominee, Monsignor Sheehy (with whom Peter Sutherland had already had contact), he received in due course a negative reaction to both the proposed amendments.

When this was reported to us in Government we were divided on our reaction. Michael Noonan and the majority favoured going ahead with the Fianna Fáil amendment, qualified by these two changes, despite the fact that this was apparently not acceptable to the Catholic hierarchy. Fianna Fáil would of course take advantage of this, leaving us no further on in avoiding conflict in the Oireachtas, where both our party and the Labour Party would be split. A minority of the Government, of whom I was one, favoured dropping this attempt to improve the Fianna Fáil wording, an attempt that we felt would bog us down in sterile debates about when pregnancy began and about the circumstances in which intervention to save the life of a mother should be permitted. Moreover, the most that Michael Noonan could say about his amendment was that 'it would meet *at least in significant part* the criticism made by the Attorney General.' It seemed to me and several others that, given the impossibility of getting agreement on a wording along these lines, we should go back to the original concept of a simple amendment that would deal with the fear originally expressed to us that the Supreme Court might follow the decision of the United States Supreme Court, precluding anti-abortion legislation.

When we brought the matter to the parliamentary party, despite the fact that I and the Government minority on this issue did not press our case, the party members demanded a full debate, and, after insisting that they hear Peter Sutherland's opinion in person, and persuaded by his view, opted by a large majority for the simple formula designed to exclude intervention by the Supreme Court, namely, 'Nothing in the Constitution shall be invoked invalidating a provision of a law on the grounds that it prohibits abortion.' This was subsequently amended on technical grounds to: 'Nothing in this Constitution shall be invoked to invalidate or to deprive of force or effect a provision of the law on the grounds that it prohibits abortion.' This wording was endorsed as being preferable by the main churches other than the Roman Catholic Church.

The eventual vote in the Dáil was extremely confused, with members of both Fine Gael and Labour splitting three ways on the wording of the Bill: some voting for and some against and some abstaining. The net result however was that, with the support of eight Fine Gael deputies and four Labour Party members, the Fianna Fáil wording was eventually adopted. Following a legal challenge that got nowhere, it was decided that the referendum be held on 7 September. The Fine Gael party as such did not campaign, although a number of us made our positions clear, setting out the grounds on which we rejected the Fianna Fáil amendment and urging the people to vote against it because of its dangers.

The campaign for the amendment was conducted on emotional lines and almost totally without regard to the actual issues at stake as set out in Peter Sutherland's opinion, issues that I presented in a speech on the subject during the campaign. The ambiguities of the Fianna Fáil wording were either ignored or were rejected without serious discussion by its supporters, apart from one intervention by the Bishop of Kerry (later to be Archbishop of Dublin), the late Dr Kevin McNamara. He dismissed our fears on the grounds that a form of words could 'be devised which by any reasonable interpretation would render highly unlikely a Court judgement that it was compatible with legalised abortion'—which is precisely what Michael Noonan had tried to do on this point but which had been rejected by Monsignor Sheehy on behalf of the hierarchy! On the danger that the Fianna Fáil amendment might be interpreted to prohibit surgical operations of a kind currently being carried out, the bishop contented himself with the comment that the fact that such practices were possible *under existing law* seemed a sufficient answer. These comments totally missed the constitutional points at issue.

In a speech on 12 April I described the evasion of the legal issues involved as 'astonishing'. Bishop McNamara's response to this was that I was 'ascribing to the law a kind of rigidity that was totally irreconcilable with the idea that the law is a flexible and developing science.' This reference to the flexibility of law ignored the fact that the whole issue arose from the manner in which the law had been flexibly interpreted in the United States and the fear that it might be interpreted in the same way in Ireland.

The only attempt made to justify Monsignor Sheehy's objections on behalf of the hierarchy to Michael Noonan's proposals was a suggestion that these objections were 'necessarily provisional and incomplete', because Monsignor Sheehy had never been shown the final wording of the amendment that we proposed. This was, however, a quibble, for in fact the two modifications of the original amendment had been put in writing to Monsignor Sheehy, and the eventual form of the amendment, including these qualifications, was thus not in the slightest doubt.

This defensive attitude on the part of the Catholic hierarchy did however suggest a certain amount of unhappiness on their part at the way they had handled the matter. I was left with the impression that they recognised that there was no intellectual basis on which to challenge the criticisms of the amendment put forward by Peter Sutherland but that, faced with pressure from right-wing lay Catholics, the hierarchy had adjudged it safer to support the proposed amendment than risk being accused by unscrupulous elements in the anti-abortion camp of themselves being 'soft' on the issue.

However that may be, on 22 August the hierarchy issued a statement that gave it as their considered opinion that the amendment would safeguard the life of both the mother and her unborn child—a remarkable excursion by the bishops into the field of constitutional law, in the course of which they clearly had no qualms about flatly contradicting the view of the Attorney General, which by this time had been reinforced by that of the Director of Public Prosecutions. Indeed, the hierarchy went on to use the existence of this contrary professional view by the relevant law officers to justify a demand for a clear majority for the Fianna Fáil amendment, an exercise in logic that frankly dizzied me: 'As some conscientiously hold a different opinion, we are convinced that a clear majority in favour of the amendment will greatly contribute to the continued protection of human life in the laws of our country.'

The amendment was carried by a two-to-one majority in a 54 per cent poll. In the end of the day no-one came well out of the affair. The Catholic hierarchy was, at best, weak in the face of extremist pressure. Fianna Fáil for its part was totally opportunist in wooing the 'pro-life' lobby. Even the Labour Party, the leaders of which had from the beginning taken up a wiser position than I had on the issue, was at the end of the day as divided as Fine Gael, with over a quarter of its deputies voting with Fianna Fáil, as some of ours also did, for the amendment that had originally been proposed by the Haughey Government.

For my part I should never have accepted the original referendum proposal put to me, however harmless it may have appeared at the time, for that commitment to introduce a constitutional amendment on the issue led me eventually into a position that, while intellectually defensible, was much too complicated to secure public understanding or acceptance. However, the truth is that, given the attitude of such a substantial minority of the members of both Government parties, no tactics of mine could have prevented the amendment from being forced through by Fianna Fáil, whatever I had proposed or failed to propose. As long as simplistic attitudes to complex moral issues persist in Ireland, and as long as unscrupulous politicians are prepared to exploit religious feeling, our society will remain vulnerable to the 'crawthumpers'.

Several months after the formation of the Government, while we were immersed in this referendum issue, a number of backbenchers, one of whom was herself a biochemist, approached me about an alleged industrial pollution problem in Co. Tipperary. It was suggested that toxic emissions from a chemical factory had affected human and animal health on a nearby farm. The issue was a complex one, and when I raised it in Government in late March it was agreed that an interdepartmental report be prepared for us to consider at an early date. (A proposal of mine that Justin Keating, a former lecturer in veterinary medicine, examine the problem on our behalf was rejected by the Government.) Despite various promises this report was not produced until July, and when I received it I found it most unsatisfactory, leaving so many loose ends that I had to raise some fifty further queries on it. The response to these further queries of mine still left outstanding some score of issues, which I sought to probe further, but because the farmer had initiated a legal process against the company that owned the factory and was not in a position to furnish us with further information until the case was heard, I could not take the matter any further.

Why did I involve myself so deeply in this issue? Because I was worried about the possibility that undue concern about the negative impact on industrial development or agricultural exports of the establishment of a link between the factory and the farm health record might have unconsciously influenced officials into taking up an overdefensive attitude on the matter. If this *had* happened, the rights of the farmer involved could have been jeopardised by our administration. A politician's job as I have conceived it is to make sure that such individual rights are protected, not undermined, by the government machine.

It was clear that the officials from the departments involved were extremely irritated by my approach, although they did their best to hide it. They asserted that there was no evidence to link the problem at the farm with emissions from the factory, and that cross-referencing of the dates on which the incinerator at the factory was operated with the dates on which odours were reported and when the animals were reported to be suffering respiratory difficulties did not indicate such a link. They also asserted that ten problems that had been reported on the farm had been satisfactorily explained by factors unrelated to possible chemical contamination.

Yet five years later the Supreme Court found that on the balance of probabilities the farmer's lung disease *was* caused by toxic emissions from the factory and that there was *uncontroverted evidence* that animals had been seen and heard to be in distress at the time the emissions had taken place. Moreover, five veterinary surgeons were of the firm opinion that what the animals were suffering from was caused by toxic emissions from the factory.

While I recognise that in such a case it is impossible to arrive at objective truth with scientific certainty—the court case hinged on issues of the burden of proof, and eventually the issue was decided on the basis of *probable* causes—nevertheless it was disturbing that the farmer won his case partly on grounds of facts as to the relationship of the timing of emissions and the timing of animals being in distress that directly and flatly contradicted what I had been told by the officials whom I had asked to examine the matter. My concern at the time lest officials' concepts of the public interest in relation to industrial promotion and the reputation of our farm exports clouded their judgement of the only real public interest—that of justice—seemed to me to have been validated in this instance.

Another case several years later in relation to which I found myself concerned about the rights of an individual arising from his relationship with the public service involved drug smuggling in Spain. I learnt that an Irishman charged with a drugs offence in Spain claimed to have been acting as an undercover agent for our customs service. When I sought information about this case I found that he was telling the truth, but was now facing a sentence of up to twenty years, because the customs officials who had been using him in the hope of trapping a member of a Tamil drug-smuggling ring had failed to tell either the Gardaí or the Spanish police about their plan. When I discovered this during a weekend I immediately summoned the heads of the relevant Government departments to my home to see what could be done for this hapless tool of our customs service, galvanising all concerned into approaching the Spanish authorities at the highest level into securing his release, which, with great difficulty, we eventually achieved. Because his life and that of his wife were now known to be at risk—a danger of which inadequate account seemed to me to have been taken by those who initiated this scheme—we subsequently had to help him start a new life in another country, a project in which John Rogers, the Attorney General, played a major part.

To the establishment, if I may call it that, my involvement in cases like these must have seemed quixotic and destabilising. I think they had become accustomed to a more passive and less interventionist political leadership so far as human issues of this kind were concerned; but the truth is that, despite my political office, I remained in a sense rather anti-establishment, especially in dealing with such issues.

In Foreign Affairs, which has a strong human rights bias, I had found less of a problem about issues of this kind, although even there I experienced some reticence about a case in which I authorised the Dutch wife of an Irishman committed to a mental hospital to have her two children put on her passport without her husband's consent (which he was then incapable of giving), so that she could take them with her to the Netherlands, where she could get employment more readily. However, departmental caution was vindicated in this case, for later on, while I was in opposition, the husband sued the department, and the court found that I had acted incorrectly in exercising what had always been believed to be an unfettered Ministerial discretion to decide passport issues of this kind; I should have asked the courts to decide the issue.

There were no legal repercussions in another case, however, where a woman whose American husband had succeeded in taking their child to the United States in defiance of a custody order in her favour asked me to add the child's name to her passport without her husband's consent, so that when she had saved enough money she could go there to take the child back to Ireland. She succeeded in this venture, escaping with the child and, with assistance from our local Consul-General, returning to Ireland. I had no compunction in assisting in this enterprise, given that our public administration, through defects of procedure, had failed to protect her legal rights in the first instance; and the Secretary of the department, Paul Keating, sharing my concern, was quite unperturbed when a newspaper headlined the mother's successful enterprise.

But to return to our early months in office in 1981: we found ourselves faced with the need to reform An Bord Pleanála. As they had done in June 1981, Fianna Fáil in December 1982 had made a number of public appointments between the time of their election defeat and the transfer of power—something I had ruled out when my first Government fell. As a result five of the nine members of An Bord Pleanála were now political appointees of Fianna Fáil, who had no apparent relevant qualifications and experience. Dick Spring, Minister for the Environment as well as Tánaiste, was gravely concerned at this, especially in view of information that suggested that some appeals were in effect being delegated to groups of board members that might include no non-political appointees. A huge backlog of three thousand cases had also accumulated.

Dick brought this matter to Government, and we authorised him to prepare a Bill that would limit the Ministerial power to make appointments to the board. The Bill confined the choice of chairman to a person nominated by a committee consisting of six ex-officio holders of prominent positions in the public and private sector. It also limited the choice of four other members of the board to panels of names to be proposed by groups of organisations representing professional, environmental, development and community interests; and one member was to be a civil servant. Word of our review of the board's position had reached the press on 4 March, and ten days later our decision to replace the board emerged, its current members being given the option of resigning or being dismissed.

This reform was of course bitterly fought by Fianna Fáil, but was equally firmly insisted on by our Government because of the vital importance of sealing off the physical planning appeals system from political influence, which, given the amounts of money at stake, could be open to accusations of corrupt use. Irish politics for most of the life of the state has been almost totally free of any suspicion of financial corruption; but since the institution of physical planning controls in 1963 doubts have been expressed whether this happy situation has continued. It is fair to add that the number of politicians about whom there has been any hint of suspicion can be counted on the fingers of one hand. Nevertheless the scale of the pressure on the physical planning system from interested parties with a major financial stake in the outcome of planning decisions and appeals is such that even a system as carefully drawn as the one we devised may not have proved totally watertight. Six years later a Garda investigation had to be instituted into aspects of corruption involving officials of Dublin local authorities, which it was alleged may have involved a small number of politicians as well as someone in An Bord Pleanála.

While we were tackling this delicate issue I was establishing a quite different kind of planning board, one that would produce proposals for a national economic plan covering the difficult deflationary years ahead. The idea of establishing such a board had been present in my mind for some time before I returned to power at the end of 1982, for during my earlier nine-month Government I had been concerned to observe how far the Department of Finance had moved from the innovative and developmental role it had played under T. K. Whitaker's leadership in the late 1950s and 1960s. Faced with the enormous increase in public spending since 1977, the Department of Finance's preoccupation with the need for expenditure cuts was understandable and laudable, but this concern was concentrated so much on each separate year's budget that there did not seem to me to be a sufficient sense of direction even for the medium term, let alone the long term.

Accordingly, when I came to form my second Government at the end of 1982 I consulted several people who had played a key role in the 1960s, including Ken Whitaker himself and Louden Ryan. (Louden Ryan, who had been responsible for my year's research stint at Trinity in 1958–59, had subsequently been deeply involved in the process of economic development, both when he had been seconded to the Department of Finance for a number of years and later when he had been chairman of the National Industrial Economic Council and its more broadly based successor, the National Economic and Social Council.)

Following my discussion with them I moved to establish on 18 March 1983 the National Planning Board, with Louden Ryan as chairman and six other members drawn from industry, the trade union movement, and academic life. The board's objective was to report to the Government through a task force of Ministers on how to maximise output and employment in competitive conditions and how to undertake and finance infrastructural public works at minimum net cost over and above unemployment payments, as well as how best to reconcile social equity and the efficient use of public resources.

I was particularly concerned that the board should operate independently of the Government machine, because it seemed to me that Fianna Fáil's late-1982 attempt at planning had suffered greatly from being undertaken—with outside assistance, it is true—within the Government framework. The text of the document they then published bore all the marks of having been filtered through processes designed to ensure that it said nothing that would be either politically embarrassing or contrary to Department of Finance orthodoxy.

I arranged, however, for a liaison committee to be established within the civil service to provide the independent board with all it needed. This system worked well at its own level, but it seems to me in retrospect that there remained a problem that was difficult to define, let alone resolve, namely ensuring that the board's recommendations would be cast in terms that could easily be accommodated within the civil service frame of reference. As it turned out, despite the close and, as far as I could see, quite amicable relationship between the board and the civil service, when it came to implementing some of its recommendations problems arose because of structural discontinuity between what it proposed and the way in which the public administration actually works.

The speed with which the board submitted to the task force of Ministers their initial 'Programme for Recovery' was impressive. We needed an early contribution from them so that we could build their initial recommendations into our departmental estimates for 1984, and we had their programme before us three months after the establishment of the board. The final version of this document, incorporating their reactions to departmental comments, was with us in September. They then went on to prepare their 'Proposals for a Plan', which they completed in March 1984. This in turn provided much of the basis for the Government's plan *Building on Reality*, published in October 1984.

This was as fast a pace of work as could possibly have been expected. But the fact that the Government's plan based on the board's proposals was eventually published almost two years into its term of office—and terms of office of Governments rarely exceed four years in practice—must in retrospect raise a question whether, given the urgency of the problems we faced in late 1982, it was wise to proceed by this rather circuitous route. By the autumn of 1984 not alone was the Government almost half way through its effective life but by that time some at least of the possible field of action had been pre-empted by events. Also, because the board had been established initially to help us tackle a particular situation, its role was not adequately built into the permanent administrative structure for decision-making. It did not therefore leave as enduring a mark on public administration as I had hoped.

Nevertheless quite a number of important recommendations were implemented. Thus we adopted their proposal to limit the burden of tax to 36.5 per cent of GNP, as well as some of their suggestions for public service reform. Other recommendations adopted included the abolition of the newly introduced 65 per cent top income tax rate, the introduction of a deposit interest retention tax, the substitution of a higher rate of children's allowances for the child allowance in the income tax code, the introduction of changes in the Farm Advisory Service, and the abolition of the Land Commission. We also set about introducing a land tax as proposed by the board, but the complex administrative arrangements for this had not been completed in early 1987 when Fianna Fáil succeeded us in office and abolished this form of farm taxation. Another recommendation of the board that we adopted and that Fianna Fáil also reversed (only to reverse it again several years later) was for a much higher level of investment in roads.

The implementation of proposals such as these provided the core of *Building on Reality*, launched with some style in the ballroom of Iveagh House in the autumn of 1984. There were several other features of the plan in relation to which I took initiatives of my own. For example, one of the board's proposals was to put to work some of the 110,000 long-term unemployed on schemes to be organised by or through local authorities. The proposal would be expensive to implement: including overheads and supervision it would cost perhaps £156 million a year over and above the saving on unemployment payments involved. The board said that this sum should be found through spending cuts beyond those the board itself had recommended. But as we were experiencing great difficulty in making even the recommended cuts, this did not seem very realistic.

Thinking over this dilemma one morning when I had woken up early—as sometimes happened to me when I was under pressure—it suddenly struck me that half a loaf being better than no bread, this financial constraint could be overcome if each unemployed person were put to work for *part* of a week. For each week's work involved, the heavy overhead of materials and supervision would thus be spread over two workers. I put this to our Government Task Force on Employment on the basis that each long-term unemployed person taken on would work for twelve months and that the number of days worked per week would be scaled in relation to the marital status and number of children of those involved. The task force judged this latter aspect to be too complex, however, and decided instead on a flat half-week's work for each long-term unemployed person, with a rate of pay that varied with family commitments—but not by enough to be attractive to people with families, whom I had been particularly anxious to help through the scheme. Another feature of my proposal that was adopted, however, was that people would be free to undertake other work during the half of each week when they were not working under the scheme. I also secured a provision that the services of those concerned be made available to voluntary bodies as well as to local authorities. Unfortunately in Dublin, where the city council had already laid off workers because of cuts in its rates support grant, the trade unions refused to allow the council to use the scheme to employ people. Nevertheless, since 1984 an enormous amount of useful work has been done through this Social Employment Scheme, which was intended to provide a year's break in the cycle of long-term unemployment for people who found themselves out of work for a prolonged period. However, when the twelve months was up most of those involved naturally wanted to remain at work, and where community organisations or other voluntary bodies were involved they in their turn normally preferred to keep the people they had become used to and had trained rather than start again with a new temporary employee. But as the whole idea of this revolving scheme had been to provide a *temporary* break for as many long-term unemployed as possible, this aspect was not open to review.

Another element of the Government's plan in which I had a direct involvement was the decision, despite the massive cuts being made in most forms of public investment other than roads, to increase investment in higher education, where in the 1980s we had to cater for a rapidly expanding number of young people. I knew from our discussions in Government that some of my colleagues were unsympathetic to priority being given to this; they took the view that in a time of financial crisis we simply could not afford to expand significantly the most expensive sector of education, especially as we already had far more graduates than we could employ at home, with the result that such an expansion would involve educating people for jobs in other countries.

I had always rejected this utilitarian, manpower-related approach to education. It seemed to me that if, in large measure because of past political mismanagement, a high proportion of those now in primary and secondary education were not going to be able to find employment in Ireland, we owed it to that generation at least to offer as many as possible of those who sought higher education, and were capable of benefiting from it, the opportunity to qualify themselves for a more rewarding career abroad. Moreover, a far higher proportion of graduates than of those who left the educational system after second level secured employment at home, and some at least of this reflected an unfulfilled demand, especially by new foreign industries, for people with a high standard of education. The more we educated to this level, the fewer would emigrate in the long run.

In a Government in which a major part of my role had to be to urge my colleagues to reduce spending, and the members of which were constantly watching each other's performance in this economy campaign, I was not well placed to argue the case for more expenditure on higher education—especially as I was myself a university lecturer on extended leave of absence and therefore suspected of being partisan.

However, my chance to achieve my objective came when Alan Dukes asked me, because of his absence abroad, to stand in for him as Minister for Finance in discussions on the provisions to be made in the *Building on Reality* medium-term proposals for certain departments, including Education. When Gemma Hussey and I came to discuss the matter—she along with her officials and I accompanied by the Finance officials—I disconcerted the Finance representatives by accepting the demographic basis of her argument and her view that this need should be met, while proceeding to counter-argue strenuously that half of it should be accommodated by increased productivity in the sector, i.e. by more intensive use of physical space and a drop in the ratio of staff to students.

The resultant increase in provision for higher education contributed notably to the eventual 38 per cent rise in educational investment in our plan. (An increase of 40 per cent in the number of third-level enrolments took place between 1980 and 1986, the years of economic crisis.)

Unhappily, some of the expansion of facilities thus planned was still to be implemented when the Government changed early in 1987, and in their vigorous attack on public spending in that year's budget a reformed and frugal Fianna Fáil cancelled many of our plans—only once again to reinstate some of them later.

Finally, in another area to which I was personally committed I got agreement to a continued expansion in the share of our GNP devoted to development assistance to the Third World during the period of our plan, a decision that was in part at least implemented during our term of office, although the new Fianna Fáil Government subsequently cut by almost two-fifths the share of GNP devoted to this purpose. I noted wryly at the time that this slashing of our aid programme to a level below that of any other western European country was greeted with far less public protest than I had met at the time for not *increasing* more rapidly the share of GNP devoted to this purpose.

How did our national plan fare? In the three-year period of the plan GNP grew, albeit by 5 per cent as against the plan figure of 7.5 per cent; our external payments and inflation rate performed much better than we had foreseen; and living standards rose much faster. Industrial output, boosted by foreign investment, had been rising rapidly since our first year in office; but although redundancies, which were mainly in indigenous industries, fell sharply after the autumn of 1984, employment failed to respond. The rise in unemployment was slowed by the various schemes we introduced, but the number out of work did not begin to decline until the end of our period in office.

One of the most notable economic achievements of our term of office was the winding down of inflation. When Fianna Fáil had left Government in mid-1981 inflation was approaching 20 per cent. While this owed much to the sharp rise in import prices following the second oil crisis, the situation had been aggravated by runaway pay increases in the public sector, where the average level of earnings had been allowed to jump by 29 per cent in the single year 1980. The public sector pay round that we negotiated during our first term had brought the annualised increase in pay rates down to 10 per cent. In the first half of 1983 we had a further very tough negotiation with the public service unions, which brought the increase down further to 6.5 per cent; and by the end of our term of office the figure was below 5 per cent. A combination of this public service pay headline with Government 'guidelines' helped to wind down pay rises in the private sector to the same levels, albeit with a time-lag of a year or so on the pay trend in the public sector.

This achievement was hard won. The trade unions, which had had such an easy time of it with Fianna Fáil in the two years before we had taken over in 1981, were clearly unhappy with our determined stand; they may have particularly resented it in view of the Labour Party's participation in our Government.

Meetings between us and the ICTU were formal, often tense, and on the whole unproductive throughout our term. Indeed, the only personal recollection I have of a genuine worthwhile discussion with the unions is of an encounter between the ICTU and the Fine Gael Ministers that took place in our party office. However that may be, Fianna Fáil inherited from us in 1987 an industrial relations situation that had been transformed, and the fruits of this were soon to be seen in the three-year national agreement for annual pay increases of around 2.5 per cent that they were able to negotiate later that year and in the future national pay agreement of early 1991.

In describing briefly—for this is not an economic text—these initiatives that we took in our early months in Government, I have jumped ahead to complete the story. I must now return to the early months of 1983. By the end of March we had behind us the budget and the resolution of the phone-tapping affair; the die had been cast on the wording of the abortion amendment; the Bord Pleanála reform was under way; the Planning Board was established; and the attack on inflation had been initiated. I had also successfully launched the New Ireland Forum, and I was engaged with Austin Deasy in the preliminary stages of the battle in the EC against the threatened milk superlevy (events that are described in a later chapter). We had, moreover, survived defections from the Labour Party on our Social Welfare Bill, and, despite many criticisms on our severe spending cuts, we were still riding high in the polls.

Some reforms that I pressed on my colleagues at this time were, however, successfully resisted at civil service level. Proposals for tackling the problem of arrears of tax were dismissed by Finance officials as inspired by 'ill-informed comments suggesting that vast sums of unpaid taxes are there for the asking'— words that came back to me when, following an initial, limited tax amnesty by our Government, our successors in office launched a large-scale amnesty that yielded £500 million in a single year. And my proposal to extend normal PRSI to the hitherto exempt category of the civil service was met by a defensive memorandum claiming that this would cost more than it would bring in, because civil servants would have to have their pay increased to compensate them for such a change and would also have to be given the opportunity to draw double pensions, both occupational and social welfare.

I had more immediate success in the area of the reform of the public service itself, where for the first time there was a Minister—and an energetic one at that—whose sole task was to tackle this issue. During the Easter break in 1983 I wrote to John Boland at some length on a range of issues, including the appointment of Secretaries of departments for a limited period rather than until retirement, and the introduction of mobility between departments. The initial response from the Department of the Public Service on the issue of mobility between professional and administrative grades and between departments of the civil service was discouraging. Several years previously they had put a great effort into this, and despite resistance from the civil service unions they had made some progress at the assistant principal officer level, although in order to overcome what they described as 'the known opposition of Departments to interdepartmental promotion schemes' they had conceded that only 20 per cent of existing posts at this level would be open to competition from other departments.

They had, however, apparently given up on the issue of mobility at higher levels, which I felt was of crucial importance, both in order to extend the principle of promotion on merit rather than seniority and also to bring fresh attitudes and ideas into various departments from other areas of the civil service, as well as, hopefully, from outside it. Partly at least because of the effects of the internal promotions system, many departments had in the absence of fresh thinking from outside become very conservative and defensive in their attitudes, pursuing traditional policies long after they had ceased to be relevant.

The lack of momentum on this issue seemed to me to be a product of trade union pressure to extend mobility beyond the home civil service to diplomatic postings. It was clear that the Department of the Public Service was itself in sympathy with this approach, with the result that its officials seemed unwilling to proceed further with the mobility issue unless Foreign Affairs was first forced to accept that diplomatic postings be covered by the new arrangement. Foreign Affairs had, in my view, been absolutely right in resisting this demand, which if conceded would have been seriously damaging to the effectiveness of our foreign policy. Our success in foreign relations since the early days of the state had depended to a high degree on the development of a corps of skilled and very experienced diplomats, whose ranks had in practice frequently been strengthened by a substantial but selective inflow of able officials from other departments.

In subsequent discussions I told John Boland, who on this issue seemed to share the view of his department about Foreign Affairs, that he should not allow the whole mobility issue at higher levels of the civil service to get bogged down by a kind of dog-in-the-manger attitude towards the Department of Foreign Affairs. He eventually accepted this, but, I later discovered, not before he had spent a whole day trying to pressure the Secretary of Foreign Affairs, Seán Donlon, to concede on the issue. Seán, knowing the strength of my views on this matter, had given him no satisfaction, however.

There remained the problem of getting through the Government a scheme combining mobility at the higher levels of the civil service on a basis of merit with a new system of appointing departmental Secretaries for seven-year terms rather than until retirement. There was bound to be resistance to these proposals from Ministers, many of whom would have an instinctive personal preference for the appointment to senior posts of officials whom they had come to know from within their own departments as against people from other departments of whom they may never even have heard. And the senior civil servants would, I feared, if they learnt of the proposal in advance, try to brainwash their Ministers against what I saw as a long-overdue reform. Accordingly, I encouraged John to bring the proposal to the Government without circulating a memorandum in advance; and while objections to the proposal were indeed raised by a number of Ministers, it eventually got through at a second meeting—some Ministers asked for a few days to reflect—by a narrow majority: a margin of a single vote, as I recall it.

The storm broke as soon as our decision was announced. The most vociferous opponent of all was the Department of Finance, with which my relations were already difficult, although I had never attempted to interfere in that department, dealing with it always through the Minister, then Alan Dukes, later John Bruton. I would have regarded any attempt to go behind the back of a Minister to his officials as quite improper. The experience of the 1979–81 period, when Charles Haughey during his first term of office as Taoiseach had appointed a weak Minister, Gene Fitzgerald, and had in effect run the department himself, with disastrous financial consequences for the country, was always present in my mind. But the Department of Finance nevertheless seemed to resent the contribution I had tried to make to policy through its Ministers.

About this time also I initiated collective Government 'brainstorming' sessions to review progress and to plan ahead. Several of these meetings were held, Barrettstown Castle in Co. Kildare being the location for all but one. Although in attractive grounds, the castle is actually quite a small building, with a drawing-room and dining-room that can just accommodate fifteen Ministers and a Government Secretary, and one other reception room: a small study that can be used as a communications room. There are, however, nine bedrooms of varying size and comfort, in which Ministers from places distant from Dublin can stay overnight.

Among the matters on which we decided to take further action at sessions in the summer of 1983 were the need in a period of limited resources to concentrate social welfare provisions on the worst-off people in society; the expansion of street policing as the strength of the Garda force increased; the problem of relieving the shortage of space in prisons; the introduction of a police complaints tribunal; and the need for a police authority—on which we made no more progress in this administration than had the 1973–77 Government. We also discussed the drugs problem, and the highly controversial issue of school transport, in respect of which we were introducing modest charges, against strong local opposition in some areas. Another issue I raised was the social undesirability of segregation of public and private housing, which was perpetuating and indeed reinforcing class divisions. Finally we discussed the legislative programme for the months ahead.

Experience showed, however, that policy initiatives arising from unstructured discussion without written policy documents on occasions like these sometimes fail to mature into action. Account was taken of this in arranging the agenda for future sessions in this location, at the next of which I succeeded in substituting a transport allowance for junior Ministers in place of state cars and Garda drivers; the saving was some £750,000 a year, and thirty to forty gardaí were released for other duties. Needless to say this reform, announced after this July Barrettstown meeting, was at the time unpopular with many junior Ministers!

The Barrettstown conferences nevertheless had, I believe, a very positive psychological effect on the solidarity of the Government. From the outset it had been clear that we were in for a very rough ride; the financial crisis we had inherited was, as I had foreseen, putting our Coalition under great pressure. While this was especially true at the level of our parliamentary parties, at Government level too there was tension, especially between Dick Spring on the one hand and Alan Dukes and John Bruton on the other. Although for the most part this tension was institutional rather than personal, both Dick and John, as distinct from Alan, had short fuses, and this occasionally led to fireworks at the cabinet table. However, these clashes, and the less emotional ones between Dick and Alan, were tempered by the mutual respect felt for each other by Dick and his two Fine Gael colleagues; and the opportunity to meet in the more relaxed atmosphere of Barrettstown, as well as from time to time for a post-cabinet drink in Seán Barrett's office beside the cabinet room, helped to keep things on an even keel.

Indeed these informal encounters developed a sense of camaraderie and warmth between members of the Government, which balanced an underlying tension that never completely disappeared. The Labour Ministers clearly feared that at some point a misjudgement on the Fine Gael side might push them over the brink, making it impossible for them to remain in Government while retaining authority within their own divided and unnerved party. At the same time among the Fine Gael Ministers there was a persistent concern that the problems faced by the Labour Ministers might at some point precipitate a split. There was, moreover, frequently irritation and at times alarm at the leaks by Labour Ministers' aides to the press, which seemed to be designed to keep their more restless TDs and non-parliamentary left wing happy. The apparent implication of many of these leaks—that only the constant vigilance of the Labour Ministers saved the country from savage cuts in public services—was particularly galling for Fine Gael Ministers, whose concern for the preservation of these services and for minimising the impact of spending cuts and tax increases on the less well-off was in fact just as great as that of their Labour Party colleagues.

The frustration of some Fine Gael Ministers with this aspect of Labour's participation in Government was intensified by the self-defeating dogmatic ideological position of the Labour Party on a small number of issues. One of these was the development of local broadcasting, where the shortsighted opposition to our proposals by one Labour backbencher close to the unions in RTE prevented any progress being made throughout the life of the Government with a scheme that would have given RTE the right to a significant minority share in all local commercial stations. As I feared at the time, this recalcitrance gave Fianna Fáil in Government in the late 1980s the opportunity to introduce legislation for commercial broadcasting, including television, that put RTE's longer-term viability at risk. In the face of so many pressures our Government would scarcely have survived if the personal relations between its members had not been so good and if my own relationship with Dick Spring had not been so solidly based.

By the time the Barrettstown meeting of July 1983 took place, this fundamental solidarity of our Government had been well established. I was happy enough with our situation when shortly after this meeting Joan and I went to Schull in Co. Cork for a few weeks' holiday. Friends of ours, Gay and Jacinta Hogan, who had stayed with us in Schull in 1975, had been so attracted to the area that in 1982 they had bought a house there near the end of a boreen that was sometimes submerged at high tide. The house was secluded, the ever-changing view from it over a tidal inlet was satisfying. Throughout this period in Government they frequently gave us refuge there.

That summer Joan was quite ill. Since June she had been suffering from a gastric complaint that was not resolved for well over a year and which in 1984 became life-threatening. Fortunately August 1983 was a glorious month in west Cork, and the Hogans arranged for Joan to spend the days in bed on the lawn overlooking the inlet. I had always had an ambition myself to lie comfortably out of doors between sheets, my head resting on pillows, and before long we were spending much of the summer days head-to-head in two beds, our faces sheltered from the sun by a huge parasol.

Our relaxation was interrupted in sad circumstances. My brother Fergus had been very ill during the previous twelve months. Since childhood we had been very close, despite the six-year age difference, and he had been a major influence on me in my youth. During his long period as an official of the FAO in Rome after 1951 we had seen less of each other: we had been able to visit Rome on only a couple of occasions, and he got home on leave only every second year; but we had kept in close touch throughout this period. After the death of his wife, Una, he moved to the EC in Luxembourg, where I saw him quite frequently. He retired from that post in 1976, however, following his marriage to Eilis Johnston, chief hostess supervisor with Aer Lingus, and came back to Ireland, settling with undisguised sentimentality in Bray, a few hundred yards from our childhood house, Fairy Hill, which was by then buried beneath a modern housing estate. There he had become an active member of Fine Gael—the only one of my brothers to involve himself politically. For the year before his death he had faced with remarkable courage the fatal consequences of lung cancer. His last engagement, linking past and future, had been my son Mark's wedding two weeks before his death. Since my parents' death he had been my strongest link with childhood; we had been able to share many pre-war memories of our parents. Now we heard that he was close to death. We broke our holiday to see him for a last time; he died next day.

Mark's wedding, though in the shadow of Fergus's impending death, had been a great joy to us. He had met his wife, Derval O'Higgins, at the Presidential inauguration in 1976, at which her father, Tom O'Higgins, officiated as Chief Justice. Mark had been accompanying Joan on that occasion, as I was absent abroad at the time, and Derval had been replacing her mother, who was unwell. In the intervening years Derval had already become part of our family.

The marriage linked two families whose members had been friends for over sixty years. Derval's great-uncle Kevin, murdered by an IRA breakaway group in 1927, had for years before that been my father's greatest and most admired friend. Kevin O'Higgins's brother, Tom, had been a member of the Coalition Government of 1948–51, as his son, Derval's father, also Tom, had been a member of the second Coalition of 1954–57, and deputy leader of Fine Gael on the front bench with me from 1965 to 1973, when our views on policy and on the party had been closely aligned.

On his marriage Mark purchased Mary's share in our house. We had already moved from the top to the lower floor, converting Mary's flat there into living accommodation for ourselves, for Joan's disablement as a result of arthritis had made it impossible for her to continue to climb the stairs. The top floor was simultaneously converted into a separate flat for Mark and Derval, in which they lived throughout my period as Taoiseach. On the middle floor the dining-room became a bedroom for Mary and Vincent when in Ireland during holiday periods, leaving us with the drawing-room on that floor as a reception area, rarely used because of Joan's disability.

This arrangement was the best we could manage during those years. It meant that our accommodation was fairly cramped: basically two rooms on the garden level, with the corridor serving as a kitchen. On this floor we never succeeded in overcoming the problem of rising damp, which we combated with a noisy dehumidifier in our bedroom, where even in summer artificial light was needed for reading because of overhanging shrubs in front. I think it was the most modest accommodation occupied by any prime minister, but it saw us through this period until I was in opposition again. We were able then, with the aid of the gratuity paid on my simultaneous belated retirement from UCD, to install a lift. We thus recovered the use of the whole house, Mark and Derval having at this stage purchased a home of their own nearby.

The question of an official Taoiseach's residence had occasionally been raised; indeed Jack Lynch had planned to build one for his successors in office in the Phoenix Park, on the site of what had for many years been the Papal Nunciature. But I have to say that even if such a residence had existed, and despite the limitations of our own accommodation at this time, I think we would have been reluctant to move there.

# TOWARDS THE ANGLO-IRISH AGREEMENT

In the following three chapters the course of the negotiations leading to the Anglo-Irish Agreement of November 1985 is charted in some detail; more detail, perhaps, than would normally be appropriate in an autobiography. But I feel this is justified by the intrinsic interest of these events and the fact that there seems little likelihood that anyone else involved in this process and having access to the records will feel free, and be prepared, to make a similar endeavour in advance of the release of this material in Ireland and Britain in the years 2013 to 2015.

Because the course of the negotiations was somewhat tortuous there may be some merit in offering at this point an outline of the different stages of this process. The New Ireland Forum was launched in late May 1983 and continued until May 1984. It was envisaged that a negotiation with Britain would start after the Forum ended and on the basis of its report; but following Margaret Thatcher's re-election in June 1983 we felt it desirable to take an initiative to ensure that when determining the priorities of her new government before the autumn parliamentary session she would include in these priorities the negotiation that we contemplated. Towards this end I agreed that Michael Lillis, acting on his own account, should suggest to the British an Irish involvement in the political and security situation in Northern Ireland. When this evoked a positive interest, I confirmed to Margaret Thatcher at Chequers in November 1983 our interest in a radical move along the lines of joint authority. She was unwilling to permit even informal talks at that time, however, pending the publication of the Forum report; accordingly we were surprised to receive a British proposal in March 1984. This proposal included an element that we made clear would be unacceptable to us: a proposed border zone within which security forces from both sides would operate.

In May 1984, following the publication of the Forum report, we presented a set of proposals to the British that were supplemented some time afterwards by an indication of our willingness to contemplate an amendment to articles 2 and 3 of the Constitution if the package emanating from the negotiation were such as to make the success of such a referendum likely.

In July the British responded to our proposal, and from then until the end of September the negotiation was carried on upon this basis. Around this time the Northern Ireland Office became involved in the negotiation. During October there were conflicting signals from the British side, with the new Northern Ireland Secretary, Douglas Hurd, seeming to prefer a less comprehensive package that would not involve a constitutional amendment on our side. Moreover, in the weeks immediately before the 18–19 November summit meeting between Margaret Thatcher and myself there was a rather sharp exchange of notes between the two governments, which augured badly for the meeting.

At Chequers I made a strong plea to Margaret Thatcher that we should work together on a 'package' that would make possible a successful referendum on articles 2 and 3; but she and Douglas Hurd argued for a less radical package and an abandonment of the referendum idea. A communiqué was agreed, however, that recognised the problem of dual identity in Northern Ireland; and in her press conference following the meeting Margaret Thatcher endeavoured to sound a very positive note. But the sharpness of her tone in rejecting, in response to a press query, the three Forum 'models' (which the media did not realise had formally ceased to be the focus of the negotiation since the previous July) created an impression that the negotiation had failed and that I had been rebuffed. This was a serious setback.

However, the political and media reaction to this in Ireland and in Britain and elsewhere, especially in the United States, was such that a major review of their position was undertaken by the British during the Christmas break. Towards the end of January they put forward a new approach, which lay intermediate between the positive July–September stance and their negative October–November one but which specifically did not require action by us on articles 2 and 3.

Between January and June the negotiation proceeded on this new basis. By June there was a considerable measure of accord on the shape of an agreement, with the exception of 'confidence-building' or associated measures to be taken by the British to reduce the alienation of the nationalist minority from the security system in Northern Ireland.

A tough argument between Margaret Thatcher and myself in the margin of the June 1985 Milan European Council meeting broke this deadlock, however, on a basis proposed by the Prime Minister that involved describing the associated measures we sought as involving 'early implementation' of the principal clauses of the agreement rather than as separate confidence-building measures.

The months from July to November 1985 were spent in refining the draft terms of the agreement; agreeing on the manner in which some of its provisions in relation to security and the administration of justice would be the subject of early implementation; and reaching agreement on the composition, functions and location of the Joint Secretariat and—somewhat less controversial—of the Ministerial Conference also. Other matters that were settled during this period included the arrangements for an international fund, and the venue and timing of the agreement, which was signed at Hillsborough, Co. Down, on 15 November 1985.

# CHAPTER FIFTEEN

# THE NEW IRELAND
# FORUM

By the time the Government changed at the end of 1982 the state of Anglo-Irish relations was little short of disastrous. In the face of the British reaction to his handling of the Falklands sanctions issue and his abortive UN intervention, Charles Haughey had taken a series of negative decisions in July to avoid or prohibit discussions with the British government. For her part Margaret Thatcher was understood to have said privately that she saw no solution to the Northern Ireland problem; and she was believed to regret the 1980 summit meetings with their emphasis on the London-Dublin axis, as these had soured her relations with the right wing of her own party.

In Northern Ireland itself Sinn Féin had gained relative to the SDLP, to the point where shortly after my return to office I was advised that at the forthcoming British general election they could conceivably win three or four seats, as against one or two for the SDLP. I was told also that the two communities in the North were more polarised than ever, and that the security situation had deteriorated.

There could scarcely be a more discouraging starting point for a new initiative than the one presented to me in these terms when Peter Barry and I met our officials to review the situation on 6 January 1983.

I have already described some of my thinking on Northern Ireland as I had developed it for my Dimbleby Lecture in May 1982. Since then I had come to the conclusion that I must now give priority to heading off the growth of support for the IRA in Northern Ireland by seeking a new understanding with the British government, even at the expense of my cherished, but for the time being at least clearly unachievable, objective of seeking a solution through negotiations with the Unionists. However, as I had suggested in a speech in

Pittsburgh at the beginning of October, I envisaged as a first stage, in advance of a negotiation with Britain, consultations that would involve all the parties in the Dáil together with 'all in Northern Ireland who might be willing to talk to us, however informally, whether they be organised in political parties or not, and whether they sought, opposed or (less probably!) were indifferent to the development of a new political relationship between North and South.' I had gone on in that speech to say that 'we must seek in discussion with all in Northern Ireland who may see merit in reducing tension within our island their help in identifying those aspects of the Constitution, laws and social arrangements of our state which pose obstacles to understanding amongst the people of this island.'

This presentation differed consciously from John Hume's idea of a nationalist Council for a New Ireland. What had happened was that while I had been working in Pittsburgh on the final version of my address Joan had rung me to say that John Hume had phoned to communicate his intention of proposing in his speech to the forthcoming SDLP conference a Council for a New Ireland, comprising constitutional nationalist parties from North and South. She had given him my Pittsburgh number, and he would be ringing me in a few minutes.

I had immediately turned back to the typewriter and hammered out the paragraph cited above, so that when John rang five minutes later I was able to respond to his proposal by reading out what I was about to say in Pittsburgh—remarking that we seemed to be working along somewhat similar lines.

I had thus come into Government at the end of 1982 with two elements of strategy in my mind: first, to organise a forum that would be wider than the SDLP's Council for a New Ireland, by being open in principle to Unionist Party participation and in practice to hearing the unionist case put to it at least semi-officially, but that would be designed in such a way that it would help to restore the SDLP's self-confidence; and second, to have through this forum a more secure base from which to move towards my objective of a new arrangement with Britain that would reduce the alienation of the Northern nationalist minority and thus strengthen constitutional nationalist politics against inroads by the IRA's political party, Sinn Féin. Then, at some further stage, such a stabilised situation might make possible, I hoped, progress towards a political entente between the two communities in Northern Ireland.

I do not think that at that stage I had a clear idea of what form an agreement with Britain during the second stage of this operation might take, beyond envisaging that as one element it might perhaps involve, as I had proposed in the Dimbleby Lecture and again in my election speech on Northern Ireland, a court and police force common to both parts of the island. Nevertheless, from private discussions with civil servants at this time I had derived a valuable clue about the direction that the negotiations I envisaged with the British government might usefully take. I learnt that in their frustration at the dead end into which Anglo-Irish relations had been driven, some British civil servants were speculating whether in the long run an Anglo-Irish approach to Northern Ireland, involving joint action of some kind there, might not provide an answer to this intractable problem. This seemed to suggest not alone that my idea for a common court and police force might be worth pursuing but that there could be merit in exploring more generally the idea of joint authority or joint sovereignty. The inclusion of such a concept in the report of the forum would have the advantage that it would provide endorsement for a 'Brits in' type of agreement and protect my flank from attacks for not having secured Irish unity, which Fianna Fáil liked to pretend was possible at that stage. The inclusion of such a model would have the defensive advantage that its presence in the report would provide endorsement for an eventual outcome that did not involve Irish unity: a result that Fianna Fáil would wish to attack. Securing acceptance of this concept by the forum as a possible model became thenceforth a key element in my strategy.

Thus it was that the concept was born of a forum that would provide me with a flexible and negotiating mandate for an Anglo-Irish agreement on Northern Ireland while at the same time offering an opportunity for the unionist viewpoint to be presented to the public in our state, an educational process that I had sought to initiate a year earlier when I had arranged the visit of the McCartney group to Dublin in September 1981.

I had to postpone any initiative on this matter, however, until after the resolution on 5 February of the challenge to Charles Haughey within his own party after the disclosure of the phone-tapping affair—a resolution that was in his favour, as it turned out. I could not wait much longer thereafter, for two reasons. The SDLP were now pressing for our reaction to their narrower proposal for a Council for a New Ireland that would bring together constitutional nationalist parties in the island, and I had not yet succeeded in persuading John Hume of the desirability of widening its composition and excluding from its title the word 'Council', which I felt would remind Unionists too forcibly of the 'Council of Ireland' proposal in the Sunningdale agreement. Also, the Fianna Fáil ard-fheis was due to meet at the end of the month, and I guessed, correctly, that Charles Haughey would take this opportunity to profess support for John Hume's Council for a New Ireland, which would pre-empt my broader proposal.

Accordingly on Tuesday 22 February I brought to the Government a proposal for a New Ireland Forum in which all constitutional parties in the island would be invited to participate, with the objective of ending violence, reconciling the two traditions in Ireland, and securing peace and stability. The terms of reference included no mention of Irish unity, as that would have made nonsense of an invitation to *all* parties, including the Unionist parties and the Alliance Party, to participate.

I was taken aback by the reaction of my Government colleagues, which was almost uniformly negative. In the course of discussion it became clear that they feared that if my proposal went ahead my deep concern about Northern

Ireland could distract me from what they saw—with some reason—as exceptionally pressing domestic problems. At the end of the discussion twelve members of the Government opposed my proposal, and only two supported it.

I was deeply upset by this outcome, and blamed myself for having too easily assumed that my colleagues would support me. After consulting some of my close advisers I decided to try to retrieve my initiative by using a procedure employed from time to time to secure without an actual meeting of Ministers rapid Government decisions on minor, non-contentious issues. This involved what is known as an 'incorporeal' meeting of the Government. (Given that the Fianna Fáil ard-fheis was starting in three days' time, there was not time to wait for another regular Government meeting.) Accordingly on Wednesday, with the help of Seán Barrett, the Chief Whip, I set about persuading my colleagues individually to reverse their negative votes on this issue. I used the political argument, which I had perhaps not sufficiently emphasised at the previous day's meeting, that if we did not move at once with my proposal Fianna Fáil would put us on the spot by announcing acceptance of John Hume's concept of a Council for a New Ireland.

I succeeded within a few hours, and on Thursday I was able to announce my proposal that discussions be held between parties in Dáil Éireann on initiating consultations about the way in which progress might be made towards the ending of violence and the reconciliation of the two traditions in Northern Ireland in the context of a new Ireland.

My initiative did not of course prevent Charles Haughey from endorsing at his ard-fheis the SDLP's Council for a New Ireland, or from presenting this as a body that would prepare a plan for 'an all-round constitutional conference to be convened on the basis that it would be a prelude to a final withdrawal of Britain from Ireland'—as if such a conference would have any possibility of coming into existence if it were proposed that Britain participate on these terms, or would have any relevance if on this account the British government opted out. However, the fact that as Taoiseach I had on the previous day written to Charles Haughey and to Tomás Mac Giolla, leader of the Workers' Party, to invite their participation in talks on the basis I had outlined meant that it was I rather than he who now held the initiative.

Four days later Haughey replied to my letter. He sought clarification on several points, while at the same time indicating his reticence about certain aspects of the terms of reference I had proposed.

Meanwhile the SDLP was pressing me to respond to its Council for a New Ireland proposal. A fortnight after my original announcement I decided that the moment had come to force the issue—with John Hume and with Charles Haughey. I asked John to return from Strasbourg via Dublin on Thursday 10 March; Peter Barry and I saw him that evening. I told him that I was not prepared to 'run' with his version of a Council for a New Ireland, but I was sending the leader of the opposition my own proposal next morning. I would be publishing this late the following afternoon, with or without a positive response from Charles Haughey. What I would be proposing would be a forum, not a council; and *all* constitutional parties would be invited to participate, not just nationalist parties. The views of people of both traditions from outside the party political system would be sought by the Forum. Would John now back this? He agreed without further demur that he would do so. Would he seek to persuade Charles Haughey to participate? He would arrange to see him for this purpose on the following day.

Next morning I sent my formal proposal to the leader of the opposition. I explained to him that the SDLP had been pressing me for a response to its proposal, as its Executive and constituency representatives were meeting the following day. Accordingly I was sending John Hume that morning the draft announcement 'which the Government would propose to make later that day.'

If Charles Haughey did not agree to participate, the SDLP would then be faced with a choice between refusing a formal invitation from the Government to join in such a body—which I was sure they would not want to reject—and participating in a body that Fianna Fáil was boycotting, about which they would be very uncomfortable. Thus John Hume now had a strong incentive to persuade Charles Haughey to agree. And for his part Haughey could scarcely afford to opt out of a forum in which the Government and the SDLP would be participating. Although presenting what amounted to an ultimatum in this way was clearly something of a gamble, I judged that my tactic would succeed. It did.

At lunchtime I had a phone call from Charles Haughey's Northern Ireland adviser, Martin Mansergh, proposing some amendments in my draft, none of which affected the essential thrust of my proposal or did any violence to my concept. What was most striking about them was that they involved no attempt to introduce into my terms of reference any mention of Irish unity as an objective. After a brief meeting at 3 p.m. with the leader of the opposition, at which these amendments were agreed, the announcement was made, as I had intended, at 5 p.m.

That evening Charles Haughey sought—with some success—to obscure the manner in which he had been outmanoeuvred. He claimed that the Forum would achieve his purpose of preparing in advance an outline plan that could be put before an all-round constitutional conference as a valuable first step in preparation for the 'final constitutional settlement'—a version that Séamus Mallon supported. I refused to get into an argument on this, as I had no desire to give the opposition leader an excuse to go back on the agreement I had extracted from him. I merely reiterated that the Forum was open to all and not just to nationalist parties.

Some members of the Alliance Party told me subsequently that it was these statements by Charles Haughey and Séamus Mallon that led to the extremely negative response from that party to the Forum, in which I had hoped they might participate. But another factor, I believe, was irritation at what they felt to have been my failure to consult them in advance or to respond to what had come as a routine request on their part to me for a meeting. I had allowed the pressure of domestic business and my preoccupation with getting my concept of the Forum accepted by the SDLP and Fianna Fáil to lead me into insensitive handling of the Alliance Party. I should have recalled from earlier relations with them their particular sensitivity to preference being shown by Governments to the SDLP at their expense.

I sought to mend these fences shortly afterwards, and relations were restored to the point where I was told that while the Alliance Party would not participate in the Forum they might later in the year make a presentation to it. In the event, however, nothing came of this.

Another negative reaction to the successful launching of the Forum came from Frank Cluskey, who protested in Government at the fact that I had gone ahead with the launching of the Forum without further consultations with my Government colleagues after I had secured from him and from them on 23 February a piecemeal and reluctant consent to my original proposal. He was so angry indeed that he said that by acting in this way I had forfeited his trust.

Meanwhile the four party leaders got down to the task of getting the Forum into operation. Our first meeting was held on 14 April in Leinster House; Charles Haughey was insistent on this venue rather than my office in Government Buildings, on the not unreasonable grounds that the discussions were not between Government and opposition but between political parties. We made considerable progress at this meeting, and were able a week later to announce decisions on a number of key issues as well as to fix the date of the first meeting of the Forum, and its venue: 30 May, in Dublin Castle.

One of the crucial issues was the chairmanship of the body. It would have been unreasonable to expect that the opposition leader would participate under my chairmanship, and from the outset therefore I had envisaged an independent chairman. Charles Haughey vetoed two of the names put forward—Declan Costello, by now a High Court judge, and T. K. Whitaker, former Secretary of the Department of Finance—but he accepted a third: Colm Ó hEocha, President of UCG. I had been a schoolmate of Colm Ó hEocha's in Ring fifty years earlier, when his father had been headmaster of the school, although I had not seen much of him since then. He is a distinguished academic who has no known political involvement but is accepted by all as someone committed to the public interest. As chairman he had the wisdom to employ a very loose rein in handling his four headstrong steeds.

The leaders also agreed, with rather more difficulty, on a membership of the Forum that gave greater relative weight to the smaller parties: Fianna Fáil was to have nine members, Fine Gael eight, Labour five, and the SDLP five; and there was also provision for a number of substitutes, who, with the partial exception of those of Fianna Fáil, participated freely in the discussion on the same basis for all practical purposes as full members. Finally we agreed that the secretary to the Forum should be the clerk of the Seanad, Jack Tobin, who had acted as recorder at our party leaders' meeting.

A number of lesser problems remained to be settled subsequently, not all of them without some acrimony. These included the choice of officials to service the Forum, the first four of whom comprised one from the Department of the Taoiseach, Wally Kirwan, to act as co-ordinator, two from the Department of Foreign Affairs, and one from the SDLP. Later it was agreed that each delegation should appoint a secretary to co-ordinate its own work. I appointed as the Fine Gael delegation secretary John Fanagan, a young teacher who had been active in the party and for whose concern about the Northern Ireland problem, intelligence and literary capacity I had a high regard.

I think there was general relief that Fianna Fáil did not appoint as its secretary Martin Mansergh, a former official of Foreign Affairs who had become Charles Haughey's political adviser and whose views seemed at times to be even more rhetorically republican that those of his boss (as I had found out at a conference on Northern Ireland the previous year in England when he had upstaged the Fianna Fáil TD representing the party).

Before describing the meetings of the Forum I must turn back for a moment to the steps I had taken to put together the civil service team that, while monitoring the Forum discussions, would also prepare the way for the negotiations with the British government that I envisaged as starting when the Forum had completed its work.

In my previous administration I had already brought Seán Donlon back from Washington to become Secretary of the Department of Foreign Affairs. He had been involved with Northern Ireland in one way or another since the early 1970s, and in Washington he had built on the achievements of Michael Lillis by establishing close relations with successive administrations and with key politicians on Capitol Hill. These contacts proved extremely useful during the course of, and particularly towards the end of, the negotiations.

In preparing for and carrying through the negotiations another key Foreign Affairs post would be that of the Ambassador in London. Noel Dorr, who had served as information officer and as political director in the department when I was Minister and who was currently Ambassador to the United Nations, was my choice for the delicate task of representing us on the spot in London and keeping us in touch with the interplay of personalities and ideas in Whitehall.

At a later stage his embassy staff would be supplemented by Richard Ryan, a young diplomat who was both a well-known poet and an excellent shot, talents that gave him a ready entrée to several segments of British society, including important sections of the Tory party. His role was to influence a wide range of MPs, particularly Conservatives, in favour of our policy. He did Trojan work 'dining for Ireland', and helped to ensure that when Margaret Thatcher eventually came to sound out whether an agreement along the lines we were seeking was 'saleable' to her party, she would receive a positive response.

There remained in Foreign Affairs the key position of Assistant Secretary in charge of the Anglo-Irish Division. Whoever held this post should, I felt, be an 'ideas' person. With this in mind I decided to add Michael Lillis, my diplomatic adviser during the period of the 1981–82 Government, to the team. But Michael was most reluctant to return to the department at this stage. He was, I believe, conscious of a negative attitude in Fine Gael circles following his move to Brussels with Dick Burke a year earlier. On this account he was uncertain how Peter Barry would receive him; he would after all be my choice for this post, not Peter's, and he could reasonably feel that Peter might resent this. In the end I virtually had to order him back, and his first meeting with Peter Barry was somewhat tense, but their relationship soon developed very positively.

So much for the Foreign Affairs part of the team. Another key participant at civil service level when the negotiations got off the ground would be the Secretary of the Department of Justice, Andy Ward, who, apart from the unique value of his advice on security matters, would be able to apply his subtle mind to seeing around corners in other aspects of the negotiations. From the Attorney General's office Declan Quigley would also join the team at that later stage.

What about my own department? Clearly the leader of the negotiating team must be Dermot Nally, the Secretary to the Government. I was delighted with the way in which the Foreign Affairs officials responded immediately to his skilful leadership. Apart from his crucial role in our administrative system there was another reason why the Government Secretary should lead our team. The British government would clearly face a dilemma in the composition of its team when negotiations actually began. Because Northern Ireland is part of the United Kingdom, such a negotiation could not easily be led by the Foreign Office, while the Northern Ireland Office for its part was not going to be in a position to lead an international negotiation with a 'foreign' government. These considerations, together with the British Prime Minister's 'hands-on' approach, meant that the British Cabinet Secretary, Sir Robert Armstrong, a man with a sense of history and a deep commitment to Anglo-Irish relations, would inevitably be the key figure in any negotiations; he had indeed played this part in such contacts as had already taken place since Margaret Thatcher had become Prime Minister. The need for Dermot Nally to take the lead on our side at the civil service level was thus from every point of view unchallengeable.

Although the end of the year was not an absolute deadline for reporting by the Forum, its terms of reference as set out in the agreed announcement envisaged it completing its work by then. I had set this target with a view to beginning negotiations with the British government early in 1984 and, I hoped, completing them by September of that year. If this timetable could be adhered to there would then be ample time for Fianna Fáil to come to terms with the new situation thus created before an election (probably in 1987) that, because of the economic problems facing us, might bring that party back to power, despite its record since 1977.

One of the matters that concerned me from the outset was how to ensure that the Forum report would in fact set out a number of models of future possible solutions to the Northern Ireland problem, including specifically a 'joint sovereignty' version. I have already explained why I saw this as perhaps the most important single result at which to aim, but there was the obvious difficulty that Fianna Fáil might refuse to accept this approach and seek to divert the Forum's discussions along other lines. Reflecting on this at an early stage, it struck me that a possible non-controversial way of building this element in to the Forum structure from the outset would be to make the different models part of the terms of reference for a study of the economic consequences of a new North-South relationship that we were commissioning.

Accordingly I suggested to Dick Spring and John Hume a scenario for one of the earlier meetings of the four leaders that would involve a proposal by me that such an economic study be undertaken, the suggestion to be made in a manner that would encourage the opening up of the question of alternative political models. Realising that if I were to be the one to suggest the joint sovereignty model, Charles Haughey might react negatively, I suggested to John Hume and Dick Spring that at that point I would propose building in to the economic study a variant based on the confederation proposal put forward by Fine Gael in 1979, and that they rather than I could perhaps propose that it also include a 'joint sovereignty' model. This tactic worked perfectly, and these alternative models were built in to the economic study entitled 'The Macro-Economic Consequences of Integrated Economic Policy, Planning and Co-ordination in Ireland', which was formally commissioned on 15 September 1983 and published before the conclusion of our proceedings.

The Forum had meanwhile been opened on schedule on 30 May.

While all this had been going on I had, of course, been re-establishing contact with the British government. The first opportunity to do so at a personal level came when I met Margaret Thatcher in the margin of the European Council meeting in Brussels on 22 March. After dealing with some security issues I told her we were interested in reactivating, without publicity, the official-level contact that had started after our 1981 meeting but had ceased at senior official level after January 1982. She agreed, but insisted it was important to move slowly. My Forum proposal, announced eleven days earlier, had, she said, complicated things. I explained to her some of the rationale of the Forum as I saw it, including the need to strengthen the position of the SDLP within the nationalist community. She commented that the SDLP could go into the Assembly if it wished, and she was not particularly receptive to my comment that if they did so this could weaken rather than strengthen their position in the nationalist community.

She then asked if I had any purpose in establishing the Forum other than to help the SDLP. I responded that by expanding the idea from a nationalist Council for a New Ireland to a forum open to unionists I had hoped that ideas might emerge that would show how their British identity could be accepted by nationalists so that unionists would feel less threatened. She was unconvinced, saying that if we pursued this it could become very, very damaging, as it would revive all the 'Sunningdale ghosts'. I urged the further advantage of providing the people of the Republic with an opportunity to hear the unionist case, adding that greater understanding of the problem of Northern Ireland on the part of the people of our state would be helpful to the SDLP in their struggle with the IRA. 'The SDLP are your problem,' the Prime Minister responded; her problem was that they were anti-unionist.

It had been a cool enough encounter. While over time I might be able to re-establish the kind of relationship that had been destroyed in 1982, she had made it quite clear that this could be a slow and perhaps difficult process.

Six weeks later Jim Prior came to see Peter Barry. He said that he had asked Margaret Thatcher to reappoint him as Northern Ireland Secretary in the event of a Conservative election victory. He thought it unfortunate that no previous Secretary of State had served more than two years, which more or less corresponded to the learning period involving the first shock of direct exposure to Unionist views and tactics. As a result his predecessors had never had a chance to make any real advances. He hoped to involve the SDLP in the second phase of the Assembly and in time to find himself in charge of a cabinet with SDLP participation. Among other matters discussed, Peter Barry raised the Dowra Affair. Prior claimed not to be fully up to date with developments in that case.

Peter Barry's impression of this discussion was that on the whole Prior was indifferent towards the SDLP and did not sufficiently appreciate the danger of allowing it to be eroded in favour of Sinn Féin.

Three months later, following her re-election to office, I had a further meeting with Margaret Thatcher in the margin of the Stuttgart European Council. In preparation for it Peter Barry, Seán Donlon and I met the previous evening in the interval between the end of the European Council meeting and the formal dinner. During our discussions I noticed that the handle of the door moved as if someone had been contemplating entering. I asked Seán to see who was outside. He came back in to say that the only person in the corridor was a British diplomat who had formerly served in Dublin and who was currently part of Margaret Thatcher's delegation. Suddenly suspicious, I told him to go out and find out what this man was doing in our delegation area, apparently trying to get into our room. He returned with a broad grin to say that the diplomat's mission had been to enquire whether we had any whiskey, as the Prime Minister wanted a drink after the Council session and there was no whiskey in the British delegation's quarters. I told him to send my private secretary to our hotel at once to fetch a bottle of whiskey and to bring it to her rooms. Next morning when I met her I started by asking her if she had enjoyed the whiskey. She looked at me quite blankly: it was clear that her delegation had not told her the source of the belated supply, and apparently she had been unaware that she had been drinking Irish rather than Scotch.

At this meeting I explained the background to the Dowra case and made certain suggestions about how it might be handled, to which the Prime Minister responded that she had taken a careful note of what had been said so that the matter could be dealt with. I then tried to give her some feel for the scale of intimidation and personation by the IRA and Sinn Féin in the recent West-minster election. In one polling booth where there were 900 registered voters an SDLP agent, ignoring threats to her life by Sinn Féin, had turned away 240 people who attempted to personate. Finally she had had to be driven away from the booth in an armoured car. Unfortunately journalists also suffered intimidation, and there was as a result a tendency to play down this element in Northern Ireland elections. I suggested that a change in the law regarding personation might help to limit the extent of the problem, adding that it might be useful for her to see John Hume, who could tell her more about this problem at first hand. When she asked if he could first write a letter to her on the subject, I suggested that it might be more appropriate for her to invite him to meet her as the leader of a major political party in Northern Ireland.

I also tried to explain to her how Sinn Féin might have gained further support if, as she and her Secretary of State had been pressing, the SDLP had entered the Northern Ireland Assembly. I then went on to describe the work of the Forum as I envisaged it developing, including the opportunity to provide for the unionist case to be presented publicly.

When I raised the question of a possible substantive meeting between us, as distinct from brief discussions in the margins of European Council meetings, she was immediately receptive to the idea and said that we should meet more often. Because of her party conference in October and the Commonwealth Con-ference in November she suggested a meeting after that, and this was agreed.

This meeting had taken place in a much more positive atmosphere than that of three months earlier; but the situation when in July I came to review it was not particularly encouraging. It is true that there had been suggestions that some senior civil servants and even Jim Prior himself had been speculating about the possibility in the long term of some kind of joint sovereignty arrangement in Northern Ireland, but the initiative being prepared in the Northern Ireland Office was, we were told, firmly limited to another attempt to achieve power-sharing. Any 'Irish dimension' had been written off by the NIO as certain to undermine the acceptance of power-sharing by the Unionists. The only other new development that could even be considered, in their view, was the pos-sibility of getting the parliamentary tier under way.

We knew that during the summer break following her election victory Margaret Thatcher was likely to fix her priorities for her new term of office. If these, once determined, excluded any significant move on Northern Ireland, then in view of the complexity of the British governmental system it would be extremely difficult, if not impossible, to secure serious attention thereafter for a major approach on our part. Given that a formal approach to initiating a major Anglo-Irish negotiation must await the completion of the work of the Forum, how were we, in the very limited time available during the forthcoming Westminster parliamentary break, to attract her attention in such a way as to ensure that in planning her new term of office she would make at least ten-tative provision for the possibility of a major Anglo-Irish initiative?

It was Michael Lillis who put forward to me at this point an imaginative proposal. He pointed out that the key to tackling the alienation of the minority in Northern Ireland lay in a radical change in the security and judicial systems. If there were a full and equal Irish role in these two areas—I had suggested in the Dimbleby Lecture one way this could be achieved, but there were other possibilities—the Northern Ireland nationalist community could be brought once again to accept the authority of the governmental institutions. True, these were regarded by the British government as fundamental areas of sovereignty involving the most basic functions of government and the most emotive symbols. But they were also the areas where Britain in Northern Ireland most needed our help. A novel and daring proposal for our direct involvement in these areas might therefore engage the Prime Minister's attention. Could something be done along these lines while perhaps assuaging Unionist objections to our involvement on the ground in Northern Ireland by some other concessions to them?

In the absence of any other practical suggestion I decided to allow Michael to pursue this strategy on a personal basis with British officials in a manner that would not engage my authority or that of the Government, which I did not wish to involve in the preparation of concrete proposals at this stage—unless of course these soundings evoked a positive response, in which case I would have to address the question of how far along this road the Government would be willing to go.

The first tentative step in this direction was taken in a discussion with NIO officials in London on 27 July, when Michael contested their assertion that the most that could be hoped for at that time would be some sort of power-sharing without any 'Irish dimension'. On a personal basis he argued that the most urgent necessity for both governments, as well as for the people of the North, was stability and order on the streets and roads of Northern Ireland. Instability had fed on the alienation and disaffection that had taken a deeper hold among nationalists during the two years since the hunger-strike than at any time in living memory. The problem was thus how to devise arrangements that would make the principle of authority in Northern Ireland and its actual application on the streets minimally tolerable to the nationalist community at large so that the SDLP could express support for the security forces and urge young people to join up. Accordingly, not because of any Dublin ideological requirement but because of the practical needs of the situation from Britain's point of view as well as ours, the principle of authority in Northern Ireland must, he argued, be given a visible Irish as well as British legitimacy.

Michael also put these general arguments forward to Brian Mawhinney MP, who was a strong advocate of a further attempt to introduce power-sharing, and to Nick Scott, Minister of State at the Northern Ireland Office. Moreover a fortnight later, when asked by the new British Ambassador, Alan Goodison, whether the introduction of the parliamentary tier would be enough to meet the requirements for an 'Irish dimension', Michael told him, once again on a personal basis, that this could be so only if the authority of the parliamentary tier were palpable on the streets, and it was not clear how this could be devised.

Alan Goodison, who had arrived in July, proved an ideal appointment as Ambassador at this critical point. Dedicated to the improvement of the Anglo-Irish relationship, he showed a sensitivity to Irish concerns that had not been universal amongst his predecessors. He won our confidence to an extent that must have enabled him to report to London more fully and accurately on our thinking than might normally have been the case. As Noel Dorr similarly won and enjoyed the confidence of Ministers and civil servants in London, there was a remarkable, and helpful, degree of transparency in the Anglo-Irish inter-governmental relationship during these crucial years.

My own initial encounter with Alan Goodison in the summer of 1983 was at the first of the annual series of theology weekends under the auspices of the *Furrow*, the Maynooth journal—a series whose initiation Joan had stimulated on the model of a Living Theology Week in Stonyhurst that she and I had attended together with some friends in 1980. As a lay reader in the Church of England, Alan Goodison shared an interest in theology with David Goodall, who at this time was on secondment to the Cabinet Office from the Foreign and Commonwealth Office and who, with his boss, Sir Robert Armstrong, the Cabinet Secretary, was the other key figure in the negotiation.

David Goodall's interest in Ireland was not merely professional: he himself came from a Co. Wexford family, and one of his ancestors had been a member of the Irish Parliament who in the middle of the eighteenth century had been actively involved in one of the earliest challenges from within the Anglo-Irish community to the Dublin Castle establishment. Despite marked differences of temperament, Michael Lillis and he struck up a warm friendship, which proved of major importance to the negotiation we were seeking to initiate.

In the formal Anglo-Irish Intergovernmental Council structure with which the Anglo-Irish relationship had been endowed by my November 1981 summit meeting with Margaret Thatcher, Sir Robert Armstrong and Dermot Nally provided the Steering Committee, while Michael Lillis and David Goodall were joint chairmen of the subsidiary Co-ordinating Commission. It was in this context, in the margin of meetings of the Steering Committee, whose frequency was deliberately increased at this point, that Michael put forward in some detail the ideas he and I had discussed.

We soon began to receive initial informal reactions through this channel to the ideas Michael Lillis had presented; and at the end of September he was told authoritatively that the problem of alienation on the nationalist side was being taken very seriously by the Prime Minister. Michael's concept of the need for an Irish legitimation of the system of public authority in Northern Ireland had been mentioned to her on the clear basis that it did not commit the Government or any member of the Government. These ideas, we were told, appeared to the British to contain two elements: a proposed involvement of Irish security forces and the Irish judiciary in the system of maintaining security and order in

Northern Ireland, together with no formal change in the position of Northern Ireland within the United Kingdom. The first of these ideas was not at that stage rejected, but for it to receive serious consideration it would be necessary that it be conveyed more authoritatively—for example by the Taoiseach to the Prime Minister at a private session during their forthcoming summit meeting.

Progress on these ideas would require from a British point of view acceptance of the constitutional position by Dublin in a form that could not be repudiated by another Irish Government. It was not clear how this could be done without a change in the Constitution. To these comments Michael Lillis, still speaking personally, responded that such a change in the Constitution could not be contemplated or with any prudence attempted unless it was very clearly seen that serious progress was being made on the first side of the equation.

We were told that the Prime Minister had also said that joint sovereignty in the formal sense was simply 'not on', and that to the extent that any civil servants or Ministers had hinted at or spoken of this as a long-term objective they had no political authority from her to do so.

A point raised by the British in the course of this informal exchange was whether joint security operations on both sides of the border were envisaged. Michael Lillis's reply, once again speaking personally, was that he would not envisage such operations. The essence of his idea was that an initiative in the security area should be embarked on only because it was, and would be seen to be, strictly necessary in the interests of security and not for political reasons or for reasons of superficial symmetry.

Thus by the end of September it was clear that our objective of interesting Margaret Thatcher in the possibility of a major initiative during her second term of office had been achieved. The problem now was to maintain and perhaps develop this interest while we waited to start official negotiations, for which, after the end of the Forum, I would require formal Government authority. Clearly much now depended upon my meeting with the Prime Minister at Chequers on 7 November.

As we came nearer to this meeting thought was given to the shape it should take. I would of course be accompanied by Dick Spring and Peter Barry, my partners in this exercise, and Margaret Thatcher would have with her Sir Geoffrey Howe and Jim Prior. The normal pattern on such occasions was to start with a tete-à-tete between the two principals accompanied by note-takers while the other participants met separately to discuss matters on the agenda that it was not proposed should be raised during the tete-à-tete. Then the two groups would combine for a plenary session, which, depending upon circumstances, might take several different shapes. Thus on some occasions the two principals might recap their discussions with a view to a general review of the issues they had been dealing with, or, alternatively, other issues requiring discussion amongst all participants might be taken up in this format. This plenary session might be long or short, depending upon the particular needs of the occasion and the amount of time available before breaking for lunch, after which normally the meeting would come to an end.

This November 1983 summit meeting was an unusual one, however, for while a number of practical issues relating both to Europe and to Northern Ireland would need to be discussed, the primary purpose from our point of view—and probably also now from the British Prime Minister's point of view—was the need to convey our expectations about the Forum and to confirm that the personal views voiced by Michael Lillis on a possible future initiative with regard to Northern Ireland had my personal approval, although this could not at that stage engage my Government. I would of course be concerned to note her reactions on these points, but at that stage the only practical issue that could arise for further action would be the question of whether, pending publication of the Forum report, she might see merit in the matters in question being pursued informally between officials.

Assuming therefore that the Ministers in their separate discussion would be able to deal satisfactorily with outstanding European issues and with some practical points in relation to the current situation in Northern Ireland, it did not seem that there would be need for a prolonged plenary session on this occasion following these two sets of separate talks. That meant that the time available for the discussion between the Prime Minister and myself could be longer than usual—up to two hours—and this in turn would make it possible for us to have an initial completely private discussion without anyone else present before pursuing our tete-à-tete in the presence of note-takers.

In the particular circumstances this seemed to me to be a good way to proceed, because for my part I felt that I might be able to make more impact in the course of a purely private discussion à deux, and I was advised that Margaret Thatcher would also be more likely to respond in a less inhibited way if no-one else were present. I was given to understand that if there were anyone else present she tended to speak for the record and even to some degree to act a role.

And so it was arranged. Our private discussions in Chequers started at 10.15 a.m., and, as I recall it, we remained together without note-takers for about three-quarters of an hour while I explained to her the thinking behind the establishment of the Forum and the features of its report that I saw as likely to be helpful in preparing a negotiation. These were the alternative models and a statement of the principles on which further progress in Northern Ireland might be made by our two governments: principles that I believed would be presented in the report in a form acceptable to the British government as a basis for our discussion.

It had been my intention also to develop with her in rather more detail the kind of joint action in Northern Ireland that might help to create conditions in which the minority could identify with the system of authority. In the event I was not able to bring this part of the discussion as far as I had intended, because of a recent media development that I had guessed, rightly, would have disturbed her. Brian Walden, for whom she had some admiration, had just presented a television programme on Northern Ireland that had focused on the issue of joint sovereignty. This may have arisen out of the work then known to be under way in the Forum. As a result, when I came to this point in my presentation she discouraged me from going much further, saying that the television programme could lead to questions in Parliament and that she must be able to say in reply to any such questions that there had been no discussion between us on joint sovereignty. And when I came to raise the question of informal discussions taking place between our officials pending the publication of the Forum report, she said that she could not authorise such discussions because, once again, if questioned in Parliament at that stage she must be in a position to say that no negotiations were taking place.

My main concern however had been to ensure that after this meeting Northern Ireland would feature on her list of priorities for her new term of office, and I felt from the kind of discussion we had had that I had succeeded in this by conveying during this private meeting something of my passion and commitment to make real progress in relation to Northern Ireland during my term of office and my willingness to take major risks towards that end.

When we were joined by note-takers (Dermot Nally always fulfilled this function for me), at her request I went over some of the ground again, so that my arguments for a significant initiative designed to deal with the alienation of the nationalist minority by providing them with an alternative focus of loyalty to authority in Northern Ireland would be on the record.

Concerning the Brian Walden broadcast I told her that we had been sensitive to the problem of public discussion of the alternative models, and had refused to put anyone on that programme; in so far as that programme had focused on the joint sovereignty concept it did not reflect any briefing on our part. Moreover I had stressed to the press in advance of our meeting that the purpose of this encounter was for us to reflect together on the nature of the problem in Northern Ireland and how it might be solved, and that on this occasion I would be looking neither for hard decisions nor conclusions.

Two other matters dealt with in this second part of our tete-à-tete were the problem of personation in Northern Ireland elections, upon which we had already spent a good deal of time when we had last met in June, and the Dowra Affair. On the latter issue she said it was important that some satisfactory conclusion be reached. Four weeks later we returned to this contentious matter yet again in the margin of the Athens European Council.

We then joined the others for the plenary session. I found afterwards that the matters I had discussed with her had also been raised at the Ministerial session. The two British Ministers had been concerned to probe, in a manner the Prime Minister had been reluctant to do, our ideas on involvement in the security process in Northern Ireland. Would this also involve an Irish role in the process of government in Northern Ireland? Could such a role be provided by representation of our Government on the Northern Ireland Police Authority? One informal suggestion from them was for a political involvement of the South in the administration of Northern Ireland through the right of a Dublin agent of some sort to be consulted: could that conceivably be accepted by Unionists? Would there be changes in our Constitution? Without changes in the Constitution, they said, there could be no chance of joint sovereignty, but there might be some possibility of a joint authority. Thought had been given to the idea of a single police force operating north and south of the border. Such a force, they suggested, might in practice be in two parts but would nevertheless be a joint force controlled by the two governments acting together—although it was recognised that this would be fraught with difficulties.

In response to these soundings from the British side Peter Barry and Dick Spring said that our participation in a political layer in Northern Ireland would also be essential. The nationalist minority could then give their loyalty to such a political structure, which would itself control any security arrangement. On articles 2 and 3 they said these would have to be looked at, but if we got to the stage we were now speculating about, a new Constitution would probably be needed anyway.

During the lunch that followed the brief plenary session Margaret Thatcher asked me to point out Michael Lillis to her. I did so, and she remarked on how lucky we were to have someone like him who was prepared to open up issues for discussion on his own initiative and authority.

Many months were to elapse, however, before we learnt that in discussions with her Ministers and senior civil servants at Chequers after our departure, Margaret Thatcher had instructed that consideration be given to preparing for a major new initiative on Northern Ireland.

On my return home I felt that in view of the Prime Minister's extreme sensitivity to the phrase 'joint sovereignty' it might be tactful for us at this point to substitute some other phrase to describe the third model in the Forum report, which was then in course of preparation. I took the matter up at the next meeting of the party leaders in the Forum—with some hesitation, for I was uncertain how Charles Haughey would respond. In the event he simply asked what alternative I suggested, and when I proposed 'joint responsibility' he put forward the alternative 'joint authority', which I immediately accepted. It is ironic that he should have christened this concept to which he later declared himself so strongly opposed.

During the summer months a large number of written submissions had come in to the Forum, of widely varying quality. Under the arrangements that we had agreed each party could request that a certain number of these written submissions be supplemented by oral presentations, to be made in public session and to be recorded for television. Fine Gael used its quota primarily to ensure that the views of Northern unionism were presented not just to the Forum but to public opinion generally, with a view to ensuring a better understanding in the Republic of the character and quality of the deep divisions in Northern Ireland. Towards this end Fine Gael asked David Harkness, Professor of History at Queen's University, Robin Glendinning of the Alliance Party, and the McGimpsey brothers of the OUP to supplement their written submissions with oral presentations. The Labour Party asked the Tory backbencher Sir John Biggs-Davison and the Women's Law and Research Group from Northern Ireland to give oral evidence; while Fianna Fáil simply invited people who would reinforce traditional nationalist views, such as Seán MacBride, Desmond Fennell, and Dr Roy Johnston.

The first of these public sessions had got off to a bad start. There were excellent presentations from two distinguished economists, Sir Charles Carter and Dr Louden Ryan, which demolished the thesis that in the absence of continuing large subsidies from the UK Northern Ireland would be better off or indeed anything like as well off as part of a united Ireland rather than the United Kingdom. It had been agreed before the session that the party leaders would make short statements thanking the two economists for their submissions. Dick Spring and I expressed our gratitude briefly. At this point a large bundle of scripts of an address by Charles Haughey was brought in, and these were circulated to everyone present. This speech, apparently prepared by Martin Mansergh during and since the lunch break, asserted that the Forum must reject positively certain concepts put before us that morning, and insisted that Britain provide the necessary finance for a united Ireland. The other delegations made clear afterwards their annoyance at this blatant propaganda ploy, and no attempt was made by the opposition leader to repeat it thereafter.

One oral presentation was prevented by Fianna Fáil vote from being recorded by television cameras: that of the Women's Law and Research Group, whose written submission had been critical of social conditions in the Republic. Such criticism could not be tolerated, in Charles Haughey's view.

A week later, during a private session on the morning of 16 December, our last meeting before Christmas, there was a dramatic episode. Our activities had been beset by a variety of leaks from private sessions, which did not help relations between the parties. Thus I had been reported, incorrectly, as suggesting that we should re-join the Commonwealth; and now there was a story—which this time, however, was correct—that Fianna Fáil was strongly supporting the unitary state model as against either federation/confederation or joint authority. When this session began I said I was fed up with the constant stream of disclosures to the press, many of which seemed aimed against the credibility of my party. Charles Haughey then spoke in similar terms, emphasising the impossibility of the Forum's work proceeding if this state of affairs were to continue.

Dick Spring, who had just arrived from the Dáil, where he had been attacking the opposition on issues of domestic policy, and was still in a combative mood, declared that he could not accept what Haughey had said, as it was plain to him that the latest leak, like some of the others, had come from the Fianna Fáil delegation. Haughey, infuriated by this onslaught—which was, I think, unwarranted in this instance—described this as an unjustified and outrageous attack on his delegation. Unless Dick Spring withdrew his allegations he would lead his party out of the Forum.

I tried to calm the storm by saying that in raising the matter initially I had had no intention of apportioning blame; but Dick still refused to withdraw his charge. At this Haughey, now looking more hurt than angry, appealed to Forum members to realise that he had been entrusted by me with confidences in relation to matters of state, which he had never betrayed, and that it was despicable to suggest that he would be the source of leaks from the Forum. 'No-one has suffered more than I have from journalists,' he said—and at that broke down.

Because I was sitting on the same side of the table as Haughey I could not see clearly what was happening, and my first impression was that he might be acting a part. I realised almost immediately, however, that this was not the case, for, in an undoubtedly emotional state, he had to be helped from the room by Ray MacSharry. It now became clear that he had arrived at the meeting already in a very upset condition because of the recent publication of a book, *The Boss*, written about him and in particular about the GUBU events of the previous year.

We adjourned at once, and Dick Spring, John Hume and myself went with the chairman to a nearby room where our leaders' meetings were held, usually over lunch. There we waited, uncertain what to do next, for about forty minutes. Then Haughey arrived, clearly still very shaken, and we sat down to an early and rather tense lunch, at which, however, Dick Spring made his peace with Haughey. After lunch I left the room to make a phone call, and when I returned I found Haughey and Dick Spring deep in conversation in a corner of the room. They asked me to leave them to it, and I did so. Dick Spring told me subsequently that Haughey had explained to him how upset his family had been, and he on their account, by the book published the previous day.

Immediately after the afternoon session Dick and I were discussing Haughey's breakdown together when we both suddenly realised that in response to queries from the *Sunday Tribune* about our likely Christmas reading we had each mentioned *The Boss* as a book that we would want to read during the break. Clearly this was not going to help the situation, and humanity as well as prudence suggested that we try to put this right. I said I would ring Vincent Browne, the editor of the *Sunday Tribune*. There was, of course, the danger that such a request would itself be featured in the *Sunday Tribune*, leading to publicity for the events of that morning that all of us were concerned to avoid, but I believed this would not happen. I was right. When I rang Vincent Browne he already knew—much to my surprise—what had happened that morning, but he agreed not to publicise it and to substitute other works in place of *The Boss* in my list and in Dick's.

When the Forum resumed after Christmas we turned to the alternative constitutional models that had formed the basis of the economic study we had commissioned, 'The Macro-Economic Consequences of Integrated Economic Policy, Planning and Co-ordination in Ireland'. It soon became clear that Fianna Fáil wanted to talk only about the unitary state model: they were virtually silent on the federal or confederal model. This was one of the most surprising features of the Forum experience. The question of the form of Irish unity, whether unitary or federal/confederal, had not in the past been made a major political issue, and for Fianna Fáil to press it virtually to the point of breaking over it three months later did not seem to me to make much sense from their point of view.

The discussion on joint authority at the Forum meeting on 12 January was opened by John Hume, who pointed out that this model had the advantage of immediately answering the need for action now, and was a logical develop- ment of the Anglo-Irish process of discussion that had begun in 1979. The unitary state was not attainable at present, and something had to be done in the meantime. Austin Currie, Eddie McGrady and Joe Hendron supported this strongly, while Séamus Mallon contented himself with asking me a series of questions about how such a model would work, which I answered. Fianna Fáil opposed joint authority vigorously; and the resultant stalemate was met by the appointment of separate subcommittees to study each of the three models, listing in each case their advantages and disadvantages. Two members were appointed from each of the four parties to every subcommittee, and a member of the secretariat was nominated to each as rapporteur.

The three committees reported back on 8 February with, save in one instance, agreed reports on the merits and demerits of each of the three models, which later formed the basis for chapters 6, 7 and 8 of the formal report. The excep- tion to this unanimity was the committee on a unitary state, chaired by Séamus Mallon, where Fine Gael, Labour and the SDLP agreed that such a state should, if it came into existence, enact laws that would immediately provide the same civil liberties in the whole island as at present existed in the North. Ray MacSharry refused to agree to this, and Brian Lenihan—reluctantly, and with obvious embarrassment—went along with him. Séamus Mallon, who on some other issues tended to support Fianna Fáil, was totally opposed to them on this point, saying with his customary bluntness that he had not waited all his life for a unitary state only to see it diluted by having different laws north and south.

The implication of MacSharry's stance seemed to be either that in a unitary state Northern Ireland would lose some of its existing civil liberties (which even the delegation of the Roman Catholic hierarchy, who appeared before us on the day after the subcommittee reports were presented to the Forum, did not propose), or alternatively that the two parts of the unitary state would continue after union to have different laws—which seemed somewhat incon- sistent with Fianna Fáil's rejection of any idea of a federal or confederal structure! The fact that Fianna Fáil's deputy leader felt obliged to go along with Ray MacSharry on a point that appeared to be either partitionist or sectarian was indicative of the influence Ray MacSharry continued to hold in the Forum, despite the fact that since the beginning of the year he had been a backbencher in Fianna Fáil.

Meanwhile work had been continuing on the early chapters of the report, which attempted to set out the historical background to the situation we now faced. Members of the Fianna Fáil delegation were very active in discussion of these chapters, seeking to ensure as far as possible a traditional Irish nationalist presentation of history. The other delegations saw this as a delaying tactic, which in part it was. My own delegation indeed found this part of the work extremely frustrating, and there were considerable tensions within our group because, in my concern to get on with the report, the delay in the preparation of which worried me greatly, I was not prepared to fight to the death every historical misrepresentation.

At this point I should perhaps explain that there was a considerable diversity of view within the Fine Gael delegation. While I was naturally inhibited in what I could say in view of the delicacy of the negotiations ahead, I had tried from the outset to get across to its members the role that I saw the Forum report playing in the future evolution of the Anglo-Irish relationship. I think a number of them were sceptical about what must have seemed to them a rather complex, grandiose and perhaps impractical design. Naturally enough they were inclined to look on the report as something to be viewed in its own right rather than as a means towards the end of an Anglo-Irish negotiation. As a result, when they saw Fianna Fáil members beavering away at what they viewed as an attempt to distort historical realities in the early chapters of the report they became disillusioned and discouraged.

Two members of our delegation seemed in any event out of sympathy with the whole venture: Paddy Harte, and the late John Kelly. Paddy Harte had devoted much of his life to a generous and dedicated attempt to open up and improve relations with Unionists in Northern Ireland, a crusade that, because of the single-minded way in which he pursued it, had made him decreasingly acceptable to the SDLP. This was indeed why, although we had worked together closely during much of our time in opposition, I had subsequently felt it wise to distance him to some degree from the Northern Ireland issue. He never quite came to terms with the Forum project.

In John Kelly's case the problem was even more acute. He seemed to be totally out of sympathy with what I was trying to do, and at meetings of the delegation when we had to discuss specific issues he would repeatedly go back to first principles, challenging the whole purpose of the endeavour. At times I found it difficult to keep patience with this persistent attempt to question the whole rationale of the Forum when I felt that so much urgency attached to bringing it to a successful conclusion as a basis for the next stage: the negotiation of a new agreement with Britain. In relation to the proposed three models in the report he said that for Unionists these three options would be 'like trying to supply liquor to a teetotal household.'

During February there had been three significant developments. The first was the appearance before the Forum of representatives of the Roman Catholic hierarchy; the second was the revelation in the *Sunday Tribune* that an attempt had been made to 'bug' the house in which Séamus Mallon stayed in Dublin; and the third was the beginning of a discussion of the crucial 'Realities and Principles' section of the report.

There had been difficulties about the appearance of a hierarchy delegation at a public session, difficulties for which the hierarchy were not primarily to blame. Through an oversight—the relevant letter to Cardinal Ó Fiaich had apparently been put to one side to be translated into Irish and had then been overlooked—they had not been asked in July 1983, as others had been, to submit their views to the Forum. The relevant letter was not in fact sent until the beginning of October, which meant that it could not be considered by the hierarchy until its November meeting.

When the chairman eventually rang the cardinal on 13 December he was told that there would be a positive response to the request to appear at the Forum, and the cardinal in fact indicated the composition of the proposed hierarchy delegation. The written presentation was not yet ready, however, and even on 3 January, when it was collected from Archbishop's House in Drumcondra, Dublin, its six sections could be seen to have been typed on six different typewriters and to differ greatly in presentation and content. It seemed that the cardinal had been anxious to get the submission to the Forum as early as possible so that an invitation to an oral session could be officially extended before these sessions drew to a close.

After some indecision on the part of the bishops the representatives of the hierarchy appeared before the Forum on 9 February. When our delegation met to consider how we should handle this session, it was proposed that John Kelly should question the representatives of the Catholic Church on behalf of Fine Gael. Given his rather negative attitude to the Forum generally, I was doubtful about the wisdom of this, but did not contest it. Perhaps understandably John was not particularly receptive to the extensive suggestions I made about questions that he might put. He reduced the original list of questions to two sheets, which were sent to me for approval. I am afraid that I came back with further suggestions, at which point I am told he threw up his hands in horror, saying, 'It's like one of those bloody biological specimens put under a microscope: take your eye away from it for a minute and it subdivides itself sixty million times!'

There was one moment when I particularly regretted that I was not questioning the hierarchy representatives myself. This was when, in reply to a question from John Kelly, Bishop Cassidy told the Forum that the Irish Episcopal Conference had considered appealing to Rome for a derogation from the church's general provisions in relation to the handling of mixed marriages, but had not done so, as they did not feel that there was even a slight chance that Rome would accede to that particular appeal. I would love to have been able to point out in reply that six years earlier, when I had been Minister for Foreign Affairs, I had raised this matter in Rome only to be told there that I should take this up with the Irish hierarchy! It would have been interesting to hear what response I would have got if I had been able to draw Bishop Cassidy's attention to the manner in which this particular ball was being kicked backwards and forwards between Rome and Ireland.

Ten days after this public session, at a moment when the other Sunday papers were saying that the Forum was on the brink of collapse because of Fianna Fáil intransigence, the *Sunday Tribune* reported that at the beginning of November a 'bugging' device had been installed in the house of an SDLP supporter near Dublin with whom Séamus Mallon stayed when in the city; that this had been reported to me several weeks later by Séamus Mallon; that the matter had not been adequately investigated by the Gardaí; and that there were suspicions that the Gardaí had themselves been responsible for the attempted bugging.

The first I had heard of this affair had been on 18 November when I had been handed two documents that Séamus Mallon had given to a civil servant for transmission to me. One was a request to lift a ban on state employment imposed on someone convicted of taking part in the British embassy riot in July 1981; the other was a statement about an attempted 'bugging', with wiring, a microphone, and a transmitter, of the house in which Séamus Mallon stayed in Dublin. I sent both documents to Michael Noonan, and at the next meeting of the Forum told Séamus Mallon I had done so.

According to reports I received in early January, the Gardaí had concluded that men who installed a wire in the house (on the pretext that they were from the Post Office and were fitting a new phone system) were in fact planning a robbery. No microphone or transmitter was found by Post Office officials who had investigated the original complaint. I gave statements by these officials to Séamus Mallon at the next Forum meeting. In regard to representations he had made to me about the participant in the British Embassy march (who, as it happened, was a relative of the bugged householder) I showed him a photograph of that person with a stave in his hand in the front row of the crowd attacking the gardaí, and I understood him to accept my view that as he was clearly far from being, as had been represented, an innocent participant in a demonstration, the ban on state employment should remain.

After the Forum meeting a week later he handed the statements back to me without comment, except for an expression of regret at the delay in doing so. I took it from this that he was satisfied, and, as I was never informed of the fact that he had subsequently asked an official if there were any further developments, I had thought no more of the matter. Nor was I told anything about a further Garda inquiry initiated by the Minister for Justice, who felt that the householder should be interviewed.

And so when I was told on the evening of Saturday 18 February that the *Sunday Tribune* was running a story that, among other things, alleged that the Gardaí now had in their possession a transmitter and microphone retrieved from the scene, I was taken totally by surprise. I summoned officials from the Department of Justice to elucidate the matter. I was shown a second Garda report that had been completed three weeks earlier but had not been transmitted to me. From this it emerged that in the course of their inquiry the Gardaí had interviewed the householder and his wife, who, they said, seemed surprised that the matter was being further pursued at this stage. A microphone and transmitter that had been found were handed over to the Gardaí. Later I learnt that the householder had told Séamus Mallon that they had not given these items earlier to the Posts and Telegraphs officials who had called to the house to investigate the complaint because they could not at that point rule out the possibility that these officials were themselves in some way involved in the affair.

This second Garda report also said that the device had been installed by someone who, although having enough knowledge to assemble it, had very little expertise, and had used as a pick-up microphone a telephone mouthpiece, which, placed under a carpet as it had been, would have been almost entirely ineffective even at close range. The whole device, they said, was extremely crude and inefficient. The conclusion they reached was that it had been placed for some purpose other than to overhear conversations.

Meanwhile in the immediate aftermath of the *Sunday Tribune* story Charles Haughey had gone on radio to link the attempted bugging with alleged attempts by 'the British establishment' to interfere with the Forum. Vincent Browne, the editor of the *Sunday Tribune*, had boosted his story with an announcement that he believed a 'Technical Support Section' of the Gardaí had been responsible for the affair. In the Dáil on the following Tuesday Haughey made the most of the affair, which was also the subject of a debate in the Dáil a week later. If, as now seems clear, the whole affair was devised by the IRA to embarrass the Government and to drive a wedge between us and Séamus Mallon, it had a fair measure of success.

In his initial reaction to the *Sunday Tribune* story Séamus Mallon had said that while he was concerned at the Garda handling of the matter he was utterly convinced that I had acted in good faith from start to finish, but he became very critical of me after my Dáil statement on the following Tuesday. He objected to my inclusion in that statement of a reference to his other request, for removal of the ban on state employment of a participant in the British Embassy riot, and he resented my explanation to the Dáil of the reasons for referring to it, namely that my response to his representations on this issue, although negative, demonstrated that I had not ignored his approach, and second, that the two matters were not quite distinct, because the subject of his representations was a relative of the householder who had been consulted by him about the device in the house.

Séamus Mallon saw this, incorrectly, as an attempt by me to smear his friend and host, and for him this false impression was reinforced by his incorrect supposition from other remarks I made that I was saying that the occupants were hostile to or uncooperative with the Gardaí. This was a complete misinterpretation, as Michael Noonan made clear in the later debate.

When Séamus Mallon and I met in the Forum two days after my reply in the Dáil to Charles Haughey's questions on the matter, his loyalty to his friends and misunderstanding of my statements led him to react very coldly to me. When I approached him in the Forum ante-room he attacked me verbally. He had already refused to come to my home for breakfast on the previous day unless he could be accompanied by a lawyer. A year was to elapse before our relationship was restored. All this did not contribute to the smooth working of the Forum or to the coherence of the SDLP delegation, who were deeply embarrassed by this affair.

Meanwhile direct contact between John Hume and Margaret Thatcher had been established in mid-February when, somewhat belatedly, she took up my proposal that she invite him to come to see her. She was able to confirm for herself that he and I were on the same wavelength with regard to a future negotiation, for John and I kept in close touch on this matter throughout, and of course after, the Forum.

By now we had finally begun to come to grips with the key issues encapsulated in what was to become chapter 5 of the Forum report: 'Present Realities and Future Requirements'. John Hume, Dick Spring and I saw this section as the potential springboard for the major negotiation that lay ahead. For us its essential elements were recognition of the equal validity of the unionist and nationalist identities—something that hitherto, for opposite reasons, both Irish nationalists and British governments had been reluctant to concede; the need to accommodate both identities in any new arrangements without domination of one by the other; and finally, the urgency of the problem, which suggested the need for an immediate reassessment of their policy by the British government and resolute action by them in the light of that reassessment.

This draft section of the report was discussed initially amongst the party leaders. At this stage it contained seven points. The third of these accepted unionists' underlying sense of Britishness, while the fourth, headed 'Acceptance of the equal validity of the two traditions', read: 'Both of these traditions must each have a secure, adequate and durable expression and protection of their identities.'

Our morning session on 16 February on this draft went well. Charles Haughey made some useful additions to the seven points and showed no sign of challenging these two crucial statements to which John Hume, Dick Spring and I attached so much importance, nor did he show any disposition to add anything that we would find unacceptable. After lunch, however, his mood was transformed. He flatly refused to discuss the 'Realities' any further, and announced to us that there could be only one recommendation from the Forum: a unitary state. He could not 'sell' the other models to his colleagues; if he tried to do so 'you'd have two Fianna Fáils.' In any event, he went on, the British would veto anything the Forum produced, so it was better to 'go for broke' and bid high for a unitary state. I told him—as I obviously could not do in a full Forum session—that there were in fact clear signs of movement from the British; but this evoked no response.

There were several theories about what had precipitated this volte-face. Some members, including certain SDLP representatives, put it down to a lunchtime meeting Haughey was supposed to have had with Séamus Mallon, who, however, denied this to John Hume. This theory might have owed something to the fact that the unitary state model was the crucial issue at stormy SDLP delegation meetings that evening, when Séamus Mallon, with one supporter, was reported to have proposed that they back this model only. The other eight delegation members rejected this attempt to exclude the other models, however, and there were unfounded reports next day that Séamus Mallon was thinking of resigning from the SDLP delegation.

Charles Haughey's own excuse for his sudden change of stance was opposition within his own delegation, an explanation that gained credibility when next day in the public session discussion of the 'Realities' document Ray MacSharry moved in like a shot to denounce it. The only reality that mattered to him, MacSharry said, was the British 'guarantee' to the Unionists, and he could not stand over any 'Realities' document that did not point this out. Frank Cluskey responded by asking whether Fianna Fáil were serious about an agreed report. If they were not, then they should say so now and we could all go home.

Stephen McGonagle, the former Northern Ireland Ombudsman and a respected non-political member of the Labour Party delegation, immediately appealed to the Southern parties to remember the suffering of the people of the North and not to fight among themselves. In the face of this appeal Fianna Fáil could not credibly persist with their attempt to impose their distorted vision on the other three parties. Faced with the cul-de-sac into which Ray MacSharry had walked him, an obviously infuriated Charles Haughey gathered up his papers and almost shouted at the chairman, 'It's half-past three.' Colm Ó hEocha responded by declaring the meeting closed.

When the leaders met again, on 22 February, in the immediate aftermath of the Mallon 'bugging' row, Haughey appeared very depressed, complaining both of leaks that made Fianna Fáil look intransigent and of the problems he said he had with his delegation—'and I'm not bluffing.'

On the following Monday, when a new version of the 'Realities' document was circulated by the secretariat, Haughey said he no longer favoured such a section appearing in the report; and after the meeting I for my part discovered that a crucial sentence had been inadvertently omitted from it. The draft was then withdrawn. We agreed, however, to circulate the draft of chapter 3 to the members; and by the end of the week it appeared, together with chapters 1 and 2, in the *Irish Press*.

As it happened Charles Haughey and I had got on well both at the private and public sessions on Friday 2 March; we even found ourselves united on one issue against the SDLP at the public session. We also agreed that to avoid further leaks the text of future chapters would be discussed initially *within* delegations and then by the leaders, without a general debate in plenary session. In addition—and this was a real breakthrough—at the leaders' meeting on the following Wednesday the leader of the opposition for the first time agreed to a specific deadline for completion of the report, namely six weeks from then. At that meeting also I showed him a copy of the section of my speech to Congress that dealt with the Forum, and I accepted an amendment he proposed. Three weeks later he reciprocated by showing me the moderately worded section of his ard-fheis speech.

In my absence in the United States in mid-March, the Fine Gael delegation revolted. They were frustrated by the fact that the final drafting was now being done by the leaders after consultation with their delegations; they felt that I had been conceding far too much to Fianna Fáil, and that they were being used to rubber-stamp a document the shape of which was being decided elsewhere. On this occasion Peter Barry eventually calmed them down.

But when I met them after my return from Washington and Brussels they had been destabilised once again by a *Belfast Newsletter* report that Fianna Fáil had made a decision to oppose joint authority. Given that this was the model most likely to provide a basis for a negotiation that they were aware I intended to initiate, they wanted to know if there was any point in continuing with the Forum. Ivan Yates said our 'bottom line' had now been reached, and Enda Kenny told me that Fianna Fáil now viewed me with contempt. For my part I insisted that if Fianna Fáil rejected the joint authority model the SDLP—except perhaps for Séamus Mallon—would support Labour and Fine Gael in insisting on its inclusion, and the Forum would split three-to-one. On this basis the delegation rallied; they would back a report containing the three models whether Fianna Fáil did so or not; and at that stage they believed that Fianna Fáil would not do so.

Fianna Fáil was also having problems. At this stage some members of the party outside the Forum, who were unhappy with the apparent intransigence of their delegation, circulated to the press copies of a 1980 post-summit press conference statement in which Charles Haughey had said that he would rule out nothing that led to political progress.

On 6 April, with his ard-fheis now behind him, Haughey produced to a leaders' meeting his version of the 'Realities' document. This was a 'green' version of the secretariat draft of 27 February, but it contained the crucial elements we had been seeking, namely rejection of violence, recognition of the Britishness of unionists and of the validity of the unionist as well as the nationalist identity, and an assertion of the urgent need for a British response. The fly in the ointment was a proposed assertion that the 'only' structure that could accommodate all the realities on a stable and permanent basis was a unitary state. But it was a fly that did not worry me too much at the time. This proposition was one that all three of the other delegations would reject, leaving it to Fianna Fáil to decide if it would 'break' on a formulation that would secure little public support.

There were other wrinkles to be ironed out; but for the following three weeks the battle was joined on the unitary state issue, specifically Charles Haughey's insistence that we should all commit ourselves to the view that a unitary state was both the best and the only constitutional model for a new Ireland. On 11 April our delegation agreed that this was a sticking point: let Fianna Fáil be isolated on this issue if it chose to insist on imposing its view on others. At a Fianna Fáil delegation meeting Ray MacSharry's hard-line stance won the day against opposition from a couple of moderates.

Next day I made our position quite clear at the leaders' meeting, where John Hume and Dick Spring supported me. However, I offered to accept a formulation describing a unitary state as the 'ideal' from a nationalist view-point, but one that could be achieved only by consent. Dick was willing to drop the phrase about 'consent' in this sentence, as it would appear elsewhere. A private meeting of the full Forum next day merely led to a referring back of the matter to the delegations.

During the weekend the Forum co-ordinator, Wally Kirwan from the Department of the Taoiseach, went to Armagh to see Séamus Mallon. This visit produced a compromise formula to the effect that a unitary state was 'the particular structure of political unity which the Forum wish to see established.' During the lunch break following a fruitless meeting of the leaders on Monday morning Charles Haughey put this formula to John Hume, linked with agree-ment on his part to the outstanding issue in the report that we regarded as essential: a statement to the effect that the Forum remained open to other views that might contribute to political development, i.e. views other than the unitary, federal/confederal and joint authority models.

With this final paragraph, together with the three models and the 'Present Realities and Future Requirements' section of the report, we would have all that we needed to initiate an open-ended negotiation with the British govern-ment. The 'Future Requirements' section, which contained nothing a British government—or indeed Unionists—could reasonably quarrel with, provided the material for a preamble to such an agreement; the joint authority model provided a rationale for an agreement that would include recognition of the British role in Northern Ireland; and the final sentence covered the possible negotiation of an agreement that did not involve formal joint authority.

The achievement of all the objectives I had set out to secure in the Forum fifteen months earlier was thus within our grasp; but I was still not happy with the suggested compromise on our attitude to the unitary state model as 'the particular structure . . . the Forum wish to see established.' I proposed the introduction into the Mallon-Kirwan compromise of the conditional verb 'would', thus describing the unitary state as 'the particular structure of political unity which the Forum would wish to see established.' Charles Haughey accepted my amendment.

The report was not yet complete, but we knew now that there would be an agreed document. A rearguard action was still to come, however. Fianna Fáil sources told us that Martin Mansergh was unhappy with his boss's cave-in on the issue of making the unitary state model our 'only' choice. On 17 April

Fianna Fáil submitted a new and much expanded draft of the chapter on the unitary state model, attributed to Martin Mansergh, which attempted to boost this model at the expense of the others and at the expense of the subsequent chapters on the federal or confederal and joint authority models. The latter of these could not easily be expanded in competition with an enlarged unitary state chapter without giving away too much of our thinking about the negotiations to come and possibly prejudicing the outcome. In the event, by expanding the federal/confederal chapter we were able to foil Martin Mansergh by ensuring that the unitary state and federal/confederal chapters were of the same length, with a somewhat shorter chapter on joint authority.

The leaders having reached agreement amongst themselves, the party delegations met in Dublin Castle on 30 April. This was the first time the delegations had had the opportunity to see all eight chapters of the report together. On the whole they were happy with the report, but with strong reservations on the part of the Labour Party and Fine Gael about the historical section in chapter 3. These reservations were shared by members of the Government, who had seen a semi-final draft a week earlier. I myself was conscious of the danger of a hostile British reaction to the propagandist tone of this chapter. Accordingly I wrote to Margaret Thatcher on 27 April indicating what seemed to me to be highly significant parts of the report.

At the leaders' lunch on this last day the first serious problem arose. Charles Haughey wanted to reintroduce the ambiguity about consent by a majority in the North to unification that we had earlier agreed to eliminate: he proposed referring to the consent of 'the Irish people north and south'. Dick Spring and I consulted our delegations—knowing well how they would react. When we reported back that they were adamant, Haughey complained about his own delegation's stubborn mood, but he finally accepted the phrase 'agreed to by the people of the North and by the people of the South,' which left no doubt about the need for the consent of a majority in Northern Ireland to unification.

But when the leaders' meeting adjourned at 5.30 p.m. the Labour Party was still refusing to accept a wording that referred to the federal or confederal and joint authority models as 'suggestions' that had been put to us. While agreeing with them that this word seemed to downgrade these two models, I felt bound by the agreement we had reached earlier on this point. Mary Robinson, now President (who was the 'toughest' of the Fine Gael and Labour members opposing the attempt to commit the Forum to the unitary state model), and Frank Cluskey were not prepared to yield, despite efforts by John Hume, Peter Barry and myself to persuade them. (It will be recalled that Mary Robinson later resigned from the Labour Party because of her opposition to the Anglo-Irish Agreement.) They felt the matter needed further reflection, and finally it was agreed that Dick Spring would decide overnight what the Labour Party would accept. Next morning he proposed the substitution of 'proposals' for 'suggestions', and this was accepted by Charles Haughey. On the morning of 1 May the report was thus finally agreed for launching at

2.30 p.m. the following day at a formal session in St Patrick's Hall attended by the resident diplomatic corps.

It had been an unprecedented episode in Irish political history. In the course of eleven months the three main political parties in the Irish state, together with the constitutional nationalist party of Northern Ireland, had met on almost a hundred occasions, including over fifty leaders' meetings, to establish a considerable measure of common ground on the most divisive national issue. The tense public relationship between Charles Haughey and myself (by contrast, at a personal level we had never clashed during the forty years we had known each other) had not impeded the successful accomplishment of our task; indeed on the whole he and I had got on well at the leaders' meetings, although he had made no secret of his desire to return to the normal political climate of parliamentary conflict.

Apart from the nationalist bias of the historical section and the ritual obeisance to the concept of a unitary state, the report conformed to the requirements I had set before the Forum was established, and gave me precisely what I needed in order to start a major negotiation with the British government. Only in one respect did it fall short of what I had wanted: its preparation had taken four months more than I had allowed for.

There remained the public launching of the report. When for the last time the leaders met before this public session, Charles Haughey told us that in his press conference at that session he would be presenting his own view of the report. He read from a note of what he proposed to say. I and, I believe, my two colleagues were not very happy with what we heard, which, as far as I can recall it, involved a restatement of Haughey and Fianna Fáil's commitment to the unitary state. But while we feared that his proposed presentation might weaken the impact of the report, we could not reasonably quarrel with what we understood from a quick hearing to be the content of his proposed remarks on his own and Fianna Fáil's position.

In my speech at the formal session I was concerned to soften the impact on the British and the Northern Unionists of the historical analysis in chapter 3, which had been so successfully 'greened' by Fianna Fáil. I referred to it as 'an Irish nationalist analysis', adding that 'others in this island or in Britain who do not share our perspective will not agree with all the details of this analysis,' but that it was right that it should be placed on the record. I went on to say that the report had, however, 'transcended this analysis and interpretation of past events.' The Forum had sought to raise its sights to new horizons and to set out ideals that could provide common ground for the two traditions and a basis for common action by the two governments to reconcile these traditions. It was not a blueprint for the island of the future, I said, but an agenda that presupposed further action.

In his speech at this session Charles Haughey confined himself to generalities; he said nothing controversial. The session was followed by a succession of fifteen-minute press conferences; I gave the first, and Haughey gave the second. In my replies to questions from the media about the Forum's handling of the unitary state issue I said that we were all Irish nationalists and that our preferred option, and the ideal we would aspire to, would be a unitary state; but we also recognised that we could not achieve this ourselves: others were involved, and for such a state to come into existence they would have to agree. We had indicated our openness to other views and had in the most specific terms resisted seeking to draw unionists into Irish unity against their will.

At the time when I was answering these questions from the media I was unaware of the manner in which, before the publication of the report, the press had been briefed by Fianna Fáil. I had not had the opportunity to watch RTE's pre-session programme, in which both of the commentators, Brian Farrell and John Bowman, had clearly been briefed to the effect that the Forum was committed to the unitary state option (a view strongly challenged by two well-informed observers whom they interviewed at this point, Mary Holland and Pádraig O'Malley).

Accordingly I was, like many others, completely unprepared for Charles Haughey's replies at his press conference. These went far beyond expressing a Fianna Fáil view on the issues at stake. In his references to the unitary state model he repeatedly misquoted the report, a process that culminated in his statement that 'the only solution is as stated in the report: a unitary state with a new constitution.' He also rejected the whole concept of the consent of a majority in Northern Ireland being a precondition of Irish unity, saying in relation to the establishment of a unitary state that 'nobody is entitled to deny the natural unity is unification of Ireland . . . The Forum wish to see established a unitary state; I don't believe that the consent or agreement of anyone is required for that.'

The value of the report as an agreed position of the four parties was clearly damaged by this episode, but the negative reaction of most people, including very many Fianna Fáil supporters, to the Fianna Fáil leader's handling of it was a counterbalancing factor. I would have preferred a different outcome but did not feel, nor I think did the Government, that the state of public opinion following this episode should inhibit us from pursuing the strategy to which we had seen the Forum as a vitally important preliminary.

I should perhaps add that I was never clear why Charles Haughey decided to make such an issue of the unitary state model, rejecting the federal or con-federal model of Irish unity. I could have understood, without agreeing with, a Fianna Fáil stance in favour of Irish unity that would have rejected joint authority as unsatisfactory, for Fianna Fáil had always conceived itself as having the particular role in Irish politics of voicing the aspirations of traditional Irish nationalism in such a way as to attract away from the IRA and to constitutional politics as large a proportion of 'republican' opinion as possible. I respect this motivation, which I knew Charles Haughey shared, and I recognise the contri-bution it has made to stabilising the Irish state from 1926 onwards. The role of Fine Gael and, since the end of the 1960s, the Labour Party is, I believe, quite different, namely to pose an alternative, pluralist concept of Irishness that would have room for unionists as well as nationalists. Neither side should dismiss the value of the other's role in securing political stability on the one hand and progress towards North-South reconciliation on the other.

But by rejecting one form of Irish unity in favour of another—a unitary state—in a way that no previous Fianna Fáil leader had done, Charles Haughey seemed to me to have weakened his party's capacity to fulfil its historic role. In so far as this served to 'take the heat' off my joint authority concept, our immediate task of securing wide acceptance of an agreement that would have joint authority aspects to it was made easier; but I remained—and remain—puzzled about why at this point in the history of his party this Fianna Fáil leader chose to narrow the issue to a unitary as against a federal or confederal state. I can only speculate that the diversionary tactics I had earlier employed to secure consideration of the joint authority model may have misled him into thinking that I was actually 'targeting' confederation, which had after all been the principal proposal in Fine Gael's 1979 Northern Ireland policy. This could have led him to support the unitary state model with a view to distinguishing Fianna Fáil's position from what he thought ours might be. If this was his approach it was, I believe, counterproductive, having the clearly unintended effect of obscuring Fianna Fáil's real commitment, which is, I think, to Irish reunification rather than to a particular form of unity.

# CHAPTER SIXTEEN

# ANGLO-IRISH AGREEMENT: NEGOTIATION

Before coming to the steps we took to follow up the Forum report with the British government I must go back two months to 1 March, when we had received an approach that, in view of Margaret Thatcher's November 1983 rejection of even informal discussions, came as a surprise to us.

On a visit to Dublin Sir Robert Armstrong put forward some suggestions on behalf of the Prime Minister and the Cabinet, the details of which, they told us, were known only to the Prime Minister and the Secretaries of State for Foreign Affairs and Northern Ireland. The proposals involved creating a 'security band' along the border, to be overseen by a Joint Security Commission and policed by joint crime squads, which could develop later into a common police force or crime squad. They also proposed a law commission for the whole island, with the possibility of an all-Ireland court, then or later. Political developments they envisaged would involve more equitable franchise arrangements in Northern Ireland as well as symbolic measures such as changes in the flags and emblems legislation. These provisions were to be accompanied by some kind of guarantee by us of the status of Northern Ireland, paying special attention to articles 2 and 3 of the Constitution.

Our officials were also told that these proposals could be viewed as building-blocks for future political arrangements, that the 'security band' proposal might also apply in west Belfast, that the European Convention on Human Rights might be incorporated in the laws of both parts of Ireland, and that a parliamentary tier as envisaged in the Anglo-Irish joint studies could be looked at.

When the meeting ended Dermot Nally asked to see me urgently. When I heard his summary of the British proposals I asked if the British emissaries were still there. They had left, he said. I told him to make contact with them as soon as they arrived back in Britain and before they could report to the British Ministers. I wanted them to be told why some aspects of their proposals, most notably the 'security band' concept, would be completely unacceptable to us.

This was done, and four days later our more formal reactions were presented in London at a meeting where the genesis of the British proposals was first explained to us. It appeared that, talking to her Ministers and officials after our departure from Chequers on 7 November, the Prime Minister had said that she had been impressed with my exposé, and accepted that doing nothing might now be worse than attempting an initiative, however risky. Some ideas should be developed, she had said, centred on a 'basic equation' involving on the one side an acknowledgement of the union of Great Britain with Northern Ireland and on the other our involvement in the government of Northern Ireland, with particular emphasis on security. When the matter had been brought to the Cabinet on 27 February the Prime Minister had been unable to speak because of laryngitis, but Jim Prior had outlined on her behalf the concept of a 'basic equation', the need to do something rather than nothing in such a dangerous situation, and the proposal that Robert Armstrong should sound out our reaction. Most Ministers had been sceptical but had not formally opposed the idea.

In our response to the proposals put forward on the British side about joint security operations we said that we were glad that the need for joint action was recognised by the British side but that some of their proposals seemed to us to involve a misconception of the idea of balance and to be likely to prove counter-productive. We could defend joint security operations within Northern Ireland only if they were placed within a wider concept of joint authority. A joint border zone could not be contemplated, for several reasons: it would create two borders not to be crossed by security forces in pursuit of the IRA instead of one; the authority and acceptability of our forces in our own state would be undermined; and in our view there was no objective need for British or Northern Ireland security forces to operate within the Republic.

We believed the two governments should first agree on the nature of the problem and then devise a framework within which practical and enduring proposals could be worked out with political confidence: arrangements that would be durable at least for a generation and that would involve a solid integration of the joint authority system with the internal government of Northern Ireland.

The British replied that they could be flexible on the security band proposal and on territorial limitations for joint security operations within Northern Ireland. They felt, however, that their proposals for a Joint Security Commission and an All-Ireland Law Commission should be of interest to us. Our suggestion that we should first agree on a set of principles as a solid framework for consideration of joint authority came up against the British preference for pragmatic proposals. They added, however, that there was now a momentum on the British side, involving openness to hitherto 'unthinkable' issues from their point of view, and that we should come up with further proposals as soon as possible.

Peter Barry visited London for St Patrick's Day. After his arrival on 15 March he saw Geoffrey Howe to strengthen our response at official level to the British initiative of 1 March. He was concerned at this meeting to be as positive as possible so that the Prime Minister would not get too discouraging a report from this discussion, while at the same time making clear our opposition to some of the ideas put to us by the British a fortnight earlier. We heard soon afterwards that he had been successful. During his talk with Geoffrey Howe he was told that, while joint sovereignty was not on, the British could contemplate joint authority, but would find 'joint responsibility' preferable.

Next day he met Jim Prior privately for almost an hour, as well as meeting him with his officials on outstanding Northern Ireland issues. In the tete-à-tete Jim Prior confirmed that the Prime Minister now had a much more open mind on the problem and was willing to consider broader and wider political ideas than had been put to us on 1 March—but for this to happen, movement by us on articles 2 and 3 was vital.

In the margin of these talks we also learnt at this time of the British 'two-track' approach to the Forum report and the impending negotiations: their reaction to the report was to be 'led' by the Northern Ireland Office in conjunction with the Foreign Office, but the other exchanges were to be handled by the Cabinet Office, with the knowledge of only two officials in the Foreign Office and of only one—the Secretary—in the NIO, in addition of course to Jim Prior himself. Shortly afterwards we learnt that the Attorney General had also been brought into the 'circle'.

When I met Margaret Thatcher three days later in the margin of the European Council meeting in Brussels (a meeting of which I no longer have a record) I was concerned to convince her that within six or eight weeks I would be putting forward a substantial proposal as the basis for a negotiation. At the same time I outlined the likely shape of the Forum report that was now emerging. I explained why the proposals put to us on her behalf on 1 March did not in our view meet the needs of the situation, and I formed the impression that she might now find acceptable a quite different and more radical approach.

I arranged that a full report on the evolving situation be submitted to the Government. This memorandum set out the concern Peter Barry and I felt at what seemed to us and to the British government to be a real danger that the IRA would achieve a political breakthrough in Northern Ireland at the local elections in a year's time. At a recent by-election in the Lower Falls area of Belfast the Sinn Féin vote had exceeded that of the SDLP by a margin of over three to one. If Sinn Féin's electoral support in Northern Ireland were to exceed that of the SDLP, the situation there could get out of control and threaten the whole island, for in those circumstances the IRA might seek a violent confrontation with the unionists and try to follow this by an attempt to destabilise the Republic.

The Government were also told that the British Cabinet now accepted our analysis of the situation and had come to the view that it might now be more dangerous to do nothing than to attempt an initiative aimed at stabilising the situation. Accordingly, following the publication of the Forum report a set of proposals for the future government of Northern Ireland would be brought to the Government for approval and then presented to the British.

I sent a copy of the draft Forum report to Margaret Thatcher on 27 April. In their public response to the report the British government said that we could not expect them to accept the nationalist interpretation of past events, which was 'one-sided'. Nevertheless they welcomed the report and the positive elements in it, which they cited at some length. But there was no reason, they said, to expect the consent of a majority in Northern Ireland to a change of sovereignty 'in any of the three forms in the Report'—an unhappy phraseology, which ignored the distinction I had sought to make between joint authority and joint sovereignty.

That said, the statement went on to acknowledge the problems of division and violence in Northern Ireland, 'including the feelings of alienation amongst the nationalist minority,' and the British government declared its continuing wish to provide a basis on which Northern Ireland citizens could live securely, peacefully and prosperously in the years immediately ahead, 'giving full expression to their identities and aspirations and playing their proper part in public affairs.' Finally there was a welcome for the statement that the parties in the Forum remained fully open to discuss other views.

Meanwhile in the immediate aftermath of the publication of the Forum report we had moved quickly to get authority to begin a negotiation. On 9 May the Government authorised an approach to the British that would involve taking up with them first the unitary state model; if that were not acceptable, the federal or confederal model; and if that in turn proved unacceptable, a set of ideas incorporating joint authority in a form that would be durable and would provide for the possibility of Irish unity. Excepted powers to be reserved to the British government would include defence, foreign policy, and finance, but these might be matters for consultation with us, and we would suggest that certain excepted powers, such as representation of some or all Northern Ireland interests in the European Community, could by agreement between the two governments and after consultation with the Northern Ireland Assembly pass from British to Irish responsibility.

The joint authority we proposed would comprise a full-time cabinet Minister from each government and would directly control certain reserved areas, including the nomination of a Northern Ireland Executive, security, and certain issues of identity such as flags and emblems, broadcasting, and posts and telegraphs. By agreement these powers could be transferred to a Northern Ireland Executive, which, in conjunction with the Assembly and subject to a series of checks and balances, would operate the remaining devolved powers. Operational arrangements would have to be made to deal with a failure of the representatives of the two governments to agree within the joint authority framework.

In the security area a system of joint command would be proposed, with alternating command at the highest level, and an all-Ireland court would be envisaged, to be appointed jointly by the Irish Government and the Northern Ireland Executive, as well as a North-South commission to harmonise the criminal law. A primary objective would be to secure acceptance of such a system by the people of Northern Ireland and as far as possible by both communities. The memorandum also proposed that we seek agreement with the British on a public statement comprising the 'Present Realities and Future Requirements' sections of the Forum report; these were in fact the only sections of the report that involved actual proposals by the Forum.

On 10 May we presented these ideas to Robert Armstrong and David Goodall in London. A fortnight was to elapse before we received an authoritative reaction at political level. Peter Barry had a meeting with Jim Prior in London on 25 May, the day following a discussion of our proposals between Jim Prior, Geoffrey Howe, and the Prime Minister. He was told by Jim Prior that the Prime Minister had been very negative towards our proposals. However, he added, Peter Carrington, on the basis of his experience in relation to Rhodesia/Zimbabwe, had told Jim Prior to expect this sort of initial reaction. Geoffrey Howe, Prior said, had a more positive and more interested attitude than the Prime Minister, and Peter Barry should encourage this interest when he met him at a forthcoming EC Foreign Ministers' 'weekend of reflection'.

Jim Prior then put forward what we viewed as a very inadequate set of proposals, but added that if changing articles 2 and 3 could be considered a lot of things might open up.

In the light of this I came to the conclusion that we should review our tactics on articles 2 and 3. In not seeking authority from the Government at the outset to open up the possibility of amending the articles I had been influenced by two considerations: a feeling that it would be unwise to put all our cards on the table at the outset, and doubts whether the Government as a whole yet accepted that a really important initiative was practicable. Until they had been convinced on that score there would certainly have been considerable reticence about proposing a referendum on articles 2 and 3, which many would believe unlikely to succeed. I now asked myself, however, whether we could or should sustain this cautious approach in circumstances where on the British side our apparent unwillingness to face the issue was clearly being interpreted as lack of commitment on our part to a serious initiative involving elements of joint authority.

Accordingly I sought the views of some of our key officials who were closely involved with these issues, and found that they shared my fears that our initiative might founder very quickly if we did not at least indicate a possibility of movement on articles 2 and 3 in return for a major package involving movement in the direction of joint authority.

Our next contact with the British at official level was to be on Wednesday 30 May in Dublin. Accordingly I asked John Hume, Dick Spring and Peter Barry to come to my home on the previous Tuesday evening to discuss this dilemma. It was agreed that we would indicate at official level on the following day that if an adequate package were agreed we would be disposed to put that package to the electorate in the Republic by way of a plebiscite or referendum, as provided for by the Constitution.

During a subsequent discussion amongst us on security arrangements in Northern Ireland I expressed the view that we should not necessarily be wedded to a system of joint security of the kind that had been aired in the autumn of the previous year if this appeared to pose insuperable problems. John Hume for his part expressed a preference for a new locally recruited police force. It was agreed that our openness on the precise character of the new security arrangements that would be acceptable to the minority should also be indicated to the British at this point.

At official level on the following day we received further confirmation of the importance attached by Margaret Thatcher to articles 2 and 3. But despite our reticence on this issue she had not given up the idea of a major initiative, we were told: she had expressed her affection for and confidence in me, but suspected that these feelings might lead her to make the wrong concessions!

The two adjustments to our position that we had agreed informally amongst the four of us on the previous evening were put forward in the course of this discussion at official level, and subsequently confirmed by Peter Barry, who at the same time, when asked how the two governments might best pursue these ideas, suggested a conference of the two governments and the Northern Ireland parties.

A week or so later we heard from Jim Prior that the Prime Minister was now in a more positive frame of mind. But as we approached my meeting with her in the margin of the Fontainebleau European Council, the plot began to thicken. We were approached confidentially and indirectly in London on behalf of Jim Prior in relation to his proposals of 25 May that we had regarded as inadequate. A similar indirect and confidential approach had been made on his behalf four months earlier, which on that occasion had apparently percolated back to Whitehall. It had been suggested to us that this could have happened as a result of a telex from the London embassy to Iveagh House being intercepted by the British government's communications monitoring centre at Cheltenham, and that we should therefore communicate between London and Dublin in future by courier rather than by telex—a suggestion that I had forthwith adopted. Arising from this incident a member of the British Cabinet subsequently asked me personally for an assurance that, given the vulnerability of our telex link to such interception, nothing he said to us in London would be transmitted by this method. A senior member of the US administration also made this point to me around the same time, also suggesting that if we wanted to communicate confidentially with him we should send someone to see him personally, in view of the fact that any message transmitted by telex could be intercepted.

What came to us now through this indirect channel, the use of which earlier in the year had sparked off this cloak-and-dagger business, was an attempt to convince us that only a very limited package could be delivered. There was no way, we were told, that our security forces could be allowed to operate north of the border unless there were reciprocal arrangements for security forces there to come south. If, however, I had reason to believe that I could somehow sell a larger package to the Prime Minister, Jim Prior would wish me well. He would, however, be grateful if I could phone him at home immediately before the European Council meeting to tell him what I intended to propose to her. Meanwhile the vital meeting between him and the Prime Minister would be on 21 June, and he would arrange for us to be told the result of that meeting so that I would be in a better position for the Fontainebleau discussion.

We viewed this approach sceptically. We suspected that Jim Prior might be seeking to limit rather than to expand the Prime Minister's willingness to contemplate action. It seemed better not to pursue the suggestion that I let him know what I proposed to say to Margaret Thatcher.

Meanwhile in the course of a discussion in the Cabinet Office on 15 June we confirmed officially our open position on articles 2 and 3 and on security in Northern Ireland, as set out informally several weeks earlier. We also suggested that it would be advantageous if the package were to emerge from a conference involving the two governments and the constitutional parties in Northern Ireland rather than from a negotiation confined to the governments alone. On this occasion we also directed attention to the function of the courts in Northern Ireland as a particular area where there was alienation of the minority.

A meeting between Noel Dorr and Jim Prior a couple of days later was notably unproductive. Now that we had responded to his original suggestion about articles 2 and 3 by agreeing to consider such an amendment, Prior seemed to be taking fright at the thought of the substantial package that would be required in order to enable us to win such a referendum. He told Noel Dorr that he felt a package of a sufficient scale to achieve this result would be unacceptable to what he described as 'the people of Northern Ireland', by which he clearly meant the unionists. He also wondered whether the Prime Minister and I would have much of substance to talk about at this stage when we met at Fontainebleau. Noel Dorr thought that the presence of a note-taker—towards whom Jim Prior kept glancing during the meeting—might have inhibited the discussion, but then if the British Minister had wanted to speak more freely or more positively he could have dispensed with having a record of the discussion as it took place.

My meeting with Margaret Thatcher at Fontainebleau took place at 9 a.m. on the second day of the European Council. At the outset I confirmed that I would be willing to move to amend articles 2 and 3 of the Constitution if there were a substantial package that seemed likely to secure political acceptance by the Northern minority, ending the problem of alienation. Then, with the support of the SDLP—a powerful influence on public opinion in our state—and with enthusiastic campaigning by Fine Gael and the Labour Party, the members of which would welcome a chance to tackle the 'republican rhetoric' of those who might oppose such an agreement, a referendum could in my view be won. The kind of changes in articles 2 and 3 that I would propose would be along the lines of substituting an aspiration for the 'territorial claim', together with an acknowledgement that the existing situation could not be changed unless and until a majority in Northern Ireland agreed to that change. When Margaret Thatcher pointed out that if we failed in such a referendum both countries would be in a far worse position, I agreed, but said that the problem would never be solved unless we were prepared to take some risks.

I then moved on to discuss our joint authority proposal. She immediately intervened to say that this involved derogation of sovereignty. I rejected this: joint authority as I saw it was simply a method that the British government might choose to adopt in the exercise of its sovereignty in order to regulate the affairs of one part of the kingdom. I added that I had gone to considerable trouble to make this distinction between joint sovereignty and joint authority in television interviews after the Forum.

Would I, she riposted, say that a joint border zone for security purposes involved no derogation of sovereignty on our part? I replied that while some might see it as such, the main objection to that proposal would be that it was unnecessary and that it would involve creating two borders instead of one, thus complicating further the problem of dealing with the IRA in those areas.

I went on to emphasise the importance of stressing the need for consent by a majority in Northern Ireland to any change of sovereignty—and the need also to emphasise the importance of any arrangement entered into being *durable*. The minority needed participation; the majority needed durability: they must not be given grounds for feeling that any arrangement we entered into was part of a continuing process that would threaten their position.

I enquired how matters under discussion should be advanced. Would she consider a conference involving all the parties, as distinct from an intergovernmental meeting? She replied ambiguously that we would have to consider at what stage the present consultations would be enlarged. In this context I also suggested that if we could agree on the direction in which we were moving perhaps a statement of principles could be prepared for joint publication. A basis for such a statement could be the common ground that existed between the Unionist document *The Way Forward* and the Forum report. And there for the moment we had to leave it.

Jim Prior's subsequent House of Commons speech on the Forum report was helpful. In London on 10 July we learnt, however, that some leaks to the press on the British side reflected the hostility on the part of NIO officials to any move being made. They had been excluded by their own side from the early stages of the Armstrong-Nally process because of their negative attitude to any initiative with a North-South dimension. Another problem in relation to the confidentiality of our discussions was the instinctive tendency of Jim Prior to seek to create a favourable climate for an initiative—not necessarily ours—by means of informal discussion with unionist politicians and journalists; he was an inveterate communicator, we were told, who had difficulty in controlling his compulsion to 'spill the beans'.

On the other hand we were also told that the Prime Minister remained very well disposed towards me and felt that our exchanges at Fontainebleau had been very useful indeed. It was remarked that there could not be enough of this: no amount of briefing, it was said, could match the value of hearing directly from me about our domestic political realities, such as the problems and possibilities of amending articles 2 and 3. She was now committed to doing something rather than nothing, but she still had doubts about our capacity to act and about her own capacity to carry a major initiative vis-à-vis her own party and the Unionists.

On 16 July we received the formal British response to our proposals of 10 May. The ideas now put forward on behalf of the British government were, we were told, ideas for further consideration and discussion rather than proposals, but they had the full authority of the Prime Minister and the knowledge and authority of the Cabinet.

At the outset, we were told, they must say 'no' to the unitary state and the federal or confederal models, but they pointed out that they had been much more cautious about the joint authority proposal. What they had really concentrated on, however, had been our openness to other views as expressed in paragraph 5.10 of the Forum report. They understood the need for some element of jointness in security operations, and their idea of a Joint Security Commission—part of their 1 March proposals—was still on the table. Perhaps a start could be made in this direction with liaison officers? They recognised that much of what they had previously proposed was not practicable and that any acceptable package would need some form of jointness at the political as well as at the security level. They believed, however, that both they and we could get into insuperable difficulties with anything that looked like joint sovereignty. The distinction I had made at Fontainebleau between joint sovereignty and joint authority as an *exercise* of sovereignty on the part of the British government would, we were told, seem very slim to unionists in Northern Ireland. However, in the period since we had submitted our proposals two months earlier the British government had been trying to find a way round this. Would it be possible, they wondered, to have a system of government for Northern Ireland in which the Irish Government would have a part but that (*a*) would not seem to involve a derogation of British sovereignty and (*b*) would be such that the minority would see in it an effective protection of their interests? In this context they considered three possibilities: first, that arrangements to give us real authority in Northern Ireland be undertaken within the ambit of the Anglo-Irish Intergovernmental Council as an additional element; second, that regular meetings be held between Belfast and Dublin outside the ambit of the Anglo-Irish Intergovernmental Council; and third, that an Irish resident presence be established in Belfast, which would be the focus for these matters.

In return for a package along these lines the British government would need to have an assurance that these arrangements, which must be durable, were not the thin end of a territorial claim. They would also need clarification of our position on articles 2 and 3 in the context of arrangements along these lines, and they would like to hear our view on what issues would not be devolved and on the idea that liaison officers could possibly develop into joint squads and later perhaps into single units under the proposed Joint Security Commission.

Our civil servants reserved their position on these proposals, which were clearly highly political in character. When it was suggested on our side that the liaison officer proposal might create problems, the response from the British side was to raise the possibility of a third type of police force, comprising elements from both North and South under a Joint Security Commission. In this connection they had registered our objections to joint security operations south of the border.

In reply to a query from our side about the legal nature of any proposed arrangement, the British side responded that it might take the form either of a treaty or of an agreement combined with an Act of Parliament. On the nature of the power the Irish Government would have in any such joint authority structure it was said that a formal and statutory right to be consulted would include the right to reject proposals and to withhold our approval, or even in extreme circumstances to withdraw from the arrangement.

At a subsequent informal discussion the two sides returned to the question of how to proceed with these proposals. We pressed the case again for agreement on a statement of principles to be made the basis for a conference of the two governments and the constitutional parties in Northern Ireland. On the British side there was some support for such a conference, but we were told that a statement of principles could not be agreed until there was a clearer common understanding of the shape an eventual agreement would take.

In the latter part of July we received the impression that Jim Prior might now regret having told us that all kinds of possibilities could open up if we were prepared to amend articles 2 and 3: he now seemed to prefer a much less substantial package. However, as we learnt that he would be retiring from the government in September we were not too seriously disturbed by this.

On 30 July a further discussion took place within the Armstrong-Nally framework to give us an opportunity to respond in a considered way to what had been put forward by the British side a fortnight earlier. Our officials started by saying that we saw two serious inadequacies in these British proposals. We told them that in our view their proposals were too gradualist either to tackle effectively the alienation of the minority or to provide for the kind of 'durability' that would reassure unionist fears of 'creeping unification'. Second, the political framework proposed was inadequate both as an actual political control mechanism for security arrangements and as a perceived response to the need to give to the minority the necessary sense of being identified with the system of political authority. By preventing the emergence of the conditions in which a referendum to amend articles 2 and 3 would be carried, these inadequacies would in turn prevent unionists from being given the sense of security that they needed and could derive from such a constitutional change.

If we were to make serious progress in tackling the alienation of the minority there would also have to be a radical change in the security arrangements in Northern Ireland. Consideration should be given to establishing a new, additional nationalist police force that would be unarmed. It and the RUC could be backed by a new joint 'security force'. These forces would be under the aegis of a Joint Security Commission, which would itself be subsidiary to and within a joint political framework. In the interim period before such new forces could be put in place we saw no option but to provide for joint security operations in Northern Ireland for a limited period.

An initial reaction from the British side was that they had difficulty with the idea of a completely unarmed police force dealing with crime in part of Northern Ireland; however, they agreed that if there were a force of the type of the German frontier police, dealing with terrorism, another force might be unarmed. They did not exclude an additional police force—possibly joint—operating in certain geographical areas or in regard to certain matters. There were precedents on the Continent for separate police forces dealing with different matters within the same geographical area. But three police forces would be too complex and too expensive. Instead, should the Joint Security Commission not be given a remit to work out ways of moving towards an all-Ireland police force in conjunction with an all-Ireland court?

The relative openness of the British side in this preliminary discussion on our proposals on policing was, however, matched by unwillingness on their part to go beyond their proposals of 16 July in relation to the political role of the Irish Government in Northern Ireland. A further submission to the Government now appeared necessary. I gave instructions for this to be drafted while I was on holiday in August with a view to presenting it at a Government meeting on 31 August. I received a draft memorandum while on holiday, and sent back my comments.

This memorandum, which was accompanied by a series of papers dealing with particular aspects of the matter, including the attitudes of Northern nationalists and unionists and the IRA's strategy, set out the developments that had taken place in the negotiation during the previous three months. It went on to outline the shape of a possible agreement that we could seek within the parameters of what had been discussed and had either been agreed or at any rate had not so far been rejected by the British side. The memorandum then put to the Government the issue of whether proposals along these lines, if agreed, would be sufficient to reverse the tide of nationalist alienation in Northern Ireland and to convince opinion in the Republic that articles 2 and 3 of the Constitution should be changed.

The proposals put to the Government envisaged the creation within the Anglo-Irish Intergovernmental Council, which Margaret Thatcher and I had established in 1981, of an Anglo-Irish Ministerial Commission, including one cabinet Minister from each government. The Irish member of the commission could have offices in Belfast and Dublin, with sub-offices at various points in nationalist Northern Ireland. In regard to excepted matters (including defence, foreign policy, and finance) the Irish Minister would have the right to seek consultation. Such a right might be exercised for example in relation to co-operation and co-ordination of North-South economic policy and some European Community issues, but not in relation to external defence. In regard to reserved matters (all or any of which could by agreement between the two governments be devolved to a Northern Ireland Executive), pending devolution the British Minister would have an obligation to consult the Irish Minister. These reserved functions would include the nomination of the Executive, security, the courts, broadcasting, posts and telegraphs, and issues of identity, for example flags and emblems, place-names, and language.

In regard to security it was put to the Government that this must be tackled with the same courage that was displayed by the first government, which had set up an unarmed police force in the early part of 1922. We envisaged the establishment of a new unarmed police force to operate in nationalist areas; an unarmed RUC in unionist areas; and a new force based on the other two to be armed and deployed to deal with terrorist crime. During the interim period while the new forces were being recruited and trained, Irish forces would be temporarily deployed in nationalist areas.

These measures would be accompanied by the establishment, it was hoped, of a Northern Ireland power-sharing Executive, which, in conjunction with the Assembly, would operate the full range of devolved powers, subject to a series of checks and balances. There would be an all-Ireland court and a North-South commission on the harmonisation of the criminal law; a bill of rights—possibly in the form of the direct application of the European Convention of Human Rights; and a parliamentary tier involving members of the Dáil and House of Commons and possibly also of the Northern Ireland Assembly.

All this would be accompanied by a change in articles 2 and 3, perhaps reaffirming the legitimate aspiration of a majority of the people of Ireland to Irish unity to be achieved peacefully and by agreement of the people of the North and of the people of the South, and also acknowledging the rights and equal validity of the two main traditions on the island. Finally it would be important to involve the main constitutional parties in Northern Ireland in a conference, if this were possible.

These proposals were discussed at length by the Government, and authority was given to us to proceed on this basis. Some Ministers were less enthusiastic than others, being concerned about the proposed temporary involvement of our security forces in Northern Ireland for a transitional period, or about the feasibility of winning a constitutional referendum, or about the possible character of unionist reaction to an agreement along these lines. But by this stage the negotiation had developed its own momentum, and no-one was prepared to say that it should not proceed.

Three days later I met Margaret Thatcher in Downing Street. We had European Community affairs to talk about; I was in the middle of my Presidency of the European Council. At the end of lunch, however, we turned to Northern Ireland. I started the discussion with some remarks about our relationship with the non-alienated section of the nationalist community, which, I said, we now had a fair chance of bringing with us. Turning to the talks that had taken place since March, I remarked on the manner in which these discussions reflected a common desire to find solutions to common problems rather than to 'negotiate' with each other. I went on to say that despite the fact that if we failed to carry a referendum our Government could not survive, we regarded this matter as taking precedence over all other considerations and were therefore prepared to take this risk.

After this introduction by me she started to present her view of the situation. We were dealing with fear, suspicion, and folklore: not a problem that would be resolved simply by reason and common sense. The problem was to find a way through the difficulties in a manner and at a rate that would not cause it to blow up in our faces. She knew full well that any suggestion of giving the Republic a right to be consulted in relation to Northern Ireland could cause violence. Joint authority was out: the unionist reaction to this would be that they were being sold down the river. 'You know the language that they use.' She recognised that the problem was how I could win a referendum in those circumstances. She added that there was no question of disarming the RUC or UDR.

I responded that there were two distinct but linked problems: in what circumstances could I win a referendum, and secondly, how could we change the security situation in Northern Ireland so as to reverse the problem of alienation?

There followed a rather confused discussion of cross-border security problems, including a reference to one murder near the border in respect of which a wanted person had in fact been extradited. I tried to bring the discussion back to the problem of what sort of security system would work effectively in Northern Ireland. I described how if the RUC came to investigate a crime in the Divis Flats in Belfast they had to be guarded by soldiers taking up a defensive position against a possible armed attack. This was not normal policing. How could we get over this?

Why, she asked, did I think 'it' (I think she meant a new policing system) would end alienation? I responded that the alienation problem was now spreading to hitherto moderate and stable sections of the community, such as doctors and lawyers, who were coming to feel that there was no possibility of justice in Northern Ireland. The situation had been aggravated by recent *obiter dicta* of High Court judges, one of whom had congratulated on his 'aim' an RUC man who had killed two unarmed IRA men in a car by emptying two magazines of his machine-gun in succession into the vehicle, and another of whom had referred to men shot by the RUC as having been 'sent to the Supreme Court of

Justice.' We had to change the police and judicial systems in Northern Ireland if we were to deal with this spreading alienation problem. The Armstrong-Nally talks must continue to seek a solution.

Yes, she replied, the talks must go on—though some would argue, by analogy with a Methodist saying, that this was 'the first step to Rome. I must not alarm my people.'

When the time came both our governments, I said, would have to decide whether they could go forward, but we should both put the people of Northern Ireland first; for fifteen years they had gone through hell. We had a duty to them. *Our* governments would survive one way or another.

We agreed on 19 November for our summit meeting, the venue being left open, with the possibility of a further meeting in April. Before concluding I raised two questions. The first was the proposed statement of principles; it would be desirable, I said, to issue that before our November meeting. 'Let's consider that,' she responded. Second, would we be able to bring in the parties in Northern Ireland rather than having an exclusively intergovernmental agreement? 'We are not at that point yet,' she replied. As we broke up she said, 'We are walking on eggs.'

Driving back to the embassy I remarked to Dermot Nally that her briefing on security had been confused, but she had not rejected at this stage either the statement of principles or the conference idea.

A couple of days later Douglas Hurd replaced Jim Prior as Secretary of State for Northern Ireland. He was a somewhat unknown quantity to us, but his Foreign Office experience would, it seemed to me, probably be helpful, and the high regard in which he was held both by his colleagues in government and by senior officials was encouraging.

At the next negotiating session on 19 September the Irish side put forward our ideas on a package of measures designed to reverse the alienation of the minority in Northern Ireland and to enable us to win a referendum on articles 2 and 3 of the Constitution. The package we proposed involved recognition of and guarantees for the unionist and nationalist identities in Northern Ireland and for their satisfactory, secure and durable expression. It also provided for the establishment of an Anglo-Irish Ministerial Commission for Northern Ireland, the Irish Minister in which would have offices in Belfast and would be a full-time Minister of cabinet rank. Defence, foreign policy and finance would be 'excepted matters' reserved to Britain but on which the Irish Government would have a right of consultation. The nomination of a power-sharing Executive, the courts, and issues of identity, such as flags and emblems and language issues, broadcasting, sport, and telecommunications, would be reserved to the British government, subject to consultation within the commission on these matters unless they were devolved to a power-sharing Executive by agreement between the two governments. Other powers would be devolved to the Assembly and Executive from the outset, subject to checks and balances, and there should be a joint court in which the judges would be nominated by the commission.

Appeals from this court would be to a higher court within the jurisdiction in which a case was heard. And there should also be a North-South law commission to harmonise the criminal law, as well as an Anglo-Irish parliamentary tier.

On security we proposed the establishment of a separate police force based in the nationalist community that would police areas of nationalist concentration. Alternatively there could be, as in countries like Belgium, a multiplicity of local police forces. These forces should be unarmed, but a separate force should be armed to deal with the terrorist threat. A Joint Security Commission should control these forces. We also urged the desirability of a statement of principles, and said that we saw merit in a conference including the constitutional parties in Northern Ireland to settle these issues, and we asked if the British government would see a role in such a conference for the opposition parties in our two states.

Apart from our security proposals these ideas did not at that point appear to pose any insuperable problems for the British side in their preliminary 'off-the-cuff' reactions. The question of whether the Irish member of the Anglo-Irish Ministerial Commission for Northern Ireland would be a Minister or a senior civil servant was seen as a matter primarily for us to decide. On the proposed court to deal with terrorist crimes, the British side felt this might be opposed by the Northern Ireland judiciary, but it was helpful to know that this was something to which we attached importance. The British side saw difficulties with our security proposals, but it was felt that it might be possible to think of a joint force with the Gardaí taking the lead in the Republic and the RUC in Northern Ireland, or that in an RUC that Catholics joined in significant numbers these new members might patrol in Catholic areas. Another idea floated in this 'brainstorming' session was that of quasi-separate county forces with their own recruitment arrangements under an RUC umbrella.

While, of course, nothing said on the British side by way of reaction to our proposals involved any commitment on their part, we were encouraged by what seemed a productive and useful exchange of views, from which at least the skeleton shape of a possible package seemed to be in process of emerging. The main outcome of this meeting, however, was agreement on a list of topics on which papers were to be prepared for a two-day meeting in October.

Ten days later we heard that Margaret Thatcher's reaction to the account she was given of this meeting had been anxious rather than critical: 'Aren't you going a bit fast?' We also heard that despite the problems we had had with Jim Prior during the months before his departure from the government his parting advice to Margaret Thatcher had been that the approach being adopted through the Armstrong-Nally discussions was essential. There was confirmation that Geoffrey Howe was keenly interested, concerned to be helpful, and pleased with the progress being made; he hoped to talk to Peter Barry about these developments during the forthcoming EC meeting with the Central American countries in Costa Rica (where the British embassy was being supplied with Barry's tea for the occasion!).

However, at this stage problems began to arise with the Northern Ireland Office, which had until now not been involved in the negotiations, although the Permanent Secretary and later four of its officials had for some time past been 'in the know'. The NIO were, we knew, totally opposed to the proposed initiative, which they had earlier on felt to be 'mad'. It was in part this negative attitude that had encouraged the British side to decide that papers should now be exchanged; this, it was suggested, would force the NIO to join in devising ways of implementing the approach to the problem that had now emerged instead of continuing to set out thousands of reasons why this approach was, or should be, unthinkable. It was at this point also that the official in charge of the Lord Chancellor's Office—another area of possible resistance—was brought into the circle.

On our side the negotiating team was also widened at this point to bring in the Secretary of the Department of Justice, Andy Ward, and Declan Quigley from the Attorney General's office. We had already extended the Ministerial group in charge of the negotiation to bring in the Minister for Justice, Michael Noonan, the Minister for Defence, Pat Cooney, and the Attorney General, Peter Sutherland. Pat Cooney was unenthusiastic about the whole venture, however, and after a time dropped out of this informal committee.

On 10 October the Government considered and endorsed a memorandum approving the position we had taken up in the talks three weeks earlier. But two days later the Brighton bombing took place. We were appalled at this atrocity, which narrowly missed killing the Prime Minister and many of her Cabinet and inflicted death or serious injury on a number of people. I immediately sent a message to Margaret Thatcher expressing the horror this outrage evoked amongst the Irish people. And as I began to recover from the initial shock of the news I could not but wonder what effect it would have on the negotiation.

The negotiating meeting planned for three days later was not postponed, although some of the documents promised by the British side were not available for it. At the outset Dermot Nally handed to Robert Armstrong a further personal note I had written to Margaret Thatcher, in which I indicated that if she preferred our next meeting to be in Britain I would not press her to come to Ireland in accordance with the normal process of alternation. I guessed that after the bombing she might prefer to meet me on her own territory.

At this meeting our side spelt out in more detail some of the ideas that had been presented four weeks earlier. Thus it was proposed that the Northern Ireland Assembly would legislate on the basis of a weighted majority and that the Executive would be made unboycottable by providing that at least initially the Secretary of State would be Chief Executive, with the power to nominate Ministers from the Assembly or, if it proved impossible to secure a balanced Executive in this way, from outside the Assembly.

The discussion revealed, however, that the British side now viewed the proposed Joint Security Commission as an advisory rather than executive body. To give it executive functions would involve an element of joint authority that they could not accept, they said. So far as the Ministerial Commission was concerned the British side saw it as a forum within which the Secretary of State would be required to formally consult the Irish representative on a range of matters. The Irish side expressed its scepticism about the adequacy of such an arrangement. What we had sought was a provision whereby both governments would accept a formal obligation to seek agreement on a range of specified issues and a formal acceptance that it must be made to work successfully in order to ensure the maintenance of stability in Northern Ireland.

When the issue of policing within Northern Ireland was discussed the reaction to our ideas was very negative. We were now told that county police forces would be counter to good organisation, and that a second police force for nationalist areas was contrary to general practice and would be 'unsaleable'. Moreover, the value of a separate force to deal with terrorism was contested on the grounds that terrorism and crime were mixed up together in Northern Ireland. The idea of three-man courts was contested on the grounds that this would require more extra judges than could readily be found from within the relatively small Northern Ireland Bar. This was rejected by the Irish side, which pointed out that the members of the court would not need to be senior judges; in the Republic the Special Criminal Court included Circuit Court judges and district justices. In the end, however, the British side agreed that the objections to three-man courts were not insuperable, with the rider that while the Lord Chancellor's department had been consulted, Lord Hailsham himself had not. Geoffrey Howe was, however, said to agree in principle with the concept while believing that the matter needed to be looked at with care.

At the end of the meeting the British side offered to prepare a paper showing the points of agreement and disagreement. An Irish enquiry whether there should be a political contribution to this process from the proposed meeting between Douglas Hurd and Peter Barry was greeted with a very firm negative answer from the British side—in part at least, we presumed, because Douglas Hurd was still finding his feet in his new post and would not yet have acquired a feel for all the complexities of the issues under discussion, but perhaps also because of fear of a negative response from the NIO at Ministerial as well as official level.

Concern was expressed on our side at what seemed to be an impasse in relation to the key area of policing. A suggestion was accordingly made by us that changes might be made in policing that would be declared to be for the short term only, in order to give both sides a breathing space. A dual policing system with separate provisions for unionist and nationalist areas could be announced as being for five or ten years only. The British side agreed to look at this.

I have to say I was depressed by the account I received of this meeting. The involvement of the NIO for the first time seemed to be having a very negative effect on the talks. The emerging scene did not seem one that would enable us to attempt with any confidence an amendment of articles 2 and 3. However, it had been pointed out by the British side that Margaret Thatcher was personally committed to trying to do something, and if she decided at the summit meeting that what was being discussed was worth going for, some of the obstacles I now saw looming up could be overcome. Nevertheless when John Hume was informed of these discussions he shared both my concern that the package as it was emerging might not 'carry' an amendment of articles 2 and 3 and my belief that a more radical change in policing than the British seemed prepared to contemplate was required.

My fears that the negotiation was rapidly going backwards were confirmed on 25 October by three simultaneous discussions: between Douglas Hurd, on his first visit as Northern Ireland Secretary to Dublin, and Peter Barry; between the NIO Permanent Secretary, Robert Andrew, who accompanied Douglas Hurd, and our officials; and, in London, between John Hume and Nick Scott, Minister of State at the NIO.

In a general discussion with Douglas Hurd, Robert Andrew and other NIO officials Peter Barry raised a series of issues that had been taken up with us by the nationalist community. Douglas Hurd was visibly uncomfortable with this part of the discussion, in the course of which he tended to refer the points raised to his officials. He ruled out any restructuring of the RUC, and subsequently over dinner with Peter Barry dismissed a power-sharing Executive as impossible, expressed his opposition to most of the proposals under discussion in the Armstrong-Nally talks, and remarked that amending articles 2 and 3 might be too difficult for us. Like Jim Prior some months earlier he wanted to confine any initiative to security co-operation, with perhaps some consultative role for us in relation to security in Northern Ireland. Peter Barry made it clear that he would not recommend such a limited approach to the Government and warned of the consequences for the survival of the SDLP and thus for stability throughout Ireland of a failure to find agreement at the forthcoming summit meeting.

The source of this negativism had become abundantly clear, as Robert Andrew had talked to our officials while the Ministers were closeted together. He was openly critical and clearly resentful of the talks that had taken place without NIO participation since March, describing them as 'academic'. He did not, however, suggest that we should abandon the idea of amending articles 2 and 3; that shaft was left to his political master.

This NIO attitude did not surprise us. After the December 1980 summit meeting a number of open-minded officials there had been replaced by people with a background exclusively in the security area. Meanwhile Nick Scott was also telling John Hume in London that several Cabinet Ministers were coming to the view that it would be difficult and perhaps dangerous for us to attempt to amend articles 2 and 3. A view was emerging that we should not be asked to attempt this; the British would content themselves with the Sunningdale formula. At the same time we heard that there were delays in the preparation of the British papers that had been promised in early October. 'There are serious problems here in London,' we were told.

Within days, however, we were told authoritatively that the Hurd-Andrew stance was unilateral and did not have the authority of either the Prime Minister or the Cabinet. Margaret Thatcher, Geoffrey Howe and Douglas Hurd had not in fact met for some weeks past to discuss the negotiation. They would, however, be meeting after the Cabinet meeting on 1 November to discuss two options: discontinuation of the exchanges, or continuation of them on the basis of the Prime Minister's basic equation involving the amendment of articles 2 and 3 in return for a package providing for our involvement in a new system of government in Northern Ireland. At that meeting they would be told that if we were to try to amend articles 2 and 3 we could not contemplate any watering down of what we were seeking. The Prime Minister was unlikely to adopt Douglas Hurd's line, and would in any event await our tete-à-tete at the summit meeting before deciding what course to pursue.

We were also told that the British side would bring with them to Dublin on 2 November a paper setting out the positions of the two sides as they understood them. This would be shown to us, but not given to us at that stage. They would also bring a draft statement of agreed objectives for possible inclusion in the communiqué. All this was more reassuring; but I felt that the battle going on within the British camp would not make our task easier.

These developments were reported to the Government at the end of the month. On 2 and 3 November the negotiators met again in Dublin to discuss the British 'statement of the position', which set out the areas of agreement between the two governments and their divergent positions on other issues. It had been 'cleared by Ministers', we were told. It was a disappointing document from our point of view. The British officials justified this step backwards as necessary to 'keep the show on the road' and to ensure that the whole process was not discontinued. So as not to frighten off Margaret Thatcher our position had been understated to her, and the parts of this Ministerial document purporting to set out our position in relation to areas of disagreement had to be extensively re-drafted at this two-day meeting in order to reflect our views adequately.

Our side was, however, particularly disturbed that a new and as we saw it negative element had now crept into British thinking: that agreement to the proposed Irish role in Northern Ireland must depend upon the introduction of an 'acceptable' system of devolved government in Northern Ireland. Acceptable to whom? Apparently to the Unionists, which would probably mean a return to majority rule. No attempt was made to disguise the fact that this was a totally new element, which, however, the British side now saw as part of the 'central concept' of the proposed agreement. It was Douglas Hurd who had insisted on this, we were told.

While this meeting had been taking place I had been in India for the funeral of the Prime Minister, Indira Gandhi, who had been assassinated by some of her Sikh guards. Before flying out via Amsterdam I discussed with my advisers the possible merits of seeking a lift back from New Delhi in the British plane on which Margaret Thatcher would be returning with Princess Anne and other members of the British party. Although this could provide an additional opportunity for a discussion with her, in the course of which I might convey our concern at the direction the Anglo-Irish talks were taking, on balance we decided against it. Nevertheless it seemed worth while to try to have a word with her in New Delhi.

When I arrived I found the city in turmoil. The area in which our embassy was situated was quiet enough and I could get from there to the funeral by a roundabout route, but there were riots in many other districts. The last part of the journey from the embassy to the funeral pyre was by bus from a building in a large square where we all met. The funeral itself was a prolonged affair, of which I had a good view, sitting in the second row, just behind Princess Anne and Margaret Thatcher. When it ended everyone rushed for the buses, led by Princess Anne, Margaret Thatcher, and the British High Commissioner, who accompanied them. Though I moved smartly, the bus they had climbed into was full by the time I reached it, but I managed to get into the second bus after an English voice had overruled the Indian in charge of the bus door: 'There's always room for you, Garret!' The British opposition leaders were on this bus.

We spilled out onto a vast empty square with no security people in sight. Passing a disconcerted President Zia of Pakistan, who had not expected to find himself so publicly vulnerable in a relatively hostile country, I hurried after Margaret Thatcher, only to see her engulfed in a sea of Arab burnouses. When she escaped from this and re-joined Princess Anne and the High Commissioner I asked her if we might meet later that evening. She said she would let me know within the hour. Forty-five minutes later the phone rang in the embassy and a British voice said, 'The plane leaves at 10.45 in the morning. Could you be at the airport at 10?' Taken aback by this, and momentarily wondering if someone at home had got the wrong end of the stick and had asked for a lift for me after all, I said 'Yes.' I never discovered why I received this invitation; no-one at home had sought it. Perhaps someone at the High Commission had misunderstood Margaret Thatcher's account of my request in the square.

I now found myself at a disadvantage, for I did not know what had happened at the Dublin negotiating meeting. However, on the plane the British gave me a copy of the telegram Margaret Thatcher had received about this meeting, which enclosed the text that had emerged from the discussions. The covering note to her from Robert Armstrong said, 'We are sending these texts for background information. We respectfully suggest that detailed discussion of the texts between the two Governments should wait until the Prime Minister and the Taoiseach have each been able to discuss matters further with their own colleagues.' Given the complexity of the situation revealed by the British text, as modified in Dublin, I was happy to agree with this.

Accordingly dinner on the flight with Margaret and Denis Thatcher and her private secretaries was largely a social occasion. However, when Enoch Powell's name came up I remarked somewhat sourly that I did not think much of the article he had recently published in the *Times* accusing me and my Government of complicity in an IRA plot to murder her. 'Did he really say that?' she asked one of her officials. 'Well, yes, Prime Minister, that was the gist of the article,' he answered. I expected some acknowledgement of the horrendous character of this allegation; but her mind was elsewhere. 'Such an intelligent man!' she remarked. I could think of no suitable response to this remarkable non sequitur.

On my return I learnt that the British side had taken up gratefully my private hint to Margaret Thatcher in the note I had sent her after the Brighton bombing that in the circumstances I would not press her to reciprocate my visit to her a year earlier. Accordingly we were to meet again at Chequers. There would be time for an extended tete-à-tete; we would start with a working dinner and continue until after lunch the following day.

Meanwhile we had decided that, rather than try to construct an Irish version of the British document that our side had amended during the meeting of 2 and 3 November, we would produce our own version of our position in a speaking note to be presented before the meeting. The first point in this note concerned the new British proposal that the implementation of the arrangements for our involvement in Northern Ireland should be conditional on the introduction of devolved government. We said bluntly that for us to attempt to amend articles 2 and 3 subject to this condition, which many in the Republic would see as a very uncertain prospect at best, would be madness, and contrary to British interests as well as Irish.

This difficulty was compounded by what seemed to us to be a British view that an Executive with political representatives from both sides of the community divide was unlikely to emerge, but that an Executive without such support would nevertheless be acceptable in Northern Ireland. A referendum on articles 2 and 3 in the face of what appeared like a British proposal to reactivate majority rule in Northern Ireland—if we had understood them correctly—would clearly be impossible. We went on to state our view that so difficult was the relationship between the UDR and the nationalist population that no prospect existed of the police winning the confidence of the minority so long as the UDR played a role in the security system. This whole question should be discussed by experts.

This speaking note was presented in London on 11 November. The British side was told that our Ministers were alarmed and resentful at the new British position on devolution, and also at an interview Douglas Hurd had given to the *Sunday Telegraph* purporting to represent our position in a manner that was not in accordance with the facts and was also contrary to the understanding between us on the confidentiality of our discussions.

It was accepted that we had reasonable grounds for complaint, but the tone of our speaking note was said to be unhelpful, and in particular the reference to the UDR. In the course of subsequent discussion it emerged clearly that, as we had indeed suspected, the idea of making the achievement of devolution a precondition of our Government's involvement in Northern Ireland had emanated from the NIO.

The British side then raised the question of a possible less ambitious initiative if either government decided that a referendum on articles 2 and 3 would be too difficult and dangerous. This was a worrying development, which seemed to confirm our feeling that the British were backing away from a major package.

In the following days we had signals from the official level that the atmosphere was not very propitious; and on the evening of 14 November we heard that the Prime Minister had rejected an extended version of the draft communiqué that we had proposed. We were also told that our speaking note of three days earlier had not gone down well with her: we were seen by the British to have hardened our position, just as we for our part had felt the British side had done at the start of the month.

On Sunday 18 November we arrived at Chequers. That evening I saw Margaret Thatcher privately, without advisers or note-takers. I told her that I believed an agreement that would enable me to achieve an amendment of articles 2 and 3 would be of immense value. These articles were seen by the unionist population of Northern Ireland as a threat to their position, and, however unjustified this belief might be, in their present form they represented major obstacles in the way of a better North-South relationship and of reconciliation between the two communities in Northern Ireland. There was a chance now to make a historic breakthrough by tackling at one blow both the growing alienation of the Northern minority and the siege mentality of the unionists. She and I had a unique opportunity that had not previously existed and might not readily recur. We should take our courage in our hands and together make this breakthrough. I was prepared to do my part by calling on the people of the Republic to amend their Constitution if she could agree to changes in Northern Ireland that would end the alienation of the minority, especially from the security forces, and would enable that minority to identify with a system of government in Northern Ireland in which we would be playing a part. She listened carefully, quizzed me on various aspects of what I was proposing, and promised to reflect overnight on all I had said.

Next morning, however, just before the meeting started we were given a British speaking note that responded to our message of 11 November. The tone was stiff. Anything suggestive of joint authority was rejected. What the British were prepared to agree to in return for our amendment of articles 2 and 3 was a right for the Irish Government 'to contribute, on a systematic and institutionalised basis, to the consideration by the United Kingdom Government of a range of policy matters, including security, as a means of strengthening the confidence of the minority community in the institutions of government.'

On devolution, however, there was a very helpful clarification of the British proposal put to us on 3 November. What had been agreed in Dublin at the beginning of the month, this note said, was that a system of devolved government was 'integral' to any new arrangements, and that such devolution would need to command the acceptance of both majority and minority communities. Such devolved government was not a necessary condition for the implementation of *any* (their emphasis) of the other proposals under discussion. If, however, it were not achieved then the range of matters for institutionalised consultation 'would need careful definition', because the acquiescence of the majority in that arrangement would be more difficult in the absence of clear progress towards devolved government.

The note went on to say, however, that if we were allowed to establish a resident official representative in the North with a formal right of consultation, the majority's refusal to participate in devolved government based on power-sharing would be likely to be further entrenched, and it was in that context that the British government would wish to examine alternative bases for devolution, which, by providing effective safeguards for the minority, might be acceptable to them.

This was the NIO line: either power-sharing or an Irish Government role in Northern Ireland, but not both.

The speaking note concluded by saying that the British side had serious reservations about a dual structure for security arrangements of which one part would be concerned only with Northern Ireland; they felt reciprocity should form an essential feature of the security arrangements. And while they noted our views on the security forces, they emphasised that any changes in the structure of the RUC or UDR would be strongly opposed by the majority community.

This was a thoroughly discouraging start to the morning's discussion, but we had little time to reflect on it before my second tete-à-tete with Margaret Thatcher. This time it took place in the presence of our two cabinet secretaries and of Seán Donlon and Charles Powell as British note-taker. (Dermot Nally, as was customary, took a note of the discussion for me.)

Was there really a chance to amend our Constitution? she asked at the outset, following up our discussion of the previous night. Might we not fail because of distortions and false accusations? Perhaps we should not be running that particular risk. And what did the SDLP want that could be given without outraging the unionists? I replied that as a result of the violence of the previous fifteen years nationalist expectations North and South had been reduced; most people now accepted that, because of this, unity was not now likely in the short run. The nationalist community in the North had suffered from harassment by Protestant paramilitaries, by the IRA, and, especially in the case of young people, by the security forces. The minority simply wanted to live in their own country in peace. Just as she was proud of being English, they took pride in their Irish identity and felt themselves cut off by an arbitrary act from the rest of the nationalist majority in the island. They could not express their identity, not being allowed even to fly the flag of their own nation in their own country. To them the security forces were those of another community: UDR guns were used to bully them. They saw hard evidence of bias in the system of justice, in the operation of the security system, and in policing. A way must be found to enable them to identify with the system of government.

Margaret Thatcher, citing the Macedonians, Croats, Serbs and Sudeten Germans as examples of minorities that were not given particular prerogatives as of right, responded that she did not understand why nationalists in Northern Ireland sought such treatment. Did the Protestants in the Republic seek representation in government as of right—if there were enough of them left? Might a possible answer to the problem not be a re-drawing of boundaries? That would be a fatal mistake, I replied. And I repeated that expectations had been lowered, and this made it possible to contemplate action short of reunification that would end alienation.

If special arrangements were made for the nationalist minority in the North, she asked, would the Sikhs of Southall demand to be allowed to fly their own flag? Not wanting to be sidetracked, I refrained from saying that as far as I knew there was no law in Britain, as there was in Northern Ireland, preventing them from doing so. I pointed out instead that analogies with minority situations in Britain or continental Europe were false: where in those countries could you find one-sixth of the population with relatives or close friends in prison? We were, moreover, talking about a situation where there had been a death toll equivalent to 100,000 people in Great Britain.

Who, she asked, was really being harassed in the North? Some 2,500 people had lost their lives there in the security forces. The vast majority of deaths, I countered, were *not* in the security forces but were civilians, the greatest number of them amongst the nationalist minority. That minority had the feeling that the security forces who stopped and searched them were alien to them; that was why we were now discussing a Joint Security Commission that would include an Irish Minister. At this the discussion became somewhat less heated. We must seek the best solution, she said. I took the opportunity to raise the concept of areas with overwhelming nationalist or unionist populations being policed by forces drawn from the dominant community in that area. Many areas were not policed at present; when I had gone to west Belfast as Minister for Foreign Affairs the RUC looking after me had as a matter of course remained behind in the centre of the city. She and I should not accept a situation in which whole areas were without normal policing. There must be a reorganisation of the RUC that would enable these areas to have such policing. This could not be achieved, as she suggested, by recruiting more Catholics to the RUC as at present constituted. Northern Ireland, like Britain, should have local police forces. Not in a capital city, she said. Brussels had forty-six police forces, I replied; we must get away from what Sir Robert Peel had thought or done in Ireland. Robert Armstrong intervened to comment helpfully that England and Wales had forty-three separate police forces.

The situation in Northern Ireland was not a normal one to be tackled in a normal way, I continued. Within Belfast 100,000 people—almost one-fifth of the population—had been forced out of their homes in the previous fifteen years: 85,000 Catholics and 15,000 Protestants. The enclaves created by this ghettoisation could not be dealt with by 'normal policing'. At present many of the nationalist areas were simply being left to the IRA with their protection rackets and knee-cappings; such patrols as existed were army, not police, patrols. That was why we supported a Joint Security Commission in which we could play a role to develop policing that would work.

The Prime Minister replied that she agreed in principle with a form of Joint Security Commission 'to advise Douglas,' and she would also like to see a commission to harmonise the criminal law, North and South. We went on to discuss the proposed joint commission. I said I envisaged it having responsibility for appointments, guidelines, and a complaints mechanism. It could not be 'sold' if it were to be merely consultative, and it would have to be part of a general political framework; on its own it would be shot down, as we would be seen as merely 'helping you along.'

Margaret Thatcher then asked why the SDLP had not entered the Assembly. Because the Unionists were insistent that they would not share power, I replied, and the party could not contemplate accepting the permanent humiliation of a situation where neither they nor their children nor their children's children could ever hope to participate in the government of where they lived. She replied that there was no-one on the Unionist side who would accept power-sharing. I referred to the concept of an unboycottable power-sharing Executive headed by the Secretary of State with members drawn if necessary from outside the Assembly, which Jim Prior had floated but had not proceeded with in early 1982. In Britain the executive was drawn from the Houses of Parliament, she responded.

Was she, I asked, abandoning the principle that a devolved Executive had to be acceptable to both communities? No, she replied, but all their attempts to get such an Executive had failed; was the animosity so fundamental that we could never get an acceptable Executive, or had they just not got the right formula? Anyway, we would never get it unless security was improved, but the Republic's role in that could only be advisory.

Again I stressed the need for an involvement of our Government at both the security and political level if we were to end the alienation of the minority. Referring back, I think, to the dual policing concept, she replied that unionists would see this as a re-partition; however, she added, she had not ruled out re-partition. Vigorously rejecting re-partition, I said we must try to create a society in which the present division would eventually disappear.

On the question of our Government's role in the political structure of Northern Ireland I said that what had been under discussion had been a system under which the British and Irish Ministers would be committed to seeking agreement on issues as they arose. One suggestion had been that if agreement were not forthcoming, an outstanding issue could go on appeal to the two prime ministers. Her reaction made it evident that she did not relish this idea.

I concluded this part of the discussion by saying that it would be impossible to amend articles 2 and 3 on the basis of a right on our part merely to be consulted. She replied that if consultation were agreed it would be genuine, but ultimately the judgement of the Secretary of State could not be fettered; she was answerable to Parliament, which was answerable for Northern Ireland. I could not resist pointing out that for fifty years Parliament had not regarded itself as answerable for Northern Ireland and had refused to allow questions about that area to be put to it; that was part of the reason for the present trouble.

After this somewhat disorganised and generally discouraging discussion, which did not suggest that my plea of the previous evening had made any impact, we adjourned, and after brief meetings with our respective delegations we met our Ministerial colleagues at 12.20.

Margaret Thatcher then asked me to open the discussion, saying I looked depressed. I said that, frankly, I was very worried. The political problem was being sidelined by an exclusively security-oriented approach. Unless a political solution was found that would enable the minority to identify with the system of government in Northern Ireland it would be impossible to solve the security problem. We were clearly having difficulty in getting our British colleagues to accept this. We were not challenging British sovereignty or seeking to unsettle the unionists, but the British side should face the fact that there had to be a political context for anything done on the security side. Yes, I was depressed.

She responded by saying there were three issues: the security issue, which they proposed addressing through a security commission with an advisory role in which the Dublin representative would have a high profile; the need for a political framework—how to get the parties in Northern Ireland to agree on one; and the judicial side, which could probably be agreed. It was clear to me from what she said that on the political framework there seemed to be a preconcerted limitation of this concept to the problem of securing agreement on devolved government as distinct from a political role for our Government.

Douglas Hurd came in to say that the proposed security commission would cover issues such as prisons and complaints as well as policing; it was accepted that we would have a right of advocacy there, without being asked to 'pay the price of a referendum'. That might be something that Northern Ireland political leaders could eventually be brought to accept.

Geoffrey Howe and Margaret Thatcher joined in to persuade us of the merits of such a security commission; but the discussion soon reverted to the issue of the exclusion of the minority from power in the North. Margaret Thatcher pointed out that the SDLP exercised power in Londonderry. I responded that nationalist politicians had a majority in five district councils, and these were fairly administered; but of the eighteen councils controlled by unionists, no fewer than eight had been found guilty by legal or administrative tribunals of discrimination, and another three had come under notice for such practices.

We returned once more to the security commission proposal—an *advisory* commission, Margaret Thatcher emphasised. I responded again that we needed more than an advisory role, for example in relation to appointments and complaints. 'We can't have that, Garret. That's joint authority. That's out,' she riposted.

I decided to test again the apparent British abandonment of the concept of an amendment to articles 2 and 3 in return for a substantial package. 'If the people can't see a package capable of providing a durable solution—' I began; before I could finish my sentence Douglas Hurd intervened to say that their proposal of an advisory role for a security commission stood on its own merits: it could be implemented without our having to change our Constitution. And Margaret Thatcher added that they had a strong reason for doing something together with us anyway.

I changed tack slightly. 'You seem to envisage arrangements for involving the Irish Government in the affairs of Northern Ireland so as to give it an opportunity to—' 'Involving?' she interrupted. 'I never used that word or authorised anyone to use it on my behalf. Robert, have you been using that word? I remember that at a previous meeting certain people'—she pointed at Dermot Nally—'slipped in words in a communiqué which subsequently got me into great difficulties: the communiqué issued after my meeting with Mr Haughey.' I calmed her down by explaining that the word 'involved' was ours; it had not been used on the British side. And I followed up by asking her what about mixed courts? That seemed to be okay, she replied, although they couldn't agree on it until they had looked into all the details.

When Peter Barry remarked that our representative on a security commission would not necessarily be the Minister for Justice, I came in to say that leaving on one side the security commission there was the question of enabling an Irish Minister to make a substantive contribution to the formulation of policy. This would be a powerful encouragement to unionists to join with nationalists in a devolved government, because such a government would take Irish Ministers *out* of Northern Ireland affairs. Douglas Hurd commented that anything wider than a security commission involving us would require something substantial from us, and while our proposal for a referendum on articles 2 and 3 was obviously a major and courageous step, he was not sure the majority in Northern Ireland would see it as all that big a step.

Peter Barry pointed out that for years we had been told that these articles of our Constitution were a serious stumbling-block; now we were being told their removal would not amount to much. Dick Spring intervened to ask where we were now. What were we going to do? Was there any reason to believe that in ten years' time six other well-meaning politicians would not be sitting in this room going over exactly the same ground again?

Margaret Thatcher responded by asking me once more whether it would not be worth going ahead with the security commission without a constitutional referendum. When Peter Barry pointed out the consequences if we returned to defend a communiqué that referred only to security matters, she said, 'Then it looks as if we won't have any communiqué.' But she added that it had been a good meeting, as for the first time we had come to grips with the problem and had talked about the real issues. We needed to keep meeting, and maybe we should put something in the communiqué (which she had just abolished!) about meeting again in the spring.

That, I replied, would be disastrously dampening. We needed to meet again very early in the new year—not in the spring. She suggested a second meeting to discuss matters other than the political framework. I said I could find a reason to come to London and have a less publicised meeting.

There followed a brief discussion about what might be put in the communiqué. Peter Barry suggested that we should say that ideas had been advanced on both sides, that there was a wide gap between us, and that we were asking our officials to explore these matters further. Geoffrey Howe proposed that it say that both of us recognised the desirability of finding a way of enabling us to make a serious input into security matters. Margaret Thatcher intervened at once to say they should be careful: they did not want to cause problems for me back home. 'We like you.'

Nevertheless both Douglas Hurd and she pressed me once again to agree to the advisory security commission. My reaction was such that she remarked, as she had done at the beginning of the meeting, 'Garret, you look depressed. Is it that bad? I am not depressed. We're now tackling the problem in detail for the first time.' She went on to say that we should concentrate on the first two items—the security and political issues—and leave the judicial side for the moment. In my view that made things even worse. Accordingly, I replied that the courts were a fundamental part of the package.

Once again she remarked that this was the best discussion we had ever had. Without enthusiasm, I agreed. But I returned one last time to the constitutional amendment issue, telling her not to underestimate the effect of such an amendment. It could release forces in unionism in a way that the earlier amendment on the special position of the Catholic Church had not done. At the same time we for our part could solidify the moderate ground in our state in a way that could not be easily undone by a subsequent Government. I did not want to lightly abandon the possibility of doing something significant.

'I understand,' she replied, adding that they would look carefully at everything we had said and would see what they could do. 'It may be that something involving articles 2 and 3 is worth going for.' Douglas Hurd then asked if, in view of the press stories about articles 2 and 3, he could give an indication of my view to the Unionists and see how they reacted. But what, asked Margaret Thatcher, was she to say to the press if they asked whether we had discussed it?

I replied that what I had said when pressed on this point was that we had asked the British government not to exclude anything in these talks; in logic, therefore, we could not exclude anything. 'Then I could say that you are not excluding anything?' the Prime Minister asked quickly. 'Yes,' I replied, 'but only if at the same time you say that *you* are not excluding anything.' 'I'd better stick to what you say,' was her answer.

Peter Barry asked if the Armstrong-Nally talks were to go ahead. 'Yes,' Margaret Thatcher and I said, emphatically and together. 'What about a conference?' asked Dick Spring. 'Don't call a conference,' she replied, 'because that would get you into the public arena, where it is impossible to get anything done.' With that the meeting broke up.

At lunch the American invasion of Grenada a month earlier came up in the conversation. Margaret Thatcher's anger at the American action was undisguised.

Before we left after lunch a communiqué had been agreed that, despite the combative tone of much of the discussion, was positive and left the way open for further progress. It described our exchanges on Northern Ireland as 'extensive', which was certainly true, and 'constructive', which was more arguable. We were agreed not only on the rejection of violence and of those who adopted or supported such methods but also on the need to recognise and respect the identities of both communities and to reflect these identities in the structures and processes of Northern Ireland in ways acceptable to both communities. Moreover, the process of government in Northern Ireland should be such as to provide the people of both communities with the confidence that their rights would be safeguarded.

We drove back to London with very mixed feelings. The negative character of much of the discussion was disturbing. It seemed clear to us that the British Ministers had decided to scale down the scope of any agreement to something that would provide no basis for an attempted amendment of articles 2 and 3, to which I had become strongly committed. Moreover, what they had in mind would have a totally inadequate impact upon the alienation of the nationalist minority in Northern Ireland.

It had been agreed that at five o'clock Margaret Thatcher would give a press conference on our meeting and that I would follow at six o'clock with a similar event at the Irish embassy. Given the unsatisfactory nature of the discussion there would not, I felt, be much for me to say; I would have to stick closely to the communiqué, emphasising the positive parts of it such as that on the need to respect the identities of both communities.

We had arranged that one of our diplomats would attend the British press conference and report to me before I went to meet the press. He had to return to brief me before the British press conference had ended, but what he had heard of it was, with one exception, very encouraging. Margaret Thatcher had described our meeting as 'the fullest, frankest and most realistic bilateral meeting I have ever had with the Taoiseach.' In reply to questions she had agreed that the two identities in Northern Ireland merited equal respect, if not equal recognition, and she had later added that the minority did not think their identity was fully reflected in the structures and processes of Northern Ireland. And she had volunteered off her own bat that the security issues we had discussed included prisons and judicial issues as well as policing. On our neutrality, she had said that we were proud of it and that it was a matter for us. Finally she had not merely shown sensitivity in these replies but had herself remarked on the need to give careful replies, because one slip of the tongue can make things more difficult.

The only reply that I could fault in all that had been said up to the time our observer left, when the press conference was four-fifths completed, was her comment that 'this word "alienation" crept into the vocabulary, which I do not think a very good one.' However, her objection seemed to be a semantic one to the word 'alienation', which I believe she thought was drawn from Marxist vocabulary.

Although this seemed to have been a heartening presentation, I said I would like to hear the BBC six o'clock news headlines before going to my press conference. Because of interference from a pirate radio station I was not able to catch much of what was said about our meeting in the opening minutes of the news, but I had the impression that near the end of the press conference she had rejected a confederation of two states and also joint authority. I went in to my press conference a few minutes late somewhat less happy than I had been before listening to the BBC—but quite unprepared for the hurricane that was about to hit me.

It very quickly became apparent that the helpful and positive comments the Prime Minister had made up to a late point in her press conference, as well as the positive elements in the communiqué itself, had been rendered totally irrelevant by the manner in which she seemed to have dealt with the three Forum models. As I had not heard her actual remarks I was completely thrown by the questions hurled at me. These were all the more difficult to handle because the journalists seem never to have grasped the full significance of the enabling clause in paragraph 5.10 of the Forum report, under which we had been negotiating since the formal rejection of the three models in the early stage of the negotiation in July; since that time the three models, as such, had ceased to be relevant to the negotiation, and I was disconcerted at their sudden reappearance as controversial issues at this stage. Moreover, as I did not know exactly what Margaret Thatcher had said or in what context her remarks were placed I could not deal with them as robustly as the press clearly expected me to do without risking a complete breakdown in a negotiation that might still, I believed, be steered towards a constructive outcome.

It was scarcely surprising in the circumstances that I found myself through-out completely at cross purposes with the journalists. To me they seemed to have missed the whole point of what was, admittedly, a fairly subtle negotiating stance on our part; to them I seemed to be ineffectively trying to obscure the reality of what they saw as a humiliating rebuff. From the point of view of those who watched this press conference on television, many of whom had also heard—as I had not—the dismissive manner in which Margaret Thatcher had shot down what were widely misconceived as our *only* negotiating proposals, my performance must have appeared extraordinarily ineffective.

It was a glum party of Ministers and officials that returned home from London. By the time we got back I had been able to assess the impact of what had happened. I heard for myself on a recording the tone of voice that had been used to dismiss each of the three models in turn: 'That is *out* . . . that is *out . . .* that is *out*,' followed by the assurance that I knew that this was the British government's view, 'cogently expressed'. I could see now why the press had homed in on this tiny fraction of Margaret Thatcher's otherwise constructive press conference, and why they had concluded that the negotiation had in effect collapsed. We were further depressed to hear that Douglas Hurd had revealed publicly some of the proposals put to us at the Chequers meeting, and had dismissed any possibility of an executive role for the Irish Government— a breach of confidence against which we lodged a strong protest.

When I came to consider how I should react to all this in my report to the Dáil and in other public comment I concluded that my best long-term course of action, regardless of the short-term humiliation involved in remaining silent, would be to ignore what had happened. Any critical comment in public by me would reduce, and possibly even eliminate, the helpful reaction I believed this debacle would evoke in Britain, a reaction that might eventually help to get the negotiations back again on a constructive path. Of course this left my supporters at a serious disadvantage in the face of the scathing attacks launched on me by a jubilant Fianna Fáil opposition, led by Charles Haughey, but that short-term price seemed worth paying for a possible long-term advantage. In licking my wounds after this debate I was encouraged by my friend Alexis FitzGerald, who sent me a poem by Yeats:

> Now all the truth is out,
> Be secret and take defeat
> From any brazen throat,
> For how can you compete,
> Being honour bred, with one
> Who, were it proved he lies,
> Were neither shamed in his own
> Nor in his neighbours's eyes?
> Bred to a harder thing
> Than Triumph, turn away
> And like a laughing string
> Where can mad fingers play
> Amid a place of stone,
> Be secret and exult,
> Because of all things known,
> That is most difficult.

The Fine Gael party meeting on Wednesday 21 November was one of the most difficult I had had to face as leader. I opened by saying that we must not be deflected from our course by Charles Haughey's determination to prevent anyone else succeeding where he had failed, destroying in the process the Anglo-Irish relationship as it was developing before he had come back to power early in 1982. We must continue to rebuild that relationship step by step, as had indeed been recognised in most of the press reaction to the summit meeting. The Thatcher press conference posed a special problem. In my own press conference immediately afterwards I had had to choose my words with care and to restrain myself in order to preserve the possibility of long-term progress. Nothing I said at the present meeting should, I added, be quoted outside.

The flood-gates opened as soon as I finished. Irreparable damage had been done, I was told; I had been insulted and thrown to the wolves and was lying down under it. Margaret Thatcher with her condescending manner had done the job of recruiting agent for the Provisional IRA. And so on. In reply I recognised that her remarks were seen as gratuitously offensive, but called on the party to continue to support my efforts for peace. Unhappily the term 'gratuitously offensive', torn from its context and attributed to me as my own comment on her remarks, leaked out, undoing my efforts to hold the line and to ensure for us an indisputable moral advantage in the situation that had arisen.

When I called in Alan Goodison next afternoon to hand him a letter to Margaret Thatcher, this leak gave him the chance to fight his corner in the face of what I, Dick Spring and Michael Noonan had to say to him. I told him first that these events had given the IRA their biggest boost for years and that the SDLP were in a state of shock, their morale shattered. Michael Noonan, joining us at this point, described the consequences as feared by the Gardaí: more tolerance of IRA activities, more safe homes for them, and less intelligence information. Dick Spring said he had never seen such anger and frustration as had been visible at his party meeting; the security of the state had been put at risk.

Alan Goodison said he noted what we had said but would be guided in what he reported by the fact that it would be injudicious to convey all of it. And he went on to say that nothing could excuse personally abusive references; unless what I was reported to have said was regretted, it would be very hard to restore the situation. I told him that I deeply regretted selective and out-of-context reporting of our party meeting, at which I had stressed positive elements of the situation. There followed a long and fairly contentious discussion.

In my letter to Margaret Thatcher I pointed out—as we had done frequently before—that the three illustrative models were *not* proposals, as she had implied; the *only* proposals in the report were those contained in the 'Future Requirements' sections. The fact that she had confined herself in her reply at the press conference to referring in the most dismissive terms to the 'models' section of the report had created a strongly negative reaction amongst nationalists and had contributed to the very misunderstanding of the report that we had worked so long and hard to eliminate from the very day it was published. It would be a tragedy if, through misunderstandings, an impression were maintained that she totally rejected the essence of the Forum report contained in the 'Future Requirements' section; this would contribute to the recurring feeling amongst nationalists that no effort on our part to work towards peace and stability would ever be appreciated.

As for alienation, both Jim Prior and Douglas Hurd had accepted its existence; we did not mind what word was used to describe this problem as long as there was acceptance of the reality whereby many thousands of people were estranged in a fundamental way from the whole system of authority, security and justice in Northern Ireland.

In her reply a week later Margaret Thatcher explained that she had answered the question asked about the three models. If her view on the report as a whole had been sought she would certainly have endorsed Jim Prior's references to the parts of it that they found helpful. As for alienation she did not like the term but she did not dispute that, although many members of the minority supported and worked within the existing system, there were others who did not have confidence in the system of authority and law and order and who looked to the Republic; therein was the problem that both of us were trying to resolve. She added that the British government were reflecting carefully on the ground covered at Chequers and hoped that they would be able before long to let us have an indication of the areas that they believed it would be fruitful to explore further with us.

It was a conciliatory response, and when we met four days later in the margin of the European Council in Dublin she opened our tete-à-tete on Northern Ireland by saying that she had been doing everything she could—she had been smiling all day! We should meet early in the new year to try to get a new framework. On the press conference *she* thought it had been all sweetness and light; what had gone wrong?

I explained that the difficulties had arisen from the manner in which she answered the questions on alienation and the Forum options; I accepted that she was not trying to be contentious. My problem had been that I had had to give my press conference without knowing exactly what she had said, with the result that I had given the worst press conference of my life. The whole thing had had a pretty serious effect on my Government and on me, which should not be minimised. Could she, I asked, now look for some phrase that would recognise that the minority did not easily or fully accept authority within Northern Ireland and that they looked to the Republic?

She was frightened to death about saying anything about nationalists in Northern Ireland, she replied very frankly. She must stick to the line that there was a problem—which was very obvious; that we were working on it; and that we would meet again early in the new year.

In her press conference next day she tried to undo some of the damage of two weeks earlier. She emphasised that in the margin of this meeting we had had a 'very successful talk'. She and I were united in abhorring violence, in wanting peace and stability, and in recognising a need for a new political framework for Northern Ireland. All of that, she added, 'is in other parts of the Forum report.' And by way of explanation of her response at the press conference to the question on the Forum options she said, 'I have a weakness, when people ask me direct questions, of giving direct answers.'

For my part, at my press conference at the end of the European Council I said that the public relations aspect of the Chequers meeting had clearly gone very much wrong but that at our meeting in the margin of the European Council we had recommitted ourselves to seek a new political framework.

Next day Douglas Hurd addressed the Northern Ireland Assembly in terms that were also clearly intended to be conciliatory towards Northern nationalists and towards us. What he said reflected a new sensitivity to Irish issues as well as his increasing self-confidence in his portfolio, and also (it was suggested to us) a reaction to the misconceived triumphalism of some Unionists after the press conference. And at another level, we understood, it also reflected an increased contribution by some NIO officials in Northern Ireland, who were better acquainted with the situation on the ground and more in tune with our thinking than NIO officials in London.

Meanwhile we had been encouraged by the reaction in Britain and abroad that had been evoked by the Prime Minister's handling of her press conference. It was clear that there was pressure on her from within her own Cabinet and party and from her advisers, as well as from foreign opinion, to modify what was seen as a negative stance vis-à-vis our Government. Knowing that she valued her relationship with President Reagan within the context of what British policy-makers saw as a special relationship between Britain and the United States, we decided to approach the President on the issue. Seán Donlon had maintained the valuable contacts he had built up during his period as Ambassador in Washington, including his close relationship with Bill Clark, the former National Security Adviser, who had paid an official visit to Ireland in 1981 and who was a close friend of Ronald Reagan. Now Seán asked Bill Clark to suggest that when Margaret Thatcher visited Washington just before Christmas the President find an opportunity to express his concern about the Anglo-Irish situation. He did so, somewhat to the surprise, I believe, of the State Department and other advisers. As I recall, we were told that he told her he looked forward to hearing when they met again in February how the Anglo-Irish relationship was going. However that may be, his expression of concern must have been a factor contributing to the more positive approach the British adopted a month or so later.

Meanwhile a meeting to maintain contact within the Armstrong-Nally framework was held in London on 17 December. In the absence of any fresh Ministerial instructions on the British side until the new year it was not a substantive session. The British side stressed at this meeting, however, that there had been a 'plus' side to the Chequers encounter. The Prime Minister's outspokenness had evoked a similar outspokenness on my part—an exchange that, however uncomfortable, was said to have been a better education for the Prime Minister than any number of British official briefs. She felt that much of what the Unionists had done in Northern Ireland was inexcusable; she could therefore accept that changes were needed for the nationalists while being able to reassure the Unionists that nothing had changed for them.

Over Christmas I reflected on the situation we now faced, and at the beginning of January I prepared an analysis, which I sent to Dermot Nally, Seán Donlon, and Michael Lillis.

In this document I contrasted the positive attitude of our public opinion on the Northern Ireland problem that had existed before the Thatcher press conference, as demonstrated by an *Irish Independent* poll on the eve of the Chequers meeting, with the negative public attitude in the aftermath of these events. The pre-Chequers poll had demonstrated an overwhelming majority of our people willing to look at solutions other than unity and feeling that solutions other than the Forum options should be considered; and there had also been evidence for the first time that a majority might support an amendment to articles 2 and 3.

It seemed to me that public opinion now doubted whether any long-term solution could be found as long as Margaret Thatcher was Prime Minister. While this could have the effect of making any agreement actually reached appear to be a 'turn-up for the books', and therefore more acceptable than might have been the case before the press conference, it was at least equally possible that *any* solution negotiated with Margaret Thatcher would simply be greeted with cynicism and disbelief. Also, as a result of the press conference a substantial agreement that would involve amending articles 2 and 3—always likely to have been a difficult 'gnat' for the SDLP to swallow—might now seem even less appetising to that party.

On the other hand, I continued, the invitation John Hume had just received on 31 December to meet Margaret Thatcher on 16 January (later changed to the seventeenth) was a potentially positive element. If publicly known it would also help to mitigate negative attitudes in our state towards Margaret Thatcher, which had become a problem for us in continuing the negotiation.

I then went on to stress the need on our side for a clear assessment of what we needed in order to create the conditions for an acceptable solution. I proposed the following elements, along the lines of which, I said, specific proposals should be worked out to be presented by us at the Armstrong-Nally talks on 21 January:

1. Unionist-SDLP power-sharing.
2. A political as well as security presence for the Irish Government in Northern Ireland—even though this would be limited in scope if accompanied by devolved power-sharing.
3. An Irish Government security role that would realistically safeguard us from the danger of involvement in shooting to kill, 'supergrass' trials, abuse of plastic bullets, harassment of the minority etc.—in other words, a joint decision-making role in security policy, and in appointments and complaints, inter alia.
4. A restructuring of the police, involving separate units, divisions or forces for such areas as Derry and Belfast.
5. Confining the UDR to barracks and replacing them temporarily with the British army while the police force was being expanded.
6. Joint courts.
7. A bill of rights.

8. A commission to harmonise at least the criminal law in relation to violence.

In the light of the outcome of the meetings of 16 and 21 January we should, I added, undertake a policy review to determine whether we should work towards a summit meeting that would produce a total package or whether we should go for a gradualist, step-by-step approach, as some were suggesting.

An information memorandum to the Government a week later reported on the efforts made by Margaret Thatcher and Douglas Hurd in December to undo some of the damage done by their statements after the Chequers summit meeting, efforts that had been largely lost in the welter of continuing unionist euphoria and nationalist dismay.

From the OUP side we had been told by a senior member of the party (not Jim Molyneaux) who had been briefed in detail by the British about the Armstrong-Nally talks that Unionists had been profoundly reassured by Margaret Thatcher's stance, but that they also knew that she would now want them to move in the direction of the nationalists. Unionists knew that the SDLP would need something by way of an 'Irish dimension', and they could now be pushed further than the British seemed to believe on this, so long as the Union was secure. They might well refuse to participate in the Irish-dimension institutions, but if these were not excessive, Unionists would work the other element, namely devolution. However, in summarising this for the Government we expressed the view that Unionists were not prepared in relation to power-sharing to go beyond their long-standing offer of committee chairmanships in the Assembly.

The Northern Ireland Committee of the Government reviewed our strategy at a meeting on 15 January, and John Hume came to see us on the sixteenth en route to his meeting in London with Margaret Thatcher. We knew that he had recently become more confident that the SDLP could hold its own against Sinn Féin in the May local elections, but we urged him not to present himself as overconfident about this and thus seeming to write off the Sinn Féin threat, for it was the perceived menace of the SDLP losing ground to Sinn Féin that had provided in the first instance the underlying logic of the agreement we were seeking with the British government.

John Hume subsequently told me that at his meeting with Margaret Thatcher she said that the Chequers meeting was one of the best she had ever had, and that she was now committed to doing something about the problem within the parameters set out in the Chequers communiqué. John Hume told her that the immediate and perhaps greatest problem was the absence of order in the nationalist areas. This problem was now such that it could not be solved within the limited context of Northern Ireland: a solution had to transcend the area, and there could not be a solution on the basis of interparty talks alone. Towards the end of the meeting she told him that when they had first met she had not understood how people could have different loyalties, but she understood this a lot better now.

All this was encouraging; a lot that I had said to her at Chequers and that she had seemed unwilling to take account of at the time had clearly been accepted, and it was obvious that she had been very concerned to be conciliatory and understanding with the SDLP leader.

Four days later the Armstrong-Nally talks resumed in Dublin. It was a relatively brief meeting of five hours, but it proved to be very significant. Clearly since the hard-hitting Chequers meeting and the subsequent disastrous Prime Ministerial press conference much had been done on the British side with a view to presenting us with a proposal on the basis of which serious negotiations could take place. It represented what the British government was now willing to offer without any quid pro quo from us in the form of an amendment to articles 2 and 3. They clearly hoped to persuade us to settle for a package along these lines and to drop our proposal to seek a constitutional amendment in return for a more radical restructuring of policy in Northern Ireland.

The British side made it clear that what they were putting to us had the full authority of the Prime Minister. Their proposal was for the establishment within the Anglo-Irish intergovernmental framework established in 1981 of a joint body to consider in relation to Northern Ireland legal matters, relations between the police and the community, prisons policy, security co-ordination, and political human rights questions, as well as other topics that might be agreed. Within it every effort would be made to resolve differences rather than simply reporting differences to the two governments. There would be a joint Secretariat in Belfast with the two Ministers as joint chairmen. In subsequent discussion it became clear that they did not now envisage an Irish Minister resident in Belfast. The question of joint or mixed courts for terrorist crimes would be considered by a subcommittee. In relation to policing, the body would put in hand a programme of action that would include among other things the establishment of local consultative machinery, improvements in the handling of complaints, and action to increase the proportion of Catholics in the RUC, the main object of all this being to make the police more readily accepted by the nationalist community.

On political and human rights issues the new structure to protect human rights and to prevent discrimination would provide opportunities to ensure that our views were 'taken into account' in making appointments to the Police Authority, Police Complaints Board, Fair Employment Agency, Equal Opportunities Commission, and Standing Advisory Committee on Human Rights. Finally the parliamentary tier proposal was still open.

The first reaction from the Irish side—without commitment, in the absence of any political guidance—was that, while noting that it was a 'narrow' package, we appreciated what was in it. It was, however, very heavily loaded on the security side; mixed courts were presented only as something to be 'examined'; and no indication had been given of how the proposed structure would operate if there were devolved government.

*t work, between Peter Barry and President Mitterrand.*

*On the balcony after the session, between Gaston Thorn and President Mitterrand.*

'I'm not doin' anythin' else,' interposed William. 'I'm sick of bein' Prime Min'ster. I'm sick of pol'tics all together. There isn't any sense in 'em. I'd sooner be a Red Indian anyday. I'll give up bein' Prime Min'ster to you an' you c'n start doin' things.'

—*William – Prime Minister, by Richmal Crompton* 19 March

*With former Fine Gael Leaders on the 60th anniversary of the foundation of Cumann na nGaedheal in 1984. James and Maura Dillon* (above), *and Liam Cosgrave* (below).

*Visiting Northern Ireland as Taoiseach:*

*In Belfast 1982 with Commissioner Christopher Tugenhat, Ted Heath and John Hume at dinner for the Silver Jubilee of the European Communities.*

*At Derry in 1985, thanking the RUC on departure.*

The New Ireland Forum in 1984:

*The Hierarchy delegation and the Party Leaders in February.*

*The Final Session in May.*

*With Margaret Thatcher signing the Anglo-Irish Agreement at Hillsborough on 15 November 1985 (above), and (below) facing the press at the conference immediately afterwards with Peter Prendergast and Bernard Ingham.*

*With Joan during the 1987 Election Tour.*

*An extending family in 1987, with Doireann, Mary, Mark, Reachbha, Ciara, Derval, Eithne, Joan, John, Iseult, and Aoife.*

*With two of my grand-daughters, Ciara and Reachbha after receiving the Japanese Order of the Rising Sun.*

Moreover it emerged from this discussion that there were now indications that there would be some trouble with the Northern Ireland judiciary about joint courts, although we were told that the British side would nevertheless happily talk about this in further discussions.

On the question of a more substantial package involving an amendment to articles 2 and 3, the British side said that they were not precluded from discussing this with us without commitment, or from going back for instructions on it. The text presented was a framework on which to build 'from the bottom up'. But there were indications that the British were less convinced than previously about the need to complete the negotiation and to announce an agreement in advance of the May local elections.

The importance of the proposals put to us on this occasion lay in the fact that in contrast to what had been said on the British side in earlier discussions, we now had a proposal to which the British government was committed that involved a regular and continuing institutionalised role for our Government in Northern Ireland, this role to be serviced by a joint Secretariat in Belfast.

On the other hand, in some important respects these proposals represented a step back from what had earlier been under discussion. Matters capable of being devolved were not to be within the competence of this new structure, and this would remove an incentive to Unionists to agree to devolution in order to reduce the role of the proposed body. This was to become thenceforth a major issue between us. Moreover, provision for full participation in decision-making on security policy, police complaints and nominations of senior police officers was not included.

At the end of this official meeting I arranged to see Robert Armstrong. I told him of our reservations, and he stressed that his government was not limiting itself to the contents of this document in its present form. There was one very significant feature in all this, he added: the Prime Minister did not want to 'stand pat'; she had said this both to John Hume and to Ronald Reagan.

I emphasised that the essential point was that there must be a structure or process sufficient to produce political involvement on the part of the minority and to carry them along to a point where they could support the security and judicial systems. If measures were devised that caught the public imagination, the IRA could become quite demoralised and could cease to be an effective force.

A memorandum on these British proposals was discussed by the Government on Thursday 31 January. The Government agreed to respond by incorporating our ideas within the structure of the British proposal; this meant that while major differences remained between the two governments, which in the event took months to resolve, henceforth both of us were operating within the same textual framework. The general lines of our response to the British proposal were discussed at this meeting, but we decided to postpone firm decisions until after Peter Barry had met Douglas Hurd and Geoffrey Howe on the following Monday in London.

At that meeting, when Peter Barry referred to our concern lest an agreement be too exclusively security-oriented, Douglas Hurd's response was a reasonably open one. They largely shared our analysis on this point, and he had tried out on the Assembly the idea that an Irish Minister should be able to put forward views on Northern Ireland. Molyneaux had initially accepted that there was a good deal in this point, and although he subsequently backed off this stance in public, Douglas Hurd's own feeling was that the Unionists would 'wear' an initiative along these lines while being publicly negative about it.

By this point it was clear that the fear that Sinn Féin might defeat the SDLP at the local elections in May no longer concerned us or the British as much as it had done; the Provisionals were not now expected to threaten the SDLP's position as had been feared in 1983 and 1984. But the negotiations had now gained a momentum of their own, and the joint fear of Sinn Féin electoral success had gradually been replaced on both sides by a positive hope of seriously undermining its existing minority support within the nationalist community.

Our alternative proposal was presented in a preliminary way through the Armstrong-Nally channel on 8 February. A constructive discussion at this meeting and subsequent contacts three days later cleared away a large number of problems. It thus identified what seemed at this stage to be the residual areas of disagreement, some of which were still significant. These included the role we might play through the joint body regarding appointments to five other bodies concerned with policing or discrimination; the joint court issue, where objections from Lord Chief Justice Lowry were now beginning to loom large; and the proposed Anglo-Irish parliamentary body.

In addition, however, and of great importance there remained outstanding a number of matters, described by the British side at this stage as 'confidence-building measures', which were designed to produce a 'visible change' in relation to the RUC and UDR. Also at issue were a review of prison sentences in the event of a drop in violence, and a proposed international fund to help areas badly affected by violence.

On our side there remained a question about possible actions in relation to security co-operation, the problem here being that at this stage the British could think of nothing specific they wanted us to do apart from reviving the Garda 'task forces' whose operations in border areas in 1982 had in our view added little to border security. Also the manner in which we would acknowledge the status of Northern Ireland remained to be determined.

In the course of this discussion we felt that we had secured acceptance of a number of important points. These included the idea that if devolution had not taken place by the time an agreement was signed we could put forward through this body views and proposals affecting the interests of the minority in regard to subsequent devolution. The body was also to have a role in relation to the promotion of social and economic reconstruction and improvement of those areas in both parts of Ireland that had suffered most severely from the violence, 'including the possibility of securing international support to that end'—a reference to the international fund that we were proposing and on which I had begun to sound out other governments.

The Government at its meeting on Tuesday 12 February confirmed that from our point of view the outstanding issues at that point were as set out above and that in other respects the text agreed represented our position at this stage of the negotiation; and with these qualifications this text was presented as our position next day to Douglas Hurd, Geoffrey Howe, and Margaret Thatcher, so that an informed discussion could take place between our two teams on the following Tuesday.

At a subsequent negotiating meeting we passed on the impression we were receiving from our contacts with Unionist politicians that they—especially the OUP—had a very good idea from briefings of what was in preparation, without, however, having seen the actual language proposed, and that they did not find these ideas as alarming as expected. The British side responded that there was not a monolithic Unionist view and they could probably guess who had been saying this to us. But, they wondered, would the OUP come up to scratch, and could they deliver the voters if Paisley sought a massive disapproval vote?

Turning to our response to the British proposal of 21 January, the British side told us that they regarded the idea of a possible international fund as useful, for they agreed with our view that remarkable benefits could accrue if our two countries approached the EC together on this. On the joint court they simply said they 'weren't there yet,' but they noted our proposal.

A new element that emerged, however—much to our surprise, given the way the discussion had gone at the previous meeting—was strong British reticence about our proposal for an Irish Government role if devolution could not be achieved or sustained on a basis that secured widespread acceptance throughout the community in Northern Ireland. We had proposed that in those circumstances the joint body could for the time being constitute a framework within which we could put forward views and proposals on policy aspects of economic and social matters affecting the interests of the minority that, pending devolution, would be the responsibility of the Secretary of State. This new area of disagreement, which had clearly arisen from the British Cabinet committee discussion, was not resolved for four months.

I should perhaps explain the significance of this provision. It was not only important in its own right but also, in our view, as an incentive to the Unionists to agree to devolution, for if and when devolution occurred, our role in Northern Ireland through the conference would be cut back to the specific issues identified in the agreement, many of which, we then hoped, would have been resolved and no longer at issue. At the same time the reference to devolution being 'sustained' should also encourage the SDLP to continue to take a positive stance in relation to devolution—which, after all, would involve their participation in a Northern Ireland Executive in a minority role. For this formulation would reassure them that if they agreed to participate in a devolved Administration and this political structure failed, they would still have a role to play in co-operation with our Government, which would then be involved once again through the conference in relation to the issues that had been, but would now no longer be, matters for a devolved Executive.

From February onwards the British side used their reticence on this issue to reintroduce as a bargaining counter the issue of the amendment of articles 2 and 3. This tactic seemed to be intended to put us off pursuing our proposal, while at the same time switching to us and away from them the onus of not amending the articles.

On confidence-building measures we raised the possibility that we might be able to sign the Convention on the Suppression of Terrorism following a Supreme Court decision that seemed to remove road-blocks in the way of extradition for certain politically motivated crimes. I had come to the conclusion that we should introduce this issue into the negotiations because by sidelining the amendment of articles 2 and 3 at the November summit meeting the British side had created a disturbingly unilateral bargaining situation, one in which they were in a position to make and withhold concessions at will because we had virtually nothing on the table to offer in turn.

We had always wanted it to be possible for our courts in appropriate cases to extradite people charged with terrorist crimes, but we had been frustrated from providing for this by High Court rulings against extradition in the case of so-called political offences. Peter Sutherland's earlier initiative in appealing such cases to the Supreme Court had paid off: that court's ruling on appeal had freed us at last to sign the European Convention on the Suppression of Terrorism and to enact its provisions into our law. In these circumstances we might as well get some credit for doing so by introducing this issue unilaterally into the present negotiation, thus improving our bargaining position when discussing measures we were seeking from the British side. The British seemed quite surprised by this initiative.

We also argued for action under the heading of confidence-building measures in relation to the UDR. The British side said that they were looking at this matter as well as at army powers of arrest and at a new study of anti-discrimination legislation. It was moreover agreed by the British side that community policing in areas like west Belfast, Derry and south Armagh would be examined. We subsequently heard from a British government source that they were giving some thought to making the UDR a more full-time force and phasing out part-timers if the force could not be abolished, and that they were also examining the possibility that all UDR patrols would be accompanied by RUC members.

In February 1985 I decided to send Seán Donlon to Washington to brief the US administration on the negotiations. Margaret Thatcher was about to pay a further visit there, so, following our successful approach in December, it seemed a good moment at which to tell the American administration how things stood. The first stage in this process had been accomplished on 15 February when Rick Burt, the Assistant Secretary of State for European Affairs, who was soon to become Ambassador to Germany, visited Dublin for bilateral talks. Peter

Barry and Seán Donlon brought him up to date on the Anglo-Irish discussions, to which I also referred during his courtesy call to my office. Given the President's interest in the issue and the constructive relationship that had been developing between the British and Irish administrations, Burt agreed to abandon the customary State Department 'hands off' attitude towards Northern Ireland and to suggest to his Secretary of State, George Schultz, that he include Ireland among the short-list of topics to be raised at the 20 February meeting between Margaret Thatcher and Ronald Reagan. The Schultz brief would include a note that, given the present crucial point in the negotiations, we felt that Margaret Thatcher should be given one more nudge, as well as an indication that the United States might be willing to give financial backing to an agreement.

Seán Donlon met John Hume in London en route to Washington and was authorised by him to tell his US contacts that the SDLP were likely to support an agreement that, he believed, if implemented fairly quickly might contribute to the emergence of a power-sharing administration in the North later in the year. In Washington Seán Donlon secured an intervention by Speaker Tip O'Neill, who agreed to urge the President to raise the issue with Margaret Thatcher, whom O'Neill also arranged to see himself in order to pledge support for a reconstruction programme at an appropriate time. The President duly brought up the Irish question and shortly afterwards told our Ambassador that the discussion had led him to believe that the Prime Minister really wanted to do something about the problem.

We had the impression that no similar briefing was given to the Americans by the British. Indeed two months later a US diplomat in London complained to us about this; the Americans had previously found the British so tight-lipped about Irish affairs, he said, that the embassy in London—which did not seem to have received any response from Washington, at any rate at the level of this particular official—concluded that something serious must be in the air. The US diplomat also added, humorously but nonetheless significantly, that we did not even put our Anglo-Irish stuff on the air any more, which was no way to help a friend! I was happy with this tribute to the efficacy of the London–Dublin courier service with which we had replaced telex communication about sensitive matters following the Jim Prior affair a year earlier.

Since January I had been disturbed by the reports we had been hearing from the British side about opposition from the Northern judiciary, and in particular from the Lord Chief Justice, Lord Lowry, to the idea of a mixed court of Northern and Southern judges that would deal with terrorist offences in both jurisdictions. I found it hard to reconcile this with my own contacts with Lord Lowry over the years. I had always found him to be what might be described as a liberal unionist who seemed well disposed towards a co-operative North-South relationship; and the respect in which he was held by both sides of the community in Northern Ireland had been demonstrated by his unanimous choice as chairman of the Northern Ireland Assembly in the mid-1970s.

After lunch in our house, to which I had invited Lord Lowry and his wife before the England-Ireland rugby international in early 1985, I broached the subject of mixed courts with him. It immediately became evident that he was more than prepared for such an initiative on my part, and was totally hostile to it. He said that he saw it as a reflection on his courts' past record, and that if this issue were pressed he would write to voice his hostility to the Prime Minister, the Lord Chancellor, and the Secretary of State for Northern Ireland. He could assure me that he was in a position to say that the senior judiciary, Catholic and Protestant, would resign if an attempt were made to establish mixed courts, even on a North-South reciprocal basis. I was shaken by the force of this reaction, which I had not expected. That these proposed letters were no idle threats soon became clear from our contacts with the British.

It now seemed desirable to inform ourselves more fully about the judiciary in the North. The information we were given by legal sources on the nationalist side some weeks later was most disturbing. We had been told by the British that a religious imbalance in the judiciary reflected the fact that it had proved impossible to persuade Catholics to accept judgeships. We now heard that on the contrary, although five years earlier one Catholic senior counsel had turned down an appointment to the ten-member High Court and Court of Appeal, in fact four Catholic senior counsel, not all of them nationalist in political terms, had since indicated their interest in appointment to that court, which included the four-member Court of Appeal, but had been passed over—two of them on three occasions. Despite the fact that there were more Catholics than Protestants at the Senior Bar, there were in fact only two Catholics among the ten members of these courts, one of whom was in the Court of Appeal. Concern was also expressed to us at the recent pattern of judicial appointments, which had been interpreted, we were told, as designed to produce in due course an all-Protestant and unionist Court of Appeal with an age composition that would ensure its continuance in this form for many years ahead. (The precise membership that was forecast to us at that time for the Court of Appeal is in fact that which actually emerged in the late 1980s.) The suggestion that Catholics would not accept judicial appointment was, we now learnt, true only in relation to County Court judgeships, which a number of senior barristers, both Protestant and Catholic, had turned down, in part at least because of the limited jurisdiction of that court.

This information, which we checked through several channels, influenced us thereafter in pursuing both the mixed court concept and also the need for balanced appointments to the Northern Ireland courts, in which we eventually made some progress, although our successors in Government seem to have failed to inhibit the predicted appointment of an all-Protestant and unionist Court of Appeal.

At the end of February Séamus Mallon had been brought into our confidence about the negotiations. We had kept in continuous touch with him since the Forum through Dáithí Ó Ceallaigh, an exceptionally able young diplomat with whom he had established ties of friendship, but we had not hitherto briefed Séamus on the negotiations. John Hume told us that this should now be done. I had some qualms about this, because Séamus was, I believed, more of a traditional Northern nationalist than John and might be less easy to convince about the merits of the kind of agreement that was likely to emerge. Moreover, my personal relationship with him had been affected for a period by the 'bugging' affair during the Forum. Nevertheless I complied with John's request, and when, after briefing him, Peter Barry brought Séamus over to my office to join John and myself for dinner, it was clear that he had taken the briefing calmly. He told me with his usual forthrightness, which I always appreciated, that he would not commit himself for or against until a conclusion had been reached. Later on, during the summer, again at John Hume's request, Joe Hendron and Eddie McGrady were also brought into the circle.

Meanwhile Geoffrey Howe and Douglas Hurd came to Dublin for discussions on the negotiation with Dick Spring and Peter Barry. I joined them for lunch and took the opportunity to express my concern at the way in which Douglas Hurd had been playing down in his public comments the significance of the negotiations. We discussed—fairly inconclusively—most of the outstanding issues: our possible role in relation to economic and social matters in the absence of power-sharing; the mixed court proposal; the parliamentary tier; and the application of the principle of respect for the identities of the two sections of the community to the operations of the security forces.

As I had to be in London that night to speak at the Diplomatic and Commonwealth Writers' Banquet, I left immediately after lunch for Baldonnell military airport. Our guests departed just after me; but I had no Garda escort, as they had, so they made much better time. I arrived to find their aircraft taking off. As the Government jet prepared to follow, the door was flung open and a figure catapulted into the cabin. It was a Foreign Office official accompanying the two Ministers who had been left in their wake and had jumped into our plane, assuming that it was the British aircraft. We had an entertaining discussion during the journey.

Next day in London I learnt that the extension of the British Cabinet group handling the negotiation that we knew was imminent had taken place. The additional members were the Lord President of the Council, Willie Whitelaw; the Lord Chancellor, Lord Hailsham; the Attorney General, Sir Michael Havers; the Minister for Industry, Norman Tebbitt; the Chancellor of the Duchy of Lancaster, John Biffen; and the Minister for the Arts, Lord Gowrie. It was felt that it would take some time for this wider group to get the feel of the complex negotiating situation, which made it even more likely that the official reaction to our document of 13 February would be considerably delayed.

While it was clearly necessary that Lord Hailsham as Lord Chancellor as well as Michael Havers as Attorney General be involved in the process as we approached a possible conclusion, the record of judicial appointments in Northern Ireland, in which Lord Hailsham had clearly had a key role, and the known strength of some of his views were matters of concern. We wondered also about Norman Tebbitt's likely reaction to the kind of agreement we were hoping would emerge—not because of the Brighton bombing but because he was known to be strongly unionist in his sympathies, having referred to the unionists in conversation on one occasion as 'our people over there'. Willie Whitelaw and Grey Gowrie, as well as Michael Havers, would, however, be likely to be more positive, we believed.

A week later, on 30 March, the morning of the second day of the Brussels European Council, Margaret Thatcher and I met in the Charlemagne Building. We talked first about the proposed international fund. It was clear that at that point she was thinking of a voluntary, charitable fund, not a programme of assistance by governments, but she eventually agreed to consider the idea of aid being given from public funds by the US government and the EC.

'What do we do now?' she then asked, rather abruptly. I said our proposal was on the table, with, however, a set of brackets in relation to mixed courts. She said she had been struck by how passionately Lord Lowry was against this idea. Robert Armstrong intervened to say that Lord Lowry had made that clear to me and to the Lord Chancellor, adding that the strength of his opposition was possibly due to the fact that he was not aware of the full context of what was envisaged. I agreed with him on this.

I went on to stress the importance of the proposed confidence-building measures, notably in relation to the UDR and RUC. It was intolerable that in Derry for example social welfare payments could no longer be made locally because the RUC could not protect the post office in the Creggan; recipients had to take a bus or taxi to collect their payments. 'Might bank accounts be used?' Margaret Thatcher asked. I replied dryly that they would not be of much use in an area like the Creggan, adding that what was needed was an unarmed police force working in conjunction with the RUC. 'You mean like the B Specials?' she asked. No, I replied, an *unarmed* force, like the Garda Síochána, which had been established during a civil war. 'You mean vigilantes?' she came back. No, I replied patiently, a fully trained local police force within a Northern Ireland Police Service. 'Is west Belfast a no-go area for the police?' she asked Robert Armstrong. Yes, he replied; when they go in they have to go in large numbers with military support. Turning back to my proposal she enquired, 'Are there people who would join such a force?' We are told there are, I answered. 'How would you know whether potential recruits were IRA people?' she demanded. I told her that on the ground everyone knew who was and was not in the IRA; the RUC and SDLP between them could identify those who should be ruled out.

It had been an atmospheric, marking-time kind of meeting. Clearly we would have to wait for any real progress on the outstanding issues until, with her new ad hoc Northern Ireland Committee, she got down to a detailed study of these matters.

While we awaited a British response in the weeks that followed we became concerned at the insensitivity of some decisions being made in or in relation to Northern Ireland. In mid-April I took some of these issues up with the British Ambassador, Alan Goodison. One such issue was the promotion of an RUC officer who had been in charge at the time of the machine-gunning of flats in Belfast by the RUC in August 1969. Another was the appointment as Commander of Land Forces in Northern Ireland of an SAS officer, later described to us by a British official as a very good officer whom one would not, however, like to meet on a dark night. We were also concerned about 'shoot-to-kill' incidents, in respect of one of which, occurring at about this time, we eventually received from British sources three different, and in our view incompatible, explanations. And we were unhappy that we were not seriously consulted before the publication of proposals for a reform of the police complaints procedure. It was around this time too that we were told by a senior Unionist of the briefing on the negotiations that he had received from an NIO official.

The first meeting of the enlarged group of British Ministers handling the negotiations did not in fact take place until 24 April. The outcome of this was a revised version of the paper under discussion. When this was produced at an Armstrong-Nally meeting on 29–30 April the Irish side reacted very critically, because it involved little more than the previous British proposal with some linguistic changes. There was no progress on the mixed courts issue, on which we were told that Lord Lowry's colleagues shared his view and that he had said he saw it as a resigning matter. The problem of our role in relation to economic and social issues if devolution did not take place or if it failed was not seriously addressed; and the language of this revised text in some places seemed to have been weakened from our point of view, leaving the main 'operational' paragraph about the joint body in a most unsatisfactory shape. Our side thought they saw the hand of the NIO rather than the Cabinet Office in this re-draft, and wondered too whether it might have reflected a negative influence arising from the widening of the British Ministerial group.

However that might be, the Irish side's reaction on these issues was carefully calculated: going close to the brink of rejecting the document but not going far enough to cause a breakdown of the talks. The result at the end of the day was a suggestion by the British side that the presenting of this text to our Ministerial group be deferred in order to give the British an opportunity of reworking it. Our officials were sceptical, however, about whether this was likely to yield progress on the two outstanding issues in the document itself, as distinct from the parallel confidence-building measures, namely the mixed courts and our role in relation to economic and social issues in the absence of devolution.

It emerged on this occasion that on the British side the non-participation of the SDLP in the Assembly was seen as an unwillingness to accept participation in devolved government. What the British did not seem to have taken cognisance of was the fact that at our meeting a month earlier I had told Margaret Thatcher 'with authority' (there was no point in concealing the fact that the two SDLP leaders were reasonably aware of what was going on through discussions with me) that the SDLP would support devolved government, involving representatives of both sections of the community in the context of an agreement signed by us with the support of that party. The text we had proposed and which had SDLP support included a link between the agreement and devolution.

In the course of this meeting we also clarified the confidence-building measures we were proposing on both sides. The issues we raised for British consideration were:

> The composition and name of the RUC and RUC Reserve; the possibility of local unarmed police forces; a declaration by the RUC of respect for the identities of the two communities; and the Police Authority.

> The UDR.

> The possibility of a prison sentence review related to a reduction in violence.

> The issue of 'supergrasses' (although this was ceasing to be a problem).

> The proposed international fund—mentioned in the draft paper, but requiring much more work.

And on our side:

> Recognition of the status of Northern Ireland.

> The ratification by us of the Convention on the Suppression of Terrorism.

> A possible reactivation of Garda task forces in border areas—although our view was that these had not been really effective.

In relation to the RUC the British side responded that the Chief Constable had not been very encouraging about our proposal for an unarmed force, although he had agreed that if a framework were set up through the agreement, issues like this could be discussed. The Irish side also referred to the need to deal with the continued presence in the reformed RUC of some 'bad apples' from the 'Strasbourg period'.

On the UDR the Irish side expressed its concern about the known association of some members with paramilitary bodies like the UDA or otherwise with crime, and about the record of their dealings with the nationalist community both on and off duty. In earlier discussions we had been told that relations with the public were to be conducted exclusively by the RUC; indeed we had understood from some of what had been said that this system was already in place. The UDR should, in our view, conduct operations only in support of the RUC, under the operational control of regular units giving military support to the RUC, and they should mount checkpoints only in the presence of and in support of the RUC, who alone should have powers of arrest.

At the end of the meeting the Irish side emphasised the potential importance of our proposal to ratify and incorporate in our domestic law the provisions of the Convention on the Suppression of Terrorism and the importance also of the proposed international fund. For their part the British side suggested that before their new document was submitted to our Government they would look at it again to see whether they could take account of the reactions of the Irish side at this meeting. They would also examine a 'Common Statement of Principles' document that we had submitted that afternoon, based on the relevant part of the Forum report.

On the same day as this meeting, 30 April, I visited Derry with Peter Barry to inaugurate a new Dublin–Derry air service. This produced the usual chorus of protests from certain Unionist political sources, and was followed by a protest from the British government. The Foreign Office complained that the advance warning to them of this visit had been 'wholly inadequate and lacking in detail'. It would have been courteous, they said, to have informed them of my intention to visit a factory and other parts of the city. The chargé d'affaires who called at Iveagh House to make these representations also said that he had been instructed to say that visits by Irish Ministers to the North, or for that matter to the rest of the UK, that were likely to command a great deal of attention should in future be discussed with the British government in advance.

In response to this it was pointed out by our side that on 26 April, four days before the visit, we *had* given notice to the embassy, and also to the RUC, to which we had indeed given full details of the visit as then proposed, together with the information that further arrangements were being made by John Hume, whom the RUC had not, however, subsequently contacted. It then transpired in the course of the discussion that the telegram from the embassy reporting this had not reached the Foreign Office until three days later, and that the RUC had not contacted the British authorities following our notification of the visit to them. Our comment on this was that we could not be responsible for the inadequacy of the British internal communication system, and that the terms of the British complaint were 'unacceptably sharp'. Moreover, the suggestion in the British démarche that, because this inaugural flight took place several weeks before the local elections, my arrival on this aircraft had been seen as an intervention in that campaign by the Irish Government was absurd. Was it suggested that my visit had caused the Unionists to lose votes? The only conceivable indirect impact of my visit on the election was a possible shift in votes from Sinn Féin to the SDLP, in which surely both governments had a shared interest. And in any event, far from my visit having been directed only towards nationalists, as had also been suggested in the démarche, some thirty Unionists had attended the reception I had given.

I was glad to hear in due course of this robust response to what had been a particularly ill-judged British approach.

A fortnight later there was a further Armstrong-Nally meeting, at which progress was made with the text of a potential agreement, but more work still had to be done on it on the British side, as a result of which an interval of a further month followed before this draft could be brought to finality.

Quite apart from the fact that in John Hume's absence in the United States Séamus Mallon had come close to coming out against the negotiations, within my Government there was by this time considerable concern on a number of important points. Ministers were seriously worried about the absence of any advance in relation to the confidence-building measures that we were seeking from the British. These concerns were put to Alan Goodison early in June; he told us he had repeatedly urged on London the necessity to clarify their position on these matters. This discussion with the Ambassador was also used to indicate my interest in having an opportunity to discuss matters with Geoffrey Howe when I met him at the signing of the Portuguese and Spanish agreements with the European Community in mid-June.

It came to our notice shortly afterwards that the confidence-building measures had hardly featured in the discussions in the British Cabinet subcommittee when drawing up its new version of a draft agreement. It was also clear that the subcommittee had no inclination to push the issue of mixed courts, lest this lead, as had been threatened, to the resignation of Lord Chief Justice Lowry. Those in the Northern Ireland judiciary who had supported him on this issue had presented themselves, we were told, to the British government as steadfast Unionists whose loyal work must not be compromised or tainted by having to work alongside judges from the Republic, and this had been sympathetically received.

It was against this background that I had my discussion in Lisbon with Geoffrey Howe. It was a very informal discussion, which took place during an interval in the signature ceremonies at the Jeronimos Monastery in Lisbon. We started talking on the outer balcony of the monastery looking out over the Tagus, with other Ministers and officials all around us, but were interrupted by a participant who clearly thought we were just having a social chat. We resumed on an internal balcony of the cloister after lunch, under the gaze of the journalists across the courtyard, and exchanged some concluding words during a reception in Madrid on the following day.

I told the Foreign Secretary that our Government was becoming sceptical about ever getting an adequate response from the British on the matters about which we wished to be satisfied. We were seriously considering whether it would not be better to terminate the negotiations than allow them to drag on indefinitely. Geoffrey Howe noted with concern these reactions, but, as he had done previously, stressed the magnitude of what was involved in the draft agreement. It would, he said, concede to us a right of involvement in Northern Ireland that he believed (sincerely, in my view) would be the start of an evolving situation of historic significance.

I said that what was proposed in the draft agreement should not be seen as a concession to *us*. It was something that, because of a series of past failures, had become necessary in order to secure peace and stability. The need for our involvement in Northern Ireland, as a means of securing Northern minority acceptance of the political authority of the security forces and of the judicial system, derived directly from these failures and not from any wish on our part. These were not things that we sought because we wanted to be more involved in the difficult situation there; on the contrary, it was with great reluctance that we were prepared to take on responsibility without power—always a dangerous thing to do.

Geoffrey Howe replied by saying that the issues we had raised were very difficult for them. On the mixed courts they had the obstacle of Lord Chief Justice Lowry, and he seemed to me to suggest that action here would best await the departure of the Lord Chief Justice. That would not be acceptable to us, I responded, as it would leave this whole issue over for a long and perhaps indefinite time. I would need an assurance that the mixed court would come into existence within a year. On the UDR I went on to point out that we had put forward practical proposals that fell short of its abolition. We had also proposed local unarmed police forces for 'no-go areas', and we had suggested the announcement of a major prison review after six months of peace. On none of these had we had a response.

The Foreign Secretary suggested that an announcement of a prison review could pose difficulties for the unionists. I replied that there were many of the majority tradition in prison also, and that an important section of unionists were concerned about them. An announcement of such a review following a sustained period of peace would be essential to put pressure on the IRA through the prisoners' families—a point that he admitted he had hitherto missed. He noted our concerns and agreed to convey them to his colleagues. The fact that he returned to the subject at Madrid seemed to indicate a degree of pre-occupation on his part with what I had said.

So far as the actual text of an agreement was concerned, the Armstrong-Nally meeting that coincided with my absence in Lisbon and Madrid had made good progress. Indeed what emerged from this meeting was a draft agreement acceptable in principle to both sides, with the exception of the paragraph on mixed courts. A 'Common Statement of Principles' that we had presented on 30 April, the terms of which had been drawn ultimately from the Forum report, had been incorporated in the text in the form of a preamble, with some drafting improvements.

The initial 'operational' paragraph about the joint body had been revised in a satisfactory way, and our concern lest our role be confined too narrowly to security issues, thus weakening the incentive to Unionists to agree to devolution, had at last been met by a new provision that reintroduced the concept that the British side had seemed to accept in January but had resisted from February onwards. This new paragraph stated that if it should prove impossible to achieve and sustain devolution on a basis that would secure widespread acceptance in Northern Ireland, the joint body would constitute a framework within which we could put forward views on proposals for major legislation on Northern Ireland on policy issues significantly and especially affecting the minority. In the settlement of this issue one of the London NIO officials involved in the negotiation, Tony Brennan, played a significant part, and the outcome owed a good deal to his ingenuity.

At this meeting agreement was also reached on a joint declaration by the two governments about the status of Northern Ireland, in terms that avoided any constitutional problem for us. Thus, apart from the mixed court issue, the only significant matters that appeared to remain outstanding at this point were the confidence-building measures or, as they had now come to be known in these discussions, 'associated unilateral measures', which as we saw it involved the restructuring and redeployment of the UDR and changes in the RUC and prisons policy. Agreement was reached at this time, however, that a code of conduct would be drafted, incorporating the principle of a declaration by members of the RUC and UDR—perhaps even by the British army—accepting and undertaking to respect the legitimacy of the nationalist as well as the unionist identity. We were told that something along these lines was under consideration already for the Metropolitan Police in relation to ethnic minorities in London. However, the Chief Constable had not yet been spoken to about this.

In the memorandum I submitted to the Government immediately after this, on 15 June, I tried to put the best face on the problem of the confidence-building measures, believing that the efforts I had made with Geoffrey Howe and the pressure from our side in the latest Armstrong-Nally talks should yield some kind of positive result when I met Margaret Thatcher at the end of the month. I was able to say that the British Prime Minister was now understood to be quite enthusiastic about the idea of an International Fund for Northern Ireland, for which we had secured support from President Reagan and Speaker O'Neill in the United States and about which recently I had personally secured positive reactions from Prime Minister Mulroney in Canada, President Mitterrand, Chancellor Kohl, and the Prime Ministers of the Netherlands and Luxembourg, as well as Jacques Delors, President of the European Commission.

In conclusion I told the Government that I believed it was worth pursuing these negotiations to a conclusion, with a view to completing the Government's set of desiderata in the overall package, but that this would probably take a further five or six weeks at least. An agreement might be signed at a summit meeting in September, after the holiday break.

The Government approved my report; there was indeed considerable satisfaction that we had reached this point, despite the worries over the confidence-building measures, which, together with the mixed courts issue, were now the outstanding matters to be discussed between Margaret Thatcher and myself in the margin of the Milan European Council. Much now clearly depended upon this meeting. That day was to prove to be crucial for the future development of Europe as well as for Northern Ireland, since later in the morning of our bilateral discussion the German Chancellor and the French President were to propose a vote on the calling of a conference to amend the Rome Treaty with a view to what became known as the Single European Act.

When Margaret Thatcher and I met and took up the question of Northern Ireland, she asked me to open the discussion. I said that a certain amount of progress had been made. 'There is a *lot* of progress,' she interrupted immediately. I agreed that the draft text now before us seemed to be more or less all right and that there appeared to be no reason why the remaining issues arising could not be sorted out.

There was, however, a lot to be done on the associated measures, I continued. I spoke first about the steps we for our part proposed to take, including the statement we were to make jointly with the British government on the status of Northern Ireland. On our proposal this was now to include for the first time a recognition of something that while seeming self-evident had nonetheless been controversial for us in the past: the fact that consent to Irish unity did not at present exist. On the proposal that we reintroduce task forces on the border I said that it posed some problems for us because of public pressure to bring gardaí back from the border to Dublin and other areas, where crime had increased sharply, including an epidemic of car-stealing. Notwithstanding all this we would set up a task force. The signing of the agreement could spark off some short-term violence, and it was important that we should be prepared for this on the border, as her government also would have to be in Northern Ireland. I referred also at this point to our decision to ratify and implement in our legislation the provisions of the Convention on the Suppression of Terrorism, which had been made possible by a recent judgement of the Supreme Court.

But, I went on to say, in all this the Northern Ireland minority community must also be brought along. What had now been worked out between our two governments was just about 'saleable' on our side *if* it secured the support of the minority community in Northern Ireland. But without that support the agreement just could not work. Even on our side of the border there would be problems in these circumstances, because we would be accused of taking on responsibility without power.

I went on to say that the associated measures we sought related to the courts, the RUC, the UDR, and the review of prison sentences in the event of a major and sustained reduction in violence. I was anxious to hear her reaction to our proposals on these items. She replied that on their side they were already afraid they might have gone too far. She had to look to the Unionist reaction, and what we had already agreed could bring out the Paisleyites. If further action were taken on associated measures there could be a very strong reaction indeed, which could put the whole thing in jeopardy. There might, however, be some possibility of things being done over time by way of implementation of the agreement.

She added at this point that Lord Chief Justice Lowry was reported to have said a lot of things that they knew nothing about. (In view of the amount we had heard from the British about things he had been saying, I found this rather puzzling.) I said that, as she knew, I had met the Lord Chief Justice socially some time ago and had outlined to him in a very broad way the mixed courts proposal. He had said he would resign if anything like that happened, and he had since made a great play of his opposition to the mixed courts, all of which had got into the newspapers in Ireland and in London—not from us. Recently, however, it appeared that the judges of the higher court in Northern Ireland had come together to ask what all this was about and, it seemed, had in the end confronted Lowry, saying that they would do whatever their constitutional duty was and that there was no question of their resigning. A letter had been written to her on behalf of the higher judiciary. (I had heard of this letter just before coming to Milan and had checked through Dermot Nally and Charles Powell before the meeting whether she had received it. It appeared she had not, and I had had to decide whether in these circumstances I would refer to it. I knew that she would not be pleased to learn that I knew of the letter before she had received it herself, but the issues we had to address were of such importance that I did not think I could let this opportunity to settle the associated measures pass without dealing fully with the mixed court issue, and I did not feel I could do so effectively if I omitted reference to the forthcoming letter.)

She immediately responded that she had no such letter; the only letter she had had was one some time back that had said that the proposal for mixed courts would bring the judiciary into politics. When I then went on to say that I understood that Lord Chief Justice Lowry had also been saying that there were not enough suitable people to act as judges, she interrupted before I could complete the sentence to say that there could be acute difficulties if I told her about what went on in her territory about the court system. All that could be done, she added, was that the agreement could say that consideration would be given to the possibility of setting up a mixed court system.

I replied that unless I knew in advance that a system of mixed courts would be set up I would be in difficulty about going ahead with the agreement, but she responded that there was no possibility of agreeing in advance to mixed courts. I said that this question had to be considered *now*. People had been saying that I was being led up the garden path, and this would be said even more strongly if this issue were not settled; I would be accused of having been fooled by the British again. She replied that the Unionists would say that this was a foot in the door, and she assured me that future consultation on this issue would be genuine.

After further fruitless discussion on the courts, she promised she would genuinely consider what I had said, but she could not say what the result would be. She then moved on to the associated measures, prefacing her remarks with the comment that Douglas Hurd was one of the best people they had ever had as Secretary of State for Northern Ireland. He believed that if announcements of associated measures were made at the same time as the agreement, it would be jeopardised. He would hope to implement them over time, but with his responsibilities he had to consider Unionist reactions.

I replied that all these measures were necessary to enable the minority to identify with institutions and systems of government; unless they happened, we would have been wasting our time. She answered that they could consider an undertaking to implement certain measures; would it be sufficient to set up arrangements that would come into force later? Unless the minority supported the new arrangements from the very first moment, I said, they would just be worthless. There was no way that the minority could stand up to the IRA without these measures. But, she replied, she was in the same position as far as the Unionists were concerned. They would say that the agreement gave us a foot in the door and that the Republic should never have come into this arrangement and that we were putting the constitution in danger.

I then told her that for the last six months my Government had been increasingly sceptical about the negotiations. They had been saying that unless these associated measures took place simultaneously they just could not back the agreement. I had persuaded them to go along with what was happening, but with difficulty. If at this stage things broke down, this would be very damaging. And I started to explain that what we wanted was something on the UDR and RUC; perhaps a code of conduct.

She responded that these things could be done, but they must have a low profile. For the last six months, I replied, we had been saying that we could not get the minority to back this agreement unless there were simultaneous changes in the UDR and RUC. What had we got? By the time the measures she mentioned were put into force in the way she was suggesting, the whole effect of the agreement would have evaporated. I had put my personal authority on the line here in the face of the deepest scepticism about the negotiation on the part of very many people in the Republic. She responded that I was getting an agreement that involved institutionalised consultation in the North.

By this time it was clear to me that I was getting nowhere on these associated measures, and the only course open to me at this point was, I felt, a make-or-break one. I must go in with all guns blazing, using more forcible language than I had ever previously used. At the worst this would lead to a break in the negotiation, but given the way our discussion had been going, that seemed inevitable anyway. And there was always the possibility that I could shock her into modifying the 'stone wall' attitude that I had met so far in the course of our discussion.

I began by telling her that she should understand that I was not seeking these things for the benefit of our people in the South; in fact our people did not want to be involved in the North. We had just had local elections in the South, and time and again people had come to us to say, 'Stop talking about Northern Ireland; we want tax down, we want unemployment cured, and we do not want to be involved in Northern Ireland.' This was the background against which I had initiated the current negotiation, because it seemed to me to be vital to try to break out of the cycle of violence in Northern Ireland, even if this involved taking risks.

I would tell her, I went on, how I saw the whole question. This business would never have started if the right thing had been done at the right time. In 1969, when the trouble had started, all the minority community had then wanted had been a right to be represented in Parliament as a constitutional opposition on the basis of equal rights. But there had been fierce opposition even to that minimal change from unionists in Northern Ireland. Then in 1974 a British government—not hers—walked away from an agreement that had been made at Sunningdale, and things that could well have worked collapsed, again in the face of Unionist opposition. And even as late as 1982 if the ideas in relation to power-sharing that Jim Prior had canvassed and then dropped had gone ahead, things might have worked out. We had always been faced with these half-solutions: too little and too late.

The consequence of doing nothing now would be to force people like supporters of the SDLP into the arms of Sinn Féin. I would use all the moral authority I had to campaign for a settlement that would stop this from happening. There was a deliberate campaign being waged by the IRA in Northern Ireland to create instability. Qadhafi was deeply involved, and was willing to put millions of pounds into a similar effort north and south. He was backing the IRA politically and trying to manipulate the Irish state in that way. For over eight hundred years English *realpolitik* had taken it as a fundamental tenet of policy that Ireland must not be allowed to become a base for attacking Britain. Now it could be allowing that very thing to happen: its government could be doing just what British policy over eight hundred years had spent every effort to prevent—at great cost to Ireland. There was now a certain current flowing. I was ready to take this opportunity and to run with it. This was a historic opportunity; I did not know what history would say if we missed it. It was something that she and I could do together: no-one else could do so now or for the foreseeable future.

As I reached this point in my extempore address I glanced across at Dermot Nally, and I had the impression from the look on his face that he thought I had gone over the top, with probably fatal results. Regardless I ploughed on.

We were not saying 'Abolish the UDR,' I told her. We were saying that it should be used in support of the police, with a number of improvements in its training and organisation. We hoped that we could get such an arrangement accepted by the minority in Northern Ireland, but without knowing if we could do so. The changes we had suggested in the RUC had been the minimum—possibly even less than the minimum—required to deal with the problem of alienation. We had exactly the same interest as she had in avoiding a Unionist reaction that could become uncontrollable. Our best assessment was that the things we suggested could be done. We knew what the minimum was to make the agreement work. We had our own contacts with the Unionists, and we had some feeling for what they could acquiesce in while protesting.

At this stage Margaret Thatcher intervened, saying that she saw what I was getting at: I wanted something visible. But we should not call these 'associated measures'; rather they should be described as 'implementing part of the agreement'. She knew just how hostile the atmosphere to this agreement could be. Both parts of Ireland could be in danger.

The two of us together could do it, I told her. This was an opportunity that might not recur. There were still some problems with the RUC, I went on. In 1976 Merlyn Rees and Frank Cooper, the Permanent Secretary to the Northern Ireland Office at that time, had told me that there were then only about twenty policemen left in the force who had misbehaved in the 1968–69 period, and that these would be gone within a year. Yet this did not seem to have happened. Looking recently at the Scarman Report we had recalled an incident in which there had been a machine-gun attack on the Divis Flats in Belfast in which a child had been killed, and a second incident in which whole streets of Catholics had been burned out. In both these incidents and in a further one later on, all of which had been mentioned in the Scarman Report, a particular police officer had been involved, although he had not been named there. We were astonished to hear recently that he had been appointed to one of the highest offices in the Northern Ireland police. What kind of sensitivity did that show? Did she think that the minority community could support a police force with that sort of thing happening?

Margaret Thatcher was clearly shocked at this. She was sure, she started to say, that Douglas Hurd would never—'But that is the very point,' I interrupted. 'Someone is not telling him the facts.' We had the fullest confidence in the Cabinet Office and in the Foreign and Commonwealth Office, but we had serious doubts about what was getting to the Secretary of State from the Northern Ireland Office.

Still disturbed at what I had just said, she asked me to tell her more. Were there any other similar incidents of which I knew? I replied that I was using these incidents simply as an illustration. I did not want to go into details; we were not engaging in a witch hunt. 'What you are talking about', she replied reflectively, 'is a code of conduct.' 'Not *just* a code of conduct,' I replied; 'a declaration of commitment to uphold the rights of both communities.' If some people in the RUC did not like this and decided to go, then we could use that opportunity to fit in other suitable people from both sections of the community. What we had been speaking about was a declaration by the UDR and the police that in their activities they would be fair to both communities.

'Go on,' she replied encouragingly, 'I want to hear all about this.'

Encouraged by her response and by the remarkable change in atmosphere that had followed my impassioned address, I went on to tell her that what was needed in the UDR was a corps of competent and professional military officers down to company level, as well as adequate numbers of experienced NCOs. The part-time membership of the UDR should be disbanded, and better control of UDR operations should be ensured.

She intervened to say that she admired their courage. Many of them had been shot. They were a remarkable group of men. I acknowledged that men had been murdered in the most appalling circumstances; but the fact was that the UDR and RUC had come to be seen as representing one section of the community. In some areas the UDR harassed local Catholic boys, many of them their neighbours with whom they had grown up. This harassment went on and on and had become a problem that in Northern Ireland tended to have the sort of end that we all knew. The UDR were seen by the minority as a hostile force. There must be visible changes. We were not suggesting anything that would make them less effective; we were making concrete suggestions so that they could act more effectively in support of the police and attract community support.

We then moved on from this to discuss the possible timing of a summit meeting at which an agreement could be signed. 'What about October?' she asked. That meeting should be in Dublin, I said. Not in Dublin, she replied; and there would be difficulties about Belfast. She was not objecting to a place in the South, but not Dublin, as that would heighten the profile too much, and we would get a very strong reaction from unionists.

I told her that as far as the location of the summit meeting was concerned, Belfast posed no problem for me; but it must in any event be in Ireland. As for the associated measures, I didn't mind what they were called so long as they attracted and sustained the confidence of the minority.

The meeting concluded rather suddenly, as we both had to turn to preparations for the start of that day's session of the European Council. I left much relieved. My deeply felt onslaught seemed to have produced the desired result. At least she was now converted in principle to the need for certain confidence-building measures; and if they were to be described as part of the implementation of the agreement, so much the better.

# CHAPTER SEVENTEEN

# ANGLO-IRISH AGREEMENT: COMPLETION

After Milan the negotiation changed in character: the primary concentration shifted to what had now come to be known as 'early implementation' (at this stage I include in this the mixed court issue) of criminal justice and security aspects of the agreement, to the role and functioning of the proposed Secretariat, and to the actual arrangements for the final summit meeting. True, work continued right up to the very end of the negotiation on improving the text, but the discussions on that issue were on the whole co-operative and largely non-contentious, while the discussion on 'early implementation' proved extremely difficult.

The frequency of the Armstrong-Nally meetings rose sharply at this stage: except for the month of August these meetings now took place at intervals of a week or ten days, and in fact there were over a dozen meetings between 9 July and 12 November, just before the actual signing of the agreement. In addition there were a number of Ministerial meetings.

The principle of taking action in the various areas we had identified at Milan was conceded at the very first Armstrong-Nally meeting after the European Council, that of 9 July. The British proposal to give effect to this was that the communiqué accompanying the agreement would announce that the first meeting of the joint body would take place on an early date, to be specified, and that, while the two governments did not envisage that in the normal course an agenda would be publicly announced, they wished it to be known that on that occasion priority would be given to the questions of criminal justice and security that fell within the committee's remit.

What would actually be announced from that meeting would be agreed in advance, including on our side the ratification of the Convention on the Suppression of Terrorism and the reintroduction of Garda task forces on our side of the border. The British team would have something ready on the question of the code of conduct of the RUC, and on enhanced training for the UDR as well as on an increase in the number of full-time British personnel working with it. On the UDR the British were also able to tell us by the end of July that they had no plans for any increase in its strength or role in relation to the regular army: in other words the policy of 'Ulsterisation' had reached a plateau. They added that in furtherance of the policy of army (including UDR) patrols being mounted at the request of the RUC, it was intended that progressively, as circumstances permitted, the number of patrols with an RUC presence would be increased.

In early September, on the Irish side, we returned to this question, pressing for a time-scale for the achievement of an RUC presence with all UDR patrols. At the following meeting the British draft of a paragraph for the summit communiqué dealing with this matter emerged in the form of a proposal that the joint body at its first meeting consider 'how the principle that the military (which includes the UDR) operate only in support of the civil power can be further implemented in the operation and deployment of the security forces in Northern Ireland, with the particular objective of achieving as rapidly as circumstances permit the full implementation of this principle in operations which involve direct contact with the community, save in the most exceptional circumstances.'

Somewhat surprisingly, at the next meeting the British side proposed the deletion of the phrase 'in operations which involve direct contact with the community, save in the most exceptional circumstances,' on the grounds that the Ministry of Defence did not feel they needed this restriction. However, in the subsequent discussion it was decided to retain the phrase in a modified form; the Irish side suggested introducing the word 'police', and this was accepted by the British, who then proposed the wording 'that there is a police presence in all operations which involve direct contact with the community.' The assurance thus given of the Ministry of Defence attitude to this issue, and the British proposal to introduce the word 'all' before 'operations which involve direct contact with the community,' were extremely reassuring to us, and the draft in this form was accepted for incorporation in the communiqué. The phrase 'the most exceptional circumstances' was explained by the British side as covering cases where an RUC man might fail to turn up for a patrol or where there was a major security crisis that prevented the RUC from providing police officers to service a patrol.

I have gone into some detail about the way in which this formulation in the communiqué was arrived at, because six years after the signing of the agreement, and despite constant pressure from the Irish side, one-third of patrols continued to be unaccompanied by an RUC presence. Nothing in the negotiations could have given reason to the Irish side to expect such an outcome.

Discussion on a code of conduct for the RUC that would commit that body to impartiality in respect of the two identities was initiated on 15 July, and we were told that the Chief Constable had started looking at the code of conduct in the London Metropolitan Police 'Blue Book'; it was suggested that something along these lines could be incorporated into the conditions of service of the RUC. At the next meeting we were told that the senior RUC people thought there was a real job that could be done in this respect and that they were bringing in religious and community leaders to say what they for their part found exasperating about RUC members who were not of their own persuasion. The code of conduct, we were told, could become part of standing orders, a breach of it being an offence. It was suggested to us that the intention to have a code of conduct should be mentioned in the communiqué, with possibly some indication of a date for its implementation—say the end of the year or earlier.

At the meeting on 3 September we were told that it had now been proposed by the Chief Constable that a formula be included on the following lines:

The task of good community relations is the responsibility of every member of the force. That means it is your responsibility—it is not that of the Community Relations Branch only. It should be carefully studied by every member of the force . . . A breach will be a prima facie disciplinary offence.

It is the declared policy of Government that the identity of both the majority and minority communities must be upheld. The process of government in Northern Ireland should be such as to provide the people of both communities with the confidence that their rights will be safeguarded. The RUC can, must and will be in the forefront of the effort to uphold these rights.

This was acceptable to us. In the event, however, the code of conduct was not issued until long after the agreement was announced. We were told that this delay arose from the Chief Constable's unhappiness with the fact that the issue had been referred to at a political level. Moreover, when it was eventually issued it was not published, although it leaked out some time later. As a result none of the impact we had hoped for from this development was achieved.

The question of a review of sentences in the event of violence ceasing for a significant period was discussed at the meeting of 15 July, when the British side said they were looking at this idea. We explained that we believed the IRA would set out to destroy the agreement by violence, and we wanted to take the ground from under them. The only force that could be used for this purpose was, as Fr Denis Faul has never tired of pointing out, the family structure, which had brought the 1981 hunger-strike to an end when everything else had failed. A formula proposed by the British was a statement to the effect that if an agreement led to a real and sustained reduction in the level of violence, that would be among the factors to be taken into account by the Secretary of State in reviewing the release of prisoners who had been convicted of terrorist crimes, and in particular of those who were very young at the time of the conviction or who had served most of their sentences. This text was later modified at our suggestion to read that action along these lines should be taken 'if a substantial and major reduction in violence was sustained over a period of months.' A year, it was felt, would be too long to be effective.

The British side proposed, and we agreed, that this measure should emerge in the parliamentary debate on the agreement rather than being announced at the summit meeting, but as it happened the Secretary of State did not use this text in his reply to the debate in the House of Commons, because of concern lest hostile Unionist reaction to the agreement might be further aggravated. We—unwisely, I think in retrospect—did not press the issue at the time, although I raised it with Margaret Thatcher shortly afterwards. Something along these lines was said later by Nick Scott in the House of Commons, but, this statement not being associated directly with the agreement around the time of signature, its impact was lost.

The introduction of mixed courts for terrorist offences on a reciprocal North-South basis had been a subject of contention since early in the year, when indications of a positive British attitude on this issue had evaporated following Lord Lowry's objections. At the 9 July meeting, however, the British side confirmed that, as I had told Margaret Thatcher at Milan, a letter had been written to her on behalf of the higher judiciary saying that the Northern Ireland judiciary would do whatever Parliament wanted. Now we learnt that despite this letter British resistance to the proposal remained. The only actual objections raised were, first, that even if the three-judge court gave a single verdict, the public might suspect that one judge, possibly ours, had dissented, and second, that it would not be possible to find extra judges from the small Northern Ireland Senior Bar. The first objection seemed to us trivial and contrived, and the second appeared perverse, since we knew of a number of prominent Catholic QCs who were willing to serve in the Supreme Court but had been passed over.

This matter was discussed repeatedly in the Armstrong-Nally forum and also between the two Attorney Generals, when John Rogers suggested to Michael Havers that a solution might be to have a 'side document' with a commitment to joint courts, binding in honour but not in law, the modalities of the new court to be worked out by a committee. But no progress was made, and in early September we were disturbed by leaks to the press and by a claim by James Molyneaux that we had sought such an arrangement but were not getting it.

The mixed court issue was eventually dealt with by a provision in the agreement that the joint body would seek ways of securing public confidence in the administration of justice, considering among other things the possibility of mixed courts in both jurisdictions for the trial of certain offences.

The composition of the Northern Ireland judiciary was a particularly important issue. The existence of an evident disproportion between the number of Catholic and Protestant judges was at one stage challenged by the NIO, which named several 'Catholic' judges, one of whom, we had to point out, was a well-known member of the Synod of the Church of Ireland. The disproportion was then blamed by the NIO on Catholic QCs feeling that they could make more money as barristers while also being at less risk. We contested this, having established that a number of Catholic QCs of a calibre that in our view would be acceptable to the Lord Chancellor in a British context had been repeatedly passed over for senior judicial appointments.

The British later returned to this issue of the composition of the higher Courts, admitting their religious imbalance but saying that there were no vacancies. Our side at once refuted this, pointing to the British legislation under the provisions of which there *was* a vacancy in the High Court. When this was then admitted we were told that 'they said' that there was no case on the grounds of the work load for having an additional judge. But under pressure the British side agreed to take the matter back for further consideration.

Eleven days later Margaret Thatcher wrote to me about a number of issues in the negotiation, to which I shall return. In this letter she said she had just learnt that the Lord Chief Justice was on the point of writing to the Lord Chancellor to propose that in view of the pressure of work in the High Court, the so-far vacant sixth seat on the court should be filled by an early appointment! I had the clear impression that both the Cabinet Office and Foreign Office and some of the senior Ministers involved, including Margaret Thatcher herself, had been extremely unhappy with the situation that our probing had eventually revealed to them. When two weeks later Dick Spring and Peter Barry met Geoffrey Howe and Tom King in London, the latter said that there was no secret about the candidate proposed to fill this vacancy: the chairman of the Northern Ireland Bar Council, Michael Nicholson.

But while the desired appointment was then made, and a further Catholic judge was later appointed to the High Court, the only change in the crucial Court of Appeal, made after my Government left office, was the replacement of a retiring Catholic judge by a Protestant unionist barrister, thus producing for the first time in many years an all-Protestant and all-unionist Court of Appeal! This was the development that had been accurately forecast to us by senior Catholic legal circles in Belfast early in 1985. I had been unwilling to believe that a British government would ever allow this to happen, but happen it did, exactly as we had been told it would.

During the discussion of these issues the timing of the signing of the agreement had slipped considerably, eventually to 15 November. As to the venue for the signing, in mid-July on my suggestion we proposed the Royal Hospital in Kilmainham, Dublin, where the ceremony could have taken place very appositely, I thought, under the portraits of King William III and Queen Mary II. While Margaret Thatcher herself had no difficulty about a signing ceremony in Ireland—after all, my three summit meetings with her had all been held in England, and it was our turn—she felt that unionists might resent a signing in Dublin. This led to the suggestion that it take place in Hillsborough,

Co. Down, or Stormont, and the former was finally chosen, with Dromoland Castle in Co. Clare, near Shannon Airport, as an alternative. (A British team had visited this castle some days earlier, and full arrangements, including security precautions, had been made in case it should be required at a late stage.)

An issue that proved very difficult to resolve, absorbing a lot of time in the closing stages of the negotiations, was the location, staffing and method of operation of the Secretariat. Our considered views on this subject were put forward at the meeting of 7 July. We argued that the person heading the Secretariat on each side should have the necessary status to deal with senior officials in various departments in relation to Northern Ireland and that both of these officials should have the confidence of the two heads of government. The idea was put forward that two 'cabinets' on the Continental model be constituted, the members of which would work together and would include people who within their own administrations would have the status to act and speak with authority. We felt that the Irish team might be able to work more effectively if it faced an authoritative British team rather than having to interact amorphously with the whole of the Northern Ireland administration. At this stage, however, apparently under NIO influence, the British side seemed to envisage the Secretariat as merely a channel to the Northern Ireland Office, which would operate under the closest scrutiny of the Permanent Secretary of the NIO, rather than as a channel between the two governments that would cover also the responsibilities of other British government departments concerned with Northern Ireland. It was clear that the British had not got in mind at this point a Secretariat headed by a senior official on their side, nor had they contemplated, as we had, the possibility of the head of the Secretariat being drawn from the Foreign Office or Cabinet Office as distinct from the NIO.

At the following meeting we made the point that, given our experience over the previous fourteen years or so of frequent late-night telephone calls about problems in the North, the Secretariat would need to be available twenty-four hours a day and 365 days a year. We saw the Secretariat as a place within which problems would be defused, thus avoiding the need to call in the British Ambassador to make formal diplomatic approaches on issues as they arose.

I was very concerned with the tendency on the British side to minimise the role of the Secretariat, and I made it clear to our team that as the primary function of the proposed joint body, as I saw it, was to resolve differences, a crucially important vehicle for this would be the Joint Secretariat, although, of course, decisions on major issues would be taken by the Ministers in the joint body. Subsequently, in a bilateral discussion with the Permanent Secretary at the NIO, agreement was reached that the Secretariat would, in addition to its normal functions as regards the agenda, minutes etc. of the joint body, also be a channel of communication, but on the NIO side there was still an unwillingness to allow it to have a life of its own, with a decision-taking responsibility. For our part we believed that, at any rate as far as the Irish side was concerned, our head of the Secretariat should have something close to plenipotentiary powers. He should be a person of considerable seniority, operating through the Department of Foreign Affairs system.

At the 13 September meeting the NIO minimalist attitude was challenged from within the British delegation, the view being expressed that the Secretariat would be a gear-wheel in the system and that, a change of gear to a new system being a very difficult task, the British head of the Secretariat should be a person of weight. There was, it was suggested, an obvious analogy with delegates to organisations such as NATO and the WEU. The NIO said that they could not tear up the entire administrative system of Northern Ireland to accommodate the new arrival; but this drew the response from others on the British side that the administration of Northern Ireland would in future be very different, because in negotiating this agreement the British government would have decided that it would be different; the Secretariat and Conference would create an additional dimension for those who now administered the area. A real change was involved in the relations between the two governments, for which there was perhaps no precedent—certainly none in the Anglo-Irish relationship. History was being created as we went along. Both governments, having put their hands to it, were going to want to make the new system work to achieve the objectives set out in the agreement in the interests of peace and stability in Northern Ireland. The Secretariat would not just be note-takers: they would be applying their experience and rank to deal with problems and would have to represent themselves and each other in the decision-making process.

This very full statement of a considered British view of the role of the Secretariat eventually evoked from the Permanent Secretary of the NIO a personal commitment on behalf of his department to make the system work.

Nevertheless, when the new Northern Ireland Secretary, Tom King, who had replaced Douglas Hurd, came to Dublin to see Peter Barry and myself he expressed the hope that the new process could start in a low-key and measured way with a 'soft launch', and that there would not be a 'great Secretariat producing a massive programme', even though he accepted that the Secretariat was an important part of the new arrangement. Peter Barry replied that he understood what King meant by a 'soft launch', but that in attempting to secure a withdrawal of support from the Provisionals, particularly in west Belfast, it would be necessary that the Irish presence be visible.

Despite this, at the following Armstrong-Nally meeting an NIO representative said that he had been directed by the Secretary of State to say that he was very concerned in regard to the presentational impact of the Secretariat. The first couple of meetings of the joint body and the location of the Secretariat should not at the outset be in Northern Ireland but rather in London, leaving open the question of where they should be located after that.

This NIO intervention came as a bombshell, not merely to us but, it was clear, to other members of the British team. The whole agreement as it had emerged over such a long period clearly hinged on the role of the Secretariat and on its location at the centre of the administration of Northern Ireland in

Belfast, and this attempt to reopen this fundamental issue was, to say the least, maladroit. Even the official who had been given the task of communicating this to the two negotiating teams appeared most unhappy with his task, but he did his best to explain that the Secretary of State was worried about getting it under way if it were opposed by a wide body of Unionist opinion. Other members of the British delegation, however, clearly felt that the idea of starting the operation of the Secretariat in London was not practical: the action, as one of them said, was in Belfast. When in response to this Tom King's spokesman remarked that London and Belfast were no more than ten minutes apart, a member of the Irish side reminded him what Reggie Maudling was supposed to have said, that there was a time difference between them of 287 years. It was agreed that the British side would reflect further.

At a later September session of the Armstrong-Nally discussions a fresh statement was made by the British side on their attitude to the location of the Secretariat. There was, they said, no doubt in their minds that the Secretariat would be in Belfast, and they were not reviving the proposal that it should start in London. The only issue was when it would happen. They felt that there should first be an assessment of reaction to the agreement in Northern Ireland, to ensure that the offices of the Secretariat did not become a focus for attack—although they would do their best to supply adequate security. The NIO view was that it would be a bad start if people had to be brought in by helicopter.

I had given firm instructions two days earlier that it was an absolute requirement that the Secretariat be in Belfast from the outset. Accordingly the Irish reaction to this was that it would be a great mistake to back off in the face of threats. It was important that whatever happened should happen on day 1. We would, of course, keep the Secretariat out of the public eye and play it low-key, but we should not make the mistake of locating it elsewhere than in Belfast from the outset. Doing it in two stages would do nothing except give two targets to fire at instead of one.

In the face of this the British side began to give ground, suggesting that perhaps the Secretariat could begin in Belfast with one Irish representative instead of a great Irish team marching in, and could then be built up gradually. We made it clear that there would be no question of having families present with officials at that stage, and this was seen by the British side as a great help.

Even as late as the meeting of the four Ministers on 6 November Tom King was quite negative, not only about the Secretariat but even about the first meeting of the joint body itself. He said he did not think that at the moment agreement could be reached on when the joint body should first meet or where the Secretariat should be located.

And when Peter Barry again stressed the importance of the Secretariat being present in Belfast from day 1 if this aspect were to have any impact on the nationalist minority in Northern Ireland, Tom King, infuriatingly, went back once again to the question of what the Secretariat would actually be doing. With whom would it be in contact? And how it would do business? These matters had of course all been settled during the previous discussions, as was pointed out.

He then tried a new tack, remarking that some State Department people who had been in Northern Ireland recently and had seen everyone had said that the one real thing that was getting the Unionists excited was the Secretariat. The way to neuter Unionist pressure was to remove it. There were already plans for picketing. The Secretariat would in effect have to be in a bunker.

Geoffrey Howe intervened at that point to say that if there were a comparable range of Anglo-French problems and they judged that it needed a continuous consultation arrangement they would not think twice about establishing an Anglo-French tourist office or operations office or travel office. He could see the need for some such thing here, and all practical considerations pointed to having such a place, to which we also attached importance. When Tom King said that if our side of the Secretariat were beleaguered and had to be protected heavily by the RUC and helicoptered in and out, this would not be quite the new voice for the minority that we had hoped for, Geoffrey Howe demurred at this picture, saying that this involved making assumptions with regard to the scale of protests that might not be justified.

After this long and inconclusive discussion, and with the proposed signing date of the agreement barely a week away, I wrote to Margaret Thatcher to summarise our position as it had evolved and to stress the urgency of speedily finding a solution to the intergovernmental differences on the issue. I told her we regarded it as essential that all meetings of the Inter-Governmental Conference (as the joint body had now been named) be held in Belfast, that the Secretariat be located in offices at Stormont from the first meeting of the Conference onwards, that offices and residential accommodation be secure and adequate, and that the two heads of the Secretariat be officials of a rank compatible with the importance to both of us of this agreement and be selected as people in whom each of us had special confidence. I went on to say that any temporising about the implementation of the Secretariat on this basis would be seen as weakness and could create the risk that our two governments would be back in the situation of May 1974, when an important and promising political effort had been damaged by divided counsels and constant hesitations. There were some difficulties that simply must be faced by both of us—and this was one.

I told her also that we envisaged that the Irish side of the Secretariat would comprise three senior officials and two posts at secretarial level. There was no question of family members being involved at that stage. And I concluded by saying that on both sides we were now approaching fundamental decisions about whether to proceed or not with what was now before us. It was only right that I should let her know in complete frankness that so far as we were concerned it was essential that clear understandings be reached now in relation to the matters addressed in my letter and that these understandings be implemented in full from the beginning. I hoped that we would have reassurance on these matters when the final Armstrong-Nally meeting took place on 12 November.

This firm communication evoked a positive response from Margaret Thatcher four days later. In her reply she said that she agreed that the Inter-Governmental Conference should normally meet in Belfast, while not precluding an occasional meeting in London or Dublin if that were convenient, and that there should be a Secretariat with British and Irish co-secretaries serving the Conference on a continual basis. Since the Conference would normally meet in Belfast it was sensible that the Secretariat should be there as well. While they remained of the view that it would be preferable not to hold the first meeting of the Conference in Belfast, in view of the strength of my feelings on this they were prepared to agree that it should be held there, probably about a fortnight after the exchange of notifications had brought the agreement into effect.

With regard to siting the Conference and the Secretariat in a permanent location, she said there was simply no room to house them in Stormont House or Stormont Castle. But they had identified an existing government building close to Stormont that could provide accommodation at a proper standard for the Conference and Secretariat, office accommodation for both sides of the Secretariat, and residential accommodation for the Irish side, in a position that could be made reasonably secure. This would facilitate rapid and easy communication between the two Secretaries, who would be the normal channel of contact, as well as easy access to the NIO and Northern Ireland departments when it was necessary for other officials to be involved. Until this building could be ready they would have to make the best temporary arrangements they could, and hoped that we would be able during this time to keep to an absolute minimum the number of officials that needed to be in Belfast on a continuing basis.

As for the two heads of the Secretariat, she agreed that both should be of a rank compatible with the importance of the agreement, although the British Secretary would still be less highly graded than ours but would nonetheless be a senior official of proven calibre and competence in whom Geoffrey Howe, Tom King and herself had confidence.

This communication brought the long saga of the Secretariat to a satisfactory conclusion.

Another issue that was not settled until a very late stage—the end of October—was the name of the joint body. Various possible titles were debated during the long negotiation, including 'committee' and 'commission'. The Irish side saw 'committee' as too minimalist a title, submitting a fascinating and semi-humorous memorandum on the use of this term in Ireland and the way in which it had been made a butt of ridicule in a television satire programme of the 1970s. The British on the other hand were unhappy with 'commission', because of its resonance on the European scene. During October the two sides gradually came to the conclusion that the word 'conference' would be preferable to either of these, and this was incorporated in the drafts of the agreement from 30 October onwards.

A matter that absorbed much of the time of the Armstrong-Nally group during the last four months of the negotiations was the international impact of the agreement and the development of the international fund to be financed by the United States, certain Commonwealth countries, and perhaps members of the European Community. While both sides wanted to maximise international support for the agreement, the impetus on this issue came mainly from the Irish.

The NIO was notably and persistently unenthusiastic about the fund, tending to view it as a reflection on their performance in Northern Ireland. Other members of the British team were, however, strongly supportive, although we were aware of a certain reticence on Margaret Thatcher's part. Her initial reaction to the idea had been to try to mobilise public support for voluntary donations in the United States rather than look for official aid; and because of her continuing efforts to cut back the EC budget she was also extremely sensitive about approaching the European Community for support.

There was also sensitivity on the British side lest the provision of official aid by the United States be interpreted as a bribe by the Americans to Britain to enter into the agreement—a reaction to Enoch Powell's conspiracy theory about Northern Ireland. We were able to counter this by pointing out that since 1977 we had secured support from successive US Presidents for the idea of aid if significant progress were made towards peace in the North. The NIO objections that there might be a problem about spending such a fund productively were met from within the British delegation by the comment that 'even the Treasury would not look a gift horse in the mouth'!

In mid-July there was agreement that my well-received approaches in May to the US and Canadian governments, and in the margin of the Milan summit meeting to almost all the EC heads of government, be supplemented by British approaches to France, Germany, and Australia. At the 21 July Armstrong-Nally meeting Seán Donlon was able to report on his recent visit to Washington. He told his colleagues that the principle of a fund to back up US support for the agreement seemed to be accepted both on Capitol Hill and in the administration. This was confirmed by the State Department. As regards the amount the United States might contribute to the fund, he had not been able to get very far, but reference had been made on a number of occasions to the Cyprus precedent, involving $250 million, and his contacts on Capitol Hill did not seem to be frightened by that figure, or even by a larger one. As to timing, any time up to mid-October would be possible; thereafter the US budgetary timetable would create problems.

It was agreed eventually that the task of getting Ronald Reagan and Tip O'Neill together to discuss the issue should be undertaken by Seán Donlon in the last week in September, when he would be in the United States in connection with Peter Barry's attendance at the UN General Assembly. An additional line of communication would be through Bill Clark, who had helped us in December and who, although no longer having a major post in Washington, continued to have an office in the White House. During a visit to Ireland the previous week he had met both Douglas Hurd and myself and had gone back convinced that there was a need for a fund, and intending to pursue the matter with the President.

When the British suggested that the President would want the issue 'staffed' (i.e. prepared by his officials), Michael Lillis replied that this would not be the case: the President and Tip O'Neill 'were two old Irishmen simply getting together on a political issue.'

When Seán Donlon talked to Tip O'Neill in New York at the end of September the Speaker said that he was meeting George Schultz on 1 October and would discuss the matter with him on that occasion, and would raise it a week or so later with the President at one of their regular breakfasts together. He would be quite happy to make a joint statement with the President.

On 30 September the question was raised of the message that Margaret Thatcher and myself might send to President Reagan about the agreement. Should it be a written message, or should we send emissaries? On the British side there was some reluctance about suggesting a draft text of a joint statement by the President and Speaker O'Neill, as they felt this would seem like teaching their grandmother how to suck eggs; but Seán Donlon made it clear that we were not so hesitant in providing drafts, for the reason that we had had some appalling experiences of what had happened when we didn't! Later I personally briefed Tip O'Neill on the situation. Margaret Thatcher also mentioned the agreement to the President during a short meeting she had had with him, and he had made it clear that he would welcome the agreement, but it did not appear that the financial side had been discussed between them.

For our part we were clear that the administration now thought that if we were ready, the time was right for a formal joint approach to them. Tip O'Neill would like to have things sewn up with the President well before the summit meeting with Gorbachev on 19–20 November; he thought it would be very unfair to the President to distract his attention with other matters close to that meeting. All this seemed to point to the need for a visit by representatives of the two governments—Robert Armstrong and Seán Donlon—very shortly before the signing of the agreement. Meanwhile, at an informal meeting of EC Foreign Ministers in Luxembourg on 26–27 October, Peter Barry and Geoffrey Howe had mentioned the agreement to their colleagues and had sought political support. They had been pleased with the reaction; but the question of the fund had not been mentioned, because of reluctance on Geoffrey Howe's part to raise the issue. Further briefing of members of the Community would be undertaken by the British; we had already briefed our ambassadors in European capitals, and they would now be asked to seek political support.

The visit by Robert Armstrong and Seán Donlon to the United States took place in the first week in November, and it achieved its objective. It was agreed that a joint statement would be issued by the President and Speaker immediately after the announcement of the agreement, and steps were taken to initiate American support for the international fund. Approaches to the various EC countries by us also evoked similar positive responses, but in these cases British reticence on the fund prevented this matter being raised by us jointly with our EC partners.

At the final Armstrong-Nally meeting on 12 November the question arose of further briefing in the United States following the signing of the agreement. It transpired that the British proposed to send Nick Scott to the United States to 'sell' the agreement there. While we had great respect for Nick Scott, whom we had always found to be very positive in respect of Northern Ireland, we were concerned lest a briefing by him directed in part at least towards Irish-Americans might prove counterproductive: past experience had shown that Irish-American opinion tended to react negatively to English Ministers, simply because they were English. With this in mind we decided to send Michael Noonan to the United States on the day the agreement was signed, so that he could undertake briefings on our behalf, directed particularly towards the Irish-American community.

All developments in connection with the agreement had of course been monitored continuously by the Northern Ireland Committee of our cabinet, and reports had been made to the Government at approximately monthly intervals. At the meeting on 19 September the Government had sought further information on political developments in Northern Ireland and in particular on the contacts we had been having with representatives of the different parties and other interests. A report on this was furnished to the meeting on 4 October. The Government were told that an important factor in assessing the current mood in Northern Ireland was that there had been widespread leaking by the British side about the progress achieved and the discussions taking place between the two governments. These leaks had included the possibility of some form of Irish presence in Belfast, of significant changes in the security area involving the RUC and UDR, and of proposals by us for a mixed court for trials of terrorist offences. The Government were also told that as Jim Molyneaux was a Privy Councillor it was very likely that the British government had kept him well informed on a Privy Council basis as the talks had progressed, and it added that numerous contacts we had had with members of the OUP and DUP had indicated that briefings of varying content had been given to a number of members of these two parties.

Paisley and Molyneaux had recently said that they concluded from a letter received from Margaret Thatcher on 13 September that British-Irish machinery for dealing with Northern Ireland was contemplated, and that they saw such proposals as clear infringements of British sovereignty. Justice dictated, they had gone on, that the people of Northern Ireland, either through their elected representatives or in some other appropriate manner, should be afforded the opportunity to accept or reject what the British government had negotiated before the agreed deal was finally struck.

In private discussion a leading DUP member had told us that they assumed the British government would try to sell an agreement to the unionists with the argument that it would help them to defeat the IRA, but this would not be enough to compensate for what unionists would see as an infringement of sovereignty. A leading member of the OUP had told us that their party would oppose any role for Dublin other than a minimal consultative one; if a Ministerial or official presence in Belfast were involved it would be very difficult for Unionists to see that as other than an infringement of sovereignty. Peter Robinson, the deputy leader of the DUP, had recently said publicly that he expected that unionists would be called upon to defy and oppose an Anglo-Irish Agreement, that an attempt to impose a settlement on them against their will would end in conflict with the security forces, and that they would not allow an Irish Government Secretariat to operate in Belfast. Jim Molyneaux had recently implied that the initial reaction of Unionists might be for some or all Westminster MPs to resign their seats and seek re-election on an anti-agreement platform.

It was, however, widely believed amongst serious observers, and among middle-class moderate unionists with whom we had been in touch, that the vast majority of the unionist population wanted peace and stability and would be prepared to accept a role for the Irish Government and some form of power-sharing for Northern nationalists if the result were to be peace in Northern Ireland. Some Unionist politicians had been more forthcoming and less belligerent in private than in public; but there was a danger that public bluster would encourage support for the loyalist paramilitaries. These, however, lacked the resources for a sustained military campaign, although they were capable of sectarian attacks and occasional bombings either within or outside Northern Ireland.

The appreciation of the situation contained in this memorandum was supplemented by a verbal briefing by me based on what we had earlier been told by the British side. Following an indication by the Irish side that we felt that there could be a case for briefing the Unionists, the British had then made the point that there was a great difference between the Unionists and the SDLP: the latter wanted the negotiations to succeed if the outcome were right in their view, but there was no similar guarantee as regards the Unionists. Our response to this had been that any briefing would require the use of judgement and discretion, but that if possible a situation should be devised where the Unionists could not say afterwards, 'Of course, if you had told us what was going on . . .' We had added that the British side might of course find, using their judgement, that it was better not to brief the Unionists, but it was the view of our Ministers that they should think about it.

To this the British had responded that they had in fact thought about it and that something had been given to Molyneaux in his role as Privy Councillor, but not to the DUP on the same scale, because of course Paisley was not a Privy Councillor. On the basis of that information and in the light of hints to us from some Unionist sources that public indignation against an agreement would be accompanied by a measure of private acquiescence, I offered a measure of reassurance to the members of the Government who were concerned about a possible Unionist political reaction, but at the same time I told them that the best information we had would suggest that there could be a significant violent backlash from paramilitaries on both sides.

In retrospect it became clear that we both overestimated the extent of the briefing that had been provided by the British to Molyneaux personally and underestimated his unwillingness to face realities—encouraged, we heard later, by Enoch Powell.

Our lack of direct contact, or even of contact through agreed intermediaries, with Jim Molyneaux in particular was a major factor in the misunderstandings that arose between the Unionist leadership and ourselves during the period of the negotiations. We were inhibited from such a contact by concern about the possible British reaction; but I doubt whether Molyneaux for his part would have welcomed an approach from us at that time.

After the signing of the agreement we were told that it had come as a great shock to him; that he had refused a Privy Council briefing; that his contacts with Enoch Powell and perhaps with a member of the British Cabinet had led him to believe that there would be no agreement or at any rate that there would be no agreement that did not include an amendment of articles 2 and 3; and that accordingly he had discounted all the media leaks. But at the time— given the information available to us about British contacts with him and with other leading unionists, the detailed leaks to the media from British government sources about the main features of the agreement, and comments to us by other leading unionists on various features of the agreement of which they were clearly aware—we believed that Jim Molyneaux 'knew the score'.

We expected the Unionist political reaction to be containable both in its intensity and its duration. Our fear, and, I believe, that of the British government, was of a renewal of violence on a substantial scale by Protestant paramilitaries and of intensification of IRA violence, a combination that in the immediate aftermath of the agreement might require a very determined response by both our governments. Preparations were made for this contingency. The paramilitary reaction turned out to be much less severe than we and the British had anticipated, whereas the Unionist political reaction was both more intense and longer-lasting than we had thought likely.

Until the eve of the signing of the agreement we remained uncertain also about the nature of the reaction to the agreement that we could expect from Northern nationalists. In providing a basis for the ending of nationalist alienation and for the acceptance by them of the institutional and security structure in Northern Ireland, the form the agreement eventually took was less helpful than we had originally hoped. Although John Hume had been fully supportive throughout the negotiation, as had Eddie McGrady and Joe Hendron, Séamus Mallon had reserved his position, while maintaining total confidentiality about our discussions. His stance left open the possibility that at the end of the day he might oppose, or at least criticise strongly, the content of the agreement when it was announced. It was only on the Monday before the signing that we received his considered reaction.

That evening Dick Spring, Peter Barry and myself met the four SDLP leaders at dinner in Iveagh House, together with some of our key civil service negotiators. Following some detailed discussion of British intentions in relation to the UDR and the action we proposed to take in regard to ratification and implementation of the Convention on the Suppression of Terrorism, John Hume told us that the main features of the agreement had been presented to and discussed at a long party meeting the previous Wednesday—one of the most successful for a long time. It had been agreed there that the party would ask the public to study the agreement in detail and not to react impetuously. At this point Séamus Mallon intervened to make a personal statement. There were things about the agreement that he liked and things he didn't like; in his public comments on the agreement he would be mentioning both. His concerns were concentrated on the areas of justice, the UDR, and extradition. This was not a criticism of the Government: he would not say anything critical about the position of the Government in a personal way. His point of departure was the position of his party on these particular issues. He added that he had thought very long about his own position: he had indeed had six months of hell on the issue. Two considerations brought him to acknowledge that we now had the machinery to work towards his party's objectives as regards security in Northern Ireland: the manner in which John Hume had presented the issue at the party meeting on Wednesday, and his own concern not to do anything to split the party.

In response to this I said that when I had first met Margaret Thatcher as leader of the opposition it had been clear to me that, if I could persuade her to address the problem of Northern Ireland, she had the qualities necessary to do something serious about the North and to stand by anything agreed, and that I had then made up my mind to make an all-out effort to influence her in that direction. What had emerged fell short of our aspirations, and in signing this agreement the Government realised that it was taking a considerable risk—as, of course, was the SDLP in supporting it. But within the agreement there was the potential for much more progress. Even if we failed I had no doubt that it had been worth trying.

To this in turn Séamus Mallon responded emotionally, in terms that went well beyond his initial somewhat reserved statement. He said that this was one of the most moving moments he had ever experienced. He would go beyond that: he would like to make it absolutely clear that he personally and his party would put their shoulder to the wheel and that I as Taoiseach, and Peter Barry as Irish permanent member of the Conference, would not find him wanting; nor would those who took on the dangerous business of serving the Secretariat. John Hume and he thanked me for taking the SDLP leadership into our confidence during the negotiations. Both Séamus and I, and indeed others present, were deeply moved during this emotional exchange.

As we had been approaching the final stages in the negotiation I had had to address the question of how the agreement should be presented. Given what had happened at Margaret Thatcher's press conference a year earlier, it was natural that this loomed large in everybody's mind. With the best will in the world there was a danger that the difference in our respective orientations—Margaret Thatcher almost exclusively towards the unionists and I primarily, but not exclusively, towards the nationalists—and in our manner of address might disturb, perhaps even seismically, the common ground involved in the agreement. What the two of us said and how we said it on the occasion of the signing—and even more so in our replies to questions at the press conference—was therefore a matter of joint concern. It would be easy enough to prepare our respective speeches for the occasion and to check them with one another to make sure they were compatible; the problem lay much more with the answering of questions. Towards this end, therefore, the two teams applied their minds during the last six weeks of the negotiation, preparing a 'catechism' for Margaret Thatcher and myself that eventually turned into a 7,000-word document containing sixty questions and answers with which we were both supposed to familiarise ourselves, so that whatever question might be asked our responses would be couched in the same language—if not always necessarily in the same tone of voice!

I do not know what Margaret Thatcher thought about this, but I must say I found it rather nerve-racking, never having been much good at learning things off by heart. Nevertheless, while I was certainly not word-perfect on the day, and I doubt that she was either, the exercise of formulating common responses to such a wide range of questions proved very useful and, I am sure, helped us to avoid many traps on this demanding occasion.

As I listened to the news on the evening of Thursday 14 November I heard of unionist crowds gathering at Hillsborough, which they had identified as the location for the signing of the agreement. This raised the question of whether we should bring into effect our contingency plan for using Dromoland Castle. At ten o'clock that night I rang Dermot Nally to say that I thought that in view of what was happening at Hillsborough we should raise with the British the question of whether this fall-back procedure should be put into effect. He rang me back shortly afterwards, however, to say that the British believed they could contain the situation at Hillsborough and did not wish for a change of plan. Accordingly next morning we took off for Aldergrove Airport, Belfast, where we changed to helicopters to fly to Hillsborough.

Margaret Thatcher and I had an hour together before the lunch that preceded the signing of the agreement and the press conference. When in the course of our preliminary conversation I told her that we would be designating Peter Barry as the permanent Irish and Ministerial representative, and that he would have a heavy work load, she interrupted to say good-humouredly that Foreign Secretaries were not overworked: they spent half their time travelling to and from meetings; they could halve the number of their meetings and do twice the work at each of them and maintain the same results as now. As a former Minister for Foreign Affairs I rejected this description of Foreign Ministers' activities, suggesting instead that we could do with half the number of European Council meetings. She did not respond to this provocation; I knew that she enjoyed these meetings of heads of government.

She then asked Dermot Nally to think of the most difficult question she might be asked at the press conference, and asked Robert Armstrong to do the same thing for me. The two cabinet secretaries took us through the 'catechism', and we gave our answers on the status of Northern Ireland, the courts, what was in the agreement for unionists and nationalists, the issue of our Government having responsibility without power, security co-operation, secret agreements, the UDR, the judiciary, the RUC, devolution, the use of the word 'consultative' to describe the arrangements, a bill of rights, and so on. We both came through this trial in reasonably good shape, and then went off together to look at the room in which the press conference was to be held and to discuss detailed arrangements for it, after which we went to lunch.

When the moment for the signing came we walked together to the room in which the ceremony was to be held. Although this was presumably the largest room in the castle, it was much too small for the many media people, including a number of television crews, who had been brought there for the occasion without knowing at the time just where they were going. We went through the process of signing the documents, and made our speeches. There followed the question-and-answer session, which, after our intensive preparations, we survived reasonably well, I thought. Then, with a great sense of relief, we moved off to celebrate the occasion with a glass of champagne.

There is, I think, no record of what was said between Margaret Thatcher and myself on this very informal occasion, but two things stand out in my recollection. The first was her obvious deep upset at the news that the late Ian Gow had resigned in protest against the agreement. I knew that she had great respect for him, and this development came as a serious personal blow that for her cast a shadow over what otherwise should have been an occasion for some celebration.

The second point I recall is that I took this opportunity to raise with her the question of pursuing with our European partners the possibility of support for the international fund, a matter that up to that time had been raised only with the United States. I was taken aback by her reaction. 'More money for these people?' she said, waving her hand in the general direction of Northern Ireland. 'Look at their schools; look at their roads. Why should they have more money? I need that money for my people in England, who don't have anything like this.' I was frankly quite nonplussed at this singular declaration of English nationalism on an occasion when I had expected rather to have to cope with what had so often been described to me as her 'unionism'. When I sought to press the matter further I came up against another obstacle. She made it clear that she feared that any approach to EC countries for contributions to the fund might in some way undermine her case for economies in the EC budget, a case that she was urging strongly at that time at meetings of the European Council.

Some eighteen months later I found myself as an opposition backbencher at an interparliamentary meeting in London, still pressing for action on the matter. In response to a question from me Geoffrey Howe told the Irish parliamentarians, with some embarrassment, I felt, that if the Irish Government wanted to look for money for Northern Ireland from the European Community we could do so on our own. This seemed a somewhat curious position to be taken up by a British government that was insistent on the maintenance of its sovereignty over Northern Ireland.

However, some two years after the agreement was signed a relatively small amount of EC money was at last secured for the fund, to supplement the major contribution from the United States and smaller contributions from several Commonwealth countries. The opportunity to secure substantial support that I had opened up in my contacts with the other EC heads of government had been lost as a result of the British Prime Minister's preoccupation with holding down the Community budget, which was in fact irrelevant to my proposal.

Within two weeks of signature the agreement had been approved by both parliaments, despite the opposition of Fianna Fáil under Charles Haughey, which to me at least was not unexpected. The negative character of that party's opposition during the 1982–87 Government on so many issues, and Charles Haughey's handling of the situation at the ending of the New Ireland Forum, had led me to expect that Fianna Fáil would vote against the agreement— although in view of the remarkable scale of public support for it this was, I think, a political mistake on their part. I calculated, however, that if, as I intended, we remained in power until early 1987, sufficient time would by then have elapsed for him to effect, as public opinion demanded, the necessary U-turn on the issue that would secure the survival of the agreement if, as seemed likely, the Government changed at that point.

In the British Parliament the opposition was minuscule: only twenty-one right-wing Tories and a small number of left-wing Labour members voted against the agreement. This reflected to a significant degree the hard work put in by our London embassy during the previous two years, and in particular by our counsellor there, Richard Ryan (whose work in this area I mentioned in an earlier chapter). With his delightful Korean wife he had charmed many members of the Conservative Party into a more positive attitude towards the agreement than they might have adopted if left to themselves. As a result, when in the autumn of 1985 the Conservative Whips came to make an assessment of the likely reaction of their party to an Anglo-Irish agreement of the kind then con-templated, they found a much more positive reaction than would have been the case had the issue arisen a year or two earlier.

Eighteen days after the signature of the agreement Margaret Thatcher and I met in the margin of the European Council meeting in Brussels. It was clear from her demeanour and what she had to say on this occasion that she had been shaken by the Unionist reaction, which she described as 'much worse than expected'. She felt that I had had all the glory and she had had all the prob-lems. I agreed with her that we must take steps to detach moderate unionists from the stance of the more extreme elements, and told her that I had already met two groups of unionists who had come to Dublin and had been encouraged by their attitude on what I had said to them. 'But they will not speak—they dare not speak,' she replied.

There must, she went on, be visible action on security. When could we ratify the Convention on the Suppression of Terrorism? The Unionists were angry, she said, that we had not gone ahead with the possibility of constitutional change in the Republic—from which she and Douglas Hurd had headed me off a year earlier! There must be political action, and convictions of more IRA men. I told her that if there was evidence against anybody, there were channels through which it could be communicated, and action would be taken.

She jumped around from point to point, saying at first we must do something about the unionists, and then commenting that a meeting between the Garda Síochána and the RUC the previous day had gone very well. Then she asked again when we would follow up with action on the Convention on the Suppression of Terrorism. She sprang from this to the Inter-Governmental Conference, saying that unionists would be furious if the Conference met in Stormont; Aldergrove was the only possible place, or perhaps London. On this she would have to take the advice of the security people.

I demurred at this, but did not pursue the matter at this point, as she was so agitated. Instead I pointed out that the by-elections precipitated by the resignations of the Westminster Unionists could provide an opportunity for changes to appear in concrete form on the ground. In Armagh Séamus Mallon could well succeed in being elected (and was), and the SDLP could also possibly win a seat in South Down (they did so in the 1987 general election). And turning back to the Convention on the Suppression of Terrorism, I said we were looking at the question of the order in which we should act: signing the convention first and then legislating, or the other way around.

Reverting to the internal situation in Northern Ireland she asked, what about John Hume? He had made an excellent speech in the Commons debate (I knew she had congratulated him on it), but what we needed was action. He had said that the SDLP would sit down and talk about devolution—could anything happen there? I said I would be meeting a delegation of the SDLP later in the week, quietly and without publicity. I would talk to them and see what they thought. They were, however, a party in their own right and must make up their own minds.

She then jumped in to change the subject again. She had been told she was treacherous and had betrayed the unionists. She must reassure them, and fast, she said. After the by-elections what would happen? Up to now they had been acting constitutionally; would there then be strikes and violence? Could I think of amending articles 2 and 3? 'You've got the glory and I've got the problems,' she again complained. Her own Parliamentary Secretary, Ian Gow, had resigned; some of her party would go over to Northern Ireland and campaign in the by-elections for the Unionists. She recognised that there was nothing the Unionists could bring down on this occasion, but she was deeply upset about the 'betrayal' charges.

Part of the problem was that unionists would hear only what they wanted to hear. It was no good saying things with an English voice: Irish voices must come in and help. They had heard it being said that this was the nearest thing we could get towards joint authority; however, she supposed on reflection that this showed that we had not got joint authority. I responded that it was notable that nobody in the South had said, 'This is a step towards a united Ireland.' Over a three-day debate in the Dáil nobody had said that. There was no triumphalism.

Turning to Charles Powell she asked, 'Could we use that? We should go through the debates and see if anything emerged . . . But then'—thinking aloud—'they would say that "you don't need to say anything about a united Ireland because it is all in the Constitution."'

I pointed out that we now had a position where between two-thirds and three-quarters of the people in the South openly supported the agreement, with its assurance on the status of Northern Ireland. At this she admitted that she had been only too relieved that the unionists had reacted constitutionally; there had been no strikes and no bombs. She seemed to calm down somewhat at this stage.

I then raised the question of the passage that had been agreed during the negotiations for inclusion in the speech by Tom King at the end of the debate in the House of Commons, in which he would indicate the possibility of a review of sentences for prisoners if there were a sustained period of reduced violence after the agreement. This had not been used in the debate. 'That would be dynamite—no, not dynamite, nuclear,' she replied. They could not think of a review for people guilty of bombing, murder, and other atrocities. Support for Sinn Féin was falling, I replied; if we could work on the families we could develop this trend. It was the only way ultimately to stop them.

'I have to look to those by-elections,' she responded. The agreement had already caused a visible swing from Sinn Féin towards the SDLP, I replied. This, after all, had been one of its main purposes.

Molyneaux and Enoch were leading the 'treachery and betrayal' charge, she said. They claimed the SDLP had known everything and the Unionists nothing. We must now let the Unionists know what was going on, and we must involve them. What about a parliamentary report every three months on the decisions of the Inter-Governmental Conference? Charles Powell intervened at once to say, 'You cannot talk about decisions. The Conference doesn't take decisions.'

But the Unionists had to be involved in some way, she said. I agreed that some system involving consultation with them seemed desirable, and asked her what she had had in mind in this respect in what she had said in a recent letter to the Alliance Party leader, John Cushnahan. Time, however, did not permit a full reply by her to this question; she simply said that they would have to consider how to consult the Unionists, and we then turned to the question of what we would say to the press.

It had certainly not been a particularly useful meeting, but I felt by the end of it that she had calmed down somewhat. But four hours later, while we were still at the European Council, a row broke out over unfortunate remarks made by Tom King at a lunch in Brussels. He had said that they had now signed an agreement in which the Prime Minister of the Republic of Ireland, notwith-standing the fact that he had to live with a constitution containing aspirations about sovereignty over Northern Ireland, had in fact accepted that for all practical purposes and in perpetuity there never would be a united Ireland.

This off-the-cuff statement was apparently a very loose version of what he had been proposing to say in a speech that night. I immediately challenged his remarks as inaccurate, inappropriate, and a mistake. The row took some time to die down.

Meanwhile the Secretariat had moved into Maryfield—the building that the British government had identified as a possible seat of the Joint Secretariat—under fairly uncomfortable conditions, and on 11 December the first meeting of the Conference was held in Belfast, as we had recommended all along. Three Ministers attended on each side, as did the Chief Constable of the RUC and the Commissioner of the Garda Síochána. Thus, less than four weeks after the signing of the agreement the structure it established was in place and operating as we had intended.

Maryfield was an office-block that had to be converted for the purpose, and the work had not been completed when this purpose became known, at which point all activity on the site stopped. The result was that the conditions in which Michael Lillis, whom I had appointed as the first Irish Secretary to the Conference, and his small team found themselves in mid-December were fairly primitive. They were not only working in monastic seclusion but also dwelling in conditions of some asceticism. The location of Maryfield, beside the Palace Barracks in Holywood, offered a measure of security, but in the early days in particular there was a good deal of tension, with mobs at times gathered out-side the gates and movement to and from the building very hazardous. Despite this an effective work pattern was quickly established in conjunction with the British Secretariat team, and over time, as conditions improved, contacts with the Northern Ireland administration gradually developed in a constructive way.

Before summarising the achievements of the new structure during the course of 1986 I should mention one issue in particular in respect of which we failed to achieve our objective. Because of the British reluctance to agree to the estab-lishment of mixed courts as part of the agreement itself, and clear indications that there would be strong opposition to the establishment of such courts in the immediate aftermath of the agreement, we decided to seek as a second-best the establishment of three-man courts within Northern Ireland, to be manned by Northern judges exclusively. It seemed to us at the time that this would bypass objections that had been made to the idea of mixed or joint courts on grounds of 'sovereignty', which we ourselves had always rejected. Since the introduction of the three-man Special Criminal Court in Dublin during the

Second World War, and subsequently during periods of IRA violence, we had found that such multi-judge courts worked effectively, the multiplicity of judges helping to avoid some of the dangers that could arise if a single judge were to seek to carry out all the functions of a jury as well as his normal judicial duties.

As no problems had ever arisen with the decision-taking mechanism under which majority verdicts are presented as single verdicts of the Special Criminal Court, we did not envisage any serious objection on the British side to a constructive reform of the Northern Ireland 'Diplock' (no-jury) courts along these lines. What we had not fully grasped was the extent to which *any* change in the court system in Northern Ireland was viewed by Lord Chief Justice Lowry as an unacceptable criticism of how these courts had operated in the past; it gradually transpired that on this account a three-man court of Northern Ireland judges would be just as unacceptable to him as a three-man court with a Southern judge (an arrangement that would of course have been reciprocated with a Northern judge on the three-man Special Criminal Court in our state).

We pursued this matter during the summer of 1986. As the months passed we were told repeatedly by British Ministers and civil servants that the difficulty in the way of accepting our proposal lay with Lord Chief Justice Lowry and the Lord Chancellor, Lord Hailsham; Margaret Thatcher, we were told, had a relatively open mind on the issue but was unhappy at the thought of overruling the Lord Chancellor on a matter of this kind. The question finally came up for decision at a Cabinet subcommittee meeting on 2 October 1986; but despite the reported support at that meeting of Sir Geoffrey Howe, Douglas Hurd, and Tom King, our efforts to persuade the British government of the need to effect this reform, which would have helped us in our difficult task of getting the extradition legislation through the Dáil in the autumn of that year, were unsuccessful.

Many other issues addressed through the Joint Secretariat during 1986 were settled satisfactorily, however. Thus, as a result of speedy action through the Secretariat many security 'flashpoints' were successfully resolved, and a major programme of change, both legislative and administrative, was carried through that was designed to remove or to mitigate many of the disadvantages under which the nationalist population in Northern Ireland had laboured, in some cases since 1920. The Flags and Emblems Act, which discriminated against the symbols of the nationalist minority, was repealed. Stricter criteria were established for decisions on the routing of controversial parades and marches. The law on incitement to hatred was strengthened. New and improved guidelines for fair employment were introduced, and there was a commitment to strengthen legislation in this area, which was later implemented. There were improvements in the representation of Catholics on a range of appointed bodies. Decisions were taken to demolish and progressively replace three nationalist ghettos—the Divis, Unity and Rossville Flats—decisions that had been sought for over a decade without success. And recognition was given to the use of Irish for place-names, which had been banned for some decades previously.

So far as the security forces were concerned, a Police Complaints Commission was established, and a document was published summarising complaints procedures in relation to the army. There was *some* progress, although nothing like what had been promised, in the accompaniment of the UDR by the RUC on patrols. And there was a notable reduction in complaints of harassment of the nationalist community by the security forces. Powers of arrest under the Emergency Powers Act became exercisable only on the basis of reasonable suspicion, and it was arranged that suspects could be held by the police on their own authority for only forty-eight hours, as against the previous seventy-two hours. Most important of all perhaps was the manner in which the RUC handled the Unionist demonstrations against the agreement, displaying by their firmness their capacity for even-handed action and the extent to which under the leadership of Jack Hermon the force had become non-political.

In relation to prisoners there were improvements in arrangements for parole and compassionate leave, and more sensitive handling of many individual cases without prejudice to the requirement of good order in prisons.

As far as the administration of justice was concerned there were a number of changes, including a shifting of the onus of proof to the prosecution in relation to bail applications. The statutory guidelines on the admissibility of confession evidence were revised to make clear that confessions obtained by the use of threats of violence were not admissible, and that confessions could be excluded in the interests of justice. A suspect in police custody became entitled to have a person outside informed of his or her arrest and whereabouts, and to have automatic access to a solicitor after forty-eight hours. And the waiting time for trial was reduced by the appointment of three additional judges and by an increase in the size of the Senior Bar, as well as by a new power for scheduled cases to be heard outside Belfast so as to ease the pressure on accommodation. The Secretary of State was also given power to set statutory time limits for the period between first remand and trial; and another new factor reducing the period between trial and appeal was the making available of transcripts of trials, delays in the provision of which in the past had been a cause of complaint. And a possibility of a reduction in the number of trials in 'Diplock' courts was created as a result of the power given to the Attorney General to certify more offences out of non-jury trial in specific cases.

A further significant result of the new process was the ending of the controversial 'supergrass' cases, which involved the joint trial of large numbers of suspects on the evidence of a single accessory. These trials had proved unsatisfactory: guilty verdicts in the court of first instance regularly had to be overturned on appeal. Now representations by the Irish Government through the Conference led to the cessation of this method of trial.

The above list—and it is no more than a list—illustrates two points: first, the range of issues that needed to be dealt with even after thirteen years of direct rule by Britain, and second, the extent to which the new Conference structure, backed up by the Secretariat, successfully handled an extraordinarily wide range of issues in its first year.

This book is not an appropriate place in which to recount these events in detail, or indeed to attempt to evaluate the working of the Conference or the Secretariat, beyond commenting that its early achievements during our last fifteen months in Government, with Michael Lillis in charge in Maryfield, have certainly been underestimated. The bitter and prolonged Unionist reaction to the agreement had one clear effect: it caused the British government to play down the activities of the Conference and Secretariat for fear of provoking the Unionists further. Perhaps mistakenly, we largely went along with this, because we shared this concern, and at the time the nationalist community were so delighted with the existence of the agreement that it seemed unnecessary for their further satisfaction to drive home its achievements. The result was that when this euphoria in the nationalist community wore off, as it inevitably did, the minority were left with no clear sense of the remarkable number of changes effected through its mechanisms, and as a result the longer-run impact of the agreement among nationalists was much less than we had intended, although it was clearly sufficient to consolidate the drop in IRA support that had begun while it was under negotiation.

One other point should perhaps be made in conclusion. Early in 1986 I was approached by intermediaries who were concerned to bring the Unionists back from their campaign of protest to constructive discussion of the issues involved. In response to suggestions put to me I indicated my willingness to arrange an interval of several months between meetings of the Conference, so as to create a window of opportunity for discussions involving the Unionist parties. Unhappily this opportunity was 'blown' in early April when Peter Robinson said publicly that I was reasonable but that Margaret Thatcher was intransigent. Such a statement created the risk that the Prime Minister might conclude that I was undermining her firm position on the agreement, and accordingly these contacts had to be allowed to lapse. Had Peter Robinson not made his unfortunate public comment, the consequences of which he did not himself realise, as I later learnt, some kind of talks might perhaps have got under way in 1986 on how the 1985 agreement might be 'transcended'—a word that I was, I believe, the first to employ to describe the process by which the dynamic created by the agreement might in time lead to a new accord that would bring into the consensus the two groups not involved in the 1985 agreement, the Unionists and Fianna Fáil. As I write these words, talks designed to achieve such an outcome have taken place but, for the time being at least, have broken down. I hope and believe that they will be resumed in due course and brought ultimately to a successful conclusion as now seems to be the wish of a majority of both communities in Northern Ireland.

# CHAPTER EIGHTEEN

# LAST LAP OVERSEAS

The relationship with the United States is of course as important for Ireland as for other countries, with, however, an additional dimension in the Irish case. Almost from the time that violence broke out in Northern Ireland in 1969 we had been faced with a problem of support for the IRA amongst certain elements of the Irish-American community, a support that was not merely financial but also involved at times significant flows of arms and ammunition. Since 1972 successive Governments had, therefore, put a considerable effort into tackling this problem by direct contact with Irish-American groups and also with legislators of Irish extraction and other members of Congress, some of whom, in the hope of maximising the Irish-American vote in their constituencies, felt it appropriate to offer support to IRA-front organisations. These efforts had been substantially successful: we had reason to believe that by the early 1980s the financial flow had been considerably reduced, and arms shipments had become more sporadic, partly because of action by American law enforcement agencies working closely with us and with the British government.

Since 1977, active support had also been given by leading members of Congress to the Irish Governments' campaign against the IRA, and in that year the Government of the day had moreover secured an offer of aid from President Carter in the event that violence ended in Northern Ireland. It was important to sustain the momentum of these efforts, and this required that I and other Ministers visit the United States to keep up the pressure against the IRA-front organisations.

Now, however, there was to be a further reason for close contact with the US administration; for with the establishment of the New Ireland Forum and the preparation for a negotiation with the British government, we needed to ensure as much sympathy and support for this policy as we could muster, including support from the President, who might at some point be helpful in influencing the British government in a positive direction. Moreover, if the negotiation were successful we would want to 'cash the cheque' that Carter had drawn in 1977 by securing American aid in support of any agreement that might emerge. It was with this combination of reasons that I paid three visits to the United States during my term of office.

Before this, however, in 1983, Vice-President George Bush had visited Ireland on the occasion of the Fourth of July. I had met him several times previously in Washington. I was glad of the opportunity to bring to his attention some of our concerns, not only in relation to Northern Ireland but also to the then difficult position of the UNIFIL force in Lebanon. This visit also provided me with the opportunity to explain what I had had in mind in initiating the New Ireland Forum. In addition, we had a considerable discussion about US policy in Central America. From my previous period in Government I knew how sensitive the Americans were to our independent line on this issue, and I was not surprised that he raised it with me; as he told a questioner at a subsequent press conference, the United States and ourselves had some differences on the subject.

The first of my visits to America as Taoiseach took place in the week before St Patrick's Day in 1984. On this occasion there was an additional special factor involved: President Reagan had indicated an interest in coming to Ireland later in the year, and it was felt that a visit by me to Washington would be an appropriate preliminary to such a trip. Joan came with me, despite a gastric problem from which she had been suffering during the previous nine months, and Mark and Derval accompanied us so as to look after her while I was fulfilling various engagements in which she was not involved.

On 15 March I addressed a joint session of Congress; the invitation was a particular honour, since Liam Cosgrave had given such an address as recently as 1976. The next day, having in the meantime met Vice-President Bush and Secretary of State Schultz, I went to the White House to meet President Reagan. Our discussion was relatively short. I opened by explaining to him the policy I was pursuing in relation to Northern Ireland. I was not sure at the time to what extent he took my points, but from the manner in which he raised this issue with Margaret Thatcher during her visit to Washington nine months later it would appear that I must have made an impact. Reagan then turned the discussion to Central America and, speaking from notes on cards, developed the American position at some length. This confirmed my impression that the Americans were quite concerned about our position on this question. We were in fact more critical of their stance than were most western European countries—an approach that reflected the sensitisation of Irish public opinion by the reports of Irish missionaries in the area.

At lunch Joan was seated at the President's table between Tip O'Neill and Reagan. She had been feeling particularly ill that morning, and I was very concerned about her as I watched her from the table where I was seated with Nancy Reagan. Her discomfort was evident, although some of it I found afterwards was due to the fact that almost the sole topic of conversation at the President's table was American football.

Early in June that year Reagan came on his visit to Ireland. It was a difficult occasion, owing to the extreme unpopularity of his Central American policy. There were protests against his visit; the main one was in Galway, but the Gardaí and protesters reached an amicable agreement on where the demonstration would be located, and the whole matter was handled in a very civilised way.

Another problem for me in relation to this visit arose from the tradition that in the absence of any official method of honouring distinguished guests (Ireland is almost unique in having no order to confer on such occasions) it had been the practice for the National University to offer an honorary degree to such visitors. For the previous decade I had been a member of the Senate of the NUI, and when I received a phone call from the registrar to tell me that it was suggested that I might invite the university to confer an honorary degree on the President, I felt I must respond positively. This became a highly controversial issue, for the proposal was then presented as if I had been its initiator and had thus imposed a controversial nomination on the university. At the time I was obviously in no position to clarify the misunderstanding.

We guessed that in the Dáil there would also be a protest walk-out by the Workers' Party members, and when I met a senior American diplomat at a Bilderberg meeting in Stockholm some time before the visit I told him to forewarn the President of this, and pinpointed the part of the Dáil chamber from which the protest would, I thought, come—as come it did.

All these problems, together with the ever-present security risk, made the visit rather nerve-racking.

The state dinner in honour of the Reagans, offered by President and Mrs Hillery, was held in Dublin Castle. As the guests arrived Joan and I were first in the receiving line, with the task of introducing them to the Reagans. We were quite unaware of the fact that this part of the occasion was being televised with the aid of a microphone quite close to us. As a result, Joan's introduction of the guests to the Reagans—she is much more adept at this kind of thing than I am—was clearly audible to the television audience, and the aplomb with which she introduced each guest and explained who they were to the President and Nancy Reagan caused a great impression. She almost took the place inadvertently of the television commentator, our friend and UCD colleague Brian Farrell.

I had to draft my speech for this occasion with particular care. On the one hand it was clearly important to show every courtesy to our visitor and as far as possible to avoid contentious areas, but on the other hand I would be expected by many people in Ireland to make some reference to our unhappiness with American policy in Central America. As was appropriate, I devoted a significant part of my speech to the report of the New Ireland Forum, which had been published just five weeks earlier. I also referred to east-west relations, commenting that as a small country with a nightmare past we were more deeply concerned than most at the violent tyranny that tore apart small countries like Afghanistan and at the repression that sought to still the powerful instinct for freedom in eastern European countries like Poland, as well as at the deprivation of human rights in so many countries in Latin America. Our people had, I said, close emotional ties with many of these latter countries through the work of our priests and nuns and lay helpers there, who sought to relieve the poverty of the people and to give them back their dignity, of which they had been deprived by repressive regimes. And our people's deep concern was that these problems be resolved peacefully by the people of the regions themselves—in Central America, along the lines proposed by the Contadora countries.

I was able to add that many people in Ireland had been most heartened by the news of Secretary Schultz's visit to Nicaragua on the previous Friday, and I expressed the hope that this might lead to the restoration of normal relations between that small country and the United States, thus enhancing the climate for peace and democracy in that troubled region.

After the dinner George Schultz commented to me that it had been an interesting speech, and asked several times for a copy, but I did not feel that serious offence had been taken at what I had said; while on the other hand the prominence I had given to the issue evoked a warm telegram from Bishop Casey of Galway, one of the main critics of American policy in this area.

After dinner I asked Joan how she had got along with the President. She told me that she had talked to him about Central America and nuclear weapons, which she felt was an appropriate response to the discussion on American football she had been faced with in the White House three months earlier.

In May 1985 I paid another visit to the United States, and this time also to Canada. In New York I had a meeting with Cardinal O'Connor, which I found particularly difficult. I had met him with some other American bishops when they visited Ireland some time previously, and I had been unhappy with the discussion we then had about Northern Ireland. On this occasion in New York our discussion was even more difficult. I had hoped to persuade him to share my view of the IRA and its activities, but he seemed to see the conflict in Northern Ireland in much more traditional Irish-American terms, to a degree that I frankly found exasperating. I think it was probably the most contentious meeting I had with anyone outside Ireland during the course of my years as Minister for Foreign Affairs and Taoiseach; and one of our officials who accompanied me remarked later that he had never previously attended a meeting like it.

The visit to Ottawa by contrast was a success. In the course of my discussions with Brian Mulroney I found him genuinely interested in the Northern Ireland problem and supportive of the idea of an international fund, if it were established in conjunction with the agreement that I hoped would emerge later in the year.

My third visit to the United States as Taoiseach was in March 1986, when I once again visited New York and Washington as well as attending a St Patrick's Eve dinner in Scranton, Pennsylvania, which I found much more enjoyable than similar functions in the major cities. On St Patrick's Day I called on President Reagan and had a brief discussion with him; but the principal feature of the visit was our attendance at the farewell dinner in honour of Tip O'Neill on the occasion of his retirement as Speaker of the House of Representatives. Apart from the Irish party, which also included John Hume, this was an entirely domestic American occasion: it would, I think, be impossible to visualise the head of government of any other country being invited to participate in such a function, at which, with the President and Senator Ted Kennedy—as well, of course, as Tip O'Neill himself—I was one of the four speakers.

During my period as Taoiseach we were on the receiving end of a number of other state visits, including those of President Cossiga of Italy, the King and Queen of Spain, the Crown Prince and Princess (now Emperor and Empress) of Japan, and the President of Israel and Mrs Herzog. On the whole I enjoyed these affairs, which provided a certain amount of relief from the normal run of political life. Some tension attached to the Herzog visit, however, because of the problems posed for our UNIFIL contingent in Lebanon by the activities of the Israeli forces and the south Lebanon militia that they organised and financed. But the President himself, with his Irish background (he was brought up in Dublin, where his father had been Chief Rabbi), was a pleasant guest, by whom I was entertained to lunch in 1990 when I visited Israel in the course of preparing a report on the Israeli-Palestinian issue for the Trilateral Commission.

Most of my involvement in foreign affairs as Taoiseach was, however, in the context of the European Community. In addition to routine participation in the European Council meetings two or three times a year, at the outset of my second term I had to play a role in seeking and securing special treatment for Ireland in relation to the milk superlevy, which had been threatened since 1981. And during the third Irish Presidency, in the second half of 1984, I had to play a part in removing the final obstacles in the way of enlargement of the Community to include Spain and Portugal, and in getting under way the process that led a year later to the Single European Act. Moreover, the final stage of the negotiation of that Act absorbed some of my attention in 1985 in parallel with the completion of work on the Anglo-Irish Agreement.

The negotiation on the milk superlevy at European Council level dominated the meeting of heads of government in 1983 and early 1984. I had already had to deal with this issue at an embryonic stage of its development in 1981, when I had sought support from President Mitterrand for special treatment for Ireland. At the end of 1982 I found that the superlevy proposal had hardened considerably in the interval; and so had the pessimism in our civil service about our capacity to secure special treatment. A number of other countries were also seeking such special treatment, I was told—some, indeed, for opposite reasons to ours. We were not the only milk-exporting country that was claiming a right to be exempted in some measure from production limitations; but Italy and Greece, as *importing* countries, were making an inverse claim to ours, seeking to increase their production as a move towards greater self-sufficiency in milk. And any solution designed to protect traditional farms against the 'factory farms' that were responsible for much of the milk surplus would be resisted by the Netherlands and Denmark. There were thus so many special cases and vested interests that our officials believed we had little chance of securing unique treatment for Ireland. To adopt a high profile on such a claim would, they thought, be to invite a politically damaging defeat at the end of the day.

I thus found myself in a position closely similar to that in which I had been as Minister for Foreign Affairs in 1976 in relation to fish quotas, when I had rejected the cautious advice of civil servants, protective as ever of their political boss, whom they did not want to see 'hung out to dry'. And the fact that I had been right in sticking my neck out in 1976 over fish quotas did not convince them that I would be right in taking this risk once again in relation to milk. Lightning might not strike twice in the same place.

However, supported by Austin Deasy, who never wanted to flinch from a fight, I rejected this advice and launched a high-profile campaign with the aim of securing for Ireland exemption from—or, more probably in the outcome, special treatment within—the proposed milk quota and superlevy regime.

But before coming to the milk negotiation I should perhaps refer to some lighter aspects of the European Councils of that period.

The German Presidency of the first half of 1983, which started just after we returned to office, involved two European Councils. The first of these was held in Brussels, and the second in Stuttgart. The Mayor of Stuttgart was Field-Marshal Rommel's son, whom we met at luncheon. At dinner that evening Helmut Kohl entertained us with an account of the various plots against Hitler, including that of July 1944, in which Field-Marshal Rommel had been implicated. He described Rommel's fate: the call by the SS at his home, and the choice offered him—of going into the nearest forest and shooting himself, in which event his wife and son would be spared, or alternatively the execution of all three of them—and Rommel's subsequent forest suicide. We were all somewhat taken aback when the silence that followed this dénouement was broken by Margaret Thatcher saying, 'I thought he died in a car accident' (the story the Nazis had propagated at the time).

This relaxed discussion after dinner was unusual: normally aspects of world affairs were discussed on these occasions; sometimes issues of nuclear policy. I recall, however, being entertained by one head of government's evaluation of the European and American Catholic hierarchy's attitudes to nuclear weapons. He saw the American bishops as 'unsound' (i.e. anti-nuclear), whereas the NATO bishops were seen in a more favourable light following some meeting of the European hierarchies in Rome at which they must have shown greater tolerance of nuclear armaments.

I was, indeed, surprised at the number of occasions on which religion was touched on in informal discussions such as at luncheons on these occasions— whether it was an Italian head of government telling humorous stories about the Vatican or, as I recall happened at luncheon at Fontainebleau, Margaret Thatcher being teased about the Catholic Church. On that occasion I heard Ruud Lubbers, the Dutch Prime Minister, telling her that no-one in the Netherlands went to Confession any longer. She seemed quite shocked, and, turning to Peter Barry, sought reassurance: 'But in Ireland I'm sure people still go.' Peter did not miss the chance to disconcert her further. 'Nobody except some old people go to Confession in Ireland now,' he replied—something of an exaggeration. 'Really,' she responded, 'I *am* surprised. When I lived in Grantham as a child they were always running in and out of the Catholic church near our house.'

On a more serious note, I was irritated by the way in which some heads of government at times dismissed texts on foreign policy issues that had been most carefully prepared by their Foreign Ministers. When these were raised, often at the end of an admittedly long meeting, one or other head of government would say, 'Oh, we haven't had time to consider these texts; we can't deal with them here.'

At the Stuttgart meeting this did not happen, however. There was a text on Central America before us that was quite a radical one by diplomatic standards. It declared that growing tensions in the area could be eliminated only by peaceful means, and that efforts towards this end should be guided by the principles of self-determination, sovereignty, non-interference, territorial integrity, and inviolability of frontiers. Moreover, it went on, the Ten fully supported the initiative of the Contadora Group. While all this may sound fairly banal, the language was not that which the US administration would have wanted to hear from the Community countries, and was clearly designed to distinguish the European position from that of the United States. I doubted if it would get past Margaret Thatcher and Helmut Kohl, who were always particularly concerned to avoid disagreements with the Americans.

At the end of the meeting, however, when the participants were about to leave the table, Lubbers proposed the adoption of this text. I seconded it at once, and Wilfrid Martens, the Belgian Prime Minister, supported us. These interventions, all in English, which took less than ten seconds, were, I think, lost on Margaret Thatcher, who was absorbed in putting papers away and did not seem to hear them. In the absence of any objections from her, Helmut Kohl in the chair, unwilling perhaps to reopen debate at such a late stage, accepted our proposal, and this text thus became, and remained thereafter, the official position of the Ten—to the annoyance of Margaret Thatcher, it was said.

A major issue at this Stuttgart European Council in June was the financial situation of the Community. It was clear that the Community's 'own resources', limited at that time to a maximum of 1 per cent of member-states' VAT, would be insufficient for its needs from 1984 onwards. A decision to increase this limit, which required unanimity amongst member-states, would, however, not be agreed by Britain, Germany and the Netherlands unless economies were accepted, especially in the financing of the Common Agriculture Policy, where growing surpluses, especially of milk, were imposing an unsustainable burden. Britain also made its agreement to any increase in own resources conditional upon agreement on what it described as 'budgetary imbalances', i.e. Britain's net contribution to the budget.

The unyielding and combative manner in which Margaret Thatcher approached her problem at this meeting created a very negative reaction from her partners towards her and her advisers. During one break in a restricted session I was on the far side of the room when Hans-Dietrich Genscher, talking to some of our colleagues near a window, began to shout. I went across and asked him what was wrong. 'It's all his fault,' he replied, pointing to Geoffrey Howe's seat beside Margaret Thatcher, momentarily occupied by Michael Butler, one of her advisers. 'What's he doing there? He has no right to be there. *He* is the problem: giving her bad advice.'

It was decided to review these three interlinked issues with a view to resolving them at the Athens European Council in December. By the autumn it was clear that the major role of milk surpluses in the growth of CAP expenditure was raising again in an acute form the superlevy issue that had first surfaced several years earlier. This threatened the continued expansion of our dairy industry, an expansion that we had always seen as the largest single potential advantage to Ireland deriving from membership of the Community.

I believed that our best approach was to communicate to our partners the unique importance of the dairy sector in our economy. With Austin Deasy and officials of the Department of Agriculture I prepared a memorandum and had it circulated by the Council Secretariat. This memorandum quantified the contribution to our economy of the dairy industry, including the multiplier effect of the spending by farmers of their income from dairying. We estimated this contribution to represent no less than 9 per cent of GNP and to account for 10 per cent of employment and exports. In other words dairying was as important to our economy as oil and gas were to the UK, oil, gas and chemicals to the Netherlands, and the automobile, textile and non-ferrous mineral industries to Germany. The share of the dairy industry in our GNP was five times the Community average for this sector and two-and-a-half times greater than that of any other member-state. At the same time the productivity of the Irish dairy industry, although it had improved since we had gained access to continental EC markets, was still only 60 per cent that of other dairy areas in the Community. The imposition of a superlevy on increased output would deprive Ireland of the opportunity of benefiting from its natural advantage in this sector in accordance with the basic principles of the Common Market.

To back up our case, and to ensure that heads of other governments would be fully apprised of it, I visited between the end of October and early December the capitals of other member-states, meeting the heads of all governments in the Community.

Following a visit to Athens (Greece held the Presidency of the Council) I was able to arrange separate meetings with the three Benelux Prime Ministers in the margin of a Christian Democrat meeting in Brussels on Saturday 26 November; I flew to Copenhagen two days later; and on the following Thursday and Friday I met Chancellor Kohl, President Mitterrand and Prime Minister Craxi in their capitals, returning to Ireland for the second inauguration of

President Hillery on the Saturday morning before flying to Athens that evening for the European Council.

My most fruitful discussions were with Helmut Kohl and President Mitterrand. I had already spoken briefly to the German Chancellor at the Christian Democrat meeting in Brussels a few days earlier, and he had then indicated his full recognition of our special problem. He now repeated this to me, saying that Germany would have no difficulty in accommodating our position with regard to the superlevy; but he asked me not to use this information. (At the subsequent European Council meetings he was in fact supportive of our position, without sticking his neck out too obviously; there were others who were also claiming special treatment whom he had no wish to alienate.)

This having been cleared at the start of our meeting, we then had a wide-ranging discussion, beginning with the general prospects for the Athens Council with its tangle of unresolved and interrelated problems, including German reunification. He had no illusions about the negative attitudes of many member-states to this issue; it must, therefore, be approached under a European umbrella. This was why Germany needed the Community more than others, and regarded its contribution as a payment in advance for the future. When I probed his thinking about the east-west situation he stressed the Soviet Union's economic difficulties, which were forcing it to turn inwards, and its growing problems with its minorities. The Soviet Union's grip on eastern Europe was no longer as tight as it had been; the Polish virus was beginning to work. I expressed concern that the Soviet Union's failures in agriculture, the population's desire for higher living standards and the minority problems might lead to instability on a scale that could disturb the military. This must concern us. So must the isolation of the United States from the opinions of its allies, whom it was unwilling to listen to or consult, thus leading to US actions in Grenada or Central America, for example, with which most European leaders were very unhappy. The trouble with the United States, he responded, was that it had the wisest constitution in the world—except for one thing: the method of election and the powers of its President.

I have given some details of part of this discussion because it is relevant to subsequent events; Kohl's thoughts on east-west relations have largely been validated by what has happened since.

That evening I met President Mitterrand in the Élysée Palace. My earlier discussion with him in December 1981 had clearly made an impact; he appreciated intellectually the objective strength of our case in relation to milk, and he promised his support for special treatment for Ireland. He was as good as his word. At Athens and at the subsequent Brussels European Council he not merely supported me but himself presented our case to the others, making it his own. Given the strength of the French dairy lobby, this was a remarkably generous gesture, which clearly surprised and puzzled the other heads of government.

My final port of call was Rome, where my case was received by Bettino Craxi with some reticence. Italy, after all, was pressing for special treatment so as to become more self-sufficient by *reducing* imports from countries like Ireland.

At the Athens European Council I pointed out that, even in the modified form that seemed now to be emerging, the impact of the superlevy on our economy would be about four to five times greater than what the UK had described as an 'unacceptable situation' for them, namely their budgetary contribution. Clearly no Irish Government could accept such a proposal. Accordingly I would have no alternative but to declare that the proposal was unacceptable and that a vital Irish national interest was involved.

An overnight Greek Presidency compromise offered some improvement on what had hitherto been proposed in relation to Italy and ourselves, but it was clear that there was no disposition on the part of other countries to accept this, and in the circumstances it seemed wise not to commit ourselves to a proposition that was going to fail.

When it became clear that there could be no agreement on the issue at Athens I commented that a fundamental error had been the failure to tackle in good time what was a market problem by market mechanisms—i.e. through the price system—and the resultant decision to try to stop the rot belatedly by an essentially arbitrary mechanism of quantitative restrictions that was incompatible with the most fundamental principles of the Community. I am not sure that if the logic of my argument had been accepted Irish farmers would have cheered; I suspect they would prefer higher prices for a frozen market share to an expanding market share at lower prices that would eventually squeeze out inefficient German farmers in particular. But there was no danger that my theoretical approach would be adopted at that stage, and by basing our position on this ideologically solid ground I converted our plea for special treatment into an argument of principle, the logic of which could not be refuted. This was where the high ground lay.

The Agriculture Council on the eve of the Brussels European Council meeting of 19–20 March agreed a general reduction of 1983 milk output by 5.3 per cent in 1984/85 and 6.3 per cent in the four subsequent years, but our position remained outstanding in this proposal; the Agriculture Council recognised that our case was a special one, which could be decided only by the European Council.

But, despite vocal support from France and less vocal support from Germany, at this European Council Britain and the Netherlands were obdurate, refusing agreement to a proposal that we be permitted to increase production by 5 per cent in 1984/85 rather than reducing it with the others, and that a review be undertaken of the level of Irish output that would be exempted from the superlevy in future years in the light of the milk situation and taking account of the possibilities being offered by the market. The only concession Margaret Thatcher made in the course of this discussion was to allow Geoffrey Howe to express British opposition in gentler terms than she would herself have been likely to employ.

Faced with this obduracy by our opponents I decided, without premeditation, to leave the meeting. I did not, as was later alleged, 'slam the door'; the door of the Council chamber is self-closing, and it closed itself quietly. I simply went to my office in the building and stayed there during the remaining hours of the meeting, issuing no statements, so that the other members of the Council were left guessing for some time whether my departure was temporary or whether I was going to absent myself for the rest of the meeting. I asked Peter Barry to remain, however, so that he could make it clear that I was maintaining our general reserve and, in the event of accord being reached amongst the others, so that he could withhold our agreement on all other issues.

This action dramatised our problem and created a climate in which the French Presidency was able to seek a compromise solution in the days that followed. This emerged from discussions at two subsequent Agriculture Council meetings and telephone conversations I had with Gaston Thorn, President of the Commission, and Michel Rocard on behalf of the French Presidency. The eventual agreement gave an average reduction of 7 per cent on 1983 production for the other countries (although Italy and Luxembourg were allowed to hold their 1983 level) and an increase in our case of 4.63 per cent; in other words we ended up with a 12.5 per cent advantage vis-à-vis the rest of the Community, being the only country to be allowed to increase output. In addition we got a commitment that we would have priority in relation to any increases in the quota that might take place in subsequent years if production in other countries were reduced as a result of the impact of the quota system on their dairy industries—a provision that never came into play, however, because of the somewhat perverse manner in which the superlevy worked, encouraging countries to produce to the maximum as well as adding an artificial element to the value of every dairy farm in the Community.

I should perhaps add that our achievement, concerning which the *Irish Times* commented that it was difficult to see how Ireland could have done better, left bruised feelings in some other member-governments. I was told at the time that our success had been achieved at a considerable cost; it would be held against us by some of our partners in our future relations with them. I did not take this too seriously, however; in international relations tempers soon cool and irritation quickly fades as new issues emerge involving new alignments between states.

With the milk issue out of the way the scene was set for the Fontainebleau European Council of 25–26 June 1984, at which the Presidency would be passed on to us. We were deeply concerned about the resolution of the British 'budgetary imbalance' problem, but fortunately a solution was found at Fontainebleau, involving a climb-down by the British in relation to the sum agreed while nonetheless giving them substantial financial relief. Unhappily, however, an ambiguity in the wording of the agreement subsequently gave rise to dispute about a supplementary budget by 1984 that we had to resolve in the months that followed.

At this Fontainebleau meeting President Mitterrand identified the principal tasks that Ireland would have to tackle in our Presidency as the conclusion of the third Lomé Convention (we had already successfully concluded and signed the first two such agreements); the achievement of agreement on enlargement of the Community by the inclusion of Spain and Portugal; the securing of a consensus on the nomination of the next President of the Commission; and the initiation of a process of strengthening the Community by establishing two committees of representatives of heads of government to look at, in one case, progress towards European union through changes in the Community's institutional structure and, in the other, progress towards a 'Europe of the Citizens' that would make the Community more meaningful to ordinary people.

Helmut Kohl spoke in support of the proposal for an Institutional Affairs Committee. We needed for this purpose, he said, a 'top-notch group' of imaginative and inspirational people who should produce for the European Council a written report identifying the weaknesses of the Community's present structure. The Belgians, Danes and Dutch also favoured a committee of the kind President Mitterrand had in mind.

Margaret Thatcher was less forthcoming. She had, she said, just fought a European election on the issue of honouring the treaties, with, however, a right to insist on discussions continuing until agreement was reached: in other words, the practice that had been followed since the issue of qualified majority voting had been challenged by France in 1965. Britain would join the working party, but, the Prime Minister said, in relation to this matter she was bound by her electoral programme.

Both the nomination of the new President of the Commission and the establishment of the two committees were clearly going to be matters of considerable delicacy. There were five known candidates for this Presidency; if views on who should be appointed to the post hardened into a serious division we could face a very difficult problem, and if we stumbled in our attempts to resolve it other countries, I knew, would be happy to pin on us responsibility for the resultant difficulties. As to the committees, and in particular the proposed Institutional Affairs Committee, the vague mandate given at the European Council, together with the indications there of possible conflicting views on the role and composition of this committee, suggested that on this matter also we could have a rough ride.

I had been reflecting on the chairmanship of the two ad hoc committees. The Committee on Institutional Affairs, as it soon came to be described in order to distinguish it from the Committee on 'Europe of the Citizens', was clearly of great potential importance, and if I were to ensure that it went in the direction I hoped it would—mainly towards a much more integrated Community that would not, however, at this stage have defence implications—it was desirable that its chairman should be Irish. I had no difficulty in deciding who this should be: Jim Dooge, who had won the respect of his Community colleagues during his brief six months as Minister for Foreign Affairs in 1981–82.

On Wednesday 11 July I embarked on a series of phone calls to other heads of government in connection with the Presidency of the Commission and the establishment of the committees. These preliminary phone calls revealed that most countries, even those that themselves had candidates in play, would accept a strong candidate from France or Germany for the Commission Presidency if such a person were on offer, Delors and Genscher being names mentioned by one head of government as 'strong candidates'. In each case I mentioned my intention to nominate Jim Dooge to the Institutional Affairs Committee and his availability to serve as chairman of that committee.

However, Margaret Thatcher expressed astonishment that the Germans should abdicate their 'turn', and concern lest there be a Franco-German deal to impose a French candidate. She pressed Etienne Davignon's candidature, remarking, however, that Franz Andriessen was also an effective Commissioner. She accepted that Jacques Delors was a strong candidate, but he should not take precedence over Davignon; and Claude Cheysson would be quite unacceptable. I told her I would ring her again on the issue when I heard from the Germans, and went on to discuss with her the two committees, mentioning Jim Dooge as our representative on the Institutional Affairs Committee and his availability to preside over it. She agreed that the membership of this committee should consist of politicians, not civil servants.

I followed this up that afternoon with letters to the various heads of government setting out proposed terms of reference for the two committees. I also formally proposed in these letters that Jim Dooge chair the Committee on Institutional Affairs for the duration of its work, and said that I envisaged that the members of the committee would be people of high political standing. With regard to the 'Europe of the Citizens' Committee I suggested that people of the highest rank associated with the administration of each country rather than politicians could appropriately be nominated, but that the chairman should be a person of European standing who would keep in direct contact with the President in office.

Some of the responses to my letter about the two committees suggested variations in the terms of reference that we had proposed; arguments about this dragged on until September. But on 20 July Margaret Thatcher wrote to me welcoming my suggestion that Jim Dooge chair the Institutional Affairs Committee, and going on indeed to suggest that, with a view to ensuring that the two committees made interim reports to the next European Council in December, it would be very appropriate if we also undertook the chairmanship of the 'Europe of the Citizens' Committee, which I had not proposed and did not think would be welcome to all our partners.

Meanwhile, when it had become clear that there was no German candidate for the Commission Presidency I had gone back to my colleagues on this question. In view of the expressed willingness of the smaller member-states (with some reluctance in the case of Belgium) to accept a strong candidate from one of the larger states, and on the other hand the reticence of several countries in respect of Claude Cheysson's nomination, I presented to them the name of Jacques Delors, and received agreement in each case. Margaret Thatcher took some convincing, arguing that the French had had the Presidency already, that the Secretary-General of the Commission was also French, and that Stevie Davignon of Belgium deserved to be promoted from membership of the Commission to its chairmanship in view of the effective way in which he had performed his duties—as indeed he had. Nevertheless she eventually rallied, subject to my clarifying that there was no question of a 'deal' having been done between the French and Germans to split the four-year term, as in practice it had come to be, between them—a clarification that Chancellor Kohl and President Mitterrand readily provided. Thus by 23 July the issue of the Presidency of the Commission had been resolved; and at a meeting of the Council of Ministers that day Peter Barry cleared with them Jim Dooge's chairmanship of the Institutional Affairs Committee, which I then announced in the course of my speech at the inaugural session of the new European Parliament two days later.

Shortly afterwards Jim Dooge's appointment provoked a reaction from the Germans. They told us that they wanted their former President, Karl Carstens, to chair the committee. This was an extraordinary development, given that Genscher had told me several weeks earlier that their representative on the committee would be the relatively junior Political Secretary of State in the Ministry of Foreign Affairs, that I had written to him confirming my suggestion of Jim Dooge as chairman, and that at the meeting of Foreign Ministers on 23 July this proposal had, I understood, been agreed. I told the Germans that I could not agree to their suggestion and that Jim Dooge's nomination as chairman stood. They reacted very negatively to this.

During August I had the opportunity of discussing this and other issues, first with Roland Dumas, the French Foreign Minister, after we arrived at the Fort of Bregançon on 21 August to spend ten days there at the invitation of President Mitterrand, and subsequently with the President himself when he came, together with Roland Dumas and his Prime Minister, Laurent Fabius, to dine with us there four days later. I was disconcerted when Dumas told me on the Tuesday that President Mitterrand had said to the Germans that he had no objection to Carstens; but when I raised this with the President on the following Saturday night he said there could be no question of going back on the decision with regard to Jim Dooge, but that it was important to try to find some way of conciliating the Germans, who had got themselves into a difficulty through their failure to find a suitable candidate for the Presidency of the Commission and then wished to retrieve this belatedly by finding some appropriate position for Carstens. However, in early September the Germans finally faced reality and accepted Jim Dooge's appointment.

Meanwhile we had had to deal with the problem created by Britain's refusal to countenance a supplementary budget to deal with the shortfall in the Community's receipts, pending the increase in own resources agreed at Fontainebleau. The British regarded the budget problem as solely due to overruns on expenditure, which should be met by spending cuts, mainly in the agriculture area, and by deferral of some spending to the following year, when the Community's own resources were due to be increased on the basis of the Fontainebleau agreement. This view had been rejected by the other member-states in mid-July in the Budget Council and the Foreign Affairs Council; and the atmosphere was not improved by a move a few days later by the European Parliament to withhold a refund of Britain's contributions that had been agreed at Fontaine-bleau unless Britain withdrew its opposition to the supplementary budget.

At the same time Germany was making the implementation of the increase in own resources conditional on enlargement being achieved, while France for its part was determined to hold up enlargement until controls on Italian wine production were imposed, which the Italians rejected—all this to the intense distress of the Spaniards and Portuguese, who were becoming increasingly impatient about the delays in the negotiations, which now appeared to be pre-judicing their proposed accession date of 1 January 1986. Everyone demanded that we disentangle this mess to their individual satisfaction.

On 27 July Gaston Thorn rang me to propose that I tackle the budget and own resources problem by seeing Helmut Kohl and Margaret Thatcher before the 5 September Budget Council meeting in Brussels. I decided to see Helmut Kohl on my way back from my French holiday, and to go to London a few days later to see Margaret Thatcher. This timetable would give me the opportunity to discuss the tangle first with Roland Dumas and President Mitterrand when I met them at Bregançon during my holiday there.

In that discussion President Mitterrand suggested that it would help with the British if we could get the Parliament to withdraw its veto on the British refund; he had already sought the support of the President of the Parliament, Pierre Pflimlin, on this. He added that he and Dumas were sceptical about getting the Germans to agree to increasing own resources in advance of enlargement, but they agreed that an attempt by me to achieve this might also help with the British. They reiterated the French position on wine, stressing that in their view the problem lay with the Italians.

The net outcome of my discussions with Helmut Kohl and Margaret Thatcher was a distinct softening in the British position. During the discussion with Margaret Thatcher there was a light moment when Jim O'Keeffe, our Minister for the Budget Council, sought to explain to her how he saw the situation. He compared the need for a supplementary budget to the situation when a thatched cottage was being built in Ireland: the roof was put on as soon as possible, to stop the rain getting into the structure so that work on the interior could proceed. She punctured his simile in a flash: 'And you're telling that to me, a Thatcher?'

At the Budget Council a couple of days later Jim O'Keeffe secured British agreement to a figure for the content of a supplementary budget, and a few days later he got the President of the Parliament's Budget Committee to agree that the British refund should be released once the supplementary budget had been transmitted to the Parliament.

Soon after this Felipe González came to Dublin to discuss the enlargement negotiation with me. In our tete-à-tete I sought flexibility from him in relation both to wine—where he was happy to rely on Italy to fight the battle against production limitations—and fish. But he was insistent that Spain would not accept discriminatory treatment of its fishing fleet, the depredations of which in the waters around our islands both the British and ourselves greatly feared. Spain accounted for one-eighth of world fish, he said, and fishing was a part of Spain's civilisation; any restriction on Spanish fishing would be incomprehensible to the people of Spain. I could see that this was going to be a difficult issue.

Four days later I paid an official visit to Portugal at the invitation of the Prime Minister, Mario Soares. My earlier visit during our first Presidency, in 1975, when the outcome of the Portuguese revolution had still lain in the balance, was remembered with great warmth—and earned me the Portuguese Order of Christ. The Portuguese were concerned lest a hitch in the Spanish negotiation would hold up, or even perhaps prevent, Portuguese membership— just as our membership application of 1961 had been shelved in January 1963 when de Gaulle had vetoed British entry. They therefore wanted a preliminary agreement that would mark the fact that their negotiation had been substantially successful. During the following weeks we secured the agreement of our partners to the signing of such a document. As soon as Soares learnt of this he asked for an immediate meeting to sign it, and a couple of days later, on 24 October, he visited Dublin for this purpose. The reaction in Portugal to the speed with which we had arranged the signature was very positive; one paper headed its report, 'The road to Europe passes through Dublin.'

Meanwhile the lack of progress on outstanding issues had led us to send Jim O'Keeffe on a tour of capitals in mid-October; this helped to secure agreement on a range of outstanding items, which narrowed the field of disagreement to two or three significant issues, including wine. By mid-November the crucial importance of wine to the negotiations had become even clearer. German proposals to deal with the wine surplus by means of a compulsory distillation of wine produced in excess of 100 million litres, which would involve price reductions of one-half or two-thirds on the wine surplus distilled, were rejected by Italy and Greece. Indeed these countries turned the tables on the Germans by pressing for a solution of which one element would be a financial penalty for the sugaring of wine that subsequently had to be distilled. (Producers in Germany and Luxembourg sugar some of their wines, because this artificially increases the quantity of drinkable wine.) Helmut Kohl, whose power base is in a wine-producing area, was shocked and furious at this counterproposal. Indeed, by the end of the third week in November the strength of the German stance on the question, combined with Kohl's obvious unhappiness with criticism by his CSU Bavarian rival, Franz-Josef Strauss, of German acceptance of the 1986 deadline for Spanish and Portuguese entry, which Strauss argued had weakened Germany's bargaining position, was leading some experienced Community officials to speculate whether Germany might not be having second thoughts about enlargement. Clearly we were in for a difficult time in the final two weeks before the European Council meeting, and possibly, if we failed to break the deadlock, at that meeting itself. And it was at precisely this moment that I had to face the domestic fall-out from Margaret Thatcher's post-Chequers press conference.

Meanwhile the Spaniards were getting upset at the position of the Irish delegation (as distinct from the Irish Presidency, for we had endeavoured to keep the two roles distinct) on fish. They could understand our concern to develop our fishing sector, but, they said, our human resource potential for this sector seemed limited. A Spanish fish enterprise in the west of Ireland that under the existing rules had to recruit 75 per cent of its labour in Ireland had, they claimed, found that 201 of 207 Irish workers had given up after two days. I could not help wondering what kind of conditions these employees had found when they had started work!

The final pre-Council meeting of Foreign Ministers took place on 26–28 November, just five days before the Dublin meeting of heads of government. It failed to resolve the crucial wine deadlock, on which the Germans and Italians remained obdurate, and Greece was furious with the UK for refusing to agree that funding for the Integrated Mediterranean Programme, involving substantial financial aid to Greece in compensation for losses expected as a result of Spanish and Portuguese membership, should be additional to normal Structural Fund money from the Community budget.

Reviewing this situation immediately after the end of the Foreign Affairs Council, I decided I would visit Paris and Rome at once with a view to working out a possible compromise on wine during the weekend before the European Council. Next day I met Mitterrand in Paris and also had a technical discussion with Roland Dumas, during which I tried out some ideas on how the Franco-Italian disagreement might be resolved. What I had in mind was a regional wine production limitation system to be implemented by national governments; the French had been unhappy about allowing such a system to be implemented at a regional level.

The French press comments after my visit were fairly downbeat. If my 'last ditch' efforts succeeded it would be a triumph for Irish diplomacy, they said, but they did not rate my chances highly.

Encouraged by Dumas's reaction to my proposals, however, I flew on to Rome, where next morning I had a meeting with Craxi, Andreotti, and the Agriculture Minister, Pandolfi, who were accompanied by a senior official, Renato Ruggiero. I found it difficult to pin the Ministers down, but from their reactions and Ruggiero's demeanour I judged that the proposals I had in mind might 'run'.

As it happened I knew Renato Ruggiero quite well. He had been George Thomson's chef de cabinet in Brussels during the sometimes acrimonious dispute I had had with George on regional policy in 1973–74. Moreover I recalled that I had then learnt that by a remarkable coincidence Ruggiero had got engaged to be married some thirty years earlier in the drawing-room of a house in Eglinton Road that we had subsequently purchased from an Italian in 1959. In the light of the discussion we had had I thought I stood a better chance of getting a sensible deal worked out with him than with his Ministers, so on leaving the meeting in Rome I lingered behind with him for a moment and got from him his home telephone number.

When I returned to Dublin my officials and I put together a concrete proposal, and on Saturday I rang Dumas and Ruggiero to tell them precisely what I would propose at the outset of the European Council. Receiving favourable reactions in principle from them, I suggested that when I turned to their delegations at the Council to ask them to react to what I was suggesting, their response should be a grudging agreement to look at my suggestion with a view to returning to it later, if the Germans and Luxembourgers meanwhile showed a willingness to compromise on the wine sugaring issue. Both Dumas and Ruggiero agreed to this tactic.

When on Monday morning the European Council turned its attention to enlargement, I put forward my compromise on wine and secured the desired responses from the French and Italians. Then I turned to the Germans and Luxembourgers, saying that there was an evident need to take a specific step in relation to wine sugaring that would ensure a contribution to reducing the cost of the Community's wine policy. My concrete proposals towards this end, which involved a version of what had already been tried out in the Foreign Affairs Council, were greeted by Helmut Kohl with undisguised hostility; he stuck to this line for most of the meeting, but agreement was eventually reached on a proposal designed to limit to some degree the cost of distilling German wine whose alcohol content had been increased by sugaring. And when we returned to the enlargement issue on the morning of the second day, the French and Italians accepted my compromise on production limitations, subject to some slight adjustments, as being a necessary step towards enlargement. The other, less difficult enlargement problems were handed back to the Council of Ministers to settle.

There was, however, a confrontation on the issue of the Integrated Mediterranean Programme, which Greece linked to enlargement; and Papandreou placed a reservation on the wine agreement (which Greece dropped shortly afterwards) and also on enlargement itself until this issue was resolved to their satisfaction. To this reservation I appended a statement, however, that negotiations would have to proceed on an *ad referendum* basis, i.e. subject to later confirmation, pending resolution of the Greek reservation. Although initially challenged, this was later accepted by Greece.

While negotiations with Spain on particular issues continued for several months thereafter before agreement was eventually reached—even on fish!—on the eve of the Brussels European Council in March, the turning point of the enlargement negotiation was undoubtedly the Dublin European Council meeting. In his report on the European Council to the Bundestag, Helmut Kohl told them that this meeting had taken important decisions in an unusually difficult situation; the Dutch described the Council as 'efficient and stimulating'; the Belgians congratulated us on an extremely skilful pursuit of a compromise; while the British commented on what they called our exceptionally skilful and highly proficient handling of the meeting.

But the aspect of this European Council in which I took most satisfaction was the agreement reached on proposals I put forward to deal with the Ethiopian and sub-Saharan famine. I had asked my colleagues to agree that the Community and its member-states should between them provide 1.2 million tonnes of grain and that it should at the same time appeal to other countries to bring this total up to 2 million tonnes, which was the aid agencies' estimate of the requirement for the years ahead. This was to be undertaken as part of a longer-term operation to combat drought. Aid on this scale was in fact provided in the months that followed, and, while there were some distribution problems, the famine was substantially alleviated by the action taken by the Community. In this connection I should, I think, mention that the issue of famine aid for Ethiopia had in fact first been raised at a European Council informally by Margaret Thatcher over dinner in Brussels nine months earlier; she had clearly been deeply moved by a television programme on the destitution and hunger of the populations involved.

The final act of our Presidency so far as I was concerned was my report to the European Parliament a week later. Hitherto reports to the Parliament after European Council meetings had been made by Foreign Ministers rather than heads of government, and my decision to attend in person and to answer questions was warmly welcomed. Having dealt with the contentious issues, I added that I had never liked the way the European Council was used as a kind of court of appeal from the Foreign Ministers' Council—a role that heads of government did not always fulfil very successfully. I would not, I added, apologise for having settled the wine problem 'on appeal' from the Foreign Ministers, but I was sorry that this had had to be done at such a high level.

I was able to tell the Parliament that, contrary to what had been suggested by some speakers during the debate, the European Council had in fact had a wide-ranging and constructive debate on an interim report received from the Dooge Committee, and would, I was convinced, have a really serious discussion on the final report at the June European Council meeting to be held in Milan, a judgement that was amply vindicated by subsequent events. I told them that I hoped a decision would be made at Milan to call an intergovernmental conference to implement the Dooge Report recommendations, which is in fact what happened.

On the eve of the March 1985 European Council in Brussels—indeed in the early hours of the day on which we met—the Foreign Affairs Council finally agreed the terms of the accession treaties for Spain and Portugal. What remained for the heads of government to do was to remove the obstacle of the Greek reservation, which derived from the unhappiness of the Greek government with the scale of compensatory aid proposed for that country in the form of its share of the Integrated Mediterranean Programme. This problem was eventually resolved after much heated debate. (Papandreou announced at one point that he had to leave early, at which Kohl exploded.) The way was thus cleared for enlargement and for the increase in own resources, to which the Germans had not been prepared to agree before enlargement.

In the months that followed there was intense diplomatic activity in relation to the proposal by a majority on the Dooge Committee, including Ireland, to call a conference that would amend the Rome Treaty so as to give effect to the report's main recommendations. The personal representative of Craxi on the committee, Mauro Ferri, visited all the capitals, and there were Kohl-Thatcher and Kohl-Mitterand meetings.

In discussion with Peter Barry at the end of May, Geoffrey Howe had said that he was wary and sceptical about the value of an intergovernmental conference, which he saw as a device for postponing substantive questions. Amending the treaty would, he felt, be extremely difficult, because this required unanimity amongst twelve countries. Britain would prefer a 'Milan Accord' on practical proposals to make the Community work better. It was clear that at that point the British were reasonably convinced that the conference idea would come to nothing.

Meanwhile I was concerned about reports that the Franco-German axis had been somewhat weakened following divergences between the two states in relation to non-EC matters. Britain was said to have been encouraged by these reported differences to intensify its opposition to the proposals for an intergovernmental conference. An Italian initiative, involving the circulation of a draft mandate for such a conference, had evoked a cool reaction, not merely from the three member-states that opposed the holding of a conference but also from France and Germany, which did not want the European Council to be pre-empted by discussions of this kind at Foreign Minister level in advance of the Milan meeting. The French were said to be perplexed by this Italian initiative, which they attributed to some requirement of Italian domestic politics.

Doubts continued to grow. A week or so before the Milan European Council I met some of my colleagues, including Helmut Kohl, at a European Christian Democrat meeting in Rome. I took the opportunity to have a bilateral meeting with Bettino Craxi, the Italian Prime Minister, who indicated to me that instead of convening the proposed conference at the Milan summit meeting it could be called at a later point, after the Foreign Ministers had reported to the European Council at the end of the year. I made it clear that we would react positively to an intergovernmental conference, although we felt it essential to create conditions first in which it could succeed.

My discussions in Rome took place during the state visit of President Chaim Herzog to Ireland, and I had to return home for the concluding part of his visit before flying to Paris to see President Mitterrand also. I found Mitterrand more sceptical than he had been earlier about the idea of a conference.

All the indications thus pointed towards a fudged result from Milan, with no decision being taken to call a conference, at any rate at that time. Thus the decision to hold a vote at the European Council on the convening of an intergovernmental conference came as a great surprise to most of the heads of government, and as a particular shock to the British. Why did it happen?

We were told subsequently that when Kohl returned from the European Christian Democrat conference in Rome he had decided, for party political reasons, to push after all for a qualitative change in Europe. He secured a measure of support from France (although Mitterrand was thought to have been unhappy about this development, as he could have lived with or without a conference). But Kohl failed to consult or to give notice to other heads of government, perhaps because he had not finally decided to take the crucial step. It has been suggested that this was decided only at the last moment, following pressure from the Italian Foreign Minister, Andreotti.

The first day of the conference was largely wasted. The Italian Presidency followed its predetermined scenario; and although Helmut Kohl spoke forcibly about the need for progress towards integration, others failed to grasp the possible significance of this. The British had proposals for the formalisation of Political Co-operation, which, however, they failed to put squarely before the meeting so as to focus discussion on them. We were happy about this, because a Franco-German text on this subject showed much greater sensitivity to our problems in the defence area.

Next day Kohl and Mitterrand cut short the discussion by formally proposing a vote on the calling of an intergovernmental conference. This caused evident astonishment all around the conference room. The meeting was interrupted to provide an opportunity for informal consultations. I was sitting immediately on the left of the Italian Presidency, and as I got up to speak to Craxi and Andreotti about this development others were doing likewise. Into the excited group that was beginning to form around the top of the table steamed Margaret Thatcher, coming from the far end of the room. As she approached, pushing her way through the crowd, she said to me something like, 'Garret, I hope you are going to oppose this. Remember our negotiation on Northern Ireland.' (A couple of hours earlier we had had our crucial meeting about the Anglo-Irish Agreement.)

When we returned to our seats the vote was taken. I had no hesitation in voting for the proposal with the six original members of the Community. Britain, Denmark and Greece voted against. Under the Rome Treaty the calling of a conference of this kind is a matter for a simple majority, so the Presidency declared that a decision had been taken to summon a conference. It was clear to me at the time that, because of the way in which discussions between member-states had gone in the weeks before the European Council, Margaret Thatcher in particular had been in no way prepared for this development, and felt that she had been tricked and trapped, as to some extent she had been.

I left the meeting exhilarated by this development and wondering what the outcome would be. Would a two-tier Community emerge from the impending conference? Or, given that the conference itself could take decisions to amend the Treaty only by unanimity, would anything at all emerge from it?

From our diplomatic contacts in the weeks that followed it was clear that even countries like the Netherlands, which were strongly in favour of amending

the Rome Treaty to achieve a greater measure of political and economic integration, were uncertain where the Community would be going from here.
Thus the Dutch Prime Minister, Ruud Lubbers, talking to the British, Danish
and Irish Ambassadors at a reception in the Hague a few days later, said that he
had hoped that the Milan meeting would take a decision on urgent and practical
measures on which there was general agreement, remitting to a subsequent
Council more ambitious and more contentious issues, but nothing of the kind
had happened, as a result of Helmut Kohl's hastily prepared plans and Margaret
Thatcher's bad tactics. And a couple of days later we were told by the Danes
that before the Council the British and French had worked out together a set
of proposals that could have been accepted at the Milan Council in relation to
the internal market, a technological Europe with certain minimal institutional
changes, and a formalisation of European Political Co-operation. But because
Helmut Kohl had spoken the day before in the Bundestag of Franco-German
agreed proposals—which, the Danes said, did not exist in detailed form at the
time—a Franco-German initiative, according to this Danish account, had to be
put together hastily, setting aside the agreement with the British.

The British view was that the Milan summit meeting had been a shambles:
the chemistry had gone wrong on the second day, and the Italian President
had, in their judgement, abandoned the role of chairman and sought to advance
an Italian interest in the calling of a conference instead of seeking consensus.
However—and this was significant—Britain did not rule out treaty amendments
if they were not extravagant but were prudent and carefully considered.

The fears that the conference would lead to the emergence of a two-tier
Community were without foundation. When the initial anger at the way they
had been taken by surprise died down, the British, together with the Danes and
Greeks, joined in the preparatory discussions. While little progress was made in
September and October, there was a clear concern all round to avoid further
confrontations of the kind that had occurred at Milan.

Our biggest concern was to advance the concept of cohesion as part of the
process of moving towards a single market. This technical term had come to
encapsulate the whole concept of measures designed to secure faster growth in
peripheral countries, which had a lower GNP per head, so that they might
gradually catch up with the more prosperous countries in the centre of the
Community. This concept had found its place in the preamble although not in
the body of the original Rome Treaty, and of course the regional policy adopted
by the Community in 1974 was in principle designed to contribute towards
this end. But in our view, and that of other peripheral countries, the commitment in the Rome Treaty to this concept was too weak, and the Regional
Policy and Fund too limited in scale; and if the Community was to move
towards creating a genuine single market it would be necessary to give cohesion
a much stronger concrete expression in the amended treaty.

Naturally enough these ideas were not entirely welcome to some of the
better-off and centrally situated countries, notably Germany, which believed

that the Community had to give priority to convergence of economic policy *before* (although I sometimes thought they really meant *instead of*) seeking the convergence of living standards. France and Britain shared this view.

I had no illusions about the difficulty we would face in getting acceptance of a concrete obligation to seek movement towards the convergence of levels of economic activity; indeed I was somewhat sceptical about what might be achieved in this respect at the end of this negotiating process. Nevertheless the battle was worth fighting; and on 21 October we submitted our views on this subject to a meeting of the intergovernmental council. At an informal meeting of Foreign Ministers a few days later Peter Barry made it clear that we wanted cohesion as a separate item on the agenda for the crucial heads of government intergovern-mental meeting. I derived some encouragement from the fact that the Presidency seemed to accept that cohesion should appear on the agenda as a separate item, and that our approach was understood, if not shared, by the Germans—in contrast to their attitude to a Greek submission on the subject, which the Germans regarded as quite unacceptable. I was also encouraged to learn that the French regarded the stand I had taken at Milan as having major significance, because it had blurred the line between old and new member-states and had thus been of importance in persuading other member-states to agree eventually to participate constructively in the intergovernmental conference.

By mid-November the Luxembourg Presidency was making it clear that they thought it essential to incorporate cohesion in a treaty revision; the French and British positions on the issue had evolved positively, with, however, the Germans and Dutch still maintaining a fairly hard-line position, although now willing to accept the inclusion of the goal of cohesion in the treaty on the basis of the Luxembourg Presidency's proposals.

The issue of cohesion was of course not the only one in relation to which we had a particular interest. On the question of establishing the internal market we strongly favoured the substitution of qualified majority voting for unanimity in respect of many important issues. Experience over twenty years had shown the impossibility of making real progress towards a single market in the absence of qualified majority voting. Only in one area were we concerned that decisions should continue to be taken on a basis of unanimity, namely the harmonisation of indirect taxation. Because the level of our indirect taxes was higher than that of most other member-countries, we would face a considerable loss of revenue if taxes were to be harmonised to an average Community level. Also, in the case of excise duties on drink and tobacco, reduction to such a level could have serious consequences for health. However, the maintenance of unanimity in respect of these decisions had already been agreed without difficulty in the earlier stages, and did not arise as an issue at the European Council.

We also had a specific problem with respect to the insurance industry. Quite apart from concern that an adequate period should be allowed for our industry to become fully competitive vis-à-vis the insurance sectors of some other European countries, we had the particular difficulty of the levy on general insurance that we had had to impose in order to finance the bail-out of the PMPA insurance company. To meet this problem I made a unilateral declaration that was noted by the conference and is contained in the Final Act; this declaration drew attention to the sensitivity of the insurance sector in Ireland and stated that the Government expected to be able to rely on a sympathetic attitude from the Commission and other member-states if it later considered it necessary to seek a special arrangement for the insurance industry in Ireland.

We were moreover concerned that the changes being effected by the proposed amendments should not interfere with our right to take national measures for the protection of health and the life of humans, animals, or plants. This was a concern that we shared with the British, particularly in relation to animal diseases, from some of which we and the British were free as a result of strict measures in the past on the control and movement of animals.

In the original Rome Treaty this provision had been covered by article 36, which also permitted national restrictions on trade on grounds of public morality, public policy, or public security. I knew that extreme right-wing opponents of abortion in Ireland (as distinct from the mass of the population who were opposed to abortion in a rational and measured way) were liable to raise a scare about any European commitment that they could present as in any way endangering our right to legislate against abortion. There would, I thought, be some advantage in covering this explicitly by having the assurance with regard to national measures being permitted in relation to the movement of animals and plants extended to the issue of public morality also; and in the course of the Council meeting I made this proposal.

I was not prepared, however, to explain my reasons for doing so, because the potential public relations advantage of having this point covered could very easily rebound against me if by any chance my proposal were not accepted by my colleagues and word got out that I had sought its inclusion because of apparent concern about the implications of the Single European Act for abortion. The result would then be that, in relation to a concern that had no concrete basis, I would have aroused quite unnecessary fears. Not unnaturally some of my colleagues wanted to know why I required this additional provision in the proposed Single European Act. When I refused to answer, Andreotti, in an endeavour to be helpful, suggested that my concern probably related to contraception, at which various prime ministers nodded their heads wisely. I refrained, for obvious reasons, from telling them that we had liberalised our law on contraceptives earlier in the year and that this was not the motivation for my proposal. On the basis of this misunderstanding they finally agreed to meet my point by deciding to make provision in the draft treaty for *all* the different exceptions contained in article 36 (which also included the right to act nationally to protect national treasures possessing artistic, historical or archaeological value) rather than to pick out two elements only of this article.

But the part of the draft treaty to which we directed most of our attention during the discussion at Luxembourg was of course the section on economic and social cohesion. The draft text before us seemed to us to be inadequate in a number of important respects, and we had quite a number of amendments down to it. Given the reticence of the Germans and Dutch in particular, and to a lesser extent of the British and French, I was sceptical about how far we would get with these amendments. But in the event we achieved a very considerable measure of success, most of our proposals being eventually adopted. The provisions on economic and social cohesion that emerged from this debate thus represented a breakthrough from the point of view of Ireland and the other peripheral countries. The objective of 'reducing disparities between the various regions and the backwardness of the least-favoured regions' was now incorporated as an objective towards which the Community had to aim. It was also provided that member-states should conduct and co-ordinate their economic policies in such a way as to attain this objective. And it was agreed that the implementation of the common policies of the internal market must take into account the achievement of this objective, the attainment of which the Community was required to support by the action it took through the Structural Funds, the European Investment Bank, and the other existing financial instruments.

All this was no pious aspiration: after the ratification of the Single Act the Commission speedily brought forward proposals for a doubling of the Structural Funds, with a view to helping the peripheral countries, and this proposal has since been put into operation. I doubt if in advance of the Luxembourg European Council any of the peripheral member-states expected such specific commitments to be entered into and to be so rapidly implemented.

So far as the European Political Co-operation aspect of the Single European Act was concerned, the provisions adopted were based on the Franco-German draft presented at Milan, which met our concerns by providing for the co-ordination of the positions of the twelve countries more closely 'on the political and economic aspects of security'; the military aspect thus continued to be excluded from European Political Co-operation.

When we came during 1986 to the question of the ratification of the Single European Act I was asked by Dick Spring to postpone introducing the necessary legislation until after a Labour Party conference in the autumn of that year. While reluctant to let the legislative process run so close to the deadline for ratification, which had been determined so as to enable the Act to be brought into force throughout the Community on 1 January 1987, I agreed with this request in order to minimise problems the Labour Party might face in mobilising support by its deputies for ratification in the Dáil. The result was that the ratification process was not completed until December. We were then taken by surprise by the decision of Raymond Crotty to challenge the constitutionality of our ratification, and we were even more surprised when in early 1987 the Supreme Court decided that the Single European Act was unconstitutional, thus requiring a referendum to be undertaken in order to make the appropriate change in the Constitution.

What was particularly surprising was that the Supreme Court decision was not taken because of any changes in the Rome Treaty but because of the part of the Single European Act dealing with European Political Co-operation. It had always been remotely possible, although I would have thought very improbable, that the amendments to the Rome Treaty could have been deemed in some respect to have gone beyond what had been authorised by the terms of the referendum on EC membership in 1972; but the reasoning that led to a decision that the Political Co-operation provisions were unconstitutional was, to say the least, unexpected and puzzling. The only obligation in relation to this issue imposed on us by the Act was to consult our colleagues in relation to foreign policy issues, with a right of veto on any decision that might be proposed. As I pointed out in the debate in the Dáil on the consequent amendment to the Constitution, if this requirement was unconstitutional, what might the same court have found if our membership of the United Nations had been brought to it for a decision, bearing in mind the obligations imposed by the UN Charter on member-states to implement, by military action if required, decisions of the Security Council in relation to breaches of the peace in the world community?

The year 1986 itself was one in which no major developments took place in the European Community. There were in fact only two European Councils that year, because business was light. However, at the second London meeting I took one initiative that proved productive. Paddy Masterson, who had recently become President of UCD, contacted me before the European Council meeting about the Erasmus programme for university student exchanges. He told me of the imminent breakdown of this project because of a reluctance by the Education Ministers of the bigger EC countries to approve spending on the scheme at the level recommended by the EC Commission. He asked me if there was anything I could do about it; I said that I would see if I could raise the matter without notice at the European Council. I decided the best way to approach the issue was informally; accordingly, during a break in the discussions I spoke to Jacques Chirac. He responded enthusiastically, clearly concerned that his Minister for Education should have taken a negative view of the proposal, and he suggested that we jointly approach Hans-Dietrich Genscher, because the German Minister for Education was another of those opposed to it. We went across the room to speak to Genscher, and secured his immediate support. I told my officials at once about this, and the project was then successfully pursued at other levels, with the result that the Erasmus programme, the survival of which had seemed threatened, got off the ground quite soon thereafter.

Such a programme is obviously of particular interest to Ireland, because of our relatively isolated position and the higher cost for students of travelling to other countries as compared with the cost for students in more central states. The response in Ireland to the scheme was indeed very large, although unfortunately the allocation of the funds between states was not related to the demand for student exchanges but was based on a predetermined quota system, with the result that the funds available to us had to be spread over a very large number of students, with very small individual payments. Nonetheless, small though these payments have been, the scheme has resulted in a very significant increase in the number of Irish students taking part of their courses abroad.

By the time this European Council took place I knew that we were most unlikely to win the impending 1987 general election, and even if we did it was my intention to resign shortly afterwards, so I knew I would not be in London again for a European Council meeting. Accordingly, at the end of the lunch in Buckingham Palace I thanked the Queen for the hospitality I had received from her since 1977, and I also told Margaret Thatcher that she would probably be dealing with my opponent, Charles Haughey, after the next election. She was obviously distressed at the prospect of a change of leadership in Ireland and was not receptive to my attempts to convince her that my opponent would not perform a U-turn on the Anglo-Irish Agreement.

# CHAPTER NINETEEN

# FINAL YEARS

My return from our August 1983 holiday in west Cork coincided with the shooting down of a South Korean airliner by the Soviet air force off the coast of Siberia in early September. Like the rest of the world, our Government reacted with a vigorous denunciation of this atrocity. The US government, however, wanted something more from friendly states than a condemnation of this act. We came under strong pressure to close down Aeroflot's operations at Shannon, where it had established the principal transatlantic stopping-place for its airliners flying to Cuba and other points in Central and South America.

Because of the scale of Aeroflot's operations at the airport and the manner in which Aer Rianta's other activities were facilitated by the availability of aviation fuel from Aeroflot at keen prices, such an action would have imposed a unique burden on us. We decided accordingly to confine ourselves to taking action similar to that of some other countries that were withdrawing temporarily Aeroflot's traffic rights, and we did not withdraw the airline's right to make technical stops at Shannon. The US government was clearly annoyed at this response.

As it happened, quite a different action in relation to the Soviet Union was required at this time for other reasons. Our intelligence services reported to me that several members of the small staff at the Soviet embassy had been engaged in improper activities that had involved the use of our territory for the secret transfer of information concerning the military affairs of another power. In the absence of Peter Barry I instructed Jim O'Keeffe, Minister of State at the Department of Foreign Affairs, to call in the Soviet Ambassador to demand the recall of two diplomats and the wife of another member of the embassy staff. This well-justified action may have had the incidental effect of calming American irritation at our refusal to respond to the demand in relation to Aeroflot's operations at Shannon. At the same time the Soviet authorities must have recognised privately that our action in relation to their diplomats was justified, and may also have given us some marks for resisting US pressure in relation to Aeroflot. In any event there were no retaliatory expulsions of Irish diplomats in Moscow.

It was a misrecollection of this episode that caused Barry Desmond years later to suggest, quite erroneously, that the US authorities had put pressure on us over the Aeroflot facility in connection with the negotiations two years later for American aid to the International Fund for Northern Ireland. This matter was in fact never raised in that context.

I naturally briefed Charles Haughey fully on this spying affair. Indeed, throughout my period as Taoiseach I kept him informed on important security issues, as well as briefing him on other sensitive matters that required the co-operation of the opposition in order to secure speedy parliamentary action. He was always helpful in matters of this kind.

Charles Haughey and I, with Dick Spring, also co-operated that autumn in persuading President Hillery to serve for a second term. Dr Hillery was notably reluctant to continue in office, and several meetings were necessary before he eventually agreed, good-humouredly commenting as he conceded on the issue that his was the only sentence in respect of which apparently one got an additional seven years for good behaviour.

I had always had a good relationship with Paddy Hillery. Joan had known him in college forty years earlier, and even when, before he had assumed the Presidential office, he and I had found ourselves on opposite sides politically we had always got on well. During my official visits to him as President I kept him well informed of what was happening on the political scene, including my developing plans for an Anglo-Irish Agreement, and I tried to help him with problems that he faced in his office. He could be touchy if he felt that officials were not treating him or his office with sufficient sensitivity, and misunderstandings occasionally had to be smoothed over. But his concern to exercise his role independently of party politics merited respect, and I would happily have provided him with further assistance had he wished to pursue more actively some suggestions that came up in discussion between us.

I have to add that having observed the frustration felt by his two immediate predecessors with the limitations on their actions imposed by successive Governments' interpretation of the constitutional relationship between the President and the executive arm, as well as President Hillery's own evident unhappiness with some aspects of his situation, I did not find myself attracted later on to the idea of standing for this office. To have done so would, for example, have inhibited me from publishing this book!

It cannot be easy for anyone who has a wish to exchange and communicate ideas publicly to accept the constraints of Presidential office, and the actual role the President can play in Irish life offers limited compensation for this deprivation. I should however add that I had other, personal reasons—a preference for continuing my own post-Government life-style and a concern to be freer to look after Joan in the years ahead—for not standing for this office in 1990.

And, writing in the aftermath of the 1990 Presidential election, I am convinced that Mary Robinson can do a far better job as President than I could ever have hoped to do.

On our return from holiday at the end of August 1983 Frank Cluskey had immediately come to me to say that a major insurance company, the Private Motorists' Protection Association, was near the point of financial collapse. The PMPA offered motorists insurance premiums lower than those of the established insurance companies. Successive Governments had worried about the longer-term viability of the company, but efforts both by the National Coalition Government of the mid-1970s and by Des O'Malley, Minister for Industry and Commerce in its Fianna Fáil successor, to satisfy themselves about the way it was run had revealed no firm grounds for action. Now an official inquiry had given Frank Cluskey good reason to believe that a collapse was imminent.

Discussing it together, Frank Cluskey and I reached two conclusions. First, because of the social consequences of what might become a large-scale aban-donment of any form of motor insurance if people chose not to transfer to firms charging higher premiums, we could not afford to let the company fail. This meant that we would have to be ready with a copperfastened take-over plan to be implemented in a lightning move when the moment came, as could happen within weeks rather than months. Second, the preparation of the neces-sary legislation had to take place in total secrecy: any hint that we were engaged in such an operation would lead instantly to the very collapse that we feared.

It was only at the end of October that all was ready; fortunately the company had survived until this point. When we brought the draft legislation before the Government there was immediate approval for our proposed action, and Frank Cluskey was congratulated by all on the manner in which he had tackled the problem and for his success in maintaining total secrecy throughout. On 30 October, as the crisis in the company reached its climax, we moved without warning, and with complete success. The company was found to have a huge deficiency in its funding, and its survival under administration required the imposition of a levy on all forms of general insurance for years thereafter; but there was general agreement that this was a price worth paying in the circum-stances. Seven years later the company had reached the stage where it was possible for the receiver to return it to private ownership.

The preparation of this legislation coincided in time with another endeavour in which Frank Cluskey also had an important role: the resolution of a crisis involving the Alliance and Dublin Consumers' Gas Company, familiarly known as the Dublin Gas Company. Disagreement with his colleagues on this matter was to be the precipitating factor in his resignation from the Government.

The Dublin Gas Company, a privately owned public utility, had a reputation for inefficiency and poor management that had permitted the development of unacceptable work practices. The company was, however, a major potential user of natural gas from the newly developed Kinsale gas field, the product of which was handled by a state enterprise, Bord Gáis Éireann. This state company had an agreement with the Dublin Gas Company to help finance the conversion of its network and its customers' appliances to natural gas. But by the latter half of 1983 it was evident that not alone was the Bord Gáis investment in a pipeline from Cork to Dublin and in the conversion of the Dublin gas network at risk but so also was the continuance of the existing gas supply to several hundred thousand Dublin homes that depended on gas for cooking. This posed the question whether and on what conditions the state, through its agent, Bord Gáis, should further subsidise the operation and development of a grossly inefficient private company. Frank Cluskey was quite clear on his position: Dublin Gas should be nationalised, which in practice meant being taken over by Bord Gáis.

There could not be, and indeed were not, any serious objections to this on ideological grounds; given the efficiency of the state-owned Bord Gáis relative to the inefficiency of the privately owned Dublin Gas Company, the usual case against state ownership made no sense in this instance. There was, however, another consideration that influenced most members of the Government, including some of Frank Cluskey's Labour Party colleagues: if Dublin Gas were to be merged with Bord Gáis, might not the Dublin Gas workers, many of whom were felt to have 'milked' that company for years, attempt to use their key position to 'milk' Bord Gáis on an even larger scale—for, as a result of the exceptionally favourable terms of the state's agreement with Marathon, the owners of the Kinsale gas field, this state company enjoyed very large profits indeed. This risk appeared to most of us to be too great, and, despite Frank Cluskey's counter-arguments, the Government decided in favour of retaining Dublin Gas in the private sector. The battle in the Government was a long-drawn-out one; there was no better man than Frank Cluskey for this kind of rearguard action. But when it was clear that he had lost, he resigned.

There was some speculation amongst his colleagues whether Dublin Gas was the real, or at any rate the only, reason for this action. As I have related earlier, Frank Cluskey had been very unhappy at the establishment of the New Ireland Forum. He was also visibly uncomfortable, to an even greater extent than the rest of us, at finding himself part of a Government that was being forced by the extravagance of its predecessor to cut spending as well as to increase taxes sharply. This was not Frank Cluskey's 'scene', and it may well have been that his general discomfort with the financial decisions being forced on us influenced him, at least subconsciously, to make the Dublin Gas issue a resigning matter.

I regretted losing a colleague whose courage, social commitment and political skill I had come to appreciate over the years and whom I regarded with affection—tinged at times with frustration at his occasional stubbornness! However, some of my colleagues did not have quite the same feeling for him and were visibly relieved that we were now to face the rest of our stormy voyage without him.

The irony of all this was that our attempt to maintain an 'arm's length' relationship between the gas field and the Dublin Gas workers eventually failed.

Despite our appointment of a number of directors to its board, the management problems of Dublin Gas were not resolved, and two-and-a-half years later we had to mount a further salvage operation. In the course of this the company was taken over by Bord Gáis, which eventually turned it into a reasonably efficient concern with a reduced work force.

Dick Spring's choice of successor to Frank Cluskey was Ruairí Quinn, whom I had known since the late 1960s, when as a student of architecture he had been involved in the successful attempt to have my eldest brother, Dem, replaced as professor of architecture at UCD. (Dem had been criticised by the students for having failed to persuade the college authorities to provide the School of Architecture with sufficient resources to ensure that recognition of its degrees in Britain would not be put at risk; he was simply too lacking in aggression to force the issue with the president of the day.) Subsequently Ruairí and I had been involved together in seeking to defuse the 'Gentle Revolution' of 1969 in the college, and I had kept in touch with him after he graduated. While he and I were constituency rivals, we remained friends, and the ideological complexion of much of the Fine Gael constituency organisation at that time favoured a co-operative relationship between us, save when in the first 1982 election Ruairí had seemed to take an anti-coalition stance.

Dick Spring proposed that Liam Kavanagh now take over the Environment portfolio from him, with Ruairí Quinn replacing Liam as Minister for Labour, while Dick would take over the Department of Energy himself. Trade, Commerce and Tourism were to be restored to the Department of Industry, where John Bruton was the Minister.

Ruairí Quinn proved to be an energetic Minister for Labour, committed to mitigating the impact of unemployment by various schemes designed for those out of work, especially the long-term unemployed. If he was not fully successful in establishing a good relationship between the Government and the trade unions, the reasons for this lay at a deeper level than he or any other Labour Party Minister could deal with, for in the wake of the Fianna Fáil Governments of 1977–81 and 1982 it had fallen to us not merely to cut spending and raise taxes but also to wind down inflation by constant pressure for more modest pay rounds, without being able during this period of deflation to offer the unions much to compensate for these measures. At the same time there seemed to me to be a deep irritation on the part of some union leaders with Labour participation in Government, which, particularly in relation to the public sector, they appeared to regard as involving a confusion of the clear-cut division between representatives of labour and management with which they were comfortable.

The period during which the Dublin Gas issue had been fought to a conclusion in the Government coincided with the early stages of the Don Tidey kidnapping affair. Don Tidey was an executive of the Quinnsworth supermarket group who was kidnapped by the IRA with a view to extorting a large sum from the Canadian owners of the group, the Westons. Almost three weeks were to elapse before he was found and rescued at the expense of two lives: a Garda recruit and a soldier were killed by the IRA in the course of the rescue operation.

We hoped that the foiling of this and other kidnap attempts by the IRA and various breakaway groups would have ensured that this possible source of funds would be barred to them. Unhappily we discovered fourteen months later that £2 million sterling had been paid to a Swiss bank, from which the great bulk of it was transferred via New York to a branch of an Irish bank in Navan. When we heard this on Wednesday 13 February 1985 we set to work at once to draft legislation that would enable us to seize this money in a manner that could not be challenged in the courts on the basis of a claim that the constitutional property rights of an alleged owner had been violated. The Bill went through more than twenty drafts in the course of the intervening weekend before the Dáil was due to meet. I had, of course, briefed Charles Haughey about the legislation and the reason for introducing it, and the opposition co-operated fully in ensuring the speedy enactment of our Bill, which by midnight had been signed by the President.

But to return to late 1983: the allowances paid to members of the Oireachtas had for many years previously been linked to basic public service pay increases through an Oireachtas approval mechanism, but the series of elections in 1981 and 1982 had held up the legislative implementation of this linkage with a series of public service pay rounds that had taken place during that period.

We decided to bring the allowances into line with the public service pay levels to which they were linked, but without any retrospection. There was a huge, and prolonged, outcry at this decision; public opinion was totally unwilling to accept that what members of the Oireachtas were now to receive represented no more than an incomplete catching up on the rest of the community. We should of course have foreseen this irrational response and should have sought to forestall it by staggering this increase over several stages, so that the 19 per cent figure did not become such an emotive issue. This error of judgement did significant damage to the popularity of our Government, both in a by-election in Dublin Central around this time and thereafter.

In the autumn of 1983 we introduced a new Criminal Justice Bill, directed against non-political crime, which had mushroomed since the 1960s, partly because of the easier availability of guns as a result of IRA activity. The Bill involved the extension of life sentences to certain firearms offences in order to bring this aspect of our law into line with the law in Northern Ireland, as well as detention for up to twelve hours for questioning, photographing, and finger-printing. The legislation also proposed the extension of majority jury verdicts to criminal cases. In recognition of public concern about the increased powers that we proposed to give to the Gardaí, we announced that these aspects of the Bill would come into force only when a proposed police complaints procedure had been put into place.

As I expected, this legislation had a mixed reception. Public opinion was, and remains, divided between a libertarian minority and a large majority principally concerned to see stronger action taken against the spread of crime, especially burglaries, the scale of which in some areas was by 1983 affecting a significant proportion of the whole population. Critical reaction in the Dáil came from a number of Government, and especially Fine Gael, backbenchers who approached the Bill from a civil liberties viewpoint. This was frustrating for the Minister, Michael Noonan, who faced—good-humouredly most of the time—many months of debate during which he had to battle with this posse of critics ranged behind him rather than in front of him. However, taking a philosophical view of this one could feel that it was good to see the Dáil working as it ought to work but often does not, because of the rigidity of the whipping system.

Towards the end of September I had endeavoured to set the scene for the 1984 budget in a speech at Carlow in which I had made it clear that further narrowing of the budgetary gap must be effected by cuts in expenditure rather than increases in tax. Perhaps because in this speech I also fired a shot across the bows of some of our more extravagant state enterprises, urging them to stop 'game-playing' and to reflect on whether at times they were serving the people or were self-serving, this produced a stronger reaction from the Labour Party than my fairly harmless budgetary comment merited. Dick Spring responded with a speech in which he diplomatically suggested that in my comments I had not pre-empted alternative solutions to spending cuts. At the same time he stressed the conditional character of the Government's commitment to phase out the current deficit in five years—'having regard to prevailing economic conditions and particularly the compatibility of this with the protection and creation of employment.'

His point was valid, but it did not help that he felt it necessary to make it in this way at this time. When the Government assembled for a weekend meeting on 30 September Dick asked for an adjournment for half an hour to enable the pair of us to discuss this situation, and when we resumed I told our colleagues that it had been agreed that there would be no further speeches by members of the Government until we had sorted out the budgetary situation. This did not, however, prevent journalists being briefed mendaciously by someone to the effect that on this budgetary issue Frank Cluskey had made 'a blistering attack' on me that had led to a fifteen-minute adjournment of the meeting—a story that Dick Spring flatly denied. Nor did it prevent leaks a day or two later from Labour Party sources to the effect that their Ministers were pressing for cuts in tax of £100 to £200 million.

The outcome of this and subsequent budgets I shall, however, leave until the end of this chapter. The saga of our efforts from 1983 to 1987 to cut the deficit and borrowing deserves to be dealt with as a whole rather than year by year.

In October we appointed the first Ombudsman. An imaginative suggestion, adopted enthusiastically by the Government, was the nomination to this post of Michael Mills, political correspondent of the *Irish Press*. Although the paper for which he wrote had been the party organ of Fianna Fáil from its foundation fifty years earlier, Michael Mills had won universal respect amongst politicians for his independent and incisive reporting of political events and for his wise comments on political matters. There was widespread agreement that he would serve the public effectively in this new role, in which he would be intimidated neither by politicians nor civil servants. Like a number of other independent agencies, the Ombudsman's office was the object of restrictive measures by Fianna Fáil after its return to office in 1987. The staff was cut back severely, which threatened to emasculate its role of watchdog over the public administration; but Michael Mills fought this measure so effectively, mobilising political and public opposition to these moves, that any undermining of the Ombudsman's role was soon averted.

The week before the 1984 budget the Ford plant in Cork had closed. Cork had already become something of an employment black-spot, especially following the closure of the Dunlop tyre factory some months before. But the closure after more than forty years of the Ford plant, which had for so long been Cork's flagship industry, had a symbolic significance over and above the immediate blow to employment. Years were to elapse before morale in Cork recovered from this disaster, and in the meantime the popularity of our Government in Cork, and of Peter Barry in particular as the Government member from the city, suffered severely. After the replacement of Jack Lynch, their favourite son, by Charles Haughey, Fianna Fáil had lost ground there; now it was our turn to lose out.

Nevertheless, despite severe criticism on economic grounds, and without much expectation of political reward, we took some very important steps to protect Cork from further disasters. Thus the modernised Irish Steel plant had a huge overhang of borrowing, the servicing of which was converting its operating profits into net losses that would soon have closed it if we had not provided a very large injection of capital before an EC deadline after which further state aid would have been impossible. We also ensured the continuance of NET, the fertiliser plant, and of the Whitegate oil refinery, the latter being kept going by requiring oil distributing companies to take its products.

In March 1984, when returning from Washington to Brussels for a European Council meeting, I heard that Dominic McGlinchey, leader of a particularly vicious breakaway IRA group, the INLA, had been recaptured by the Gardaí. Having absconded when on bail pending a Supreme Court hearing of an extradition process against him, he had been on the run for many months. His case was in fact the first political extradition case that, on Peter Sutherland's initiative in 1981–82, had been successfully taken on appeal to the Supreme Court. That court had departed from the pattern of previous decisions on political offence extradition cases and had decided that when recaptured he should be extradited.

Before leaving for the United States I had directed that, if arrested, McGlinchey should be extradited at once on foot of the Supreme Court's decision. Having learnt of his capture I tried on landing at London Airport, where I was to change planes, to phone Dublin from a VIP lounge to confirm that the extradition was being carried out. To my astonishment I was refused permission to make this call, on the grounds that only local calls could be made from the VIP lounge. I blew up at this lunatic piece of British red tape and told the British Airports Authority representative what I would say to Margaret Thatcher when I met her at lunch in Brussels in a couple of hours' time. This left the official quite unmoved; but fortunately an Irish embassy official who had come to meet me found a coin-box phone and produced a 10p piece, which enabled me to contact my office in Dublin.

In the event, before McGlinchey could be got to the border a habeas corpus action was initiated; but an emergency sitting of the Supreme Court that evening reaffirmed its earlier decision, and late that night he was handed over to the RUC at the border. That was not to be the end of the story. The evidence in relation to the particular murder for which he was extradited did not stand up in the Northern Ireland courts, and in October 1985 we had to re-extradite him from Northern Ireland in order to try him for another offence in our state, for which he was given a long sentence.

In mid-1984 we faced the European Parliament election. This we could do with reasonable equanimity, because the freak result of the 1979 European election had left us with only four seats—one in each constituency—and we could only improve on this. In that year the Labour Party, with 14 per cent of the votes to our 33 per cent, had secured by a fluke the same number of seats as we had—four out of fifteen—and it was bound to lose ground on this occasion. As it happened, although our share of the vote dropped slightly we in fact gained two seats; Fianna Fáil, its vote still under 40 per cent, gained three; and the Labour Party lost all four of its seats, as did the republican independent Neil Blaney. While this result was demoralising for Labour and increased anti-coalition sentiment within that party, in the short term it naturally had a beneficial impact upon Fine Gael morale.

In conjunction with the European election we had initiated a constitutional referendum to enable us to reciprocate the British provision under which, despite our departure from the Commonwealth in 1949, our citizens had retained the right to vote in elections to Westminster. This was something that I had agreed at the time of my first summit meeting with Margaret Thatcher in November 1981. The proposal, expressed in the form of an amendment to the Constitution enabling the Government to grant parliamentary voting rights to citizens of other countries that gave our citizens similar rights, was adopted by a popular majority of almost three to one; this arrangement and the size of the majority in favour of reciprocation illustrate the unique character of the Anglo-Irish relationship.

This marked the beginning of a period in which some of our reforms began to emerge from the frustratingly long legislative pipeline. For example, the legislation for the establishment of an independent Garda Complaints Tribunal was published on the day after the European election and referendum. There had been resistance in the Garda Síochána to the establishment of an independent tribunal, but this had been mitigated by linking the establishment of this tribunal with the new Criminal Justice Bill that had been progressing through the Oireachtas during the first half of the year. Nevertheless the tribunal was not established until 1986, and unhappily its effectiveness was somewhat limited in the late 1980s because the number of complaints received was almost two-and-a-half times as great as we had expected, and extra staff to handle this was not provided for several years. (I should add, however, that the proportion of complaints actually found to have substance and to require disciplinary or other action has been small: less than 5 per cent.)

At the end of July the first fruits of Gemma Hussey's negotiations with the European Community on allocating resources from the Social Fund to the educational sector emerged: grants of £300 a year were provided for up to one-third of school leavers who undertook courses on preparation for employment at the end of the their school careers.

In May 1984 it had transpired that our balance of payments figures were seriously defective. What was instantly christened a 'black hole' emerged in the form of a huge unexplained jump in the residual figure of current payments unaccounted for. Further investigation revealed serious defects in the sampling of foreign companies earning large profits; the proportion of these profits being repatriated had apparently risen sharply during the recent recession, but this development had been missed. The error was soon rectified, but it drew attention to the fact that the Central Statistics Office had for many years been underresourced. It seemed a good moment to review its operations, in which I had had a particular interest for decades previously.

Jim O'Leary, my economic adviser during my period as leader of Fine Gael in 1982, had accompanied me into Government at the end of that year. In 1983, however, he had decided to leave to join the National Planning Board. I had heard that Patrick Honohan, who had been my economic adviser in 1981–82, would be willing to take on this role again, and in February 1984 he re-joined me in the Department of the Taoiseach. It was Patrick who now pointed out to me that the Act establishing the CSO in 1926 had made provision for a Statistical Council, which, however, had never been set up. With his expert assistance I established such a council to review the working of the CSO; and it recommended the establishment of the office as a state body outside the civil service, together with a National Statistical Board with co-ordinating functions in relation to all official statistics. This recommendation was implemented in February 1986 and has since greatly extended computerisation of the work in the office and improved its system of publication.

In mid-1984 a new control system on public expenditure that I had introduced, which involved monthly reports on the cumulative total of spending under each departmental vote, revealed that spending was currently running ahead of the level we had provided for. There had to be emergency spending cuts. The National Planning Board had recommended the abolition of the food subsidies that the National Coalition Government had introduced in the mid-

1970s with a view to securing a renegotiation of grossly excessive national pay agreements. The Government had already decided to accept this recommendation, and so at the end of July it was agreed that we should deal with the overspending problem by eliminating half of these subsidies forthwith. This would not alone cut public spending in the current year but would also phase the impact on consumer prices of these removal of the subsidies.

Because of the timing of this decision at the end of July it was decided that news of it should be released during the August holiday weekend rather than held over until the following week; this, we thought, might have the advantage of reducing adverse public reaction to the announcement. At the end of this Government meeting John Boland, to whom we had delegated responsibility for liaison about our decisions with Peter Prendergast, the Government Press Secretary, told Peter what we had decided. Peter pressed strongly that we should not appear to seek to evade criticism of this announcement and that a senior Minister, preferably myself, should be available to deal with the press on the matter.

We had come to the end of a very tiring session, and John Boland knew that I was fairly exhausted and about to leave for my holiday. He decided, compassionately but unwisely, not to come back to me with this strong recommendation, which would have involved postponing my departure. The result was that when the announcement was made neither Dick Spring nor myself was available to deal with the press, and this produced, as Peter Prendergast had rightly calculated, a highly negative press and public response. This proved to be one of the major public relations miscalculations of our period in Government.

Part of our holiday that year was spent in the south of France, some of it with friends of ours who had taken a house inland and the second part of it, as I mentioned in the previous chapter, in the Fort of Bregançon on the coast to the east of Toulon. With Mary and several friends, Joan and I were the guests there of President Mitterrand, who, in conversation earlier that summer, had enquired where we were spending our holiday that year and had invited us to stay in this official residence, which had once housed Napoleon at an early stage of his career.

I had accepted the invitation after enquiring from several people who had stayed there whether there were many steps, a matter that concerned me because of Joan's disability. I had been assured that there were only a few steps from the car to the guest accommodation, but in fact I counted no less than 168! Nevertheless, because the accommodation at the higher level of the fort opened onto lawns surrounded by battlements, once Joan had managed to get there, with considerable difficulty, she was able to remain at that level in comfort during our stay, descending to the formal reception level only once, when President Mitterrand and his wife, together with Prime Minister Fabius and Foreign Minister Dumas and their wives, came to dinner.

The dinner was, incidentally, a most entertaining occasion. The fortieth anniversary celebration of the liberation of Paris had just taken place, and Mitterrand enlivened the evening with many stories of his experiences at that time. His aide-de-camp was named Barry, which happened also to be the name of one of Mary and Vincent's friends, the composer Gerald Barry, who was staying with us but did not speak French. When a phone call came in the middle of the night from the Élysée Palace for the aide-de-camp it was unfortunately put through to Gerald, whom we had coached to explain in French when addressed in that language that he did not speak it. This response, apparently from the President's aide-de-camp, must have had a fairly shattering effect on the caller from the Élysée.

In the summer and early autumn of 1984 the relationship between Dick Spring and myself came under unexpected strain. We had to nominate a member of the European Commission for the period 1985–88. Fine Gael, restive about what it saw—or at times imagined—to be a Labour Party tail persistently wagging the Coalition dog, was in no mood to concede this European appointment to a Labour nominee, and while the name of Justin Keating was advanced by that party, it was not pressed.

I had reflected on whom I should propose from Fine Gael. Conscious of the need to field an outstanding candidate who might become a really influential member of the European Commission, I felt at the same time that I could not spare one of my Ministerial 'heavyweights', nor did I wish to face a by-election that we might easily lose.

It was Joan who came up with the answer when I put the dilemma to her one morning; she suggested Peter Sutherland. He was an ideal choice: someone who could, and did, become a leading member of one of the more successful Commission teams for many years, and who increased immensely our reputation in Europe. When I brought his name forward Dick Spring was prepared to agree, but on one condition: that *he* would nominate Peter's successor as Attorney General.

Hitherto the Attorney General had always been the personal choice of the Taoiseach of the day; the relationship between Taoiseach and Attorney General is a particularly close one, partly because of the delicacy of the legal issues that arise under a Constitution that so tightly controls the actions of both executive and legislature. The Attorney General's office, indeed, was until recently sited on the floor immediately below that of the Taoiseach, and, at any rate in my experience, the Attorney is a frequent and valued visitor to the Taoiseach's office. To have my Attorney General chosen for me was something that I instinctively resisted, and Dick's choice, John Rogers, was not known to me, although I soon learnt that before moving to Labour he had been a member of the Fine Gael Youth Movement who apparently had approached me, with others, in 1969 in an attempt to persuade me to move against Liam Cosgrave.

I reflected for some weeks on the matter and consulted several legal people to get their views before I finally agreed, with some qualms, to Dick's proposal. I need not have worried. John Rogers turned out to be excellent, and enormously helpful to me on political as well as legal matters. Because of the nature of my personal relationship with Dick Spring, which soon recovered from the tensions temporarily created by this issue, no problems of divided loyalty arose, and John Rogers was often able to help smooth over problems between the two parties in Government. His relative lack of experience in constitutional matters was fully compensated for by his qualities of judgement and his willingness to draw on the advice of his office or others with special skills. He shared my commitment to the achievement of an Anglo-Irish Agreement and played an important role in its negotiation—albeit not without occasional tensions with my advisers in the Department of Foreign Affairs.

When at the end of July I had talked to Jacques Delors about my possible nomination of Peter Sutherland, I had told him something of Peter's exceptional qualities and legal skills and had suggested that he might consider him for the Competition portfolio in the Commission. This is a particularly important portfolio, the holder of which has personal power to determine on his own account what state aids governments may give to their industrial sectors. By virtue of this power the Commissioner for Competition tends to carry considerable weight in the Commission, and Peter's appointment to this portfolio, together with his own qualities, seemed to me to be likely to provide him with the opportunity to become an outstanding member of the next Commission.

Jacques Delors, whose appointment as President of the Commission I had recently secured in my capacity as President of the European Council, took my recommendation seriously, and when the time came several months later to make his appointments he nominated Peter Sutherland for this position. Peter's success in his appointment, and his emergence as one of the key figures in that Commission, are a matter of record.

The summer and autumn of 1984 were also a period marked by a number of developments in the security area, including the extradition of Séamus Shannon, accused of the murder of the former Speaker of the Stormont Parliament, Sir Norman Stronge, and his son, who, like McGlinchey, was subsequently acquitted of the charge in Northern Ireland. In mid-November came the escape of a suspected IRA woman, Evelyn Glenholmes, as a result of a story in the *Sunday Times* that alerted her to the fact that she was being sought. There were also the seizures of the *Marita Ann* with 109 tonnes of arms for the IRA off the Co. Kerry coast and of another boat in Boston suspected of being involved in a similar attempt; the murder of a guard during an armed robbery in Co. Meath; and, in mid-October, the Brighton bombing, to which I referred in an earlier chapter.

The third of the corporate crises that faced us during this term of office declared itself in November 1984. This time it was a state company, Irish Shipping, which had been established in 1941 to provide us with a wartime strategic shipping fleet and which had been retained in state ownership thereafter, operating on the whole with success over the intervening decades. Unhappily the key posts of chairman, chief executive and chief accountant had been allowed to be cumulated in the hands of one person, who made a grave error of judgement in chartering vessels on a long-term basis at charter rates that proved unsustainable outside periods of strong shipping demand. With the collapse in the recent period of shipping rates the entire operation became immensely vulnerable. We now found ourselves faced with an insolvent company whose debts were state-guaranteed to the tune of £40 million but which also had long-term liabilities of over £140 million that were not so guaranteed. We had no alternative but to allow the company to go into liquidation and its staff of almost four hundred people to be made redundant. The most tragic part of the affair was that we were unable to supplement the meagre statutory redundancy payments for staff without risking an extension of our legal liability to include the additional £140 million of debts, for which the state simply could not afford to take responsibility. Understandably the staff and their dependants could not easily grasp why they alone of those found redundant in the state sector during these years had to be confined to statutory redundancy payments, receiving no adequate compensation for their loyal service to the company. This was one of the most painful decisions that we had to take while in Government.

Four months later we were to face yet another corporate crisis that, although this time in the private sector, was of such a character that we could not avoid becoming involved in its resolution. Associated with Irish Shipping throughout much of its life had been an insurance company, the Insurance Corporation of Ireland, originally established to provide cover for the shipping fleet. However, this company had developed a much wider range of business and had eventually been privatised. Allied Irish Banks had purchased a minority interest in the company in 1981, acquiring ownership of 100 per cent of the capital in September 1983.

In the week beginning 4 March 1984 it was discovered that the ICI had incurred huge and, in the short term at least, unquantifiable liabilities in the London insurance market as a result of the activities of its London manager. These losses were known to be so great that they appeared to endanger the stability of Allied Irish Banks, which accordingly approached the Government to seek help to save the bank.

In mid-March, when the matter was brought to the attention of the Government, I was temporarily laid up. It was Alan Dukes as Minister for Finance and John Bruton as Minister for Industry and Commerce who had to deal with the crisis, together with their civil servants and the Central Bank. The advice the two Ministers received was that unless the Government acted to relieve AIB of the liabilities of the ICI, the bank itself might not survive, and the collapse of AIB could endanger the other major banking group, the Bank of Ireland, and indeed the credit of the state and the stability of the currency. If this crisis were to be avoided, not merely would the state have to act in an unprecedented way but it would be necessary not to disclose the full rationale for this action lest such a disclosure precipitate panic.

When Alan Dukes and John Bruton came to tell me of this at home I was horrified at the scale of the disaster and shocked that the banking system, of which I had made an intensive study in 1965, could since then have become so vulnerable to mismanagement in a single subsidiary. I was told that this extraordinary situation had arisen because, since I had undertaken my study, the arrangements for bank equity had been modified so as to treat as equity certain loans from other banking institutions, which could be withdrawn without notice if any subsidiary of the bank became insolvent. I could not understand, and have never since had explained to me, how such an element of inherent instability had been allowed to creep into the system without the Government being alerted to this dangerous development—the Government that was now being told that if it did not acquire the ICI from AIB, and take responsibility for the ICI's unknown liabilities, these loans to AIB from other banks were likely to be withdrawn, leading to its collapse and perhaps that of the whole financial system.

When we enquired about how the mounting crisis in the ICI had failed to be detected by the supervisory body of insurance companies, the Department of Industry and Commerce, we were informed that that department had been unhappy with the London insurance activities of the ICI and had made enquiries five months earlier but had been assured that all was well by the British Department of Trade and Industry, which apparently had responsibility for supervision of the company's activities in London. In other words nobody in Ireland appeared to be to blame, but our Government had to carry the can.

While the opposition supported the necessary legislative provisions in the Dáil to deal with the crisis, involving the acquisition of the ICI by a company established by the Department of Industry and Commerce for this purpose, together with funding of the deficiency by the Central Bank out of its reserves, Fianna Fáil soon began to criticise us severely for our handling of the affair. To this criticism we could not respond adequately at the time without casting dangerous doubts on the state of the whole banking system. We also suffered from the fact that, while I was determined that none of the ultimate financial cost of this salvage operation should be borne by the taxpayer, it was not possible in advance of sorting out the mess to give assurances that this could be achieved. I insisted that the Central Bank should return to this problem later in the year, working out a scheme under which the temporary assistance it was providing would over time be refunded by AIB, with some assistance from other banks and insurance companies. This was eventually done, so that the taxpayer was eventually protected from carrying any part of the burden. Unhappily we never succeeded in convincing public opinion of this, and as a result the myth has persisted ever since that the exchequer, i.e. the taxpayer, carried the burden of bailing out AIB.

Nevertheless I shared to the full the sense of frustration and indignation about the manner in which this affair had been handled by AIB, and was frankly shocked at the provocative way in which the bank shortly afterwards announced that its results for the year would be unaffected by this development and that no reduction would be made in the dividend payable to shareholders. Its concern to reassure its shareholders seemed to me and to many other people in public life to take precedence over any sense of public responsibility on this occasion; and the effect on the credibility of the banking system with the broader public was certainly very negative.

Shortly before the ICI-AIB crisis broke we had put through the Dáil a Bill reforming the law on contraception. In 1979 Charles Haughey, then Minister for Health, had produced what he described as 'an Irish solution to an Irish problem': the legalisation of the sale of contraceptives on prescription, for family planning purposes only. This had followed a judgement of the European Court of Human Rights in Strasbourg that had impugned the ban on contraception in the case of a married woman whose health would have been in jeopardy in the event of a further pregnancy.

I was determined to replace this anachronistic and disreputable piece of legislation, which sounded like a late flowering of mediaeval ecclesiastical law, with a straightforward legalisation of the open sale of contraceptives by pharmacies and by health boards, although I recognised that to get this through the Dáil, which was certainly not going to be easy, there would have to be a (somewhat theoretical) limitation on the sale of contraceptives to people of eighteen years and over.

The day before I was due to announce this legislation I received a courtesy call from the new Archbishop of Dublin, Dr McNamara, following his installation a fortnight earlier. I reflected on whether I should tell him of my intention to act in this matter, but decided that whatever view the Catholic Church might hold on the morality of contraception, legislation on the subject was strictly a matter for the Oireachtas—unlike divorce, which, if introduced, would have implications for a marriage ceremony carried out jointly by church and state and which *would* be an appropriate matter for consultation with the churches. This was possibly a somewhat rigid application of the doctrine of separation of church and state; on reflection, I might perhaps have mentioned the matter in passing to the archbishop on the occasion of his call. Perhaps not surprisingly in the circumstances, my announcement of the legislation on the following day evoked immediate criticism of the Bill from Dr McNamara.

I had decided to push the Bill through as rapidly as possible; there were bound to be problems both in my party and in Labour, and the less time we gave these problems to emerge the more effectively they would be overcome. In the outcome three of our deputies and one Labour Party deputy voted against the Bill, and another Labour deputy abstained. On the opposition side, however, Des O'Malley also abstained, as a result of which he was expelled from Fianna Fáil; this was the first move along the road towards the formation of the Progressive Democrats, the existence of which was eventually to deprive Fianna Fáil of the possibility of an overall majority at subsequent elections. The Fine Gael whip was withdrawn from the three of our TDs who had voted against the Bill, but was restored later on in the life of the Dáil.

A few days later I had the pleasure of seeing published the only substantial Bill that I had the opportunity of personally introducing and steering through the Oireachtas during my time in Government: the National Archives Bill. This Bill provided for combining the Public Record Office and the State Paper Office to form the National Archives, and made provision for the lodging therein after a period of thirty years of the papers of central government. Up to that time there had been no provision of this kind, although in the 1970s Liam Cosgrave had lodged the government papers for the first quarter of a century of the existence of the state in the Public Record Office, where they had been made accessible.

In drafting this legislation I had been concerned to make it as liberal as possible, limiting very strictly indeed the categories of papers that could be withheld, and setting up a system of checks designed to ensure that these liberal provisions would be adhered to. In January 1991 the great bulk of pre-1960 central government records were released to historians—an estimated one million files. Two departments failed to make a transfer of their files by this deadline but were committed to doing so during the course of the year.

Other reforming measures undertaken during 1985 included the ending of the banking cartel and the introduction of competition between the leading banks; a decision to eliminate jury trials in car insurance cases, with a view to reducing the excessive cost of car insurance; and the introduction of tax incentives for the development of the Dublin inner city area. This measure was later extended to the other principal cities, and it helped in varying degrees the subsequent revival of run-down areas in those centres.

In July 1985, following the announcement of a merger of two major building societies (which in the event did not happen), I appointed a committee chaired by Patrick Honohan to examine the legislation and regulations governing the activities of these bodies. Within three months the committee reported, recommending the abolition of certain restrictive practices but allowing the building societies to undertake some types of banking business. Some of these recommendations were incorporated in one of the last Bills passed during our term of office. Other unpublished recommendations were given effect in the 1986 budget, including the introduction of the deposit interest retention tax. And other suggestions in the report for improved supervision of the building societies were implemented by our successors in Government.

In June 1985 I lost a valued friend, Alexis FitzGerald, who had been ill for some time previously. We had known each other for almost forty years, sharing many common interests although often with differing viewpoints, and I had drawn heavily on his advice and assistance throughout my political career, both when he had been a senator and also as a special adviser to my first short-lived Government of 1981–82. In the closing years of my premiership I greatly missed his advice and support.

A few days after his death the local elections were held, which, against my advice, had been postponed the previous year. During the preceding twelve months the continuing deflation of the economy had inevitably reduced our popularity, and in these elections, for the first time since the 1960s, we lost a significant amount of ground in many city and county councils. The inevitable weakening of morale in Fine Gael was temporarily mitigated by the signing of the Anglo-Irish Agreement in November.

One of the short-term domestic political consequences of this agreement was the resignation of Mary Harney from Fianna Fáil. A year earlier I had heard that she was very disillusioned with that party under Charles Haughey and was thinking of leaving and possibly joining Fine Gael. I had suggested to her at the time that the announcement of the Anglo-Irish Agreement, which I believed Haughey would oppose, would provide a more appropriate occasion for such a resignation. The consequence of this, however, was that with such a prominent member of Fianna Fáil, Des O'Malley, already 'on the loose' as an independent, Mary Harney did not in fact join our party but at the end of that year joined with him in the establishment of the Progressive Democrats. For myself I would have preferred if Des O'Malley and she had joined Fine Gael. The establishment of a new political party was, I felt, a second-best; but whatever the short-term consequences for Fine Gael—and I have to say I never contemplated a drift of our voters to the new party on the scale that actually occurred in 1987—it seemed a good thing at the time that a new rallying point be established against Fianna Fáil under Charles Haughey that would ensure that he would not become leader of a Government with an absolute majority in Dáil Éireann.

The closing months of 1985 saw the emergence of two other issues that were to loom very large during 1986, our last year in Government. These were the early stages of the teachers' pay dispute, and growing pressure for the introduction of divorce.

The teachers' unions have always been a powerful force, and their efforts had led to a higher valuation being put on the work of teachers in Ireland than in many other countries. I believe that over the years this had been one of a number of factors contributing to the quality of Irish education. We were now, however, faced with a serious dilemma. We were experiencing great difficulty in reducing the level of the budget deficit and of Government borrowing below that to which we had cut them quite sharply between 1981 and 1983, and the exchequer was certainly in no position to take on the burden of a very large increase in teachers' pay, which, it was proposed, should be back-dated and which could all too easily prove a headline for similar claims from other groups in the public sector. Accordingly we felt we had no alternative but to plead inability to pay the proposed award, and by mid-January 1986 talks on the issue had collapsed.

Gemma Hussey had been actively pursuing a whole range of reforms in the educational sector, a number of which were, however, being frustrated by lack of resources. She was distressed at the idea that sums many times in excess of those needed to provide the resources for a significant improvement in the quality of education in various sectors were now being sought to improve teachers' pay at a time when the community as a whole was going through a period of intensive belt-tightening. As a result, in a radio interview she had been moved to raise the question of the morality of a pay claim of this magnitude being pressed at a time of national difficulty. My sympathies were with her as she met a flood of almost hysterical denunciation from indignant teachers; I could so easily have made the same comment myself.

Now, just as the teachers' pay dispute reached its climax, Gemma was hit by another torpedo. In view of the pending rapid decline in the number of primary pupils—due to fall by some 135,000, or almost 25 per cent, by the end of the century—a decision we had had to take in Government was to close one of the training colleges for primary teachers, Carysfort College in Dublin. There was already considerable overcapacity in the system; before the end of the 1980s the remaining training colleges would have four times as many places as would be needed. When the decision was finally taken that Carysfort should close, unhappily this information leaked out and reached the college head prematurely, just before she was officially informed, thus unleashing another storm around Gemma Hussey, who was accused of discourtesy as well as, absurdly, of sabotaging the training of teachers.

I had always envisaged a reshuffle of the Government in the second half of our term of office. The delay in the conclusion of the Anglo-Irish Agreement had led me to postpone consideration of such a move until early in 1986. Whether we won the next election or not, I intended to retire as party leader in the early part of the next Dáil, and I was concerned to leave behind me a party in which the leading figures would have as wide a range of experience as I could manage to secure for them, and one in which the various potential future leaders of the party would as far as possible find themselves starting from positions of equal strength; I wanted to make sure that none would be disadvantaged by virtue of the roles they had had to play in my Government. I was convinced that it would be wrong of me to try to influence in any way the outcome of that leadership contest; on the contrary my duty to the party was to ensure the widest and most open choice possible. I was also concerned, as I had been in December 1982, when I did not reappoint some of the junior Ministers who had served in my previous brief administration, to give an opportunity to several younger backbenchers to serve in Government for a time before the next general election.

To these considerations was now added concern lest several Ministers find their future political prospects damaged by being identified in the public mind with financial cuts made necessary by our extremely difficult economic situation, and I was anxious that those concerned should have an opportunity to recover ground in other, less controversial departments before our Government came to the end of its term in 1987.

These various worthy motivations led me now into a reshuffle whose consequences proved damaging to me personally and to our Government.

The two Ministers whom I had decided some time previously to move with a view to minimising the political damage that participation in this Government might have done them were Alan Dukes, who had the most unpopular job of all in Finance, and Barry Desmond, who had handled the Health portfolio with great skill but at the cost of considerable unpopularity because of the cuts he had been forced to make. Dick Spring agreed with me about his party colleague, Barry Desmond, who had a marginal seat.

Gemma Hussey also had a very marginal seat, and for her to remain in her post while the teachers' dispute continued to rage would, I now felt, put her re-election also at risk. On the pay issue itself I was totally supportive of her stand, and in moving her I had no intention whatever of easing the way for a Government climb-down, as subsequent events were misleadingly to suggest.

As to the others, John Bruton had, I knew, been upset by not being reappointed to Finance in December 1982, but this had given him an opportunity to widen his experience, and he could, I felt, now return to the job to which I knew he aspired, without the danger of being typecast as the man who had taken all the unpopular decisions over a six-year period.

Michael Noonan had done an excellent job in Justice and was entitled to be given experience in some other major post. John Boland had carried through a number of key reforms that I had wanted to see implemented in the civil service structure, and deserved a chance to apply his talents to a 'heavy' department where his toughness and drive might achieve worthwhile results in the year ahead.

Peter Barry, my deputy leader, had told me that if I wished to move him from Foreign Affairs he would go, but he clearly preferred to stay where he was, and there was a case for maintaining continuity here in the early stages of the implementation of the Anglo-Irish Agreement.

Jim Mitchell was doing a remarkable job in Communications, and already had experience in another post; I decided to let him stay to complete the task he was undertaking of 'turning around' the previously loss-making enterprises under his control. And Austin Deasy should, I felt, remain in Agriculture, where he had won the respect of the farming community without bending to their often excessive demands.

Another question I had to consider in the context of a reshuffle was whether I should offer one or two junior Ministers an opportunity to serve in the cabinet. On balance, however, I decided against such a move. There had been no tradition in Ireland of dropping Ministers from the cabinet, and the disturbance this would cause in the closing stages of a Government that was under pressure in the Dáil and had yet to face the hazards of legislation on divorce and extradition did not seem worth while. I could give a couple of backbenchers a taste of office by replacing one or two junior Ministers, as I had made clear at the start of the Government I intended to do. That was as far as it seemed wise to go in terms of dropping Ministers.

As to where the reshuffled Ministers were to be relocated, there were many options. Once I had decided to move Gemma Hussey, Alan Dukes emerged as a possible replacement in Education. He would not want to concede on the teachers' pay claim, and I believed he would carry on the reforms she had initiated. John Boland seemed well suited for the Environment portfolio, but he could equally well take on Health and Social Welfare if Barry Desmond were to be moved to Environment. As for Gemma Hussey, I had been contemplating for some time previously the allocation of a second cabinet Minister to Foreign Affairs to look after European Community matters and perhaps also development aid, and this now seemed a matter of some urgency, because in the months ahead Peter Barry would have his hands full with Northern Ireland as well as the rest of Foreign Affairs. In tentative sketches of the possible reshuffle ante-dating my late decision to move Gemma Hussey I had considered allocating Alan Dukes provisionally to this new post, but Gemma's move from Education opened up the alternative scenario I have just outlined. The other significant change I proposed at this point was a move of Michael Noonan to Industry and Commerce, replacing him in Justice with Barry Desmond or, if Barry went to Environment, with Dick Spring.

This was the rough outline of the reshuffle I initiated on the evening of Wednesday 12 February. Most of the changes were accepted without too much demur by those concerned, although Gemma Hussey was clearly, and under-standably, upset by being asked to move from Education. However, she was obviously attracted by the proposed European Affairs post. Both that evening and next morning she rang me back to clarify aspects of the new arrangements; I did my best to reassure her. When the last such call came on the following morning my reshuffle was at that time in grave difficulties, and I had to cut our conversation short.

Two problems had arisen. Barry Desmond had refused to move, preferring, he said, to lose his seat if that were the price to be paid than to abandon his portfolio at this time. And Dermot Nally had that morning informed me that if I appointed Gemma Hussey as European Affairs Minister in the cabinet I would have to divide the Department of Foreign Affairs in two and to appoint a separate Secretary of a new European Affairs Department. The Barry Desmond crisis, which soon began to leak to the media, prevented me from probing this advice as deeply as I might otherwise have done. By midday Dick Spring, who had supported my proposal to move Barry Desmond, was in my office telling me that he had been unable to resolve the problem and that in the circum-stances he felt he must resign from the Government together with his colleagues. I should prepare to establish a Fine Gael Government without the Labour Party, he said.

Shattered by this totally unexpected consequence of my concern, and Dick's, for Barry Desmond's political future, and aware of the growing atmosphere of rumour outside, I sat down to prepare a Fine Gael alternative Government. However, within half an hour Dick Spring was back with the news that Barry Desmond would relinquish his Social Welfare portfolio if he could keep Health; he had always given most of his time to health matters.

As the rumours of a crisis rapidly grew I undertook a quick reshaping of my original proposal. The emergence of a vacant Social Welfare portfolio, virtually coinciding with the effectual disappearance of my putative European Affairs post (for I was not prepared to damage the Department of Foreign Affairs by splitting it in two with two departmental Secretaries) provided a possible solution to the problem of safeguarding Gemma Hussey's seat. Barry Desmond's over-concentration of his attention on the Department of Health in the past couple of years had left room, I thought, for a reforming Minister for Social Welfare, and Gemma Hussey would, I felt, be as effective in this role as she had been in Education. She would, I hoped, be willing to explore the possibility of creating a single income transfer system, combining social welfare and taxation. Patrick Honohan at my request had already investigated the feasibility of such a unified basic income system, and his analysis suggested that it was within the realm of practical possibility, although there were significant problems that might be very difficult to resolve at a time when we had no leeway for tax cuts. Labour Party Ministers take a conservative view on issues of this kind, tending to shy away from fundamental changes because of their attachment to the traditional social insurance system, and a Minister of that party might, I felt, have been disinclined to contemplate a basic income system.

With Barry Desmond not available for the Environment or Justice portfolios, I allocated Environment to John Boland—which had been my first preference for him and, I suspected, his own preference also—and Alan Dukes to Justice rather than Education. This left a vacancy in Education. Of the Ministers not so far placed Pat Cooney was the senior, and I offered him Education, on this basis rather than because I felt he had a particular aptitude for this portfolio. By this time I felt under pressure to complete the process before the rumours about the reshuffle got totally out of hand. The process was then completed by moving Liam Kavanagh to Forestry and Fisheries, with Paddy O'Toole replacing Pat Cooney in Defence while retaining the Gaeltacht portfolio.

The result was not really satisfactory. Gemma Hussey was deeply distressed at being moved from Education and then losing the European Affairs portfolio, to the prospect of which she had begun to look forward. She saw Social Welfare as a bed of nails rather than as an opportunity to initiate a fundamental reform of income redistribution, for which, indeed, there was very little time before the already impending general election. While Pat Cooney was happy to move to Education, being of a conservative bent he did not have Gemma Hussey's deep commitment to educational reform. Moreover, in my view he turned out to be too easily convinced by his civil servants of the need to concede to some of the teachers' union demands, although in fairness I should add that they ended up persuading me also, against my better judgement, to agree to these concessions on the basis that the cost would be covered by a combination of savings on the salaries of teachers who had been on strike and a claim for a graduates' allowance that was due to be settled but could be subsumed in settlement of the dispute. I subsequently came to doubt the validity of this calculation.

Moreover, quite apart from the Hussey-Cooney dimension of the reshuffle, the public impact of what was seen as a badly executed move was damaging, and the mess was made worse by a subsequent error of mine with respect to the reshuffling of the Fine Gael junior Ministers. When I had appointed the junior Ministers in 1982 I had made it clear to them that I intended to reshuffle them at some point and that I would be introducing some new blood during the lifetime of this Government. In line with this policy I decided to replace two of my older Ministers of State with two backbenchers in their mid-thirties. I was given to understand that one of the Ministers of State to be replaced already expected to return to the back benches, and when I saw him he accepted my decision without demur. The other protested. Not wishing to rub salt in their wounds, however, I did not (as Dermot Nally had warned me I should do) specifically ask them to put their resignations in writing; I foolishly assumed that they would do this automatically. I suffered the consequences of this moment of unwise compassion, for when they returned to their constituencies after I had announced their resignations and the names of their replacements in the Dáil, they repudiated my statement, declaring that they had not resigned, as technically they had not. I was then forced to implement the procedure for termination of their appointments, and also to apologise to the Dáil the next time it met for having inadvertently misled it.

Thus ended an unhappy episode, the memory of which may have been a factor influencing Charles Haughey to abandon a planned reshuffle of his Government in early 1991.

Two further changes of junior Ministers took place subsequently. One Labour Minister of State resigned and was replaced by a colleague, and I had to replace a Fine Gael junior Minister in unhappy circumstances. Through inadvertence and clearly without any improper intent, Eddie Collins, a Minister of State in the Department of Industry and Commerce, who was an exceptionally hard-working and effective member of our team, had attended some meetings of the board of a family company from which he had quite properly resigned on appointment to his Ministerial post. He was present at such a meeting when an application for assistance from a state financial institution was discussed.

My request for his resignation was a painful decision, taken after a personal examination by me of the events in question. He clearly found my decision hard to accept. I felt, however, that if I were to uphold integrity in public life I must ensure not only that no impropriety occurred—which in my view was clearly the case—but that no suspicion of impropriety be allowed to exist. Justice, in terms of integrity in public life, must be seen to be done as well as actually being done. Some of my colleagues, I believe, felt that I was acting more strictly than necessary in this case; and for my own part it was perhaps the most painful personal decision I had to take as Taoiseach, and one that has left me most unhappy ever since.

The issue of divorce had been a live one within Fine Gael since 1978, when at a very well-attended meeting during my first ard-fheis as leader the participants had given strong support to the removal of the constitutional ban on the dissolution of marriage. During my first period in Government I had sought to have this matter discussed by an all-party committee, but this had been rejected by Fianna Fáil, and a few days before the budget on which the Government fell I had written to the leader of the opposition to say that I regretted that it had not been possible to set up this committee by agreement and that in the circumstances I proposed bringing forward a motion in the Dáil to establish a select committee of the Oireachtas for this purpose as soon as the Dáil resumed.

Because of the fall of the Government nothing came of this; but when we returned to Government at the end of 1982 we took the matter up again with the Fianna Fáil opposition, and in July 1983 we secured agreement to the establishment of a Joint Committee on Marital Breakdown to consider the protection of marriage and of family life and to examine the problems arising from the breakdown of marriage, and to report within a year. In the event, because of Fianna Fáil obstruction, two years were to elapse before the committee reported, but it eventually came up with a majority recommendation that the prohibition on the dissolution of marriage in the Constitution should be replaced with a positive provision authorising divorce in certain circumstances.

It would have been possible, I suppose, to stall more or less indefinitely on this issue, but this carried the risk that divorce would feature largely in the eventual general election to be held in 1987. This seemed to me highly undesirable; that election should, I believed, be fought as clearly as possible on the issue of fiscal policy, with a view to pinning Fianna Fáil down to facing the need for continued action to reduce borrowing should they, as seemed possible, return to power at that election. If the issue of divorce were not faced now we could find ourselves facing an election in which this crucial economic issue might be sidetracked by a campaign in which we would be under attack both from liberals for not having initiated a divorce referendum and from Fianna Fáil for allegedly intending on re-election to introduce divorce on demand. My feeling that this matter should be addressed without further delay was reinforced by the fact that public opinion, as recorded by various polls, appeared to favour a move to introduce a restricted form of divorce, although I would prefer the margin in favour of this to have been somewhat larger.

Irish marriage law as it evolved in the nineteenth century, with some amendments in 1972, is uniquely complex, with different provisions for different religious denominations as well as provision for civil marriages before a registrar. Clearly, as the great majority of marriages are solemnised in churches of one denomination or another, with a subsequent civil registration of the marriage, any move to modify the provision in relation to the indissolubility of such marriages must involve consultation with the churches in question. There were moreover other issues in relation to marriage itself that needed to be addressed and that were of legitimate concern to the churches, quite apart from the question of an amendment to the Constitution with a view to making possible legislation dissolving marriages.

Accordingly, on 14 February 1986 I wrote to the heads of the various churches to tell them that in view of the common interest of the state and the churches in the stability of marriage, and more specifically in view of the fact that the vast majority of marriages are solemnised in churches and are registered as civil marriages by the clergyman concerned, I was anxious to have the views of the principal churches on the recommendations of the Joint Oireachtas Committee on Marriage Breakdown and on matters that might arise from these recommendations, before bringing to the Government proposals in relation to these matters.

I went on to list the issues on which I was particularly anxious to have the views of the churches, namely the minimum age of marriage; the possible desirability of providing for a minimum period of notice before marriage; counselling for married couples having matrimonial difficulties; the legal grounds for separation; the enforcement of the law proscribing bigamy; possible changes in the law of nullity; the possible establishment of family tribunals to deal with all types of marriage cases; and, in cases where a marriage had irretrievably broken down, the question of divorce and remarriage.

I also told them I would prefer to arrange these consultations generally on a joint basis should this prove acceptable to all the churches concerned, although even if this were acceptable I recognised that on particular points separate consultations with an individual church or churches might be considered desirable. However, most of the churches preferred not to participate in a joint consultation, asking me to receive them separately. Moreover, the Irish Episcopal Conference of the Roman Catholic Church asked to add several items to the agenda, namely better financial support for the family in marriage; the rights of the parents vis-à-vis their own children in the light of proposals to safeguard children from abuse and neglect; and the Domicile and Recognition of Foreign Divorces Act, which we had introduced some time previously.

I started the series of meetings with the churches following my return from my American visit in mid-March, and concluded them after Easter, when I met the Church of Ireland and the Roman Catholic Church.

The meetings with the churches were in fact very constructive and contributed significantly to the proposals we subsequently produced. Thus our decision to propose a minimum age of eighteen for marriage, subject to the possibility of authorisation of marriage in exceptional circumstances by a proposed family court for people between the ages of sixteen and eighteen, reflected the thinking of most of the churches; and our proposal to introduce a new requirement of a minimum of three months' notice for marriage was influenced by our discussions with representatives of the Catholic hierarchy in particular. The decision to allow divorce only where a marriage had failed and the failure had continued for a period or periods of at least five years reflected the thinking of several churches, including in particular the Church of Ireland.

It had been expected that the discussions with representatives of the Roman Catholic hierarchy would be the most difficult, because of their objection to the introduction of any form of divorce, but in fact that part of our discussion proved relatively straightforward, in that we agreed to differ on that issue. Some tension did arise, however, in the course of this meeting on a different issue, which perhaps requires some background explanation.

The Irish law of nullity derives from the ecclesiastical law of the Church of Ireland, which always remained very restrictive by comparison with the developing provisions for declarations of nullity by ecclesiastical tribunals of the Roman Catholic Church. This produced the uncomfortable situation where the same marriage in civil and ecclesiastical law is subject to two quite different nullity processes, so that a certain number of Irish marriages that have been annulled by the Roman Catholic Church in circumstances that permit of remarriage in that church remain valid marriages in the eyes of the state. In these cases remarriage in a Catholic church constitutes bigamy, although, because of the difficulty of securing evidence of the second marriage, prosecutions for bigamy do not take place. This is an uncomfortable position both for church and state, and it was a matter that had to be addressed in the context of our discussions, which, in conjunction with Alan Dukes, the new Minister for Justice, I undertook with the representatives of the Roman Catholic hierarchy.

When we reached this point on the agenda I remarked that the problem could be tackled by separating the civil and religious ceremonies but that I was reluctant to contemplate such a separation if it could be avoided, in view of what I believed to be the attachment of most Irish people to the traditional joint ceremony. The member of the hierarchy allocated by their delegation to deal with this matter then raised the possibility of a new arrangement, under which a church remarriage of someone who had benefited from a church decree of nullity would constitute a purely religious event, which would make no claim and give no appearance of a civilly valid marriage. It was suggested that the hierarchy and the Government might co-operate in the development of such a new arrangement.

In retrospect I think that perhaps in their concern to find a solution to the conflict of laws that would enable the Catholic Church to continue with its existing practice of making declarations of nullity, the representatives of the hierarchy may not have considered the implications of this proposal for Alan Dukes and myself. As a result they were, I think, taken aback by the strength of our reaction to a proposal that appeared to us to suggest that, instead of amending the Constitution to provide a means for dealing with this as well as other marriage breakdown problems (which the representatives of the hierarchy were strongly opposing), we should collaborate in undermining the existing constitutional protection of marriage. For as long as this clause remained in the Constitution, we were committed as officers under the Constitution to uphold it.

In the face of our very negative reaction to their initial suggestion the representatives of the hierarchy did not proceed to elaborate the suggestions they had in mind about how such an arrangement might be implemented on their side; instead we passed on to other matters. However, some years later this matter surfaced publicly when, in an interview as leader of Fine Gael, Alan Dukes expressed forcibly, and, it must be said, in inappropriate language, his feelings about the proposal made to us by the hierarchy. For my part, in

December 1989 in an article in the magazine *Alpha* I wrote: 'There was even a suggestion by the hierarchy delegation that we "bend" our civil marriage laws so as to accommodate these bigamous marriages, a suggestion that was, in my view, quite improper.'

This comment evoked a letter to me from the late Cardinal Ó Fiaich in which he took issue with my comments. He went on to explain that what the representatives of the hierarchy had been intending to propose to us at that meeting was that in the case of Catholics whose earlier marriage had been annulled in the ecclesiastical court they be remarried either by way of a religious marriage accompanied by a disclaimer of any civil significance for the ceremony or by way of a marriage ceremony in the absence of an episcopally ordained minister, with a lay person delegated instead to assist at the marriage, or perhaps even by a marriage taking place in the presence of witnesses alone and without any representative of the Catholic Church present.

I responded to this letter several months later, pointing out that from our point of view what the hierarchy delegation had started to propose to us would have involved an arrangement between the Government and the hierarchy of one church designed to facilitate the entry by some people into arrangements that at the very least would in the eyes of the public purport to displace the existing joint civil-religious marriage, which enjoyed the protection of the Constitution. And I went on to raise a number of other aspects of the matter that concerned me. At the end of the letter I suggested that publication of this exchange of letters on a matter of considerable interest would be appropriate, with a view to clarifying for the public the complex issues at stake; but because of Cardinal Ó Fiaich's tragic death some time later, before he had an opportunity to reply to my letter, I did not pursue this matter. The two letters are, however, reproduced as an appendix to this book.

A fortnight after this series of meetings with the churches, Dick Spring, Alan Dukes and myself launched our proposals for a referendum on an amendment to the Constitution to remove the ban on the dissolution of marriage. In conjunction with this press conference we published the text of the Bill and a statement of our intentions with regard to separation and divorce. This statement was designed to meet a genuine and widely held concern that in introducing a restricted form of divorce we might be starting on a slippery slope towards 'easy divorce'. The proposed constitutional amendment itself provided that a dissolution could be granted only where these conditions were fulfilled, i.e. that the marriage had failed and the failure had continued for a period or periods amounting to at least five years, that there was no possibility of reconciliation between the parties to the marriage, and that moreover the court was satisfied that adequate and proper provision, having regard to the circumstances, would be made for any dependent spouse or for any child who was dependent on either spouse.

In the Bill that we announced simultaneously with the proposed constitutional amendment we also proposed that a divorce would have to be preceded by a judicial separation at least two years previously, and new grounds were introduced for such separations, namely desertion, including constructive desertion, separation for up to three years, or separation for one year with the consent of the respondent. Separation and divorce cases were to be heard by a Family Court, to be presided over by a judge or judges of the Circuit Court specially assigned for this purpose, and this court would have power to adjourn proceedings for a separation if it thought it necessary or appropriate that a mediation process, to be conducted by a registered counselling agency, should be undergone before the legal proceedings.

In the course of our press conference I made it clear that our two parties would be supporting the amendment to the Constitution in the Dáil and before the electorate, while accepting that individual members might on grounds of conscience not wish to participate in the campaign if they held a contrary view on the amendment.

The basis on which we were proceeding to introduce the provision for divorce was our belief that the balance of social good would be served by making this provision, for while it was accepted that any divorce provision might have a negative effect on some existing marriages, on the other hand the number of people now in irregular unions and the number of children adversely affected by this situation was, in the considered view of our parties, even more desta-bilising. During the press conference one journalist remarked that the campaign on the referendum had already been predicted to be a dirty and divisive one, and asked how I would be trying to sell the referendum when I went out to the country to campaign on it, to which I replied, 'Less luridly.' She was right about the campaign, however.

A poll was carried out a few days later that showed that at that point 57 per cent were in favour of our constitutional amendment and 36 per cent against, with 7 per cent not holding an opinion. There was a majority in favour in all four regions, in rural as well as urban areas, and in all political parties (although by a small margin in the case of Fianna Fáil supporters), and only the oldest age group and large farmers contained a majority against the referendum at that point.

The campaign against the proposed amendment was launched on 9 May, and a few days later the hierarchy set out their opposition to the legislation and their intention to publish and distribute one million copies of a pastoral letter against divorce. I was disturbed to hear around this time that Pat Cooney, now Minister for Education, had attacked the proposed legislation at a private meeting of his Longford-Westmeath constituency. We had secured agreement in our party that the amendment would not be opposed, although I had made it clear that no-one would be required to campaign for divorce if they had a conscientious objection to its introduction.

By early June a poll showed that about one-fifth of those who had previously favoured the amendment had clearly become undecided about it, with no change at that point in the proportion against divorce. As the anti-divorce campaign gained momentum with a formal statement by the hierarchy on 11 June, support for the amendment eroded rapidly, and a poll taken shortly before the referendum, which was held on 27 June, showed that opinion had by that time swung conclusively against it.

The suddenness and magnitude of this shift in opinion during the first half of June was unexpected, and indeed unprecedented. Two factors seem to have played a major part in it. The first was the fact that an earlier commitment by the Catholic hierarchy not to tell people how to vote but to confine themselves to stating the Catholic moral position on the issue was not adhered to. Immense pressure from the pulpit was put on people to oppose the referendum. The second fact was the skilful and unscrupulous way in which some opponents of divorce sought to spread alarm about the possible effect on property rights of the introduction of divorce.

These two elements, combined with the strong opposition to the amendment from Fianna Fáil throughout the country, despite that party's stated neutral stance, and with unenthusiastic campaigning by many supporters of our party in particular, had produced a swing in opinion on the part of something like a quarter of the total electorate, which led to a 63 per cent majority against the proposed constitutional amendment.

I found the debate itself extremely depressing. Given the Catholic Church's stated position that it did not seek to impose its theological views on the civil law of the state, it seemed to me that the only relevant consideration was whether the balance of social good would or would not be served by the restricted form of divorce. I recognised that there could of course be divided views on this issue—it was essentially a matter of judgement—but the fact that the two sides of this crucial question were never addressed by the church during the course of the campaign disturbed me.

Quite unconnected with the divorce question was the introduction of legislation at around the same time to abolish the concept of illegitimacy. This was a matter that Young Fine Gael had taken up some years earlier, running a national campaign on the issue that had awoken people's consciences and had stimulated us to address the question in Government. It turned out, however, that the legal complexities of the issue were far greater than they, or indeed I, had envisaged. The memorandum for the Government on the proposed legislation ran to almost a hundred pages, and this did not include any padding but comprised detailed analysis of many consequential legal effects of the changes that we proposed to make. This Status of Children Bill effected a major and long-overdue reform in our law, and while the enactment of the legislation took several years, coming to fruition only in the following Dáil, I was happy that we had initiated and drafted such a significant measure of social reform.

The last few months of 1986 proved to be our most traumatic time in Government. Our small majority in the Dáil evaporated, and our Government found itself at the mercy of half a dozen members of our two parties who on one issue or another threatened to withdraw their support. At the same time expenditure for the first time during our period in Government began to exceed the level provided for in the estimates, leading to a sudden sharp rise in interest rates; moreover, the implementation of EC sex equality legislation, which had negative effects on some social welfare beneficiaries, led to a revolt in our two parties, necessitating a series of climb-downs by the Government, with serious financial implications. The ratification of the Single European Act, postponed at Labour's request until after its party conference in early November, was placed in doubt. The highly contentious legislation to ratify the Convention on the Suppression of Terrorism with a view to strengthening our extradition law had to be got through a Dáil in which we no longer had a majority. And while all this was happening our two parties found themselves unable to agree on budgetary proposals, a development that eventually led to a break-up of the Government. I doubt if any other Government since the end of the Civil War in 1923 faced such a catalogue of difficulties crowding in on it one after the other in such a short space of time.

Despite defections by Fine Gael and Labour Party deputies that eventually eliminated the combined majority in the Dáil, we continued to introduce reforming measures, including an Adoption Bill to extend adoptions to legitimate children who had been abandoned by their parents—a cause to which I had been strongly committed since an experience I had in an orphanage during the 1979 European election but one that required particularly careful handling because of possible constitutional difficulties. We also proceeded with the establishment of the Dublin Transportation Authority, a long-overdue measure of transport rationalisation in an area that had been neglected for decades. And this was followed by a Bill to establish a Dublin Metropolitan Streets Authority to take over from the city council the central part of the city, the appearance of which was suffering from long neglect. (Both these measures were cancelled by Fianna Fáil after its return to power.)

A personal initiative of my own around this time that upset some of my colleagues because I had not consulted them was the announcement that I was not prepared to see the old-established firm of Bewley's Oriental Cafés disappear, as was then threatened. By alerting other private interests to the potential of this business, thus precipitating a take-over of Bewley's, my action saved one of Dublin's great attractions without the need for any actual state intervention.

Meanwhile during September I had endeavoured to concentrate the minds of potentially dissident backbenchers by announcing that TDs who did not obey the party whip during the session ahead would not be ratified as candidates in the next general election.

Turning now to the financial difficulties that eventually brought down the Government, the publication at the end of September of exchequer returns for the first nine months revealed a deterioration in the balance of expenditure and revenue that pointed towards a £180 million overrun in exchequer borrowing in the calendar year. This raised serious doubts in the minds of the financial community about our capacity to survive as a Government and fears of a return to power of a Fianna Fáil Government that might, it was then believed, abandon financial restraint as it had done in 1977–81 and again in early 1982.

Massive sales of Government stock followed, the yield on Government funds rose sharply, and interest rates rose by three to four percentage points, although the increase in bank and building society rates was held at 2 per cent.

In mid-October, in an effort to steady the markets and to restore confidence in our determination to maintain the process of reducing the deficit and borrowing, I put to the Government a proposal that we should announce that the current deficit for 1987 would be held at the current year's budgeted level of 7.4 per cent of GNP and that exchequer borrowing in 1987 would be less than the budgeted figure of 11.8 per cent for the current year, which in that year seemed about to be exceeded by one percentage point. I also proposed that we make it clear that we would not increase the burden of taxes.

The clear implication of any such announcement was that significant expenditure cuts would be effected; this naturally presented problems for our Labour partners. Nevertheless the threat to interest rates in particular posed by the decline in confidence in financial circles was such that I felt it necessary on this occasion to do what I had never previously done: to press for a majority decision, despite the opposition of our four Labour Party colleagues.

While warning that this could put at risk their continued participation in the Government when we came to take decisions on the estimates for 1987, the Labour Party Ministers agreed to accept this majority decision without public dissent in order to deal with the immediate crisis. Nevertheless, the fact that we were forced into this unprecedented course of action made it virtually certain that our Government would not survive in its current form to present the 1987 budget.

I shall return later to the discussions that ensued, setting them against the background of the budgetary measures we had taken in the years since 1984; but first I must sketch the way in which other events developed during the two months between mid-October and Christmas.

The first test came in the opening week of the session when, on 23 October, we faced a vote of confidence, which we won by 83 votes to 81. It was clear by this time, however, that one of our biggest problems in the weeks ahead would be to retain the support of one of our backbenchers, Liam Skelly, who was now pressing the Government to accept a scheme put forward by Canadian developers to build a bus station and an associated shopping centre in the middle of Dublin in conjunction with a proposed underground railway. I was not prepared to agree to anything that was not fully justified on its merits, or by departing from the normal procedures for Government negotiations with the promoters of such projects; but as some aspects of the project seemed to have some potential merit I agreed that they should be further examined, and on this basis Skelly's continued support was secured for the time being. However, we remained under threat of a defection by him until the end of the year.

Next, major problems arose in relation to a Social Welfare Bill designed to implement EC requirements in respect of equality for women. Because this new system cut across traditional social welfare arrangements it threatened to *reduce* very substantially the payments being received by some 20,000 social welfare recipients. The cost of providing the new benefits without any loss to existing recipients would be many tens of millions, which, given the extraordinarily difficult budgetary situation facing us, we felt we could not accommodate. However, the pressure on Fine Gael Ministers from our backbenchers, and the pressure on the Labour Party from its backbenchers, was such that we were forced into a series of climb-downs, involving eventually agreement to changes that would cost £36 million in the following year—and even this package got through the Dáil only on the casting vote of the Ceann Comhairle following an 80/80 vote on 26 November.

Two days later one of our dissident backbenchers, a right-wing conservative Catholic, Alice Glenn, failed to secure reselection at the constituency convention in Dublin Central. I discussed the situation with her, but she resigned the whip, leaving us in a minority in the Dáil.

A couple of days later Fianna Fáil made it clear that they would oppose our Extradition Bill because it did not require prima facie evidence against the accused in our courts and did not reserve to the Government a right to refuse extradition if it had reason to believe that a person extradited would not receive justice in the courts of the country to which he was to be sent. We were now at risk both in relation to the Single European Act legislation and the Extradition Bill; but the Labour members rallied on the Single European Act, and with support from the three Progressive Democrat members it was passed against Fianna Fáil opposition by a margin of 70 to 63 on 11 December, with Alice Glenn joining Fianna Fáil in the vote against us on this occasion.

The final hurdle was the Extradition Bill, on which a series of votes was decided on the Ceann Comhairle's casting vote after Alice Glenn had abstained. It was eventually passed on the basis that in order to leave time for the various procedures under the Bill to be sorted out it would not come into effect until 1 December 1987. Two deputies who were ill—David Andrews of Fianna Fáil and Oliver Flanagan on our side—attended; the appearance of Oliver Flanagan, who everyone knew had not long to live and who had been a stormy petrel in Irish politics during his forty-three years in the Dáil, evoked a spontaneous round of applause from the whole Dáil.

The final act of the Dáil on 18 December was the defeat by a margin of one vote of a Fianna Fáil amendment calling for its dissolution.

To conclude my account I must return now to our handling of the economy during the years following our first budget in 1983, the preparation of which I outlined in an earlier chapter together with the manner in which we later implemented recommendations of the National Planning Board.

But first I should say that the strain on Ministers created by the financial pressures that we had to face was considerable. The truth is that the most debilitating venture one can undertake in politics is identifying and deciding on cuts in public spending. It is difficult for individual Ministers to approach this issue with objectivity: they are bound to be concerned both about possible damage to the public services for which they have been given responsibility and about the political implications of cuts for their electoral support. Moreover, few Ministers are able to escape from a sense of obligation to defend their department's spending; their own self-esteem is at stake, and their civil servants keep them under intense pressure to defend their corners. Finally, concern not to do less well than their colleagues causes them to eye with suspicion the cuts being made—or, more important, *not* being made—by these colleagues.

Most Governments hit a patch when tough decisions of this kind must be taken; but when through the life of two Governments over a period of almost six years this dreary process has to be repeated annually, the morale of all concerned is bound to suffer. The heritage of our predecessors' incredible extravagance was a heavy burden for our Ministers to bear.

The fact that our Ministers were drawn from two different parties, with different sectoral support, aggravated the problem, but this was only a contributing factor. The real difficulty lay with the situation we had to face, and with the realisation, gradually borne in upon us, that there was unlikely to be any light for us at the end of the tunnel. The breakthrough to a normal political situation, in which there would be real political choices to be made between different courses of action rather than a single one-course menu of cuts followed by cuts followed by cuts, was not going to come in the lifetime of *our* Government, whether we went in for a 'big bang' massive deflation or tried to keep the economy on a reasonably even keel while chipping away at the problem.

The measures we took to monitor spending during 1983 had, however, been highly successful. In contrast to preceding years, spending in 1983 was kept within 0.25 per cent of the budgeted level. It is true that tax revenue fell short of the projected figure by just over 1 per cent, but the resultant overrun on the current budget was partly offset by a reduction in capital spending. All in all this was an encouraging start, especially as in one year we had cut exchequer borrowing by a further three percentage points.

Adjusting for the impact on public revenue and expenditure of the withdrawal of the postal and telecommunications services from the civil service (they had been constituted as separate state enterprises with their own budgets), exchequer borrowing was down from a threatened 21 per cent to just over 14 per cent of GNP. But now, in line with EC Commission guidelines, we had to reduce it by a further 1 to 1.5 per cent in 1984, i.e. to around 12.75 per cent of GNP.

In October–November 1983 we went through the painful process of reducing proposed expenditure by some £250 million, or almost 5 per cent—cuts, however, that left public spending slightly above the previous year's level as a percentage of GNP. But, together with some £110 million of additional taxes, mainly on expenditure, these measures enabled us to meet out current deficit and borrowing targets in the 1984 budget while easing the income tax burden slightly and increasing social benefits, including children's allowances, by 7 per cent. This increase more than compensated for inflation, for in the twelve months covered by these increases the rise in the consumer price index proved to be only 5 per cent.

The National Planning Board had not recommended an explicit target for exchequer borrowing, and in preparing our National Plan during 1984 in the absence of such guidance we had to define for ourselves an appropriate budgetary framework. We did this by making our goal a stabilisation by 1987 of the debt/GNP ratio, which had been rising at a most alarming rate since 1977—and this required a reduction of the current deficit to 5 per cent of GNP by the target year and a cut in exchequer borrowing to 9.75 per cent of GNP by the same year. This significant modification of our original objective of eliminating the current deficit within four or five years of our return to office at the end of 1982 was justified in our plan on the grounds of adverse international economic development since 1981. At prevailing high real interest rates in international markets an attempt to achieve our original target of a current budgetary balance by 1987 would, we said, have so great a deflationary effect as to damage severely for many years to come the vitality of the economy. The merits of this decision are naturally arguable, but it should be seen against the background of the fact that in our budgets of the previous three years we had reduced the threatened level of borrowing by nearly £1,000 million—almost 7 per cent of GNP.

During these discussions in Government on the implementation of the plan we had faced the problem of securing a reduction in the proportion of GNP absorbed by public spending, and had decided that, rather than make further major cuts in public services, we would approach this problem by two other routes. In the 1983 and 1984 budgets we had overindexed social welfare payments by a substantial margin, partly accidentally as a result of underestimating our own ability to 'talk down' pay claims and thus to reduce rapidly the rate of inflation. In the context of the plan it was agreed that we would underindex 1985 payments by 1.5 per cent, which would still leave social welfare beneficiaries better off vis-à-vis their position in any earlier year. Secondly, it was also agreed that we would limit the cost of public service pay increases to 1 per cent in 1985 and 3 per cent in 1986. Some members of the Government were unhappy with these decisions, suspecting that in practice they would not be adhered to.

They were right. When the time came to make the 1985 budget decisions the Labour Party Ministers were not able to stand over the underindexation agreement, fearing the reaction of their deputies. Social welfare benefits were accordingly increased by the expected inflation rate of 6 to 6.5 per cent, but once again we underestimated our success against inflation: prices rose by barely 3 per cent between July 1985 and July 1986, so we ended up with a further unintended substantial overindexation of social welfare payments.

At the same time, if we tried to hold public service pay to a 1 per cent increase in 1985 an all-out strike in the public service was likely. Faced with this danger the Government eventually decided by a majority to concede a public service pay claim of 4.5 per cent: a not unreasonable figure in itself, but one that, in conjunction with the social welfare decision, cost us almost £100 million.

Nevertheless we had the satisfaction of starting our 1985 budget from the basis of a 1984 outturn that had improved upon our budget forecast; the current deficit and exchequer borrowing for 1984 were £50 million below our target figures. Both industry and agriculture had experienced substantial increases in output, as a result of which GDP had risen by almost 4 per cent—although over half of this growth had been absorbed by higher debt interest payments and an increase in the outflow of profits, so that the increase in GNP was much smaller.

This 1985 budget contained some radical measures, including a rationalisation of income tax and VAT rates. One of the six income tax bands had been eliminated in the previous year; now they were reduced to three, with a top rate of 60 per cent; over a quarter of taxpayers had their marginal tax rates reduced. The six VAT bands were reduced to two, the top rate being cut from 35 to 23 per cent; and VAT on newspapers was reduced from 23 to 10 per cent.

(There had been representations on this question for some time previously, but urgency was given to them by reports that without such an adjustment the *Irish Press* might close. Already in 1981 I had secured the abolition of price control on newspapers, because I was told that otherwise this newspaper might disappear. Despite the fact that the *Irish Press* had been the Fianna Fáil flagship since it was founded by de Valera almost fifty years earlier, there was no hesitation in the Government on either occasion. The desirability of maintaining a plurality of newspapers took precedence in all our minds over political considerations, although some of my colleagues speculated ruefully whether Fianna Fáil in Government would have taken a similar approach in relation to an organ established to support Fine Gael or the Labour Party.)

On the face of it, in the particular circumstances of that year the postponement of a reduction in the current deficit and in exchequer borrowing was not unreasonable. But it ignored one glaring political reality: we were boxing ourselves into a position in which the planned targets were now going to have to be achieved in the two pre-election budgets of 1986 and 1987, at the expense of a reduction of no less than one-quarter in the current deficit within this two-year period.

In a memorandum to me in mid-1985 Patrick Honohan pointed out some of the factors that had led us into this impasse. He took the view that in our first two budgets we had placed insufficient emphasis on expenditure cuts. This had happened in 1983 because of inadequate time to prepare a budget, which had to be based on our predecessors' Book of Estimates (Fianna Fáil faced exactly the same problem when they returned to office in 1987). But, possibly because of uncertainties about our majority in the Dáil after Frank Cluskey's December 1983 resignation, we had once again made fewer cuts in the proposed 1984 spending than would have been desirable, with the result that public spending as a proportion of GNP had drifted slightly upwards for the second successive year. The non-implementation of the agreement on under-indexation of social welfare payments and on an effective pay pause in 1985 had now left us with little room for manoeuvre, especially as economic growth in 1985 was disappointing, leading to a revenue shortfall and higher expenditure on unemployment than had been foreseen.

Patrick Honohan went on to point out that in the light of these develop-ments the prospect for the 1986 budget was notably unfavourable, with the danger of a current deficit over £200 million greater than that provided for in the National Plan. In fact 1985 turned out to be somewhat better than expected, because of savings on the capital budget and buoyancy of non-tax revenue. Nevertheless a tough 1986 budget was required to bring us back in line with the planned targets.

Substantial expenditure cuts were made in that budget; expenditure taxes were raised again, by £120 million; a deposit interest retention tax was introduced; and a 15 per cent tax was imposed on the gross investment income of life assurance companies. These measures brought our budgetary figures broadly into line with the planned targets—save for non-tax revenue, which was estimated to fall short of these targets because of a drop in the surplus income of the Central Bank that may have been due to the short-term impact of the ICI salvage operation and to a drop in Bord Gáis profits as a result of its having to bail out Dublin Gas.

Nevertheless we seemed now to be on course for our objectives, although we knew the 1987 pre-election budget would pose serious difficulties for us. If these could be resolved, however, then despite the ground lost because of Fianna Fáil's brief return to power in 1982, when taxes had been cut and spending increased, in comparable terms, we would have reduced exchequer borrowing from the threatened figure of 21.5 per cent of GNP for 1982 that had faced us on coming into office in mid-1981 to 9.75 per cent five-and-a-half years later. This would have been a remarkable achievement. But 1986 was to prove thoroughly disappointing.

First of all, even though as late as May 1986 the Central Bank was projecting a 3.5 per cent rise in GDP, by early 1987 it was clear that there had in fact been no growth at all in the economy during the year. Tourism was having a bad year, because American tourists were avoiding Europe, fearing retaliation for the US bombing of Libya; agricultural output was being affected adversely by weather for the second successive year; and the rise in industrial output had been halted as export growth had flagged. A sudden and sharp depreciation of sterling at a time when the dollar had also fallen was clearly beginning to put undue competitive pressure on our already depressed economy.

At the beginning of August John Bruton, now back in Finance, and myself, in consultation with Patrick Honohan, decided to tackle this latter problem by a unilateral devaluation of the Irish pound within the EMS. This was a controversial decision. Since the formation of the EMS in 1979 the Irish pound had occasionally been allowed to move down with the franc and the lira during general realignments, but on other occasions it had stayed in the middle of the band. As a result our currency had strengthened relative to all the EMS currencies except the Deutschmark and the guilder, and substantially so relative to the franc and the lira. This had stood to us during our domestic financial difficulties, helping to maintain international confidence. To reverse this policy now was, to say the least of it, adventurous.

Nevertheless I was convinced that, although a once-and-for-all devaluation within the EMS band might have negative short-term effects on confidence, it would put us in a position where, regardless of any further devaluation of sterling or the dollar, we would be able without fear of a significant loss of competitiveness to keep our currency in line with the Deutschmark and thus gradually to command the long-term confidence of the international financial markets. An 8 per cent devaluation of the Irish pound was agreed with our EMS partners without the need for a weekend meeting of Ministers. This produced no significant upward pressure on consumer prices; indeed prices remained stable for some months thereafter, and rose only 3 per cent in the whole of the succeeding twelve months; nor did it have any impact on pay levels.

Thereafter the Irish pound remained closely linked to the Deutschmark. Indeed after the general realignment in January 1987 it fluctuated during the following four years by only 1 per cent on either side of a rate of 2.66 Deutschmarks to the pound. This stability contributed to a major influx of funds that helped to bring Irish interest rates down and to keep them at a level much nearer to the German than the British level. In the spring of 1991 the three-month Euro-currency interest rate was over seven percentage points nearer to the German rate than in 1982, and four points below the British rate, whereas in 1982 it was five points higher than in Britain: a relative improvement of nine percentage points.

Meanwhile the unexpected and sharp deterioration in our domestic economy had affected the outcome of our 1986 budget. Given the severity of the sudden recession, the extent to which we were knocked off course was relatively small. A combination of an overrun of current spending and a shortfall of budgeted non-tax revenue (because the impact of the Dublin Gas crisis on Bord Gáis profits had been greater than had earlier been foreseen) pushed the current deficit up from 7.4 to 8.1 per cent of GNP, but unfortunately a statistical under-estimation of GNP at the time made it seem as if the deficit had been increased by more than a full percentage point, to 8.5 per cent of GNP. Nevertheless, although the real deterioration was small, the effect on a Government committed to reducing the current deficit to 5 per cent in an election year proved fatal.

We recognised of course that we could not now hope to achieve this planned target for 1987, but the Fine Gael members of the Government believed that to preserve confidence the current deficit and borrowing must be reduced by more than 1 per cent of GNP, and, as mentioned earlier, we announced this in mid-October after a Government decision in which for the first and only time the Labour Party members were placed in a minority.

After endless painful meetings we succeeded in cutting the departmental spending demands by £350 million and reducing the threatened current deficit from 10 per cent to just over 8 per cent of GNP. To get below that figure required further cuts, however, mainly in the provisions for Health, which Barry Desmond and his Labour colleagues were not prepared to concede. The Fine Gael Ministers for their part were not prepared to achieve our deficit and borrowing targets by increasing the burden of tax above the level at which it had been fixed in the National Plan. By mid-December it was clear that the two parties had reached an impasse, which was unlikely to be resolved, although we would continue to make the attempt.

I think that by this time we all knew that the end had come, but there was no point in giving up at that point and precipitating a break before Christmas. We agreed to review the position in January; but when we did so the conclusion was evident. We agreed amicably that the parting of the ways would be on 20 January, when Labour would leave the Government, explaining that they could not accept the proposed health and social welfare measures. Fine Gael for its part would stand by its determination to reduce the deficit and borrowing to a level significantly below that to which it had risen in 1986 as a result of the recession in that year. Each of us could thus appeal to our own constituency.

Shortly before the day came for Labour to leave the Government my eldest brother, Dem, died of Alzheimer's disease. Pierce, who was two years younger, had died in Rome nine months earlier after a long visit home at Christmas 1985, half of which he had to spend in hospital. With their deaths the last close family links with my childhood snapped, almost simultaneously with the end of the active phase of my political career.

When the day came for Labour to leave the Government it was a sad moment. We had soldiered together in this Government for over four years, restoring confidence in the political independence of the Gardaí and in the integrity of public life and introducing many social and tax reforms despite the financial pressures under which we operated. We had initiated the New Ireland Forum and had negotiated the Anglo-Irish Agreement. We had just passed through the Dáil, by the Ceann Comhairle's casting vote, the extradition legislation. And we had together come very close indeed to the point of halving the level of borrowing/GNP ratio that Fianna Fáil had left behind in mid-1981. Moreover, although our two parties responded to somewhat different economic constituencies, we shared a deep concern for social justice, liberal values, and integrity in public life.

We knew that in parting thus it was unlikely that we should find ourselves shoulder to shoulder again in the near future, and I knew that if and when that day came I would not be leading that Government. After Dick had handed me his own and his colleagues' formal resignations we all shook hands with each other warmly and with considerable emotion; Gemma Hussey was embraced by several of our Labour colleagues. Then at noon Dick and his colleagues told the press outside Government Buildings that they had resigned, and they went across to a conference room in the Setanta Building in Kildare Street to explain to the media the reasons for their decision.

(After the election, during the interval before the Dáil met to elect a new Government, my Fine Gael cabinet colleagues suggested that there should be a dinner for 'the real Government'. I found I was entitled to hold such a function at my own expense in Barrettstown Castle, and there on 3 March the Coalition Ministers of both parties, the former Attorney General, John Rogers, and the Chief Whip, Seán Barrett, celebrated until a late hour a Government in whose record we all took pride.)

As Labour were announcing their departure from the Government I was preparing for our press conference three hours later in Iveagh House. There I presented Fine Gael's uncompromising estimates and budget proposals. They included policy changes involving expenditure cuts of £210 million on top of the pruning of departmental estimates, combined with increases in expenditure taxes and a limit of 3 per cent on welfare increases, which were to take effect from November 1987, much later than usual. The expenditure cuts were set out in the greatest detail: no-one could accuse us of fudging any of the issues.

On the basis of the then prevailing forecast of GNP for the year ahead, these measures fulfilled the commitment we had entered into in mid-October with regard to the size of the current deficit and exchequer borrowing. In the event, as the outturn of the (only marginally different) budget eventually introduced by Fianna Fáil was to demonstrate, the recovery in the economy that occurred during 1987, which the Central Bank had forecast, would have reduced borrowing under our budget to something like 10.75 per cent of GNP or precisely half the figure we had faced when we had come to power in June 1981. Thus, contrary to the popular myth, to which even some academic economists have succumbed, well over half the painful financial adjustment effected between mid-1981 and the budget of 1991, with its planned exchequer borrowing figure of 1.9 per cent of GNP, was undertaken by our two Governments, operating under very adverse circumstances, especially towards the end of our period in office. (In saying this I have no desire, however, to minimise the contribution made by the subsequent Fianna Fáil administration in its cost-cutting budgets of 1988 and 1989.)

In presenting this uncompromising budget to the people I had two objectives in mind. First of all I wanted to ensure that in the subsequent election campaign we would be placed firmly on the high ground and in a position to challenge Fianna Fáil day by day to match our approach. My guess, which proved well founded, was that Charles Haughey would not have the courage to face this issue. Accordingly I made provision for an exceptionally long campaign—four weeks instead of three—in order to give plenty of time to hammer home to the electorate the contrast between our approach and his. This tactic proved successful, and produced during the course of the campaign a swing of about 5 per cent from Fianna Fáil to Fine Gael as between the first public opinion polls, taken at the beginning of February, and the eventual result of the election on 17 February.

My second purpose was to ensure that the budget Fianna Fáil would bring in when they came to power, as I believed they were likely to do, would keep the economy on the right course as the recovery predicted for 1987 took place. I knew that a Government coming to power on 10 March (the date on which the Dáil was to resume) would be unable for practical reasons to effect further significant reductions in public expenditure on that occasion, while possibly making some adjustments on the tax side, and in this I proved correct. I felt comfortable fighting an election on a strategy that would in practice determine the shape of Fianna Fáil's first budget but was likely to leave them at a disadvantage during the election campaign, because they would be unwilling to commit themselves to this strategy before the electorate.

Meanwhile I had allocated to the existing Fine Gael Ministers the portfolios relinquished by Labour, appointing Peter Barry as Tánaiste, and had launched the campaign with a helicopter tour of the midlands and the west.

Particularly for Ministers, including former Labour Party Ministers, all of them exhausted by the strain of Government during such a difficult period, and in particular by the trauma of the last three months, the campaign was a very tiring one, and I think we showed considerable signs of wear and tear. Nevertheless the tactic of having a long campaign, giving the electorate time to take account of the crucial budgetary issue, proved correct; successive polls showed a steady decline in Fianna Fáil support.

During the last week of the campaign I faced the test of a television debate with Charles Haughey. It had been agreed that the discussion on this occasion would follow a certain pattern, opening with 'harmless' questions to be addressed to Haughey and myself by the moderator, Brian Farrell, then moving through various aspects of the economic and financial situation and on to the issue of Northern Ireland policy. Whatever question Brian asked me totally disconcerted me, however; I lost the thread of the discussion, and could not thereafter follow properly the different stages of the debate. All I could do was keep on demanding that the leader of the opposition explain where he stood on the budgetary issue, which he had avoided throughout the campaign. After what seemed an eternity the discussion turned to Northern Ireland.

Just before the debate started I had recalled something Charles Haughey had said on radio the previous day about renegotiating part of the Anglo-Irish Agreement because of what he saw as its constitutional implications; the words he had used had been hastily scribbled down for me on a piece of paper. Now that we were discussing Northern Ireland I put it to my opponent that his commitment to renegotiate the Agreement would put at risk all that had been achieved. He proceeded to deny that he had ever said anything of the kind, claiming repeatedly that the remarks to which I referred related to emigration, although this made no sense whatever.

I searched for the scrap of paper on which I had written down the words he had actually used. At first I could not find it; but just as Charles Haughey once again repeated his denial I spotted it on the desk in front of me, and, picking it up, proceeded to read it out, unaware of the fact that a camera over my shoulder was focused on it so that the viewers could see the words themselves: 'We would strive by diplomatic and political action to see if we can change these constitutional implications to which we take exception.'

It was now his turn to be disconcerted, and the viewers could see that his attempt to suggest that the quotation related to emigration had been complete nonsense. The negative impact of this on his credibility was reinforced visually by the manner in which the camera had focused on the note of his words that I had read out.

Thus when I emerged from the studio I found to my astonishment that I was seen as having been victorious in this debate; even my panic-driven reiteration over and over again of the demand that my opponent clarify his position on the budget had come across to the viewers as a masterly tactic to put him on the spot, and the collapse of his credibility over his Northern Ireland statement appeared as a climax to what was seen as my successful handling of the debate.

It seems likely that this debate helped to boost Fine Gael's fortunes and to damage Fianna Fáil in the closing stages of the campaign, for the vote actually recorded in the election gave us several percentage points more, and Fianna Fáil several points less, than any poll up to that point.

However, there was one further development in the campaign that I think had a significant impact on the result. Two days before election day my team told me that there had been contacts with Des O'Malley's new party, the Progressive Democrats, and that they were willing to engage in a reciprocal exchange of transfers between our two parties, which, if effective, could have a significant impact on the eventual result, the Irish electorate being traditionally open to persuasion by their parties about the destination of their later-preference votes.

I was willing to accede to this preference exchange proposal, confidently expecting that in accordance with what had been agreed between our two election teams an offer of such an arrangement by me would be reciprocated. It wasn't; a number of the former Fianna Fáil members of that party immediately phoned in to its head office a demand that my offer be rejected, and rejected it was, to the fury of those in our election headquarters who had negotiated the arrangement. Nevertheless PD transfers, of which there were a large number (for many of their candidates were eliminated), came to us rather than Fianna Fáil, in a ratio of three to one, and this disproportion in the transfers gave us four, or perhaps even five, additional seats.

I listened to the election results coming in at our headquarters; and although the figures were better than the polls had led us to expect, and it soon became clear that, as I had hoped, Fianna Fáil was not going to secure the overall majority of which, given the events of the months immediately preceding the election, it had been confident, it was highly unlikely that anyone else but Charles Haughey could form a Government. With the outcome still uncertain that evening, I could have taken the line that in its minority position Fianna Fáil might not be capable of forming a Government, but this would have seemed like whistling in the dark, and would have deprived me of the opportunity of ensuring that Fine Gael rather than other parties would control the performance of Fianna Fáil in the next Dáil.

Accordingly, on the television results programme that night I conceded the election, and announced that we would support Fianna Fáil if they pursued similar fiscal policies to ours and if they accepted and worked the Anglo-Irish Agreement. By this tactic I hoped to ensure that even though in order to secure a majority Fianna Fáil would have to get the support of some independent deputies, Charles Haughey would know that in Government he need not depend on these independents for electoral support or be influenced by mavericks into pursuing the kind of irresponsible policies he had adopted in 1982 when his minority Government had been at the mercy of the Workers' Party. Perhaps on this, his third occasion as Taoiseach, he would in any event have adopted the strategy I was seeking to impose on him; but in view of past experience there was no harm in making sure that he did so, especially as not alone the responsible handling of the economy but the survival of the Anglo-Irish Agreement depended on this.

When the Dáil came to meet on 10 March the issue of the election of a Taoiseach was still in doubt. It was clear that my nomination as Taoiseach would be defeated, but it was not clear that Charles Haughey's nomination would be endorsed. The possibility of a deadlock existed. Indeed, given the stance adopted by the socialist independent Tony Gregory, such a result might have been deemed probable. For this deputy informed four of our backbenchers that he would be voting against Charles Haughey's nomination, which would have led to his defeat. I judged, however, that the fact that he had taken the trouble of communicating this, not just by chance to one of our backbenchers but deliberately to four of them, meant that he was seeking to put tactical pressure on Fine Gael to break the deadlock by abstaining as a party on Charles Haughey's nomination; and that was something I had no intention of doing. I believed that when it came to the point Gregory would not vote against my opponent as he saw our party going into the lobbies against his nomination.

Nevertheless I could not be certain that this would happen, and I had to consider what steps I would take if a deadlock did in fact emerge. I decided to discuss the matter with President Hillery, who would have a crucial role to play in resolving such a deadlock. He suggested to me a course of action that would put maximum pressure on the Dáil to elect a Taoiseach, if not on this occasion then shortly afterwards. I was to prepare two alternative speeches to be made after the vote on Charles Haughey's nomination: one to be used in the event of his election to office, announcing that I was going to Áras an Uachtaráin to present my resignation to the President, and the other to be used if Charles Haughey, like myself, were rejected by the Dáil, to say that I would discuss with the President the situation that had emerged. Under no circumstances, the

President advised, should I suggest that in the event of a deadlock I would seek a dissolution, although I would of course have to resign following the defeat of my nomination as Taoiseach.

Then, after visiting him, I was to go back to the Dáil and attempt, by knocking heads together, to get a resolution of the deadlock. If I failed in this attempt I was to return to the President once again, at which point he would publicly instruct me to make a further effort, acting on his authority. We both hoped that the mounting pressure thus created would resolve the problem, should it arise.

I was very appreciative of the manner in which President Hillery approached the problem, and I was entertained also by the irony of the situation in which I might find myself: seeking to cajole the Dáil into electing Charles Haughey as Taoiseach! There was, of course, the possibility that arising from a deadlock Charles Haughey might come under pressure to stand down with a view to another Fianna Fáil nominee being put forward, but this seemed to me extremely unlikely in view of the failure of all earlier attempts to shift him.

In the event it all worked out as I had expected. Faced with the responsibility for deciding the issue one way or the other, Tony Gregory abstained on the vote, and Charles Haughey thus became Taoiseach for the fourth time, in a Government that depended thereafter for its survival on the support of Fine Gael. This support was subsequently accorded to it on an appropriate conditional basis by my successor, Alan Dukes.

Meanwhile, during the interval between the election and the assembly of the Dáil I had several meetings with Charles Haughey to prepare for the almost certain transfer of power. As had always been the case in relation to our private contacts, these were amicable encounters. During these meetings we discussed practical matters, and at the end of the first I asked him to let me know if he would wish to have my views on key diplomatic postings related to the Anglo-Irish Agreement. At the second meeting he said he would be glad to hear my views on this, and I suggested names to him for three of these posts, two of which featured in the decisions he later made on this matter, although in a slightly different form than I had suggested.

When he had been elected Taoiseach we had a third brief discussion, during which I explained to him the layout of the Taoiseach's office, which had replaced in 1983 the original office in another part of the building. He remarked on this occasion that any Government would have been unlucky to have had to face even one of the commercial crises that had arisen during our term of office in relation to the Dublin Gas Company, the PMPA, Irish Shipping, and the ICI, but we had had extremely bad luck in having to face all of these in turn.

Meanwhile I had been reflecting on my own personal position. When I had taken on the leadership of Fine Gael in July 1977 I had said then that I would undertake this task for a period of ten years, of which nine-and-three-quarter years had now elapsed. If, as seemed likely, Charles Haughey were elected Taoiseach there was a fair chance that his Government would run for four years, and if I sought to remain leader during that period with a view to the possibility of returning to office at the end of the next Dáil, I would by then have been leader of the party for fourteen years and would be sixty-five years of age. This seemed to me to make no sense, either for me or for the party. I could, of course, remain on for some time after the new Government was formed, choosing a moment later in the life of the Dáil to retire from the leadership; but the only result of this would be to shorten my successor's period of preparation for the task of taking on Fianna Fáil at the next election, which in view of the close result might be much less than four years away. Moreover, given the fact that I had found the wear and tear of office fairly gruelling, especially in recent months, I did not think I had the physical or moral stamina to provide the kind of dynamic leadership the party would need in order to recover from the defeat that it had just suffered.

Finally there was Joan to consider. She had never been enthusiastic about my political career but had supported me loyally throughout, despite the fact that during the whole of the period of my leadership she had been disabled, increasingly as time went on, by arthritis. It would not, I felt, be fair to impose a further strain on her; at this stage she deserved more of my time and attention, as did my grandchildren.

She raised the question with me shortly after the election, and I asked her to let me reflect on it for a period so that I could satisfy myself that if I retired at this stage it would be the best thing not merely for the two of us but also for the party and for the country. I discussed the matter with none of my parliamentary colleagues, although I did speak to one or two other people who were closely involved with me in the political arena. Ten days later I made up my mind: everything pointed to an immediate resignation once a new Government had been formed.

Accordingly, immediately after the election of Charles Haughey I called meetings of the front bench and the parliamentary party for the following morning. Although in the previous couple of weeks there had inevitably been some speculation that I might resign after the election of the new Taoiseach, there had not been time overnight for members of the party to address this issue, and I think almost everyone was taken by surprise when I told first the front bench and then the parliamentary party of my intention to resign, and proposed that the election of my successor take place in eleven days' time.

That afternoon I held a press conference and was highly entertained to receive from the political correspondents a framed illustration from one of Richmal Crompton's 'William' books. It showed a disgruntled William telling his friends, 'I don't want to be Prime Minister. You can keep your old Prime Ministership.'

Some time previously I had received an invitation to lecture at Tulane University in New Orleans, and I had allowed my acceptance of this engagement to stand, despite the election, feeling that I might want to take it up whether or not I was Taoiseach. I had in fact arranged that Joan and I would leave for the

United States on the morning after my resignation, to return on the morning of 22 March, when the election of my successor was to take place. This had the great advantage that I would be absent throughout whatever campaign for the leadership might take place. I had always thought it of crucial importance that I should not attempt to influence the outcome of such an election in any way; indeed it was in part this concern that had led me to attempt the abortive reshuffle of my Government a year earlier.

Three candidates entered the ring: Peter Barry, John Bruton, and Alan Dukes. Returning on the morning of Saturday 22 March I went to the party meeting, curious to see what the outcome of the election would be. I found that the three candidates had agreed that the tellers for the election should be the chairman of the party, Kieran Crotty, and myself, and they proposed that when we announced the winner we should give no details of the votes cast, lest a narrow majority for whomever was elected might weaken his authority, or a poor vote for one or other candidate might adversely affect his subsequent standing in the party. We agreed to this, and, having counted the votes, simply announced that Alan Dukes had been elected.

Ironically, despite my determined neutrality, reinforced by my absence during the entire campaign, a belief subsequently developed that I had been actively promoting the candidature of Alan Dukes. I never succeeded in dispelling this particular rumour, which soon hardened into an accepted myth; to have attempted to do so with the vigour necessary to carry conviction could have misled people into thinking that I was unhappy with the new leader.

From then on, Joan and I lived happily ever after.

# EXCHANGE OF LETTERS
# WITH CARDINAL Ó FIAICH

Ara Coeli
Ard Mhacha/Armagh

January 9, 1990.

Dear Doctor FitzGerald,

I note in your article in the December 21 issue of ALPHA that you make the following statement about the meeting at which we were both present on Monday 7 April 1986:

> "Indeed, there was even a suggestion by the Hierarchy delegation that we 'bend' our civil marriage laws so as to accommodate these bigamous marriages, a suggestion that was, in my view, quite improper."

No such suggestion was made by the delegation or by any member of it.

The discussion on this matter began, as you will recall, with your own raising of the possibility of the complete separation of civil and religious marriage, with distinct ceremonies, such as is the practice in several continental countries. We indicated that we had no objection in principle to this suggestion. As a matter of fact, we welcomed the recognition implied in the suggestion that civil and sacramental marriages are distinct, if closely related realities and that there can be sacramental marriages which have no civil effect.

This suggestion of yours was the only occasion on which a change in the civil law was proposed as a way of dealing with this question.

The meeting then turned to the possibility of finding a way, short of the complete separation of all civil and religious marriages, in which it could be made clear that, in this small number of instances, a purely religious event was taking place which made no claim and gave no appearance of a civilly valid marriage.

Our delegation had discussed this matter in detail before the meeting and we are absolutely clear about the points which we wished to make, and which we did make.

We explicitly stated that what we had in mind was an exploration of ways whereby the Sacrament could be celebrated in a manner which would remove any ambiguity. We said, in particular, that we felt that there were possibilities in *Canon Law* which were worth examining.

The possibilities which we had in mind ranged from a formal declaration at the time of, or even as part of, the ceremony, disclaiming any civil significance, to the conducting of the ceremony in the absence of an episcopally ordained minister as provided in Canon 1112 (the delegation of a lay person to assist at marriage) or in Canon 1116 (marriage in the presence of witnesses alone).

At no time did the delegation representing the Episcopal Conference, or any member of the delegation, suggest that a change in the civil law would be a sensible way to approach this question. Still less did anybody suggest that the law should be 'bent'. Furthermore, the surviving Bishops who were present wish to place it on record that such suggestions do not represent the views of any of them and would not have represented the views of any of them at the time of the meeting.

The draft Report of the meeting, which was never agreed, contains one sentence which may reflect or give rise to your misunderstanding:

> "It was additionally suggested that, in the case of a Church remarriage following annulment by the Catholic Marriage Tribunals, consideration be given to a change in the civil law to provide that where a sacramental marriage could not be a legal civil marriage because under the civil law a prior marriage still bound one of the parties, the sacramental marriage would not constitute a civil marriage."

It is not indicated who made this suggestion. The only reference to a change in civil law which would accomplish this was your own suggestion of complete separation.

The sentence is, as you will see, completely incoherent. If the sacramental marriage in these cases 'could not be a civil marriage' this is because the law *already* provides that it 'would not constitute a civil marriage'.

If the sentence is trying to say that civil law should be altered to provide for some process whereby a Church marriage could in some cases be designated as 'non-civil', that was not a proposal made by us.

The preferable course of action in our view was, and is, the one we put forward, namely that the ceremony be conducted in such a way that it would not have even the appearance of a valid marriage under the existing civil law.

This might, we believe, take account of both of the elements which must concern the State—the avoidance of any confusion or ambiguity about the civil status of parties in purely sacramental marriages and the vindication of their constitutional rights to the free practice of religion subject to public order and morality.

With kind personal regards and all good wishes for 1990,

Yours very sincerely,
✠ Tomás Ó Fiaich
Cardinal Archbishop of Armagh

Dáil Éireann
Baile Átha Cliath, 2.
(Dublin, 2).

13th March 1990

His Eminence Cardinal Tomas O Fiaich,
Ara Coeli,
Armagh.

Your Eminence,

Thank you for your letter of 9th January.

The part of the discussions between the Government and the Hierarchy delegation about which you have written to me relates to the issue of bigamy arising from cases where a sacramental marriage is solemnised in Ireland by the Roman Catholic Church following a declaration of nullity by the authorities of that Church in respect of an earlier joint civil/religious marriage.

As you say, I opened this part of our discussion with a reference to the possibility of tackling this problem by separating the civil and religious ceremonies; I believe I indicated, however, that because of what I believed to be the attachment of most Irish people to the traditional joint ceremony, I was reluctant to contemplate such a separation if it could be avoided. I note, however, that you have no objection in principle to such a change.

The discussion then turned to a suggestion from your side that a way might be found to secure that in such cases, in your words, "a purely religious event was taking place which made no claim and gave no appearance of a civilly valid marriage". I do not, however, think that we discussed the specific suggestions with respect to Canon Law contained in your letter.

On the other hand I have a clear recollection of the sense of shock I felt, which I believe was shared by the Minister for Justice, as members of a Government obliged to uphold the constitutional provision for the protection of marriage unless and until, as we were then suggesting might be done, it was modified by [the] Oireachtas and the people. For, as we saw it, what was being suggested by the Hierarchy delegation—now developed in greater detail in your letter—would have involved an arrangement between the Government and the Hierarchy of one Church designed to facilitate the entry by some people into arrangements which at the very least would in the eyes of the public purport to displace an existing joint civil-religious marriage enjoying the protection of the Constitution.

Moreover, quite apart from this constitutional issue, your proposals raised a possible legal difficulty. For, as your delegation's detailed discussions on the problems posed by the law of bigamy will presumably have disclosed, the crime of bigamy may be committed even where the forms and ceremonies of marriage gone through by someone who is already married and whose marriage has not been dissolved, are for one reason or another void or invalid. And if a change were to be made in the law in order to clarify this issue in relation to what you were proposing, such a change could be open to constitutional challenge as being specifically directed towards undermining valid legal marriages enjoying the protection of the Constitution, by encouraging people to enter into a second union while the first marriage subsisted in civil law.

It would appear from your letter that the Hierarchy delegation was aware that any ceremony carried out with the assistance of a priest, even with disclaimers as to its possible civil effect, would almost certainly be bigamous. That consideration would appear to underly your delegation's decision, (which, however, did not emerge clearly to me at the time), to propose alternatives based on Canons 1112 or 1116, involving the abandonment of the presence of a priest at this proposed religious ceremony.

If such a wide interpretation of Canon Law were employed here, involving the recognition as sacramental marriages of ceremonies at which priests even though physically available do not assist—and I understand that there are precedents for this, in South Africa, for example—would some people not then be likely to raise the question of why the Catholic Church feels it necessary to insist that civil ceremonies at which State registrars assist are necessarily invalid marriages in its eyes? This insistence has unhappily also brought the Church into potential conflict with the constitutional provisions in Ireland for the protection of marriage under the law. For, not recognising such civil marriages, the Catholic Church has claimed the right to solemnise a sacramental marriage involving a party to such an undissolved civil marriage; I recall one such case receiving much publicity several decades ago.

There is, moreover, the further potential problem which, given the growing number of people in Ireland who for one reason or another are unbaptised, may become an actual one in the years ahead—of the Catholic Church's claim to have the power to dissolve marriages involving such persons while simultaneously opposing the exercise by the State of such a power of dissolution.

The problem of bigamous second marriages solemnised by the Catholic Church that arises or may arise in Ireland in these different cases has been avoided in some other countries through the introduction by the Church authorities of a requirement that any prior marriage recognised by the State must be dissolved by civil process before the Church authorities will authorise a sacramental marriage. For the time being, however, because of the defeat of our referendum proposal, this solution to an unhappy Church/State conflict of laws is not available to us in Ireland.

It was, of course, in the context of this referendum proposal that these matters came up in discussion between us. I can see that your suggestions, which were not developed in detail on that occasion, were designed to suggest ways of avoiding in one of these cases a Church/State conflict in the absence of a provision for divorce which, where it exists, the Church requires its members to avail of in such cases in order to avoid the problem of bigamy. From our point of view, on the other hand, this approach appeared disconcerting. For, while facing opposition on the part of the Hierarchy to a strictly limited constitutional change that would have resolved this problem in Ireland in the same way as elsewhere, we were, as we saw it, being asked simultaneously by the delegation to collaborate in a process that appeared to us designed to undermine the constitutional protection of marriage, which, in the absence of a constitutional change, we were obliged to uphold!

Please forgive the length of this letter, which necessarily also suffers from the defect of being written by a double layman—lay in relation to the civil law as well as in relation to the clerical state! I felt, however, that in view of the obvious danger of mutual misunderstanding between us and the trouble you have taken to set out your position in relation to this matter in some detail, I owed it to you to do likewise.

In view of the public response made on behalf of the Hierarchy to this part of my article in Alpha, which questioned the aptness of my comment on this matter in the columns of that journal, I feel that publication of this exchange of letters on a matter of considerable interest would be appropriate with a view to clarifying for the public the complex issues at stake.

Yours sincerely,
Garret FitzGerald, T.D.

# Address at the Memorial Service for Christopher Ewart-Biggs

[The following address was given by Garret FitzGerald as Minister for Foreign Affairs at the memorial service for the British Ambassador, Mr Christopher Ewart-Biggs, and Miss Judith Cooke in St Patrick's Cathedral, Dublin, on Wednesday 28 July 1976.]

*Death be not proud, though some have called thee*
*Mighty and dreadful, for thou art not so,*
*For those whom thou think'st thou dost overthrow,*
*Die not, poor death . . .*
*Why swell'st thou then?*
*One short sleep past, we wake eternally,*
*And death shall be no more; death, thou shalt die.*

He came to Ireland as a guest, and a friend. At the personal request of the Prime Minister of his country, he undertook the task of representing the United Kingdom in Ireland, at a time when the relations between our two countries are of singular importance to both. He brought with him a conviction of the evil and futility of violence and a dedication to the task of strengthening the links that bind our peoples together in the face of the common threat to both. He also brought a belief that cynics may mock, but true statesmen rightly maintain, that between governments and peoples, as between individuals, truth and honesty provide the only sure foundation for a solid and lasting relationship.

We in Ireland welcomed Christopher and Jane Ewart-Biggs with instinctive warmth, recognising their informed goodwill, their absolute sincerity, their quality as people, and an element of humour and indeed gaiety which struck an instant chord amongst all who met them here.

For myself, from the moment I first met him in Oxford four short weeks ago, I looked forward to a personal and diplomatic relationship which I knew would be positive and constructive, open and uninhibited. I knew that, given the problems that exist at times in the relations between our two countries, we were bound to have some difficult encounters, but I knew also that such momentary difficulties—always to be seen in any event in the wider context of the profound common interests of Ireland and Britain—would be eased by the kind of relationship that we would be able to establish between us.

The shock, and for us the shame, of his murder, and of that of Judith Cooke, have had profound effects for all of us. No doubt the perpetrators calculated, with their unfailing lack of insight or understanding, that Anglo-Irish relations would be severely weakened, perhaps permanently damaged, by such an atrocity. That the opposite has been the case is now evident to all. Our two peoples, whose pasts have been so closely linked for ill and for good throughout eight centuries, have confounded our common enemy by responding to this tragedy with a deepened sense of our close interdependence, and of our common interest in combating violence and averting anarchy. Politicians, press and people in our two islands have instinctively understood the trap set for them by evil men, and have been drawn closer together in the aftermath of this murder.

Perhaps for the first time the Irish people have been brought to appreciate fully those qualities of dignity, calm and restraint on which Britons rightly pride themselves. Perhaps for the first time also the British people have understood the depth of abhorrence of violence that animates our people.

Whatever ill-conceived and twisted objective the perpetrators of these murders may have had in mind, it was certainly not the outcome that we observe. For they have brought about a strengthening of the ties that link Ireland with Britain in friendship, and a re-animation of our joint and unequivocal determination once and for all to destroy this conspiracy against freedom and against life—which in Northern Ireland has already wrought such universal tragedy.

The tragedy of this moment in Ireland touches all. It touches the young— the young like Judith Cooke, courageous, talented, attractive. The promise of her generation is a prey to those who respect neither age, nor frailty, nor sex, nor youth, in their urge to destroy those whom they seem in their blindness to conceive only as impersonal symbols, never as living people. What kind of world can they be dreaming of, in which living vital people like Judith have no place, save in the grave?

Christopher Ewart-Biggs brought to this country a total commitment against this callous insensate violence, a belief in truth and peace. He could not have conceived that within two brief weeks of his arrival he would have made, at the cost of his own gallant life, a unique contribution to the aims he sought to serve—a contribution which, had he lived, he would have dedicated himself to achieving by the slower process of diplomatic action. His widow and children, to whom every Irish heart goes out at this moment, can hope at least that in this way his death has not been in vain.

Ireland, shamed by the deeds of men with minds twisted by the myths that for too many in this country have displaced history, will not forget this moment.

We ask Christopher's family for their compassion. We are grateful that his widow, generous of spirit as he was, has found the courage and charity to understand and to maintain the full dedication of her husband's commitment to peace in this island. We can humbly learn from her.

I am honoured, and through me I believe the Irish people for whom I speak are honoured, that she should have asked me to address you at this, for her, most tragic moment. I do so on behalf of a country which with one mind and heart offers her its love and sympathy.

# INDEX

corporal punishment, 74
Corrymeela Reconciliation Centre,
    Belfast, 200
Cosgrave, Liam, 27, 136, 191, 192,
    248, 276, 325, 348, 361, 614
  elected TD, 34
  chairs Policy Committee, 68
  FG leader, 70, 71
  appoints G. F. to Seanad, 72
  relations with G. F., 73, 76, 77,
    174, 196–7, 293–4
  coalition talks, 78–9
  NI policy, 91, 98–100, 102–3,
    105, 203–6, 209, 287
  and Arms Trial, 93, 94–5
  tensions within party, 93
  'mongrel foxes' speech, 105–6
  and Offences Against the State
    Bill, 106–9, 292
  becomes Taoiseach, 112–14
  presides over European Council,
    155
  and EP representation, 166–7
  fisheries policy debate in
    European Council, 170
  US Congress speech, 182–3, 577
  and Holy See, 188–9
  and O'Brien, 197, 198
  Sunningdale talks, 211–12, 217
  Sunningdale interview, 226, 227
  meets Faulkner, 227–8
  post-Sunningdale meeting,
    228–30
  meetings with Wilson, 232–4,
    250, 252–3, 277–8
  and UWC strike, 241
  correspondence with Wilson,
    258, 266
  response to British talks with
    IRA, 260
  statement on NI power-sharing,
    267
  and SAS arrests, 281
  as leader of party, 292–3
  ministerial appointments by,
    293–5
  as Taoiseach, 295–6
  social reform speech, 298, 304
  and contraception bill, 308–9
  and 'Heavy Gang' allegations,
    314
  endorses O Dalaigh for
    President, 315
  and O Dalaigh resignation,
    316–17
  calls election, 1977, 320
  resigns FG leadership, 322
Cosgrave, W. T., 27, 34, 76, 182,
    294
Cossiga, President, 580
Costa Rica, 508
Costello, Declan, 29, 70, 79, 106,
    198, 235, 362
  UCD student, 31
  FG activity, 67, 76
  Just Society movement, 68–9,
    73, 93
  High Court judge, 174, 467
  Sunningdale talks, 213, 216, 237
  and extradition, 232
  SAS intrusion, 281
  Attorney General, 294

Costello, John A., 31, 45, 47, 60,
    68, 127, 294, 363
  and G. F., 74, 86
  retirement, 85
Coughlan, Stephen, 78
Council of Europe, 283
Council of Ireland (Sunningdale),
    207, 210, 239, 464
  proposed, 202, 205–6
  finances of, 209, 225
  functions, 212–13
  policing, 214, 216–21
  discussed at Hillsborough,
    228–30
  Consultative Assembly, 230
  Rees' attitude to, 231
  Faulkner seeks deferral, 234
  Faulkner seeks changes, 236
  NIE discussions on, 240–41
Council of State, 316
Court of Appeal, NI, 555
courts. see legal system
Coyle, Fr, SJ, 21, 24, 28
Craig, Bill, 238, 274, 379
Craig, James, 2
Cravinho, Sr, 158
Craxi, Bettino, 583, 584–5, 592,
    595, 596
Cremin, Con, 127
Cresson, Edith, 390–91
Criminal Justice Bill, 1983, 608–9,
    612
Criminal Law (Jurisdiction) Act,
    278–9, 290
Crosland, Susan, 177
Crosland, Tony, 142, 145, 168,
    176–7, 261, 283, 287
  fisheries policy dispute, 172–3,
    174–5
cross-border security, 229, 230,
    232–3, 256–7, 291, 381, 506
  map-reading errors, 201–2
  British Army incursions, 230–31,
    257
  Rees and G. F. discuss, 274
  SAS intrusion, 281
  security zone proposal, 384,
    494–6
  in Anglo-Irish Agreement, 532,
    552
Crotty, Kieran, 406, 647
Crotty, Raymond, 600
Crotty, Tom, 31
Crowther, Sir Geoffrey, 59
Cubbon, Brian, 282
Cuddy, Miss, 14, 17, 32
Cumann na mBan, 8
Cumann na nGaedheal, 11, 17–18,
    294
  and Irish language, 306
Curriculum and Examinations
    Board, 354, 387
Currie, Austin, 90–91, 99, 231, 481
  Sunningdale talks, 219
  after UWC strike, 249
  pressures within SDLP, 283
Cusack, Cyril, 315
Cushnahan, John, 571
Custom House Dock, 403
Cyprus, 161, 181
Czechoslovakia, 124–5

Dail Eireann, 8, 11, 72–3
  Treaty split, 9
  First Dail commemorated, 65
  G. F. elected to, 85–8
  Arms Trial debates, 94–6
  Bloody Sunday debate, 103–4
  Offences Against the State Bill,
    1972, 106–9
  Soviet loan, 1920, 127
  size increased, 308, 343
  need for reform, 337
  legislative bottlenecks, 385
  FF tries to prevent dissolution,
    398–9
  Reagan protest, 578
  ratifies SEA, 600
  Criminal Justice Bill, 1983, 609
  election of Taoiseach, 1987, 644–5
Daily Telegraph, 140, 164, 184,
    273, 333, 349
Daly, Dr, Bishop of Derry, 188
Davern, Noel, 108
Davignon, Etienne, 588
Dawnflights, 40
de Gaulle, General, 30, 32, 591
de Valera, Eamon, 7, 18, 46, 63, 81,
    113, 117
  forms first government, 11
  wins 1944 election, 34
  and Seanad Eireann, 60
  Presidential election, 76
  Constitution, 1937, 176
  and Irish language, 306
  and Irish Press, 637
  dying, 270
de Valera, Dr Eamonn, 57
de Valera, Vivion, 27
Deane, Vincent, 110, 111, 423,
    459, 614
Deasy, Austin, 408, 429, 622
  Minister for Agriculture, 430
  milk superlevy, 454, 581, 583
Deaver, Mike, 373
Decimal Currency Bill, 1969, 87
Defence, Dept of, 96
Defence, Ministry of, 552
Defence Council (Emergency), 27
Defence Forces, 27, 48, 232, 257,
    271, 314, 316
Delors, Jacques, 544, 588–9, 615
Democratic Unionist Party (DUP),
    330, 379, 563–4
Dempsey, Gerry, 41–2
Dempsey, Jerry, 40–41, 51
Den Uyl, Joop, 166
Denmark, 124, 129–30, 150, 164,
    391, 580, 596–7
  official visit to, 137–8
  EC Presidency, 146
  and Portugal's EEC application,
    156
  EP representation, 166–7
  and fisheries policy, 173
  deposit interest retention tax, 619
Derry, 201, 218
  G. F. visits, 91, 271
  Bloody Sunday, 102–4, 271
  army harassment, 247
  Dublin–Derry air service, 541
Desmond, Barry, 78, 428–9, 604,
    640
  and reshuffle, 622–4

Prohibition of Forcible Entry Act, 107
property tax, 436–7
proportional representation
   referendum, 77–9
protectionism, 49–50, 58
Provisional IRA. *see* Irish
   Republican Army
Public Accounts Committee (PAC),
   4, 96, 339
Public Administration, Institute of
   (IPA), 53–4, 59
Public Prosecutions, Director of,
   281, 445
Public Record Office, 619
public sector, 44–5, 53–4, 62. *see
   also* civil service
   merit system, 79–80
   employment, 336, 353
   recruitment embargo, 385
   need for reform, 430, 450, 454–6
   Oireachtas pay increases, 608
   pay increases, 453, 636–7
Public Service, Dept of the, 225,
   430, 454–5
Puerto Rico, 142
   summit, 183
Purser, Sarah, 18
Pym, Francis, 210, 215–16, 228,
   229, 233

Qadhafi, Colonel, 284, 548
Queen's College, Belfast, 2, 3
Queen's University, Belfast, 58, 261
Quigley, Declan, 469, 509
Quinn, Gerry, 58
Quinn, Ruairi, 607

Radio Telefís Eireann (RTE), 74,
   174, 312, 358
   first election coverage, 69–70, 72
   ban on subversives, 318–19
   G. F./Haughey debates, 401,
      420, 642–3
   appointment of Authority, 433
   and local broadcasting, 457
Rambouillet
   summit, 183
Ramphal, Sridi, 152
Rathmines School of Commerce, 43
Rawlinson, Sir Peter, 213–14
Reagan, Nancy, 577, 578
Reagan, President Ronald, 31, 527,
   531, 535, 544, 561–2
   and hunger-strikes, 372–3
   Irish visit, 577–9
Red Hand, 289
Redmond, John, 6, 77
Rees, Merlyn, 105, 228, 231, 252,
   282, 283, 549
   NI Secretary, 230
   and IRA, 231, 259–60, 267–8
   meets Irish delegations, 232–4,
      250, 252
   and Law Enforcement
      Commission, 235, 236
   meets G. F. and Costello, 237–8
   and UWC strike, 239–45
   meets Cooney, 256
   Green Paper, 257, 258
   detainees released, 261
   and Northern Ireland
      Convention, 264–7

ends meetings with Irish
   government, 269–70
G. F. attempts meeting with,
   272–4
meets G. F., 274–5
discusses Convention collapse,
   276–8
meets G. F. and Cooney, 278–9
approach to Unionists, 289
refuse disposal strike, 338
Regional Fund, EC, 162, 163–5,
   208, 597
Relief Advisory Services, NI, 248
Republic of Ireland
   declared, 45–6, 47
   economy of, 49–50
   anti-intellectualism, 66
   role in EC, 146–77
   and EC financial policies, 162–5
   and EC Fisheries Policy, 169–75
   Third World aid, 189–91
   reactions to Sunningdale, 225–8
   franchise extended to British
      citizens, 382, 611
   and EC cohesion, 598–600
   ratification of SEA, 600–601
Revenue Commissioners, 299,
   393–4
Rey, Jean, 73
Rhodesia, 243. *see also* Zimbabwe
Riad, Mahmud, 160–61
Ring College, Co. Waterford, 16,
   21, 45
roads, investment in, 451, 452
Robinson, Mary, 146, 323, 398,
   490, 605
Robinson, Nick, 323
Robinson, Peter, 564, 575
Rocard, Michel, 586
Roche, Dr Louis, 36
Rogers, John, 447, 554, 614–15,
   641
Rogers, William, 124
Rome
   European Council meetings,
      140, 142, 165–6, 184, 186
   Foreign Ministers meeting, 142
Rome, Treaty of, 50, 120, 138, 599
   unanimity requirement, 147–8
   amendment conference
      proposed, 595–8
Rommel, Field-Marshal, 581
Rooney, Major Eamonn, 46, 47
Rooney, Michael, 47–8
Rossi, Hugh, 334
Royal Hospital, Kilmainham, 555
Royal Irish Academy, 344
Royal Ulster Constabulary (RUC),
   98, 229, 252, 268, 419, 541,
   559, 611. *see also*
   interrogation techniques
   reforms proposed, 90, 201, 208,
      214
   internment, 97
   and Garda Siochana, 217, 570
   in Sunningdale talks, 217–18
   and British Army, 232–3, 274
   call for nationalists to back, 236
   and sectarian intimidation, 238
   Reserve, 271, 279, 540
   and UUAC strike, 289–90
   strengthened, 290–91

Dowra Affair, 414, 471, 477
promotion of machine-gunning
   officer, 439
in Anglo-Irish Agreement,
   504–6, 508, 511, 516–17,
   532, 540, 544–9, 552, 563
distrusted by nationalist
   community, 506–7
need for more Catholics, 530
and UDR, 534, 538, 552–3, 574
complaints of, 549
code of conduct, 552, 553
and Maryfield Secretariat, 572
Rugby, Lord, 26
Ruggiero, Renato, 592–3
Rumor, Mariano, 122, 137, 138,
   166, 212
Ryan, Dermot, 29
Ryan, Eoin, 27
Ryan, Dr Louden, 51, 58, 449, 479
Ryan, Richard, 468, 569
Ryan, Richie, 92–3, 98, 99, 101,
   107, 225, 237, 293–4, 308,
   319, 323, 324, 327
   and NI, 102, 331
   wealth tax proposal, 298–301

Sabbatarianism, 166, 219–20
Sadat, President, 362
St Brigid's school, Bray, 16–17
Sanfey, Commdt Jim, 325
SAS, 276
   border intrusion, 281, 290
   promotion of officer, 539
Sauvagnargues, Jean, 132–4, 137,
   138, 143, 156, 390
   and world economic summit, 141
   on Portugal, 157
Scally, Willy, 310
Scarman Report, 549
Scheel, Walter, 132
Schmidt, Helmut, 137–8, 155, 175,
   192, 193, 344
Schultz, George, 124, 535, 562,
   577, 579
Scoil Bhride, 29–30
Scollard, William, 4
Scotland, 164
   EP representation, 167, 168–9
   and fisheries policy, 172–3
Scott, Nick, 473, 511, 554, 563
Seanad Eireann, 13, 55, 80, 87, 359,
   440
   Desmond FitzGerald in, 22
   Electoral Law Commission, 60
   election campaign, 1965, 70–72
   G. F. in, 72–4
   ministers from, 363–4
   G. F. discusses constitutional
      crusade, 379–80
   role of, 385
security policy, 311–15, 354
   Security Committee, 310
   Emergency Powers Bill, 312–13,
      315–18
   'Heavy Gang', 313–15, 318, 330
Shannon, Seamus, 615
Shannon Airport, 603
Shannon Free Airport Development
   Company (SFADCo), 191
Sharp, Mitchell, 124
Shaw, George Bernard, 3, 6, 15